Our Favorite Recipes

At *Cooking Light*, only those recipes that have passed muster with our Test Kitchens staff make it into our pages. The staff tests each recipe to ensure that it's healthy, tasty, easy to prepare, and has that all-important quality we call the "yum factor." So which of our 2001 recipes pack the most flavor? Well, they're the ones readers keep calling about and the ones our staff loves to whip up for their own families and friends. They're the most delicious of the delicious, and we've gathered them for you here.

Oven-Roasted Sea Bass with Couscous and Warm Tomato Vinaigrette *(page 161):*

Buttery sea bass, moist, lemon-infused couscous, and a sweet, tart vinaigrette star in this almost effortless, fresh-tasting dish.

More of
Our Favorite Recipes

◄ Cooking Light's Ultimate Roasted Turkey *(page 341)*:

One taste and it was unanimous: This is our best holiday turkey ever.

Spice-Crusted Salmon with Lime-Orange Salsa *(page 302)*:

The refreshing taste of citrus complements the robust cumin and coriander crusted fish.

Roasted Asparagus with Balsamic Browned Butter *(page 262)*:

A simple sauce made with browned butter, soy sauce, and balsamic vinegar lends a nutty, salty, and pungently sweet flavor.

◄ Pesto *(page 285)*:

We can think of no better use for a bumper crop of fresh basil. Freeze this lightened classic to enjoy all year long.

◄ Jamaican Jerk Beef Kebabs *(page 221)*:

Bring the Caribbean to your table with tender cubes of beef and bell peppers marinated in a spicy-hot mixture of cinnamon, nutmeg, and allspice.

◄ Raspberry Jelly Roll with Apricot Coulis *(page 279)*:

Delicate flavors from apricots and raspberries complement this tender cake that's ready for the most elegant of dinner parties.

◄ Potato Gratin with Goat Cheese and Garlic *(page 291)*:

With the pronounced flavors of goat cheese and garlic, this comfort dish reaches new heights.

◀ **Asparagus, Ham, and Fontina Bread Pudding** *(page 353):*

It just might be our favorite bread pudding. Nutty, creamy fontina and savory ham yield a bona fide taste sensation.

◀ **Cinnamon-Beef Noodles** *(page 32):*

Cinnamon spices beef stew meat in this classic Chinese dish, a delicious departure from run-of-the-mill soups and stews. Your kitchen will smell wonderful while it simmers.

◀ **Vanilla Bean Crème Brûlée** *(page 44):*

A deep, rich vanilla flavor, a crunchy topping, and a creamy custard in this lightened favorite delight the senses.

▲ **Sauternes-Poached Apricots with Fresh Berries and Vanilla Crème Fraîche** *(page 216):*

Buttery, slightly tart crème fraîche rounds out the concentrated sweetness of poached apricots.

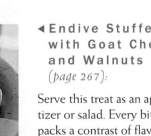

◀ **Cookies-and-Cream Ice Cream** *(page 138):*

Who'd believe tofu would play a part in our favorite ice cream of the year? One taste and you'll be sold, too.

◀ **Spiced Basmati Pilaf with Garden Peas** *(page 324):*

Cardamom and cloves add just the right amount of spice to this side—a terrific balance for highly seasoned entrées.

◀ **Endive Stuffed with Goat Cheese and Walnuts** *(page 267):*

Serve this treat as an appetizer or salad. Every bite packs a contrast of flavors and textures—salty, sweet, tangy, bitter, creamy, and crunchy.

◀ **Chambord Granita** *(page 199):*

You'll marvel at how just four ingredients can come together for so much refreshing flavor.

Sichuan-Style Stir-Fried Chicken with Peanuts (*page 33*):

Also known as kung pao chicken, this Sichuan classic is multidimensional. The hot-sweet and salty-sour flavors reflect true regional style.

Cooking Light®

ANNUAL RECIPES 2002

Oxmoor House®

©2001 by Oxmoor House, Inc.
Book Division of Southern Progress Corporation
P.O. Box 2463, Birmingham, Alabama 35201

ISBN: 0-8487-2450-X
ISSN: 1091-3645

Printed in the United States of America
First printing 2001

Be sure to check with your health-care provider before making any changes in your diet.

Oxmoor House, Inc.

Editor-in-Chief: Nancy Fitzpatrick Wyatt
Executive Editor: Katherine M. Eakin
Art Director: Cynthia R. Cooper

Cooking Light® Annual Recipes 2002

Editor: Heather Averett
Copy Editor: Jacqueline B. Giovanelli
Copy Assistant: Jane Lorberau Gentry
Editorial Assistant: Suzanne Powell
Designer: Carol Damsky
Publishing Systems Administrator: Rick Tucker
Director, Production and Distribution: Phillip Lee
Books Production Manager: Greg Amason
Production Assistant: Faye Porter Bonner
Contributing Indexer: Mary Ann Laurens

WE'RE HERE FOR YOU!

We at Oxmoor House are dedicated to serving you with reliable information that expands your imagination and enriches your life. We welcome your comments and suggestions. Please write us at:
Oxmoor House, Inc.
Editor, *Cooking Light® Annual Recipes*
2100 Lakeshore Drive
Birmingham, AL 35209

To order additional publications, call 1-205-445-6560.

For more books to enrich your life, visit
oxmoorhouse.com

Cooking Light ®

Editor: Mary Kay Culpepper
Executive Editor: Billy R. Sims
Managing Editor: Hillari Dowdle
Senior Editors: Kelly Caudle (Healthy Living), Jill G. Melton, M.S., R.D. (Food)
Senior Writer: Robin Mather Jenkins
Projects Editor: Mary Simpson Creel, M.S., R.D.
Editorial Coordinator: Carol C. Noe
Associate Editor: Phillip Rhodes
Associate Food Editor: Krista Ackerbloom, M.S., R.D.
Assistant Editor: Melissa Ewey Johnson
Assistant Food Editors: Julie Grimes, Ann Taylor Pittman
Contributing Beauty Editor: Linda Mooney
Senior Editor/Food Development Director: Ellen Templeton Carroll, M.S., R.D.
Art Director: Susan Waldrip Dendy
Assistant Art Director: Maya Metz Logue
Designers: Fernande Bondarenko, J. Shay McNamee
Assistant Designer: Brigette Mayer
Senior Photographer: Becky Luigart-Stayner
Photographer: Randy Mayor
Senior Photo Stylist: Lydia DeGaris-Pursell
Photo Stylists: Melanie J. Clarke, Jan Gautro
Photography Assistant: Karry Hosford
Test Kitchens Director: Vanessa Taylor Johnson
Food Stylist: Kellie Gerber Kelley
Test Kitchens Staff: Sam Brannock, Kathryn Conrad, M. Kathleen Kanen, John Kirkpatrick, Tiffany Vickers, Mike Wilson
Copy Chief: Maria Parker Hopkins
Senior Copy Editor: Ritchey Halphen
Copy Editor: Jennifer Southall
Production Editors: Hazel R. Eddins, Liz Rhoades
Production Assistant: Joanne McCrary
Research Assistant: Dani Leigh Clemmons
Editorial Assistants: Cindy Hatcher, Reinaldo Ramos, Jr.
Correspondence Editor: Michelle Gibson Daniels
Interns: Paige Boyle, Leah Griffin
CookingLight.com
Editor: Maelynn Cheung
Managing Editor: Jason Burnett
Assistant Editor: Jennifer Middleton

Cover: *Chocolate-Walnut Cake (page 88)*

contents

Our Year at Cooking Light.

Dear Reader,

At the risk of sounding forward, I feel as if I know you. For years, I've been an avid reader of *Cooking Light*. At the same time, I've also been a faithful collector of *Cooking Light Annual Recipes*. I've always loved this book series because it offers such a convenient way for me to find my favorite recipes. In fact, *Cooking Light Annual Recipes* is always the first cookbook I reach for whenever I need a fresh menu, a fast solution for dinner, or just want to lose myself in reading about food.

This year, though, I quit being just a reader. I became editor of *Cooking Light* in January 2001. As a result, I've had the singular experience of getting to know the magazine from the inside out. Let me share some of the highlights that have made 2001 special for *Cooking Light*—and this cookbook:

- Our January-February feature on the essential elements of a well-balanced life highlighted nine must-have recipes (beginning on page 14) to tempt your palate all year long.

- A story in March called "The New Light" (page 81) detailed the healthy-food revolution that continues to define how people cook, eat, and think about food.

- The magazine's popular "Cooking Class" series focused this year on global cuisine, offering dishes from Italy to India. At the same time, we continued the successful "Back to the Best," the last-page reprise of our highest-rated dishes.

- "Dinner Tonight" revamped the magazine's "30 Minutes or Less" column with complete menus that come together in about half an hour. And our new "Superfast" feature delivered healthful recipes that are ready in just about 20 minutes—including prep time.

- Staffers at *Cooking Light* joined some of the country's finest Latino journalists in producing *¡Gusto!* magazine, which highlighted recipes, workouts, and feature stories geared to a Hispanic audience. (For a sampling of recipes, see page 103.)

- Our Web site, CookingLight.com, sparked extraordinary reader interaction. One of the brightest spots: Reader exchanges on the bulletin boards resulted in more than 100 new *Cooking Light* supper clubs springing up around the country. We celebrated in a special supper club series in September, complete with menus, recipes, party themes, wine suggestions, and get ahead guides (starting on page 261).

- We wrapped up the year in December with a comprehensive soup-to-nuts holiday cookbook (beginning on page 346) and recipes from the winners of the *Cooking Light*-Hershey's Chocolate Pro-Am contest—a sweet way to celebrate the holidays (page 370).

In short, it's been an exciting year at the magazine, and I think that's reflected in this year's *Cooking Light Annual Recipes*. I'm especially pleased to add this edition to my collection, and I hope you, too, find it useful, informative, entertaining, and utterly indispensable in your pursuit of living well.

Very truly yours,

Mary Kay Culpepper

Editor

january ◆ february

45 Essentials & 9 Gotta-Have Recipes for a Healthy Kitchen

Here are the top ideas, products, ingredients, techniques, tools, and recipes to keep you eating smart—and well.

The dawn of a new year has always seemed so perfect for lofty pronouncements about what's in, what's out, or on its way from one to the other. (Heaven knows we have produced our share of top-10 lists.) This year, however, we decided to take a different approach. Instead of focusing on ephemeral trends and fads, we asked dozens of experts on our staff and around the world about what they consider most essential to a healthy lifestyle. We then distilled their collected wisdom into our top picks—45 of the most indispensable ideas, products, ingredients, techniques, and tools we've ever found—and added nine special recipes that should be essential to any healthy kitchen. Our recipes combine good nutrition with great flavor to help you eat smart and well.

This isn't just about what's hot this month, or even next year. It goes beyond calendars and prognostications to identify things we believe can help you live a better life. So read on, and here's to a happy, healthy new year—for this and all the years to come.

LIGHT PRODUCTS THAT SACRIFICE NO TASTE

Fat-free caramel sauce, virtually indistinguishable from its high-fat cousin. Our favorite is Smucker's caramel topping in a jar.

50% light white cheddar cheese. Less fat—not *no* fat—means better flavor and better texture. We like Cabot the best.

Light coconut milk, Thai and other Asian-influenced cuisine's new best friend.

Low-fat mayonnaise can stand in for regular in most uses, and is just as creamy. We like Hellmann's.

Flavored chicken sausages, precooked links that add a lower-fat gourmet touch to any recipe (who wants to clean the stove after frying up pork sausage?). We like Aidells and Gerhard's brands.

SUPER FOODS THAT ARE SUPER TO EAT

Edamame (eh-dah-MAH-meh), the Japanese name for fresh whole soybeans, is a trendy snack with major nutritional credentials. Look for the pods in the produce section or frozen in Asian markets and health-food stores.

Dried mango, a sweet treat that's loaded with beta carotene and vitamin C.

Flaxseed adds a tasty, crunchy spin to breads, cookies, and muffins; it's high in phytoestrogens and omega-3 fatty acids.

Tofu, the emperor of soy superfoods, has literally hundreds of applications, often as a substitute—in place of sour cream in your favorite dip, for example.

Fruit juice with calcium. Two are better than one, and you need both calcium and vitamin C in a balanced diet. Excellent alternative calcium source for people who don't drink milk.

CONVENIENCE PRODUCTS ALMOST LIKE THE REAL THING

Frozen bread dough saves the trouble of measuring and kneading. Use in place of higher-fat doughs in tarts, rolls, and breads, or as a base for flavored breads like our Olive Bread (recipe on page 16).

Bottled roasted red bell peppers. Save yourself the fuss of roasting and peeling peppers. Another plus: You can find this item year-round.

Ready-to-eat polenta. Its handy tube shape makes it easy to slice and layer into lasagna and casseroles (see our Polenta Lasagna with Wild Mushrooms on page 15).

Pizza crusts, refrigerated and prebaked. Making your own pizza couldn't be easier; just get creative with the toppings (which is half the fun anyway). We like Pillsbury and Boboli brands.

Pesto in a jar. When you don't have time to make it using fresh basil, Alessi's or Crespi & Figli's pesto will stand in nicely.

SPICES NICE TO KEEP IN STOCK

Cinnamon may seem common, but don't limit it to sweets. It's great with savory dishes, too, especially when used with other allies such as chili powder, coriander, and cumin.

Cumin is a must-have for many international-style dishes. If you don't have any now, you'll need to get some very soon.

Coriander. An up-and-coming flavor that's particularly crucial to Middle Eastern dishes.

Curry powder adds ethnic flavor to ordinary dishes. Try sprinkling some into your favorite chicken salad recipe.

Spice blends can be such time-savers. We especially like Spice Islands' new blends—try the Cajun, Jamaican Jerk, and Thai seasonings.

SNACKS TOO GOOD NOT TO KEEP ON HAND

Mini candy bars. Keep pint-size versions on hand, and not just for Halloween.

Edy's Whole Fruit Sorbet. The creamy, rich flavor comes from real fruit, not a juice concentrate as in some other brands.

Terra Chips. With up to 50% less fat than regular potato chips and available in exotic varieties such as Spiced Taro, Jalapeño Sweet Potato, and Yogurt and Green Onion Yukon Gold, these chips are irresistible.

Pretzels, the old-fashioned snack, still rule. We like Snyder's of Hanover and Rold Gold.

Soy nuts. Not as common as potato chips yet, but these nutritious nuggets are gaining popularity. Look for them near gourmet produce or with nuts and snacks in your supermarket or local health-food store.

THROW-TOGETHER MEAL MUSTS

Dried pasta. It's obvious. So is oxygen. You need both.

Garlic. You could cook without it, but why bother?

Parmigiano-Reggiano cheese. It's sharper and more flavorful than domestic Parmesan.

Low-sodium soy sauce. You'll never find a kitchen in China without soy sauce. That's because few sauces go as well with so many foods.

Green onions. These can fill in for leeks, onions, garlic, or chives.

MEDIA WITH A MESSAGE

Food FAQs (FAQs Press, 2000; $12.95). Don't have fish sauce? Find out what to use instead in this handy paperback. (It's soy sauce and anchovy paste, by the way.)

The New Food Lover's Companion (Barron's, 1995; $13.95). It's not a cookbook, but it tells you everything you might want to know about the foods you're cooking with. Knowing makes it more fun.

Tufts University Health & Nutrition Letter. A great source for accurate, cutting-edge nutrition information each month. (Details: 800-274-7581 or www.healthletter.tufts.edu.)

The Food Network keeps us entertained all day. Our favorite shows: *Cooking Live, East Meets West with Ming Tsai,* and *Molto Mario.*

Cook's Illustrated (as a secondary read—after *Cooking Light,* of course). It's a competitor, sure, but we like the detail, quirkiness, and passion of this magazine.

5 BEST FLAVOR-BOOSTING TECHNIQUES

Toasting creates the most intense flavor as well as a great-smelling kitchen. Toss whole spices and nuts into a dry skillet and put them over medium-high heat for about a minute.

Indoor grilling. Invest in a heavy-duty stovetop grill pan for smoky, grilled flavors all year long. We especially like All-Clad, KitchenAid, and Lodge pans.

Roasting, a labor-saver because food cooks unattended, makes everything taste better. (See *Cooking Light Annual Recipes 2001* for more information on this technique.)

Braising. Long, slow cooking is the ideal way to make inexpensive, leaner meats melt-in-your-mouth tender.

Deglazing takes those browned morsels that stick to the bottom of the pan and turns them into a flavorful sauce. Just add wine or stock to the pan, scrape, and stir.

KITCHEN TOOLS YOU'LL REALLY USE

OXO's Good Grips Silicone Turner ($8.99; 800-545-4411 or www.oxo.com) looks like a rubber spatula, but its 600-degree heat resistance means you can cook with it, too. It sports a notch for scraping under jar rims, plus an extension that acts as a spoon rest.

Bash 'N Chop, Graham Kerr's nifty device ($5.99; 800-426-7101), scoops up chopped ingredients so deftly you'll use it constantly. It also has handy inch markings on the edge.

Kitchen shears cut just about anything from canned tomatoes to pizza.

Garlic press, the easiest and most efficient method of mincing garlic for recipes.

Chef's knife. Honestly, you just *have* to have one, and you have to keep it sharp. It'll make almost everything easier and better looking.

❶ Juicy Apple Crisp

(pictured on page 39)

½ cup regular oats
⅓ cup packed brown sugar
1 tablespoon all-purpose flour
1½ tablespoons butter, melted
1 tablespoon thawed apple juice concentrate
½ teaspoon ground cinnamon
2 tablespoons granulated sugar
1 tablespoon cornstarch
½ teaspoon ground cinnamon
⅛ teaspoon salt
8 cups sliced peeled Granny Smith apple (about 2 pounds)
¼ cup thawed apple juice concentrate, undiluted
2 tablespoons water
¾ cup vanilla light ice cream

1. Preheat oven to 425°.
2. Combine first 6 ingredients.
3. Combine granulated sugar, cornstarch, ½ teaspoon cinnamon, and salt. Place apple slices in an 11 x 7-inch baking dish, and sprinkle with cornstarch mixture. Pour ¼ cup juice concentrate and water over apple mixture. Top with oat mixture. Bake at 425° for 25 minutes or until bubbly and golden brown. Let stand 15 minutes. Serve with ice cream. Yield: 6 servings (serving size: 1 cup apple crisp and 2 tablespoons ice cream).

CALORIES 258 (16% from fat); FAT 4.6g (sat 2.4g, mono 1.2g, poly 0.5g); PROTEIN 2.2g; CARB 55.2g; FIBER 3.4g; CHOL 10mg; IRON 1.2mg; SODIUM 101mg; CALC 56mg

---

menu

Sweet-and-Tangy Roasted Pork Tenderloin

Mashed Potatoes with Blue Cheese and Parsley

Tossed salad with Balsamic Vinaigrette (page 15)

---

❷ Sweet-and-Tangy Roasted Pork Tenderloin

(pictured on page 38)

Cumin is one of our essential spices. Here, it's combined with chili powder, vinegar, and brown sugar to create a zesty flavor. The pork can marinate for up to 24 hours, so you can prep it the night before Sunday dinner.

¼ cup packed brown sugar
2 tablespoons cider vinegar
1 tablespoon tomato paste
1½ teaspoons chili powder
1 teaspoon ground cumin
¼ teaspoon black pepper
1 (1-pound) pork tenderloin, trimmed
Cooking spray

1. Combine first 6 ingredients in a shallow dish; add pork, turning to coat. Cover and marinate in refrigerator 1 hour.
2. Preheat oven to 450°.
3. Remove pork from dish, reserving marinade.
4. Place pork on a broiler pan coated with cooking spray. Brush with reserved marinade. Insert a meat thermometer into thickest portion of pork. Bake at 450° for 20 minutes or until thermometer registers 155° (slightly pink). Remove from oven; cover and let stand 5 minutes. Yield: 4 servings (serving size: 3 ounces).

CALORIES 193 (17% from fat); FAT 3.6g (sat 1.1g, mono 1.5g, poly 0.7g); PROTEIN 24.2g; CARB 15.4g; FIBER 0.6g; CHOL 74mg; IRON 2.4mg; SODIUM 74mg; CALC 29mg

❸ Mashed Potatoes with Blue Cheese and Parsley

(pictured on page 38)

2 pounds red potatoes, cut into 2-inch chunks
2 garlic cloves, peeled
1 cup (4 ounces) crumbled blue cheese
½ cup 1% low-fat milk
2 tablespoons chopped fresh parsley
¼ teaspoon freshly ground black pepper

1. Place potato and garlic in a large saucepan; cover with water. Bring to a boil; cook 15 minutes or until tender. Drain. Place potato mixture and remaining ingredients in a large bowl. Mash to desired consistency. Yield: 4 servings (serving size: 1 cup).

CALORIES 284 (28% from fat); FAT 8.7g (sat 5.6g, mono 2.3g, poly 0.3g); PROTEIN 12.2g; CARB 40.5g; FIBER 4.2g; CHOL 22mg; IRON 3.2mg; SODIUM 428mg; CALC 223mg

---

menu

serves 4

Tuscan White Bean Soup with Prosciutto

Citrus-and-romaine salad*

*Combine 4 cups torn romaine lettuce, 1 cup fresh orange sections, and ½ cup sliced red onion in a bowl. Combine ¼ cup red wine vinegar, 2 teaspoons olive oil, and 2 teaspoons honey in a bowl; stir with a whisk. Drizzle over salad; toss gently.

---

❹ Tuscan White Bean Soup with Prosciutto

The canned beans allow you to prepare this soup in just over 30 minutes. While the soup is simmering, assemble a salad and toast some Italian bread. Or try serving this soup with Olive Bread (recipe on page 16).

2 teaspoons olive oil
½ cup chopped prosciutto or ham (about 2 ounces)
1 cup chopped onion
¾ cup chopped celery
¾ cup chopped carrot
1 garlic clove, minced
1 cup water
2 (19-ounce) cans cannellini beans or other white beans, undrained
1 (15.75-ounce) can fat-free, less-sodium chicken broth
2 bay leaves
2 tablespoons minced fresh parsley
2 tablespoons sherry (optional)
¼ teaspoon black pepper

1. Heat oil in a large stockpot over medium heat. Add chopped prosciutto, and sauté 2 minutes. Add chopped onion, celery, carrot, and minced garlic; sauté 2 minutes or until soft.

2. Add water, beans, broth, and bay leaves, and bring soup to a boil. Partially cover, reduce heat, and simmer 20 minutes.

3. Add parsley, sherry, if desired, and pepper; cook 1 minute. Discard bay leaves. Yield: 4 servings (serving size: 1½ cups).

CALORIES 356 (20% from fat); FAT 7.8g (sat 1.3g, mono 3.3g, poly 2.4g); PROTEIN 20.4g; CARB 53.4g; FIBER 7.8g; CHOL 8mg; IRON 5.4mg; SODIUM 817mg; CALC 111mg

⑤

Polenta Lasagna with Wild Mushrooms

We've substituted polenta slices for lasagna noodles in this essential make-ahead meatless entrée. The lasagna can be assembled up to two days in advance, covered, and stored in the refrigerator. If you make it ahead, bake an additional 10 minutes while still covered.

- 1 (½-ounce) package dried porcini mushrooms
- ½ cup hot water
- 1 teaspoon olive oil
- 1 cup chopped onion
- 5 cups chopped portobello mushroom caps (about ¾ pound)
- 4 cups chopped shiitake mushroom caps (about ½ pound)
- 3 cups chopped button mushroom caps (about ½ pound)
- ¼ teaspoon salt
- ¼ cup dry red wine
- 3 tablespoons tomato paste
- 1 teaspoon dried rosemary
- 1 teaspoon dried oregano
- 2 (14.5-ounce) cans no-salt-added diced tomatoes, undrained
- 2 cups (8 ounces) shredded part-skim mozzarella cheese, divided
- 1 teaspoon dried thyme
- 1 (15-ounce) carton part-skim ricotta cheese
- 2 large egg whites, lightly beaten
- 2 (16-ounce) tubes polenta, each cut into 20 (¼-inch-thick) slices
- Cooking spray

1. Combine porcini and hot water in a small bowl. Let stand 30 minutes. Drain in a sieve over a bowl, reserving ¼ cup mushroom liquid. Rinse and drain porcini; finely chop.

2. Preheat oven to 375°.

3. Heat oil in a large nonstick skillet over medium-high heat. Add onion; sauté 2 minutes. Add porcini, portobello, shiitake, and button mushrooms. Sprinkle mushrooms with salt; sauté 8 minutes.

4. Combine reserved mushroom liquid, wine, tomato paste, rosemary, oregano, and tomatoes in a medium saucepan. Bring to a boil; reduce heat, and simmer 5 minutes.

5. Combine 1 cup mozzarella, thyme, ricotta cheese, and egg whites in a bowl.

6. Arrange 15 polenta slices in bottom of a 13 x 9-inch baking dish coated with cooking spray. Top with 2½ cups mushroom mixture, 1 cup tomato sauce, and 1¼ cups ricotta mixture. Repeat procedure with 15 polenta slices, remaining mushroom mixture, 1 cup tomato sauce, and remaining ricotta mixture. Top with remaining polenta slices and tomato sauce. Sprinkle lasagna with 1 cup mozzarella. Cover and bake at 375° for 45 minutes.

7. Uncover and bake an additional 15 minutes. Let stand 5 minutes. Yield: 8 servings.

CALORIES 301 (30% from fat); FAT 10.1g (sat 5.7g, mono 3g, poly 0.7g); PROTEIN 19.4g; CARB 33.5g; FIBER 4.3g; CHOL 33mg; IRON 3.1mg; SODIUM 506mg; CALC 380mg

⑥

Balsamic Vinaigrette Chicken over Gourmet Greens

(pictured on page 37)

If we could have just one salad, this hearty, refreshing main dish would be it. The vinaigrette is so versatile that it doubles as a marinade and a dressing. Serve the salad with Olive Bread (recipe on page 16).

Balsamic Vinaigrette, divided
- 4 (4-ounce) skinless, boneless chicken breast halves
Cooking spray
- 8 cups gourmet salad greens

1. Combine ½ cup Balsamic Vinaigrette and chicken in a shallow dish. Cover and marinate in refrigerator 1 hour.

2. Preheat broiler.

3. Remove chicken from dish; discard marinade. Place chicken on broiler pan coated with cooking spray; cook 6 minutes on each side or until done.

4. Combine remaining Balsamic Vinaigrette and salad greens; toss well. Divide greens mixture evenly among 4 plates; top each serving with 1 chicken breast half. Yield: 4 servings.

(Totals include Balsamic Vinaigrette) CALORIES 221 (23% from fat); FAT 5.6g (sat 0.9g, mono 3g, poly 1g); PROTEIN 28.5g; CARB 14.2g; FIBER 2g; CHOL 66mg; IRON 2.5mg; SODIUM 86mg; CALC 67mg

BALSAMIC VINAIGRETTE:

- ½ cup basil leaves
- ⅓ cup balsamic vinegar or sherry vinegar
- ⅓ cup finely chopped shallots
- ¼ cup water
- 2 tablespoons honey
- 1 tablespoon olive oil
- ¼ teaspoon freshly ground black pepper

1. Place all ingredients in a blender; process until smooth. Yield: 1 cup (serving size: 2 tablespoons).

NOTE: Vinaigrette will keep in refrigerator for up to 1 week.

CALORIES 37 (41% from fat); FAT 1.7g (sat 0.2g, mono 1.3g, poly 0.2g); PROTEIN 0.3g; CARB 5.8g; FIBER 0.1g; CHOL 0mg; IRON 0.2mg; SODIUM 1mg; CALC 7mg

❼ Artichoke-Crab Dip with Cumin-Dusted Pita Chips

We've added nutrition powerhouse tofu to this popular combination of crabmeat and artichoke hearts. You can combine the ingredients for this essential appetizer a day ahead of baking; just keep it covered and in the fridge during that time.

- ½ cup finely chopped soft tofu (about 4 ounces)
- 6 tablespoons (1½ ounces) grated fresh Parmesan cheese, divided
- 1 tablespoon Dijon mustard
- 1 teaspoon dried oregano
- ¼ teaspoon black pepper
- 1 (16-ounce) carton reduced-fat sour cream
- ¾ cup (6 ounces) lump crabmeat, shell pieces removed
- 1 (14-ounce) can artichoke hearts, drained and chopped
- 2 tablespoons dry breadcrumbs
- ½ teaspoon paprika
- Cumin-Dusted Pita Chips

1. Preheat oven to 350°.
2. Combine tofu, ¼ cup cheese, mustard, oregano, pepper, and sour cream in a large bowl. Gently fold in crabmeat and chopped artichokes. Spoon crabmeat mixture into a 1-quart baking dish, and sprinkle with 2 tablespoons cheese, breadcrumbs, and paprika. Bake at 350° for 20 minutes or until browned. Serve dip with Cumin-Dusted Pita Chips. Yield: 16 servings (serving size: ¼ cup dip and 3 chips).

(Totals include Cumin-Dusted Pita Chips) CALORIES 165 (28% from fat); FAT 5.1g (sat 2.7g, mono 1.4g, poly 0.6g); PROTEIN 8.2g; CARB 21.3g; FIBER 0.8g; CHOL 27mg; IRON 1.4mg; SODIUM 360mg; CALC 132mg

CUMIN-DUSTED PITA CHIPS:
Use a variety of pitas—onion, plain, and wheat—and make extras to keep on hand for snacks.

- Cooking spray
- 8 (6-inch) pitas, each cut into 6 wedges
- 1 teaspoon ground cumin
- ½ teaspoon salt

1. Preheat oven to 350°.
2. Coat a baking sheet with cooking spray. Place pita wedges on pan; coat with cooking spray. Sprinkle with cumin and salt. Bake at 350° for 8 minutes or until lightly browned. Yield: 4 dozen chips (serving size: 3 chips).

NOTE: Chips can be made ahead and stored in an airtight container for up to 4 days.

CALORIES 84 (5% from fat); FAT 0.5g (sat 0.1g, mono 0.1g, poly 0.2g); PROTEIN 2.8g; CARB 16.8g; FIBER 0.7g; CHOL 0mg; IRON 0.9mg; SODIUM 234mg; CALC 27mg

❽ Basmati Pilaf with Almonds and Cilantro

What inevitably comes to mind when you think of side dishes? Rice, no doubt. There are a lot of varieties out there, but we like basmati—known as "popcorn rice" because of its unique flavor and aroma—the best. It's the perfect foundation for the bold flavors of cilantro and green onions.

- 2 teaspoons olive oil
- ⅓ cup sliced almonds
- 1 cup uncooked basmati rice
- 1 garlic clove, minced
- ¾ cup water
- 1 (10½-ounce) can beef broth
- ¼ cup chopped fresh cilantro
- ¼ cup chopped green onions
- ¼ teaspoon salt
- ¼ teaspoon black pepper

1. Heat oil in a medium saucepan over medium heat. Add almonds, and sauté 2 minutes or until lightly browned. Add rice and garlic, and sauté 2 minutes. Stir in water and broth, and bring to a boil. Cover, reduce heat, and simmer 15 minutes or until liquid is absorbed. Remove from heat; stir in cilantro and remaining ingredients. Yield: 4 servings (serving size: 1 cup).

CALORIES 258 (23% from fat); FAT 6.7g (sat 0.8g, mono 4.4g, poly 1.1g); PROTEIN 8.4g; CARB 40.7g; FIBER 1.8g; CHOL 0mg; IRON 3mg; SODIUM 540mg; CALC 51mg

❾ Olive Bread

Here, we've filled thawed bread dough with a flavorful olive paste. The resulting savory essential bread is perfect with soup or a salad.

- 1 (1-pound) loaf frozen white bread dough
- ½ cup pitted kalamata olives
- 3 tablespoons capers
- 3 tablespoons fresh lemon juice
- 1 teaspoon dried thyme
- 4 canned anchovy fillets
- 2 garlic cloves, peeled
- Cooking spray

1. Thaw dough in refrigerator 12 hours.
2. Combine olives and next 5 ingredients in a food processor; process until well blended.
3. Roll dough into a 12 x 8-inch rectangle on a lightly floured surface. Spread olive mixture onto dough, leaving a ½-inch border. Starting from short end, roll up jelly-roll fashion; pinch seam and ends to seal. Place roll, seam side down, in an 8 x 4-inch loaf pan coated with cooking spray. Cover and let rise in a warm place (85°), free from drafts, 2½ hours or until doubled in size. (Press two fingers into dough. If indentation remains, dough has risen enough.)
4. Preheat oven to 375°.
5. Uncover dough and bake at 375° for 25 minutes or until lightly browned. Cool in pan 10 minutes on a wire rack; remove from pan. Cool completely on wire rack. Yield: 1 loaf, 12 slices (serving size: 1 slice).

CALORIES 163 (17% from fat); FAT 3g (sat 0.5g, mono 1g, poly 1.3g); PROTEIN 5.7g; CARB 28.4g; FIBER 1.1g; CHOL 1mg; IRON 1.7mg; SODIUM 423mg; CALC 46mg

Chicken Most Tender

We help one couple rescue a true love—and revive a succulent memory.

Lynn and Barry Brand used to rendezvous at a restaurant known for its Chicken Français. But when the eatery closed, this couple thought that it was all but a memory. Lynn tracked down the recipe, hoping to recreate the food at home. One glance at the ingredients and she knew she'd fallen into a destructive relationship. Loaded with fat and cholesterol, it was far from heart-healthy.

By replacing the whole eggs with egg substitute and cutting all but 2 tablespoons of butter, we trimmed 11.5 grams of fat and 96 calories from each serving.

Chicken Français

- ¾ cup egg substitute
- ¼ cup (1 ounce) grated fresh Parmesan cheese
- ¼ cup chopped fresh parsley
- ¼ cup dry white wine
- 2 tablespoons fresh lemon juice
- ¼ teaspoon salt
- ⅛ teaspoon hot pepper sauce
- 3 garlic cloves, minced
- 8 (4-ounce) skinless, boneless chicken breast halves
- ¼ cup all-purpose flour
- 1 tablespoon olive oil, divided
- Cooking spray
- 2 tablespoons butter
- ¼ cup dry white wine
- 3 tablespoons fresh lemon juice

1. Combine first 8 ingredients in a shallow dish.
2. Place each chicken breast half between 2 sheets of plastic wrap, and pound to ¼-inch thickness using a meat mallet or rolling pin. Dredge chicken in flour, and dip in egg substitute mixture.
3. Heat 1½ teaspoons oil in a large nonstick skillet coated with cooking spray over medium heat. Add 4 chicken breast halves; cook 4 minutes on each side or until done. Remove chicken from pan, and keep warm. Wipe drippings from pan with a paper towel. Repeat procedure with 1½ teaspoons oil and remaining chicken.
4. Melt butter in pan; add ¼ cup wine and 3 tablespoons juice. Bring to a boil; cook 10 seconds. Serve immediately over chicken. Yield: 8 servings (serving size: 1 chicken breast half and 2 teaspoons sauce).

CALORIES 211 (30% from fat); FAT 7g (sat 3g, mono 2.7g, poly 0.7g); PROTEIN 30.3g; CARB 5g; FIBER 0.2g; CHOL 76mg; IRON 1.6mg; SODIUM 269mg; CALC 70mg

BEFORE	AFTER
SERVING SIZE	
1 chicken breast half with sauce	
CALORIES PER SERVING	
307	211
FAT	
18.5g	7g
PERCENT OF TOTAL CALORIES	
54%	30%
CHOLESTEROL	
241mg	76mg
SODIUM	
380mg	269mg

Chiles Rellenos Casserole

Fluffy, yet dense; flavorful, yet mild; complex, yet uncomplicated.

This Chiles Rellenos Casserole, which first appeared in our January-February 1995 issue, is a study in contradictions. Somehow, though, it works on every level—which is why it's on our list of all-time favorites.

Chiles Rellenos Casserole

- ½ pound ground turkey
- 1 cup chopped onion
- 1¾ teaspoons ground cumin
- 1½ teaspoons dried oregano
- ½ teaspoon garlic powder
- ¼ teaspoon salt
- ¼ teaspoon black pepper
- 1 (16-ounce) can fat-free refried beans
- 2 (4-ounce) cans whole green chiles, drained and cut lengthwise into quarters
- 1 cup (4 ounces) preshredded Colby-Jack cheese, divided
- 1 cup frozen whole-kernel corn, thawed and drained
- ⅓ cup all-purpose flour
- ¼ teaspoon salt
- 1⅓ cups fat-free milk
- ⅛ teaspoon hot sauce
- 2 large eggs, lightly beaten
- 2 large egg whites, lightly beaten
- Red onion slices (optional)
- Chopped cilantro (optional)

1. Preheat oven to 350°.
2. Cook turkey and chopped onion in a nonstick skillet over medium-high heat until browned, stirring to crumble. Remove from heat; add cumin and next 5 ingredients. Stir well; set aside.
3. Arrange half of green chiles in an 11 x 7-inch baking dish, and top with ½ cup cheese. Spoon mounds of turkey mixture onto cheese, and spread gently, leaving a ¼-inch border around edge of dish. Top with corn. Arrange remaining green chiles over corn; top with ½ cup cheese.
4. Combine flour and salt in a bowl; gradually add milk, hot sauce, eggs, and egg whites, stirring with a whisk until blended. Pour over casserole. Bake at 350° for 1 hour and 5 minutes or until set; let stand 5 minutes. Garnish with onion slices and cilantro, if desired. Yield: 6 servings.
NOTE: Two (4.5-ounce) cans chopped green chiles can be substituted for whole chiles, if desired.

CALORIES 335 (24% from fat); FAT 9g (sat 4.5g, mono 2.7g, poly 1.6g); PROTEIN 26.9g; CARB 37.7g; FIBER 5.5g; CHOL 112mg; IRON 3.8mg; SODIUM 825mg; CALC 280mg

That Resolutionary Spirit

Broaden your culinary horizons with these quick, easy recipes that'll start your New Year right.

Familiarity breeds contentment for only so long. The best way to keep favorite dishes fresh is to introduce new recipes into your recipe repertoire.

Chicken Mole with Green Beans

PREPARATION TIME: 5 MINUTES
COOKING TIME: 18 MINUTES

Cooking two things simultaneously will get dinner on the table in half the time. While the chicken thighs cook in the microwave, prepare the mole sauce on the stovetop. And though chocolate and cinnamon might seem odd in a savory dish, it's a traditional combination in Mexican cooking.

8   chicken thighs (about 2 pounds), skinned
1   pound green beans, trimmed
Cooking spray
2   teaspoons olive oil
1   cup finely chopped onion
1   tablespoon chili powder
2½ teaspoons bottled minced garlic
2   teaspoons unsweetened cocoa
2   teaspoons ground cinnamon
2   teaspoons dried thyme
½   teaspoon sugar
¼   teaspoon salt
¾   cup fat-free, less-sodium chicken broth

1. Heat a large nonstick skillet over medium-high heat. Add chicken; cook 3 minutes on each side. Place chicken and beans in an 11 x 7-inch baking dish coated with cooking spray, and cover with plastic wrap. Microwave at HIGH 12 minutes or until chicken is done, turning after 6 minutes.
2. While chicken mixture cooks, heat oil in skillet over medium-high heat. Add onion and next 7 ingredients; cook 3 minutes or until onion is soft, stirring frequently. Add broth, and cook until thick (about 2 minutes). Spoon sauce over chicken mixture. Yield: 4 servings (serving size: 2 thighs and about 1 cup beans).

CALORIES 367 (29% from fat); FAT 11.8g (sat 2.8g, mono 4.5g, poly 2.7g); PROTEIN 48.5g; CARB 16.5g; FIBER 4.3g; CHOL 188mg; IRON 5.3mg; SODIUM 460mg; CALC 114mg

Superfast Salisbury Steak

(pictured on page 40)

PREPARATION TIME: 5 MINUTES
COOKING TIME: 26 MINUTES

We used a blend of two kinds of ground meats for the patties. The turkey breast brings the total fat down while the ground round adds moistness and flavor. Serve with roasted vegetables, such as potatoes and carrots.

¾   pound ground turkey breast
¾   pound ground round
⅓   cup dry breadcrumbs
2   large egg whites
Cooking spray
¾   cup water
3   tablespoons tomato paste
2   tablespoons Madeira wine or dry sherry
1½ teaspoons Worcestershire sauce
¼   teaspoon freshly ground black pepper
1   (10½-ounce) can condensed French onion soup (such as Campbell's)

1. Combine first 4 ingredients. Divide meat mixture into 6 equal portions, shaping each into a ½-inch-thick patty. Heat a large nonstick skillet coated with cooking spray over medium-high heat. Add patties; cook 6 minutes or until browned, turning after 3 minutes. Remove patties from pan; keep warm. Stir in water and remaining 5 ingredients. Bring to a boil; add patties. Cover, reduce heat, and simmer 10 minutes. Uncover and cook until wine mixture is reduced to ¾ cup (about 10 minutes). Yield: 6 servings (serving size: 1 patty and 2 tablespoons sauce).

CALORIES 210 (25% from fat); FAT 5.9g (sat 2g, mono 1.9g, poly 0.8g); PROTEIN 27.4g; CARB 10g; FIBER 0.9g; CHOL 64mg; IRON 2.4mg; SODIUM 621mg; CALC 38mg

menu

serves 4

Fennel-Crusted Pork Tenderloin

Black-eyed pea salad*

*Combine 2 cups chopped seeded tomato, ¼ cup chopped onion, ½ cup chopped green bell pepper, ¼ cup chopped fresh cilantro, 1 tablespoon chopped seeded jalapeño pepper, and 1 (15-ounce) can black-eyed peas, drained, in a medium bowl. Cover and chill.

Fennel-Crusted Pork Tenderloin

PREPARATION TIME: 15 MINUTES
COOKING TIME: 10 MINUTES

Butterflying a pork tenderloin shortens the cooking time and allows the spice mixture to coat more surface area.

2   tablespoons fennel seeds
1   tablespoon coriander seeds
6   tablespoons fat-free, less-sodium chicken broth, divided
1   tablespoon Worcestershire sauce
1   teaspoon bottled minced garlic
¼   teaspoon salt
⅛   teaspoon freshly ground black pepper
1   (1-pound) pork tenderloin, trimmed
2   teaspoons olive oil

1. Place fennel and coriander in a spice or coffee grinder; process until coarsely ground. Place spice mixture in a blender or food processor. Add 2 tablespoons broth, Worcestershire sauce, garlic, salt, and pepper; process until well blended.

2. Slice pork tenderloin horizontally into 2 equal pieces. Slice each piece of pork lengthwise, cutting to, but not through, other side; open flat. Rub spice mixture over pork.

3. Heat oil in a large nonstick skillet over medium heat. Add pork; cook 5 minutes on each side or until done. Remove pork from pan; keep warm. Add ¼ cup broth to pan, and cook until liquid almost evaporates, scraping pan to loosen browned bits. Pour over pork. Yield: 4 servings (serving size: 3 ounces pork with pan juices).

CALORIES 168 (30% from fat); FAT 5.7g (sat 1.3g, mono 3.4g, poly 0.6g); PROTEIN 24.9g; CARB 3.5g; FIBER 0.9g; CHOL 74mg; IRON 2.3mg; SODIUM 288mg; CALC 58mg

Blackened Catfish

PREPARATION TIME: 8 MINUTES
COOKING TIME: 10 MINUTES

When you find a spice mixture you like, double or triple the recipe, and save the extra to use with other seafood (such as shrimp), chicken, pork, or even potatoes.

　2　tablespoons paprika
　1　tablespoon dried oregano
　½　teaspoon salt
　½　teaspoon freshly ground black pepper
　¼　teaspoon ground red pepper
　4　(6-ounce) farm-raised catfish fillets
　2　teaspoons olive oil

1. Combine first 5 ingredients in a small bowl. Sprinkle both sides of fillets with paprika mixture.

2. Heat oil in a large cast-iron skillet over high heat. Add fillets; cook 4 minutes on each side or until fish flakes easily when tested with a fork. Yield: 4 servings.

CALORIES 232 (39% from fat); FAT 10.1g (sat 2.1g, mono 4.5g, poly 2.3g); PROTEIN 31.6g; CARB 2.9g; FIBER 1g; CHOL 99mg; IRON 3.1mg; SODIUM 402mg; CALC 93mg

Hoisin Halibut

PREPARATION TIME: 10 MINUTES
COOKING TIME: 12 MINUTES

Update your pantry with a few Asian ingredients such as rice sticks, hoisin sauce, rice vinegar, and chile paste with garlic. They'll come in handy in many other dishes, too.

　8　ounces uncooked rice sticks (rice-flour noodles) or ¾ pound vermicelli
　¼　cup hoisin sauce, divided
　1　cup sliced green onions
　½　cup fat-free, less-sodium chicken broth
　3　tablespoons rice vinegar
　3　tablespoons low-sodium soy sauce
　1　tablespoon vegetable oil
　1　tablespoon grated peeled fresh ginger
　1　teaspoon chile paste with garlic
　⅛　teaspoon freshly ground black pepper
　8　(6-ounce) halibut steaks (about 1 inch thick)
Cooking spray

1. Preheat broiler.

2. Cook noodles according to package directions, omitting salt and fat. Combine noodles, 2 tablespoons hoisin sauce, and next 8 ingredients in a large bowl, and keep warm.

3. Rub fish with 2 tablespoons hoisin sauce. Place fish on a broiler pan coated with cooking spray; broil 4 minutes on each side or until fish flakes easily when tested with a fork. Serve over noodles. Yield: 8 servings (serving size: 1 halibut steak and ¾ cup noodles).

CALORIES 323 (17% from fat); FAT 6.3g (sat 0.9g, mono 1.9g, poly 2.3g); PROTEIN 37.5g; CARB 27.6g; FIBER 0.5g; CHOL 53mg; IRON 1.9mg; SODIUM 455mg; CALC 109mg

Chicken with Chipotle-Tomato Sauce and Ziti

PREPARATION TIME: 12 MINUTES
COOKING TIME: 16 MINUTES

Canned chipotle chiles in adobo sauce give foods a hot, smoky flavor.

　8　ounces uncooked ziti (short tube-shaped pasta)
　2　teaspoons olive oil
　¾　pound skinless, boneless chicken breast, cut into bite-size pieces
　2　cups chopped onion
　2　teaspoons bottled minced garlic
　2　cups green bell pepper strips
　1　(8-ounce) package presliced mushrooms
　1　cup canned crushed tomatoes, undrained
　½　cup fat-free, less-sodium chicken broth
　½　teaspoon salt
　1　canned chipotle chile in adobo sauce, minced (about 1 tablespoon)

1. Cook pasta according to package directions, omitting salt and fat.

2. While pasta cooks, heat oil in a large nonstick skillet over medium-high heat. Add chicken; cook 3 minutes or until lightly browned. Add onion and garlic; cook 2 minutes. Add bell pepper and mushrooms; cook 5 minutes or until tender. Stir in remaining 4 ingredients; cook 6 minutes or until thoroughly heated. Serve over pasta. Yield: 4 servings (serving size: 1 cup chicken in chipotle sauce and 1 cup pasta).

CALORIES 407 (11% from fat); FAT 5.1g (sat 0.8g, mono 2.1g, poly 1.2g); PROTEIN 30.7g; CARB 59.4g; FIBER 4.8g; CHOL 49mg; IRON 4.7mg; SODIUM 533mg; CALC 71mg

Curried Shrimp in Peanut Sauce

PREPARATION TIME: 13 MINUTES
COOKING TIME: 12 MINUTES

    8   ounces uncooked fettuccine
   ⅔   cup fat-free, less-sodium chicken
        broth
   ½   cup creamy peanut butter
    2   tablespoons balsamic vinegar
   ½   teaspoon salt
   ⅛   teaspoon black pepper
    1   (½-inch) piece peeled fresh
        ginger, thinly sliced
    1   tablespoon olive oil
   1½ cups sliced green onions
    2   teaspoons curry powder
   1½ teaspoons bottled minced garlic
   1½ pounds large shrimp, peeled and
        deveined
    2   tablespoons chopped fresh cilantro

1. Cook pasta according to package directions, omitting salt and fat.
2. While pasta cooks, place broth and next 5 ingredients in a blender or food processor, and process until smooth.
3. Heat oil in a large nonstick skillet over medium heat. Add onions, curry, and garlic; sauté 3 minutes. Add shrimp; cook 6 minutes or until shrimp are done. Stir in peanut sauce; cook 1 minute or until thoroughly heated. Serve over pasta, and sprinkle with cilantro. Yield: 4 servings (serving size: 1 cup shrimp in peanut sauce, 1 cup pasta, and 1½ teaspoons cilantro).

CALORIES 385 (29% from fat); FAT 12.5g (sat 2g, mono 5.5g, poly 3.6g); PROTEIN 33.5g; CARB 35g; FIBER 2.8g; CHOL 172mg; IRON 5.2mg; SODIUM 504mg; CALC 98mg

cooking light profile

The Family Way

To anyone who steps inside their house in St. Paul, Minnesota, it's apparent that doing things together is what Ali Selim and his family of five are all about—whether it be cross-country skiing, hiking, biking, or cooking.

Thai Fish-and-Noodle Soup

The Selims make this family favorite with salmon, but halibut also works well.

   ¼   pound uncooked pad thai noodles
        (wide rice stick noodles)
    4   cups water
    3   tablespoons fresh lime juice
    2   tablespoons finely chopped
        seeded jalapeño pepper
    2   tablespoons thinly sliced peeled
        lemon grass
    2   tablespoons fish sauce
    1   tablespoon minced peeled fresh
        ginger
   ½   teaspoon salt
    6   cups thinly sliced shiitake
        mushroom caps (about 1 pound
        mushrooms)
    2   cups julienne-cut red bell pepper
    1   cup (1-inch) sliced asparagus
    1   cup thinly sliced carrot
    4   (4-ounce) skinned halibut fillets or
        other firm white fish fillets
   ⅛   teaspoon salt
  Dash of black pepper
   10 cups coarsely chopped spinach
        (about 8 ounces)
   1½ cups thinly sliced green onions
   ¼   cup chopped fresh cilantro

1. Preheat broiler.
2. Place noodles in a bowl; cover with hot water. Let stand 3 minutes; drain.
3. Combine 4 cups water and next 6 ingredients in a Dutch oven; bring to a boil. Add noodles, mushrooms, bell pepper, asparagus, and carrot, and bring mixture to a boil. Reduce heat, and simmer 7 minutes.
4. Sprinkle fillets with ⅛ teaspoon salt and black pepper. Place fillets on a broiler pan; cook 6 minutes or until fish flakes easily when tested with a fork.
5. Stir spinach, onions, and cilantro into noodle mixture. Return to a boil; cook 1 minute or until spinach wilts. Ladle soup into serving bowls; top each serving with a fillet. Yield: 4 servings (serving size: 2 cups soup and 3 ounces fish).

CALORIES 338 (11% from fat); FAT 4g (sat 0.6g, mono 0.8g, poly 1.6g); PROTEIN 32.7g; CARB 46.8g; FIBER 10.5g; CHOL 53mg; IRON 8.9mg; SODIUM 1,261mg; CALC 264mg

reader recipes

Fit for a King

A freewheeling father serves up a vegetable-rice soup that's a crowning achievement.

Chip Reeves of Midland, Michigan, decided to put together something new for dinner. On hand to sample his creation—a tasty vegetable-and-rice soup—were his two sons, known at times to be noble-minded eaters with eclectic tastes.

Chip immediately took note when five-year-old Ken Edward asked for seconds—and then for thirds. The moral of the story: "This is a great way to get kids to eat their vegetables."

Chip crowned the dish with the name "King Edward Soup," after his son, and has since made it many times for the residents of his domestic kingdom. Variations on the theme include using less water or more rice to create a risotto, or adding Creole seasoning upon serving.

King Edward Soup

    2   teaspoons olive oil
    2   cups sliced mushrooms
   1½ cups chopped onion
    2   garlic cloves, minced
   1½ cups finely chopped yellow squash
   1½ cups finely chopped zucchini
   2½ cups water
    2   cups cooked long-grain rice
    1   tablespoon fresh basil
    6   plum tomatoes, halved and sliced
        (about ¾ pound)
    2   (10½-ounce) cans beef consommé

1. Heat oil in a Dutch oven over medium-high heat. Add mushrooms, onion, and garlic; sauté 6 minutes or until tender. Add squash and zucchini; sauté 5 minutes. Add water and remaining ingredients; bring to a boil. Reduce heat, and simmer 20 minutes or until vegetables are tender. Yield: 6 servings (serving size: 1½ cups).

CALORIES 158 (11% from fat); FAT 2g (sat 0.3g, mono 1.2g, poly 0.3g); PROTEIN 8g; CARB 28.1g; FIBER 2.8g; CHOL 0mg; IRON 2mg; SODIUM 525mg; CALC 44mg

Roasted Chicken with Wild Rice Soup

"I came up with this recipe one night when company showed up unexpectedly. It has become one of my most requested recipes by both family and friends. It's a thick soup, with a wonderfully hearty and nutty taste. It has lots of stuff in it, too, so every bite is a new flavor. It's also very easy to prepare, and it tastes even better the next day."

—Lynn McPherson, Hillsboro, Oregon

1   (6-ounce) box long-grain and wild rice mix (such as Uncle Ben's)
1   tablespoon olive oil
1½ cups chopped red onion
1   cup chopped celery
1   cup chopped carrot
2   garlic cloves, chopped
1   (8-ounce) package mushrooms, halved
¼   cup all-purpose flour
½   teaspoon dried tarragon
¼   teaspoon dried thyme
2   cups water
2   tablespoons dry sherry
2   (15.75-ounce) cans fat-free, less-sodium chicken broth
1   (12-ounce) can fat-free evaporated milk
3   cups shredded roasted skinless chicken

1. Prepare rice according to package directions; set aside.
2. Heat oil in a large Dutch oven over medium-high heat. Add chopped onion and next 4 ingredients, and sauté 6 minutes or until onion is tender. Lightly spoon flour into a dry measuring cup, and level with a knife. Stir flour, tarragon, and thyme into onion mixture, and cook 1 minute, stirring frequently. Add 2 cups water, sherry, broth, and evaporated milk; bring mixture to a boil. Reduce heat, and simmer 20 minutes or until slightly thick. Stir in cooked rice and chicken; cook 10 minutes or until thoroughly heated. Yield: 8 servings (serving size: 1½ cups).

CALORIES 246 (22% from fat); FAT 6g (sat 1.9g, mono 2.6g, poly 0.9g); PROTEIN 16.4g; CARB 31.2g; FIBER 2.1g; CHOL 43mg; IRON 2.2mg; SODIUM 690mg; CALC 173mg

Spicy Chicken-and-Pumpkin Stew

"I love to create recipes with unique ingredient combinations, things you wouldn't necessarily expect to go together. I made this for the first time this past Thanksgiving by combining a couple of recipes. My guests expected a pumpkin pie and were surprised to find that the pumpkin was part of the main course instead. The dish got rave reviews."

—Lydia Butler, Ottawa, Canada

1½ pounds skinless, boneless chicken breast, cut into bite-size pieces
½   teaspoon salt
¼   teaspoon black pepper
1   tablespoon olive oil, divided
4   cups sliced onion
1   cup chopped red bell pepper
1   tablespoon minced peeled fresh ginger
1   tablespoon minced seeded jalapeño pepper
2   teaspoons curry powder
4   garlic cloves, minced
6   cups cubed peeled fresh pumpkin or other winter squash (such as acorn)
1   cup water
1   (14-ounce) can light coconut milk
¼   cup chopped cilantro
5   cups hot cooked long-grain rice

1. Sprinkle chicken with salt and black pepper. Heat 1 teaspoon oil in a Dutch oven over medium heat. Add half of chicken, and sauté 8 minutes or until browned. Remove chicken from pan. Repeat procedure with 1 teaspoon oil and remaining chicken; set aside.
2. Heat 1 teaspoon oil in pan over medium-high heat. Add onion and next 5 ingredients; sauté 2 minutes. Stir in pumpkin, water, and coconut milk; bring to a boil. Reduce heat, and simmer 30 minutes or until pumpkin is tender. Return chicken to pan; cook 10 minutes or until heated. Stir in cilantro; serve over rice. Yield: 10 servings (serving size: 1 cup stew and ½ cup rice).

CALORIES 267 (16% from fat); FAT 4.7g (sat 2.4g, mono 1.4g, poly 0.4g); PROTEIN 19.3g; CARB 36.4g; FIBER 2.6g; CHOL 39mg; IRON 2.8mg; SODIUM 181mg; CALC 50mg

Supa Ya N Dizi
Curried Chicken-and-Banana Stew

"The original version of this recipe wasn't healthy. It called for frying a whole chicken, then adding more oil, but I was intrigued by the combination of bananas, curry, and chicken. So I came up with this low-fat version, which goes great with sourdough bread. The trick is to use very firm, almost green bananas, and not to overcook them."

—Rick Glisson, Schertz, Texas

2   teaspoons olive oil, divided
2   pounds skinless, boneless chicken breast, cut into bite-size pieces
2   cups chopped celery
1   cup chopped red onion
5   garlic cloves, minced
2   tablespoons curry powder
1   teaspoon black pepper
¾   to 1 teaspoon ground red pepper
¼   teaspoon salt
1   cup water
½   cup shredded sweetened coconut
2   (15.75-ounce) cans fat-free, less-sodium chicken broth
2   (10-ounce) cans diced tomatoes with green chiles, undrained (such as Rotel)
2   cups sliced banana (about 2 large)

1. Heat 1 teaspoon oil in a Dutch oven over medium-high heat. Add chicken; stir-fry 12 minutes or until golden. Remove chicken from pan; set aside.
2. Heat 1 teaspoon oil in pan. Add celery, onion, and garlic; sauté 3 minutes or until tender. Stir in curry powder, peppers, and salt; cook 1 minute. Stir in water, coconut, broth, and tomatoes. Return chicken to pan; bring to a boil. Cover, reduce heat, and simmer 30 minutes. Stir in banana; simmer 10 minutes or until thoroughly heated. Yield: 12 servings (serving size: 1 cup).

CALORIES 165 (19% from fat); FAT 3.4g (sat 1.6g, mono 0.9g, poly 0.4g); PROTEIN 19.4g; CARB 12.9g; FIBER 2.3g; CHOL 44mg; IRON 1.6mg; SODIUM 485mg; CALC 45mg

Chicken Noodle Soup

"My grandmother passed this recipe down to my mom, who created a healthier version she makes for me whenever I'm sick—it's the ultimate comfort food. Nothing cures colds better than my mother's homemade chicken noodle soup. The recipe was difficult for me to write down, since Mom never measures her ingredients, but I watched carefully the last time she made it."

—Amanda Janesick,
Huntington Beach, California

      8 cups water
      4 (6-ounce) skinless chicken breast
         halves
      1 cup chopped onion
      1 cup chopped celery
      1 cup chopped carrot
    ¾ cup chopped parsnip
      1 tablespoon chicken-flavored
         bouillon granules
    ¼ teaspoon salt
    ¼ teaspoon black pepper
      1 (15.75-ounce) can fat-free,
         less-sodium chicken broth
      5 cups cooked egg noodles (about 8
         ounces uncooked)

1. Combine water and chicken in a Dutch oven, and bring to a boil. Reduce heat, and simmer 15 minutes or until chicken is done. Remove chicken from pan with a slotted spoon, reserving liquid in pan. Remove chicken from bones; shred with 2 forks to measure 2½ cups meat. Discard bones.
2. Add chicken, onion, and next 7 ingredients to pan; bring to a boil. Reduce heat, and simmer 20 minutes or until vegetables are tender. Stir in noodles; cook over medium heat until thoroughly heated. Yield: 8 servings (serving size: 1¾ cups).

CALORIES 206 (10% from fat); FAT 2.4g (sat 0.6g, mono 0.7g, poly 0.7g); PROTEIN 18.7g; CARB 27g; FIBER 2.1g; CHOL 60mg; IRON 2mg; SODIUM 563mg; CALC 36mg

Tortilla Soup

"I created this soup after enjoying a similar dish."

—Jenny Thompson, Newton, Iowa

      2 cups tomato sauce
    1½ cups water
      1 cup bottled salsa
      1 cup frozen whole-kernel corn
      1 teaspoon dried oregano
      1 teaspoon dried basil
      1 teaspoon instant minced garlic
      1 (15.75-ounce) can fat-free,
         less-sodium chicken broth
      1 (15-ounce) can kidney beans,
         rinsed and drained
      1 cup (4 ounces) shredded
         reduced-fat sharp cheddar cheese
    30 fat-free baked tortilla chips

1. Combine first 9 ingredients in a large saucepan. Bring to a boil; cover, reduce heat, and simmer 12 minutes. Serve with cheese and tortilla chips. Yield: 6 servings (serving size: 1⅓ cups soup, about 3 tablespoons cheese, and 5 tortilla chips).

CALORIES 248 (17% from fat); FAT 4.7g (sat 2.2g, mono 1.1g, poly 0.4g); PROTEIN 14.7g; CARB 39.8g; FIBER 5.5g; CHOL 13mg; IRON 3.1mg; SODIUM 1,158mg; CALC 238mg

Focaccia Garlic Bread

"I serve this garlic bread as an appetizer at parties and for dinner at home. In both cases, it always disappears fast."

—Melissa Kiser, Fort Wayne, Indiana

      1 (1-pound) Italian cheese-flavored
         pizza crust (such as Boboli)
         Cooking spray
      1 tablespoon olive oil
      3 tablespoons fresh or 1 tablespoon
         dried basil
      3 tablespoons fresh or 1 tablespoon
         dried oregano
      1 tablespoon minced garlic
    ¼ cup (1 ounce) grated fresh
         Parmesan cheese

1. Preheat oven to 400°.
2. Place crust on a baking sheet coated with cooking spray; brush with olive oil.

Sprinkle with basil and oregano. Top with garlic and Parmesan. Bake at 400° for 12 minutes or until browned. Yield: 12 servings (serving size: 1 wedge).

CALORIES 131 (27% from fat); FAT 3.9g (sat 1.2g, mono 1g, poly 0.1g); PROTEIN 5.7g; CARB 17.5g; FIBER 0.8g; CHOL 5mg; IRON 1.3mg; SODIUM 237mg; CALC 82mg

Low-Fat Albóndigas Soup

"This recipe came from my mother-in-law a long time ago, and I have done things to make it healthier, like substituting ground turkey for ground beef. I'm also a big fan of cilantro, which adds a lot to the great flavor of this soup."

—Kathi Galloway, Santa Maria, California

    ¼ cup cooked long-grain rice
      2 tablespoons chopped fresh parsley
      1 tablespoon chopped fresh cilantro
      1 teaspoon dried oregano
    ¼ teaspoon black pepper
      8 ounces ground turkey
      3 garlic cloves, minced
      1 large egg white
      1 teaspoon vegetable oil
    ½ cup chopped onion
      1 cup chopped seeded peeled
         tomato
      1 cup water
      2 (15.75-ounce) cans fat-free,
         less-sodium chicken broth
      2 cups sliced celery
      2 cups sliced carrot
      1 cup frozen whole-kernel corn,
         thawed and drained
    ¼ teaspoon ground cumin (optional)
      3 tablespoons chopped fresh
         cilantro

1. Combine first 8 ingredients in a bowl, and shape mixture into 24 (¾-inch) meatballs.
2. Heat oil in a Dutch oven over medium-high heat. Add onion; sauté 4 minutes or until tender. Stir in tomato, water, and broth; bring to a boil. Add celery, carrot, corn, and, if desired, cumin. Return to a boil; add meatballs. Cover, reduce heat, and simmer 30 minutes or until vegetables are tender and meatballs are cooked. Stir in 3

tablespoons cilantro. Yield: 9 servings (serving size: 1 cup).

CALORIES 97 (28% from fat); FAT 3g (sat 0.9g, mono 1.1g, poly 1g); PROTEIN 7g; CARB 11g; FIBER 2.2g; CHOL 21mg; IRON 1mg; SODIUM 169mg; CALC 34mg

Chicken-and-Spinach Pasta with Sun-Dried Tomatoes

"When I created this recipe, I wanted a dish that would not only be healthy but also quick to prepare after working all day."

—Cara Maglione, Smyrna, Georgia

¼ cup oil-packed sun-dried tomato halves
2½ cups hot cooked farfalle (about 2 cups uncooked bow tie pasta)
1 cup cubed roasted skinless, boneless chicken breast (about 1 breast)
½ cup fat-free Caesar dressing
¼ cup (1 ounce) grated fresh Parmesan cheese
1 (10-ounce) package frozen leaf spinach, thawed, drained, and squeezed dry

1. Drain tomatoes in a colander over a bowl, reserving 1 tablespoon oil. Combine tomatoes, oil, pasta, and remaining ingredients in a bowl; toss well. Microwave at HIGH 2 minutes or until warm. Yield: 4 servings (serving size: 1½ cups).
NOTE: One 10-ounce bag of fresh spinach may be substituted for frozen spinach, if desired.

CALORIES 240 (16% from fat); FAT 4.2g (sat 1.7g, mono 1.4g, poly 0.7g); PROTEIN 16.5g; CARB 34.4g; FIBER 3.9g; CHOL 22mg; IRON 2.9mg; SODIUM 660mg; CALC 217mg

Man with a Pan

After decades of failed diets, Don Mauer, author of *A Guy's Guide to Great Eating* finally figured out the not-so-secret secret to healthy food.

Don Mauer knows that foods can be prepared in a lot of ways, so why not find the ones that maximize flavor while slashing fat and calories? He got miserly with high-fat, high-calorie ingredients and downright philanthropic with flavor.

For example, he learned to ratchet up the flavor of lean meats, chicken, and seafood by soaking them in seasoned salt water, which adds the twin virtues of flavor and moisture. And substituting drained unsweetened applesauce for shortening in dessert batters produces unexpectedly moist results almost identical to the high-fat versions. He tests and tastes every new recipe until he gets mouthwatering aromas, peak flavors, and maximum visual appeal. Because fat, by weight, has more than twice the calories of protein or carbohydrates, his new approach allows him to simultaneously downsize the calories and upsize the servings. Having it both ways—is this a guy's dream or what?

Atsa Spicy Pizza Sausage

It's as bold as the name implies. Use some now and freeze the rest for a quick pizza later.

1 pound ground turkey
1 pound ground pork
½ cup dry red wine
⅓ cup minced fresh parsley
2 tablespoons grated Parmesan cheese
1 tablespoon fennel seeds
1½ teaspoons crushed red pepper
1 teaspoon salt
¼ teaspoon dried thyme
¼ teaspoon freshly ground black pepper
4 garlic cloves, crushed

1. Combine all ingredients in a large bowl. Cook sausage in a large nonstick skillet over medium heat until browned, stirring to crumble. Drain. Yield: 5 cups (serving size: ½ cup).
NOTE: Sausage can be frozen in zip-top plastic bags for up to 3 months.

CALORIES 203 (61% from fat); FAT 13.7g (sat 4.6g, mono 5.8g, poly 2.1g); PROTEIN 17.6g; CARB 1.2g; FIBER 0.3g; CHOL 68mg; IRON 1.5mg; SODIUM 319mg; CALC 42mg

Chicago-Style Pizza

"I make my own leaner sausage for this pizza," Mauer says, "because pizza just ain't pizza unless there's sausage sittin' on it."

2 (10-ounce) cans refrigerated pizza crust dough
Cooking spray
¾ cup (3 ounces) shredded part-skim mozzarella cheese
1¼ cups cooked Atsa Spicy Pizza Sausage (recipe at left)
3 tablespoons thinly sliced fresh basil
1 (14.5-ounce) can no-salt-added diced tomatoes, drained
½ cup (2 ounces) grated fresh Parmesan cheese
⅛ teaspoon black pepper

1. Preheat oven to 450°.
2. Unroll dough portions onto a large baking sheet coated with cooking spray, slightly overlapping edges. Pinch edges together to seal. Pat dough into a 15 x 12-inch rectangle. Sprinkle mozzarella cheese over dough, leaving a
Continued

½-inch border, and top with sausage, basil, and tomatoes. Sprinkle with Parmesan cheese and pepper. Bake at 450° for 2 minutes. Reduce oven temperature to 425° (do not remove pizza from oven), and bake an additional 12 minutes or until cheese melts. Yield: 8 servings (serving size: 1 piece).

CALORIES 313 (30% from fat); FAT 10.3g (sat 4.2g, mono 3.7g, poly 1.8g); PROTEIN 17.2g; CARB 36.5g; FIBER 0.7g; CHOL 32mg; IRON 2.5mg; SODIUM 743mg; CALC 180mg

Blueberry Buttermilk Pancakes

Blueberries, either fresh or frozen, give ordinary pancakes a big flavor boost, not to mention a healthy dose of antioxidants.

  2 cups all-purpose flour
  1 tablespoon sugar
  1 teaspoon baking powder
  1 teaspoon salt
  ½ teaspoon baking soda
 1½ cups low-fat buttermilk
  ½ cup 1% low-fat milk
  1 tablespoon vegetable oil
  1 large egg, lightly beaten
Cooking spray
  2 cups blueberries

1. Lightly spoon flour into dry measuring cups, and level with a knife. Combine flour, sugar, baking powder, salt, and baking soda in a large bowl. Combine buttermilk, milk, oil, and egg in a bowl, and add to flour mixture, stirring until smooth.
2. Spoon ¼ cup pancake batter onto a hot nonstick griddle or large nonstick skillet coated with cooking spray, and top with 2 heaping tablespoons blueberries. Turn pancake when top is covered with bubbles and edges look cooked. Repeat procedure with remaining batter and blueberries. Yield: 12 (5-inch) pancakes (serving size: 2 pancakes).

CALORIES 261 (18% from fat); FAT 5.3g (sat 1.5g, mono 4.5g, poly 1.7g); PROTEIN 8.6g; CARB 45g; FIBER 2.4g; CHOL 38mg; IRON 2.2mg; SODIUM 536mg; CALC 159mg

---

Apple Appreciation

We've rarely replaced fat with applesauce in *Cooking Light* recipes because the results have seldom met our standards. So we were admittedly skeptical of Don Mauer's reliance on the method. How he does it makes all the difference, though, and now we're sold. His secret is draining the applesauce, either by paper towel or by strainer. Here's how.

The Paper-Towel Approach
1. *Spoon applesauce onto several layers of heavy-duty paper towels; spread to a ½-inch thickness.*
2. *Cover with additional paper towels; let stand 5 minutes.*
3. *Scrape applesauce into a bowl using a rubber spatula; cover and refrigerate.*

The Strainer Approach
1. *Place a fine sieve into a bowl large enough so that the sieve doesn't touch the bottom of the bowl.*
2. *Spoon applesauce into sieve. Let stand 15 minutes.*

Ultradecadent Double-Chip Brownies

The only fat comes from egg yolks and baking chips. Using drained applesauce instead of oil or butter produces a surprisingly rich, moist brownie.

 1¼ cups applesauce
 2½ cups sugar
  2 teaspoons vanilla extract
  2 large eggs, lightly beaten
  2 large egg whites, lightly beaten
 1½ cups all-purpose flour
  1 cup unsweetened cocoa
  ¾ teaspoon salt
  ½ cup semisweet chocolate minichips
  ½ cup vanilla-flavored baking chips (such as Ghirardelli)
Cooking spray

1. Preheat oven to 350°.
2. Spoon applesauce into a fine sieve over a bowl; let stand 15 minutes. Discard liquid. Scrape drained applesauce into a large bowl. Add sugar, vanilla, eggs, and egg whites; stir well.
3. Lightly spoon flour into dry measuring cups, and level with a knife. Combine flour, cocoa, and salt, stirring well with a whisk. Add to applesauce mixture; stir just until moist. Fold in baking chips.

4. Spoon batter into a 13 x 9-inch baking pan coated with cooking spray, and bake at 350° for 45 minutes. Cool on a wire rack. Yield: 2 dozen (serving size: 1 brownie).

CALORIES 175 (17% from fat); FAT 3.3g (sat 1.8g, mono 1.1g, poly 0.2g); PROTEIN 3.1g; CARB 34.4g; FIBER 0.4g; CHOL 19mg; IRON 1.2mg; SODIUM 89mg; CALC 18mg

---

Puffed-Up Chocolate-Chip Cookies

This is one of the best chocolate-chip cookies you'll ever make—and it doesn't scrimp on chocolate. Applesauce is the secret.

 1¼ cups all-purpose flour
 1½ teaspoons baking powder
  ¾ teaspoon salt
  ½ cup applesauce
  1 cup packed brown sugar
  ¼ cup butter, softened
  1 tablespoon vanilla extract
  1 large egg
  1 cup semisweet chocolate chips
Cooking spray

1. Preheat oven to 375°.
2. Lightly spoon flour into dry measuring cups; level with a knife. Combine

flour, baking powder, and salt in a small bowl; stir well with a whisk.

3. Spoon applesauce into a fine sieve over a bowl; let stand 15 minutes. Discard liquid. Scrape drained applesauce into a large bowl. Add sugar and butter; beat with a mixer at medium speed until light and fluffy (about 2 minutes). Beat in vanilla and egg. Add flour mixture; beat at low speed until well blended. Fold in chips.

4. Drop by level tablespoons 2 inches apart onto baking sheets coated with cooking spray. Bake at 375° for 10 minutes or until almost set. Cool on pan 2 to 3 minutes or until firm. Remove cookies from pan; cool on wire racks. Yield: 3 dozen (serving size: 1 cookie).

CALORIES 78 (33% from fat); FAT 2.9g (sat 1.7g, mono 0.9g, poly 0.2g); PROTEIN 0.8g; CARB 12.8g; FIBER 0.2g; CHOL 10mg; IRON 0.5mg; SODIUM 87mg; CALC 20mg

Half-the-Fat Carrot Cake with Cream Cheese Frosting

CAKE:

¾ cup applesauce
5 cups shredded carrot (about 1 pound)
¾ cup granulated sugar
¾ cup packed dark brown sugar
½ cup butter, softened
1 teaspoon vanilla extract
1 teaspoon coconut extract
2 large eggs
2 large egg whites
2 cups all-purpose flour
2 teaspoons baking powder
1 teaspoon baking soda
½ teaspoon ground nutmeg
½ teaspoon ground cinnamon
¼ teaspoon salt
1 cup golden raisins
Cooking spray

FROSTING:

4 cups sifted powdered sugar
2 teaspoons vanilla extract
1 (8-ounce) block fat-free cream cheese, chilled
1 (8-ounce) block ⅓-less-fat cream cheese, chilled

1. To prepare cake, spoon applesauce into a fine sieve over a bowl; let stand 15 minutes. Discard liquid. Scrape drained applesauce into a bowl; cover and refrigerate.

2. Combine carrot and granulated sugar in a colander. Drain 20 minutes.

3. Preheat oven to 350°.

4. Beat brown sugar and butter with a mixer at medium speed until well blended (about 2 minutes). Add applesauce, 1 teaspoon vanilla, and coconut extract; beat until well blended (about 2 minutes). Add eggs and egg whites, 1 at a time, beating well after each addition (batter will have a slightly curdled look).

5. Lightly spoon flour into dry measuring cups, and level with a knife. Combine flour and next 5 ingredients; stir well with a whisk. Add brown sugar mixture to flour mixture, stirring just until moist. Fold in carrot mixture and raisins (batter will be very thick). Spoon batter into a 13 x 9-inch baking pan coated with cooking spray.

6. Bake at 350° for 40 minutes or until a wooden pick inserted in center comes out clean. Cool completely on a wire rack.

7. To prepare frosting, beat powdered sugar, 2 teaspoons vanilla extract, and cheeses with a mixer at low speed just until well blended (do not overbeat). Spread frosting over cake; cover and chill 1 hour. Yield: 20 servings (serving size: 1 slice).

CALORIES 322 (23% from fat); FAT 8.1g (sat 4.8g, mono 2.3g, poly 0.5g); PROTEIN 5.6g; CARB 57.7g; FIBER 1.7g; CHOL 45mg; IRON 1.2mg; SODIUM 327mg; CALC 91mg

Iceberg Lettuce Wedges with Thousand Island Dressing

1 cup low-fat mayonnaise
¼ cup water
2 tablespoons bottled sweet pickle relish
2 tablespoons bottled chili sauce
2 tablespoons ketchup
1 teaspoon Dijon mustard
¼ teaspoon freshly ground black pepper
1 head iceberg lettuce, cored and cut into 6 wedges

1. Combine first 7 ingredients in a medium bowl. Drizzle dressing over lettuce wedges. Yield: 6 servings (serving size: 1 lettuce wedge and ¼ cup salad dressing).

CALORIES 97 (27% from fat); FAT 3g (sat 0.4g, mono 0.7g, poly 1.7g); PROTEIN 1.2g; CARB 17.2g; FIBER 0.9g; CHOL 0mg; IRON 0.6mg; SODIUM 583mg; CALC 20mg

One-Pan Whiskey-Flavored Pork Chops

⅔ cup fat-free sour cream
½ cup water
2 tablespoons all-purpose flour
½ teaspoon salt
½ teaspoon dried rubbed sage
¼ teaspoon black pepper
4 (6-ounce) bone-in center-cut pork chops, trimmed
¼ teaspoon salt
⅛ teaspoon black pepper
1 teaspoon olive oil
½ cup chopped onion
1 (8-ounce) package presliced mushrooms
½ cup whiskey

1. Preheat oven to 300°.

2. Combine first 6 ingredients in a small bowl.

3. Sprinkle pork with ¼ teaspoon salt and ⅛ teaspoon pepper. Heat oil in a large nonstick skillet over medium-high heat. Add pork; sauté 5 minutes on each side or until golden. Remove pork from pan. Add onion and mushrooms to pan; sauté 3 minutes. Carefully add whiskey to pan; cook 1 minute or until liquid almost evaporates. Stir sour cream mixture into pan. Return pork to pan; spoon sauce over pork.

4. Wrap handle of skillet with foil. Cover and bake at 300° for 1 hour. Serve immediately. Yield: 4 servings (serving size: 1 pork chop and about ⅓ cup sauce).

CALORIES 310 (28% from fat); FAT 9.6g (sat 3g, mono 4.5g, poly 1.1g); PROTEIN 29.5g; CARB 24.3g; FIBER 1.3g; CHOL 71mg; IRON 2mg; SODIUM 546mg; CALC 16mg

Herb-Crumb Crusted Chicken

Enough crumb mixture will be left over to make the recipe another time, or you can use it in place of dry breadcrumbs in your meat loaf recipe. To save it, freeze in a zip-top plastic bag. The sour cream marinade keeps the chicken moist and the breadcrumb coating in place.

 1 cup reduced-fat sour cream
 3 tablespoons lemon juice
 ½ teaspoon salt
 ¼ teaspoon freshly ground black pepper
 ¼ teaspoon hot sauce
 1 garlic clove, minced
 6 (6-ounce) skinless chicken breast halves
 2 teaspoons dry mustard
 1½ teaspoons salt
 1½ teaspoons dried thyme
 1 teaspoon paprika
 ½ teaspoon freshly ground black pepper
 1 (5-ounce) package melba toast
  Cooking spray

1. Combine first 6 ingredients in a large zip-top plastic bag. Add chicken; seal and marinate in refrigerator 2 hours, turning bag occasionally.
2. Preheat oven to 375°.
3. Combine mustard and next 5 ingredients in a blender or food processor; process until finely ground. Place ½ cup crumb mixture in a shallow dish; reserve remaining crumb mixture for another use.
4. Remove chicken from bag; dredge in crumb mixture. Place chicken, meaty sides up, on a jelly-roll pan coated with cooking spray. Bake at 375° for 40 minutes or until done. Yield: 6 servings (serving size: 1 chicken breast half).

CALORIES 192 (29% from fat); FAT 6.2g (sat 3.2g, mono 1.7g, poly 0.4g); PROTEIN 20.2g; CARB 10.9g; FIBER 0.8g; CHOL 59mg; IRON 1.1mg; SODIUM 603mg; CALC 64mg

Spicy Pan-Fried Sirloin Steak with Noodles

 2 teaspoons chili powder
 2 teaspoons dried oregano
 1 teaspoon ground cumin
 1 teaspoon paprika
 ½ teaspoon salt
 ¼ teaspoon ground red pepper
 1 tablespoon olive oil
 1 (1¾-pound) boneless sirloin steak, trimmed and cut into ½-inch-thick strips
 2 cups sliced onion
 2 cups chopped red bell pepper
 2 tablespoons all-purpose flour
 2 garlic cloves, minced
 2 tablespoons ketchup
 1 tablespoon tomato paste
 2 teaspoons fresh lime juice
 1 (14¼-ounce) can low-salt beef broth
 5 cups cooked medium egg noodles (8 ounces uncooked pasta)

1. Combine first 6 ingredients in a small bowl.
2. Heat oil in a large nonstick skillet over medium-high heat. Add half of beef; cook 1 minute on each side. Remove from pan. Repeat procedure with remaining beef; set aside.
3. Add onion and bell pepper to pan; sauté 5 minutes. Stir in chili powder mixture, flour, and garlic, and sauté 1 minute. Stir in ketchup, tomato paste, juice, and beef broth; bring to a boil. Reduce heat, and simmer 5 minutes, stirring occasionally.
4. Return beef to pan, and cook 3 minutes or until thoroughly heated. Serve over egg noodles. Yield: 6 servings (serving size: ¾ cup beef mixture and about ¾ cup noodles).

CALORIES 383 (24% from fat); FAT 10.2g (sat 2.9g, mono 4.6g, poly 1.2g); PROTEIN 33.9g; CARB 38.5g; FIBER 3g; CHOL 105mg; IRON 6.5mg; SODIUM 698mg; CALC 53mg

inspired vegetarian

Go with the Grain

Since the dawn of civilization, grains and grain-based dishes have put rich flavor and balanced nutrition into memorable meals.

The endurance of grains and their culinary kin isn't difficult to explain. Not only are they easily grown and prepared, but they're also highly nutritious—rich in complex carbohydrates, vitamins, minerals, and fiber. They fill you up—yet they're almost fat-free. Also, they provide a neutral background against which you can highlight other ingredients.

Asian Broth with Tofu and Rice

 2¾ cups water
 2 (14½-ounce) cans vegetable broth
 1½ cups frozen green peas, thawed
 1 cup cubed firm tofu (about 6 ounces)
 1 tablespoon minced peeled fresh ginger
 3 cups hot cooked converted rice
 2 tablespoons chopped fresh cilantro
 2 tablespoons low-sodium soy sauce
 2 tablespoons rice vinegar
 2 tablespoons dark sesame oil

1. Bring water and broth to a boil in a large saucepan; add peas, tofu, and ginger. Reduce heat; simmer 5 minutes. Stir in rice and cilantro; cook 3 minutes or until thoroughly heated. Ladle 1⅓ cups soup into each of 4 bowls. Drizzle each serving with 1½ teaspoons soy sauce, 1½ teaspoons rice vinegar, and 1½ teaspoons oil. Yield: 4 servings.

CALORIES 330 (27% from fat); FAT 10g (sat 1.5g, mono 3.5g, poly 4.4g); PROTEIN 9.8g; CARB 49g; FIBER 1.4g; CHOL 0mg; IRON 4.7mg; SODIUM 1,248mg; CALC 76mg

Wheat Berry-Stuffed Winter Squash

Wheat berries are whole unprocessed wheat kernels. They require an extended period of cooking to tenderize the grain, so use that time to cook your squash.

    1   tablespoon vegetable oil
 1½   cups finely chopped onion
    1   cup uncooked wheat berries
  ½   teaspoon mustard seeds
  ¼   cup chopped dry-roasted cashews
    1   tablespoon grated peeled fresh ginger
    1   jalapeño pepper, seeded and minced
    2   cups water
  ¼   teaspoon salt
    1   (14½-ounce) can vegetable broth
    2   tablespoons minced fresh cilantro
    1   tablespoon fresh lemon juice
    2   acorn squash (about 1 pound each)
    1   tablespoon maple syrup
  ⅛   teaspoon ground cinnamon
       Cooking spray
       Cilantro sprigs (optional)

1. Preheat oven to 350°.
2. Heat oil in a medium saucepan over medium-high heat. Add onion, wheat berries, and mustard seeds; sauté 3 minutes or until onion is tender. Add nuts, ginger, and jalapeño; sauté 1 minute. Add water, salt, and broth; bring to a boil. Cover, reduce heat, and simmer 2 hours or until tender. Stir in minced cilantro and juice. Remove from heat; keep warm.
3. While wheat mixture cooks, prepare squash. Cut squash lengthwise in half; discard seeds. Combine syrup and cinnamon; brush over squash. Place squash halves, cut sides down, on a baking sheet coated with cooking spray. Bake at 350° for 40 minutes or until tender. Divide wheat berry mixture evenly among squash halves. Garnish with cilantro sprigs, if desired. Yield: 4 servings (serving size: 1 stuffed squash half).

CALORIES 319 (23% from fat); FAT 8.2g (sat 1.5g, mono 3.6g, poly 2.7g); PROTEIN 8.6g; CARB 51.3g; FIBER 9.3g; CHOL 0mg; IRON 2.5mg; SODIUM 706mg; CALC 57mg

Kasha with Leeks and Toasted Pecans

You can omit the cooked egg whites, and this dish still will taste delicious. If you prefer small-grain kasha, increase the water to ½ cup.

    1   cup uncooked medium-grain kasha (buckwheat groats)
    2   large egg whites
  ¼   cup water
  ¼   teaspoon salt
    1   (14½-ounce) can vegetable broth
    4   hard-cooked large eggs
    1   tablespoon olive oil, divided
    4   cups thinly sliced leek, separated into rings (about 3 leeks)
    2   tablespoons water
    1   teaspoon sugar
  ¼   cup chopped pecans, toasted

1. Place kasha in a medium saucepan; cook over medium-low heat 3 minutes, stirring often. Gradually add uncooked egg whites, stirring to coat. Add ¼ cup water, salt, and broth; bring to a boil. Cover, reduce heat, and simmer 15 minutes or until liquid is absorbed. Remove from heat. Cut cooked eggs in half; remove yolks, and reserve for another use. Finely chop cooked egg whites. Add cooked egg whites and 1½ teaspoons oil to kasha mixture; stir well.
2. Heat 1½ teaspoons oil in a medium nonstick skillet over medium-high heat. Add leek; sauté 5 minutes. Add 2 tablespoons water and sugar; cover, reduce heat, and cook 2 minutes. Spoon 1 cup kasha into each of 4 bowls. Top each serving with ½ cup leek mixture and 1 tablespoon pecans. Yield: 4 servings.

CALORIES 33 (3% from fat); FAT 0.1g (sat 0.1g, mono 0g, poly 0g); PROTEIN 0.3g; CARB 8.9g; FIBER 0.9g; CHOL 0mg; IRON 0.2mg; SODIUM 74mg; CALC 5mg

Brown-and-Wild Rice Pilaf with Date Chutney

Basmati is a delicate, aromatic rice that lends a softer texture than the chewy wild rice. To streamline preparation, cook the onions while the rice is simmering.

    3   cups water
  ¾   cup uncooked wild rice
  ½   teaspoon salt
  ¼   teaspoon ground turmeric
 1¼   cups uncooked brown basmati rice
  ¾   cup frozen green peas, thawed
    1   tablespoon olive oil
 1½   cups vertically sliced onion
       Date Chutney
    6   tablespoons slivered almonds, toasted

1. Combine first 4 ingredients in a large saucepan; bring to a boil. Cover, reduce heat, and simmer 15 minutes. Add basmati rice. Return to a boil; cover, reduce heat, and simmer 25 minutes. Stir in green peas; cook 5 minutes. Remove from heat; let stand, covered, 5 minutes.
2. Heat oil in a large nonstick skillet over medium-high heat. Add onion; sauté 20 minutes or until golden brown, stirring frequently.
3. Divide rice mixture evenly among 6 plates; top each serving with caramelized onions, chutney, and almonds. Yield: 6 servings (serving size: about ¾ cup rice, about 1½ tablespoons onion, about 2½ tablespoons chutney, and 1 tablespoon almonds).

(Totals include Date Chutney) CALORIES 383 (16% from fat); FAT 6.9g (sat 0.9g, mono 4.2g, poly 1.4g); PROTEIN 9.2g; CARB 74.7g; FIBER 6.5g; CHOL 0mg; IRON 2mg; SODIUM 419mg; CALC 52mg

DATE CHUTNEY:

    1   cup chopped pitted dates (about 16 dates)
  ½   cup fresh lemon juice (about 3 lemons)
  ¼   cup water
    2   tablespoons chopped fresh cilantro
    1   tablespoon chopped seeded jalapeño pepper
  ½   teaspoon salt

Continued

1. Combine all ingredients in a blender or food processor; process until thick and smooth. Yield: 1 cup (serving size: 1 tablespoon).

NOTE: Chutney will keep in refrigerator for up to 2 days.

CALORIES 326 (28% from fat); FAT 10.3g (sat 1.2g, mono 6.1g, poly 2.1g); PROTEIN 12g; CARB 50.1g; FIBER 5.5g; CHOL 0mg; IRON 3.3mg; SODIUM 688mg; CALC 74mg

Spinach Corn Bread with Mango Salsa

The sweetness of the mango and heat from the jalapeño allow the salsa to balance nicely with the corn bread. Serve with a salad and soup for a light meal.

  1 cup all-purpose flour
  1 cup yellow cornmeal
  2 tablespoons sugar
  2 teaspoons baking powder
  ½ teaspoon baking soda
  ½ teaspoon salt
  1¼ cups low-fat buttermilk
  3 tablespoons vegetable oil
  3 large egg whites, lightly beaten
  1 cup frozen whole-kernel corn
  1 (10-ounce) package frozen chopped spinach, thawed, drained, and squeezed dry
  1 jalapeño pepper, seeded and minced
Cooking spray
Mango Salsa

1. Preheat oven to 375°.
2. Lightly spoon flour into a dry measuring cup; level with a knife. Combine flour and next 5 ingredients in a large bowl; make a well in center of mixture. Combine buttermilk, oil, and egg whites; stir well with a whisk. Stir in corn, spinach, and jalapeño. Add to flour mixture, stirring just until moist.
3. Spoon batter into an 8-inch round cake pan coated with cooking spray. Bake at 375° for 35 minutes or until a wooden pick inserted in center comes out clean. Cool 10 minutes in pan on a wire rack; remove from pan. Cool completely on wire rack. Cut into 9 wedges. Serve with Mango Salsa. Yield: 9 servings

(serving size: 1 corn bread wedge and about ¼ cup salsa).

(Totals include Mango Salsa) CALORIES 235 (23% from fat); FAT 6g (sat 1.3g, mono 1.7g, poly 2.6g); PROTEIN 6.8g; CARB 40.3g; FIBER 3.2g; CHOL 0mg; IRON 2.3mg; SODIUM 435mg; CALC 148mg

MANGO SALSA:

  2 cups diced peeled mango (about 2 large)
  ¼ cup fresh lime juice
  2 tablespoons minced fresh cilantro
  2 teaspoons minced peeled fresh ginger
  2 teaspoons sugar
  ½ teaspoon ground cumin
  ¼ teaspoon salt
  1 jalapeño pepper, seeded and minced

1. Combine all ingredients in a bowl. Yield: 2 cups (serving size: about ¼ cup).

CALORIES 31 (3% from fat); FAT 0.1g (sat 0g, mono 0.1g, poly 0g); PROTEIN 0.3g; CARB 8g; FIBER 0.6g; CHOL 0mg; IRON 0.2mg; SODIUM 67mg; CALC 7mg

Warm Barley and Soybean Salad

Whole-grain barley is the most nutritious kind because only the outer husk has been removed. Look for it in health-food stores.

  3 cups water
  ¾ cup whole-grain barley
  1½ cups frozen soybeans or lima beans, thawed
  1 cup finely chopped red bell pepper
  1 cup chopped onion
  ½ cup thinly sliced celery
  2 tablespoons light mayonnaise
  2 tablespoons fresh lemon juice
  ½ teaspoon salt
  2 tablespoons chopped fresh cilantro

1. Bring water to a boil in a medium saucepan; add barley. Reduce heat, and simmer 50 minutes or until tender; drain. Cook beans according to package directions, omitting salt and fat.

2. Combine barley, beans, pepper, and next 5 ingredients in a large bowl, and toss well. Sprinkle with cilantro. Yield: 5 servings (serving size: about 1 cup).

CALORIES 222 (23% from fat); FAT 5.6g (sat 0.8g, mono 1.2g, poly 2.7g); PROTEIN 10.5g; CARB 35.2g; FIBER 6.1g; CHOL 2mg; IRON 2.7mg; SODIUM 295mg; CALC 103mg

well-equipped

Bread-Machine Winners

With these recipes and today's easier-to-use machines, getting your daily bread is all pleasure.

Ingredients Primer

Bread flour is a high-gluten, high-protein flour that produces a light, springy loaf. Gluten creates an elastic network in the dough that traps gas created by the yeast and makes the bread rise. (All-purpose flour has less gluten, so it's not a good substitute.) It's critical to measure flour correctly: Lightly spoon—don't scoop—flour into dry measuring cups, and level off the excess with the straight edge of a knife.

Bread machine yeast is finely granulated to disperse well during mixing and kneading. It's not temperature-sensitive, so it can grow without first being proofed in warm water; just add it with the dry ingredients in your machine. You can substitute instant, rapid-rise, or quick-rise yeast.

Sugar feeds the yeast, allowing it to grow. It also helps bread retain moisture, adds flavor and tenderness, and helps brown the crust.

Salt is needed for flavor and to control yeast by delaying fermentation so the dough rises at a slower rate, allowing the gluten to strengthen.

Ham-and-Swiss Stromboli Step-by-Steps

1. *Place filling on half of dough, leaving enough of a border so you can seal edges.*

2. *Fold dough until edges meet, and crimp to seal.*

3. *Roll dough over, and place it, seam side down, on pan.*

Ham-and-Swiss Stromboli

The fillings are baked into the bread, making it a perfect make-ahead handheld lunch. To vary this recipe, use prosciutto and mozzarella cheese.

```
  3   cups bread flour
  1   cup warm water (100° to 110°)
  1   tablespoon nonfat dry milk
  1   tablespoon olive oil
2½   teaspoons bread machine yeast
  1   teaspoon salt
  ½   teaspoon dry mustard
  ½   cup (3 ounces) chopped ham
  ½   cup (2 ounces) cubed Swiss cheese
1½   teaspoons cornmeal
  1   large egg, lightly beaten
```

1. Lightly spoon flour into dry measuring cups; level with a knife. Follow manufacturer's instructions for placing flour and next 6 ingredients into bread pan, and select dough cycle; start bread machine.

2. Remove dough from machine (do not bake). Turn dough out onto a floured surface, and knead 30 seconds. Cover dough, and let rest 10 minutes.

3. Roll into a 10 x 8-inch oval on a lightly floured surface. Sprinkle ham and cheese onto half of oval, lengthwise, leaving a 1-inch border. Fold dough over filling; press edges and ends together to seal.

4. Cover a large baking sheet with parchment paper; dust with cornmeal.

Place loaf, seam side down, on prepared pan. Make 3 diagonal cuts ¼-inch deep across top of loaf using a sharp knife. Cover and let rise in a warm place (85°), free from drafts, 1 hour or until doubled in size.

5. Preheat oven to 350°.

6. Uncover dough; brush with egg. Bake at 350° for 35 minutes or until browned. Cool slightly. Yield: 1 (1-pound) loaf, 8 servings (serving size: 1 slice).

CALORIES 262 (20% from fat); FAT 5.8g (sat 2g, mono 2.4g, poly 0.7g); PROTEIN 12.1g; CARB 39.1g; FIBER 0.4g; CHOL 40mg; IRON 2.8mg; SODIUM 453mg; CALC 93mg

Orange Bubble Bread

```
  1   cup 2% reduced-fat milk
  ¼   cup butter
  ¼   cup granulated sugar
  ¼   cup water
  1   teaspoon salt
  4   cups bread flour
2½   teaspoons bread machine yeast
  1   large egg, lightly beaten
  ½   cup granulated sugar
  2   tablespoons grated orange rind
  ¼   cup butter, melted
Cooking spray
  ½   cup powdered sugar
  1   tablespoon orange juice
```

1. Combine first 5 ingredients in a 2-cup glass measure. Microwave at HIGH 3 minutes. Cool 5 minutes. Lightly spoon flour into dry measuring cups; level with a knife. Follow manufacturer's instructions for placing milk mixture, flour, yeast, and egg into bread pan, and select dough cycle; start bread machine.

2. Remove dough from machine (do not bake). Turn dough out onto a floured surface, and knead 30 seconds. Cover dough; let rest 10 minutes. Divide dough into 24 equal portions, shaping each into a ball (cover remaining dough to keep from drying). Combine ½ cup granulated sugar and rind. Dip each ball into ¼ cup melted butter, and roll in sugar mixture. Place balls in bottom of a
Continued

10-inch tube pan coated with cooking spray. Cover and let rise in a warm place (85°), free from drafts, 45 minutes or until doubled in size.

3. Preheat oven to 350°.

4. Bake at 350° for 35 minutes. Cool in pan 5 minutes on a wire rack; remove bread from pan. Cool bread 15 minutes on wire rack.

5. Combine ½ cup powdered sugar and orange juice. Drizzle mixture over bread, and serve warm. Yield: 2 dozen (serving size: 1 roll).

CALORIES 161 (26% from fat); FAT 4.7g (sat 2.6g, mono 1.3g, poly 0.4g); PROTEIN 3.6g; CARB 26.2g; FIBER 0.1g; CHOL 20mg; IRON 1.1mg; SODIUM 145mg; CALC 19mg

Asiago-Pepper Bread

This flavorful loaf is great for sandwiches or toasted and served with an Italian meal.

    3   cups bread flour
    1   cup warm water (100° to 110°)
    ½   cup nonfat dry milk
    ½   cup (2 ounces) grated Asiago cheese
 1½   tablespoons minced green onions
    1   tablespoon sugar
    1   tablespoon butter, melted
 2½   teaspoons bread machine yeast
 1¼   teaspoons salt
    ½   teaspoon coarsely ground black
        pepper
    1   large egg

1. Lightly spoon flour into dry measuring cups; level with a knife. Follow manufacturer's instructions for placing flour and remaining ingredients into bread pan, and select bake cycle; start bread machine. Yield: 1 (1½-pound) loaf, 16 servings (serving size: 1 slice).

CALORIES 136 (17% from fat); FAT 2.5g (sat 1.2g, mono 0.7g, poly 0.3g); PROTEIN 6.2g; CARB 21.9g; FIBER 0.2g; CHOL 20mg; IRON 1.3mg; SODIUM 258mg; CALC 92mg

Chocolate Bread

Ideal for peanut butter-and-jelly sandwiches, this sweet bread is also good toasted and spread with jam.

    3   cups bread flour
    1   cup warm water (100° to 110°)
    ⅓   cup sugar
    ¼   cup Dutch process cocoa
    1   tablespoon butter
    2   teaspoons bread machine yeast
    1   teaspoon salt
    4   ounces bittersweet chocolate,
        coarsely chopped
    1   large egg yolk

1. Lightly spoon flour into dry measuring cups; level with a knife. Follow manufacturer's instructions for placing flour and remaining ingredients into bread pan, and select bake cycle; start bread machine. Yield: 1 (1¾-pound) loaf, 14 servings (serving size: 1 slice).

CALORIES 183 (21% from fat); FAT 4.3g (sat 2.3g, mono 1.3g, poly 0.4g); PROTEIN 4.7g; CARB 32.2g; FIBER 0.2g; CHOL 18mg; IRON 2mg; SODIUM 178mg; CALC 12mg

Smoked-Salmon Pizza with Mascarpone and Capers

    3   cups bread flour
    1   cup warm water (100° to 110°)
    1   tablespoon olive oil
 2½   teaspoons bread machine yeast
    ½   teaspoon salt
        Cooking spray
    2   cups sliced green onions (about
        2 bunches)
    ½   teaspoon cracked black pepper
    6   tablespoons (about 3 ounces)
        mascarpone cheese
    6   ounces thinly sliced smoked
        salmon
    1   tablespoon capers
    6   lemon wedges

1. Lightly spoon bread flour into dry measuring cups, and level with a knife. Follow manufacturer's instructions for placing flour and next 4 ingredients into bread pan, and select dough cycle; start bread machine.

2. Remove dough from machine (do not bake). Turn dough out onto a floured surface, and knead 30 seconds. Cover dough; let rest 10 minutes.

3. Preheat oven to 425°.

4. Divide dough into 6 equal portions. Roll each portion into a 9-inch circle on a lightly floured surface. Cover baking sheets with parchment paper, and place dough rounds on pans. Lightly coat top of dough with cooking spray. Cover and let rise in a warm place (85°), free from drafts, 15 minutes or until puffy.

5. Divide onions and pepper evenly among rounds. Bake at 425° for 10 minutes. Remove from oven; drop 3 teaspoonfuls of cheese onto each round. Arrange 1 ounce smoked salmon on each pizza; divide capers evenly among pizzas.

6. Bake pizzas an additional 8 minutes or until cheese melts. Serve pizzas with lemon wedges. Yield: 6 servings (serving size: 1 pizza).

CALORIES 390 (27% from fat); FAT 11.8g (sat 4.3g, mono 4.4g, poly 1.5g); PROTEIN 15.7g; CARB 54g; FIBER 1.3g; CHOL 19mg; IRON 4.1mg; SODIUM 486mg; CALC 69mg

Multigrain Bread

Like an English muffin, this bread is excellent for butter, jams, or other spreads.

 3½   cups bread flour
    1   cup warm water (100° to 110°)
    ½   cup low-fat buttermilk
    ¼   cup yellow cornmeal
    ¼   cup regular oats
    ¼   cup wheat bran
    ¼   cup packed brown sugar
    2   tablespoons honey
 2½   teaspoons bread machine yeast
    2   teaspoons salt

1. Lightly spoon flour into dry measuring cups; level with a knife. Follow manufacturer's instructions for placing flour and remaining ingredients into bread pan, and select bake cycle; start bread machine. Yield: 1 (2-pound) loaf, 16 servings (serving size: 1 slice).

CALORIES 150 (5% from fat); FAT 0.8g (sat 0.1g, mono 0.1g, poly 0.3g); PROTEIN 4.7g; CARB 31g; FIBER 0.8g; CHOL 0mg; IRON 1.8mg; SODIUM 299mg; CALC 19mg

How to Cook Chinese

China is home to more than a fifth of the world's population—a country so vast and ancient that unique regional styles were bound to develop.

And they did, shaped by climate, geography, and ingredient availability, to the point that "Chinese cooking" is now not one but many different cuisines.

It's not unusual to find specialties from one area prepared in all parts of China. But the traditions of each area endure, so that a devotee of Chinese cooking is always aware of a dish's origin, flavors, ingredients, and techniques. Because of that, it helps to understand the four primary regions, or schools, of Chinese cooking. These regions include the Northern, Eastern, Western, and Southern schools.

The Northern School of Chinese Cooking

• **The Northern School** includes Beijing, the northern provinces, and Inner Mongolia. Its cuisine is the most eclectic, incorporating refined cooking of palace kitchens and Shandong province (where classic Chinese cuisine originated), as well as Mongolian and Muslim dishes.
Claim to fame: Noodles, steamed breads, and pancakes are served instead of rice.
Cooking styles: Stir-frying, pan-frying, braising, and barbecuing.
Favorite seasonings: Garlic, chives, leeks, star anise, and sweet bean sauces.
Signature dish: Moo Shu Pork with Mandarin Pancakes (recipe below).

Moo Shu Pork with Mandarin Pancakes

(pictured on page 40)

In northern China, wheat-based staples such as pancakes, noodles, and steamed buns replace rice. Moo Shu Pork is typical: It's a stir-fried dish made with pork, green onions, mushrooms, and scrambled eggs, all rolled into small, thin pancakes. If you like, substitute flour tortillas brushed with a little sesame oil for the pancakes.

2 tablespoons low-sodium soy sauce
2 tablespoons rice wine or sake
1 teaspoon dark sesame oil
2 teaspoons cornstarch
1 (1½-pound) boneless pork loin, trimmed and cut into 1 x ¼-inch strips
10 dried shiitake mushrooms
½ cup (1-inch) sliced green onions
3 tablespoons minced garlic (about 12 cloves)
2 tablespoons minced peeled fresh ginger
¼ cup dried wood ear mushrooms (about ¼ ounce)
3 tablespoons rice wine or sake
3 tablespoons low-sodium soy sauce
½ teaspoon cornstarch
½ teaspoon sugar
¼ teaspoon black pepper
1 tablespoon vegetable oil, divided
2 large eggs, lightly beaten
3 cups thinly sliced napa (Chinese) cabbage stalks
4 cups thinly sliced napa (Chinese) cabbage leaves
2 tablespoons rice wine or sake
½ cup hoisin sauce
1 tablespoon low-sodium soy sauce
16 Mandarin Pancakes (recipe at right)

1. Combine first 4 ingredients in a zip-top plastic bag. Add pork; seal and marinate in refrigerator 1 hour, turning occasionally. Remove pork from bag; discard marinade.
2. Combine boiling water and dried shiitake mushrooms in a bowl; cover and let stand 20 minutes. Drain; discard mushroom stems, and thinly slice mushroom caps. Combine sliced mushroom caps, green onions, garlic, and ginger in a small bowl; set aside.
3. Combine boiling water and wood ear mushrooms in a bowl; cover and let stand 20 minutes. Drain; cut mushrooms into thin slices. Set aside.
4. Combine 3 tablespoons rice wine and next 4 ingredients in a small bowl; stir well with a whisk. Set aside.
5. Heat 1½ teaspoons vegetable oil in a wok or large nonstick skillet over medium-high heat. Add pork, and stir-fry 3 minutes. Remove pork from pan. Add 1½ teaspoons vegetable oil to pan. Add eggs; stir-fry 30 seconds or until soft-scrambled. Add shiitake mushroom mixture; stir-fry 1½ minutes. Add cabbage stalks; stir-fry 30 seconds. Add wood ear mushrooms, cabbage leaves, and 2 tablespoons rice wine; stir-fry 1 minute. Add pork and cornstarch mixture; stir-fry 2 minutes or until sauce is thick. Place pork mixture on a platter.
6. Combine hoisin sauce and 1 tablespoon soy sauce. Spread about 1½ teaspoons hoisin sauce mixture on uncooked surface of each Mandarin Pancake. Top each pancake with ½ cup pork mixture; roll up. Yield: 8 servings (serving size: 2 filled pancakes).

(Totals include Mandarin Pancakes) CALORIES 418 (29% from fat); FAT 13.6g (sat 3.5g, mono 6.1g, poly 2.8g); PROTEIN 24.7g; CARB 46.2g; FIBER 2.8g; CHOL 107mg; IRON 3mg; SODIUM 710mg; CALC 85mg

MANDARIN PANCAKES:

2 cups all-purpose flour
1 cup boiling water
1½ tablespoons dark sesame oil

1. Lightly spoon flour into dry measuring cups; level with a knife. Combine flour and water in a large bowl. Stir until a soft dough forms. Turn dough out onto a lightly floured surface. Knead until smooth and elastic (about 3 minutes).
Continued

Mandarin Pancakes Step-by-Steps

1. *Shape dough into a 1½-inch-thick log. Divide dough into 16 portions. Roll each into a 6-inch circle on a lightly floured surface.*

2. *Brush 8 pancakes with oil; top each with a plain pancake, gently pressing them together.*

3. *Place 1 pancake stack in a heated nonstick skillet. Cook 1 minute on each side or until slightly puffed.*

Shape dough into a 1½-inch-thick log. Divide dough into 16 equal portions. Roll each dough portion into a 6-inch circle on a lightly floured surface. Brush 8 pancakes evenly with oil. Top each with one of remaining pancakes, gently pressing together.

2. Heat a medium nonstick skillet over medium-high heat. Place 1 pancake stack in pan, and cook 1 minute on each side or until slightly puffed. Remove from pan, and cool. Peel pancakes apart. Repeat procedure with remaining pancake stacks. Yield: 16 pancakes (serving size: 1 pancake).

CALORIES 64 (20% from fat); FAT 1.4g (sat 0.2g, mono 0.5g, poly 0.6g); PROTEIN 1.5g; CARB 11g; FIBER 0.4g; CHOL 0mg; IRON 0.7mg; SODIUM 0mg; CALC 2mg

The Eastern School of Chinese Cooking

•**The Eastern School of Chinese Cooking** encompasses two centers, Shanghai and Fuzhou, and the eastern provinces. Nicknamed Heaven on Earth and The Land of Fish and Rice, it's renowned for vegetarian specialties and subtle, refined flavors.
Claim to fame: Source of China's best soy sauces and rice wines.
Cooking styles: Red-cooking (braising in a soy sauce-based mixture), stir-frying, steaming, and quick simmering.
Signature dishes: Cinnamon-Beef Noodles (recipe at right) and Steamed Vegetarian Dumplings (recipe at right).

Cinnamon-Beef Noodles

- 5 cups water
- 1½ cups rice wine or sake
- ¾ cup low-sodium soy sauce
- ¼ cup sugar
- 2 teaspoons vegetable oil, divided
- 2 pounds beef stew meat, cut into 1½-inch cubes
- 8 green onions, cut into 1-inch pieces
- 6 garlic cloves, crushed
- 2 cinnamon sticks
- 1 (1-inch) piece peeled fresh ginger, thinly sliced
- 1 (10-ounce) package fresh spinach, chopped
- 4 cups hot cooked wide lo mein noodles or vermicelli (about 8 ounces uncooked pasta)

1. Combine first 4 ingredients in a large bowl; stir with a whisk. Set aside.
2. Heat 1 teaspoon oil in a large Dutch oven over medium-high heat; add half of beef, browning on all sides. Remove from pan. Repeat procedure with 1 teaspoon oil and remaining beef. Return beef to pan; add water mixture, onions, garlic, cinnamon, and ginger. Bring to a boil; cover, reduce heat, and simmer 2 hours or until beef is tender. Discard ginger slices and cinnamon. Stir in spinach; cook 3 minutes or until wilted. Serve over noodles. Yield: 8 servings (serving size: 1 cup beef mixture and ½ cup noodles).

CALORIES 403 (14% from fat); FAT 6.2g (sat 2.3g, mono 3.3g, poly 1.3g); PROTEIN 30.5g; CARB 50.4g; FIBER 2.9g; CHOL 44mg; IRON 5.2mg; SODIUM 1,080mg; CALC 80mg

Steamed Vegetarian Dumplings

Dumplings have a prominent place in Chinese cuisine and are prepared in many different ways for holidays and festivals. They vary by region, and the ingredients depend on area availability.

- ½ pound firm tofu, drained and cut into ½-inch slices
- ½ cup dried wood ear mushrooms (about ½ ounce)
- ½ cup drained, sliced water chestnuts
- ¾ cup shredded carrot
- 1 tablespoon minced peeled fresh ginger
- 1 tablespoon minced green onions
- 1 teaspoon salt
- 2 teaspoons low-sodium soy sauce
- ½ teaspoon dark sesame oil
- 1 large egg, lightly beaten
- 4 teaspoons cornstarch
- 50 won ton wrappers or gyoza skins
- 1 teaspoon cornstarch
- Cooking spray
- ½ cup low-sodium soy sauce
- ¼ cup water

1. Place tofu on several layers of paper towels; cover with additional paper towels. Let stand 30 minutes, pressing down occasionally. Place tofu in a large bowl, and mash with a fork until smooth. Set tofu aside.
2. Combine boiling water and mushrooms in a bowl; cover and let stand 20 minutes or until soft. Drain. Place

mushrooms and water chestnuts in a food processor; pulse 5 times or until minced. Add mushroom mixture, carrot, and next 7 ingredients to tofu; stir well.

3. Working with 1 won ton wrapper at a time (cover remaining wrappers to keep them from drying), spoon 1 teaspoon tofu mixture into center of each wrapper. Moisten edges of wrapper with water; bring 2 opposite corners to center, pinching points to seal. Bring remaining 2 corners to center, pinching edges together to seal. Place dumplings, seam sides up, on a large baking sheet sprinkled with 1 teaspoon cornstarch (cover loosely with a towel to keep them from drying).

4. Arrange one-third of dumplings in a single layer in a vegetable steamer coated with cooking spray. Steam dumplings, covered, 15 minutes. Remove dumplings from steamer; set aside, and keep warm. Repeat procedure with remaining dumplings.

5. Combine ½ cup soy sauce and ¼ cup water in a small bowl. Serve with dumplings. Yield: 50 appetizers (serving size: 1 dumpling and about ¾ teaspoon sauce).

CALORIES 35 (15% from fat); FAT 0.6g (sat 0.1g, mono 0.1g, poly 0.2g); PROTEIN 1.5g; CARB 5.8g; FIBER 0.2g; CHOL 5mg; IRON 0.6mg; SODIUM 179mg; CALC 10mg

Steamed Vegetarian Dumplings Step-by-Steps

1. *Working with 1 won ton wrapper at a time, spoon 1 teaspoon tofu mixture into center of each wrapper (keep remaining wrappers covered to prevent drying).*

2. *Moisten edges of wrapper with water, and bring 2 opposite corners to center, pinching points to seal. Bring other 2 corners to center, pinching points together.*

3. *Place dumplings on a large baking sheet sprinkled with cornstarch; cover loosely with a towel to keep from drying.*

4. *Arrange one-third of dumplings in a single layer in a vegetable steamer coated with cooking spray.*

Sichuan-Style Stir-Fried Chicken with Peanuts

This is also known as kung pao chicken. Serve with rice and a steamed vegetable.

MARINADE:
- 2   tablespoons low-sodium soy sauce
- 2   tablespoons rice wine or sake
- 1   teaspoon cornstarch
- 1   teaspoon dark sesame oil
- 1½ pounds skinless, boneless chicken breast, cut into bite-size pieces

STIR-FRYING OIL:
- 2   tablespoons vegetable oil, divided

SAUCE:
- ½   cup fat-free, less-sodium chicken broth
- 2   tablespoons sugar
- 2½ tablespoons low-sodium soy sauce
- 2   tablespoons rice wine or sake
- 1   tablespoon Chinese black vinegar or Worcestershire sauce
- 1¼ teaspoons cornstarch
- 1   teaspoon dark sesame oil
- 2   tablespoons minced green onions
- 1½ tablespoons minced peeled fresh ginger
- 1½ tablespoons minced garlic (about 7 cloves)
- 1   teaspoon chile paste with garlic

Continued

REMAINING INGREDIENTS:

1½ cups drained, sliced water chestnuts
1 cup (½-inch) sliced green onion tops
¾ cup unsalted, dry-roasted peanuts
6 cups hot cooked long-grain rice

1. To prepare marinade, combine first 5 ingredients in a medium bowl; cover and chill 20 minutes.
2. Heat 1 tablespoon vegetable oil in a wok or large nonstick skillet over medium-high heat. Add chicken mixture; stir-fry 4 minutes or until chicken is done. Remove from pan; set aside.
3. To prepare sauce, combine broth and next 6 ingredients; stir well with a whisk. Heat 1 tablespoon vegetable oil in pan. Add 2 tablespoons green onions, ginger, garlic, and chile paste, and stir-fry 15 seconds. Add broth mixture, and cook 1 minute or until thick, stirring constantly.
4. Stir in cooked chicken, water chestnuts, sliced onion tops, and peanuts; cook 1 minute or until thoroughly heated. Serve over rice. Yield: 6 servings (serving size: ¾ cup stir-fry and 1 cup rice).

CALORIES 590 (25% from fat); FAT 16.7g (sat 2.7g, mono 6.8g, poly 6g); PROTEIN 36.9g; CARB 71.4g; FIBER 3.3g; CHOL 66mg; IRON 3.8mg; SODIUM 591mg; CALC 75mg

The Southern School of Chinese Cooking

•**The Southern School** includes Canton—praised by some as the haute-cuisine capital of China—and Hong Kong, known for combining Cantonese cooking with contemporary techniques and ingredients from the West. The Cantonese are considered some of China's most adventurous diners, relishing all sorts of exotica.
Claim to fame: Masters of *dim sum* (snacks).
Cooking style: Ingenious blending of superb ingredients and refined techniques.
Signature dishes: Steamed Salmon with Black Bean Sauce (recipe at right), Hoisin Barbecued Chicken (recipe at right), Stir-Fried Broccoli with Oyster Sauce (recipe on page 36), and Shrimp Fried Rice (recipe on page 36).

Steamed Salmon with Black Bean Sauce

Salmon isn't traditional in Chinese cooking, but since it's common in the United States and works so beautifully with the black bean sauce, we chose it for this recipe. Steaming accentuates the fresh flavor of the ingredients. The sumptuous sauce is redolent of garlic and ginger; it will highlight the flavor of any seafood, meat, or vegetable dish.

MARINADE:

2 tablespoons rice wine or sake
1 (½-inch) piece peeled fresh ginger, thinly sliced
2 (1-pound) salmon fillets (about 1½ inches thick)
Cooking spray

SAUCE:

1½ cups fat-free, less-sodium chicken broth
¼ cup low-sodium soy sauce
¼ cup rice wine or sake
1 tablespoon sugar
1½ teaspoons cornstarch
1 tablespoon vegetable oil
3 tablespoons fermented black beans, rinsed, drained, and chopped
3 tablespoons minced green onions
2 tablespoons minced peeled fresh ginger
2 tablespoons minced garlic (about 8 cloves)
1 teaspoon crushed red pepper

REMAINING INGREDIENT:

2 tablespoons minced green onion tops

1. To prepare marinade, combine first 3 ingredients in a large zip-top plastic bag, and seal. Marinate in refrigerator 20 minutes. Remove fillets from bag, and discard marinade. Place fillets, skin sides down, on a jelly-roll pan coated with cooking spray.
2. Preheat oven to 450°.
3. To prepare sauce, combine broth and next 4 ingredients in a small bowl. Heat oil in a wok or large nonstick skillet over medium-high heat. Add beans and next 4 ingredients; stir-fry 10 seconds. Add broth mixture; bring to a boil, and cook 1 minute or until thick.
4. Pour black bean mixture over fillets; cover pan with foil. Bake at 450° for 17 minutes or until fish flakes easily when tested with a fork. Cut fillets into 6 portions; serve with sauce, and sprinkle with onion tops. Yield: 6 servings (serving size: about 5 ounces fish, about ⅓ cup sauce, and 1 teaspoon onion tops).

CALORIES 340 (40% from fat); FAT 15.2g (sat 2.6g, mono 6.8g, poly 4g); PROTEIN 32.6g; CARB 13.5g; FIBER 0.3g; CHOL 99mg; IRON 1mg; SODIUM 547mg; CALC 23mg

menu
serves 8

Hoisin Barbecued Chicken

Steamed zucchini and yellow squash

Brown rice with sesame seeds*

*Sauté 2 cups short-grain brown rice and 6 garlic cloves, minced, in 1 tablespoon oil in a large skillet. Add 1 cup water and 2 (15.75-ounce) cans fat-free, less-sodium chicken broth, and bring to a boil. Cover and cook 45 minutes or until liquid is absorbed. Fluff with a fork, and sprinkle with 1 tablespoon toasted sesame seeds.

Hoisin Barbecued Chicken

BARBECUE SAUCE:

⅔ cup hoisin sauce
3 tablespoons rice wine or sake
3 tablespoons low-sodium soy sauce
3 tablespoons ketchup
2 tablespoons brown sugar
1 tablespoon minced garlic

REMAINING INGREDIENTS:

8 chicken drumsticks, skinned and trimmed (about 2 pounds)
8 chicken thighs, skinned and trimmed (about 2 pounds)
Cooking spray

1. To prepare barbecue sauce, combine first 6 ingredients in a medium bowl.

Place ¾ cup sauce in a large bowl; cover and chill remaining barbecue sauce.

2. Add chicken to barbecue sauce in large bowl; toss to coat. Cover and marinate chicken in refrigerator 8 hours or overnight.

3. Preheat oven to 375°.

4. Remove chicken from bowl; reserve marinade. Place chicken on a broiler pan coated with cooking spray. Bake at 375° for 30 minutes. Turn chicken; baste with reserved marinade. Bake an additional 20 minutes or until done. Discard marinade.

5. Bring remaining ¾ cup barbecue sauce to a boil in a small saucepan; reduce heat, and cook until slightly thick and reduced to about ½ cup (about 5 minutes). Drizzle chicken with sauce. Yield: 8 servings (serving size: 1 drumstick, 1 thigh, and about 1 tablespoon sauce).

CALORIES 241 (23% from fat); FAT 6.1g (sat 1.5g, mono 1.9g, poly 1.8g); PROTEIN 26.6g; CARB 17.8g; FIBER 0.7g; CHOL 97mg; IRON 1.7mg; SODIUM 727mg; CALC 26mg

A Chinese Pantry

Chinese-cooking lovers will want to keep these ingredients on hand. Many can be found in well-stocked supermarkets; all are available in Asian markets or online at sites such as www.ethnicgrocer.com. Unless otherwise specified, all condiments should be refrigerated after opening.

Black vinegar A kind of rice vinegar that tends to be lighter and sweeter than Western vinegars. Has a mellow flavor and is used in sauces and dressings. A good substitute is Worcestershire sauce.

Chile paste or sauce A spicy seasoning made of crushed chile peppers, oil, vinegar, garlic, and other flavorings. You can substitute crushed red pepper, but because it's more potent, start with one-third the amount and add more to taste.

Dark sesame oil Nutty and rich, it's made from roasted or toasted sesame seeds and is not interchangeable with the pressed sesame seed oil found in health-food stores. Because it smokes at high temperatures, it's primarily used as a seasoning and not for stir-frying.

Dried chile peppers Available in a range of sizes in Asian markets. The smaller the pepper, the more intense its heat. While both fresh and dried peppers are used in Chinese cooking, the dried ones are used to infuse oils, sauces, and dressings with their spicy flavor. They are normally left whole, cut in half lengthwise, or finely ground. Seeds may be left in or discarded, but remember that they increase the intensity or hotness of the chile flavor.

Dried Chinese mushrooms Pungent dried shiitake mushrooms (also called black mushrooms) impart a strong smoky flavor. Another variety, dried wood ear mushrooms, is relished for its crunchy texture.

Fermented or salted black beans Used to season sauces, these are black soybeans that have been fermented with seasonings like ginger, orange peel, and licorice and then dried. The beans should be rinsed and drained before using; they refrigerate indefinitely. Look for beans in packages or plastic bags rather than in cans or jars.

Ginger When buying fresh ginger, look for hefty, smooth, shiny knobs. Ginger also comes in crystallized and pickled forms for other applications.

Hoisin sauce A sauce made with soybeans, sugar, vinegar, and spices. Sweet and fairly thick, its main uses are in marinades for barbecuing and roasting, and in dipping sauces.

Oyster sauce A Cantonese staple, usually sold in bottles, that's made from oysters, salt, and seasonings. It's often used in sauces for seafood, meat, and vegetable dishes. You can substitute an equal amount of soy sauce.

Plum sauce Also known as duck sauce, this is made from plums, apricots, vinegar, and sugar. In China, it's often served with roasted goose or duck; in the United States, it's the ubiquitous table sauce in American-Cantonese restaurants.

Rice wine An all-purpose cooking wine made from fermented rice. Sake or Japanese rice wines are acceptable substitutes, as is a very high-quality dry sherry (dry, fino, or manzanilla, but not cream sherry). The best variety of rice wine is Shaohsing.

Soy sauce Made from fermented soybeans and wheat, its flavor varies by manufacturer and aging process. Regular soy sauce contains 1,030 milligrams of sodium per tablespoon; light or low-sodium versions have 484.

Stir-Fried Broccoli with Oyster Sauce

The garlicky oyster sauce not only goes well with broccoli, but also with asparagus, zucchini, green beans, or cauliflower.

    2 pounds broccoli
    6 cups water
    ½ cup fat-free, less-sodium chicken broth
    3 tablespoons oyster sauce
    1½ tablespoons rice wine or sake
    1½ teaspoons cornstarch
    1½ teaspoons sugar
    1 teaspoon low-sodium soy sauce
    1 teaspoon dark sesame oil
    1½ tablespoons vegetable oil
    ¼ cup minced green onions
    1½ tablespoons minced peeled fresh ginger
    2 tablespoons minced garlic (about 8 cloves)

1. Cut broccoli florets and stems into bite-size pieces to measure 10 cups.
2. Bring water to a boil in a large Dutch oven; add broccoli. Cook broccoli 4 minutes or until crisp-tender; drain.
3. Combine broth and next 6 ingredients; stir well with a whisk. Heat vegetable oil in a large nonstick skillet over medium-high heat. Add onions, ginger, and garlic; sauté 15 seconds. Add broth mixture; bring to a boil. Cook 1 minute or until thick, stirring constantly. Add broccoli, and cook 30 seconds, tossing to coat. Yield: 8 servings (serving size: 1 cup).

CALORIES 80 (40% from fat); FAT 3.5g (sat 0.6g, mono 1g, poly 1.7g); PROTEIN 3.8g; CARB 10.3g; FIBER 3.6g; CHOL 0mg; IRON 1.1mg; SODIUM 275mg; CALC 62mg

Shrimp Fried Rice

Fried rice is an extremely versatile dish that can be made with all kinds of meat, seafood, and vegetables. In this and other fried-rice recipes, the cooked rice must be chilled to prevent its grains from sticking. To chill, spread the cooked rice on a jelly-roll pan; cover and refrigerate 8 hours or overnight.

    2 tablespoons fat-free, less-sodium chicken broth
    2 tablespoons rice wine or sake
    1 tablespoon low-sodium soy sauce
    1 teaspoon dark sesame oil
    ½ teaspoon salt
    ¼ teaspoon freshly ground black pepper
    2 tablespoons vegetable oil
    2 large eggs, lightly beaten
    2 cups chopped green onions
    1 tablespoon minced peeled fresh ginger
    5 cups cooked long-grain rice, chilled (recipe at right)
    1 pound medium shrimp, cooked, peeled, and coarsely chopped
    1 (10-ounce) package frozen green peas, thawed

1. Combine first 6 ingredients in a small bowl.
2. Heat vegetable oil in a wok or large nonstick skillet over medium-high heat. Add eggs; stir-fry 30 seconds or until soft-scrambled. Add onions and ginger; stir-fry 1 minute. Add rice, shrimp, and peas; stir-fry 3 minutes or until thoroughly heated. Add broth mixture; toss gently to coat. Yield: 6 servings (serving size: 1⅓ cups).

CALORIES 380 (19% from fat); FAT 7.9g (sat 1.7g, mono 2.5g, poly 3.1g); PROTEIN 20.8g; CARB 53.3g; FIBER 1.7g; CHOL 184mg; IRON 4.8mg; SODIUM 527mg; CALC 83mg

Long-Grain Rice

In America, most people don't normally rinse their rice before cooking, but it's routine in China. Doing this removes the white powder from polishing and allows the grains to separate during cooking, creating a fluffier effect.

    2¼ cups uncooked long-grain rice (such as jasmine or basmati)
    4 cups water

1. Place rice in a fine sieve, and rinse with cold running water, stirring with fingers, until water runs clear.
2. Combine rice and 4 cups water in a saucepan, and bring to a boil. Cover, reduce heat, and simmer 17 minutes or until liquid is absorbed. Fluff rice with a fork. Yield: 6 cups (serving size: 1 cup).

CALORIES 253 (2% from fat); FAT 0.5g (sat 0.1g, mono 0.1g, poly 0.1g); PROTEIN 4.9g; CARB 55.5g; FIBER 0.9g; CHOL 0mg; IRON 3mg; SODIUM 3mg; CALC 19mg

---

How We Did It

Most classic Chinese cuisine is inherently healthful because of its reliance on vegetables, vegetable oils, stir-frying, and fat-free condiments. But sodium levels can get pretty high because many condiments such as soy, oyster, and hoisin sauces are higher in sodium. Our solution? Low-sodium soy sauce. We also kept the fat down by using less vegetable oil than traditional recipes call for.

Tropical Fruit Salad, page 42

Balsamic Vinaigrette
Chicken over Gourmet
Greens, page 15

Double-Chocolate Soufflé
Torte with Raspberry
Sauce, page 43

Sweet-and-Tangy Roasted
Pork Tenderloin and
Mashed Potatoes with
Blue Cheese and Parsley,
page 14

Juicy Apple Crisp,
page 14

Superfast Salisbury Steak,
page 18

Moo Shu Pork with Mandarin
Pancakes, page 31

Helping-Hands Meals

Transportable dishes for those who need a little extra help at mealtime.

Chipotle Tamale Pie

1¾ cups chopped onion
¾ cup chopped green bell pepper
¾ pound ground round
½ cup bottled salsa
1 to 2 tablespoons bottled chipotle sauce (such as La Preferidia) or hot sauce
1 (15½-ounce) can pinto beans in zesty sauce (such as S&W), undrained
1 (14.5-ounce) can no-salt-added diced tomatoes, drained
¾ cup chopped fresh cilantro, divided
1 cup all-purpose flour
¾ cup yellow cornmeal
2 tablespoons sugar
2 teaspoons baking powder
½ teaspoon salt
⅔ cup 1% low-fat milk
1½ tablespoons butter, melted
1 large egg, lightly beaten

1. Preheat oven to 400°.
2. Heat a large nonstick skillet over medium-high heat. Add onion, bell pepper, and beef; cook 5 minutes or until meat is browned, stirring to crumble. Stir in salsa, chipotle sauce, beans, and tomatoes; cook 5 minutes, stirring occasionally. Stir in ½ cup cilantro. Spoon beef mixture into a 3-quart casserole.
3. Lightly spoon flour into a dry measuring cup; level with a knife. Combine flour and next 4 ingredients in a large bowl. Add ¼ cup cilantro, milk, butter, and egg; stir until well blended. Spoon batter over beef mixture; spread evenly. Bake at 400° for 35 minutes or until golden. Yield: 8 servings (serving size: 1 cup).

CALORIES 329 (30% from fat); FAT 11g (sat 4.7g, mono 4.2g, poly 0.8g); PROTEIN 16g; CARB 41.7g; FIBER 5.8g; CHOL 64mg; IRON 4.2mg; SODIUM 655mg; CALC 157mg

Tangy Tuna-Salad Sandwiches

½ cup chopped red bell pepper
¼ cup bottled pickled vegetables, drained and chopped (such as Vigo Giardinera)
¼ cup finely chopped red onion
¼ cup fat-free mayonnaise
1 (12-ounce) can albacore tuna in water, drained and flaked
8 (1-ounce) slices multigrain bread
2 cups trimmed arugula or spinach

1. Combine first 5 ingredients in a medium bowl. Spread ½ cup tuna salad over 4 bread slices. Top each slice with ½ cup arugula and 1 bread slice. Yield: 4 servings (serving size: 1 sandwich).

CALORIES 272 (14% from fat); FAT 4.3g (sat 1g, mono 1.4g, poly 1.3g); PROTEIN 21.3g; CARB 32g; FIBER 5.1g; CHOL 33mg; IRON 2.9mg; SODIUM 876mg; CALC 71mg

Vegetable Lasagna

1 teaspoon olive oil
¾ cup sliced mushrooms
¾ cup chopped zucchini
½ cup sliced carrot
½ cup chopped red bell pepper
½ cup thinly sliced red onion
1 (26-ounce) bottle fat-free tomato-basil pasta sauce
2 tablespoons commercial pesto
1 (15-ounce) carton part-skim ricotta cheese
Cooking spray
6 hot cooked lasagna noodles (about 6 ounces uncooked), cut in half
¾ cup (3 ounces) shredded part-skim mozzarella cheese

1. Preheat oven to 375°.
2. Heat oil in a medium saucepan over medium heat. Add mushrooms and next 4 ingredients; cook 5 minutes, stirring frequently. Add pasta sauce; bring to a boil. Reduce heat, and simmer 10 minutes.
3. Combine pesto and ricotta in a small bowl. Spread ½ cup tomato mixture in bottom of an 8-inch square baking dish or pan coated with cooking spray. Arrange 4 noodle halves over tomato mixture. Top noodles with half of ricotta mixture and 1 cup tomato mixture. Repeat layers, ending with noodles. Spread remaining tomato mixture over noodles; sprinkle with mozzarella.
4. Cover and bake at 375° for 30 minutes. Uncover and bake an additional 20 minutes. Let stand 10 minutes. Yield: 6 servings.
NOTE: To make ahead, assemble as directed. Cover and refrigerate overnight. Let stand 30 minutes at room temperature; bake as directed.

CALORIES 328 (30% from fat); FAT 10.9g (sat 5.4g, mono 3.8g, poly 0.9g); PROTEIN 18.2g; CARB 39g; FIBER 3.7g; CHOL 31mg; IRON 2.9mg; SODIUM 491mg; CALC 418mg

Caramelized Onion and Canadian Bacon Strata

1 teaspoon butter
1½ cups vertically sliced onion
1⅓ cups finely chopped red bell pepper
¾ cup chopped Canadian bacon
6 cups (1-inch) cubed sourdough bread (about 12 ounces)
Cooking spray
2 cups 1% low-fat milk
1½ tablespoons spicy brown mustard
¼ teaspoon salt
¼ teaspoon freshly ground black pepper
4 large egg whites
2 large eggs
1 cup (4 ounces) shredded Swiss cheese

1. Melt butter in a large nonstick skillet over medium-high heat. Add onion, and sauté 4 minutes. Reduce heat; cook 10 minutes or until golden brown, stirring occasionally. Add bell pepper; cook 1 minute. Remove from heat; stir in bacon.
2. Arrange 3 cups bread in an 11 x 7-inch baking dish coated with cooking spray; top with half of onion mixture. Repeat with remaining bread and onion mixture.
3. Combine milk and next 5 ingredients in a medium bowl; stir well with a whisk. Pour egg mixture over bread mixture, and top with cheese. Cover and refrigerate at least 8 hours or overnight.

Continued

4. Preheat oven to 375°.

5. Let casserole stand 30 minutes at room temperature. Uncover and bake at 375° for 40 minutes or until golden brown. Let stand 5 minutes before serving. Yield: 6 servings.

CALORIES 340 (30% from fat); FAT 11.5g (sat 5.7g, mono 3.7g, poly 1.1g); PROTEIN 21.8g; CARB 37g; FIBER 2g; CHOL 105mg; IRON 2.4mg; SODIUM 926mg; CALC 358mg

Rice, Bean, and Spinach Salad

Cooking spray
    4 ounces andouille sausage, halved lengthwise and sliced
    2 garlic cloves, minced
    1 cup fat-free, less-sodium chicken broth
    ½ cup sliced carrot
    ⅓ cup golden raisins
    1 teaspoon ground cumin
    ½ teaspoon paprika
    ¼ teaspoon salt
    ¼ teaspoon ground cinnamon
    ⅛ teaspoon ground red pepper
    1 (16-ounce) can kidney beans, drained
    3 cups cooked long-grain rice
    3 cups spinach leaves
    2 tablespoons sherry vinegar or red wine vinegar
    1 tablespoon olive oil

1. Heat a large saucepan coated with cooking spray over medium heat. Add sausage and garlic, and sauté 1 minute. Add broth and next 8 ingredients; bring to a boil. Reduce heat, and simmer 10 minutes. Combine sausage mixture and rice in a bowl; cover and chill. Stir remaining ingredients into salad just before serving. Yield: 6 servings (serving size: 1 cup).

CALORIES 274 (21% from fat); FAT 6.5g (sat 1.7g, mono 3.3g, poly 1g); PROTEIN 9.9g; CARB 43.8g; FIBER 5.9g; CHOL 13mg; IRON 3.3mg; SODIUM 581mg; CALC 67mg

Sour Cream Coffee Cake

    ½ cup packed brown sugar
    ¼ cup chopped walnuts
    2 teaspoons ground cinnamon
    1 cup granulated sugar
    ¼ cup butter, softened
    2 large egg whites
    1 cup reduced-fat sour cream
    1 teaspoon vanilla extract
  1¾ cups all-purpose flour
    1 teaspoon baking powder
    1 teaspoon baking soda
    ½ teaspoon salt
Cooking spray

1. Preheat oven to 350°.

2. Combine first 3 ingredients; set aside.

3. Place granulated sugar and butter in a large bowl; beat with a mixer at medium speed until well blended. Add egg whites, 1 at a time, beating well after each addition. Beat in sour cream and vanilla. Lightly spoon flour into dry measuring cups; level with a knife. Combine flour, baking powder, baking soda, and salt; stir well. Gradually add flour mixture to sugar mixture; beat well. Spread half of batter into an 8-inch square baking pan coated with cooking spray. Sprinkle half of streusel over batter. Spread remaining batter over streusel. Top with remaining streusel.

4. Bake at 350° for 45 minutes or until a pick inserted in center comes out clean. Cool on a wire rack. Yield: 12 servings.

CALORIES 243 (30% from fat); FAT 8.1g (sat 4g, mono 2.2g, poly 1.4g); PROTEIN 3.6g; CARB 40g; FIBER 0.7g; CHOL 18mg; IRON 1.2mg; SODIUM 253mg; CALC 54mg

Tropical Fruit Salad

(pictured on page 37)

    2 cups (1-inch) cubed fresh pineapple
    1 cup chopped peeled papaya or mango
    1 cup sliced peeled kiwifruit (about 3 kiwifruit)
    1 cup red seedless grapes
    ⅔ cup (¼-inch-thick) slices carambola (star fruit; about 1)
    ¼ cup flaked sweetened coconut
    3 tablespoons honey
    2 tablespoons fresh lime juice

1. Combine first 6 ingredients in a medium bowl. Chill at least 30 minutes.

2. Combine honey and juice in a small bowl; toss with fruit just before serving. Yield: 6 servings (serving size: 1 cup).

CALORIES 128 (13% from fat); FAT 1.9g (sat 1.3g, mono 0.1g, poly 0.2g); PROTEIN 1.1g; CARB 29.7g; FIBER 2.9g; CHOL 0mg; IRON 0.6mg; SODIUM 14mg; CALC 24mg

Swedish Meatballs with Shiitake Mushrooms

    1 pound ground round
    ¾ cup dry breadcrumbs
    ½ cup fat-free milk
    ½ teaspoon salt
    ¼ teaspoon ground ginger
    ¼ teaspoon ground allspice
    ¼ teaspoon black pepper
    1 large egg white
Cooking spray
  4½ cups thinly sliced shiitake mushroom caps (about 8 ounces)
  1½ cups thinly sliced carrot
    ½ cup thinly sliced shallots
    2 tablespoons all-purpose flour
    1 (10½-ounce) can beef consommé
    ½ cup water
    ½ cup reduced-fat sour cream
    ¼ cup chopped fresh parsley
    6 cups hot cooked yolk-free wide egg noodles (about 10 ounces uncooked pasta)

1. Combine first 8 ingredients in a bowl. Shape into 30 (1-inch) meatballs. Heat a nonstick skillet coated with cooking spray over medium heat. Add meatballs; cook 8 minutes, browning on all sides. Remove from pan.

2. Add mushrooms, carrot, and shallots to pan; sauté 5 minutes. Stir in flour; cook 1 minute. Gradually add consommé, stirring with a whisk; bring to a boil. Return meatballs to pan. Cover, reduce heat, and simmer 8 minutes. Add water; cook 2 minutes. Remove from heat, and stir in sour cream and parsley. Serve over pasta. Yield: 6 servings (serving size: 5 meatballs, about ½ cup mushroom mixture, and 1 cup pasta).

CALORIES 497 (30% from fat); FAT 16.8g (sat 6.9g, mono 6.7g, poly 0.9g); PROTEIN 29.1g; CARB 55.7g; FIBER 4.5g; CHOL 60mg; IRON 5.1mg; SODIUM 686mg; CALC 105mg

Winter Wonderful

Five great desserts to get you through the coldest months of the year.

The holidays may be over and the new year rung in, but that doesn't mean all the good cheer has to stop for the duration of winter. Here are five incredible desserts to make these blustery months bearable. From Maple-Pear Upside-Down Cake to Vanilla Bean Crème Brûlée, each is reason to celebrate all over again.

Maple-Pear Upside-Down Cake

Maple syrup, cooked down to a glaze with fresh pears, is the topping for this dessert.

- ⅓ cup maple syrup
- 3 peeled Bartlett or Anjou pears, each cored and cut into 8 wedges
- 1 cup all-purpose flour
- ¾ teaspoon baking powder
- ¼ teaspoon baking soda
- ¼ teaspoon ground ginger
- ¼ teaspoon salt
- ⅔ cup sugar
- ⅓ cup butter, softened
- 1 teaspoon vanilla extract
- 2 large eggs
- ½ cup low-fat buttermilk

1. Preheat oven to 350°.
2. Bring syrup to a boil in a medium nonstick skillet over medium-high heat; cook 2 minutes. Remove from heat; arrange pears in pan in a spokelike fashion. Place pan over medium-high heat, and cook until syrup thickens (about 4 minutes), gently shaking pan frequently.
3. Lightly spoon flour into a dry measuring cup; level with a knife. Combine flour and next 4 ingredients, stirring well with a whisk. Place sugar, butter, and vanilla in a large bowl; beat with a mixer at medium speed until well blended (about 2 minutes). Add eggs, 1 at a time, beating well after each addition. Stir in flour mixture alternately with buttermilk, beginning and ending with flour mixture.
4. Pour batter evenly over pear mixture in prepared pan; wrap handle of skillet with foil. Bake at 350° for 30 minutes or until cake springs back when touched lightly in center. Loosen cake from sides of pan using a narrow metal spatula. Cool in pan 5 minutes. Place a plate upside down on top of cake; invert onto plate. Serve warm. Yield: 8 servings (serving size: 1 wedge).

CALORIES 288 (30% from fat); FAT 9.6g (sat 5.3g, mono 2.8g, poly 0.6g); PROTEIN 4.1g; CARB 47.9g; FIBER 1.9g; CHOL 76mg; IRON 1.3mg; SODIUM 262mg; CALC 71mg

Double-Chocolate Soufflé Torte with Raspberry Sauce

(pictured on page 38)

The key to soufflé success lies in the beating of the egg whites. Use spotless utensils, beating the whites until stiff peaks form—firm enough to stand up yet still able to slide around the bowl when gently swirled. Beat them too much, and they'll be too dry to create air pockets. Egg whites must be gently folded into the batter—don't overdo it. The sauce can be prepared a day ahead and chilled.

SAUCE:
- 1 cup water
- ½ cup sugar
- 1 tablespoon cornstarch
- ⅛ teaspoon salt
- 1 (10-ounce) package frozen raspberries in light syrup, thawed and undrained
- 1 tablespoon Grand Marnier (orange-flavored liqueur)

TORTE:
- 3 ounces semisweet chocolate, chopped
- 2 tablespoons Grand Marnier (orange-flavored liqueur)
- 3 tablespoons butter, softened
- ¾ cup sugar, divided
- 1 large egg
- ¼ cup fat-free milk
- ¼ cup Dutch process cocoa or unsweetened cocoa
- 2 tablespoons cornstarch
- 4 large egg whites
- ¼ teaspoon cream of tartar
- ⅛ teaspoon salt
- Cooking spray

1. To prepare raspberry sauce, combine first 4 ingredients in a medium, heavy saucepan; stir well with a whisk. Bring to a boil over medium heat, stirring frequently. Cook 2 minutes. Stir in raspberries; cook 4 minutes, stirring gently. Remove from heat. Stir in 1 tablespoon liqueur. Pour sauce into a bowl; cover and chill 1 hour.
2. Preheat oven to 300°.
3. To prepare torte, combine chocolate and 2 tablespoons liqueur in a small, heavy saucepan; cook over low heat until chocolate melts and mixture is smooth, stirring occasionally with a whisk. Place butter and ½ cup sugar in a medium bowl; beat with a mixer at medium speed 1 minute or until fluffy. Add 1 egg; beat 1 minute. Gradually add milk; beat at low speed (mixture will look curdled). Add chocolate mixture, cocoa, and 2 tablespoons cornstarch; beat at low speed until combined.
4. Place egg whites, cream of tartar, and ⅛ teaspoon salt in a medium bowl; beat with a mixer at high speed until soft peaks form using clean, dry beaters. Gradually add ¼ cup sugar, 1 tablespoon at a time, beating until stiff peaks form. Gently fold one-fourth of egg white mixture into chocolate mixture; gently fold in remaining egg white mixture. Spoon chocolate mixture into an 8-inch springform pan coated with cooking spray. Bake at 300° for 45 minutes or until a wooden pick inserted in center comes out almost clean; loosen
Continued

torte from sides of pan using a narrow metal spatula. (Torte falls as it cools.) Cool on a wire rack. Serve with raspberry sauce. Yield: 8 servings (serving size: 1 wedge and ¼ cup sauce).

NOTE: Grand Marnier adds a wonderful depth of flavor to this indulgent-tasting dessert. But if you want to go alcohol-free, substitute water or orange juice.

CALORIES 298 (26% from fat); FAT 8.7g (sat 5.2g, mono 2.6g, poly 0.4g); PROTEIN 4.1g; CARB 53g; FIBER 1.7g; CHOL 34mg; IRON 1.2mg; SODIUM 155mg; CALC 28mg

Butter Crunch Lemon-Cheese Bars

CRUST:

- ⅓ cup butter, softened
- ¼ cup packed dark brown sugar
- ¼ teaspoon salt
- ¼ teaspoon ground mace or nutmeg
- 1 cup all-purpose flour
- Cooking spray

FILLING:

- 1 cup 1% low-fat cottage cheese
- 1 cup granulated sugar
- 2 tablespoons all-purpose flour
- 1 tablespoon grated lemon rind
- 3½ tablespoons fresh lemon juice
- ¼ teaspoon baking powder
- 1 large egg
- 1 large egg white

1. Preheat oven to 350°.

2. To prepare crust, place first 4 ingredients in a large bowl, and beat with a mixer at medium speed until smooth. Lightly spoon 1 cup flour into a dry measuring cup, and level with a knife. Add 1 cup flour to butter mixture, and beat at low speed until well blended. Press crust into an 8-inch square baking pan coated with cooking spray. Bake at 350° for 20 minutes.

3. To prepare filling, place cottage cheese in a food processor; process 2 minutes or until smooth, scraping sides of bowl once. Add 1 cup granulated sugar and remaining 6 ingredients, and process until well blended. Pour filling over crust. Bake at 350° for 25 minutes or until set (edges will be lightly browned), and cool. Cover and chill 8 hours. Yield: 8 servings (serving size: 1 bar).

CALORIES 281 (29% from fat); FAT 9g (sat 5.2g, mono 2.6g, poly 0.6g); PROTEIN 6.7g; CARB 44.5g; FIBER 0.5g; CHOL 49mg; IRON 1.1mg; SODIUM 298mg; CALC 40mg

Butterscotch-Amaretti Parfaits

This is a great make-ahead dessert, especially for entertaining. To make cookie crumbs, place cookies in a plastic bag and crush with a rolling pin, or pulse them in a food processor.

- 1½ cups 2% reduced-fat milk
- ¾ cup packed dark brown sugar
- 2 tablespoons cornstarch
- ⅛ teaspoon salt
- 2 large egg yolks
- 2 tablespoons butter
- 2 teaspoons vanilla extract
- 1½ cups frozen reduced-calorie whipped topping, thawed and divided
- 16 cakelike ladyfingers
- ½ cup amaretti cookie crumbs (about 8 cookies)

1. Combine first 5 ingredients in a medium saucepan. Bring to a simmer over medium heat, stirring frequently, and cook until thick and bubbly (about 2 minutes). Remove from heat; stir in butter and vanilla. Pour into a bowl; cover surface of pudding with plastic wrap, and chill. Remove plastic wrap, and fold in 1 cup whipped topping.

2. Split ladyfingers in half lengthwise. Line each of 8 parfait glasses with 4 ladyfinger halves, standing halves upright. Spoon 2 tablespoons pudding into center of each glass, and top each portion with 2 teaspoons cookie crumbs. Spoon ¼ cup pudding on top of crumbs in each glass. Top each parfait with 1 tablespoon whipped topping, and sprinkle each serving with 1 teaspoon crumbs. Yield: 8 servings (serving size: 1 parfait).

CALORIES 286 (29% from fat); FAT 9.3g (sat 5.1g, mono 2.5g, poly 0.7g); PROTEIN 5.3g; CARB 45g; FIBER 0.2g; CHOL 146mg; IRON 1.4mg; SODIUM 143mg; CALC 99mg

Vanilla Bean Crème Brûlée

Crème brûlée, French for "burned cream," is a custard whose brown sugar topping is melted and crystallized under a broiler.

- 4 large egg yolks
- 1 teaspoon granulated sugar
- ⅛ teaspoon salt
- 2 cups 2% reduced-fat milk
- 1 (3-inch) piece vanilla bean, split lengthwise, or 1 teaspoon vanilla extract
- 3 tablespoons granulated sugar
- ¾ cup nonfat dry milk
- ¼ cup packed light brown sugar
- 1½ teaspoons water

1. Preheat oven to 300°.

2. Combine first 3 ingredients in a medium bowl; stir well with a whisk. Set aside.

3. Pour reduced-fat milk into a medium saucepan. Scrape seeds from vanilla bean; add seeds, bean, 3 tablespoons granulated sugar, and dry milk to pan. Heat mixture over medium heat to 180° or until tiny bubbles form around the edge (do not boil), stirring occasionally with a whisk. Discard bean.

4. Gradually add hot milk mixture to egg mixture, stirring constantly with a whisk. Divide milk mixture evenly among 6 (4-ounce) ramekins or custard cups. Place ramekins in a 13 x 9-inch baking pan; add hot water to pan to a depth of 1 inch. Bake at 300° for 1 hour or until center barely moves when ramekin is touched. Remove ramekins from pan; cool completely on a wire rack. Cover and chill at least 4 hours or overnight.

5. Combine brown sugar and water in a 1-cup glass measure. Microwave at HIGH 30 seconds; stir until sugar dissolves. Microwave at HIGH 60 seconds; pour evenly over desserts, quickly tipping ramekins to coat tops of brûlées. (There will be a thin layer of melted sugar.) Let harden. Yield: 6 servings (serving size: 1 custard).

CALORIES 185 (25% from fat); FAT 5.2g (sat 2.1g, mono 1.8g, poly 0.5g); PROTEIN 10g; CARB 24.7g; FIBER 0g; CHOL 155mg; IRON 0.6mg; SODIUM 177mg; CALC 309mg

march

Breakfast Unscrambled

Whether you're running out the door or relaxing at home, here are easy strategies for the first meal of the day.

For a morning meal on the run try a quick breakfast smoothie. All you need are fat-free milk, banana, mango, and a blender. Or with only a few minutes of preparation the night before, you can wake up to crunchy fruit granola or a sausage calzone that you can heat while getting dressed. Fresh muffins are always great, especially when you've filled them with cream cheese and jelly or preserves.

When there's finally time to relax on the weekend, give breakfast the attention you give to other meals. Brew some coffee or tea, sit by the window, and savor a Spinach-and-Potato Frittata or a tortilla strata rich with cheese and beans. Don't forget the soul-sustaining virtues of pancakes, either—they make the perfect breakfast partner.

Breakfast Tortilla Strata

Putting this dish together and chilling it the night before gives the tortillas time to soak up the batter, which makes the strips puff when baked the next day.

    1 cup bottled salsa
    1 cup canned black beans, rinsed and
       drained
   10 (6-inch) corn tortillas, cut into
       1-inch strips
   Cooking spray
    1 cup (4 ounces) preshredded
       reduced-fat Mexican blend or
       Monterey Jack cheese, divided
    1 cup low-fat sour cream
    1 cup fat-free milk
   ½ teaspoon salt
    2 large eggs
    2 large egg whites
   ¼ cup thinly sliced green onions

1. Combine salsa and beans in a bowl. Place one-third of tortilla strips in an 11 x 7-inch baking dish coated with cooking spray. Top with ⅓ cup cheese and about 1 cup salsa mixture. Repeat procedure with one-third of tortilla strips, ⅓ cup cheese, and remaining salsa mixture; top with remaining tortilla strips.
2. Combine sour cream and next 4 ingredients; stir with a whisk. Stir in onions. Pour over tortilla strips; sprinkle with ⅓ cup cheese. Cover and chill 8 hours or overnight.
3. Preheat oven to 350°.
4. Remove dish from refrigerator. Let stand at room temperature 10 minutes. Cover and bake at 350° for 20 minutes. Uncover and bake an additional 15 minutes or until lightly browned. Yield: 6 servings.

CALORIES 292 (28% from fat); FAT 9.2g (sat 4.5g, mono 2.7g, poly 1.1g); PROTEIN 17.7g; CARB 36.5g; FIBER 4.7g; CHOL 93mg; IRON 2.2mg; SODIUM 755mg; CALC 335mg

Oven-Puffed Pancake

This quick-to-mix pancake puffs up nicely in the oven, but don't be alarmed when it deflates as soon as you take it out—it's supposed to. Serve with sliced fruit.

   ½ cup all-purpose flour
   ½ cup fat-free milk
    2 tablespoons granulated sugar
   ¼ teaspoon salt
    1 large egg
    1 large egg white
    1 tablespoon butter
   Powdered sugar (optional)

1. Preheat oven to 425°.
2. Lightly spoon flour into a dry measuring cup; level with a knife. Combine flour and next 5 ingredients, and stir until moist.
3. Melt butter in a 10-inch cast-iron skillet over medium heat. Pour batter into pan; cook 1 minute (do not stir). Bake at 425° for 18 minutes or until golden. Sprinkle with powdered sugar, if desired. Cut into quarters; serve immediately. Yield: 4 servings.

CALORIES 141 (28% from fat); FAT 4.4g (sat 2.3g, mono 1.4g, poly 0.4g); PROTEIN 5.2g; CARB 19.9g; FIBER 0.4g; CHOL 64mg; IRON 0.9mg; SODIUM 222mg; CALC 48mg

Strawberry-and-Cream Cheese-Filled Muffins

A slather of cream cheese and jelly on top of muffins is too messy to eat on the way to work, so we tucked the goodies inside. Any flavor of fruit preserves will work. The muffins can be made ahead and stored in an airtight container overnight or in a heavy-duty zip-top plastic bag in the freezer. Just thaw at room temperature and eat. This recipe can also be doubled or tripled to feed the family for an entire week. And, it's great with our Banana-Mango Smoothie (recipe on page 47).

   ¼ cup (2 ounces) ⅓-less-fat cream
       cheese
    2 tablespoons strawberry preserves
   2¼ cups all-purpose flour
   ⅓ cup sugar
    2 teaspoons baking powder
    2 teaspoons poppy seeds
   ½ teaspoon baking soda
   ¼ teaspoon salt
   1¼ cups low-fat buttermilk
    3 tablespoons vegetable oil
    2 large egg whites
    1 large egg
   Cooking spray

1. Preheat oven to 375°.
2. Combine cream cheese and preserves; stir with a whisk.
3. Lightly spoon flour into dry measuring cups; level with a knife. Combine flour and next 5 ingredients in a medium bowl; make a well in center of mixture. Combine buttermilk, oil, egg whites, and egg; stir well with a whisk. Add to flour mixture, stirring just until moist.

4. Spoon batter into 12 muffin cups coated with cooking spray, filling one-third full. Top each with about 1 teaspoon cream cheese mixture; spoon remaining batter evenly over cream cheese mixture. Bake at 375° for 25 minutes or until muffins spring back when touched lightly in center. Remove muffins from pans immediately, and cool on a wire rack. Yield: 1 dozen (serving size: 1 muffin).

CALORIES 182 (29% from fat); FAT 5.9g (sat 1.7g, mono 1.6g, poly 2g); PROTEIN 5g; CARB 27.4g; FIBER 0.7g; CHOL 23mg; IRON 1.3mg; SODIUM 231mg; CALC 94mg

Banana-Mango Smoothie

Freeze the cubed mango overnight in an airtight container to make this smoothie a snap to throw together (for variety, try substituting frozen berries for the mango). Remember to let frozen mango thaw for 15 minutes to soften slightly. The dry milk is optional, but one tablespoon provides about 100 milligrams of calcium. Try this smoothie with our Strawberry-and-Cream Cheese-Filled Muffins (recipe on page 46).

 1 cup cubed peeled ripe mango
 ¾ cup sliced ripe banana (about
     1 medium)
 ⅔ cup fat-free milk
 1 tablespoon nonfat dry milk
     (optional)
 1 teaspoon honey
 ¼ teaspoon vanilla extract

1. Arrange mango cubes in a single layer on a baking sheet; freeze until firm (about 1 hour). Place frozen mango and remaining ingredients in a blender. Process until smooth. Yield: 2 servings (serving size: 1 cup).

CALORIES 160 (4% from fat); FAT 0.7g (sat 0.3g, mono 0.2g, poly 0.1g); PROTEIN 5.1g; CARB 36.1g; FIBER 2.6g; CHOL 2mg; IRON 0.3mg; SODIUM 65mg; CALC 160mg

---

Soup-and-Sandwich Supper

Broccoli-Sausage Calzones

Tomato soup with basil cream*

Mixed greens

Cantaloupe wedges and gingersnaps

*Prepare 2 (10¾-ounce) cans condensed reduced-fat, reduced-sodium tomato soup according to directions. Combine ⅓ cup low-fat sour cream and 2 teaspoons commercial pesto; swirl about 1 tablespoon into each serving of soup.

Broccoli-Sausage Calzones

Assemble the calzones the night before, cover, and refrigerate. The next morning, just follow the baking instructions; in about half an hour, you'll be ready to run out the door with an easy-to-eat handheld breakfast.

 ⅔ cup chopped broccoli florets
 ⅔ cup (about 3½ ounces) diced
     chicken and sun-dried tomato
     sausage (such as Gerhard's)
 ½ cup part-skim ricotta cheese
 ¼ cup (1 ounce) shredded sharp
     provolone cheese
 ¼ teaspoon freshly ground black
     pepper
 1 (10-ounce) can refrigerated pizza
     crust dough
Olive oil-flavored cooking spray

1. Preheat oven to 350°.
2. Steam broccoli, covered, 3 minutes or until tender.
3. Combine broccoli, sausage, ricotta, provolone, and black pepper in a bowl. Divide pizza dough into 4 equal portions on a lightly floured surface; cover and let rest 10 minutes. Shape each piece into a ball. Roll each ball into a 6-inch circle. Place about ⅓ cup sausage mixture on half of each circle, leaving ½-inch borders. Fold pizza dough over sausage mixture until edges almost meet. Bring bottom edge of dough over top edge of dough; crimp edges of dough with fingers to form a rim.

---

4. Place calzones on a baking sheet coated with cooking spray. Pierce tops with a fork. Lightly spray tops with cooking spray. Bake at 350° for 35 minutes or until golden brown. Yield: 4 servings (serving size: 1 calzone).

CALORIES 306 (30% from fat); FAT 10.3g (sat 4g, mono 3.5g, poly 2g); PROTEIN 16g; CARB 30g; FIBER 0.5g; CHOL 37mg; IRON 2.5mg; SODIUM 733mg; CALC 145mg

Fruit-and-Nut Granola

Serve with low-fat milk or sprinkled over yogurt for a quick breakfast. Stored in an airtight container, the granola will keep for up to 2 weeks. You can also double or triple this recipe to feed the entire family.

 4   cups regular oats
 ½   cup toasted or honey-crunch
      wheat germ
 ½   cup sliced almonds
 ¼   cup nonfat dry milk
 ¼   cup sunflower seed kernels
 2   tablespoons sesame seeds
 1½ teaspoons ground cinnamon
 ¼   teaspoon salt
 ½   cup honey
 ¼   cup orange juice
 2   teaspoons vegetable oil
 1   teaspoon vanilla extract
Cooking spray
 1   cup chopped dried mixed fruit
 1   cup golden raisins
 ½   cup sweetened dried cranberries

1. Preheat oven to 350°.
2. Combine first 8 ingredients in a large bowl. Combine honey and orange juice in a small saucepan over medium heat, and cook 4 minutes or until warm. Add oil and vanilla; stir with a whisk. Pour honey mixture over oat mixture; toss well.
3. Spread oat mixture onto a jelly-roll pan coated with cooking spray. Bake at 350° for 15 minutes; stir. Bake an additional 10 minutes or until crisp. Cool in pan. Place oat mixture in a large bowl; stir in dried fruits. Yield: 8 cups (serving size: ½ cup).

CALORIES 242 (20% from fat); FAT 5.5g (sat 0.8g, mono 2.1g, poly 2.3g); PROTEIN 6.6g; CARB 44.6g; FIBER 3.8g; CHOL 0mg; IRON 2.1mg; SODIUM 52mg; CALC 69mg

Spinach-and-Potato Frittata

A frittata is an open-faced omelet. It's easier to make than traditional omelets because all the ingredients are combined at once so you don't have to fuss with flipping it over. Leftover cooked potatoes or frozen hash brown potatoes will also work in this recipe.

1½ cups finely chopped peeled baking potato (about 6 ounces)
6 large egg whites
3 large eggs
¼ cup chopped Canadian bacon (about 2 slices)
½ teaspoon salt
¼ teaspoon freshly ground black pepper
1 (10-ounce) package frozen chopped spinach, thawed, drained, and squeezed dry
Cooking spray
½ cup chopped onion
2 tablespoons shredded reduced-fat sharp cheddar cheese

1. Preheat oven to 400°.
2. Cook potato in boiling water 5 minutes or until tender; drain.
3. Combine egg whites and eggs in a large bowl, stirring with a whisk. Stir in potato, Canadian bacon, salt, pepper, and spinach.
4. Coat a 9-inch cast-iron skillet with cooking spray; place over medium-high heat. Add onion; sauté 4 minutes or until tender. Add potato mixture to pan; cook over medium heat 5 minutes or until almost set. Sprinkle with cheese. Bake at 400° for 6 minutes or until set. Let stand 3 minutes; cut into 4 wedges. Yield: 4 servings (serving size: 1 wedge).

CALORIES 187 (29% from fat); FAT 6.1g (sat 2g, mono 2.2g, poly 0.9g); PROTEIN 17.4g; CARB 16.2g; FIBER 3.5g; CHOL 175mg; IRON 2.6mg; SODIUM 704mg; CALC 142mg

Wake-Up Shake

¾ cup prune juice, chilled
¾ cup 2% reduced-fat milk, chilled
½ cup vanilla low-fat yogurt
¾ teaspoon vanilla extract
Dash of ground allspice
8 bite-size pitted prunes
1 ripe banana, cut into chunks

1. Combine all ingredients in a blender; process until smooth. Serve immediately. Yield: 3 servings (serving size: 1 cup).

CALORIES 215 (11% from fat); FAT 2.6g (sat 1.1g, mono 1.1g, poly 0.3g); PROTEIN 4.9g; CARB 45.2g; FIBER 1.9g; CHOL 7mg; IRON 1.5mg; SODIUM 71mg; CALC 161mg

Wheat Germ Pancakes

Wheat germ provides a nutty flavor and boosts the iron, zinc, and folate in these pancakes. Top them with fresh berries or bananas and toasted pecans.

1¼ cups all-purpose flour
¼ cup whole wheat flour
½ cup toasted or honey-crunch wheat germ
2 teaspoons sugar
1 teaspoon baking soda
¼ teaspoon salt
2 cups low-fat buttermilk
2 large egg whites
Cooking spray

1. Lightly spoon flours into dry measuring cups, and level with a knife. Combine flours and next 4 ingredients in a large bowl. Combine buttermilk and egg whites; add to flour mixture, stirring until smooth.
2. Spoon about ¼ cup batter for each pancake onto a hot nonstick griddle or a large nonstick skillet coated with cooking spray. Turn pancakes when tops are covered with bubbles and edges look cooked; cook 1 to 2 minutes or until golden. Yield: 6 servings (serving size: 2 pancakes).
NOTE: To freeze, cool cooked pancakes completely on a wire rack. Place in a heavy-duty zip-top plastic bag, separating pancakes with wax paper. To reheat,

microwave pancakes at HIGH 45 seconds, or place in toaster at medium-high heat for 2 cycles or until hot.

CALORIES 198 (12% from fat); FAT 2.7g (sat 0.7g, mono 0.4g, poly 0.8g); PROTEIN 9.7g; CARB 34g; FIBER 2.8g; CHOL 3mg; IRON 2mg; SODIUM 369mg; CALC 111mg

Lemon-Poppy Seed Muffins

To save time in the morning, you can prepare the flour mixture in a large bowl the night before, then leave it covered on the counter. This recipe can also be doubled or tripled.

2 cups all-purpose flour
2 tablespoons powdered sugar
1½ tablespoons grated lemon rind
1 tablespoon poppy seeds
2 teaspoons baking powder
½ teaspoon baking soda
¼ teaspoon salt
¾ cup low-fat buttermilk
½ cup honey
3 tablespoons butter, melted
1 large egg, lightly beaten
Cooking spray
2 tablespoons powdered sugar
2 tablespoons honey
2 teaspoons fresh lemon juice

1. Preheat oven to 375°.
2. Lightly spoon flour into dry measuring cups, and level with a knife. Combine flour and next 6 ingredients in a large bowl, and make a well in center of mixture. Combine buttermilk, ½ cup honey, butter, and egg; stir well with a whisk. Add to flour mixture, stirring just until moist.
3. Spoon batter into 12 muffin cups coated with cooking spray. Bake at 375° for 19 minutes or until muffins spring back when touched lightly in center.
4. Combine 2 tablespoons powdered sugar, 2 tablespoons honey, and lemon juice in a small bowl. Brush glaze over tops of muffins. Cool muffins on a wire rack. Yield: 1 dozen (serving size: 1 muffin).

CALORIES 184 (21% from fat); FAT 4.2g (sat 2.2g, mono 1.1g, poly 0.5g); PROTEIN 3.5g; CARB 34.3g; FIBER 0.6g; CHOL 26mg; IRON 1.3mg; SODIUM 227mg; CALC 83mg

Spilling the Beans

Versatile dishes you can prepare in a snap.

For most vegetarians, beans have long been required eating. They are, without a doubt, the friendliest source of protein for anyone trying to cut back on meat. Luckily, they're also as adaptable and versatile as a food can be—possibly even more so than chicken.

Chickpea, Red Pepper, and Basil Sauté

Sautéing the cumin seeds intensifies their flavor.

- 1 tablespoon olive oil
- 2 cups vertically sliced onion
- ½ teaspoon cumin seeds
- 1 cup red bell pepper strips
- 1 tablespoon water
- ½ cup chopped green onions
- ¼ teaspoon salt
- 2 (15½-ounce) cans chickpeas (garbanzo beans), drained
- 2 cups chopped fresh basil (about 4 bunches)
- ¼ cup garlic-and-herb seasoned breadcrumbs
- 2 cups hot cooked long-grain brown rice

1. Heat oil in a large nonstick skillet over medium-high heat. Add onion and cumin; sauté 10 minutes or until onion is lightly browned. Add bell pepper and water; cover, reduce heat, and simmer 3 minutes. Add green onions, salt, and beans; cover and cook 2 minutes or until thoroughly heated, stirring occasionally. Remove from heat; stir in basil. Sprinkle with breadcrumbs, and serve over rice. Yield: 4 servings (serving size: 1 cup chickpea mixture and ½ cup rice).

CALORIES 435 (16% from fat); FAT 7.8g (sat 0.9g, mono 3.4g, poly 2.2g); PROTEIN 17.3g; CARB 76.5g; FIBER 8.3g; CHOL 0mg; IRON 6.7mg; SODIUM 499mg; CALC 148mg

Swiss Chard-and-Bean Frittata

Beans add body and a creamy texture to this frittata. Serve with salsa.

- 7 large egg whites, lightly beaten
- 2 large eggs, lightly beaten
- ½ teaspoon salt
- ¼ teaspoon black pepper
- 1 tablespoon finely chopped jalapeño pepper
- 1 tablespoon chopped fresh mint (optional)
- 4 chopped pitted kalamata olives
- 1 (16-ounce) can cannellini beans or other white beans, rinsed and drained
- 1 teaspoon olive oil
- 2 cups torn Swiss chard or spinach
- 1½ cups chopped onion

1. Preheat broiler.
2. Place egg whites, eggs, salt, and black pepper in a large bowl, and stir well with a whisk. Stir in jalapeño, mint if desired, olives, and beans.
3. Heat oil in a large nonstick skillet over medium-high heat. Add Swiss chard and onion; sauté 3 minutes or until Swiss chard is tender. Pour egg mixture into pan; reduce heat to medium-low, and cook 10 minutes or until almost set.
4. Wrap handle of skillet with foil. Broil egg mixture 4 minutes or until golden brown. Yield: 4 servings (serving size: 1 wedge).

CALORIES 193 (21% from fat); FAT 4.6g (sat 1.2g, mono 2.2g, poly 0.7g); PROTEIN 16.3g; CARB 22.6g; FIBER 4g; CHOL 110mg; IRON 2.5mg; SODIUM 637mg; CALC 90mg

Black Bean Salad with Lime-Cumin Dressing

This makes a great lunch; try serving it with vegetable pizza.

SALAD:
- 1 cup thinly sliced celery
- ¾ cup vertically sliced red onion
- 2 (15-ounce) cans black beans, rinsed and drained

DRESSING:
- ¼ cup fresh lime juice
- 1 tablespoon sugar
- 1 tablespoon olive oil
- ¼ teaspoon ground cumin

1. To prepare salad, combine celery, onion, and black beans in a large bowl; toss well.
2. To prepare dressing, combine lime juice, sugar, oil, and cumin in a small bowl; stir mixture with a whisk until blended. Pour over bean mixture, tossing to coat. Yield: 4 servings (serving size: about 1 cup).

CALORIES 245 (17% from fat); FAT 4.5g (sat 0.7g, mono 2.6g, poly 0.7g); PROTEIN 13.1g; CARB 41g; FIBER 6.9g; CHOL 0mg; IRON 3.3mg; SODIUM 316mg; CALC 59mg

Curried Kidney Bean Burritos

- 1 tablespoon olive oil
- 1½ cups finely chopped onion
- 1 tablespoon chopped jalapeño pepper
- 1 teaspoon sugar
- ½ teaspoon curry powder
- 2 (14.5-ounce) cans diced tomatoes, drained
- 2 (15-ounce) cans kidney beans, drained
- 1 tablespoon minced fresh cilantro
- 4 (8-inch) flour tortillas

1. Heat oil in a large nonstick skillet over medium-high heat. Add onion; sauté 6 minutes or until lightly browned. Add jalapeño, sugar, curry, and tomatoes; cover, reduce heat, and simmer 10 minutes. Add beans; cover and cook 3 minutes or until thoroughly heated, stirring occasionally. Remove from heat; stir in cilantro.
2. Warm tortillas according to package directions. Spoon 1¼ cups bean mixture down center of each tortilla, and roll up. Yield: 4 servings (serving size: 1 burrito).

CALORIES 414 (17% from fat); FAT 8g (sat 1.6g, mono 3.1g, poly 2.7g); PROTEIN 18.4g; CARB 70.3g; FIBER 9.2g; CHOL 0mg; IRON 6.4mg; SODIUM 710mg; CALC 182mg

Carrot-Lentil Loaf

Serve with mashed potatoes or on toasted bread as a sandwich filling.

- 2 cups sliced carrot
- 1 tablespoon olive oil
- 2 cups vertically sliced onion
- 1 tablespoon minced peeled fresh ginger
- 2 cups cooked lentils
- 2 tablespoons chopped fresh cilantro
- 2 tablespoons ketchup
- 2 large egg whites
- 1 large egg
- ½ cup quick-cooking oats
- ½ cup garlic-and-herb breadcrumbs
- ⅓ cup coarsely chopped walnuts
- ½ teaspoon salt
  Cooking spray

1. Preheat oven to 350°.
2. Steam carrot, covered, 15 minutes or until tender.
3. Heat oil in a large nonstick skillet over medium-high heat. Add onion and ginger; sauté 7 minutes or until golden.
4. Combine carrot, onion mixture, lentils, and next 4 ingredients in a food processor, and process until smooth. Combine carrot mixture, oats, bread-crumbs, walnuts, and salt in a large bowl. Spoon mixture into an 8 x 4-inch loaf pan coated with cooking spray. Bake at 350° for 45 minutes. Yield: 6 servings.

CALORIES 250 (30% from fat); FAT 8.2g (sat 1.1g, mono 3.1g, poly 3g); PROTEIN 12.3g; CARB 33.8g; FIBER 6g; CHOL 37mg; IRON 3.6mg; SODIUM 477mg; CALC 60mg

Warm Potato, Soybean, and Cucumber Salad

Look for frozen soybeans in Asian markets and some health-food stores.

SALAD:
- 3¾ cups cubed red potato (about 1 pound)
- 1 cup frozen soybeans, thawed
- 1 cup vertically sliced red onion
- ¾ cup cubed seeded peeled cucumber

DRESSING:
- ¼ cup red wine vinegar
- 1 tablespoon minced peeled fresh ginger
- 1 tablespoon Dijon mustard
- 1 tablespoon olive oil
- 1 teaspoon sugar
- ¼ teaspoon black pepper
- 1 garlic clove, minced

1. To prepare salad, steam potato and soybeans, covered, 12 minutes or until tender. Combine potato mixture, onion, and cucumber in a large bowl.
2. To prepare dressing, combine vinegar and remaining 6 ingredients in a bowl; stir with a whisk until well blended. Pour over potato mixture, tossing to coat. Yield: 5 servings (serving size: 1 cup).

CALORIES 184 (30% from fat); FAT 6.2g (sat 0.9g, mono 2.8g, poly 2.1g); PROTEIN 7.8g; CARB 26g; FIBER 2g; CHOL 0mg; IRON 2.2mg; SODIUM 48mg; CALC 49mg

cooking light profile

Naturally Healthy

Debra Stark realizes a dream with a community store devoted to wellness.

In these days of superdupermarkets and national natural-foods chains, Debra Stark has managed to create a community store, a throwback to a time when the town general store was a place for the neighborhood to congregate. Debra's Natural Gourmet, a natural foods store in West Concord, Massachusetts, is, in fact, located on Main Street. And at the center of the store, and of most customers' attention, is Debra herself, a tall, slim redhead in her early 50s.

Debra's Natural Gourmet has been open more than a decade and boasts a supplement section staffed by a registered nurse, as well as a catering service. Debra hosts cooking classes, social events, and theme sales; arranges for guest speakers; and writes a monthly newsletter. She successfully fosters the feeling of community she envisioned.

Tofu, Asparagus, and Red Pepper Stir-Fry with Quinoa

One of Debra Stark's favorites: Quinoa packs iron, fiber, and potassium into this meatless main dish.

DRESSING:
- 2 tablespoons rice vinegar
- 2 tablespoons low-sodium soy sauce
- 2 teaspoons dark sesame oil
  Dash of crushed red pepper

STIR-FRY:
- 1½ cups water
- 1½ cups uncooked quinoa
- 1 tablespoon dark sesame oil
- 1 cup chopped onion
- 2 garlic cloves, minced
- 2 cups red bell pepper strips
- 2 cups sliced mushrooms
- 2 cups (1-inch) sliced asparagus (about 1 pound)
- ½ teaspoon salt
- 1 (12.3-ounce) package reduced-fat firm tofu, drained and cubed
- 2 tablespoons sesame seeds

1. To prepare dressing, combine first 4 ingredients in a small bowl; stir with a whisk. Set aside.
2. To prepare stir-fry, bring water to a boil in a small saucepan. Stir in quinoa; cover, reduce heat, and simmer 10 minutes. Remove from heat. Let stand, covered, 10 minutes; fluff with a fork.
3. Heat 1 tablespoon oil in a large nonstick skillet over medium-high heat. Add onion and garlic, and stir-fry 5 minutes. Add bell pepper, mushrooms, asparagus, salt, and tofu; stir-fry 3 minutes. Stir in dressing. Serve over quinoa, and sprinkle evenly with sesame seeds. Yield: 6 servings (serving size: 1 cup stir-fry and ½ cup quinoa).

CALORIES 273 (29% from fat); FAT 8.8g (sat 1.2g, mono 2.9g, poly 3.8g); PROTEIN 11.9g; CARB 38.7g; FIBER 8.2g; CHOL 0mg; IRON 6.1mg; SODIUM 435mg; CALC 96mg

How to Cook Italian

Fresh ingredients and simple techniques are key to one of the world's most loved cuisines.

I t's true that Italians have a passion for life, and one of life's great pleasures is good food. Because Italian cuisine runs the gamut from rich and complex to light and simple, you'll always find it interesting.

Italian cooking is healthful, and so is the Italian way of eating. A typical meal consists of several courses, none of which dominates the meal, so that portion sizes need not be as large. The first course (*primo piatto*) is usually a soup, pasta, or risotto. The second course (*secondo piatto*) is a meat, fish, or chicken dish that's accompanied by a vegetable and followed by a salad. The meal often ends with fruit rather than a dessert (although occasionally Italians do like to indulge in something sweet).

Few cuisines have the breadth and influence of Italy's, so it was no small chore to select the following recipes. They represent the different courses of a typical meal and exemplify the essential qualities of Italian food.

Zuppa di Farro e Fagioli
Tuscan Bean-and-Barley Soup

This hearty Tuscan soup is typically made with *farro*, an ancient Etruscan grain. We've substituted barley in its place; it works like a charm.

- 2 tablespoons olive oil
- ½ cup finely chopped onion
- 1½ teaspoons chopped fresh rosemary
- 5 cups chopped escarole
- ½ teaspoon salt
- ¼ teaspoon black pepper
- 5 cups water
- 1 cup canned cannellini beans or other white beans, drained
- ½ cup uncooked pearl barley
- 1 beef-flavored bouillon cube

1. Place oil and onion in a large saucepan over medium heat. Cook 5 minutes or until lightly browned, stirring occasionally. Stir in rosemary, escarole, salt, and pepper; cook until escarole wilts and liquid evaporates. Add water, beans, barley, and bouillon cube. Bring to a boil; reduce heat, and simmer 30 minutes or until barley is tender. Yield: 4 servings (serving size: 1½ cups).

WINE NOTE: A classic Tuscan comfort food such as this dish calls for Tuscany's famous comfort wine: Chianti. Brolio's affordable 1997 Chianti Classico ($16) befits the humbleness of this soup.

CALORIES 232 (30% from fat); FAT 7.9g (sat 1.2g, mono 5g, poly 0.9g); PROTEIN 7.9g; CARB 35.3g; FIBER 7.1g; CHOL 0mg; IRON 3.1mg; SODIUM 836mg; CALC 85mg

Spaghetti Alla Norma
(pictured on page 57)

This is the classic Sicilian pasta sauce. The combination of eggplant and tomato is quintessentially Italian.

- 2 tablespoons olive oil
- 3 garlic cloves, minced
- 1½ pounds coarsely chopped peeled tomato (about 2 cups)
- 1 teaspoon salt
- 1 pound eggplant, peeled and cut into ½-inch cubes (about 4 cups)
- ¼ cup thinly sliced fresh basil
- ¾ pound uncooked spaghetti
- 6 ounces fresh mozzarella cheese, cut into ¼-inch cubes (about 1 cup)

1. Place oil and garlic in a large skillet; cook over medium-high heat 30 seconds or until garlic begins to sizzle. Add tomato and salt; cook 15 minutes or until liquid evaporates. Add eggplant; cover, reduce heat, and cook 15 minutes or until eggplant is tender. Stir in basil, and set aside.

2. Cook pasta in boiling water 9 minutes; drain. Toss with sauce and cheese. Serve immediately. Yield: 7 servings (serving size: 1 cup).

WINE NOTE: A classic Sicilian dish calls for a classic Sicilian wine, but these can be hard to find. So opt for something with the same warm Mediterranean flavors: Librandi's red wine known as Ciro ($12). From the southern province of Calabria, it's spicy, juicy, and perfect for bold, savory flavors of basil, garlic, eggplant, and mozzarella.

CALORIES 329 (29% from fat); FAT 10.5g (sat 3.9g, mono 4.6g, poly 1g); PROTEIN 12.2g; CARB 47.3g; FIBER 4.1g; CHOL 19mg; IRON 2.8mg; SODIUM 444mg; CALC 149mg

---

Cooking Pasta

Pasta should be cooked in a generous amount of boiling water. It's not necessary to add oil to prevent it from sticking. Simply follow these rules: Use at least four quarts of water for one pound of pasta, stir as soon as the pasta goes in and periodically while it's cooking, and make sure the water is always at a rolling boil. Drain the pasta when it's al dente (firm and chewy but not crunchy), and never rinse it. Toss with the sauce right away to prevent it from sticking, and allow it to absorb as much flavor from the sauce as possible.

Risotto with Clams Step-by-Steps

1. *Cooking fresh clams provides a flavorful broth that is then used to make risotto.*

2. *Combine oil, parsley, and garlic in a saucepan, and cook over medium-high heat until garlic sizzles. Add rice; sauté 5 minutes. This coats the grains with oil.*

Sautéing

The purpose of sautéing is to intensify and draw out flavor. Unlike most recipes that tell you to heat the oil until hot, with Italian cooking you want the onions and garlic, for example, to cook very slowly. Not only does this minimize the chances of burning the garlic, but you'll also get a richer flavor with a slower, more patient approach.

Risotto Alle Vongole
Risotto with Clams

In Italy, clams are as small as thumbnails and so flavorful that they hardly need any seasoning. Using the juice the clams give off as part of the cooking liquid for the rice imbues the risotto with clam flavor.

    3   dozen littleneck clams (about
        2½ pounds)
 8½   cups water, divided
    3   tablespoons olive oil, divided
    2   tablespoons chopped fresh
        flat-leaf parsley
    2   teaspoons minced garlic
 1½   cups Arborio rice or other
        short-grain rice
    ¼   teaspoon salt
    ¼   teaspoon freshly ground black
        pepper
    Chopped fresh parsley (optional)

1. Place clams and ½ cup water in a large skillet over medium-high heat; cover and cook 4 minutes or until shells open. Remove clams from pan, reserving cooking liquid. Discard any unopened shells. Cool clams. Remove meat from shells, and set aside.
2. Bring 8 cups water to a simmer in a large saucepan (do not boil). Keep warm over low heat. Place 2 tablespoons olive oil, parsley, and garlic in a large saucepan; cook over medium-high heat until garlic sizzles. Add rice, and stir until coated; sauté 5 minutes. Stir in reserved clam liquid; cook until liquid is absorbed, stirring constantly. Add water, 1 cup at a time, stirring constantly until each portion of water is absorbed before adding next. Continue cooking until rice is tender. Season with salt and pepper. Add clams; cook 3 minutes or until thoroughly heated. Stir in 1 tablespoon olive oil, and sprinkle with parsley, if desired. Serve immediately. Yield: 4 servings (serving size: 1 cup).
NOTE: To substitute canned clams for fresh, use 3 (6-ounce) cans clams, undrained, and use 7 cups water.
WINE NOTE: Risotto, a northern Italian dish, and the inclusion of clams make the case for a white wine. You could opt for a Pinot Grigio here, but the creaminess of the risotto would make a terrific foil for something zesty, lively, and fresh. Try a Prosecco, a slightly sparkling white (but not as fizzy as Champagne) that's a favorite in Venice. Zardetto makes a good one ($14).

CALORIES 422 (24% from fat); FAT 11.3g (sat 1.6g, mono 7.7g, poly 1.2g); PROTEIN 15.4g; CARB 62.4g; FIBER 1.2g; CHOL 28mg; IRON 14.7mg; SODIUM 194mg; CALC 47mg

Weeknight Italian Menu

While the chicken cooks, prepare the pasta and heat up the garlic bread.

Chicken Breast Fillets with Red and Yellow Peppers

Lemon-pepper linguine*

Garlic bread

Fresh strawberries tossed with balsamic vinegar

*Combine 3 cups hot cooked linguine, 2 teaspoons freshly ground black pepper, 1 tablespoon lemon juice, and 1 tablespoon olive oil, and toss well.

Chicken Breast Fillets with Red and Yellow Peppers

The sauce for these chicken breasts—with tomatoes, olives, and oregano—is reminiscent of the classic puttanesca sauce.

    1   tablespoon olive oil
    3   cups sliced onion
    1   large yellow bell pepper, cut into
        ¼-inch strips
    1   large red bell pepper, cut into
        ¼-inch strips
 2⅓   cups coarsely chopped tomato
    ½   teaspoon salt
    ¼   teaspoon freshly ground black
        pepper
    2   tablespoons finely chopped fresh
        flat-leaf parsley
    1   teaspoon chopped fresh oregano
 20   kalamata olives
    Cooking spray
    6   (4-ounce) skinless, boneless
        chicken breast halves, cut in half
        horizontally

1. Place oil and onion in a large nonstick skillet over medium-high heat. Cook 5 minutes, stirring frequently. Reduce heat; cook 10 minutes or until golden brown, stirring occasionally. Increase heat to medium-high. Add bell peppers; cook 10 minutes or until bell peppers are tender. Add tomato, salt, and black pepper; cook 7 minutes or until liquid evaporates. Add parsley, oregano, and olives; cook 1 minute. Pour tomato mixture into a large bowl; keep warm.

2. Wipe pan clean with a paper towel; heat pan coated with cooking spray over medium-high heat. Add 4 chicken breast pieces; cook 3 minutes on each side or until done. Remove from pan; repeat procedure with remaining chicken.

3. Return chicken to pan; add tomato mixture, and cook 1 minute or until thoroughly heated. Yield: 6 servings (serving size: 2 chicken breast pieces and ½ cup tomato mixture).

WINE NOTE: Pair this second-course dish with an equally spicy and dramatic wine like intense, medium-bodied Allegrini's Valpolicella Classico ($15), which is possibly the best Valpolicella in Italy.

CALORIES 211 (23% from fat); FAT 5.3g (sat 0.9g, mono 2.7g, poly 1.1g); PROTEIN 28.1g; CARB 12.6g; FIBER 3.1g; CHOL 66mg; IRON 2.1mg; SODIUM 344mg; CALC 47mg

Lombo di Maiale Coi Porri
Pan-Roasted Pork Loin with Leeks

Leeks, a mild, sweet member of the onion family, are cooked slowly along with the pork until they form a rich, delectable sauce for this supereasy pan roast.

    4 large leeks (about 2¼ pounds)
    ½ cup water
    1 tablespoon butter, divided
    ½ teaspoon salt, divided
    ½ teaspoon black pepper, divided
    1 (2-pound) boneless pork loin,
       trimmed
    ½ cup dry white wine
    Chopped fresh parsley (optional)

1. Remove roots and tough upper leaves from leeks. Cut each leek in half lengthwise. Cut each half crosswise into ½-inch-thick slices (you should have about 6 cups). Soak in cold water to loosen dirt.

2. Place sliced leek, ½ cup water, 1 teaspoon butter, ¼ teaspoon salt, and ¼ teaspoon pepper in a large Dutch oven or deep sauté pan, and place over medium-high heat. Cook 10 minutes or until leek is wilted. Pour leek into a bowl.

3. Heat 2 teaspoons butter in pan over medium-high heat. Add pork, and cook 5 minutes, browning on all sides. Add ¼ teaspoon salt, ¼ teaspoon pepper, and wine, and cook 15 seconds, scraping pan to loosen browned bits. Return sliced leek to pan. Cover, reduce heat, and simmer 2 hours or until pork is tender. Remove pork from pan; increase heat to reduce leek mixture if too watery. Cut pork into ¼-inch-thick slices. Serve with leek mixture; garnish with parsley, if desired. Yield: 6 servings (serving size: about 3 ounces pork and about 2½ tablespoons leek mixture).

WINE NOTE: Pork matches well with both white and red wines, but leeks in this dish suggest a vibrant, herbal white. Go for a Pinot Grigio from the north of Italy. Zenato ($10) is an affordable favorite.

CALORIES 246 (39% from fat); FAT 10.7g (sat 4.2g, mono 4.4g, poly 1.1g); PROTEIN 24.8g; CARB 12.1g; FIBER 1g; CHOL 73mg; IRON 2.8mg; SODIUM 306mg; CALC 60mg

Pan-Roasted Pork Loin with Leeks Step-by-Steps

1. *Cook leeks in water and butter to preserve their delicate flavor.*

2. *Brown pork on all sides to develop a deep, rich flavor.*

Pan Roasting

In Italy, meats are more often pan-roasted than oven-roasted. Most recipes that involve roasting follow a basic technique: Meat is first browned in either olive oil or butter, and a cooking liquid (usually a dry white or red wine) is added to the pan. Once the alcohol has evaporated and the tasty brown bits have been loosened from the bottom of the pan, the heat is lowered, and the meat cooks with a cover slightly ajar until it's very tender.

Sautéed Mushrooms with Porcinis

    1 cup dried porcini mushrooms
       (about 1 ounce)
    1 cup water
    1 tablespoon olive oil
    2 garlic cloves, minced
    2 tablespoons minced fresh flat-leaf
       parsley
    2 (8-ounce) packages presliced
       button mushrooms
    ½ teaspoon salt
    ¼ teaspoon black pepper

Continued

1. Soak porcini mushrooms in 1 cup water in a bowl; cover and let stand 15 minutes or until soft. Drain mushrooms in a fine sieve over a bowl, reserving liquid.
2. Place oil and garlic in a large skillet over medium-high heat; sauté until garlic sizzles. Add porcinis, reserved mushroom liquid, and parsley; cook until liquid evaporates. Add button mushrooms, salt, and pepper; cook 15 minutes or until liquid evaporates. Yield 6 servings (serving size: ½ cup).

WINE NOTE: This dish is practically begging for a good Chianti, which would magnify the earthiness of the mushrooms. Try Ruffino's Riserva Ducale Gold Label Chianti Classico Riserva ($35).

CALORIES 55 (43% from fat); FAT 2.6g (sat 0.4g, mono 1.7g, poly 0.3g); PROTEIN 2.1g; CARB 7.5g; FIBER 1.6g; CHOL 0mg; IRON 1.1mg; SODIUM 199mg; CALC 7mg

Broccolini Sautéed with Olive Oil and Garlic

Broccolini is a hybrid between Chinese broccoli and regular broccoli (which can be used as a substitute).

    4   quarts water
    1   tablespoon salt
    1   pound broccolini, trimmed
    2   teaspoons olive oil
    2   garlic cloves, minced

1. Bring water to a boil in a stockpot; add salt and broccolini. Cook 5 minutes or until tender; drain.
2. Place olive oil and garlic in a large skillet over medium-high heat. Sauté until garlic just begins to color. Add broccolini; sauté 5 minutes. Yield: 4 cups (serving size: ½ cup).

WINE NOTE: The olive oil and garlic demand a wine with earthiness and good acidity, like the fresh, silky Villa Antinori Chianti Riserva ($20).

CALORIES 54 (43% from fat); FAT 2.6g (sat 0.4g, mono 1.7g, poly 0.4g); PROTEIN 3.5g; CARB 6.4g; FIBER 3.6g; CHOL 0mg; IRON 1mg; SODIUM 470mg; CALC 57mg

Arugula, Fennel, and Avocado Salad

    6   cups trimmed arugula (about
        4 ounces)
    4   cups thinly sliced fennel bulb
        (about 2 small bulbs)
  1¾   cups sliced peeled avocado (about
        1 small)
    ⅓   cup fresh lemon juice
    1   tablespoon extra-virgin olive oil
    ½   teaspoon salt
    2   tablespoons shaved Parmigiano-
        Reggiano cheese

1. Combine all ingredients except cheese; toss gently to coat.
2. Divide salad among 8 salad plates. Sprinkle evenly with cheese. Yield: 8 servings.

CALORIES 93 (72% from fat); FAT 7.4g (sat 1.3g, mono 4.5g, poly 0.8g); PROTEIN 2.9g; CARB 6.1g; FIBER 2.2g; CHOL 1mg; IRON 1.8mg; SODIUM 186mg; CALC 93mg

Zuppa Inglese

This dessert (pronounced ZOO-puh in-GLAY-zay) literally translates as "English soup." It's a classic Italian trifle made with custard and chocolate layered with liqueur-soaked cake.

    1   cup powdered sugar
    6   large egg yolks
    6   tablespoons all-purpose flour
    3   cups 2% reduced-fat milk
    2   teaspoons grated lemon rind
    1   (10-ounce) loaf angel food cake,
        cut into ¼-inch-thick slices
    ¼   cup grenadine or raspberry syrup
    2   tablespoons Drambuie or cognac
    2   tablespoons cognac
    1   tablespoon white rum
    2   ounces semisweet chocolate,
        melted
    ¼   cup coarsely chopped almonds

1. Place sugar and yolks in a large bowl, and beat with a mixer at high speed until pale yellow. Gradually add flour, beating until smooth.
2. Heat milk over medium-high heat in a medium, heavy saucepan to 180° or

until tiny bubbles form around edge (do not boil). Gradually add hot milk to sugar mixture, stirring constantly with a whisk. Return milk mixture to pan. Cook mixture over medium heat until thick (about 8 minutes), stirring constantly. Remove from heat. Stir in rind.
3. Spoon ¼ cup custard into bottom of a 2-quart soufflé dish or compote. Arrange one-third of cake slices in a single layer over custard. Combine grenadine, Drambuie, cognac, and rum. Brush grenadine mixture over cake slices until wet. Spread 1¼ cups custard over cake slices. Arrange one-third of cake slices in a single layer over custard. Brush grenadine mixture over cake slices until wet. Combine 1¼ cups custard and chocolate, and spread over cake slices. Arrange remaining cake slices over custard. Brush with remaining grenadine mixture. Spread remaining custard over cake slices. Sprinkle with almonds. Cover and chill at least 4 hours. Yield: 9 servings (serving size: ⅔ cup).

CALORIES 306 (26% from fat); FAT 8.8g (sat 3.5g, mono 3.4g, poly 1g); PROTEIN 7.9g; CARB 45.1g; FIBER 1g; CHOL 152mg; IRON 1.2mg; SODIUM 283mg; CALC 170mg

Macedonia di Frutta
Mixed Marinated Fruit

    2   cups chopped cantaloupe
    1   cup chopped peeled peaches
    1   cup chopped strawberries
    1   cup blueberries
    ⅔   cup chopped peeled nectarines
    ½   cup fresh orange juice (about 1
        orange)
    ¼   cup sugar
    2   tablespoons grappa (Italian
        brandy) or brandy
  1½   teaspoons grated lemon rind
    2   peeled kiwifruit, halved
        lengthwise and thinly sliced

1. Place all ingredients in a large bowl; toss gently to combine. Cover and chill 2 hours. Yield: 5 servings (serving size: 1 cup).

CALORIES 154 (4% from fat); FAT 0.7g (sat 0.1g, mono 0.1g, poly 0.3g); PROTEIN 1.8g; CARB 34.8g; FIBER 4.2g; CHOL 0mg; IRON 0.5mg; SODIUM 10mg; CALC 27mg

30 minutes or less

Curries in a Hurry

India's most widely adapted dish inspires quick American meals.

Curries—spicy sauces with vegetables, meat, or fish usually served over rice—originated in India. Some are fiery-hot, others mild. Some end up as creamy gravies, others tomato-based stews. They can be red, green, yellow, or any combination thereof.

But all are marked by the distinctive flavor of curry powder, which consists of up to 20 spices, herbs, and seeds, and usually includes cardamom, cloves, coriander, cumin, nutmeg, red and black pepper, saffron, tamarind, and turmeric. Curries offer the same depth of flavor as marinating or slow-roasting, but in a fraction of the time.

Shrimp-and-Apple Curry with Golden Raisins

PREPARATION TIME: 10 MINUTES
COOKING TIME: 14 MINUTES

Serve over basmati rice to catch every drop of the sauce.

1   tablespoon butter
1   cup chopped peeled Granny Smith apple
¾   cup chopped shallots
⅔   cup chopped celery
1   teaspoon bottled minced garlic
2   tablespoons all-purpose flour
1   tablespoon curry powder
1⅓   cups 2% reduced-fat milk
½   cup golden raisins
1   (15.75-ounce) can fat-free, less-sodium chicken broth
1½   pounds large shrimp, peeled and deveined
¼   teaspoon salt
¼   teaspoon freshly ground black pepper

1. Melt butter in a large nonstick skillet over medium-high heat. Add apple, shallots, celery, and garlic; sauté 5 minutes or until lightly browned. Stir in flour and curry powder; cook 1 minute, stirring frequently. Gradually add milk, raisins, and broth, stirring constantly with a whisk; bring to a boil, stirring frequently. Reduce heat, and simmer until thick (about 5 minutes). Stir in shrimp, salt, and pepper; cook 3 minutes or until shrimp are done. Yield: 4 servings (serving size: 1 cup).

CALORIES 381 (19% from fat); FAT 7.9g (sat 3.4g, mono 1.8g, poly 1.4g); PROTEIN 41.1g; CARB 36.3g; FIBER 2.6g; CHOL 273mg; IRON 5.7mg; SODIUM 734mg; CALC 231mg

Curried Lamb Kebabs with Raita

PREPARATION TIME: 15 MINUTES
COOKING TIME: 14 MINUTES

Raita (RY-*tah*), a refreshing Indian condiment made from yogurt and mixed with vegetables and seasonings, balances the spiciness of the curry paste on the lamb.

1   cup uncooked couscous

RAITA:
2   tablespoons chopped seeded peeled cucumber
2   tablespoons chopped fresh mint
1   teaspoon lemon juice
⅛   teaspoon salt
1   (8-ounce) carton plain fat-free yogurt
1   garlic clove, minced

KEBABS:
1   pound boneless leg of lamb, trimmed and cut into 1-inch pieces
1   tablespoon curry powder
2   teaspoons olive oil, divided
1   teaspoon brown sugar
½   teaspoon salt
½   teaspoon ground red pepper
1   cup (½-inch) pieces yellow bell pepper
16   large cherry tomatoes
Cooking spray

Continued

1. Prepare couscous according to package directions, omitting salt and fat. Set aside.

2. While couscous is standing, prepare raita. Combine cucumber and next 5 ingredients in a small bowl; cover and chill.

3. Prepare broiler or grill.

4. To prepare kebabs, combine lamb, curry, 1 teaspoon oil, sugar, ½ teaspoon salt, and red pepper in a medium bowl; toss well. Combine 1 teaspoon oil, bell pepper, and tomatoes in a bowl; toss well. Thread lamb, bell pepper, and tomatoes alternately onto 4 (10-inch) skewers.

5. Place kebabs on broiler pan or grill rack coated with cooking spray; cook 7 minutes on each side or until done. Serve kebabs with raita and couscous. Yield: 4 servings (serving size: 1 lamb kebab, ¼ cup raita, and ¾ cup couscous).

CALORIES 388 (23% from fat); FAT 10.1g (sat 2.8g, mono 4.8g, poly 1g); PROTEIN 33.6g; CARB 40.7g; FIBER 3.1g; CHOL 77mg; IRON 3.8mg; SODIUM 479mg; CALC 135mg

Red Curried Tofu

PREPARATION TIME: 10 MINUTES
COOKING TIME: 15 MINUTES

1   cup uncooked long-grain rice
2   teaspoons dark sesame oil
2½ cups vertically sliced red onion
1   cup yellow bell pepper strips
1½ teaspoons curry powder
1   teaspoon ground coriander
½   teaspoon ground turmeric
½   teaspoon salt
1   tablespoon low-sodium soy sauce
1   tablespoon honey
½   teaspoon chile paste with garlic
1   (14.5-ounce) can no-salt-added diced tomatoes, undrained
1   (12.3-ounce) package reduced-fat firm tofu, drained and cut into 1-inch cubes
¼   cup minced fresh cilantro
¼   cup chopped dry-roasted cashews

1. Prepare rice according to package directions, omitting salt and fat.

2. While rice is cooking, heat oil in a nonstick skillet over medium-high heat.

Add onion and bell pepper; sauté 4 minutes or until tender. Stir in curry, coriander, turmeric, and salt; cook 2 minutes. Add soy sauce and next 4 ingredients. Bring to a boil; reduce heat, and simmer 2 minutes or until thoroughly heated. Serve tofu mixture over rice, and sprinkle with cilantro and cashews. Yield: 4 servings (serving size: 1¼ cups tofu mixture, ½ cup rice, 1 tablespoon cilantro, and 1 tablespoon cashews).

CALORIES 292 (24% from fat); FAT 7.7g (sat 1.4g, mono 3.6g, poly 2.4g); PROTEIN 10.7g; CARB 46.2g; FIBER 3.5g; CHOL 0mg; IRON 3.7mg; SODIUM 559mg; CALC 107mg

Thai Coconut-Curried Salmon with Greens

PREPARATION TIME: 14 MINUTES
COOKING TIME: 16 MINUTES

2   teaspoons vegetable oil
1   cup thinly sliced onion
2   teaspoons curry powder
1   cup light coconut milk
2   tablespoons sugar
1   tablespoon lime juice
1   tablespoon bottled minced ginger
1   tablespoon fish sauce
2   teaspoons bottled minced garlic
½   teaspoon chile paste with garlic
1   (8-ounce) bottle clam juice
1   (1-pound) salmon fillet, skinned and cut into ¾-inch cubes
6   cups trimmed watercress (about 2 bunches)

1. Heat vegetable oil in a large nonstick skillet over medium-high heat. Add onion and curry powder; sauté 4 minutes. Add coconut milk and next 7 ingredients. Bring to a boil; reduce heat, and simmer 3 minutes. Add fish; cover and cook 4 minutes. Arrange watercress over fish; cover and cook 4 minutes or until fish flakes easily when tested with a fork. Yield: 4 servings (serving size: 1 cup).

CALORIES 271 (43% from fat); FAT 12.8g (sat 4.2g, mono 3.3g, poly 4.1g); PROTEIN 24.8g; CARB 13.9g; FIBER 2.2g; CHOL 64mg; IRON 2mg; SODIUM 571mg; CALC 102mg

Lamb Curry with Apples

PREPARATION TIME: 5 MINUTES
COOKING TIME: 25 MINUTES

1   pound lean lamb stew meat, trimmed
1   tablespoon all-purpose flour
1   teaspoon vegetable oil
3   cups vertically sliced onion
2   teaspoons curry powder
1   teaspoon ground ginger
¼   teaspoon ground red pepper
1½ cups chopped peeled Golden Delicious apple
2   teaspoons bottled minced garlic
1   (14.5-ounce) can diced tomatoes, undrained
1   (14.5-ounce) can low-salt beef broth

1. Place lamb in a medium bowl. Sprinkle with flour, tossing to coat.

2. Heat oil in a large nonstick skillet over medium-high heat. Add lamb; cook 4 minutes or until browned, stirring frequently. Stir in onion, curry, ginger, and pepper; cook 5 minutes or until onion is tender. Stir in apple, garlic, tomatoes, and broth. Bring mixture to a boil; cover, reduce heat, and simmer 15 minutes. Yield: 4 servings (serving size: 1½ cups).

CALORIES 265 (26% from fat); FAT 7.8g (sat 2.5g, mono 2.9g, poly 1.3g); PROTEIN 25.7g; CARB 22.2g; FIBER 3.6g; CHOL 74mg; IRON 3.4mg; SODIUM 248mg; CALC 67mg

Curry Powder Blends

In India, cooks often blend their own curry powders, but premixed versions are available at most grocery stores, in varying degrees of spiciness. Pick up a jar, and you'll understand why India's love affair with curries has gone forth and multiplied so prodigiously.

Chicken Lettuce Wraps
with Peanut-Miso Sauce,
page 73

Spaghetti Alla Norma,
page 51

Barbecue Turkey Burgers, page 77 with
Spicy Grilled Sweet Potatoes, page 78

Rosemary Potatoes, page 61

Gingerbread Cake with
Blueberry Sauce, page 81

Chunky Potato-and-Swiss
Chowder, page 83

Grilled Salad Pizza, page 76

Microwave Virtues

Sure, it's great for reheating leftovers. But your microwave can cook great food the first time around, too.

It's surprising that even though most of us have microwave ovens, we use them so little. Of course, we rely on them to warm coffee, thaw chicken, melt butter and chocolate, steam a vegetable or two, and reheat leftovers. But what has been forgotten along the way is that the microwave provides unsurpassed speed for cooking everything from soup to potatoes to risotto.

And speed is only one of its virtues. The microwave is also perfect for those who are watching their fat intake—since microwave cooking doesn't require fat, any used in a recipe is needed only to add flavor. Using the microwave also saves on dirty pots and preparation time because it often allows you to cook all parts of a dish at the same time. So what's your microwave good for? Plenty, if you use it to its best advantage.

Asian Flounder

Since fillets of flounder are quite thin, they often end up overcooked and dry when baked or sautéed. Steaming the fish in the microwave cooks it quickly so that it stays moist. The unusual method of folding and arranging the fish is necessary because the food toward the edge of the dish cooks more rapidly than the food in the center.

  8 green onions
  ¼ cup minced fresh cilantro
  1 tablespoon minced peeled fresh ginger
  2 teaspoons dark sesame oil, divided
  4 (6-ounce) flounder fillets, skinned
  2 teaspoons rice vinegar
  2 teaspoons low-sodium soy sauce
  ⅛ teaspoon salt
  4 lemon slices

1. Remove green tops from onions; slice onion tops into 1-inch pieces to measure ¼ cup; set aside. Reserve remaining onion tops for another use. Cut white portions of onions into 2-inch pieces.
2. Combine cilantro, ginger, and 1 teaspoon oil in a 9-inch pie plate. Fold each fillet in half crosswise. Arrange fillets spokelike with thinnest portions pointing toward center of dish. Arrange white onion pieces between fillets. Combine ¼ cup green onion tops, 1 teaspoon oil, vinegar, soy sauce, and salt; pour over fillets. Cover with heavy-duty plastic wrap. Microwave at HIGH 4 minutes or until fish flakes easily when tested with a fork. Garnish each fillet with a lemon slice. Yield: 4 servings (serving size: 1 fillet).

CALORIES 188 (21% from fat); FAT 4.4g (sat 0.8g, mono 1.3g, poly 1.5g); PROTEIN 32.8g; CARB 2.7g; FIBER 0.9g; CHOL 82mg; IRON 1.3mg; SODIUM 299mg; CALC 57mg

Rosemary Potatoes
(pictured on page 58)

These potatoes taste as if they were roasted in the oven—but take only half the time.

  1 tablespoon butter
  1 teaspoon bottled minced garlic
  1 teaspoon dried rosemary
  ½ teaspoon kosher salt
  ¼ teaspoon black pepper
  1½ pounds red potatoes, quartered (about 4 cups)

1. Place butter and garlic in an 8-inch square baking dish. Microwave at MEDIUM-HIGH (70% power) 45 seconds or until butter melts. Add rosemary, salt, pepper, and potatoes; toss well. Cover and microwave at HIGH 15 minutes or until potatoes are tender. Yield: 4 servings (serving size: ¾ cup).

CALORIES 155 (18% from fat); FAT 3.1g (sat 1.9g, mono 0.8g, poly 0.2g); PROTEIN 3.9g; CARB 29g; FIBER 3.2g; CHOL 8mg; IRON 2.4mg; SODIUM 182mg; CALC 30mg

Sun-Dried Tomato Dip

The microwave works well for reconstituting dried foods such as apricots, mushrooms, and—in this case—sun-dried tomatoes.

  1 cup sun-dried tomatoes, packed without oil
  ¾ cup water
  ½ teaspoon dried oregano
  ½ teaspoon dried thyme
  3 garlic cloves, crushed
  2 cups chopped seeded tomato
  3 tablespoons olive oil
  ¼ teaspoon salt
  72 (½-inch-thick) slices diagonally cut French bread baguette, toasted (about 18 ounces)

1. Combine first 5 ingredients in a 1-quart casserole, and cover with lid. Microwave at HIGH 7 minutes or until sun-dried tomatoes are tender, stirring after 3½ minutes. Combine sun-dried tomato mixture, chopped tomato, oil, and salt in a blender or food processor; process until well blended. Serve with toasted baguette slices. Yield: 24 servings (serving size: 1 tablespoon dip and 3 bread slices).
NOTE: Dip will keep in refrigerator for up to 2 weeks.

CALORIES 83 (27% from fat); FAT 2.5g (sat 0.4g, mono 1.5g, poly 0.3g); PROTEIN 2.4g; CARB 13.2g; FIBER 1.1g; CHOL 0mg; IRON 0.9mg; SODIUM 205mg; CALC 21mg

Chicken-Vegetable Soup with Orzo

This homey soup shows just how quickly you can make chicken broth in the microwave. It also shows off the microwave's fabulous way with vegetables; they not only keep more color but also retain more vitamins.

- 5 cups water
- 2 pounds chicken drumsticks, skinned
- 2 cups small broccoli florets
- 2 cups presliced mushrooms
- 1½ cups sliced carrot
- 1 cup chopped onion
- ¼ cup chopped fresh basil
- ¼ cup uncooked orzo (rice-shaped pasta)
- 1 teaspoon salt
- ⅛ teaspoon black pepper
- 6 tablespoons (1½ ounces) grated fresh Parmesan cheese

1. Combine water and chicken in a 3-quart casserole. Cover with lid; microwave at HIGH 30 minutes or until chicken is done, stirring after 15 minutes. Drain in a colander over a bowl, reserving cooking liquid. Cool chicken slightly. Remove chicken from bones, and discard bones. Shred chicken with 2 forks to measure 2½ cups.
2. Combine broccoli and next 4 ingredients in casserole. Cover; microwave at HIGH 8 minutes or until tender, stirring after 4 minutes. Add reserved cooking liquid, chicken, pasta, salt, and pepper. Cover; microwave at HIGH 6 minutes or until pasta is tender. Ladle soup into 6 bowls. Sprinkle each serving with cheese. Yield: 6 servings (serving size: 1 cup soup and 1 tablespoon cheese).

CALORIES 277 (24% from fat); FAT 7.5g (sat 2.6g, mono 2.2g, poly 1.5g); PROTEIN 36.9g; CARB 14.5g; FIBER 3g; CHOL 121mg; IRON 2.8mg; SODIUM 658mg; CALC 134mg

Chicken with Duxelles

Duxelles is a thick mixture of finely chopped mushrooms, shallots, and seasonings cooked slowly to evaporate the liquid and intensify the mushroom flavor. Drizzling half-and-half over the chicken at the end pulls the flavors together.

- 3 cups fresh parsley leaves (about 1 bunch)
- 2 large shallots, peeled and quartered
- 4 cups coarsely chopped mushrooms (about ¾ pound)
- 1 tablespoon olive oil, divided
- ½ teaspoon salt, divided
- ¼ teaspoon black pepper, divided
- ⅛ teaspoon ground red pepper
- 2 teaspoons bottled minced garlic
- 4 (4-ounce) skinless, boneless chicken breast halves
- ¼ cup half-and-half

1. Place parsley and shallots in a food processor, and process until shallots are finely chopped. Add chopped mushrooms, and process until finely chopped, scraping sides of bowl occasionally. Place mushroom mixture in a deep-dish 10-inch pie plate. Microwave at HIGH 12 minutes, stirring every 4 minutes. Stir in 1 teaspoon oil, ¼ teaspoon salt, ⅛ teaspoon black pepper, and red pepper.
2. Combine 2 teaspoons oil, ¼ teaspoon salt, ⅛ teaspoon black pepper, garlic, and chicken in a bowl; toss well. Arrange chicken spokelike on top of mushroom mixture. Drizzle with half-and-half. Cover with plastic wrap, and vent. Microwave at HIGH 7 minutes or until done. Yield: 4 servings (serving size: 1 chicken breast half and about ½ cup duxelles).

CALORIES 213 (30% from fat); FAT 7.1g (sat 2g, mono 3.4g, poly 0.9g); PROTEIN 29.5g; CARB 8.1g; FIBER 2.5g; CHOL 71mg; IRON 3.8mg; SODIUM 393mg; CALC 79mg

Speedy Focaccia with Fennel and Thyme

A handy, time-saving trick: Use the microwave to make yeast bread dough rise. (You still have to bake the bread in the oven, though.)

- 1 tablespoon olive oil, divided
- ¾ cup chopped fennel bulb
- 1 (1-pound) loaf frozen white bread dough
- ½ teaspoon dried thyme
- ⅛ teaspoon black pepper
- Cooking spray
- ¼ teaspoon kosher salt

1. Heat 2 teaspoons oil in a small skillet over medium-high heat. Add fennel; sauté 3 minutes or until golden brown.
2. Cover bread dough loosely with plastic wrap. Microwave at MEDIUM-LOW (30% power) 6 minutes or until bread dough is completely thawed, turning dough over every 2 minutes. Let stand, covered, 3 minutes.
3. Preheat oven to 375°.
4. Place dough on a lightly floured surface; pat to a ½-inch thickness. Combine fennel, thyme, and pepper; sprinkle over dough. Knead 1 minute or just until fennel mixture is incorporated into dough.
5. Place dough in a large microwave-safe bowl; cover loosely with plastic wrap. Place bowl in microwave; place a small bowl of warm water beside large bowl. Microwave at MEDIUM-LOW 2 minutes; let rest 3 minutes. Microwave at MEDIUM-LOW 3 minutes. (Press two fingers into dough. If indentation remains, dough has risen enough.) Let dough rest 9 minutes.
6. Pat dough into an 8-inch round; place on a baking sheet coated with cooking spray. Brush with 1 teaspoon oil, and sprinkle with salt. Bake at 375° for 25 minutes or until lightly browned. Remove from pan. Cool slightly on a wire rack. Cut into 8 wedges. Yield: 8 servings (serving size: 1 wedge).

CALORIES 148 (21% from fat); FAT 3.5g (sat 0.6g, mono 2.1g, poly 0.7g); PROTEIN 4.7g; CARB 24.4g; FIBER 1.2g; CHOL 0mg; IRON 1.5mg; SODIUM 294mg; CALC 40mg

Polenta Pudding with Blueberry Topping

1 cup frozen blueberries
½ cup sugar, divided
2 cups 2% reduced-fat milk
6 tablespoons yellow cornmeal
¾ teaspoon lemon rind
½ teaspoon vanilla extract
¼ teaspoon salt

1. Combine blueberries and ¼ cup sugar in a medium microwave-safe bowl. Cover with wax paper; microwave at HIGH 3 minutes or until thoroughly heated and sugar dissolves, stirring after 1½ minutes.
2. Combine ¼ cup sugar, milk, cornmeal, and lemon rind in a 2-quart glass measure; stir with a whisk. Microwave at HIGH 7 minutes or until thick and bubbly, stirring every 2 minutes. Stir in vanilla and salt. Serve with blueberry topping. Yield: 4 servings (serving size: ½ cup pudding and about 3 tablespoons topping).

CALORIES 226 (11% from fat); FAT 2.8g (sat 1.5g, mono 0.8g, poly 0.3g); PROTEIN 5.3g; CARB 45.7g; FIBER 1.7g; CHOL 10mg; IRON 0.7mg; SODIUM 209mg; CALC 153mg

Poached Pears with Raspberry-Balsamic Sauce

The microwave cooks the pears with just a bit of liquid, so they don't lose any of their sweetness.

2 cups frozen unsweetened raspberries
1 tablespoon balsamic vinegar
2 teaspoons honey
⅛ teaspoon freshly ground black pepper
4 peeled firm Bosc pears (about 1¾ pounds)
1 tablespoon lemon juice

1. Place raspberries in a 3-quart casserole. Cover with lid; microwave at HIGH 2½ minutes or until thoroughly heated. Press raspberries through a fine sieve over a small bowl, reserving liquid;

discard solids. Add vinegar, honey, and pepper to reserved raspberry liquid.
2. Rub pears with lemon juice. Place pears in casserole, and drizzle with raspberry sauce. Cover with lid. Microwave at HIGH 8 minutes or until pears are tender, stirring and spooning sauce over pears after 4 minutes. Yield: 4 servings (serving size: 1 pear and 2 tablespoons sauce).

CALORIES 239 (3% from fat); FAT 0.9g (sat 0g, mono 0.2g, poly 0.3g); PROTEIN 1.5g; CARB 61.1g; FIBER 4.4g; CHOL 0mg; IRON 1.3mg; SODIUM 2mg; CALC 38mg

Italian Risotto with Shrimp

3½ cups fat-free, less-sodium chicken broth
½ cup dry white wine
1 cup chopped onion
2 teaspoons olive oil
1⅓ cups Arborio rice or other short-grain rice
1 pound medium shrimp, peeled and deveined
1 cup frozen whole-kernel corn
⅓ cup chopped bottled roasted red bell peppers
1 tablespoon chopped fresh basil
1 tablespoon chopped fresh oregano
¾ cup (3 ounces) grated Asiago cheese

1. Combine broth and wine in a 2-quart glass measure. Microwave at HIGH 5 minutes or until mixture boils. Remove from oven; keep warm.
2. Combine onion and oil in a 2-quart casserole. Microwave at HIGH 4 minutes. Stir in broth mixture and rice. Microwave at HIGH 15 minutes or until liquid is almost absorbed, stirring every 5 minutes.
3. Stir in shrimp, corn, bell peppers, basil, and oregano. Microwave at HIGH 4 minutes or until shrimp are done, stirring mixture every 2 minutes. Stir in cheese. Yield: 5 servings (serving size: about 1¼ cups).

CALORIES 409 (18% from fat); FAT 8.2g (sat 3.5g, mono 3g, poly 0.9g); PROTEIN 26.2g; CARB 55g; FIBER 2.2g; CHOL 121mg; IRON 4.3mg; SODIUM 722mg; CALC 233mg

Indian Shrimp Stir-Fry

We love the aromatic basmati rice with this microwave version of a stir-fry.

1½ pounds large shrimp, peeled and deveined
1½ tablespoons olive oil, divided
1 tablespoon curry powder
½ teaspoon ground coriander
¼ teaspoon ground red pepper
1 cup red bell pepper strips
1 cup diagonally sliced green onions
2 garlic cloves, minced
1 cup light coconut milk
¼ cup orange juice
1½ tablespoons cornstarch
1 tablespoon low-sodium soy sauce
½ teaspoon ground ginger
¼ teaspoon salt
¼ cup raisins
¼ cup sliced almonds, toasted
¼ cup shredded sweetened coconut
3 cups hot cooked basmati rice

1. Combine shrimp, 1 tablespoon oil, curry powder, coriander, and ground red pepper; set aside.
2. Combine 1½ teaspoons oil, bell pepper, onions, and garlic in a 1-quart glass measure. Cover with plastic wrap; microwave at HIGH 2 minutes, stirring after 1 minute. Set aside.
3. Combine coconut milk and next 5 ingredients in an 8-inch square baking dish; stir with a whisk. Microwave at HIGH 4 minutes or until thick, stirring after 2 minutes.
4. Stir in shrimp mixture and bell pepper mixture. Cover and microwave at HIGH 8 minutes or until shrimp are done, stirring after 4 minutes. Stir in raisins. Sprinkle with almonds and coconut. Serve with rice. Yield 6 servings (serving size: ⅔ cup shrimp mixture and ½ cup rice).

CALORIES 345 (28% from fat); FAT 10.7g (sat 3.5g, mono 4.3g, poly 1.4g); PROTEIN 21.3g; CARB 40.7g; FIBER 2.5g; CHOL 129mg; IRON 4.4mg; SODIUM 334mg; CALC 91mg

Warming Trend

International influences make hearty stews, casseroles, and soups even better.

When the temperature stubbornly defies spring overtures, there's nothing better for raising your spirits than the soul-warming pleasures of comfort food. And you can make a good thing even better by adding an ethnic spin from warmer climes. Whether it's a hearty soup or stew or a bubbling casserole of macaroni and cheese, adding ingredients redolent of Africa, South America, or Asia can wake up frozen taste buds and shake off the chill of late winter. These globally inspired recipes are simple to prepare, and most have plenty of make-ahead possibilities.

Zucchini Casserole with Red-Pepper Aïoli

We've added red peppers to the traditional French aïoli.

    2   teaspoons olive oil
    3   cups sliced onion
    6   (½-inch-thick) slices diagonally
        cut Italian bread (about 6 ounces),
        toasted and divided
    2   (14.5-ounce) cans no-salt-added
        diced tomatoes, undrained
    ½   teaspoon dried basil
    ½   teaspoon dried thyme
    ¼   teaspoon black pepper
    3   garlic cloves, minced
Cooking spray
    1   pound zucchini, halved
        lengthwise and thinly sliced
        (about 3 cups)
    2   cups (8 ounces) shredded
        part-skim mozzarella cheese
    1   (15.75-ounce) can fat-free,
        less-sodium chicken broth
    ¼   cup Red-Pepper Aïoli

1. Preheat oven to 375°.
2. Heat oil in a large nonstick skillet over medium-high heat. Add onion; sauté 15 minutes or until golden brown.
3. Cut 2 bread slices into 1-inch cubes; set aside. Drain tomatoes in a colander over a bowl, reserving ½ cup liquid; discard remaining liquid. Place tomatoes in a medium bowl. Stir in basil, thyme, pepper, and garlic.

4. Place ½ cup onion in bottom of a 3-quart casserole dish coated with cooking spray. Arrange 2 bread slices, half of remaining onion, half of tomato mixture, half of zucchini, and half of cheese over onion in dish. Repeat layers; top with bread cubes. Pour ½ cup reserved tomato liquid and broth over casserole. Cover and bake at 375° for 30 minutes. Uncover casserole, and bake an additional 25 minutes or until top begins to brown.
5. Spoon 2 cups casserole into each of 4 shallow bowls; top each serving with 1 tablespoon Red-Pepper Aïoli. Yield: 4 servings.

(Totals include Red-Pepper Aïoli) CALORIES 397 (28% from fat); FAT 12.5g (sat 6.3g, mono 4.5g, poly 1.1g); PROTEIN 23.6g; CARB 49.1g; FIBER 3.6g; CHOL 33mg; IRON 2.9mg; SODIUM 959mg; CALC 487mg

RED-PEPPER AÏOLI:

    3   garlic cloves, peeled
    ½   cup fat-free mayonnaise
    ½   teaspoon salt
    ¼   teaspoon crushed red pepper
    1   (7-ounce) bottle roasted red bell
        peppers, drained

1. Drop garlic through food chute with food processor on. Process until finely minced. Add remaining ingredients, and process until well-combined. Yield: 1 cup (serving size: 1 tablespoon).

CALORIES 10 (9% from fat); FAT 0.1g (sat 0g, mono 0g, poly 0g); PROTEIN 0.1g; CARB 2.3g; FIBER 0.1g; CHOL 0mg; IRON 0.1mg; SODIUM 173mg; CALC 2mg

Vietnamese Chicken Noodle Soup

Vietnamese cooking often calls for adding herbs and sauces to a dish at the end. These ingredients allow you to tailor the final product to your taste.

    4   cups water
    ½   cup sliced shallots
    ¼   cup minced peeled fresh ginger
    5   teaspoons minced garlic (about 2
        large cloves)
    1   tablespoon Thai fish sauce
    ½   teaspoon salt
    ½   teaspoon black pepper
    2   (15.75-ounce) cans fat-free,
        less-sodium chicken broth
    1½ pounds skinless, boneless chicken
        thighs
    ¼   pound uncooked rice sticks
        (rice-flour noodles) or vermicelli
    1   cup fresh bean sprouts
    2   tablespoons thinly sliced green
        onions
    2   tablespoons chopped fresh cilantro
    2   tablespoons thinly sliced fresh
        basil
    2   tablespoons thinly sliced fresh
        mint
    4   lime wedges
Chopped hot red or Thai chile
    (optional)
Fish sauce (optional)
Chili oil (optional)

1. Combine first 9 ingredients in a large Dutch oven; bring to a boil. Reduce heat, and simmer 15 minutes or until chicken is done. Remove chicken from pan; cool slightly. Cut into bite-size pieces.
2. Cook rice sticks in boiling water 5 minutes; drain.
3. Divide chicken and noodles evenly among 4 large bowls. Ladle 2 cups soup into each bowl. Top each serving with ¼ cup sprouts and 1½ teaspoons each of onions, cilantro, basil, and mint. Serve with lime wedges; garnish with chopped chile, fish sauce, or chili oil, if desired. Yield: 4 servings.

CALORIES 346 (18% from fat); FAT 7.1g (sat 1.7g, mono 2.1g, poly 1.7g); PROTEIN 40.4g; CARB 29.1g; FIBER 1.1g; CHOL 141mg; IRON 2.6mg; SODIUM 1279mg; CALC 61mg

Mac 'n' Cheese with Chipotles

Chipotle chiles are dry, smoked jalapeños found in cans or jars in the Mexican food section of most supermarkets.

- 1 (1-ounce) slice white bread
- ⅓ cup all-purpose flour
- 4 cups fat-free milk
- ¼ cup (1 ounce) grated fresh Parmesan cheese, divided
- 1 cup (4 ounces) shredded reduced-fat sharp cheddar cheese
- ½ cup (2 ounces) shredded Monterey Jack cheese
- 1 tablespoon Dijon mustard
- ½ teaspoon salt
- 2 drained canned chipotle chiles in adobo sauce, seeded and chopped
- 8 cups hot cooked cavatappi (about 5 cups uncooked pasta)
- ½ cup chopped green onions
- 1 (10-ounce) can diced tomatoes and green chiles, drained
  Cooking spray

1. Preheat oven to 375°.
2. Place bread in a food processor, and pulse until coarse crumbs form to measure ½ cup; set aside.
3. Lightly spoon flour into a dry measuring cup, and level with a knife. Place flour in a large saucepan. Gradually add milk, stirring constantly with a whisk. Bring to a boil; reduce heat, and simmer mixture 2 minutes or until thick. Remove from heat; stir in 2 tablespoons Parmesan and next 5 ingredients, stirring until cheese melts. Combine cheese sauce, pasta, onions, and tomatoes in a bowl.
4. Spoon mixture into a 13 x 9-inch baking dish coated with cooking spray. Combine 2 tablespoons Parmesan and breadcrumbs; sprinkle over pasta mixture.

Cover and bake at 375° for 10 minutes. Uncover and bake for an additional 10 minutes or until mixture is bubbly. Yield: 8 servings (serving size: about 1 cup).
NOTE: To make ahead, assemble casserole as directed, but stop before adding breadcrumb topping. Cover and refrigerate overnight. Let stand 30 minutes at room temperature; sprinkle with breadcrumb topping, and bake as directed.

CALORIES 328 (20% from fat); FAT 7.3g (sat 3.8g, mono 2g, poly 0.6g); PROTEIN 17.7g; CARB 46g; FIBER 1.8g; CHOL 20mg; IRON 2.4mg; SODIUM 638mg; CALC 415mg

Peruvian Chicken Stew with Sweet Potatoes and Peanuts

Cornmeal and potatoes are two of Peru's ancient staples; this recipe incorporates both. We also use a Peruvian technique: thickening the broth with ground peanuts.

- ½ cup dry-roasted peanuts
- 1 tablespoon vegetable oil
- 1½ cups thinly sliced onion
- 6 cups water
- ½ cup yellow cornmeal
- 1 teaspoon salt
- 1 teaspoon ground cumin
- ⅛ teaspoon ground allspice
- 4 cups julienne-cut peeled sweet potato (about 1 pound)
- 1½ pounds skinless, boneless chicken breast, cut into bite-size pieces
- ¼ cup chopped fresh cilantro

1. Place peanuts in a spice or coffee grinder; process until medium ground.
2. Heat oil in a large Dutch oven over medium-high heat. Add onion; sauté 10 minutes or until lightly browned. Stir in ground peanuts, water, and next 5 ingredients; bring to a boil. Reduce heat, and simmer 15 minutes. Stir in chicken; cook 10 minutes or until chicken is done. Stir in cilantro. Yield: 6 servings (serving size: 1⅔ cups).
NOTE: To make ahead, prepare soup as directed, but stop before adding cilantro. Cover soup, and refrigerate for up to 2 days. Let soup stand 30 minutes at room temperature; place in a saucepan over

medium heat. Cook soup until thoroughly heated; stir in cilantro.

CALORIES 350 (26% from fat); FAT 10.2g (sat 1.7g, mono 4.1g, poly 3.5g); PROTEIN 32g; CARB 32.4g; FIBER 4.6g; CHOL 66mg; IRON 2.4mg; SODIUM 478mg; CALC 53mg

Baked Ziti with Vegetables and Mushrooms

A favorite in many homes on "Italian night," baked ziti is usually laden with meat and cheese. This version relies on the flavors of mushrooms and spinach instead.

- 1 tablespoon vegetable oil
- 1 cup chopped onion
- 1 cup chopped green bell pepper
- 1 cup chopped red bell pepper
- 1½ cups chopped portobello, cremini, or button mushrooms
- 4 garlic cloves, chopped
- 1 teaspoon dried basil
- ½ teaspoon salt
- ¼ teaspoon black pepper
- 1 (14½-ounce) can stewed tomatoes, undrained and chopped
- 1 (8-ounce) can tomato sauce
- 7 cups torn spinach (about ½ pound)
- 3 cups hot cooked ziti (about 2¼ cups uncooked short tube-shaped pasta)
  Cooking spray
- 1 cup part-skim ricotta cheese
- ¼ cup (1 ounce) grated fresh Parmesan cheese

1. Preheat oven to 375°.
2. Heat oil in a large nonstick skillet over medium-high heat. Add onion and bell peppers; sauté 5 minutes. Add mushrooms and garlic; sauté 2 minutes. Stir in basil, salt, black pepper, tomatoes, and tomato sauce; bring to a boil. Reduce heat; simmer 5 minutes or until slightly thick. Stir in spinach; cook 1 minute or until spinach wilts. Stir in pasta. Spoon into a 13 x 9-inch baking dish coated with cooking spray. Dollop with ricotta.
3. Cover and bake at 375° for 20 minutes. Uncover; sprinkle with Parmesan. Bake an additional 5 minutes or until
Continued

lightly browned. Yield: 8 servings (serving size: 1 cup).

NOTE: To make ahead, assemble casserole as directed. Cover and refrigerate overnight. Let stand 30 minutes at room temperature, and bake as directed.

CALORIES 237 (24% from fat); FAT 6.3g (sat 2.5g, mono 2.4g, poly 0.8g); PROTEIN 11.6g; CARB 35g; FIBER 4.5g; CHOL 12mg; IRON 3.8mg; SODIUM 588mg; CALC 213mg

Curried Tuna Noodle Casserole

Here's a classic with a touch of Indian curry.

    2 teaspoons butter
    5 cups sliced cremini or button
       mushrooms (about ¾ pound)
    ¾ cup frozen green peas, thawed
    ¾ cup sliced green onions
    ⅔ cup chopped red bell pepper
    2 teaspoons curry powder
    3 tablespoons all-purpose flour
 1½ cups 1% low-fat milk
    4 cups hot cooked medium egg
       noodles (3¼ cups uncooked pasta)
    ¼ cup chopped fresh flat-leaf parsley
    ½ teaspoon salt
    1 (12-ounce) can solid white tuna in
       water, drained and flaked
    ¼ cup crushed reduced-fat round
       buttery crackers (such as Ritz;
       about 7 crackers)

1. Preheat oven to 375°.
2. Melt butter in a large nonstick skillet over medium heat. Add mushrooms; sauté 6 minutes or until soft. Add peas, onions, bell pepper, and curry; sauté 5 minutes or until vegetables are tender.
3. Place flour in a small bowl; gradually add milk, stirring with a whisk. Add to mushroom mixture; bring to a boil. Reduce heat; simmer 2 minutes or until thick, stirring frequently. Remove from heat; stir in pasta, parsley, salt, and tuna. Spoon into a 2-quart casserole dish. Sprinkle with crushed crackers. Cover and bake at 375° for 20 minutes. Yield: 7 servings (serving size: 1 cup).

CALORIES 275 (16% from fat); FAT 4.9g (sat 1.7g, mono 1.3g, poly 1g); PROTEIN 20.8g; CARB 36.4g; FIBER 4.1g; CHOL 54mg; IRON 3.5mg; SODIUM 437mg; CALC 100mg

Vegetable-Beef Stew in Pumpkinseed Sauce

In Africa, toasted pumpkin seeds are ground and stirred into soups and stews.

    2 tablespoons roasted salted
       pumpkinseed kernels
    1 teaspoon ground cumin
    ½ teaspoon ground coriander
    ½ teaspoon ground allspice
    ¼ teaspoon ground cloves
    ¼ teaspoon ground cinnamon
    ¼ teaspoon salt
    ¼ teaspoon black pepper
    2 teaspoons vegetable oil, divided
    1 (8-ounce) boneless sirloin steak,
       cut into 1-inch cubes
    1 cup chopped onion
    ½ cup chopped red bell pepper
    2 teaspoons finely chopped seeded
       pickled jalapeño pepper
 1½ cups (¼-inch-thick) slices carrot
 1½ cups canned crushed tomatoes,
       undrained
    2 tablespoons molasses
    1 (14¼-ounce) can low-salt beef broth
 1½ cups (2-inch) cut green beans
    2 cups thinly sliced kale or spinach

1. Cook pumpkinseeds in a Dutch oven over medium-high heat 3 minutes or until kernels are toasted and begin to pop. Remove from heat, and cool. Place kernels in a spice or coffee grinder; process until finely ground.
2. Combine cumin and next 6 ingredients in a small bowl. Heat 1 teaspoon oil in pan over medium-high heat. Add beef; sauté 3 minutes or until browned. Remove beef from pan.
3. Add 1 teaspoon oil to pan. Add onion, bell pepper, and jalapeño; sauté 4 minutes. Add ground kernels and cumin mixture to pan; cook 1 minute. Stir in beef, carrot, tomatoes, molasses, and broth; bring to a boil. Partially cover, reduce heat, and simmer 15 minutes. Add beans; partially cover, and simmer 30 minutes or until meat is tender. Stir in kale; cook 4 minutes or until kale wilts. Yield: 6 servings (serving size: 1 cup).

CALORIES 176 (27% from fat); FAT 5.3g (sat 1.3g, mono 1.7g, poly 1.6g); PROTEIN 14.4g; CARB 19.5g; FIBER 3g; CHOL 23mg; IRON 3.7mg; SODIUM 583mg; CALC 104mg

back to the best

Irish Bread Pudding with Caramel-Whiskey Sauce

We couldn't imagine a more fitting nod to St. Patrick's Day than Irish Bread Pudding with Caramel-Whiskey Sauce, which has been one of our favorite desserts since it first appeared in the March 1998 issue.

Its whiskey-soaked raisins, hint of cinnamon, and decadent caramel sauce make it so special, in fact, that Norwegian Cruise Line offers the dish to its half-million passengers. We suspect that bread-pudding converts are won each time it's served.

Irish Bread Pudding with Caramel-Whiskey Sauce

    ¼ cup light butter, melted
    1 (10-ounce) French bread baguette,
       cut into 1-inch-thick slices
    ½ cup raisins
    ¼ cup Irish whiskey
 1¾ cups 1% low-fat milk
    1 cup sugar
    1 tablespoon vanilla extract
    1 (12-ounce) can evaporated
       fat-free milk
    2 large eggs, lightly beaten
       Cooking spray
    1 tablespoon sugar
    1 teaspoon ground cinnamon
       Caramel-Whiskey Sauce

1. Preheat oven to 350°.
2. Brush melted butter on one side of French bread slices; place bread, buttered sides up, on a baking sheet. Bake at 350° for 10 minutes or until lightly toasted. Cut bread into ½-inch cubes; set aside.
3. While bread is toasting, combine raisins and whiskey in a small bowl; cover and let stand 10 minutes or until soft (do not drain).

4. Combine 1% milk and next 4 ingredients in a large bowl; stir well with a whisk. Add bread cubes and raisin mixture, pressing gently to moisten; let stand 15 minutes. Spoon bread mixture into a 13 x 9-inch baking dish coated with cooking spray. Combine 1 tablespoon sugar and cinnamon, and sprinkle over pudding. Bake at 350° for 35 minutes or until pudding is set. Serve warm with Caramel-Whiskey Sauce. Yield: 12 servings (serving size: 1 [3-inch] square and 2 tablespoons sauce).

NOTE: Substitute ¼ cup apple juice for Irish whiskey, if desired.

(Totals include Caramel-Whiskey Sauce) CALORIES 360 (18% from fat); FAT 7.3g (sat 3.2g, mono 1.9g, poly 0.5g); PROTEIN 7.3g; CARB 65.9g; FIBER 1g; CHOL 57mg; IRON 1.1mg; SODIUM 275mg; CALC 164mg

CARAMEL-WHISKEY SAUCE:

1½   cups sugar
⅔   cup water
¼   cup light butter
¼   cup (2 ounces) ⅓-less-fat cream
      cheese
¼   cup Irish whiskey
¼   cup 1% low-fat milk

1. Combine sugar and water in a small, heavy saucepan over medium-high heat; cook until sugar dissolves, stirring constantly. Cook 15 minutes or until golden (do not stir). Remove from heat. Carefully add butter and cream cheese, stirring constantly with a whisk (mixture will be hot and bubble vigorously). Cool slightly, and stir in whiskey and milk. Yield: 1½ cups (serving size: 2 tablespoons).

NOTE: You can substitute 1 tablespoon imitation rum extract and 3 tablespoons water for Irish whiskey, if desired.

CALORIES 138 (22% from fat); FAT 3.3g (sat 1.3g, mono 0.6g, poly 0.1g); PROTEIN 0.6g; CARB 25.9g; FIBER 0g; CHOL 11mg; IRON 0mg; SODIUM 45mg; CALC 11mg

Masquerading Mushrooms

Aided and abetted by portobellos, an executive chef delights in deceiving the masses.

If you think planning dinner for your family is hard, try setting a daily menu for up to 15,000 people. That's the challenge Howie Velie faces every day as district executive chef at the National Institutes of Health (NIH) in Bethesda, Maryland.

Howie, a former vegan who once worked as a chef in a vegetarian restaurant, strives to provide his clients with low-fat, meatless alternatives.

"I enjoy developing and preparing vegetarian dishes that meat eaters don't realize are meat-free," he says, adding that portobello mushrooms are a fantastic aid in this deception. "I love to work with portobellos. They're big, thick, and substantial, with a real meaty taste and texture. Eating one is like eating a burger or a steak." Thus the origin of the succulent Portobello "Steak" Burger with Caramelized Onions, a popular feature on the NIH menu.

Portobello "Steak" Burger with Caramelized Onions

1   cup balsamic vinegar
2   tablespoons olive oil
1   teaspoon dried basil
¼   teaspoon kosher salt
¼   teaspoon ground white pepper
2   garlic cloves, minced
6   portobello mushroom caps (about
      1½ pounds)
Cooking spray
1   tablespoon olive oil
1½   cups sliced onion
¼   cup low-fat mayonnaise
1   teaspoon bottled minced roasted
      garlic
6   (2-ounce) whole wheat Kaiser rolls
      or hamburger buns
6   curly leaf lettuce leaves
6   large (¼-inch-thick) slices tomato

1. Combine first 6 ingredients in a large zip-top plastic bag. Add mushroom caps; seal and marinate in refrigerator 24 hours.

2. Prepare grill or broiler.

3. Remove mushroom caps from bag, discarding marinade. Place mushroom caps on grill rack or broiler pan coated with cooking spray; cook 5 minutes or until tender.

4. Heat oil in a medium nonstick skillet over medium-high heat. Add onion; cover and cook 10 minutes or until golden brown, stirring frequently.

5. Combine mayonnaise and roasted garlic in a small bowl. Spread 1½ teaspoons mayonnaise mixture over top half of each bun; top each bottom half with 1 lettuce leaf, 1 tomato slice, 1 mushroom cap, 1 tablespoon caramelized onion, and top half of bun. Yield: 6 servings.

CALORIES 274 (30% from fat); FAT 9.3g (sat 1.4g, mono 3.9g, poly 3.1g); PROTEIN 8.9g; CARB 40.4g; FIBER 3.7g; CHOL 3mg; IRON 3.7mg; SODIUM 420mg; CALC 74mg

Wasabi Mashed Potatoes

"My fiancé and I love superspicy foods, so that's what inspired me to create this recipe. The potatoes go great with fish. I like to serve them with Chilean sea bass steamed in sake."

—Amanda Kruzich, Burbank, California

1   pound cubed peeled Yukon gold
      potato
1   tablespoon wasabi powder (dried
      Japanese horseradish)
2   teaspoons butter
1   (8-ounce) carton plain low-fat
      yogurt

1. Place potato in a saucepan, and cover with water; bring to a boil. Reduce heat, and simmer 20 minutes or until tender; drain. Return potato to pan. Add remaining ingredients, and mash with a potato masher. Yield: 5 servings (serving size: ½ cup).

CALORIES 116 (19% from fat); FAT 2.5g (sat 1.5g, mono 0.7g, poly 0.2g); PROTEIN 4.4g; CARB 19.7g; FIBER 1.5g; CHOL 7mg; IRON 0.8mg; SODIUM 109mg; CALC 93mg

Turkey Meat Loaf

"If you're making this for a red meat lover, it's OK to replace one pound of the ground turkey with ground round."

—Vivian F. Stewart, Pembroke Pines, Florida

    2   pounds ground turkey breast
    1   cup quick-cooking oats
    ½   cup ketchup
    ¼   cup chopped fresh parsley
    ¼   cup (1 ounce) grated fresh Parmesan
        cheese
    1   tablespoon dried oregano
    3   tablespoons Worcestershire sauce
    2   tablespoons low-sodium soy sauce
    2   teaspoons dried basil
    1   teaspoon garlic powder
        Cooking spray
    ¼   cup ketchup

1. Preheat oven to 400°.
2. Combine first 10 ingredients in a large bowl.
3. Place mixture in a 9 x 5-inch loaf pan coated with cooking spray. Top with ¼ cup ketchup. Bake at 400° for 1 hour and 15 minutes or until done. Let stand 10 minutes before slicing. Yield: 6 servings.

CALORIES 272 (11% from fat); FAT 3.5g (sat 1.3g, mono 0.9g, poly 0.9g); PROTEIN 39.1g; CARB 20.4g; FIBER 2.1g; CHOL 97mg; IRON 3.3mg; SODIUM 728mg; CALC 114mg

Middle Eastern Eggplant Dip

"This dip, which is really low in calories, is delicious and takes no time to make. It's versatile, too—tastes great hot or cold. I like to serve it with pita bread."

—Aimee Bower, Alstonville, Australia

    4½ cups (1-inch) cubed peeled
        eggplant (about 1¼ pounds)
    1   cup chopped red bell pepper
    1   cup chopped red onion
    1   tablespoon olive oil
    1   garlic clove, chopped
        Cooking spray
    1   tablespoon tomato paste
    ½   teaspoon salt
    ¼   teaspoon freshly ground black
        pepper

1. Preheat oven to 350°.
2. Combine first 5 ingredients in a 13 x 9-inch baking dish coated with cooking spray; stir well to coat. Bake at 350° for 1 hour or until vegetables are tender. Cool slightly.
3. Place vegetables and remaining ingredients in a food processor; process until smooth. Yield: 1¼ cups (serving size: 2 tablespoons).

CALORIES 41 (39% from fat); FAT 1.8g (sat 0.2g, mono 1.1g, poly 0.3g); PROTEIN 1g; CARB 6.2g; FIBER 2.1g; CHOL 0mg; IRON 0.5mg; SODIUM 121mg; CALC 10mg

Baked Egg Rolls

"When dipped in traditional Vietnamese sauce and served with rice noodles on the side, these make an easy, low-fat, and delicious main meal."

—Teresa Martin, North Aurora, Illinois

EGG ROLLS:

    ⅔   cup coarsely chopped celery
    ⅔   cup coarsely chopped carrot
    2   cups shredded cabbage
    ½   teaspoon vegetable oil
    ⅔   cup chopped onion
    ½   teaspoon minced peeled fresh
        ginger
    1   garlic clove, minced
    ½   pound ground turkey breast
    1½ tablespoons low-sodium soy sauce
    ¼   teaspoon black pepper
    14 egg roll wrappers
    1   large egg white
        Cooking spray

SAUCE:

    ¾   cup low-sodium soy sauce
    6   tablespoons rice vinegar
    2   tablespoons dark sesame oil
    1   tablespoon minced peeled fresh
        ginger
    ⅓   cup thinly sliced green onions
        (optional)

1. Preheat oven to 425°.
2. To prepare egg rolls, combine celery and carrot in a food processor, and pulse 10 times or until finely chopped.
3. Combine celery mixture and cabbage in a medium bowl. Cover with plastic wrap; vent. Microwave at HIGH 5 minutes; drain.
4. Heat vegetable oil in a large nonstick skillet over medium-high heat. Add chopped onion, ½ teaspoon ginger, and garlic; sauté 2 minutes. Add turkey; cook 5 minutes. Remove from heat; stir in cabbage mixture, 1½ tablespoons soy sauce, and pepper. Cover and chill 15 minutes.
5. Place 1 egg roll wrapper at a time onto work surface with 1 corner pointing toward you (wrapper should look like a diamond). Trim 1 inch off right and left corners of wrapper. Spoon 3 tablespoons turkey mixture into center of wrapper. Fold lower corner of wrapper over filling. Fold in trimmed corners. Moisten top corner of wrapper with egg white; roll up jelly-roll fashion. Repeat procedure with remaining wrappers, turkey mixture, and egg white.
6. Lightly coat egg rolls with cooking spray, and place, seam side down, on a baking sheet coated with cooking spray. Bake at 425° for 18 minutes or until golden brown.
7. To prepare sauce, combine ¾ cup soy sauce, vinegar, sesame oil, and 1 tablespoon ginger; serve with egg rolls. Garnish with green onions, if desired. Yield: 14 servings (serving size: 1 roll and about 1 tablespoon sauce).

CALORIES 79 (29% from fat); FAT 2.5g (sat 0.4g, mono 0.9g, poly 1.1g); PROTEIN 5.7g; CARB 8g; FIBER 0.7g; CHOL 11mg; IRON 0.9mg; SODIUM 532mg; CALC 18mg

Asian Turkey Burgers

"I usually serve these with a side salad topped with sesame dressing."

—Lisa Edwards, Hoboken, New Jersey

    1   pound ground turkey
    ¼   cup chopped green onions
    ¼   cup dry breadcrumbs
    2   tablespoons hoisin sauce
    1   teaspoon ground ginger
    ¼   teaspoon low-sodium soy sauce
    ¼   teaspoon ground red pepper
        Cooking spray
    4   (2-ounce) hamburger buns

1. Combine first 7 ingredients in a large bowl. Divide turkey mixture into 4 equal portions, shaping each into a ½-inch-thick patty.

2. Prepare grill or broiler.

3. Place patties on grill rack or broiler pan coated with cooking spray; cook 5 minutes on each side or until done. Serve on buns. Yield: 4 servings.

CALORIES 487 (30% from fat); FAT 16.5g (sat 4.1g, mono 5.2g, poly 5.3g); PROTEIN 31.8g; CARB 50.7g; FIBER 2.7g; CHOL 87mg; IRON 5mg; SODIUM 751mg; CALC 162mg

Bulgur-Bean Salad

"I came up with this recipe while in the kitchen experimenting with bulgur and some leftover ingredients from a salad. It's really important to chill this dish before serving to allow the flavors to blend."

—Jenni Fox, Venice, Florida

    2   cups water
    ½   cup uncooked bulgur
    2   teaspoons olive oil
    1   cup chopped spinach
    ½   cup (2 ounces) crumbled feta cheese
    ½   cup presliced mushrooms
    ½   cup drained canned kidney beans
    ½   cup drained canned chickpeas
        (garbanzo beans)
    ½   cup drained canned artichoke
        hearts, coarsely chopped
    ¼   cup drained canned sliced black
        olives
 1 ½   teaspoons dried basil
    1   teaspoon black pepper
    ½   teaspoon dried oregano
    2   garlic cloves, minced

1. Bring water to a boil in a medium saucepan; add bulgur. Cover and let stand 30 minutes. Fluff with a fork.

2. Heat oil in a medium skillet over medium-high heat. Add spinach. Sauté 1 minute or until spinach wilts; remove from heat. Combine bulgur, spinach, feta, and remaining ingredients in a large bowl. Cover and chill 1 hour. Yield: 5 servings (serving size: 1 cup).

CALORIES 168 (30% from fat); FAT 5.6g (sat 2.3g, mono 1.7g, poly 1.4g); PROTEIN 7.1g; CARB 24.3g; FIBER 6.7g; CHOL 10mg; IRON 2.2mg; SODIUM 374mg; CALC 114mg

in season

The Beet Goes On

Fresh beets are back in style, and this is the best month to find out why.

Fresh beets have lately become as common on fine-restaurant menus as they once were in sensible root cellars. With hues ranging from yellow to purple, they lend themselves to dramatic presentations as few other vegetables do. Factor in their texture, which holds up well when baked, boiled, roasted, or julienned raw, and their sweetness, which pairs equally well with butter or vinegar and citrus, and you have a vegetable destined to become a star.

Beet Cake with Cream Cheese Frosting

CAKE:

    1   pound beets (about 2 medium)
        Cooking spray
    ⅔   cup granulated sugar
    ⅔   cup packed dark brown sugar
    ½   cup vegetable oil
    2   large eggs
 2 ½   cups all-purpose flour
    2   teaspoons baking powder
    1   teaspoon ground ginger
    1   teaspoon ground cinnamon
    ½   teaspoon baking soda
    ¼   teaspoon salt
    ½   cup 1% low-fat milk

FROSTING:

    2   teaspoons grated orange rind
    1   teaspoon vanilla extract
    1   (8-ounce) block ⅓-less-fat cream
        cheese, chilled
    3   cups sifted powdered sugar
    2   tablespoons finely chopped
        walnuts, toasted

1. Preheat oven to 350°.

2. To prepare cake, peel beets using a vegetable peeler. Grate beets, using large holes of a grater, to measure 2 cups.

3. Coat 2 (9-inch) round cake pans with cooking spray; line bottoms of pans with wax paper. Coat wax paper with cooking spray.

4. Combine granulated sugar, brown sugar, oil, and eggs in a large bowl; beat with a mixer at medium speed until well blended. Add beets; beat well. Lightly spoon flour into dry measuring cups; level with a knife. Combine flour and next 5 ingredients in a large bowl, stirring well with a whisk. Add flour mixture to sugar mixture alternately with milk, beginning and ending with flour mixture. Pour batter into prepared pans; sharply tap pans once on counter to remove air bubbles.

5. Bake at 350° for 30 minutes or until a wooden pick inserted in center comes out clean. Cool in pans 10 minutes on wire racks; remove from pans. Carefully peel off wax paper, and cool cake completely on wire racks.

6. To prepare frosting, beat orange rind, vanilla, and cream cheese with a mixer at high speed until fluffy. Add powdered sugar; beat at low speed just until blended (do not overbeat).

7. Place 1 cake layer on a plate, and spread with ½ cup frosting; top with remaining cake layer. Spread remaining frosting over top and sides of cake. Sprinkle nuts over top of cake. Store cake loosely covered in refrigerator. Yield: 18 servings (serving size: 1 piece).

CALORIES 312 (30% from fat); FAT 10.5g (sat 3.3g, mono 3g, poly 3.6g); PROTEIN 4.5g; CARB 51.2g; FIBER 0.7g; CHOL 34mg; IRON 1.4mg; SODIUM 198mg; CALC 65mg

---

Picking the Best

More beet varieties are becoming available, with golden-hued roots appearing most recently. A new favorite at L'Etoile restaurant in Madison, Wisconsin (a beet Mecca), is the candy-striped Chioggia.

When selecting fresh beets, buy small to medium globes with stems and leaves attached; firm, smooth skin; and no soft spots. If storing, immediately trim stems to about one inch. Beets will keep in plastic bags in the refrigerator for up to two weeks.

Roasting Beets Step-by-Steps

1. *Wash beets whole, and trim to one inch from the stem to minimize bleeding before placing on a foil-lined baking sheet.*

2. *After cooking, trim off about ¼ inch of beet roots.*

3. *Rub off skins. They should slip off easily after cooking.*

Risotto with Beet Greens and Leeks

5 cups fat-free, less-sodium chicken broth
1 tablespoon olive oil
2 cups thinly sliced leek (about 2 large)
1½ cups uncooked Arborio or other short-grain rice
¼ cup dry white wine
3 cups coarsely chopped beet greens
¼ cup (1 ounce) grated fresh Parmesan cheese
⅛ teaspoon black pepper
6 lemon wedges

1. Bring broth to a simmer in a medium saucepan (do not boil). Keep warm over low heat.
2. Heat oil in a large saucepan over medium heat. Add leek; sauté 4 minutes or until tender. Add rice; cook 1 minute, stirring constantly. Stir in wine; cook 1 minute or until liquid is nearly absorbed, stirring constantly. Reduce heat to low; stir in greens. Add broth, ½ cup at a time, stirring constantly until each portion of broth is absorbed before adding next (about 25 minutes total). Stir in cheese and pepper. Serve with lemon wedges. Yield: 6 servings (serving size: about ¾ cup).

CALORIES 260 (14% from fat); FAT 3.8g (sat 1.2g, mono 2.1g, poly 0.4g); PROTEIN 8.3g; CARB 46.4g; FIBER 1.4g; CHOL 3mg; IRON 3.5mg; SODIUM 522mg; CALC 101mg

Beet Soup with Potatoes and Beet Greens

Add the greens to the soup at the end for a nutritious boost. If you prefer, you can use less than the four cups called for.

1 tablespoon olive oil
1 cup chopped onion
1 cup diagonally sliced carrot
½ cup finely chopped celery
1½ cups finely chopped peeled beets (about ¾ pound)
1½ cups finely chopped red potatoes (about ½ pound)
1½ cups water
2 tablespoons tomato paste
⅛ teaspoon black pepper
2 (10½-ounce) cans beef broth
1 (14.5-ounce) can no-salt-added diced tomatoes, undrained
4 cups coarsely chopped beet greens (about 1 pound)
1 tablespoon brown sugar

1. Heat oil in a large Dutch oven over medium-high heat. Add onion, carrot, and celery; sauté 5 minutes or until tender. Stir in beets and next 6 ingredients. Bring to a boil; reduce heat, and simmer 35 minutes or until vegetables are tender. Stir in beet greens and sugar; cook 5 minutes. Yield: 6 servings (serving size: 1⅓ cups).

CALORIES 135 (17% from fat); FAT 2.5g (sat 0.4g, mono 1.7g, poly 0.3g); PROTEIN 7.5g; CARB 22.2g; FIBER 2.8g; CHOL 0mg; IRON 2.7mg; SODIUM 625mg; CALC 88mg

Roasted-Beet Salad with Feta Dressing

3 medium beets (about 1½ pounds)
¼ cup (1 ounce) crumbled feta cheese
¼ cup fat-free sour cream
2 tablespoons 1% low-fat milk
2 tablespoons low-fat mayonnaise
1½ teaspoons white wine vinegar
⅛ teaspoon salt
⅛ teaspoon black pepper
6 cups gourmet salad greens
4 teaspoons minced red onion
4 teaspoons chopped fresh parsley

1. Preheat oven to 425°.
2. Leave root and 1 inch stem on beets; scrub with a brush. Place beets on a baking sheet lined with foil. Bake at 425° for 45 minutes or until tender. Cool beets slightly. Trim off beet roots; rub off skins. Cut each beet into 8 wedges.
3. Combine feta cheese and next 6 ingredients; stir well with a whisk.
4. Divide greens evenly among 4 plates, and top with beet wedges. Spoon dressing over salad. Sprinkle with onion and parsley. Yield: 4 servings (serving size: 1½ cups greens, 6 beet wedges, 2 tablespoons dressing, 1 teaspoon onion, and 1 teaspoon parsley).

CALORIES 98 (22% from fat); FAT 2.4g (sat 1.2g, mono 0.5g, poly 0.5g); PROTEIN 5.2g; CARB 14.3g; FIBER 2.2g; CHOL 7mg; IRON 1.8mg; SODIUM 312mg; CALC 91mg

Sweet-and-Sour Beets

This dish goes well with pork or chicken.

    2   large beets (about 1½ pounds)
    1   tablespoon butter
    2   tablespoons red wine vinegar
    1   tablespoon sugar
    ¼   teaspoon salt
    ⅛   teaspoon black pepper
    2   tablespoons finely chopped fresh
        parsley

1. Leave root and 1 inch stem on beets;
scrub with a brush. Place beets in a large
saucepan; cover with water. Bring to a
boil; cover, reduce heat, and simmer 40
minutes or until tender. Drain and rinse
with cold water. Drain and cool. Trim
off beet roots; rub off skins. Cut beets
into ¼-inch-thick strips.

2. Melt butter in a large nonstick skillet
over medium heat. Add beets, vinegar,
sugar, salt, and pepper; cook 2 minutes
or until liquid almost evaporates. Sprinkle with parsley. Yield: 6 servings (serving size: ½ cup).

CALORIES 75 (25% from fat); FAT 2.1g (sat 1.2g, mono 0.6g,
poly 0.1g); PROTEIN 1.9g; CARB 13.2g; FIBER 1g; CHOL 5mg;
IRON 1mg; SODIUM 206mg; CALC 21mg

Potato-and-Beet Greens Frittata

    2   cups finely chopped red potatoes
        (about 1 pound)
    1   cup chopped beet greens
    ⅓   cup fat-free milk
    2   tablespoons grated fresh Parmesan
        cheese
    ¼   teaspoon salt
    ¼   teaspoon black pepper
    4   large eggs
    3   large egg whites
    1   teaspoon butter
        Cooking spray
    ⅓   cup (about 1½ ounces) shredded
        part-skim mozzarella cheese
    4   beet greens leaves (optional)

1. Preheat broiler.
2. Place potatoes in a medium saucepan,
and cover with water; bring to a boil.

Reduce heat, and simmer 8 minutes. Add
chopped beet greens; cook 2 minutes or
until tender. Drain.
3. Combine milk and next 5 ingredients
in a large bowl; stir with a whisk. Stir in
potato mixture. Melt butter in a medium
nonstick skillet coated with cooking spray
over medium heat. Pour egg mixture into
skillet; cook 15 minutes or until top is just
set. Sprinkle with mozzarella.
4. Wrap handle of skillet with foil; broil
5 minutes or until golden brown. Garnish with beet greens leaves, if desired.
Yield: 4 servings (serving size: 1 wedge).

CALORIES 188 (42% from fat); FAT 8.8g (sat 3.8g, mono 3.1g,
poly 1.1g); PROTEIN 14.7g; CARB 12.1g; FIBER 1.2g; CHOL 232mg;
IRON 1.9mg; SODIUM 395mg; CALC 174mg

lighten up

Potatoes Pronounced Perfect

*A grandmother's beloved recipe gets a next-
generation makeover.*

Mix a child's pronunciation with his
grandmother's beloved potato dish, and
you get a deliciously cheesy concoction
known as Aw Maw's Potatoes.

Hazel Robertson has served this rich
and creamy dish for a good portion of her
80 years. After her husband had bypass
surgery several years ago, Hazel—known
as "Aw Maw" to grandson Chris, who as a
toddler couldn't pronounce "grandma"—
made several unsuccessful attempts to
lighten the delicious dish before daugh-
ter, Becky, called on *Cooking Light* for help.

Made with a half-pound of butter, a
pint of cream, and a third-pound of
cheese, this dish was the ultimate in
comfort food (and in fat and calories).

By substituting fat-free milk for
half-and-half, using reduced-fat cheese,
and cutting two-thirds of the butter and
a third of the salt, we stripped 152 calories, 17.8 grams of fat, and 310 milligrams of sodium per serving from the
original.

Aw Maw's Potatoes

    4   pounds unpeeled baking potatoes
        Cooking spray
    ⅓   cup butter
    3   cups fat-free milk
    1   cup (4 ounces) shredded reduced-
        fat sharp cheddar cheese, divided
    2   teaspoons salt
    ¼   teaspoon freshly ground black
        pepper

1. Place potatoes in a Dutch oven, and
cover with water. Bring to a boil; reduce
heat, and simmer 20 minutes or until
tender. Drain. Cover and chill.
2. Preheat oven to 350°.
3. Peel and shred potatoes. Place in a
13 x 9-inch baking dish coated with
cooking spray. Melt butter in a large
saucepan over medium heat. Stir in
milk, ½ cup cheese, salt, and pepper.
Cook 8 minutes or until cheese melts,
stirring occasionally. Pour over potatoes, and stir gently. Bake at 350° for
45 minutes. Sprinkle with ½ cup
cheese. Bake an additional 15 minutes
or until cheese melts. Yield: 12 servings (serving size: ⅔ cup).

CALORIES 213 (30% from fat); FAT 7g (sat 4.5g, mono 1.9g,
poly 0.3g); PROTEIN 8g; CARB 30.2g; FIBER 2.4g; CHOL 20mg;
IRON 1.2mg; SODIUM 541mg; CALC 174mg

BEFORE	AFTER
SERVING SIZE	
⅔ cup	
CALORIES PER SERVING	
365	213
FAT	
24.8g	7g
PERCENT OF TOTAL CALORIES	
61%	30%
SODIUM	
851mg	541mg

No-Miss Miso

This soybean paste is a classic ingredient in Japanese cooking that couples well with American ingenuity.

When Jean Patterson was working as an English teacher in Taiwan she would often hold class in a restaurant's private tatami room, feasting on sushi, sashimi, broiled eel, and her newfound favorite: miso soup.

After moving back to the States, she tried to duplicate the foods she'd enjoyed in Asia, especially the miso soup. With help from her roommate's mother, who had trained as a chef in her native Japan, Jean learned to use miso as a basic seasoning in many other Japanese dishes. Jean also learned of miso's subtle variations. Light miso is sweeter, whereas red miso has a stronger, saltier flavor.

But miso isn't just for Japanese food. Used sparingly, it can add depth to dressings, marinades, and sauces. Jean likes to swirl light miso into vegetable soup just before serving to provide an extra flavor boost. The richer red miso lends an exotic flair to fish and tofu marinades.

Grilled Fennel, Leeks, and Eggplant with Garlic-Miso Sauce

Mirin is a low-alcohol sweet wine common in Japanese cuisine. It's available in Asian food markets and can often be found in the gourmet sections of some supermarkets.

- 4 small leeks, trimmed and halved lengthwise and crosswise
- 4 small Japanese eggplants, halved lengthwise and crosswise (about 1¼ pounds)
- 1 fennel bulb, trimmed and cut into 8 wedges
- 5 garlic cloves, unpeeled
- ⅓ cup mirin (sweet rice wine)
- ¼ cup water
- ⅓ cup yellow miso (soybean paste)

1. Prepare grill or broiler.
2. Place leeks, eggplants, fennel, and garlic in a grill basket on a grill rack or broiler pan; cook 10 minutes or until tender, turning frequently. Remove leeks, eggplant, and fennel from heat, and cook garlic 5 minutes.
3. Combine mirin and water in a small saucepan over medium heat; bring to a boil. Reduce heat; simmer 3 minutes.
4. Squeeze garlic cloves to extract pulp; place pulp in a blender. Add mirin mixture and miso; process until smooth. Pour sauce over vegetables, and toss well to coat. Yield: 8 servings (serving size: 1 cup vegetables and 1½ tablespoons sauce).

CALORIES 88 (4% from fat); FAT 0.4g (sat 0.1g, mono 0g, poly 0.2g); PROTEIN 2.6g; CARB 19.3g; FIBER 2.7g; CHOL 0mg; IRON 2.4mg; SODIUM 375mg; CALC 75mg

Miso Soup with Enoki Mushrooms

Look for bonito at Asian food markets or in the ethnic section of the supermarket. If you can't find it, it's okay to omit it—just be aware that you'll lose the seafood flavor in the broth.

- 6 cups boiling water
- ¼ cup dried shaved bonito (dry fish flakes)
- 2 tablespoons yellow miso (soybean paste)
- 2 tablespoons red miso (soybean paste)
- ½ teaspoon low-sodium soy sauce
- ½ cup enoki mushrooms
- 4 ounces firm tofu, drained and cubed

1. Combine water and bonito; let stand 2 minutes. Strain liquid through a fine sieve into a bowl; discard solids. Bring liquid to a boil in a large saucepan. Add yellow and red miso and soy sauce; stir well with a whisk until smooth. Divide enoki mushrooms and tofu evenly among 6 soup bowls, and ladle 1 cup soup into each bowl. Yield: 6 servings.

CALORIES 40 (21% from fat); FAT 0.9g (sat 0.1g, mono 0.2g, poly 0.5g); PROTEIN 2g; CARB 5.1g; FIBER 0.2g; CHOL 1mg; IRON 1mg; SODIUM 407mg; CALC 20mg

Shrimp-and-Asparagus Salad with Orange-Miso Vinaigrette

- 6 cups water
- 2 pounds asparagus, cut into 2-inch pieces
- 1 pound large shrimp, peeled and deveined (about 20 shrimp)
- ¾ cup chopped red bell pepper
- ¼ cup yellow miso (soybean paste)
- 2 tablespoons fresh lemon juice
- 2 teaspoons grated orange rind
- ½ cup fresh orange juice (about 1 orange)
- 2 tablespoons vegetable oil
- 1 tablespoon rice vinegar

1. Bring water to a boil in a large saucepan. Add asparagus; cook 4 minutes or until crisp-tender. Remove with a slotted spoon. Plunge into ice water, and drain. Add shrimp to boiling water; cook 3 minutes or until shrimp are done. Drain and plunge into ice water; drain.
2. Place asparagus, shrimp, and bell pepper in a large bowl; chill.
3. Combine miso and lemon juice; stir with a whisk until smooth. Add orange rind and remaining 3 ingredients; stir well. Pour over asparagus mixture, and toss well to coat. Yield: 4 servings (serving size: 1½ cups).

CALORIES 250 (30% from fat); FAT 8.3g (sat 1.6g, mono 2.2g, poly 3.9g); PROTEIN 23.4g; CARB 22g; FIBER 5.3g; CHOL 166mg; IRON 5mg; SODIUM 737mg; CALC 87mg

---

Choose Your Miso

Miso comes in several varieties, but we've narrowed the options to just two for these recipes: the lighter colored miso, which has a sweeter, more mellow flavor; and the darker, saltier, and more fragrant red miso. Per tablespoon, both have about 30 calories and no fat. But the red miso has 630 milligrams of sodium compared to 540 milligrams in the yellow. Miso has the consistency of peanut butter; it will keep for up to two months when refrigerated in an airtight container.

Lettuce Wraps Step-by-Steps

1. *To make lettuce leaves more pliable, trim off raised portion of main vein of each leaf.*

2. *Arrange chicken and vegetables on lettuce leaf; roll up, and secure with a pick.*

Chicken Lettuce Wraps with Peanut-Miso Sauce

(pictured on page 57)

These are similar to summer rolls, but we used lettuce leaves in place of rice paper wrappers.

⅓ cup reduced-fat peanut butter
¼ cup honey
3 tablespoons yellow miso (soybean paste)
2 tablespoons water
2 teaspoons fresh lime juice
⅛ teaspoon ground red pepper
Cooking spray
1 pound skinless, boneless chicken breast halves
12 romaine lettuce leaves
2 cups (2-inch) julienne-cut carrot
2 cups (2-inch) julienne-cut peeled jícama
1 cup (2-inch) julienne-cut seeded peeled cucumber
1 cup fresh bean sprouts
1 cup shredded red cabbage

1. Combine first 6 ingredients in a bowl; stir well with a whisk. Set aside.
2. Heat a large nonstick skillet coated with cooking spray over medium-high heat. Add chicken; cook 4 minutes on each side or until done. Cut chicken into ⅛-inch-thick slices.
3. Cut off raised portion of main vein of each lettuce leaf. Divide chicken evenly among lettuce leaves; top evenly with carrot, jícama, cucumber, bean sprouts, and cabbage. Roll up, and secure with picks. Serve with sauce. Yield: 6 servings (serving size: 2 wraps and 2 tablespoons sauce).

CALORIES 285 (24% from fat); FAT 7.7g (sat 1.7g, mono 3.3g, poly 2.2g); PROTEIN 23.1g; CARB 31.8g; FIBER 5g; CHOL 48mg; IRON 1.8mg; SODIUM 431mg; CALC 43mg

Chopped Salad with Ginger-Miso Dressing

SALAD:

1½ cups halved cherry tomatoes
1 cup chopped seeded peeled cucumber
¾ cup shredded peeled butternut squash or carrot
¾ cup diagonally sliced snow peas
⅓ cup sliced green onions

DRESSING:

2 tablespoons seasoned rice vinegar
2 tablespoons yellow miso (soybean paste)
1 tablespoon toasted sesame seeds
1 tablespoon vegetable oil
1 tablespoon minced peeled fresh ginger
½ teaspoon sugar
½ teaspoon Dijon mustard

1. To prepare salad, combine first 5 ingredients in a large bowl.
2. To prepare dressing, combine vinegar and remaining 6 ingredients; stir well with a whisk. Pour over salad, tossing to coat. Yield: 8 servings (serving size ½ cup).

CALORIES 50 (45% from fat); FAT 2.5g (sat 0.4g, mono 0.7g, poly 1.1g); PROTEIN 1g; CARB 6.5g; FIBER 1g; CHOL 0mg; IRON 0.7mg; SODIUM 149mg; CALC 27mg

Miso-Marinated Trout with Lime-Ginger Glaze

The intensely sweet-and-salty flavor of the marinade pairs well with a higher-fat fish such as trout. If you want to substitute tuna steaks, be sure to cook them longer because they're thicker. Steamed rice and stir-fried bok choy or Chinese cabbage make good side dishes.

¼ cup red miso (soybean paste)
2 tablespoons brown sugar
2 tablespoons mirin (sweet rice wine)
4 (6-ounce) skinless butterfly-cut trout fillets
⅓ cup honey
⅓ cup fresh lime juice
2 tablespoons minced peeled fresh ginger
Cooking spray
1 tablespoon black or white sesame seeds, toasted

1. Combine first 3 ingredients in a small bowl. Brush fillets with miso mixture. Cover and chill 30 minutes. Combine honey, lime juice, and ginger in a small saucepan over medium heat, and bring to a boil. Cook 10 minutes or until mixture thinly coats back of a spoon; set aside.
2. Preheat broiler.
3. Place fillets on a broiler rack coated with cooking spray, and broil 3 minutes on each side or until fish flakes easily when tested with a fork. Drizzle honey mixture over fillets. Sprinkle with toasted sesame seeds. Yield: 4 servings (serving size: 1 fillet, about 1½ tablespoons glaze, and ¾ teaspoon sesame seeds).

CALORIES 364 (26% from fat); FAT 10.7g (sat 1.8g, mono 3.9g, poly 3.9g); PROTEIN 30.1g; CARB 36.3g; FIBER 0.1g; CHOL 82mg; IRON 2.7mg; SODIUM 708mg; CALC 91mg

The Red Season

It's no heresy to reach for canned tomatoes, especially this time of year.

Though summer tomatoes fresh from the vine have mass appeal, don't discount the seasonless variety—canned. Stewed or diced, in puree or paste, canned tomatoes are as varied as their uses. Whether put in a pasta sauce or a fish stew, they should be among your most reached-for pantry items.

But you get more than convenience. Canned tomatoes are packed with lycopene, the antioxidant that not only gives the tomato its color but is also a powerful ally in the fight against heart disease and other chronic illnesses.

Beef with Rosemary-Mushroom Sauce

1 (8-ounce) package presliced mushrooms
1 cup dry red wine
1 pound boneless top sirloin steak (about ¾ inch thick)
Cooking spray
1 cup chopped green onions
¼ cup chopped fresh parsley, divided
1½ teaspoons chopped fresh or ½ teaspoon dried rosemary
1 teaspoon balsamic vinegar
4 garlic cloves, minced
1 (10½-ounce) can beef consommé
1 (8-ounce) can no-salt-added tomato sauce

1. Combine presliced mushrooms, wine, and steak in a large zip-top plastic bag; seal. Marinate in refrigerator 30 minutes, turning occasionally.
2. Remove steak from bag, reserving marinade. Place a large nonstick skillet coated with cooking spray over medium-high heat. Add steak; cook 6 minutes or until desired degree of doneness, turning after 3 minutes. Remove from pan.
3. Combine onions, 2 tablespoons parsley, rosemary, and remaining 4 ingredients.

Add onion mixture and reserved marinade to pan. Bring to a boil; cook until reduced to 2 cups (about 15 minutes), stirring frequently.
4. Cut beef diagonally across grain into thin slices. Place beef on a serving platter. Spoon mushroom sauce over beef. Sprinkle with 2 tablespoons parsley. Yield: 4 servings (serving size: 3 ounces beef and ½ cup sauce).

CALORIES 229 (26% from fat); FAT 6.6g (sat 2.3g, mono 2.5g, poly 0.7g); PROTEIN 30g; CARB 12.4g; FIBER 1.7g; CHOL 69mg; IRON 5.1mg; SODIUM 479mg; CALC 55mg

Fiery Chipotle Rice and Sausage

1 pound sweet turkey Italian sausage (about 5 links)
1 teaspoon olive oil
Cooking spray
1 (16-ounce) package frozen pepper stir-fry with yellow, green, and red peppers and onions, thawed (such as Birds Eye)
1 cup uncooked converted rice
¾ cup thinly sliced celery
1 teaspoon dried thyme
¾ teaspoon sugar
1 (14.5-ounce) can no-salt-added diced tomatoes, undrained
1 (10½-ounce) can beef broth
1 to 2 drained canned chipotle chiles in adobo sauce, minced

1. Remove casings from sausage. Heat oil in a Dutch oven coated with cooking spray over medium-high heat. Add sausage; cook 7 minutes or until browned, stirring to crumble. Remove from pan, and drain.
2. Add pepper stir-fry mix and remaining 7 ingredients to pan, and bring mixture to a boil. Cover, reduce heat, and simmer 20 minutes or until rice is tender. Remove from heat, and stir in sausage. Cover and let stand 10 minutes. Yield: 6 servings (serving size: 1 cup).
NOTE: Store remaining chipotles in an airtight container; freeze for later use.

CALORIES 323 (27% from fat); FAT 9.8g (sat 2.4g, mono 3.9g, poly 2.5g); PROTEIN 21.8g; CARB 35.3g; FIBER 3g; CHOL 75mg; IRON 3.2mg; SODIUM 872mg; CALC 58mg

Chicken, Artichoke, and Tomato Ragoût

1 pound skinless, boneless chicken breast, cut into bite-size pieces
¼ teaspoon black pepper
1 tablespoon olive oil
1 cup coarsely chopped onion
2 garlic cloves, minced
1 cup fat-free, less-sodium chicken broth
¼ cup dry white wine
3 tablespoons tomato paste
½ teaspoon dried basil
1 (28-ounce) can diced tomatoes, undrained
1 bay leaf
1 (9-ounce) package frozen artichoke hearts

1. Sprinkle chicken with pepper. Heat oil in a Dutch oven over medium-high heat. Add chicken, onion, and garlic; sauté 6 minutes or until chicken is lightly browned. Stir in broth and next 5 ingredients; bring to a boil. Reduce heat, and simmer 20 minutes or until thick, stirring occasionally. Stir in artichoke hearts. Cook 5 minutes or until thoroughly heated. Discard bay leaf. Yield: 4 servings (serving size: 1½ cups).

CALORIES 252 (19% from fat); FAT 5.3g (sat 0.9g, mono 2.9g, poly 0.8g); PROTEIN 31.3g; CARB 21g; FIBER 1.9g; CHOL 66mg; IRON 2.6mg; SODIUM 960mg; CALC 110mg

Middle Eastern Stuffed Cabbage Rolls

8 large green cabbage leaves
6 ounces sweet turkey Italian sausage (about 2 links)
2 cups chopped onion
1½ tablespoons pine nuts
Cooking spray
½ cup uncooked converted rice
½ teaspoon sugar
½ teaspoon ground cinnamon
¼ teaspoon ground allspice
¼ teaspoon ground cumin
½ cup water
1 (8-ounce) can tomato sauce

1. Steam cabbage leaves, covered, 3 minutes or until tender. Keep warm.

2. Remove casings from sausage. Cook sausage, onion, and nuts in a large nonstick skillet coated with cooking spray over medium heat 6 minutes or until sausage is browned, stirring to crumble. Stir in rice and next 4 ingredients; cook 2 minutes. Remove from heat. Place mixture in a medium bowl; cool slightly.

3. Place ¼ cup sausage mixture in center of each cabbage leaf. Fold in edges of leaves; roll up. Place cabbage rolls, seam sides down, in pan. Combine water and tomato sauce; pour over rolls. Bring to a boil; cover, reduce heat, and simmer 20 minutes or until rice is done. Yield: 4 servings (serving size: 2 cabbage rolls).

CALORIES 276 (29% from fat); FAT 9g (sat 1.9g, mono 3.2g, poly 3g); PROTEIN 14.1g; CARB 37g; FIBER 5.4g; CHOL 43mg; IRON 3mg; SODIUM 672mg; CALC 88mg

Gnocchi with Garlicky Red Clam Sauce

  1 (16-ounce) box vacuum-packed gnocchi with potato (such as Bellino)
  2 teaspoons olive oil
  ½ cup chopped onion
  2 tablespoons minced garlic
2½ cups canned crushed tomatoes, undrained
  2 (6½-ounce) cans chopped clams, drained
  ½ cup chopped fresh basil

1. Prepare gnocchi according to package directions, omitting salt.

2. While gnocchi are cooking, heat oil in a large nonstick skillet over medium heat. Add onion and garlic; cook 5 minutes or until soft, stirring frequently. Stir in tomatoes and clams. Bring to a boil; reduce heat, and simmer 10 minutes or until thick. Stir in basil; cook 30 seconds. Serve over gnocchi. Yield: 4 servings (serving size: ¾ cup gnocchi and about ¾ cup sauce).

CALORIES 350 (11% from fat); FAT 4.4g (sat 1.5g, mono 1.8g, poly 0.8g); PROTEIN 17.6g; CARB 64.5g; FIBER 4.7g; CHOL 22mg; IRON 5.1mg; SODIUM 988mg; CALC 137mg

Orange-Saffron Shrimp-and-Snapper Stew

    Cooking spray
  1 cup chopped green onions, divided
  ½ teaspoon sugar
  ½ teaspoon dried thyme
  ¼ teaspoon grated orange rind
  ⅛ teaspoon ground red pepper
  ⅛ teaspoon saffron threads
  1 (14.5-ounce) can diced tomatoes, undrained
  1 (8-ounce) bottle clam juice
  ½ pound red snapper or other firm white fish fillet, cut into 1-inch pieces
  ½ pound large shrimp, peeled
  1 tablespoon butter

1. Heat a large saucepan coated with cooking spray over medium-high heat. Add ¾ cup onions; cook 2 minutes or until tender. Add sugar and next 6 ingredients; bring to a boil. Cover, reduce heat, and simmer 15 minutes.

2. Increase heat to medium; add fish and shrimp. Cook 5 minutes or until shrimp are done (do not stir). Remove from heat; stir in ¼ cup onions and butter. Yield: 4 servings (serving size: 1 cup).

CALORIES 179 (27% from fat); FAT 5.4g (sat 2.3g, mono 1.3g, poly 1.2g); PROTEIN 24.8g; CARB 7.5g; FIBER 1.4g; CHOL 117mg; IRON 2.9mg; SODIUM 443mg; CALC 104mg

Spinach-Feta Stuffed Shells

  1 cup 1% low-fat cottage cheese
  ½ cup (2 ounces) crumbled feta cheese with basil and tomato, divided
  ¼ cup chopped fresh parsley, divided
  ¼ teaspoon salt
  ⅛ teaspoon ground nutmeg
  1 (10-ounce) package frozen chopped spinach, thawed, drained, and squeezed dry
  1 garlic clove, minced
 16 hot cooked large seashell pasta
2½ cups bottled fat-free marinara sauce
  2 tablespoons chopped fresh or 2 teaspoons dried basil

1. Combine cottage cheese, ¼ cup feta cheese, 3 tablespoons parsley, salt, nutmeg, spinach, and garlic in a large bowl. Spoon 2 tablespoons cheese mixture into each pasta shell.

2. Combine sauce and basil in a large nonstick skillet. Arrange stuffed shells in pan, and bring to a boil over medium-high heat. Cover, reduce heat, and simmer 15 minutes. Remove from heat, and sprinkle with ¼ cup feta and 1 tablespoon parsley. Yield: 4 servings (serving size: 4 stuffed shells and ½ cup sauce).

CALORIES 293 (14% from fat); FAT 4.5g (sat 2.6g, mono 0.9g, poly 0.4g); PROTEIN 18.3g; CARB 44.5g; FIBER 5.7g; CHOL 15mg; IRON 4.1mg; SODIUM 966mg; CALC 323mg

Penne with Roasted-Pepper Marinara Sauce

Stirring in extra-virgin olive oil at the very end rounds out the flavors.

    Cooking spray
1½ cups finely chopped onion
  4 garlic cloves, minced
  2 cups coarsely chopped bottled roasted red bell peppers
  1 tablespoon dried basil
  ¾ teaspoon sugar
  ¼ teaspoon crushed red pepper
  ¼ teaspoon salt
  2 (14.5-ounce) cans diced tomatoes, undrained
  2 tablespoons extra-virgin olive oil
  6 cups hot cooked penne (about 3 cups uncooked tube-shaped pasta)

1. Place a large nonstick skillet coated with cooking spray over medium-high heat. Add onion and garlic; sauté 6 minutes or until tender. Add bell peppers and next 5 ingredients; bring to a boil. Reduce heat, and simmer 20 minutes, stirring occasionally. Remove from heat; stir in oil. Serve over pasta. Yield: 6 servings (serving size: ¾ cup sauce and 1 cup pasta).

CALORIES 315 (18% from fat); FAT 6.4g (sat 0.9g, mono 3.6g, poly 1.4g); PROTEIN 9.6g; CARB 55.9g; FIBER 3.7g; CHOL 0mg; IRON 3.6mg; SODIUM 330mg; CALC 76mg

Eggplant Parmesan

- 1 cup dry breadcrumbs
- ½ cup (2 ounces) finely grated fresh Parmesan cheese
- ¼ cup chopped fresh parsley
- 1 tablespoon dried Italian seasoning
- 1 teaspoon salt-free lemon pepper
- ½ teaspoon salt
- 2 (1-pound) eggplants, each peeled and cut crosswise into 6 slices
- 1 cup all-purpose flour
- 2 large egg whites, lightly beaten
- 1 large egg, lightly beaten
- Cooking spray
- 1 (25.5-ounce) jar fat-free marinara sauce
- 1 cup (4 ounces) shredded part-skim mozzarella cheese
- 3 cups hot cooked angel hair pasta (about 6 ounces uncooked pasta)

1. Preheat oven to 350°.

2. Combine first 6 ingredients in a shallow dish. Dredge eggplant slices in flour. Combine egg whites and egg. Dip eggplant slices in eggs; dredge in breadcrumb mixture. Arrange eggplant slices in a single layer on a jelly-roll pan coated with cooking spray. Bake at 350° for 25 minutes. Pour sauce evenly over eggplant slices; sprinkle with cheese. Bake an additional 10 minutes or until cheese melts. Serve over pasta. Yield: 4 servings (serving size: 3 eggplant slices and ¾ cup pasta).

CALORIES 472 (17% from fat); FAT 8.8g (sat 4.3g, mono 2.4g, poly 0.9g); PROTEIN 24.4g; CARB 72.8g; FIBER 8.7g; CHOL 73mg; IRON 7.7mg; SODIUM 721mg; CALC 380mg

A Closer Look at Lycopene

A Harvard School of Public Health report suggests that men who eat 10 or more servings of tomato products per week are at least 30% less likely to develop prostate cancer. Cooked tomato products are a good source of this much-acclaimed antioxidant. There is more available lycopene in tomato sauce than in an equivalent amount of fresh tomatoes; cooking tomatoes in a heart-healthy fat, such as olive oil, is a plus—it helps with absorption.

well-equipped

Grilling in Any Season

With grill pan in hand, neither rain, sleet, nor snow can stop you from making these meals.

Grilling makes just about any food taste great, but what if it's too frigid to cook outside? Or it's raining? Or you're out of charcoal?

The solution: a stovetop grill pan. With ridges that elevate food so air can circulate underneath and fat can drip away, a grill pan adds more than just pretty grill marks and smoky flavors. Your food doesn't sauté or steam as it does in a plain skillet; instead, flavor is seared into the food. Meat and fish turn out juicy, with no need for added fat. Vegetables stay crisp-tender, and their nutrients don't leach out into the cooking water.

Greek Tuna Steaks

- 1½ teaspoons chopped fresh or ½ teaspoon dried oregano
- 1 teaspoon olive oil
- ¾ teaspoon chopped fresh or ¼ teaspoon dried thyme
- ½ teaspoon salt
- ¼ teaspoon black pepper
- 4 (6-ounce) tuna steaks (about ¾ inch thick)
- Cooking spray
- 4 lemon wedges

1. Combine first 5 ingredients in a small bowl. Place tuna steaks on a plate; rub herb mixture evenly over tuna steaks. Cover tuna steaks, and marinate in refrigerator 15 minutes.

2. Heat a large grill pan coated with cooking spray over medium-high heat. Add tuna steaks; cook 5 minutes on each side or until desired degree of doneness. Serve tuna steaks with lemon wedges. Yield: 4 servings (serving size: 1 steak).

CALORIES 250 (35% from fat); FAT 9.7g (sat 2.3g, mono 3.6g, poly 2.7g); PROTEIN 38.2g; CARB 0.2g; FIBER 0.1g; CHOL 63mg; IRON 1.8mg; SODIUM 357mg; CALC 4mg

Grilled Salad Pizza

(pictured on page 60)

A great way to get a cool, crisp salad and cheese pizza all in one. If you have a square grill pan, roll the dough into a square for a better fit.

- 1 package dry yeast (about 2¼ teaspoons)
- ⅔ cup warm water (100° to 110°)
- 3½ teaspoons olive oil, divided
- 1⅔ cups all-purpose flour
- 1 teaspoon sugar
- ½ teaspoon salt
- ½ teaspoon dried oregano
- ¼ teaspoon dried thyme
- Cooking spray
- ½ cup (2 ounces) shredded part-skim mozzarella cheese, divided
- ¼ cup (1 ounce) grated fresh Parmesan cheese, divided
- 2½ cups coarsely chopped trimmed arugula (about 4 ounces)
- 1½ cups chopped seeded tomato
- ¼ cup chopped fresh basil
- 2 teaspoons balsamic vinegar
- 1½ teaspoons Dijon mustard
- 1 (14-ounce) can artichoke hearts, drained and chopped

1. Dissolve yeast in warm water in a large bowl; let stand 5 minutes. Stir in 1½ teaspoons oil. Lightly spoon flour into dry measuring cups; level with a knife. Combine flour, sugar, salt, oregano, and thyme. Add to yeast mixture; stir well. Turn dough out onto a lightly floured surface. Knead until smooth and elastic (about 10 minutes).

2. Place dough in a large bowl coated with cooking spray, turning to coat top. Cover and let rise in a warm place (85°), free from drafts, 45 minutes or until doubled in size. (Press two fingers into dough. If indentation remains, dough has risen enough.) Punch dough down; cover and let rest 5 minutes. Divide in half. Roll each half into a 9-inch circle on a floured surface.

3. Heat a grill pan coated with cooking spray over medium heat. Place one dough portion on pan; cook 10 minutes. Turn dough over; sprinkle with ¼ cup mozzarella and 2 tablespoons Parmesan.

Cook 10 minutes; remove from pan. Repeat procedure with remaining dough and cheeses.

4. Combine 2 teaspoons oil, arugula, and remaining 5 ingredients in a medium bowl. Spoon 2 cups salad onto each pizza crust using a slotted spoon. Cut each pizza into 4 wedges. Serve immediately. Yield: 4 servings (serving size: 2 wedges).

CALORIES 357 (25% from fat); FAT 9.8g (sat 3.3g, mono 4.4g, poly 1.1g); PROTEIN 15.5g; CARB 53.5g; FIBER 3.8g; CHOL 13mg; IRON 4.2mg; SODIUM 572mg; CALC 269mg

Barbecue Turkey Burgers
(pictured on page 58)

¼ cup chopped onion
¼ cup barbecue sauce, divided
2 tablespoons dry breadcrumbs
2 teaspoons prepared mustard
¾ teaspoon chili powder
½ teaspoon garlic powder
¼ teaspoon salt
1 pound ground turkey
Cooking spray
4 large leaf lettuce leaves
4 (¼-inch-thick) slices tomato
4 (1½-ounce) hamburger buns

1. Combine onion, 2 tablespoons barbecue sauce, breadcrumbs, and next 5 ingredients in a medium bowl. Divide turkey mixture into 4 equal portions, shaping each into a 1½-inch-thick patty.
2. Heat a grill pan coated with cooking spray over medium-high heat. Place patties in pan; cook 7 minutes on each side or until done.
3. Place 1 lettuce leaf, 1 tomato slice, and 1 patty on bottom half of each bun. Spread each patty with 1½ teaspoons barbecue sauce. Cover with top halves of buns. Yield: 4 servings (serving size: 1 burger).

CALORIES 310 (22% from fat); FAT 7.6g (sat 2.1g, mono 1.7g, poly 2.8g); PROTEIN 29.9g; CARB 28.5g; FIBER 2.1g; CHOL 65mg; IRON 3.5mg; SODIUM 642mg; CALC 102mg

Garlic Toasts

2 teaspoons olive oil
12 (½-inch-thick) slices diagonally cut French bread baguette
1 garlic clove, halved

1. Heat a grill pan over medium-high heat. Brush olive oil evenly over cut sides of bread. Place bread in grill pan, and cook 1 minute on each side or until lightly browned. Rub garlic halves on 1 side of each bread slice. Yield: 4 servings (serving size: 3 bread slices).

CALORIES 79 (33% from fat); FAT 2.9g (sat 0.4g, mono 1.9g, poly 0.3g); PROTEIN 1.9g; CARB 11.3g; FIBER 0.7g; CHOL 0mg; IRON 0.6mg; SODIUM 130mg; CALC 17mg

GARLIC-TOMATO TOASTS VARIATION:
After rubbing garlic on bread slices, rub with 1 halved plum tomato.

CALORIES 86 (31% from fat); FAT 3g (sat 0.5g, mono 1.9g, poly 0.4g); PROTEIN 2.2g; CARB 12.7g; FIBER 1g; CHOL 0mg; IRON 0.7mg; SODIUM 133mg; CALC 19mg

Tequila-Marinated Beef-and-Pepper Fajitas

¼ cup tequila
2 tablespoons chopped fresh cilantro
2 tablespoons fresh lime juice
1 tablespoon Worcestershire sauce
1 teaspoon ground cumin
½ teaspoon vegetable oil
¼ teaspoon ground red pepper
2 garlic cloves, minced
1 pound flank steak, trimmed
1 green bell pepper, cut into 4 wedges
1 red bell pepper, cut into 4 wedges
4 (¼-inch-thick) slices red onion
¼ teaspoon salt
¼ teaspoon black pepper
Cooking spray
4 (8-inch) fat-free flour tortillas

1. Combine first 9 ingredients in a large zip-top plastic bag. Seal and marinate in refrigerator 1 hour. Remove steak from bag; discard marinade.
2. Sprinkle bell peppers and onion with salt and black pepper.

3. Heat a large grill pan coated with cooking spray over medium-high heat. Add bell peppers; cook 5 minutes. Turn bell peppers over, and add onion. Cook 5 minutes, turning onion once. Remove bell peppers and onion, and keep warm. Add steak to pan, and cook 5 minutes on each side or until desired degree of doneness. Cut steak diagonally across grain into thin slices.
4. Warm tortillas according to package directions. Arrange about 3 ounces steak, 2 bell pepper wedges, and 1 slice onion down center of each tortilla. Fold sides of tortillas over filling. Yield: 4 servings (serving size: 1 fajita).

CALORIES 346 (30% from fat); FAT 11.7g (sat 4.6g, mono 4.5g, poly 0.7g); PROTEIN 26.1g; CARB 28.4g; FIBER 2g; CHOL 58mg; IRON 4mg; SODIUM 577mg; CALC 19mg

---

Our Favorites

We tested all types of grill pans—round and square, nonstick and stainless steel, with lids and without—with prices ranging from less than $20 to more than $100. We actually liked the least expensive pan the most: Lodge's 10½-inch, cast-iron Square Grill Pan ($16.95; available at major retail and discount stores, or at www.lodgemfg.com). It produced the best grill marks and conducted heat most evenly. We also liked KitchenAid's 12-inch Round Stainless Steel Grill Pan (model 128498, $89.95; available at Cooking.com).

Some things to look for when selecting a grill pan:

• High ridges produce results similar to those of an outdoor grill. If the ridges are too low, you might as well be using a regular skillet.

• Low sides make flipping burgers and removing food with a spatula much easier.

• A pan with a square or oblong shape fits more food than a round pan.

• A lidless pan is a good choice, since there's no reason to lock in moisture when grilling.

Spicy Grilled Sweet Potatoes

(pictured on page 58)

Try this side dish with our Barbecue Turkey Burgers (recipe on page 77).

    ¾   teaspoon ground cumin
    ½   teaspoon garlic powder
    ¼   teaspoon salt
    ⅛   teaspoon ground red pepper
    1   tablespoon olive oil
    1   pound peeled sweet potatoes, cut
        into ¼-inch-thick slices
Cooking spray
    2   tablespoons chopped fresh cilantro

1. Combine first 4 ingredients in a bowl.
2. Combine oil and sweet potato in a medium bowl; toss to coat. Heat a large grill pan coated with cooking spray over medium heat. Add potato, and cook 10 minutes, turning occasionally. Place potato in a large bowl; sprinkle with cumin mixture and cilantro. Toss gently. Yield: 4 servings (serving size ½ cup).

CALORIES 157 (25% from fat); FAT 4.3g (sat 0.6g, mono 2.7g, poly 0.7g); PROTEIN 2g; CARB 28.1g; FIBER 3.5g; CHOL 0mg; IRON 1.1mg; SODIUM 163mg; CALC 31mg

Grilled Eggplant, Zucchini, and Red Onion Sandwiches

    6   tablespoons low-fat mayonnaise
    ¼   cup chopped bottled roasted red
        bell peppers, drained
    1   tablespoon olive oil
   12   (½-inch-thick) slices zucchini
        (about ¾ pound)
    8   (¼-inch-thick) slices peeled
        eggplant (about ½ pound)
    1   large red onion, cut into 4 slices
    ½   teaspoon salt
    ¼   teaspoon black pepper
Cooking spray
    2   teaspoons balsamic vinegar
    8   (1-ounce) slices hearty white bread
    4   garlic cloves, peeled and halved

1. Place mayonnaise and bell pepper in a blender or food processor, and process until smooth.

2. Brush oil over zucchini, eggplant, and onion; sprinkle with salt and black pepper. Heat a large grill pan coated with cooking spray over medium-high heat. Add zucchini, and cook 3 minutes on each side or until tender. Place in a large bowl; keep warm. Add eggplant to pan, and cook 3 minutes on each side or until done. Add to zucchini; keep warm. Add onion to pan; cook 3 minutes on each side or until done. Add to eggplant mixture; drizzle with vinegar.

3. Lightly coat bread with cooking spray. Place 2 bread slices in pan; cook 1 minute on each side or until toasted. Repeat procedure with remaining bread. Rub 1 garlic half on 1 side of each bread slice. Spread 1 tablespoon mayonnaise mixture over garlic-rubbed side of each of 4 bread slices; layer each with 3 slices zucchini, 2 slices eggplant, and 1 slice onion. Spread 1 tablespoon mayonnaise mixture over 1 side of each remaining bread slice; place on top of sandwiches. Yield: 4 servings (serving size: 1 sandwich).

CALORIES 271 (26% from fat); FAT 7.8g (sat 1.3g, mono 3.9g, poly 2g); PROTEIN 6.9g; CARB 44.7g; FIBER 4g; CHOL 1mg; IRON 2.5mg; SODIUM 815mg; CALC 92mg

---

Seasoning a Cast-Iron Pan

Seasoning is the process of oiling and heating cast iron to protect its porous surface from moisture. The oil is absorbed, creating a rustproof, nonstick surface. Generally, you need to season your pan only once (make sure to do it before using). If the pan ever develops rust spots, though, repeat the process, scrubbing any stubborn spots with fine steel wool. Follow these steps:

1. Preheat oven to 350°.
2. Wash the pan, and make sure to dry it completely.
3. Coat the entire surface of the pan (inside and out) with vegetable oil or melted vegetable shortening.
4. Bake at 350° for 1 hour.
5. Allow the pan to cool slowly in the oven.
6. Pour off any excess oil.

Wholly Satisfying

Whole wheat flour adds a healthy twist to cookies, cakes, and cobblers.

When it comes to desserts, whole wheat flour has been woefully neglected—and that's a shame. It lends a nutty flavor and earthy texture to desserts, all the while delivering the kind of fiber boost that traditional treats can only dream of (a cup of whole wheat flour has 14.6 grams of fiber versus white flour's 3.4 grams).

In baking, whole wheat flour can be tricky to use, but it's at its best when used in conjunction with white flour. The combination produces more tender, moister results than desserts created with whole wheat flour alone.

Try adding your favorite fruits or chocolate to whole wheat desserts to mollify your sweet tooth. For instance, you can use dried cranberries and tangy oranges to add color and flavor to a whole wheat tea cake, or enliven whole wheat biscotti with chocolate and cherries to make after-meal coffee an event.

Apricot-Oat Squares

Substitute your favorite fruit preserves in place of the apricot.

    ½   cup all-purpose flour
    ½   cup whole wheat flour
   1½   cups regular oats
    ⅓   cup packed brown sugar
    6   tablespoons chilled butter, cut
        into small pieces
    ¼   teaspoon ground nutmeg
Cooking spray
    ¾   cup apricot preserves

1. Preheat oven to 350°.
2. Lightly spoon flours into dry measuring cups, and level with a knife. Combine flours, oats, sugar, butter, and nutmeg in a food processor, and pulse

5 times or until oat mixture resembles coarse meal.

3. Press two-thirds of oat mixture into bottom of an 8-inch square baking pan coated with cooking spray. Bake at 350° for 10 minutes. Spread preserves over warm crust. Sprinkle with remaining oat mixture, and press gently. Bake an additional 25 minutes or until lightly browned and bubbly. Cool completely in pan on a wire rack. Yield: 16 servings (serving size: 1 square).

CALORIES 148 (30% from fat); FAT 5g (sat 2.8g, mono 1.4g, poly 0.4g); PROTEIN 2.3g; CARB 24.9g; FIBER 1.5g; CHOL 12mg; IRON 0.8mg; SODIUM 52mg; CALC 14mg

Oatmeal-Apple Crisp

The slight nuttiness of whole wheat flour is a perfect addition to the streusel topping.

½   cup whole wheat flour
¾   cup quick-cooking oats
¾   cup packed dark brown sugar, divided
¾   teaspoon ground cinnamon, divided
½   cup chilled butter, cut into small pieces
6   cups chopped peeled Granny Smith apple (about 2½ pounds)
½   cup raisins
Cooking spray
3   cups vanilla fat-free frozen yogurt

1. Preheat oven to 375°.
2. Lightly spoon flour into a dry measuring cup; level with a knife. Combine flour, oats, ½ cup sugar, and ½ teaspoon cinnamon in a medium bowl; cut in chilled butter with a pastry blender or 2 knives until oat mixture resembles coarse meal.
3. Combine ¼ cup sugar, ¼ teaspoon cinnamon, apple, and raisins in a 13 x 9-inch baking dish coated with cooking spray. Sprinkle with oat mixture. Bake at 375° for 30 minutes or until apple is tender. Top each serving with about ⅓ cup frozen yogurt. Yield: 10 servings.

CALORIES 307 (30% from fat); FAT 10.2g (sat 5.9g, mono 2.9g, poly 0.7g); PROTEIN 4.7g; CARB 52.7g; FIBER 3.4g; CHOL 26mg; IRON 1mg; SODIUM 138mg; CALC 86mg

Mixed-Fruit Cobbler

In this cobbler, whole wheat flour does double duty. We've used it as the basis of a truly tender "cobbled" topping and as a thickener for the juicy fruit filling.

FILLING:
¼   cup whole wheat flour
4   cups frozen blackberries, thawed
4   cups frozen raspberries, thawed
1¼   cups sugar
1   teaspoon lemon juice
Cooking spray

TOPPING:
½   cup all-purpose flour
½   cup whole wheat flour
¼   cup sugar
1   teaspoon baking powder
¼   teaspoon baking soda
¼   teaspoon salt
6   tablespoons chilled butter, cut into small pieces
⅔   cup low-fat buttermilk
½   teaspoon grated orange rind
2   teaspoons sugar

1. Preheat oven to 400°.
2. To prepare filling, lightly spoon ¼ cup whole wheat flour into a dry measuring cup, and level with a knife. Combine ¼ cup whole wheat flour and next 4 ingredients in a 13 x 9-inch baking dish coated with cooking spray. Let stand 10 minutes.
3. To prepare topping, lightly spoon all-purpose flour and ½ cup whole wheat flour into dry measuring cups, and level with a knife. Combine flours and next 4 ingredients in a bowl; cut in butter with a pastry blender or 2 knives until mixture resembles coarse meal. Add buttermilk and rind, stirring just until moist. Drop dough onto fruit mixture to form 12 mounds; sprinkle with 2 teaspoons sugar.
4. Bake at 400° for 35 minutes or until bubbly. Let stand 10 minutes before serving. Yield: 12 servings.

CALORIES 268 (23% from fat); FAT 6.8g (sat 3.8g, mono 1.8g, poly 0.6g); PROTEIN 3.3g; CARB 51.7g; FIBER 6.1g; CHOL 16mg; IRON 1.4mg; SODIUM 183mg; CALC 74mg

Chocolate-Cherry Biscotti

Our Test Kitchens staff found that using a serrated knife works best for cutting the rolls after the first bake time. If you're a fan of dried cranberries, they make a great substitute for dried cherries.

2   cups all-purpose flour
1   cup whole wheat flour
¼   teaspoon salt
1   cup sugar
3   large eggs
2   tablespoons vegetable oil
2   teaspoons vanilla extract
1½   teaspoons almond extract
⅔   cup dried tart cherries
½   cup semisweet chocolate chips
Cooking spray

1. Preheat oven to 350°.
2. Lightly spoon flours into dry measuring cups, and level with a knife. Combine flours and salt in a bowl; stir well with a whisk.
3. Beat sugar and eggs with a mixer at high speed until thick and pale (about 4 minutes). Add oil and extracts, beating mixture until well blended. Add flour mixture, beating at low speed just until blended. Stir in dried cherries and chocolate chips.
4. Divide dough in half; turn out onto a baking sheet coated with cooking spray. Shape each portion into a 10-inch-long roll, and flatten to 1-inch thickness. Bake at 350° for 25 minutes or until lightly browned. Remove rolls from pan; cool 10 minutes on a wire rack. Reduce oven temperature to 325°.
5. Cut each roll diagonally into 20 (½-inch) slices. Place slices, cut sides down, on pan. Bake at 325° for 10 minutes. Turn cookies over, and bake an additional 10 minutes (cookies will be slightly soft in center but will harden as they cool). Remove from pan; cool completely on wire rack. Yield: 40 biscotti (serving size: 1 biscotto).

CALORIES 81 (22% from fat); FAT 2g (sat 0.7g, mono 0.6g, poly 0.5g); PROTEIN 1.6g; CARB 14.6g; FIBER 0.6g; CHOL 17mg; IRON 0.5mg; SODIUM 20mg; CALC 6mg

Cinnamon-Spiced Date Cookies

While dates come in many different forms in the market, we suggest using the boxed variety that's prechopped and lightly coated with sugar. It makes quick work of these cookies—and the sugar adds just the right amount of sweetness.

1½   cups all-purpose flour
  1   cup whole wheat flour
  ¾   cup chopped pitted dates
  1   teaspoon baking powder
  ½   teaspoon baking soda
  ½   teaspoon salt
  ⅛   teaspoon ground ginger
  ⅛   teaspoon ground cinnamon
1¼   cups sugar, divided
  ½   cup vegetable oil
  ½   cup applesauce
  1   tablespoon water
  ¼   teaspoon vanilla extract
Cooking spray

1. Preheat oven to 350°.
2. Lightly spoon flours into dry measuring cups, and level with a knife. Combine flours and next 6 ingredients in a large bowl; make a well in center of mixture. Combine 1 cup sugar, oil, applesauce, water, and vanilla in a bowl; add to flour mixture, stirring just until moist. Cover and chill 1 hour or until firm.
3. Shape dough into 36 balls, and roll balls in ¼ cup sugar. Place balls 2 inches apart on baking sheets coated with cooking spray. Bake at 350° for 15 minutes or until lightly browned. Cool 1 minute on pans. Remove from pans, and cool on a wire rack. Yield: 3 dozen (serving size: 1 cookie).

CALORIES 96 (30% from fat); FAT 3.2g (sat 0.6g, mono 0.9g, poly 1.5g); PROTEIN 1.1g; CARB 16.5g; FIBER 0.9g; CHOL 0mg; IRON 0.4mg; SODIUM 64mg; CALC 11mg

Double-Ginger Cake

Look for crystallized ginger on the spice aisle at your supermarket.

  ¼   cup packed brown sugar
  2   tablespoons vegetable oil
  1   large egg white
  ½   cup molasses
  ¾   cup all-purpose flour
  ½   cup whole wheat flour
2½   teaspoons ground ginger
  ½   teaspoon baking soda
  ½   teaspoon ground cinnamon
  ½   teaspoon ground allspice
  ⅓   cup low-fat buttermilk
Cooking spray
  2   tablespoons chopped crystallized ginger

1. Preheat oven to 350°.
2. Place first 3 ingredients in a large bowl; beat with a mixer at medium speed until well blended. Add molasses; beat 1 minute. Lightly spoon flours into dry measuring cups; level with a knife. Combine flours and next 4 ingredients in a small bowl, stirring well with a whisk. Add flour mixture and buttermilk alternately to sugar mixture, beginning and ending with flour mixture; beat mixture well after each addition.
3. Pour batter into an 8-inch round cake pan coated with cooking spray; sharply tap pan once on counter to remove air bubbles. Sprinkle with crystallized ginger. Bake at 350° for 25 minutes or until cake springs back when touched lightly in center. Cool cake in pan 10 minutes on a wire rack. Remove cake from pan, and serve warm. Yield: 8 servings (serving size: 1 slice).

CALORIES 191 (20% from fat); FAT 4.2g (sat 0.8g, mono 1.1g, poly 1.9g); PROTEIN 3.1g; CARB 36.4g; FIBER 1.4g; CHOL 0mg; IRON 2.1mg; SODIUM 102mg; CALC 68mg

Cranberry-Orange Tea Cake

The word "dessert" can mean many different things. In our Test Kitchens, we had trouble deciding whether to consider this a dessert or a sweet bread. One thing we did all agree on—call this what you may, whole wheat never tasted better.

  1   cup all-purpose flour
  ¾   cup whole wheat flour
  ¾   cup granulated sugar
  ⅔   cup sweetened dried cranberries, coarsely chopped
1½   teaspoons baking powder
  ¼   teaspoon salt
  ¾   cup 1% low-fat milk
  2   tablespoons butter, melted
  1   tablespoon grated orange rind
  1   large egg
Cooking spray
  ½   cup powdered sugar
  1   tablespoon orange juice

1. Preheat oven to 350°.
2. Lightly spoon flours into dry measuring cups, and level with a knife. Combine flours and next 4 ingredients in a large bowl, and make a well in center of mixture. Combine milk, butter, rind, and egg; add to flour mixture, stirring just until moist. Spoon batter into an 8 x 4-inch loaf pan coated with cooking spray.
3. Bake at 350° for 45 minutes or until a wooden pick inserted in center comes out clean. Cool 5 minutes in pan on a wire rack, and remove from pan. Cool completely on wire rack. Combine powdered sugar and orange juice; drizzle over bread. Yield: 12 servings (serving size: 1 slice).

CALORIES 184 (14% from fat); FAT 2.9g (sat 1.5g, mono 0.8g, poly 0.3g); PROTEIN 3.3g; CARB 37.8g; FIBER 1.5g; CHOL 24mg; IRON 1mg; SODIUM 123mg; CALC 53mg

The New Light

The revolution that redefined how people cook, eat, and think about food is far from finished.

At *Cooking Light* and in homes nationwide, there's been a revolution in the way people cook, eat, and think about food. This revolution has already redefined the country's restaurant scene and its food marketplace. And it's far from finished—with nothing less at stake than your health and well-being.

"People want delight at the table, maybe even a thrill. That's why lighter food has to have an edge; it has to look good, taste great, be authentic—and, by the way, be good for you, too, " says senior editor Jill Melton, summing up the *Cooking Light* philosophy.

Gingerbread Cake with Blueberry Sauce
(pictured on page 59)

Crystallized ginger deepens the flavor in this moist cake (although it is fine without it).

    2 cups all-purpose flour
   1/3 cup chopped crystallized ginger
       (optional)
  1 1/2 teaspoons ground ginger
  1 1/2 teaspoons ground cinnamon
    1 teaspoon baking powder
    1 teaspoon baking soda
   1/2 teaspoon salt
   1/8 teaspoon ground cloves
   3/4 cup low-fat buttermilk
   1/2 cup sugar
   1/2 cup molasses
   1/4 cup 1% low-fat milk
   1/4 cup vegetable oil
    2 large eggs
  1 1/2 cups frozen blueberries,
       thawed
Cooking spray
Blueberry Sauce
   3/4 cup frozen reduced-calorie
       whipped topping, thawed

1. Preheat oven to 350°.
2. Lightly spoon flour into dry measuring cups; level with a knife. Combine flour and next 7 ingredients in a large bowl, stirring well with a whisk; make a well in center of mixture.

3. Combine buttermilk and next 5 ingredients; stir well with a whisk. Add buttermilk mixture to flour mixture, stirring just until moist. Fold in blueberries. Spoon into an 11 x 7-inch baking dish or a 9-inch square baking pan coated with cooking spray. Bake at 350° for 45 minutes or until a wooden pick inserted in center comes out clean. Cool in dish 10 minutes on a wire rack; remove from dish. Cool completely on wire rack.
4. Spoon Blueberry Sauce over top of individual pieces; dollop with whipped topping. Yield: 12 servings (serving size: 1 cake piece, about 2 tablespoons sauce, and 1 tablespoon whipped topping).

(Totals include Blueberry Sauce) CALORIES 284 (22% from fat); FAT 7g (sat 1.8g, mono 1.8g, poly 2.6g); PROTEIN 4.4g; CARB 52.4g; FIBER 1.9g; CHOL 38mg; IRON 3mg; SODIUM 277mg; CALC 105mg

BLUEBERRY SAUCE:
   1/2 cup orange juice
   1/3 cup sugar
    2 tablespoons chopped crystallized
       ginger or 1 teaspoon ground ginger
    2 cups frozen blueberries, thawed

1. Combine first 3 ingredients in a medium saucepan. Bring to a boil; add blueberries. Return to a boil, and cook 1 minute. Cool. Yield: 1 2/3 cups (serving size: about 2 tablespoons).

CALORIES 44 (4% from fat); FAT 0.2g (sat 0g, mono 0g, poly 0.1g); PROTEIN 0.2g; CARB 11g; FIBER 0.7g; CHOL 3mg; IRON 0.3mg; SODIUM 1mg; CALC 6mg

Layered Chili, Cheese, and Roasted-Corn Dip

Throw this simple dip together and serve it at your next party. Reheat the leftovers and spoon them into a warmed flour tortilla for a flavorful bean burrito.

    2 (16-ounce) cans pinto beans,
       drained, rinsed, and divided
   1/2 teaspoon ground cumin
   1/4 teaspoon hot sauce
   1/8 teaspoon black pepper
    1 (8-ounce) block fat-free cream
       cheese
Cooking spray
    1 (11-ounce) can no-salt-added
       whole-kernel corn, drained
    2 garlic cloves, minced
    2 cups cooked basmati or other
       long-grain rice
   1/2 cup minced fresh cilantro
    1 (4.5-ounce) can chopped green
       chiles
    1 cup bottled salsa
   1/2 cup (2 ounces) shredded
       reduced-fat sharp cheddar cheese
    8 cups baked tortilla chips (about 8
       ounces)

1. Preheat oven to 375°.
2. Combine 2 cups beans, cumin, hot sauce, black pepper, and cream cheese in a food processor; process until smooth. Place bean mixture in a medium bowl; stir in remaining beans. Set aside.
3. Place a medium nonstick skillet coated with cooking spray over medium-high heat. Add corn and garlic, and sauté 3 minutes or until lightly browned. Remove from heat, and stir in rice, cilantro, and chiles.
4. Spread half of bean mixture in bottom of a shallow 2-quart baking dish coated with cooking spray. Spread half of salsa over bean mixture. Spread rice mixture over salsa. Top with remaining salsa and bean mixture, and sprinkle with cheese. Cover and bake at 375° for 30 minutes or until thoroughly heated. Serve with chips. Yield: 16 servings (serving size: 1/2 cup dip and 1/2 cup chips).

CALORIES 174 (10% from fat); FAT 1.9g (sat 0.6g, mono 0.6g, poly 0.6g); PROTEIN 8.5g; CARB 31.8g; FIBER 3g; CHOL 5mg; IRON 1.5mg; SODIUM 446mg; CALC 120mg

Pork Medallions in Caribbean Nut Sauce

The new approach to cooking is more sophisticated, more worldly. Curry, ginger, soy sauce, and coconut milk are virtually staples in the pantry of the new millennium.

  6 garlic cloves, peeled
  4 teaspoons chopped peeled fresh ginger
  2 teaspoons cumin seeds
  ¼ teaspoon curry powder
  ¼ teaspoon crushed red pepper
  ¼ cup unsalted, dry-roasted peanuts
  1 tablespoon hot water
  1 (1-pound) pork tenderloin, trimmed
Cooking spray
  2 tablespoons low-sodium soy sauce
  6 tablespoons water, divided
  2 cups thinly sliced red onion
  3 tablespoons light coconut milk
  1 tablespoon brown sugar
  ½ teaspoon salt
  ⅛ teaspoon black pepper
  4 cups hot cooked long-grain rice

1. Place garlic cloves in a food processor, and process until minced. Add ginger, cumin, curry, and red pepper, and process until blended. Add peanuts and hot water, and pulse until well blended, scraping sides of bowl occasionally.
2. Cut pork crosswise into 1-inch slices. Place each piece between 2 sheets of heavy-duty plastic wrap; flatten each piece to ½-inch thickness using a meat mallet or rolling pin. Coat pork with cooking spray. Heat a large nonstick skillet over medium-high heat. Add pork; sauté 2 minutes on each side or until browned. Place pork in a shallow bowl. Add soy sauce and 2 tablespoons water to pan, scraping pan to loosen browned bits. Add soy sauce mixture to pork; keep warm.
3. Add onion to pan; sauté 3 minutes. Add ¼ cup peanut mixture; cook 4 minutes. Stir in ¼ cup water, coconut milk, sugar, salt, and black pepper. Return pork mixture to pan; bring to a boil. Reduce heat; simmer 1 minute. Combine remaining peanut mixture with rice.

Serve pork with sauce and rice. Yield: 4 servings (serving size: 3 ounces pork, ½ cup sauce, and 1 cup rice).

CALORIES 460 (16% from fat); FAT 8.9g (sat 2.1g, mono 3.9g, poly 2.1g); PROTEIN 31.5g; CARB 61.2g; FIBER 3.1g; CHOL 74mg; IRON 4.5mg; SODIUM 554mg; CALC 69mg

Lazy Gourmet Menu

Spice- and seed-encrusted salmon stars in this easy supper that's elegant enough for a small dinner party.

Pepper, Coriander, and Sesame Seed-Crusted Salmon

Roasted small red potatoes

Spinach salad with mushrooms

Pound cake

Pepper, Coriander, and Sesame Seed-Crusted Salmon

  1 tablespoon sesame seeds
  1 teaspoon black peppercorns
  1 teaspoon coriander seeds
  ¼ teaspoon salt
  4 (6-ounce) salmon fillets (about 1 inch thick), skinned
  1 teaspoon olive oil
  ⅔ cup apricot nectar
  ½ cup diced red bell pepper
  ¼ cup cider vinegar
  1 teaspoon minced peeled fresh ginger

1. Combine first 4 ingredients in a heavy-duty zip-top plastic bag. Seal; crush seeds with a meat mallet or rolling pin. Place seed mixture in a large shallow dish. Coat 1 side of each fillet with seed mixture.
2. Heat oil in a large nonstick skillet over medium-high heat. Add fillets, seed sides down; sauté 4 minutes on each side or until fish flakes easily when tested with a fork. Remove fish from pan; keep warm.
3. Add apricot nectar and remaining 3 ingredients to pan, and bring to a boil, scraping pan to loosen browned bits. Cook 1 minute. Reduce heat; return fish to pan. Baste with nectar mixture. Cover

and simmer 1 minute. Yield: 4 servings (serving size: 1 fillet).

CALORIES 332 (44% from fat); FAT 16.4g (sat 2.8g, mono 8.1g, poly 3.7g); PROTEIN 35.7g; CARB 9.1g; FIBER 0.9g; CHOL 111mg; IRON 1.7mg; SODIUM 233mg; CALC 41mg

Sweet Potato Bread with Flaxseed and Honey

  ⅓ cup flaxseed
  2 cups all-purpose flour
  1 teaspoon baking powder
  ½ teaspoon baking soda
  ¼ teaspoon salt
  ¼ cup (2 ounces) ⅓-less-fat cream cheese, softened
  3 tablespoons butter, softened
  ½ cup packed brown sugar
  ¼ cup honey
  1 large egg
  1 large egg white
  1 cup mashed cooked sweet potato
Cooking spray

1. Preheat oven to 350°.
2. Place flaxseed in a clean coffee grinder or blender; process until coarsely ground. Lightly spoon flour into dry measuring cups; level with a knife. Combine flaxseed, flour, baking powder, baking soda, and salt in a large bowl; make a well in center of mixture. Place cream cheese and next 5 ingredients in a bowl; beat with a mixer, and stir in sweet potato. Add to flour mixture, stirring just until moist.
3. Spoon batter into an 8 x 4-inch loaf pan coated with cooking spray. Bake at 350° for 50 minutes or until a wooden pick inserted in center comes out clean. Cool 10 minutes in pan on a wire rack; remove from pan. Cool completely on wire rack. Yield: 16 servings (serving size: 1 [½-inch] slice).
NOTE: To freeze bread for up to 1 month, place in an airtight container, or wrap in heavy-duty plastic wrap or foil. Thaw at room temperature.

CALORIES 171 (27% from fat); FAT 5.1g (sat 2.1g, mono 1.3g, poly 1.4g); PROTEIN 3.6g; CARB 29g; FIBER 1.8g; CHOL 22mg; IRON 1.4mg; SODIUM 157mg; CALC 44mg

Chunky Potato-and-Swiss Chowder

(pictured on page 60)

What does the new light mean for *Cooking Light* recipes? It means eliminating our old no-no ingredients list, for one thing. Used with balance and moderation, even half-and-half is fine for healthy eating. A little goes a long way in this rich-tasting soup that's a meal in itself.

Cooking spray
2 cups thinly sliced leek (about 2 large)
2 garlic cloves, minced
4 cups cubed peeled Yukon gold potato (about 1½ pounds)
1 cup cubed carrot (about ½ pound)
1 cup cubed yellow squash
2 (15.75-ounce) cans fat-free, less-sodium chicken broth
2 bay leaves
1 cup hot cooked wild rice
1 cup half-and-half
½ cup (2 ounces) shredded Swiss cheese
½ teaspoon salt
¼ teaspoon black pepper
Fresh chopped parsley (optional)

1. Heat a large Dutch oven coated with cooking spray over medium-high heat. Add leek and garlic; sauté 3 minutes or until tender. Stir in potato and next 4 ingredients; bring to a boil. Cover, reduce heat, and simmer 20 minutes or until tender. Discard bay leaves. Place half of potato mixture in a blender, and process until smooth. Return pureed potato mixture to pan; stir in rice and remaining ingredients except parsley. Cook over medium heat until cheese melts. Sprinkle with parsley, if desired. Yield: 5 servings (serving size: 1½ cups).

CALORIES 302 (28% from fat); FAT 9.5g (sat 5.6g, mono 2.6g, poly 0.8g); PROTEIN 12.4g; CARB 43g; FIBER 4.2g; CHOL 28mg; IRON 2.3mg; SODIUM 693mg; CALC 209mg

Pan-Seared Chicken with Artichokes and Pasta

Four food groups, great taste, and great nutrition—all in one bowl. Since everything is cooked in one pan, the larger the pan, the better.

1 (6-ounce) jar marinated artichoke heart quarters, undrained
8 skinless, boneless chicken thighs (about 1½ pounds)
¼ teaspoon salt
¼ teaspoon black pepper
Cooking spray
½ cup sliced green onions
1 garlic clove, minced
½ cup dry white wine
4 cups hot cooked cavatappi (about 2½ cups uncooked spiral tube-shaped pasta) or fusilli (short twisted spaghetti)
1 tablespoon chopped pitted kalamata olives
1 (14.5-ounce) canned diced tomatoes, drained
2 tablespoons grated fresh Parmesan cheese

1. Drain artichokes in a colander over a bowl, reserving marinade.
2. Sprinkle chicken with salt and pepper; coat with cooking spray. Heat a large nonstick skillet over medium-high heat. Add chicken; sauté 3 minutes on each side. Add onions and garlic; sauté 1 minute. Stir in reserved artichoke marinade and wine, scraping pan to loosen browned bits. Bring to a boil; reduce heat, and stir in artichokes, pasta, olives, and tomatoes. Cook 2 minutes or until thoroughly heated. Sprinkle with cheese. Yield: 4 servings (serving size: 2 thighs and about 1¾ cups pasta mixture).

CALORIES 436 (29% from fat); FAT 14g (sat 3.4g, mono 4.6g, poly 4.4g); PROTEIN 34.4g; CARB 39g; FIBER 1.9g; CHOL 115mg; IRON 3.9mg; SODIUM 594mg; CALC 96mg

Golden Raisin-Rosemary Muffins

If you love rosemary, use 1 teaspoon; if you're a little hesitant, use ½ teaspoon.

¾ cup 1% low-fat milk
½ cup golden raisins
1 teaspoon dried rosemary
¼ cup butter, cut into small pieces
1½ cups all-purpose flour
⅔ cup sugar
2 teaspoons baking powder
¼ teaspoon salt
1 large egg, lightly beaten
Cooking spray
1 tablespoon sugar

1. Preheat oven to 350°.
2. Combine first 3 ingredients in a 2-cup glass measure. Microwave at HIGH 2 minutes; let stand 2 minutes. Add butter, stirring until melted. Cool to room temperature.
3. Lightly spoon flour into dry measuring cups, and level with a knife. Combine flour, ⅔ cup sugar, baking powder, and salt in a large bowl; make a well in center of mixture. Combine milk mixture and egg, and add to flour mixture, stirring just until moist. Spoon batter into 12 muffin cups coated with cooking spray. Sprinkle 1 tablespoon sugar evenly over muffins.
4. Bake at 350° for 20 minutes or until muffins spring back when touched lightly in center. Remove muffins immediately, and place on a wire rack. Yield: 1 dozen (serving size: 1 muffin).
NOTE: Store muffins in a heavy-duty zip-top plastic bag in freezer for up to 2 months. Thaw at room temperature.

CALORIES 174 (25% from fat); FAT 4.8g (sat 2.7g, mono 1.4g, poly 0.4g); PROTEIN 2.9g; CARB 30.6g; FIBER 0.7g; CHOL 29mg; IRON 1mg; SODIUM 184mg; CALC 74mg

Simple Sunday Supper

Make the potato recipe and steam the asparagus; pick up the rest.

**Potatoes Anna
with Bacon and Romano**

Rotisserie roast chicken

Steamed fresh asparagus

French baguette

Low-fat ice cream with
chocolate syrup

Potatoes Anna with Bacon and Romano

Placing a heavy pan on top of the potatoes compresses the slices, which makes the finished dish easier to cut into wedges. Serve as an accompaniment to roasted chicken, pork, or beef.

  3 bacon slices
  ½ cup chopped onion
  ¼ teaspoon black pepper
  2 garlic cloves, minced
  2½ pounds peeled baking potato, cut into ¼-inch-thick slices
  ¾ teaspoon salt
  ¼ cup (1 ounce) grated fresh Romano cheese
  ¼ cup fat-free, less-sodium chicken broth
  Cooking spray

1. Preheat oven to 375°.
2. Cook bacon in a 9-inch cast-iron skillet over medium heat until crisp. Remove bacon from pan; crumble. Reserve 2 tablespoons drippings, and set aside. Add onion, pepper, and garlic to pan; sauté 3 minutes or until tender. Add onion mixture to bacon.
3. Add reserved drippings to pan. Arrange one-third of potato slices in a single layer in pan; sprinkle with ¼ teaspoon salt. Spread half of onion mixture over potato slices; sprinkle with 2 tablespoons cheese. Repeat layers with potato slices, salt, onion mixture, and cheese, ending with potato slices. Sprinkle with ¼ teaspoon salt. Pour broth over top of potato slices.

4. Lightly coat 1 side of foil with cooking spray. Cover pan with foil, coated side down. Bake at 375° for 45 minutes. Place a heavy ovenproof pan on top of foil. Bake an additional 55 minutes or until potatoes are tender. Remove pan from oven; cool 20 minutes on a wire rack. Uncover and gently loosen potatoes from pan with a spatula; invert onto a serving plate. Yield: 6 servings (serving size: 1 wedge).

CALORIES 253 (28% from fat); FAT 7.9g (sat 3.2g, mono 3.3g, poly 1g); PROTEIN 6.4g; CARB 38.5g; FIBER 2.9g; CHOL 12mg; IRON 0.7mg; SODIUM 439mg; CALC 64mg

Red-Hot Tomato Pesto

Serve with toasted French baguette slices, or toss with hot cooked pasta and Parmesan cheese for a quick dinner.

  3 tablespoons water
  1 teaspoon crushed red pepper
  2 garlic cloves, peeled
  1 (8-ounce) bottle oil-packed sun-dried tomato halves, undrained
  2 tablespoons grated fresh Parmesan cheese
  2 tablespoons finely chopped walnuts
  1 (14.5-ounce) can diced tomatoes, drained

1. Combine water and pepper in a small bowl or custard cup. Cover with plastic wrap; vent. Microwave at HIGH 45 seconds or until mixture boils. Cool completely. Drain mixture through a sieve over a small bowl, reserving liquid; discard pepper.
2. Drop garlic cloves through food chute with food processor on, and process until minced. Add sun-dried tomatoes, and pulse until minced, scraping sides of bowl occasionally. Place tomato mixture in a medium bowl. Stir in reserved pepper liquid, cheese, nuts, and canned tomatoes. Yield: 1¾ cups (serving size: 1 tablespoon).

CALORIES 31 (46% from fat); FAT 1.6g (sat 0.2g, mono 0.9g, poly 0.4g); PROTEIN 1.2g; CARB 3.6g; FIBER 0.9g; CHOL 0mg; IRON 0.4mg; SODIUM 53mg; CALC 9mg

Grapefruit, Beet, and Blue Cheese Salad

You can substitute regular brown balsamic vinegar for the white, but the salad won't be as attractive or have the same great taste. For tips on working with beets, see the step-by-steps on page 70.

  ¾ pound beets (about 2 medium)
  3 pink grapefruit
  ¼ cup (1 ounce) crumbled blue cheese
  2 tablespoons white balsamic vinegar
  2 teaspoons olive oil
  2 teaspoons Dijon mustard
  ⅛ teaspoon salt
  ⅛ teaspoon freshly ground black pepper
  6 cups torn romaine lettuce

1. Leave root and 1 inch stem on beets; scrub with a brush. Place in a medium saucepan; cover with water. Bring to a boil; cover, reduce heat, and simmer 35 minutes or until tender. Drain and rinse with cold water. Drain; cool. Trim off beet roots; rub off skins. Cut beets into ½-inch cubes.
2. Peel and section grapefruit over a bowl, and squeeze membranes to extract juice. Set 1½ cups sections aside, and reserve 2 tablespoons juice. Discard membranes.
3. Place cheese in a small bowl; mash with a fork until smooth. Add reserved grapefruit juice, vinegar, and next 4 ingredients; stir well with a whisk.
4. Pour dressing over lettuce, tossing gently to coat. Divide lettuce mixture evenly among 6 plates. Top each serving with ¼ cup beets and ¼ cup grapefruit sections. Yield: 6 servings.

CALORIES 106 (28% from fat); FAT 3.3g (sat 1.1g, mono 1.6g, poly 0.3g); PROTEIN 3.6g; CARB 17.4g; FIBER 2.8g; CHOL 4mg; IRON 1.3mg; SODIUM 191mg; CALC 70mg

april

The Good Fats

Not all fats are nutritional bad guys. Some benefit our health—as well as our taste buds.

Recent studies have proven a diet rich in certain kinds of fat can be perfectly compatible with heart health. According to the American Heart Association (AHA), saturated fats and trans fatty acids should be minimized in your diet. At the same time, studies are finding that monounsaturated fats and some polyunsaturated fats are not simply neutral but have the potential to *boost* your health.

But simply adding a food high in monounsaturated fats to your diet won't help you. Why? Because total fat still counts. *All* fats—polys, monos, and otherwise—are concentrated sources of calories, with about 125 calories a tablespoon.

So how do you cut down on saturated fat while incorporating the "good" fats into your diet—and still keep from adding too many calories? The answer is to include the good fats *judiciously*, using just enough to satisfy your taste buds without piling on the pounds.

Warm Salmon Salad à la Provençal

1   (¾-pound) salmon fillet
⅛   teaspoon salt
⅛   teaspoon freshly ground black pepper
Cooking spray
¼   cup fresh lemon juice
3   tablespoons Caesar Dressing with Flaxseed
10 cups gourmet salad greens
½   cup finely chopped red onion
4   teaspoons capers
4   (1½-ounce) slices French bread, toasted
¼   cup finely chopped black olives

1. Preheat broiler.
2. Sprinkle fillet with salt and pepper. Place fillet, skin side down, on a broiler pan coated with cooking spray; broil 12 minutes or until fish flakes easily when tested with a fork. Remove skin from fillet; discard skin. Break fillet into chunks.
3. Drizzle juice and Caesar Dressing with Flaxseed over salad greens, tossing to coat. Add onion and capers; toss gently to combine. Divide salad evenly among 4 plates. Divide fish evenly among salads. Top each bread slice with 1 tablespoon olives, spreading with a knife. Cut each slice in half. Serve immediately. Yield: 4 servings (serving size: 2 cups salad and 2 bread pieces).

(Totals include Caesar Dressing with Flaxseed) CALORIES 334 (35% from fat); FAT 13g (sat 2.1g, mono 6.7g, poly 2.9g); PROTEIN 24.3g; CARB 29.9g; FIBER 4.7g; CHOL 56mg; IRON 3.4mg; SODIUM 630mg; CALC 104mg

CAESAR DRESSING WITH FLAXSEED:
Ground flaxseed contributes a nutty flavor, as well as omega-3 fatty acids, to salad dressings. The flaxseed mixture thickens as it stands and gives the dressing its texture. Try tossing it with romaine lettuce, Parmesan cheese shavings, and toasted bread cubes for a classic Caesar salad.

1   tablespoon flaxseed
¼   cup water
2   tablespoons white wine vinegar
2   tablespoons extra-virgin olive oil
1   teaspoon Worcestershire sauce
½   teaspoon Dijon mustard
½   teaspoon anchovy paste
¼   teaspoon salt
¼   teaspoon freshly ground black pepper
1   garlic clove, crushed

1. Place flaxseed in a clean coffee grinder or blender, and process until finely ground. Place flaxseed meal in a medium bowl; add water, stirring with a whisk. Let stand 5 minutes. Add vinegar and remaining ingredients; stir with a whisk. Yield: ½ cup (serving size: 1 tablespoon).

NOTE: Store dressing in an airtight container in refrigerator for up to 2 days. Store remaining flaxseed in refrigerator; since it's high in fat, it can go rancid easily.

CALORIES 40 (89% from fat); FAT 4g (sat 0.5g, mono 2.6g, poly 0.6g); PROTEIN 0.4g; CARB 0.8g; FIBER 0.4g; CHOL 0mg; IRON 0.1mg; SODIUM 133mg; CALC 5mg

Split-Pea Spread

If you're ever going to spring for great olive oil, now is the time—flavorful extra-virgin olive oil, which is high in monounsaturated fat, brings this simple spread to life. Serve with warm whole-wheat pita triangles, sesame crackers, olives, and feta cheese.

2¼   cups water
¾   cup yellow split peas
⅛   teaspoon crushed red pepper
6   garlic cloves, crushed
3   tablespoons fresh lemon juice
3   tablespoons extra-virgin olive oil, divided
1½   teaspoons ground cumin
¾   teaspoon salt
2   tablespoons finely chopped red onion
2   tablespoons chopped fresh dill

1. Combine first 4 ingredients in a medium, heavy saucepan, and bring to a boil. Partially cover, reduce heat, and simmer 40 minutes or until peas are tender and most of liquid is absorbed, stirring occasionally (pea mixture will have consistency of very thick split pea soup). Cool slightly.
2. Place pea mixture in a food processor or blender. Add lemon juice, 2 tablespoons olive oil, cumin, and salt; process until smooth.
3. Place pea puree in a shallow dish. Drizzle 1 tablespoon olive oil over pea puree, and sprinkle with chopped onion and dill. Yield: 2 cups (serving size: 2 tablespoons).

CALORIES 58 (42% from fat); FAT 2.7g (sat 0.4g, mono 1.9g, poly 0.3g); PROTEIN 2.4g; CARB 6.5g; FIBER 0.6g; CHOL 0mg; IRON 0.6mg; SODIUM 112mg; CALC 12mg

Easy Salmon Supper

Salmon with Grainy Mustard-and-Herb Sauce

Long-grain rice

Green beans

French bread

Salmon with Grainy Mustard-and-Herb Sauce

Serve with sautéed spinach or broccoli.

SALMON:

4   (6-ounce) salmon fillets (about 1 inch thick)

Cooking spray

2   tablespoons dry white wine

¼   teaspoon salt

¼   teaspoon freshly ground black pepper

2   tablespoons finely chopped shallots

SAUCE:

¼   cup low-fat mayonnaise

¼   cup fat-free, less-sodium chicken broth

1   tablespoon chopped fresh chives

1   tablespoon chopped fresh parsley

1   tablespoon spicy brown mustard

1   tablespoon fresh lemon juice

¼   teaspoon freshly ground black pepper

REMAINING INGREDIENT:

2   cups hot cooked long-grain and wild rice

1. Preheat oven to 425°.

2. To prepare fish, arrange fillets, skin sides down, in a 9-inch pie plate coated with cooking spray. Sprinkle with wine, salt, and ¼ teaspoon pepper; top with shallots. Cover with foil; bake at 425°

for 30 minutes or until fish flakes easily when tested with a fork.

3. To prepare sauce, combine mayonnaise and broth in a small skillet, stirring well with a whisk. Cook over medium-low heat until thoroughly heated (about 2 minutes). Remove from heat; stir in chives, parsley, mustard, juice, and ¼ teaspoon pepper. Serve fillets and sauce over rice. Yield: 4 servings (serving size: 1 fillet, about 3 tablespoons sauce, and ½ cup rice).

CALORIES 420 (35% from fat); FAT 16.2g (sat 2.9g, mono 7.4g, poly 4.1g); PROTEIN 38.7g; CARB 28.4g; FIBER 1.1g; CHOL 111mg; IRON 2mg; SODIUM 982mg; CALC 42mg

Quick Vegetarian Chili with Avocado Salsa

(pictured on page 96)

2   teaspoons canola oil

1   cup chopped onion

1   cup chopped red bell pepper

2   teaspoons chili powder

1   teaspoon ground cumin

1   teaspoon dried oregano

3   garlic cloves, minced

1   (4.5-ounce) can chopped green chiles

⅔   cup uncooked quick-cooking barley

¼   cup water

1   (15-ounce) can black beans, drained

1   (14.5-ounce) can no-salt-added diced tomatoes, undrained

1   (14½-ounce) can vegetable broth

3   tablespoons chopped fresh cilantro

6   tablespoons reduced-fat sour cream

6   lime wedges

18   baked tortilla chips

Avocado Salsa

1. Heat oil in a Dutch oven over medium-high heat. Add onion and bell pepper; sauté 3 minutes. Add chili powder and next 4 ingredients; cook 1 minute. Stir in barley and next 4 ingredients; bring to a boil. Cover, reduce heat, and simmer 20 minutes or until barley is tender. Stir in cilantro. Serve with sour cream, lime wedges, chips, and Avocado Salsa. Yield: 6 servings (serving size: 1 cup chili, 1 tablespoon sour cream, 1 lime wedge, 3 chips, and about 2½ tablespoons Avocado Salsa).

NOTE: Store chili in an airtight container in refrigerator for up to 2 days.

(Totals include Avocado Salsa) CALORIES 313 (29% from fat); FAT 10.1g (sat 2.2g, mono 4.8g, poly 1.6g); PROTEIN 9.6g; CARB 50.4g; FIBER 9.5g; CHOL 6mg; IRON 3.4mg; SODIUM 814mg; CALC 100mg

AVOCADO SALSA:

Store the chopped avocado with the seed until ready to combine with the remaining ingredients. Discard the seed before serving.

½   cup finely chopped peeled avocado

⅓   cup chopped seeded tomato

2   tablespoons finely chopped onion

1   tablespoon finely chopped seeded jalapeño pepper

1   tablespoon chopped fresh cilantro

1   tablespoon fresh lime juice

⅛   teaspoon salt

1. Combine all ingredients, and toss mixture gently. Serve salsa immediately. Yield: 1 cup (serving size: about 2½ tablespoons).

CALORIES 59 (79% from fat); FAT 5.2g (sat 0.8g, mono 3.2g, poly 0.7g); PROTEIN 0.8g; CARB 3.7g; FIBER 1.9g; CHOL 0mg; IRON 0.5mg; SODIUM 54mg; CALC 6mg

Asian Peanut Dip

Serve this dip with crudités or as a spread for grown-up peanut butter sandwiches with whole wheat country bread, grated carrots, sliced cucumber, and lettuce.

½   cup natural-style peanut butter (such as Smucker's)

⅓   cup reduced-fat firm silken tofu

3   tablespoons light brown sugar

2   tablespoons fresh lime juice

2   tablespoons low-sodium soy sauce

½   to ¾ teaspoon crushed red pepper

2   garlic cloves, crushed

1. Place all ingredients in a blender, and process until smooth, scraping sides. Store in an airtight container in refrigerator for up to 2 days. Yield: 1 cup (serving size: 2 tablespoons).

CALORIES 122 (57% from fat); FAT 7.7g (sat 1.5g, mono 3.8g, poly 2.5g); PROTEIN 5.4g; CARB 7.4g; FIBER 0.5g; CHOL 0mg; IRON 0.4mg; SODIUM 131mg; CALC 19mg

Apricot-Almond Muffins

These muffins are a good source of monounsaturated fat. The muffin cups will be full, but don't be alarmed—they shouldn't overflow.

½ cup apricot preserves
¼ teaspoon almond extract
1 cup all-purpose flour
1 cup whole wheat flour
1½ teaspoons baking powder
½ teaspoon baking soda
½ teaspoon salt
½ cup packed brown sugar
1 large egg
1 large egg white
1 cup low-fat buttermilk
3 tablespoons canola oil
2 teaspoons grated orange rind
1 teaspoon vanilla extract
Cooking spray
2 teaspoons granulated sugar
¼ cup sliced almonds

1. Preheat oven to 400°.
2. Combine preserves and almond extract in a small bowl.
3. Lightly spoon flours into dry measuring cups, and level with a knife. Combine flours, baking powder, baking soda, and salt in a large bowl; make a well in center of mixture.
4. Combine brown sugar, egg, and egg white in a medium bowl, and stir well with a whisk. Stir in buttermilk, canola oil, orange rind, and vanilla. Add to flour mixture, stirring just until moist.
5. Spoon 2 tablespoons batter into each of 12 muffin cups coated with cooking spray. Spoon apricot mixture evenly into centers of muffin cups (do not spread over batter), and top with remaining batter. Sprinkle batter evenly with 2 teaspoons granulated sugar and almonds.
6. Bake at 400° for 20 minutes or until muffins spring back when touched lightly in center. Run a knife or spatula around outer edge of each muffin cup. Carefully remove muffins immediately, and place on a wire rack. Yield: 1 dozen (serving size: 1 muffin).

CALORIES 209 (26% from fat); FAT 6.1g (sat 0.8g, mono 3.3g, poly 1.6g); PROTEIN 4.7g; CARB 35.3g; FIBER 2g; CHOL 18mg; IRON 1.3mg; SODIUM 242mg; CALC 85mg

Chocolate-Walnut Cake

(pictured on front cover and page 96)

CAKE:

Cooking spray
½ cup chopped pitted dates
½ cup unsweetened cocoa
½ cup boiling water
1 teaspoon instant coffee granules
1 (1-ounce) slice firm white bread
½ cup walnut halves, toasted and divided
⅓ cup all-purpose flour
¼ teaspoon salt
⅔ cup granulated sugar, divided
2 tablespoons canola oil
1 teaspoon vanilla extract
1 large egg
3 large egg whites

GLAZE:

⅓ cup unsweetened cocoa
¼ cup semisweet chocolate chips
¼ cup boiling water
1 tablespoon dark corn syrup
1 teaspoon instant coffee granules
½ teaspoon vanilla extract
1 cup powdered sugar

1. Preheat oven to 350°.
2. Coat a 9-inch round cake pan with cooking spray, and line bottom of pan with wax paper. Coat wax paper with cooking spray.
3. To prepare cake, combine dates, ½ cup cocoa, ½ cup boiling water, and 1 teaspoon coffee granules; let stand 20 minutes. Place bread in a food processor, and pulse 10 times or until coarse crumbs

---

Cooking Up Good Fats

Here are the two types of fat you want to emphasize in your diet: monounsaturated fats and omega-3 fatty acids (which are a type of polyunsaturated fat). Both are good for your heart. Here's where they're found and how you can use these foods more in your cooking.

• **Canola and Safflower Oils.** Canola is a good all-purpose oil for cooking; it also has omega-3s. Safflower is another good all-purpose oil, but it's milder in flavor than canola. It's as high in monounsaturated fat as olive oil.

• **Almonds.** About two-thirds of the fat is monounsaturated in these delicate, sweet nuts.

• **Avocado.** The buttery texture and rich flavor of an avocado go a long way. Thinly slice one for a sandwich, or chop up to top your favorite Mexican dish. More than half the fat in an avocado is monounsaturated.

• **Olive Oil.** Used as much for its flavor as its nutrition profile. It's one of the oils highest in monounsaturated fats.

• **Natural Peanut Butter.** Discernible by the layer of oil on top. We've found natural peanut butter works better in cookies and sauces than the hydrogenated stuff because it has more peanut flavor. Brands not labeled natural—basically what we all grew up on, like Jif, Skippy, and Peter Pan—contain trans fatty acids. Is a source of monounsaturated fat.

• **Olives.** A flavor powerhouse, and easy to incorporate in most any dish. Get the imported ones such as kalamata, niçoise, picholine, or Greek for the most flavor. Is also a source of monounsaturated fat.

• **Salmon.** The best source of omega-3s you'll find. It's probably the most popular, definitely the most versatile, fish available today. With its firm, meaty texture, you can serve it like a steak or flaked and put into pasta and salads. It makes a great sandwich, stands up to grilling, and takes to even the boldest of flavors. Beneficial monounsaturated and omega-3 fats make up more than half its fat content.

• **Flaxseed.** These incredible little seeds lend a nutty flavor to bread, muffins, and pilafs; think of them as wheat germ for the new millennium. More than half of the fat in these tiny seeds comes from omega-3s.

• **Walnuts.** Just as great in savory dishes as sweet ones. They can be ground for a pesto, tossed into muffins and cookies, or cracked and eaten out of the shell. Walnuts are the only nuts that contain both monounsaturated fats and omega-3s.

form to measure ½ cup. Place crumbs in a large bowl. Reserve 10 walnut halves for garnish. Place remaining walnuts in a food processor. Lightly spoon flour into a dry measuring cup, and level with a knife. Add flour and salt to food processor, and process until walnuts are finely ground. Add to breadcrumbs. Place date mixture, ⅓ cup granulated sugar, oil, 1 teaspoon vanilla, and 1 egg in food processor, and process until smooth, scraping sides of bowl once. Add date mixture to breadcrumb mixture, stirring well.

4. Beat egg whites with a mixer at high speed until soft peaks form. Gradually add ⅓ cup granulated sugar, 1 tablespoon at a time, beating until stiff peaks form. Gently stir one-fourth of egg white mixture into batter; gently fold in remaining egg white mixture. Spread batter into prepared pan. Bake at 350° for 25 minutes or until cake springs back when lightly touched. Cool in pan 10 minutes on a wire rack, and remove from pan. Remove wax paper. Cool completely on wire rack.

5. To prepare glaze, combine ⅓ cup cocoa and next 4 ingredients, stirring until smooth. Stir in ½ teaspoon vanilla. Cover and chill 1 hour. Gradually add powdered sugar to cocoa mixture, beating with a mixer at medium speed until smooth and thick.

6. Place cake layer on a plate. Spread glaze evenly over top and sides of cake. Arrange reserved walnut halves on top. Yield: 10 servings (serving size: 1 wedge).

CALORIES 280 (30% from fat); FAT 9.2g (sat 2.2g, mono 3.4g, poly 3g); PROTEIN 6.1g; CARB 45.5g; FIBER 1.2g; CHOL 22mg; IRON 2mg; SODIUM 103mg; CALC 26mg

30 minutes or less

Mood Soothers

No matter how your day goes, these easy menus, timesaving tips, and streamlined recipes are guaranteed to make dinner a mood soother.

Creamy Chicken and Mushrooms

Roasted asparagus*

*Toss 1 pound trimmed asparagus with 1 tablespoon olive oil, ¼ teaspoon salt, and ¼ teaspoon black pepper. Bake at 400° for 5 minutes.

Low-fat chocolate ice cream with praline sauce*

*Combine ½ cup fat-free caramel sauce and 2 tablespoons chopped toasted pecans. Serve over ice cream.

Creamy Chicken and Mushrooms

TOTAL TIME: 25 MINUTES

  2 cups uncooked medium egg noodles
Cooking spray
  1 pound skinless, boneless chicken breast, cut into bite-size pieces
  1 teaspoon olive oil
 ½ cup chopped shallots
  1 (8-ounce) package presliced mushrooms
 ½ cup dry white wine
  1 cup fat-free milk
  2 teaspoons all-purpose flour
 ⅓ cup (3 ounces) spreadable cheese with garlic and herbs (such as Alouette)
  2 tablespoons chopped fresh parsley
 ¼ teaspoon black pepper
Chopped fresh parsley (optional)

1. Cook pasta according to package directions, omitting salt and fat.
2. While pasta cooks, heat a large nonstick skillet coated with cooking spray over medium-high heat. Add chicken; sauté 4 minutes or until done. Remove chicken from pan; set aside.
3. Heat oil in pan over medium-high heat. Add shallots; sauté 1 minute. Add mushrooms; sauté 4 minutes. Add wine, and cook 3 minutes or until liquid almost evaporates.
4. Combine milk and flour in a small bowl; stir well with a whisk. Add milk mixture to pan; cook 3 minutes or until

slightly thick. Add chicken, cheese, 2 tablespoons parsley, and pepper; reduce heat, and simmer 3 minutes or until thoroughly heated. Serve over pasta; sprinkle with parsley, if desired. Yield: 4 servings (serving size: ¾ cup chicken mixture and ¾ cup pasta).

CALORIES 338 (18% from fat); FAT 6.9g (sat 2.5g, mono 1.7g, poly 1.1g); PROTEIN 37.1g; CARB 31.3g; FIBER 2.9g; CHOL 101mg; IRON 3.5mg; SODIUM 241mg; CALC 116mg

Pork Chops in Mustard Sauce

Cheddar mashed potatoes*

Broccoli

*Prepare 1 (22-ounce) bag frozen mashed potatoes according to package directions, using 1% low-fat milk. Stir in ½ cup spreadable cheese with garlic and herbs (such as Alouette) and ¼ cup (1 ounce) shredded reduced-fat sharp cheddar cheese.

Pork Chops in Mustard Sauce

TOTAL TIME: 27 MINUTES

QUICK TIP: When measuring syrupy ingredients like honey, coat the measuring spoon or cup with cooking spray. The ingredient will slip out easily, and cleanup will be simpler.

  4 (6-ounce) bone-in center-cut pork chops (about ¾ inch thick)
 ¼ teaspoon salt
 ⅛ teaspoon black pepper
  2 teaspoons olive oil
1½ cups dry white wine
 ⅓ cup honey
 ¼ cup Dijon mustard

1. Sprinkle pork with salt and pepper. Heat oil in a large nonstick skillet over medium-high heat. Add pork; cook 3 minutes on each side or until browned. Remove pork from pan.
2. Add wine, honey, and mustard to pan; bring to a boil, and cook 3 minutes.
3. Add pork; reduce heat, and simmer mixture 12 minutes, turning pork after

Continued

6 minutes. Yield: 4 servings (serving size: 1 pork chop and 3 tablespoons sauce).

CALORIES 308 (33% from fat); FAT 11.3g (sat 3.5g, mono 6.1g, poly 1.2g); PROTEIN 25.2g; CARB 25.3g; FIBER 0g; CHOL 72mg; IRON 1.4mg; SODIUM 675mg; CALC 15mg

Menu 3

serves 6

Spaghetti with Meat Sauce

Caesar salad*

*Combine 8 cups torn romaine lettuce with ⅓ cup bottled light Caesar dressing or Simple Caesar dressing. Top with 3 tablespoons grated fresh Parmesan cheese and 1 cup commercial croutons.

Simple Caesar dressing*

*Combine ⅓ cup plain fat-free yogurt, 2 teaspoons lemon juice, 1½ teaspoons anchovy paste, ½ teaspoon minced garlic, and ¼ teaspoon Worcestershire sauce.

Breadsticks

Spaghetti with Meat Sauce

TOTAL TIME: 28 MINUTES

QUICK TIP: Water comes to a boil faster in a covered pot.

12 ounces uncooked spaghetti
¾ pound ground sirloin
1 cup chopped onion
1½ teaspoons bottled minced garlic
¾ cup dry red wine
1 (26-ounce) bottle low-fat spaghetti sauce (such as Healthy Choice Traditional Pasta Sauce)
⅔ cup 2% reduced-fat milk
½ teaspoon salt
¼ teaspoon black pepper

1. Cook pasta according to package directions, omitting salt and fat.
2. While pasta cooks, heat a large nonstick skillet over medium-high heat. Add beef; cook until browned, stirring to crumble. Drain beef, and set aside.
3. Add onion and garlic to pan; sauté 3 minutes. Add wine; cook 3 minutes or until liquid almost evaporates.
4. Stir in beef and spaghetti sauce; bring to a boil. Reduce heat, and simmer

5 minutes, stirring occasionally. Stir in milk, salt, and pepper; cook 3 minutes, stirring occasionally. Serve sauce over pasta. Yield: 6 servings (serving size: about 1 cup pasta and ⅔ cup sauce).

CALORIES 401 (15% from fat); FAT 6.9g (sat 1.8g, mono 2.9g, poly 1.1g); PROTEIN 22.8g; CARB 60.1g; FIBER 4.9g; CHOL 37mg; IRON 4.7mg; SODIUM 544mg; CALC 77mg

Menu 4

serves 4

Sausage and Red Cabbage

Roasted potatoes*

*Toss 2 pounds quartered new potatoes with 1 tablespoon each of olive oil and bottled minced garlic, and ½ teaspoon each of salt, dried rosemary, and black pepper in a large cast-iron skillet or baking dish. Bake at 425° for 30 minutes, stirring occasionally.

Corn bread

Sausage and Red Cabbage

TOTAL TIME: 29 MINUTES

½ (12-ounce) package chicken apple sausage, cut into ½-inch pieces (such as Gerhard's)
2 cups chopped Granny Smith apple (about 8 ounces)
1 cup frozen chopped onion, thawed
1 (10-ounce) package or 6 cups thinly sliced red cabbage
1 cup apple juice or apple cider
1 cup dry red wine
1½ tablespoons brown sugar
¼ teaspoon salt

1. Heat a large nonstick skillet over medium-high heat. Add sausage; sauté 4 minutes. Remove from pan.
2. Add apple, onion, and cabbage to pan; cook 5 minutes, stirring frequently. Add sausage, juice, wine, sugar, and salt; bring to a boil. Reduce heat, and simmer 10 minutes. Yield: 4 servings (serving size: 1¼ cups).

CALORIES 188 (28% from fat); FAT 5.8g (sat 1.6g, mono 2.4g, poly 1.3g); PROTEIN 8.5g; CARB 28.4g; FIBER 3.8g; CHOL 38mg; IRON 1.6mg; SODIUM 426mg; CALC 61mg

Soup and the City

Cynthia, Lucia, Lisa, Rebecca, Katherine, and Sharon: six 20-something professional women from New York who for the past four years have met once a month to create healthy home-cooked dinners.

So while most people are putting together classic stick-to-your-ribs Sunday dinners, Cooking Club NYC—as they call themselves—is craving just the opposite. This month's hot and steamy feature—Carrot-Ginger Soup.

Carrot-Ginger Soup

2 tablespoons olive oil
¾ cup chopped onion
½ cup chopped green onions
4 cups finely chopped carrot (about 1¼ pounds)
3 cups cubed peeled baking potato (about 1 pound)
1 tablespoon grated peeled fresh ginger
¾ teaspoon salt
¼ teaspoon curry powder
¼ teaspoon ground cinnamon
¼ teaspoon ground nutmeg
¼ teaspoon black pepper
⅛ teaspoon ground cloves
3 (15.75-ounce) cans fat-free, less-sodium chicken broth
2 bay leaves

1. Heat oil in a large Dutch oven over medium heat. Add ¾ cup onion and ½ cup green onions; sauté 3 minutes. Add carrot and potato, and cook 1 minute. Add ginger and next 8 ingredients; bring to a boil. Cover. Reduce heat; simmer 1 hour. Discard bay leaves. Place 6 cups carrot mixture in a food processor; process until smooth. Return to pan, and stir well. Yield: 9 servings (serving size: 1 cup).

CALORIES 109 (26% from fat); FAT 3.2g (sat 0.5g, mono 2.2g, poly 0.3g); PROTEIN 3.8g; CARB 16.5g; FIBER 2.8g; CHOL 0mg; IRON 0.8mg; SODIUM 537mg; CALC 25mg

That's Entertainment

A Las Vegas reader puts on a show in her kitchen every week.

While Christine Datian's house doesn't feature chorus lines or megastars, it does boast some classy culinary acts.

One of Christine's specialties includes her famous Pasta Salad with Shrimp, Peppers, and Olives. It's a real crowd pleaser.

Pasta Salad with Shrimp, Peppers, and Olives

2½   cups cooked angel hair (about 5 ounces uncooked pasta)
¾   cup chopped plum tomato
½   cup chopped red bell pepper
½   cup chopped yellow bell pepper
⅓   cup chopped green onions
2   tablespoons fresh lemon juice
1   tablespoon chopped pitted kalamata olives
1   tablespoon olive oil
1½   teaspoons chopped fresh or ½ teaspoon dried thyme
½   teaspoon white pepper
¼   teaspoon dried oregano
¾   pound cooked medium shrimp, peeled and deveined
1   garlic clove, minced
½   cup (2 ounces) crumbled feta cheese
1   tablespoon chopped fresh parsley

1. Combine first 13 ingredients in a large bowl. Sprinkle with cheese and parsley. Yield: 5 servings (serving size: 2 cups).

CALORIES 252 (26% from fat); FAT 7.2g (sat 2.4g, mono 2.9g, poly 1.1g); PROTEIN 19.8g; CARB 26.7g; FIBER 1.8g; CHOL 114mg; IRON 3.6mg; SODIUM 249mg; CALC 111mg

Easy Pesto Salmon

"The salmon tastes wonderful served with grilled or steamed vegetables."
—Lori Fredrich, Germantown, Wisconsin

2   cups fresh spinach leaves
½   cup basil leaves
¼   cup fat-free, less-sodium chicken broth
1   tablespoon olive oil
¼   teaspoon salt
3   garlic cloves, peeled
Cooking spray
2   (6-ounce) salmon fillets, skinned
⅔   cup hot cooked brown rice

1. Preheat oven to 400°.
2. Place first 6 ingredients in a food processor or blender, and process until smooth. Spoon 3 tablespoons pesto into bottom of an 8-inch square baking dish coated with cooking spray. Top with salmon fillets; spread with remaining pesto.
3. Bake at 400° for 20 minutes or until fish flakes easily when tested with a fork. Serve with rice. Yield: 2 servings (serving size: 1 salmon fillet and ⅓ cup rice).

CALORIES 443 (45% from fat); FAT 22.1g (sat 3.5g, mono 12g, poly 4.4g); PROTEIN 38.7g; CARB 20.6g; FIBER 3.1g; CHOL 111mg; IRON 3.2mg; SODIUM 483mg; CALC 96mg

Shrimp Barbara

"I got the idea for this recipe from some delicious shrimp tacos I had in California. The combination of textures and temperatures is as pleasing to look at as it is to eat. For the best taste, it's important to use fresh shrimp, not frozen."
—Mark D. Watson, Limerick, Pennsylvania

1   cup reduced-fat Thousand Island dressing
½   cup water
Cooking spray
3   garlic cloves, minced
1   pound medium shrimp, peeled and deveined
7   cups packaged cabbage-and-carrot coleslaw
2   tablespoons chopped fresh cilantro

1. Combine salad dressing and water in a small saucepan. Cook over medium heat 3 minutes or until thoroughly heated; remove from heat.
2. Heat a medium nonstick skillet coated with cooking spray over medium heat. Add minced garlic; cook 1 minute. Add shrimp, and cook 3 minutes or until done. Remove shrimp mixture from heat, and stir in dressing mixture.
3. Arrange 1¾ cups coleslaw on each of 4 plates. Spoon ¾ cup shrimp mixture over each serving, and sprinkle evenly with cilantro. Yield: 4 servings.

CALORIES 292 (32% from fat); FAT 10.5g (sat 1g, mono 5.1g, poly 3.4g); PROTEIN 24.4g; CARB 21.7g; FIBER 0.7g; CHOL 172mg; IRON 3.3mg; SODIUM 787mg; CALC 112mg

Fresh Tuna Stir-Fry with Cilantro and Lime

"As a grad student, I'm a big fan of the ease and speed of stir-frying. I love this recipe because the lime and cilantro don't cover the taste of the tuna; they accentuate it. For a different flavor, I will use whole wheat couscous cooked in a mixture of vegetable broth and wine in place of the rice."
—Camilla Saulsbury, Bloomington, Indiana

3   tablespoons lime juice
1¼   pounds tuna, cut into 1-inch cubes
¼   cup low-sodium teriyaki sauce
1½   teaspoons cornstarch
1   tablespoon vegetable oil
1   cup vertically sliced onion
2   teaspoons minced peeled fresh ginger
3   garlic cloves, minced
3   cups hot cooked long-grain rice
2   tablespoons chopped fresh cilantro

1. Combine lime juice and fish in a medium bowl. Combine teriyaki sauce and cornstarch in a small bowl, stirring with a whisk.
2. Heat oil in a large nonstick skillet over medium-high heat. Add onion, ginger, and garlic; stir-fry 2 minutes. Add fish mixture, and stir-fry 2 minutes. Add teriyaki mixture; stir-fry 30 seconds
Continued

or until slightly thick. Serve over rice, and sprinkle with cilantro. Yield: 4 servings (serving size: ¾ cup fish mixture, ¾ cup rice, and 1½ teaspoons cilantro).

CALORIES 435 (22% from fat); FAT 10.6g (sat 2.5g, mono 3g, poly 4.1g); PROTEIN 37.3g; CARB 44.7g; FIBER 1.4g; CHOL 54mg; IRON 3mg; SODIUM 313mg; CALC 29mg

Broiled Salmon Burgers

"Even friends who don't usually eat fish like these burgers. I top them with red onion and romaine lettuce, and I serve roasted vegetables such as zucchini on the side. You can also use dinner or egg twist rolls in place of the hamburger buns for smaller sandwiches."

—Joy DePhillis, Franklin Lakes, New Jersey

½ cup low-fat mayonnaise
¼ cup lemon juice, divided
1 garlic clove, minced
1 cup dry breadcrumbs
¼ cup fat-free milk
2 tablespoons minced shallots
2 tablespoons Dijon mustard
5 (4-ounce) salmon fillets (about 1 inch thick)
Cooking spray
5 (2-ounce) hamburger buns with sesame seeds, toasted

1. Preheat broiler.
2. Combine mayonnaise, 2 tablespoons lemon juice, and minced garlic in a small bowl.
3. Place breadcrumbs in a shallow dish. Combine 2 tablespoons lemon juice, milk, shallots, and mustard in a medium bowl. Dip each fillet in milk mixture, and dredge in breadcrumbs. Place fillets on a broiler pan coated with cooking spray, and broil 7 minutes on each side or until fish flakes easily when tested with a fork.
4. Place fillets on bottom halves of buns; spread each with 2 tablespoons mayonnaise mixture, and cover with a bun top. Yield: 5 servings (serving size: 1 burger).

CALORIES 493 (29% from fat); FAT 15.8g (sat 2.9g, mono 6.3g, poly 5g); PROTEIN 31.3g; CARB 53.5g; FIBER 2.1g; CHOL 74mg; IRON 3.7mg; SODIUM 888mg; CALC 152mg

Shrimp Sauté

"I like to serve this dish as an entrée, with steamed broccolini topped with lemon pepper on the side, although it works beautifully as an appetizer."

—Kristy Rea, Naples, Florida

1 tablespoon butter
2 garlic cloves, minced
2 tablespoons fresh lemon juice
2 teaspoons Worcestershire sauce
¼ teaspoon salt
⅛ teaspoon black pepper
2 pounds large shrimp, peeled and deveined
⅓ cup minced fresh parsley
1 tablespoon minced fresh chives

1. Melt butter in a large nonstick skillet over medium-high heat; sauté garlic 30 seconds. Add juice and next 4 ingredients; cook 6 minutes or until shrimp are done. Remove from heat. Sprinkle with parsley and chives. Yield: 5 servings (serving size: about ¾ cup shrimp).

CALORIES 219 (23% from fat); FAT 5.5g (sat 2g, mono 1.1g, poly 1.3g); PROTEIN 37.1g; CARB 3.2g; FIBER 0.2g; CHOL 282mg; IRON 4.6mg; SODIUM 431mg; CALC 105mg

back to the best

White Russian Tiramisu

Tiramisu means "carry me up," and White Russian Tiramisu is, without a doubt, an uplifting treat.

This version of the classic Italian dessert takes its name from the popular White Russian drink—the two have the rich taste of Kahlúa in common. It's perfect as a make-ahead dessert, because it only gets better as the flavors meld.

The recipe first appeared in our July-August 1999 issue. Mascarpone cheese is a soft triple-cream cheese that comes in small tubes. You can use regular cream cheese in its place, if you prefer. Look for ladyfingers in the bakery aisle or frozen-food case of your supermarket.

White Russian Tiramisu

(pictured on page 93)

½ cup ground coffee beans
1¾ cups cold water
¼ cup Kahlúa (coffee-flavored liqueur), divided
½ cup (3½ ounces) mascarpone cheese
1 (8-ounce) block fat-free cream cheese, softened
⅓ cup packed brown sugar
¼ cup granulated sugar
24 cake-style ladyfingers (2 [3-ounce] packages)
2 teaspoons unsweetened cocoa

1. Assemble drip coffeemaker according to manufacturer's directions. Place ground coffee in coffee filter or filter basket. Add cold water to coffeemaker; brew to make 1½ cups. Combine brewed coffee and 2 tablespoons Kahlúa in a shallow dish; cool.
2. Combine cheeses in a large bowl. Beat with a mixer at high speed until smooth. Add 2 tablespoons Kahlúa and sugars; beat until well blended.
3. Split ladyfingers in half lengthwise.
4. Quickly dip 24 ladyfinger halves, flat sides down, into coffee mixture. Place halves, dipped sides down, in bottom of an 8-inch square baking dish (halves will be slightly overlapping). Spread half of cheese mixture over ladyfingers; sprinkle with 1 teaspoon cocoa. Repeat procedure with remaining ladyfinger halves, coffee mixture, cheese mixture, and 1 teaspoon cocoa.
5. Place 1 toothpick in each corner of dish and 1 in center of tiramisu (to prevent plastic wrap from sticking to cheese mixture); cover with plastic wrap. Chill 2 hours. Yield: 12 servings.

CALORIES 134 (30% from fat); FAT 4.5g (sat 2.2g, mono 1.5g, poly 0.4g); PROTEIN 3.3g; CARB 21.7g; FIBER 0g; CHOL 31mg; IRON 0.3mg; SODIUM 139mg; CALC 77mg

White Russian Tiramisu, page 92

Double-Mango Salad, page 116

Spring Vegetable Lasagna,
page 117

Tea-Crusted Tofu over Greens,
page 113

Empanaditas de Guayaba y
Queso, page 104

Quick Vegetarian Chili with Avocado Salsa, page 87

Chocolate-Walnut Cake,
page 88

The Ultimate Pantry

No need to stop at the store for the makings of dinner—if your pantry's prepared. These strategies and recipes will get you stocking.

A pantry filled with old standbys guarantees your menus will be dated and tired. If you stock it as we suggest, however, you'll almost always be able to cook at least one of your favorite *Cooking Light* recipes. And if you're savvy, you'll figure out what you need to keep on hand to get something good on the table without stopping at the store on the way home from work.

Fettuccine and Tofu with Finger-Licking Peanut Sauce

This dish has endless variations. Substitute chicken, pork, or shrimp for the tofu and almost any kind of pasta for the fettuccine. Or add vegetables of your choice.

- ½ cup fat-free, less-sodium chicken broth
- ¼ cup chunky peanut butter
- ¼ cup low-sodium soy sauce
- 3 tablespoons brown sugar
- 2 tablespoons rice vinegar
- 2 teaspoons grated peeled fresh ginger
- 2 teaspoons chile paste with garlic
- 4 garlic cloves, minced
- 8 ounces uncooked fettuccine
- 1 pound firm tofu, drained and cubed
- 1 cup (2-inch) sliced green onions
- 1 cup shredded carrot

1. Combine first 8 ingredients in a small saucepan. Cook over medium heat 5 minutes or until smooth, stirring frequently. Remove from heat.
2. Cook pasta in boiling water 8 minutes, omitting salt and fat. Add tofu, onions, and carrot; drain. Place pasta mixture in a large bowl. Add peanut butter mixture; toss gently. Yield: 4 servings (serving size: 2 cups).

CALORIES 465 (29% from fat); FAT 14.5g (sat 2.3g, mono 5.3g, poly 6g); PROTEIN 23g; CARB 60.8g; FIBER 4.5g; CHOL 1mg; IRON 9.6mg; SODIUM 713mg; CALC 174mg

Sicilian Stuffed Chicken Breasts with Marsala

- 1 tablespoon olive oil, divided
- ½ teaspoon crushed red pepper
- ½ teaspoon dried oregano
- ¼ teaspoon salt
- 1 (10-ounce) package frozen chopped spinach, thawed, drained, and squeezed dry
- 3 garlic cloves, minced
- 1 cup Marsala, divided
- 3 tablespoons grated fresh Romano or Parmesan cheese
- 2 tablespoons golden raisins
- 2 tablespoons capers
- 4 (4-ounce) skinless, boneless chicken breast halves
- ¼ cup Italian-seasoned breadcrumbs
- 2 tablespoons sherry vinegar
- 2 tablespoons water
- ½ teaspoon cornstarch

1. Heat 1 teaspoon oil in a medium skillet over medium heat. Add red pepper, oregano, salt, spinach, and garlic; cook 3 minutes. Place spinach mixture in a medium bowl. Stir in 1 tablespoon Marsala, cheese, raisins, and capers.
2. Cut a horizontal slit through thickest portion of each breast half to form a pocket. Stuff about ⅓ cup spinach mixture into each pocket. Secure each chicken breast with wooden picks. Dredge breasts in breadcrumbs, turning to coat; shake off excess breadcrumbs.
3. Heat 2 teaspoons oil in skillet over medium heat. Add chicken breasts, and cook 12 minutes or until chicken is browned, turning after 6 minutes. Remove from pan; keep warm. Add remaining Marsala and vinegar to pan. Combine water and cornstarch in a small bowl. Add cornstarch mixture to pan; bring to a boil. Cook 1 minute, stirring constantly; add chicken to pan. Cover, reduce heat, and simmer 6 minutes or until chicken is done. Drizzle sauce over chicken. Yield: 4 servings (serving size: 1 stuffed chicken breast half).

CALORIES 262 (23% from fat); FAT 6.8g (sat 1.9g, mono 3.3g, poly 0.8g); PROTEIN 31.7g; CARB 16.7g; FIBER 2.5g; CHOL 71mg; IRON 2.9mg; SODIUM 696mg; CALC 170mg

Spring Tortellini Salad

DRESSING:

- ¼ cup red wine vinegar
- 2 tablespoons extra-virgin olive oil
- 4 teaspoons spicy brown or Dijon mustard
- 2 teaspoons fresh lemon juice
- ½ teaspoon salt
- ¼ teaspoon freshly ground black pepper
- 4 garlic cloves, minced

SALAD:

- 1 (9-ounce) package fresh cheese tortellini, uncooked
- 2 cups frozen medium shrimp
- ¾ cup thinly sliced carrot
- 2 cups finely chopped tomato
- 1 cup frozen green peas, thawed
- ½ cup finely chopped red onion

1. To prepare dressing, combine first 7 ingredients in a small bowl, and stir well with a whisk.
2. To prepare salad, cook tortellini in boiling water 6 minutes. Add shrimp and carrot; cook 3 minutes. Drain well. Combine pasta mixture, tomato, peas, and onion in a large bowl; pour dressing over salad, tossing gently to coat. Cover and chill 30 minutes. Yield: 6 servings (serving size: 1⅓ cups).

CALORIES 277 (29% from fat); FAT 8.8g (sat 3.8g, mono 4.5g, poly 1g); PROTEIN 18.5g; CARB 30g; FIBER 2.3g; CHOL 91mg; IRON 2mg; SODIUM 504mg; CALC 123mg

Crispy Salmon Cakes with Lemon-Caper Mayonnaise

Chilling the patties for these croquettes keeps them from falling apart when you cook them in the skillet. The lemon-caper mayonnaise is also great with other fish.

FLAVORED MAYONNAISE:

- 6 tablespoons fat-free mayonnaise
- 2 teaspoons capers
- ½ teaspoon grated lemon rind
- ½ teaspoon lemon juice
- ¼ teaspoon freshly ground black pepper
- ⅛ teaspoon crushed red pepper

SALMON CAKES:

- 1 tablespoon vegetable oil, divided
- ¼ cup finely chopped onion
- ¼ cup finely chopped celery
- ¾ cup crushed fat-free saltine crackers (about 20 crackers), divided
- 1 tablespoon Dijon mustard
- ¼ teaspoon freshly ground black pepper
- 2 (7.5-ounce) cans salmon, drained, flaked, and bone pieces removed
- 1 large egg, lightly beaten

1. To prepare flavored mayonnaise, combine first 6 ingredients in a small bowl; cover and chill.

2. To prepare salmon cakes, heat 1 teaspoon oil in a medium nonstick skillet over medium heat. Add onion and celery; sauté 4 minutes or until tender. Combine onion mixture, ½ cup crackers, mustard, ¼ teaspoon black pepper, salmon, and egg in a medium bowl. Divide salmon mixture into 4 equal portions, shaping each into a ½-inch-thick patty. Coat each patty with 1 tablespoon crackers. Cover and chill 20 minutes.

3. Heat 2 teaspoons oil in a large nonstick skillet over medium heat until hot. Add patties; cook 5 minutes on each side or until lightly browned. Serve salmon cakes with flavored mayonnaise. Yield: 4 servings (serving size: 1 cake and 1½ tablespoons mayonnaise mixture).

CALORIES 306 (32% from fat); FAT 11g (sat 2.6g, mono 3.4g, poly 3.9g); PROTEIN 22.8g; CARB 27.3g; FIBER 1.1g; CHOL 55mg; IRON 3mg; SODIUM 1,214mg; CALC 215mg

Monterey Jack, Corn, and Roasted Red Pepper Risotto

We never seem to run out of ways to make risotto. Here, the creamy rice dish takes on a Southwestern flavor with corn, Monterey Jack cheese, and cumin. You probably have coriander in your spice rack. It's optional; if you leave it out, the dish will still have plenty of flavor.

- 1¾ cups water
- 2 (14½-ounce) cans vegetable broth
- 2 teaspoons olive oil
- 1 cup uncooked Arborio or other short-grain rice
- 1 teaspoon ground cumin
- 1 teaspoon ground coriander (optional)
- 4 garlic cloves, minced
- 1 cup thinly sliced green onions
- ¾ cup (3 ounces) shredded Monterey Jack cheese with jalapeño peppers
- ¼ to ½ teaspoon hot sauce
- 2 cups frozen whole-kernel corn
- ¾ cup chopped bottled roasted red bell peppers

1. Combine water and broth in a medium saucepan; bring to a simmer (do not boil). Keep broth mixture warm over low heat.

2. Heat oil in a large saucepan over medium-high heat. Add rice, cumin, coriander, if desired, and garlic; sauté 1 minute. Stir in ½ cup broth mixture; cook 2 minutes or until liquid is nearly absorbed, stirring constantly. Add remaining broth mixture, ½ cup at a time, stirring constantly until each portion of liquid is absorbed before adding the next (about 20 minutes total). Stir in onions, cheese, hot sauce, corn, and bell peppers; cook 3 minutes or until thoroughly heated. Yield: 4 servings (serving size: 1 cup).

CALORIES 383 (24% from fat); FAT 10.4g (sat 4.6g, mono 3.9g, poly 0.9g); PROTEIN 12g; CARB 63.3g; FIBER 3.8g; CHOL 17mg; IRON 3.6mg; SODIUM 583mg; CALC 198mg

Spiced Chicken with Couscous Pilaf

Jarred spices are really the heart of all pantries, whether beginner or advanced. Here they combine for a zesty rub that's equally as good on pork, beef, or turkey.

- 2½ teaspoons paprika
- 1 teaspoon dried thyme
- ¾ teaspoon garlic powder
- ½ teaspoon dried oregano
- ½ teaspoon salt
- ¼ teaspoon black pepper
- ⅛ teaspoon ground red pepper
- 4 (4-ounce) skinless, boneless chicken breast halves
- 1 tablespoon vegetable oil, divided
- ½ cup chopped onion
- 1 garlic clove, minced
- 1 cup uncooked couscous
- 1 cup fat-free, less-sodium chicken broth
- 1 cup frozen whole-kernel corn
- 2 tablespoons minced fresh cilantro
- 1 tablespoon lime juice
- Cilantro sprigs (optional)

1. Combine first 7 ingredients in a shallow dish. Dredge chicken in paprika mixture.

2. Heat 2 teaspoons oil in a large nonstick skillet over medium heat. Add chicken, and cook 5 minutes on each side or until done. Remove chicken from pan. Keep warm.

3. Heat 1 teaspoon oil in pan over medium-high heat. Add onion and garlic; sauté 1 minute. Stir in couscous and broth; bring to a boil. Remove from heat. Stir in corn; cover and let stand 5 minutes or until liquid is absorbed. Stir in minced cilantro and lime juice. Serve with chicken. Garnish with cilantro sprigs, if desired. Yield: 4 servings (serving size: 1 chicken breast half and 1 cup couscous mixture).

CALORIES 398 (18% from fat); FAT 8g (sat 1.3g, mono 4.7g, poly 1.2g); PROTEIN 34.5g; CARB 46.5g; FIBER 4.1g; CHOL 66mg; IRON 2.6mg; SODIUM 642mg; CALC 48mg

How to Build Your Ultimate Pantry

The majority of these ingredients can be found at your local supermarket. For some of the items, though, you may need to find an Asian market or gourmet grocery store.

The Beginner's Pantry

THE FOUNDATIONS
white rice
pastas: spaghetti, penne, couscous
canned beans: black, pinto, great Northern
canned tuna

THE FLAVOR BUILDERS
vinegars: red wine, balsamic
extra-virgin olive oil
dark sesame oil
low-sodium soy sauce
Dijon mustard
salsa
capers
fresh garlic
dried herbs
peanut butter

THE ASSISTANTS
fat-free, less-sodium chicken and
   vegetable broth
whole and diced canned tomatoes,
   tomato paste
pasta sauce

SWEET RETURNS
honey
brown sugar
granulated sugar
cocoa

COOL STUFF
boneless, skinless chicken breasts
cheeses: Parmesan, mozzarella
frozen spinach
eggs, egg substitute
fresh parsley
slivered almonds
butter
jellies and preserves
lemons
limes

The Intermediate Pantry
Add to our beginner's pantry:

EXTRA FOUNDATIONS
pastas: cavatappi, fusilli, farfalle, angel hair
beans: cannellini, garbanzo
rice: Arborio, basmati, wild
canned salmon

EXTRA FLAVOR BUILDERS
anchovy paste
bottled roasted red bell peppers
chile paste with garlic
mustards: stone-ground, honey
chipotle chiles in adobo sauce
vinegars: sherry, rice
golden raisins
spirits: red and white wine (dry), sherry
fish sauce, hoisin sauce, oyster sauce
sun-dried tomatoes

EXTRA ASSISTANTS
canned crushed tomatoes

SWEETER RETURNS
molasses
powdered sugar
semisweet chocolate
maple syrup

MORE COOL STUFF
cheeses: Romano, Asiago
fresh herbs: basil, cilantro, thyme,
   rosemary
pork tenderloin
fresh fish: catfish, salmon, shrimp
nuts: pecans, walnuts
fresh chiles: jalapeño, serrano
tubes of polenta
olives: kalamata, niçoise
tofu: firm, soft

The Advanced Pantry
Everything contained in the beginner's and intermediate pantries, plus:

EXTRA FOUNDATIONS
cornmeal, grits, semolina flour
beans: fava, soybeans
grains: barley, millet, quinoa,
   bulgur
rice: sticky, sweet, jasmine

EXTRA FLAVOR BUILDERS
specialty oils: walnut,
   truffle-scented
specialty vinegars: herbed,
   Champagne
mustards: spicy brown,
   coarse-ground
spirits: Marsala, Madeira, sake,
   mirin, port
fermented black beans
espresso powder
apricot and raspberry preserves
orange marmalade
sun-dried tomato paste
curry paste

VERY COOL STUFF
homemade stocks (chicken,
   vegetable)
fresh fish: grouper, monkfish,
   amberjack
broader selection of cheeses:
   fontina, provolone, Gorgonzola
refrigerated fresh pastas: tortellini,
   ravioli
nuts: pine nuts, macadamia nuts,
   hazelnuts

Pasta, Beans, 'n' Greens

- 2 teaspoons olive oil
- ½ cup finely chopped carrot
- ½ cup finely chopped onion
- 1 garlic clove, minced
- ½ teaspoon dried oregano
- ¼ teaspoon salt
- ¼ teaspoon freshly ground black pepper
- 1 (15.75-ounce) can fat-free, less-sodium chicken broth
- 1 (14.5-ounce) can Italian-style diced tomatoes, undrained
- ½ cup uncooked penne (tube-shaped pasta)
- 1 (16-ounce) can cannellini beans or other white beans, rinsed and drained
- ½ (10-ounce) package frozen chopped spinach, thawed, drained, and squeezed dry (about ⅓ cup)
- ¼ cup (1 ounce) grated fresh Parmesan cheese

1. Heat oil in a medium saucepan over medium-high heat. Add carrot, onion, and garlic; sauté 5 minutes. Add oregano, salt, pepper, broth, and tomatoes; bring to a boil. Cover, reduce heat, and simmer 10 minutes.

2. Increase heat to medium-high. Add pasta, beans, and spinach; cook 14 minutes or until pasta is done, stirring occasionally. Sprinkle each serving with cheese. Yield: 4 servings (serving size: 1 cup pasta mixture and 1 tablespoon cheese).

CALORIES 300 (21% from fat); FAT 6.9g (sat 1.8g, mono 2.8g, poly 1.6g); PROTEIN 16.8g; CARB 45.2g; FIBER 7.8g; CHOL 5mg; IRON 5.8mg; SODIUM 901mg; CALC 238mg

Florentine Frittata

Frozen hash browns are great to have on hand and pair well with the feta cheese and spinach. For a new twist next time, try a combination of broccoli and sharp cheddar or Swiss cheese.

- 2 tablespoons water
- ½ teaspoon dried basil
- ½ teaspoon freshly ground black pepper
- ¼ teaspoon salt
- ¼ teaspoon dried oregano
- 1 (16-ounce) carton egg substitute
- 1 (10-ounce) package frozen chopped spinach, thawed, drained, and squeezed dry
- 2 teaspoons butter
- 2 cups thinly sliced Vidalia or other sweet onion
- 2 cups frozen shredded hash brown potatoes
- 1 (7-ounce) bottle roasted red bell peppers, drained and sliced
- ¾ cup (3 ounces) crumbled feta cheese

1. Combine first 7 ingredients in a medium bowl; set aside.

2. Melt butter in a 10-inch cast-iron or nonstick skillet over medium heat. Add onion; sauté 5 minutes. Add potatoes; cook 9 minutes or until lightly browned, stirring occasionally. Pour egg mixture over onion mixture. Arrange bell pepper slices on top of frittata. Cook 7 minutes or until set. Sprinkle with cheese. Wrap handle of pan with foil.

3. Preheat broiler.

4. Broil 5 minutes or until cheese is lightly browned. Cut into 4 wedges. Yield: 4 servings (serving size: 1 wedge).

CALORIES 265 (26% from fat); FAT 7.6g (sat 4.6g, mono 1.6g, poly 0.7g); PROTEIN 19.6g; CARB 31.3g; FIBER 5.7g; CHOL 24mg; IRON 5.1mg; SODIUM 800mg; CALC 251mg

Cheesy Polenta Casserole with Roasted Bell Pepper Sauce

The roasted bell peppers and kalamata olives, found in our Intermediate Pantry (list on page 99), make the marinara sauce come alive. Try substituting any Italian cheeses in place of the mozzarella and Parmesan—provolone and Romano in particular.

- 2 cups tomato-and-basil pasta sauce (such as Muir Glen)
- ¼ cup chopped pitted kalamata olives
- 1 tablespoon balsamic vinegar
- ¼ teaspoon freshly ground black pepper
- 1 (7-ounce) bottle roasted red bell peppers, drained and sliced
- Cooking spray
- 1 (16-ounce) tube of polenta, cut into 12 slices
- ¾ cup (3 ounces) shredded part-skim mozzarella cheese
- 2 tablespoons grated fresh Parmesan cheese

1. Preheat oven to 350°.

2. Combine first 5 ingredients in a medium saucepan. Bring to a simmer over medium heat; cook 10 minutes, stirring sauce occasionally. Spread ½ cup sauce in bottom of a 13 x 9-inch baking dish coated with cooking spray. Arrange polenta slices over sauce; spread remaining sauce over polenta. Sprinkle with cheeses. Bake casserole at 350° for 20 minutes or until bubbly. Yield: 4 servings.

CALORIES 221 (28% from fat); FAT 6.9g (sat 3.5g, mono 2g, poly 0.7g); PROTEIN 10.8g; CARB 31.3g; FIBER 2.7g; CHOL 15mg; IRON 2.4mg; SODIUM 800mg; CALC 232mg

Feijoada

Feijoada is a hearty Brazilian stew.

2½ teaspoons olive oil
2 cups chopped onion
1 teaspoon dried thyme
4 garlic cloves, minced
1 (15.75-ounce) can fat-free,
 less-sodium chicken broth
4 (15-ounce) cans black beans,
 rinsed and drained
2 canned chipotle chiles in adobo
 sauce, chopped
1 pound turkey kielbasa, thinly sliced
2 tablespoons chopped fresh parsley

1. Heat oil in a nonstick skillet over
medium-high heat. Add onion, thyme,
and garlic; sauté 5 minutes. Stir in broth,
scraping pan to loosen browned bits.
Add beans, chiles, and kielbasa. Cover,
reduce heat, and simmer 45 minutes,
stirring occasionally. Sprinkle with parsley. Yield: 7 servings (serving size: 1 cup).

CALORIES 415 (26% from fat); FAT 12.2g (sat 3.5g, mono 4.9g,
poly 3.1g); PROTEIN 28.6g; CARB 50.6g; FIBER 8.9g; CHOL 43mg;
IRON 5.3mg; SODIUM 1250mg; CALC 86mg

in season

Fruit of the Desert

*Another staple of the Mexican kitchen has
arrived—the tender pads of the* nopal, *or
prickly pear cactus.*

When cooked, the oblong green pads
(also called paddles) have the texture and
taste of sautéed bell pepper with a hint of
green bean flavor. Nopal also contains a
sticky substance, making it a natural
thickener when added to soups and stews.

Creamy Rice with Nopalitos

3 *nopales* (cactus paddles), trimmed
 (about 9 ounces)
2 poblano or Anaheim chiles (about
 8 ounces)
 Cooking spray
1½ teaspoons olive oil
½ cup chopped onion
2 garlic cloves, minced
1½ cups uncooked basmati or other
 long-grain rice
3 cups fat-free, less-sodium chicken
 broth
1 (8-ounce) carton plain fat-free
 yogurt
1 (8-ounce) carton fat-free sour cream
1 (4-ounce) jar diced pimiento,
 drained
1½ cups (6 ounces) shredded
 Monterey Jack cheese

1. Preheat oven to 375°.
2. Place nopales and chiles on a baking
sheet coated with cooking spray; bake at
375° for 20 minutes or until chiles are
blackened and nopales are tender, turning nopales once. Place chiles in a zip-
top plastic bag; seal. Let stand 15
minutes. Peel chiles; cut in half lengthwise. Discard seeds and membranes;
chop chiles to measure ½ cup. Chop
nopales to measure 1 cup.
3. Reduce oven temperature to 350°.
4. While nopales and chiles cook, prepare rice. Heat oil in a Dutch oven over
medium heat. Add onion and garlic;
sauté 5 minutes or until tender. Add rice,
and sauté 2 minutes. Add chicken broth;
bring to a boil. Cover, reduce heat, and
simmer 25 minutes or until liquid is absorbed. Cool slightly.
5. Add nopalitos (chopped nopales),
chiles, yogurt, sour cream, and pimiento
to rice mixture; stir until well blended.
Spoon mixture into an 11 x 7-inch baking dish coated with cooking spray, and
sprinkle with cheese. Bake at 350° for 12
minutes. Broil 8 minutes or until lightly
browned. Yield: 8 servings (serving size:
1 cup).

CALORIES 274 (26% from fat); FAT 7.8g (sat 4.3g, mono 2.6g,
poly 0.5g); PROTEIN 13.2g; CARB 35.9g; FIBER 1.2g; CHOL 17mg;
IRON 2.2mg; SODIUM 344mg; CALC 297mg

Confetti Cactus Salad

You can also serve this salad as a chunky
salsa with baked tortilla chips.

SALAD:

1 cup *nopalitos* (about 3 chopped
 nopales [cactus paddles])
1 cup chopped red onion
1 cup fresh corn kernels (about 2 ears)
¼ cup finely chopped fresh cilantro
1 (15-ounce) can black beans, rinsed
 and drained

VINAIGRETTE:

2 tablespoons balsamic vinegar
1 tablespoon sugar
1 tablespoon fresh lime juice
1 teaspoon vegetable oil
¼ teaspoon salt

1. To prepare salad, cook nopalitos in
boiling water 10 minutes. Drain. Place
nopalitos in a medium bowl; cool. Add
onion, corn, cilantro, and beans; toss
gently.
2. To prepare vinaigrette, combine vinegar and remaining 4 ingredients in a jar;
cover tightly, and shake vigorously. Pour
vinaigrette over salad; toss gently to
coat. Cover and chill. Yield: 4 servings
(serving size: 1 cup).

CALORIES 163 (12% from fat); FAT 2.2g (sat 0.4g, mono 0.5g,
poly 1g); PROTEIN 8g; CARB 31.1g; FIBER 5.6g; CHOL 0mg;
IRON 2.1mg; SODIUM 293mg; CALC 94mg

Cactus Pointers

- The cactus paddles or pads are
 called *nopales* when whole and
 nopalitos when diced or cut into strips.
- Select nopales that are firm and
 about the size of your hand.
- Wrapped in a plastic bag or plastic
 wrap, nopales will keep for a week in
 the refrigerator.
- Much like okra, nopales tend to be a
 bit gooey; this can be minimized with
 the right cooking technique. We tried
 roasting, blanching, and boiling, and
 found that boiling gave us the best
 result.

1. *Cut off spines with a vegetable peeler or knife, and remove green nubs with a scrubbing pad or cloth.*

2. *Trim away any bruised or dried parts.*

Nopalitos con Huevos
Cactus with Eggs

⅓ cup *nopalitos* (about 1 chopped
   nopal [cactus paddle])
3 large eggs
3 large egg whites
1 tablespoon fat-free milk
⅛ teaspoon salt
⅛ teaspoon black pepper
Cooking spray
½ cup finely chopped onion
½ cup chopped tomato
4 (6-inch) corn tortillas
2 teaspoons minced fresh
   cilantro

1. Cook nopalitos in boiling water 10 minutes. Drain.
2. Combine 3 eggs and next 4 ingredients; stir well with a whisk.

3. Heat a medium nonstick skillet coated with cooking spray over medium heat. Add onion, and sauté 2 minutes or until tender. Add egg mixture; cook until bottom begins to set, stirring gent-ly to scramble. Stir in tomato and nopalitos, and cook 1 minute.
4. Warm tortillas according to package directions. Spoon about ½ cup egg mixture onto each tortilla. Sprinkle evenly with minced cilantro; fold in half. Yield: 2 servings (serving size: 2 filled tortillas).

CALORIES 288 (30% from fat); FAT 9.7g (sat 2.7g, mono 3.4g, poly 1.9g); PROTEIN 19.2g; CARB 31.9g; FIBER 4.5g; CHOL 332mg; IRON 2.4mg; SODIUM 413mg; CALC 192mg

Tomatillo-and-Cactus Soup

4 (6-inch) corn tortillas, divided
Cooking spray
1 pound tomatillos (about 16 medium)
1 cup *nopalitos* (about 3 chopped
   nopales [cactus paddles])
¼ cup chopped Vidalia or other
   sweet onion
2 garlic cloves, minced
1 tablespoon honey
½ teaspoon ground cumin
¼ teaspoon salt
1 (15.75-ounce) can fat-free,
   less-sodium chicken broth
5 tablespoons fat-free sour cream
Cilantro sprigs (optional)

1. Preheat oven to 375°.
2. Cut 1 corn tortilla into ¼-inch-wide strips. Place tortilla strips on a baking sheet coated with cooking spray. Bake at 375° for 5 minutes or until browned.
3. Discard husks and stems from tomatillos. Cook whole tomatillos and nopalitos in boiling water 10 minutes or until tender; drain.
4. Heat a medium saucepan coated with cooking spray over medium-high heat. Add onion and garlic, and sauté 3 minutes or until tender. Cut 3 corn tortillas into 4 wedges each. Place tortilla wedges, tomatillos, nopalitos, onion mixture, honey, ground cumin, salt, and broth in a blender; process until smooth.
5. Place mixture in pan, and cook over low heat 15 minutes or until thoroughly heated. Spoon 1 cup soup into each of 5 bowls. Divide baked tortilla strips evenly over servings. Top each serving with 1 tablespoon sour cream. Garnish with cilantro sprigs, if desired. Yield: 5 servings.

CALORIES 110 (7% from fat); FAT 0.9g (sat 0.1g, mono 0.2g, poly 0.4g); PROTEIN 5.2g; CARB 21.2g; FIBER 2.8g; CHOL 0mg; IRON 1.1mg; SODIUM 371mg; CALC 122mg

Pupusa Casserole

A *pupusa* is a patty of masa harina dough filled with meat and cheese, flattened, and baked. This easier version eliminates having to fill and shape individual patties.

FILLING:

2 cups *nopalitos* (about 6 chopped
   nopales [cactus paddles])
2 (4-ounce) skinless, boneless
   chicken breast halves
½ teaspoon salt
½ teaspoon ground cumin
¼ teaspoon black pepper
Cooking spray
¾ cup finely chopped onion
2 garlic cloves, minced
1 cup (4 ounces) shredded Monterey
   Jack cheese with jalapeño peppers,
   divided

DOUGH:

2¼ cups masa harina
1 cup water
¾ teaspoon salt

1. Preheat oven to 375°.
2. To prepare filling, cook nopalitos in boiling water 10 minutes. Drain.
3. Sprinkle chicken with ½ teaspoon salt, cumin, and pepper. Heat a medium nonstick skillet coated with cooking spray over medium heat. Add chicken; cook 4 minutes on each side or until done. Remove chicken from pan; cool slightly, and shred with 2 forks.
4. Heat pan coated with cooking spray over medium heat. Add onion and garlic; sauté 4 minutes or until tender. Stir in nopalitos, chicken, and ⅔ cup cheese. Cook 5 minutes or until thoroughly heated.
5. To prepare dough, combine masa harina, water, and ¾ teaspoon salt in a

medium bowl. Turn dough out onto a lightly floured surface; knead lightly. Press one-third of dough into an 11 x 7-inch baking dish coated with cooking spray. Spread filling over dough. Gently press remaining dough into a 4-inch square on heavy-duty plastic wrap. Cover with additional plastic wrap. Roll, still covered, into an 11 x 7-inch rectangle. Remove bottom sheet of plastic wrap; fit dough over filling. Remove top sheet of plastic wrap. Bake at 375° for 20 minutes. Sprinkle with ⅓ cup cheese. Bake an additional 5 minutes or until cheese melts. Yield: 8 servings.

CALORIES 234 (27% from fat); FAT 7g (sat 3.2g, mono 1.9g, poly 1g); PROTEIN 16g; CARB 26.8g; FIBER 1.6g; CHOL 35mg; IRON 3.3mg; SODIUM 474mg; CALC 244mg

taste of america

Great ¡Gusto!

A special edition from Cooking Light *captures the essence of sabores Latinos.*

The recipes in *¡Gusto!* emphasize Latino authenticity and flavor while reflecting our signature philosophies of nutrition and accessibility.

Sangría

1   cup fresh orange juice (about 2 oranges)
⅓   cup sugar
1   (750-milliliter) bottle Merlot or other dry red wine
4   whole cloves
1   (8 x 1-inch) orange rind strip
2   (3-inch) cinnamon sticks
1   orange, thinly sliced and seeded
1   lemon, thinly sliced and seeded
2   cups club soda

1. Combine first 3 ingredients in a large pitcher, stirring mixture until sugar dissolves.
2. Press cloves into rind strip. Add strip, cinnamon, and fruit to wine mixture. Chill at least 30 minutes. Stir in club soda just before serving. Yield: 1½ quarts (serving size: 1 cup).

CALORIES 160 (0% from fat); FAT 0.1g; PROTEIN 1g; CARB 20.3g; FIBER 1.1g; CHOL 0mg; IRON 1.2mg; SODIUM 30mg; CALC 36mg

Asopao de Pollo
Traditional Chicken Asopao

The Puerto Rican dish *asopao*, a cross between soup and paella, is an easy, hearty one-dish meal. *Alcaparrado* is a mixture of whole green olives, pimientos, and capers; look for it in the Latin section of the supermarket.

1   teaspoon dried oregano
¼   teaspoon salt
¼   teaspoon freshly ground black pepper
2   garlic cloves, minced
10   chicken thighs (about 3 pounds), skinned
2   tablespoons Annatto Oil (recipe at right) or olive oil
1½   cups Sofrito (recipe at right)
¾   cup diced plum tomato
1½   cups uncooked medium-grain rice
⅔   cup dry white wine
½   cup diced lean ham (about 2 ounces)
1   (4.4-ounce) bottle *alcaparrado* (such as Goya), drained, or
¾   cup pitted green olives and
¼   cup capers
4   cups water
1   (15.75-ounce) can fat-free, less-sodium chicken broth
1   cup frozen green peas, thawed

1. Combine first 4 ingredients in a small bowl. Sprinkle chicken with oregano mixture.
2. Heat Annatto Oil in a large nonstick skillet over medium-high heat. Add chicken; cook 8 minutes, turning once. Reduce heat to medium. Add Sofrito and tomato; cook 3 minutes, stirring frequently. Add rice, wine, ham, and alcaparrado; cook 1 minute, stirring constantly. Add water and chicken broth; bring to a boil. Cover, reduce heat, and simmer 20 minutes. Stir in peas, and cook 5 minutes or until rice is tender. Yield: 5 servings (serving size: 2 thighs and 1¾ cups rice mixture).

CALORIES 561 (27% from fat); FAT 17g (sat 3.2g, mono 9.7g, poly 2.8g); PROTEIN 37.3g; CARB 63.2g; FIBER 5.1g; CHOL 118mg; IRON 6.5mg; SODIUM 999mg; CALC 72mg

Aceite de Achiote
Annatto Oil

Although annatto doesn't add much flavor, it gives the oil a bright orange-red color.

2   cups olive oil
½   cup annatto (achiote seed)

1. Combine oil and seeds in a small saucepan, and bring to a simmer over medium heat. Reduce heat to low; cook 5 minutes. Cool. Strain through a sieve into a bowl; discard seeds. Yield: 2 cups (serving size: 1 tablespoon).

CALORIES 119 (100% from fat); FAT 13.5g (sat 1.8g, mono 10g, poly 1.1g); PROTEIN 0g; CARB 0g; FIBER 0g; CHOL 0mg; IRON 0.1mg; SODIUM 0mg; CALC 0mg

Sofrito

This mixture is akin to the French *mirepoix* and a basic building block for many recipes.

2   tablespoons Annatto Oil (recipe above) or olive oil
3   cups finely chopped onion
1½   cups finely chopped red bell pepper
1½   cups finely chopped green bell pepper
4   garlic cloves, minced
½   cup chopped fresh cilantro
1   tablespoon tomato paste
¼   teaspoon salt
¼   teaspoon black pepper

1. Heat Annatto Oil in a large nonstick skillet over medium-high heat. Add onion; sauté 1 minute. Add bell peppers and garlic. Cook 10 minutes; stir frequently. Stir in cilantro and remaining ingredients. Yield: 3 cups (serving size: ¼ cup).

CALORIES 49 (50% from fat); FAT 2.5g (sat 0.4g, mono 1.7g, poly 0.3g); PROTEIN 1g; CARB 6.4g; FIBER 1.6g; CHOL 0mg; IRON 0.8mg; SODIUM 54mg; CALC 17mg

Empanaditas de Guayaba y Queso
Sweet Empanaditas
(pictured on page 95)

Masa de Empanadas (*Empanada Dough*)
- ½ cup (4 ounces) tub-style light cream cheese
- 4 ounces guava paste (such as Goya), cut into 24 cubes
- 1 teaspoon water
- 1 large egg, lightly beaten
- Cooking spray
- 1 tablespoon sugar

1. Preheat oven to 400°.

2. Cut Empanada Dough into 24 circles using a 3-inch biscuit cutter.

3. Spoon 1 teaspoon cream cheese onto half of each circle, leaving a ¼-inch border. Top cheese with 1 cube of guava paste. Combine water and egg; brush egg mixture around edge of each circle. Fold dough over filling; press edges together with a fork or fingers to seal.

4. Place empanaditas on a baking sheet coated with cooking spray. Pierce tops of empanaditas several times with a fork. Brush with remaining egg mixture.

5. Sprinkle with sugar, and bake at 400° for 17 minutes or until golden. Yield: 2 dozen (serving size: 1 empanadita).

CALORIES 104 (42% from fat); FAT 4.8g (sat 1.3g, mono 1.6g, poly 1.5g); PROTEIN 1.9g; CARB 13.3g; FIBER 0.3g; CHOL 12mg; IRON 0.5mg; SODIUM 79mg; CALC 11mg

MASA DE EMPANADAS (EMPANADA DOUGH):
Most easy empanada recipes we found call for a commercial piecrust; by making our own lower-fat crust, we cut 230 calories and about 25 grams of fat.

- 2 cups all-purpose flour, divided
- 6 tablespoons ice water
- 1 teaspoon cider vinegar
- 2 tablespoons powdered sugar
- ½ teaspoon salt
- ½ cup vegetable shortening

1. Lightly spoon flour into dry measuring cups; level with a knife. Combine ½ cup flour, water, and vinegar, stirring with a whisk until well blended to form a slurry.

2. Combine 1½ cups flour, sugar, and salt in a bowl, stirring with a whisk; cut in shortening with a pastry blender or 2 knives until mixture resembles coarse meal. Add slurry; toss with a fork until flour mixture is moist.

3. Gently press mixture into a 4-inch circle on heavy-duty plastic wrap, and cover with additional plastic wrap. Roll dough, still covered, into an 18 x 12-inch rectangle; freeze 10 minutes or until plastic wrap can be easily removed. Remove 2 sheets plastic wrap, and place dough on a lightly floured surface; let stand 1 minute. Cut dough as directed according to specific recipe. Chill cut dough until ready to use. Yield: 1 empanada dough recipe.

CALORIES 1,690 (46% from fat); FAT 87.3g (sat 17.4g, mono 31.6g, poly 33.3g); PROTEIN 25.8g; CARB 198.5g; FIBER 6.8g; CHOL 0mg; IRON 11.6mg; SODIUM 1,177mg; CALC 39mg

Llapingachos Ecuatorianos
Ecuadorean Potato-and-Cheese Patties

- 1½ teaspoons kosher salt
- 2 medium peeled baking potatoes, quartered (about 1¼ pounds)
- 6 tablespoons (1½ ounces) shredded *queso fresco* or Monterey Jack cheese
- 2 tablespoons minced green onions
- ¼ teaspoon kosher salt
- ¼ teaspoon freshly ground black pepper
- 1 tablespoon olive oil
- ¾ cup diced tomato
- ½ cup julienne-cut red onion

1. Place 1½ teaspoons salt and potato in a saucepan, and cover with water. Bring to a boil; reduce heat, and simmer 15 minutes or until tender. Drain and mash with a potato masher until smooth. Cool.

2. Add cheese, green onions, ¼ teaspoon salt, and pepper to potato mixture, stirring well. Divide potato mixture into 6 balls (about ½ cup per ball). Flatten balls into ½-inch-thick patties (about 3-inch diameter). Place on a baking sheet; cover and refrigerate 20 minutes or until firm.

3. Heat oil in a large nonstick skillet over medium heat. Place potato-and-cheese patties in pan; cook 5 minutes or until bottoms are browned. Turn patties; cook 3 minutes. Remove patties from pan. Top patties with tomato and red onion. Yield: 6 servings (serving size: 1 patty).

CALORIES 157 (26% from fat); FAT 4.6g (sat 1.8g, mono 1.3g, poly 1.2g); PROTEIN 4.2g; CARB 24.9g; FIBER 2.1g; CHOL 6mg; IRON 0.6mg; SODIUM 279mg; CALC 64mg

Tres Leches Cake

Tres leches ("three milks") is a cake drenched in sweet, milky syrup and topped with meringue.

CAKE:
- Cooking spray
- 1 tablespoon all-purpose flour
- ¼ teaspoon salt
- 4 large egg whites
- ⅔ cup sugar
- 1 teaspoon vanilla extract
- 3 large eggs
- ⅔ cup all-purpose flour

MILK MIXTURE:
- 1 cup half-and-half
- 1 (14-ounce) can fat-free sweetened condensed milk
- 1 (12-ounce) can fat-free evaporated milk

MERINGUE:
- 3 large egg whites
- 1 cup sugar
- ⅓ cup water
- 1 teaspoon lemon rind
- 1 teaspoon vanilla extract

1. Preheat oven to 350°.

2. To prepare cake, coat a 13 x 9-inch baking dish with cooking spray; dust with 1 tablespoon flour.

3. Place salt and 4 egg whites in a large bowl; beat with a mixer at high speed until soft peaks form. Gradually add ⅔ cup sugar, 1 tablespoon at a time, beating until stiff peaks form. Place 1 teaspoon vanilla and 3 eggs in a large bowl; beat until thick and pale (about 3 minutes). Gently fold egg white mixture into egg mixture. Lightly spoon ⅔ cup flour into dry measuring cups; level with a knife. Gently fold flour into egg mixture. Spoon batter into prepared dish. Bake at 350° for 20 minutes or until cake springs back when touched lightly in center. Cool 5 minutes in pan on a wire rack.

4. To prepare milk mixture, combine half-and-half, condensed milk, and evaporated milk. Pierce entire top of cake with a fork, and pour milk mixture over cake.

5. To prepare meringue, beat 3 egg whites with a mixer at high speed until foamy, using clean, dry beaters. Combine 1 cup sugar and ⅓ cup water in a saucepan; bring to a boil. Cook, without stirring, until candy thermometer registers 238°. Pour hot sugar syrup in a thin stream over egg whites, beating at high speed. Stir in rind and 1 teaspoon vanilla. Spread over cake. Yield: 12 servings (serving size: 1 slice).

CALORIES 309 (11% from fat); FAT 3.9g (sat 1.9g, mono 1.2g, poly 0.4g); PROTEIN 9.7g; CARB 58.5g; FIBER 0.2g; CHOL 68mg; IRON 0.7mg; SODIUM 171mg; CALC 197mg

lighten up

A Cake That Soars

When this reader hijacked her favorite cake recipe, she was left stranded on the runway by its fat and calories.

Flight attendant Kim Henry has enjoyed her share of great food from around the world. But for the Dallas resident, nothing compares to the Strawberry-and-Cream Cake she sampled at a party.

Eager to produce the strawberry delight herself, Kim nabbed a copy of the recipe. Knowing this version simply wouldn't fly, she turned to *Cooking Light* for help.

By cutting out almost a cup of butter and switching to reduced-fat cream cheese, we were able to slash more than 1,600 calories and 187 grams of fat. Additionally, we steered away from whipping cream—which had contributed a quarter of the fat—to a fat-free whipped topping that's just as tasty.

Strawberry-and-Cream Cake

CAKE:
Cooking spray
¾ cup sliced strawberries
2 cups granulated sugar
6 tablespoons butter, softened
1 (3-ounce) package strawberry-flavored gelatin
3 large eggs
2¼ cups all-purpose flour
2½ teaspoons baking powder
1¼ cups 1% low-fat milk
1 teaspoon vanilla extract

FILLING:
1½ cups frozen fat-free whipped topping, thawed
2 tablespoons granulated sugar
½ teaspoon vanilla extract

FROSTING:
1 (8-ounce) block ⅓-less-fat cream cheese
¼ cup butter, softened
¼ teaspoon vanilla extract
1 cup powdered sugar

REMAINING INGREDIENTS:
¾ cup sliced strawberries
1½ cups quartered strawberries

1. Preheat oven to 350°.

2. To prepare cake, coat 2 (9-inch) round cake pans with cooking spray; line bottoms of pans with wax paper. Coat wax paper with cooking spray.

3. Place ¾ cup sliced strawberries in a blender; process until smooth.

4. Place 2 cups granulated sugar, 6 tablespoons butter, and gelatin in a large bowl; beat with a mixer at medium speed until blended (about 5 minutes). Add eggs, 1 at a time, beating well after each addition.

5. Lightly spoon flour into dry measuring cups; level with a knife. Combine flour and baking powder, stirring well with a whisk. Add flour mixture to sugar mixture alternately with milk, beginning and ending with flour mixture. Stir in pureed strawberries and 1 teaspoon vanilla.

6. Pour batter into prepared pans; sharply tap pans once on counter to remove air bubbles. Bake at 350° for

45 minutes or until a wooden pick inserted in center comes out clean. Cool in pans 10 minutes on a wire rack, and remove from pans. Peel off wax paper, and cool completely on a wire rack.

7. To prepare filling, combine whipped topping, 2 tablespoons granulated sugar, and ½ teaspoon vanilla in a small bowl.

8. To prepare frosting, beat cream cheese, ¼ cup butter, and ¼ teaspoon vanilla in a medium bowl with a mixer at low speed just until well blended (do not overbeat). Gradually add powdered sugar, and beat just until well blended (do not overbeat).

9. Place 1 cake layer on a plate; spread with ¾ cup filling. Arrange ¾ cup sliced strawberries over filling; top with remaining cake layer. Spread remaining filling over top of cake. Spread frosting over sides of cake. Arrange quartered strawberries on top of cake. Store cake loosely covered in refrigerator. Yield: 18 servings (serving size: 1 slice).

CALORIES 322 (30% from fat); FAT 10.6g (sat 6.3g, mono 3.1g, poly 0.6g); PROTEIN 5.1g; CARB 51.6g; FIBER 1g; CHOL 64mg; IRON 1.1mg; SODIUM 255mg; CALC 80mg

BEFORE	AFTER
SERVING SIZE	
1 slice	
CALORIES PER SERVING	
470	322
FAT	
28.9g	10.6g
PERCENT OF TOTAL CALORIES	
55%	30%

How to Cook French

Fabulous dishes from surprisingly commonplace ingredients characterize real French cooking.

French cuisine is based on a few simple tenets. The most important of these is a total devotion to using the finest possible ingredients at their peak of freshness. The techniques are mostly simple, the use of ingredients based firmly on the belief that less is more. For instance, it's not a matter of slapping in more butter and cream but in knowing when to add a bit of either or both in order to elevate a dish to the sublime.

French cuisine is most commonly associated with sophisticated, complex, and sometimes fussy dishes, the sort of food you'd get in starred restaurants. But the simple, hearty cooking presented here is the real basis of all French cuisine, for it is the cuisine of the hearth and of the land.

Coquilles St. Jacques with Curry

Coquilles, or scallops, are a winter and spring delicacy in France, served for special occasions.

- 4 teaspoons butter, divided
- 3 cups finely chopped leek (about 3 leeks)
- ¼ teaspoon kosher or sea salt
- ¼ teaspoon white pepper
- 2 cups Sauvignon Blanc or other dry white wine
- 10 thyme sprigs
- 5 black peppercorns
- 1 bay leaf
- 1 pound sea scallops
- 1 tablespoon all-purpose flour
- ¼ cup half-and-half
- ¼ teaspoon curry powder

1. Melt 2 teaspoons butter in a medium nonstick skillet over medium heat. Add leek, salt, and pepper; cover and cook 10 minutes, stirring frequently. Set aside; keep warm.

2. Combine wine, thyme, peppercorns, and bay leaf in a medium saucepan. Bring to a boil; cover, reduce heat, and simmer 5 minutes. Add scallops to wine mixture. Remove from heat, and let stand 5 minutes. Remove scallops with a slotted spoon; keep warm. Strain wine mixture through a sieve into a bowl, reserving 1 cup. Discard remaining wine mixture.

3. Melt 2 teaspoons butter in a small saucepan over medium heat. Stir in flour with a whisk; cook 2 minutes. Gradually add reserved wine mixture, stirring constantly with a whisk. Cook 5 minutes. Add half-and-half and curry, stirring with a whisk; cook 2 minutes or until thick. Add scallops to curry mixture; cook 1 minute or until thoroughly heated.

4. Divide leek mixture evenly among 4 plates. Top with scallop mixture. Yield: 4 servings (serving size: ⅓ cup leek mixture, 3 ounces scallops, and about ¼ cup sauce).

WINE NOTE: In this recipe, the meatiness of the scallops is enriched by half-and-half and emboldened by curry. Choose a wine that's round in the mouth and slightly buttery, but with a refreshing acidity running through it. A white Burgundy would be perfect. If price is no object, try the Chassagne-Montrachet from Bernard Morey ($28.50); if it is, try Louis Jadot's Mâcon-Villages ($11).

CALORIES 215 (28% from fat); FAT 6.7g (sat 3.6g, mono 1.7g, poly 0.7g); PROTEIN 21.2g; CARB 17.7g; FIBER 1.1g; CHOL 53mg; IRON 2.6mg; SODIUM 400mg; CALC 101mg

Tarte aux Pommes
Apple Tart

- 1½ cups all-purpose flour
- ¼ teaspoon salt
- 5 tablespoons chilled unsalted butter, cut into small pieces
- 6 tablespoons ice water
- 6 cups sliced peeled Granny Smith apple (about 2 pounds)
- ⅓ cup sugar or vanilla sugar
- 1 large egg white, lightly beaten

1. Lightly spoon flour into dry measuring cups; level with a knife. Combine flour and salt in a food processor; pulse 2 times. Add butter; pulse 4 times or until mixture resembles coarse meal. With processor on, slowly add ice water through food chute, processing just until combined (do not form a ball). Gently press mixture into a 4-inch circle on plastic wrap; cover. Chill 15 minutes. Slightly overlap 2 lengths of plastic wrap on a slightly damp surface. Unwrap chilled dough; place on plastic wrap. Cover with 2 additional lengths of overlapping plastic wrap. Roll dough, still covered, into a 14-inch circle. Place dough in freezer 5 minutes or until plastic wrap can be easily removed. Remove bottom sheets of plastic wrap. Fit chilled dough into a 10-inch tart pan, pressing dough against sides of pan and allowing it to extend over edge of pan. Remove top sheets of plastic wrap.

2. Preheat oven to 425°.

3. Arrange half of apple slices in bottom of tart pan; sprinkle with half of sugar. Repeat layers. Fold dough over apple slices (dough will partially cover apple slices). Brush dough with egg white. Place pan on a baking sheet.

4. Bake at 425° for 45 minutes or until apple is tender and crust is lightly browned (shield tart with foil if it becomes too brown). Cool on a wire rack. Yield: 8 servings (serving size: 1 wedge).

CALORIES 249 (29% from fat); FAT 8g (sat 3.5g, mono 2.6g, poly 0.7g); PROTEIN 3.1g; CARB 43g; FIBER 2.8g; CHOL 23mg; IRON 1.2mg; SODIUM 168mg; CALC 11mg

Pommes Anna Step-by-Steps

1. *Melt butter in a 10-inch cast-iron or heavy skillet. A heavy skillet is a must because it conducts heat well, producing the traditional crisp, browned crust—the hallmark of this dish.*

2. *Layer potatoes in an overlapping fashion for a total of six layers. They might be slightly mounded in center.*

3. *Press down on finished layers with bottom of a clean, heavy pan or your hands. You want potatoes to be dense and compact so that they hold together.*

Pommes Anna
Potatoes Anna

    1 teaspoon kosher or sea salt
    ½ teaspoon black pepper
   2½ tablespoons unsalted butter
    3 pounds peeled baking potatoes,
       cut into ⅛-inch-thick slices
    1 tablespoon unsalted butter, melted
       and divided
    1 tablespoon chopped fresh flat-leaf
       parsley (optional)

1. Preheat oven to 450°.
2. Combine salt and pepper in a bowl.
3. Melt 2½ tablespoons butter in a 10-inch cast-iron or ovenproof heavy skillet over medium heat. Arrange a single layer of potato slices, slightly overlapping, in a circular pattern in pan; sprinkle with ¼ teaspoon salt mixture. Drizzle ½ teaspoon melted butter over potatoes. Repeat layers 5 times, ending with butter. Press firmly to pack. Cover and bake at 450° for 20 minutes.
4. Uncover and bake an additional 25 minutes or until potatoes are golden. Loosen edges of potatoes with a spatula. Place a plate upside down on top of pan; invert potatoes onto plate. Sprinkle with parsley, if desired. Yield: 8 servings (serving size: 1 wedge).

CALORIES 208 (23% from fat); FAT 5.2g (sat 3.2g, mono 1.5g, poly 0.3g); PROTEIN 3.4g; CARB 36.7g; FIBER 2.6g; CHOL 14mg; IRON 0.7mg; SODIUM 353mg; CALC 11mg

Savory Onion Tart

    ½ teaspoon dry yeast
    ½ teaspoon sugar
    ¾ cup warm water (100° to 110°)
   2¼ cups all-purpose flour, divided
    1 teaspoon kosher or sea salt, divided
       Cooking spray
   1½ teaspoons olive oil
    6 cups thinly sliced onion
    2 tablespoons half-and-half
   1½ tablespoons chopped fresh thyme,
       divided
    ¼ teaspoon black pepper

1. Dissolve yeast and sugar in warm water in a large bowl; let stand 5 minutes. Lightly spoon flour into dry measuring cups, and level with a knife. Add 2 cups flour and ½ teaspoon salt to yeast mixture, stirring until smooth. Turn dough out onto a floured surface. Knead until smooth and elastic (about 5 minutes), and add enough of remaining flour, 1 tablespoon at a time, to prevent dough from sticking to hands (dough will feel tacky).
2. Place dough in a large bowl coated with cooking spray, turning to coat top. Cover and let rise in a warm place (85°), free from drafts, 1 hour or until doubled in size. (Press two fingers into dough. If indentation remains, dough has risen enough.) Punch dough down; cover and let rest 5 minutes. Roll dough into a 12-inch circle on a floured surface. Fit into a 10-inch round removable-bottom tart pan. Press dough against bottom and sides of pan.
3. Preheat oven to 425°.
4. Heat oil in a large nonstick skillet over medium heat. Add onion; cover and cook 20 minutes or until golden brown, stirring frequently. Remove from heat; stir in ½ teaspoon salt, half-and-half, and 1 tablespoon thyme. Spread mixture over dough in pan. Bake at 425° for 25 minutes or until crust is golden brown. Sprinkle with 1½ teaspoons thyme and pepper. Let stand 5 minutes. Cut into 6 wedges. Yield: 6 servings.

CALORIES 238 (10% from fat); FAT 2.7g (sat 0.7g, mono 1.2g, poly 0.6g); PROTEIN 6.6g; CARB 46.7g; FIBER 3.7g; CHOL 2mg; IRON 2.7mg; SODIUM 327mg; CALC 39mg

How We Lightened French

Aside from removing a teaspoon or two of oil or butter, these recipes are as authentic as any you might find in a French home or bistro. Though it may be surprising, no artifice, stretching, or extreme efforts were necessary to make these recipes low-fat. They are presented here as they are typically made, with the freshest possible seasonal ingredients, used as carefully and simply as possible.

Artichoke-and-Spinach Tian

Tian is the Provençal name for *gratin*, which is usually a vegetable dish but occasionally includes meat. Traditionally made with small purple artichokes of Provence called *poivrades*, it's also flavorful made with the more common, larger artichokes.

2   (10-ounce) bags fresh spinach
2   garlic cloves, minced
6   cups water
2   tablespoons fresh lemon juice
8   large artichokes
½   teaspoon kosher or sea salt
¼   teaspoon black pepper
    Cooking spray
1¼ cups (5 ounces) grated Gruyère cheese, divided

1. Heat a large nonstick skillet over medium heat. Add spinach in batches, turning frequently until wilted (about 7 minutes). Drain spinach (it should be neither wet nor dry, but moist). Combine spinach and garlic in a medium bowl.
2. Combine water and lemon juice. Working with 1 artichoke at a time, cut off stem to within 1 inch of base; peel stem. Remove bottom leaves and tough outer leaves, leaving tender heart and bottom. Cut artichoke in half lengthwise. Remove fuzzy thistle from bottom with a spoon. Thinly slice artichoke heart; place in lemon water. Repeat procedure with remaining artichokes. Drain. (You should have about 4 cups sliced artichoke.) Sprinkle artichoke with salt and pepper.
3. Preheat oven to 375°.
4. Arrange 3 cups artichoke in an 11 x 7-inch baking dish coated with cooking spray. Sprinkle with ½ cup cheese. Arrange remaining artichoke and spinach over cheese.
5. Cover and bake at 375° for 15 minutes. Uncover and bake 30 minutes. Sprinkle with ¾ cup cheese. Bake an additional 10 minutes or until artichoke is tender. Yield: 6 servings (serving size: about 1 cup).

CALORIES 252 (31% from fat); FAT 8.8g (sat 4.7g, mono 2.4g, poly 0.8g); PROTEIN 16.5g; CARB 34g; FIBER 16.8g; CHOL 26mg; IRON 6.7mg; SODIUM 514mg; CALC 455mg

---

French Bistro Menu
Côtes de Porc
Baked French fries*
Romaine leaves with low-fat Dijon dressing
Fresh sliced pears with chopped pistachios

*Slice 2 pounds red potatoes into ¼-inch cubed strips; place strips in a large zip-top plastic bag. Add 2 tablespoons olive oil and ½ teaspoon salt; toss well. Arrange on baking sheets; bake at 450° for 20 minutes, turning once.

Côtes de Porc

Cornichons, French for "gherkins," are tart pickles made from tiny gherkin cucumbers.

6   (6-ounce) bone-in loin pork chops (about ½ inch thick), trimmed
½   teaspoon kosher or sea salt, divided
½   teaspoon black pepper, divided
1   tablespoon olive oil, divided
½   cup minced shallots (about 4)
⅔   cup fat-free, less-sodium chicken broth
⅔   cup white wine
1   teaspoon Dijon mustard
¼   cup thinly sliced *cornichons*
¼   cup chopped fresh flat-leaf parsley

1. Sprinkle pork chops with ¼ teaspoon salt and ¼ teaspoon pepper. Heat 2 teaspoons oil in a large nonstick skillet over medium-high heat. Add pork; cook 8 minutes or until golden brown, turning after 4 minutes. Remove pork from pan; keep warm. Add 1 teaspoon oil and shallots to pan; cook 1 minute or until soft, stirring constantly. Stir in broth and wine, scraping pan to loosen browned bits. Bring to a boil; cook until reduced to ½ cup (about 8 minutes). Stir in ¼ teaspoon salt, ¼ teaspoon pepper, and mustard. Remove from heat; stir in cornichons. Arrange pork on a platter; pour sauce over pork. Sprinkle with parsley. Yield: 6 servings (serving size: 1 pork chop and about 1½ tablespoons sauce).

CALORIES 165 (42% from fat); FAT 7.7g (sat 2.2g, mono 4.2g, poly 0.8g); PROTEIN 17.5g; CARB 5.4g; FIBER 0.3g; CHOL 48mg; IRON 1.2mg; SODIUM 375mg; CALC 16mg

---

Baguette

Nothing symbolizes France better than its breads, particularly the long, thin baguette. The key to success is not to add too much flour to the dough, and to let it rise for the required time and slowly.

1   package dry yeast (about 2¼ teaspoons)
1   cup warm water (100° to 110°)
3   cups all-purpose flour, divided
2   teaspoons kosher or sea salt
2   teaspoons yellow cornmeal
¼   cup water

1. Dissolve yeast in warm water in a large bowl, and let stand 5 minutes. Lightly spoon flour into dry measuring cups; level with a knife. Stir 2½ cups flour and salt into yeast mixture. Turn dough out onto a floured surface. Knead dough until smooth and elastic (about 10 minutes), and add enough of remaining flour, 1 tablespoon at a time, to prevent dough from sticking to hands (dough will feel tacky).
2. Place dough in a large bowl. Cover and let rise in a warm place (85°), free from drafts, 45 minutes or until doubled in size. (Press two fingers into dough. If indentation remains, dough has risen enough.) Punch down; cover and let rest 5 minutes. Divide in half. Working with 1 portion at a time (cover remaining dough to keep it from drying), roll each portion into a 16-inch rope on a floured surface. Place ropes on a large baking sheet sprinkled with cornmeal. Cover and let rise 30 minutes or until doubled in size. Uncover dough. Cut 3 slits in top of each loaf to allow steam to escape.
3. Preheat oven to 450°.
4. Throw ¼ cup water on floor of oven (avoiding heating element). Place loaves in oven. Quickly close oven door. Bake at 450° for 20 minutes or until loaves are golden brown and sound hollow when tapped. Remove from pan, and cool on wire racks. Cut each baguette into 12 slices. Yield: 2 loaves, 12 servings per loaf (serving size: 1 slice).

CALORIES 59 (4% from fat); FAT 0.3g (sat 0g, mono 0g, poly 0.1g); PROTEIN 1.7g; CARB 12.2g; FIBER 0.5g; CHOL 0mg; IRON 0.8mg; SODIUM 240mg; CALC 3mg

Baekeoffe
Alsatian Meat Stew

4 cups thinly sliced onion
1½ cups (1-inch) sliced carrot
1 cup thinly sliced leek (about
  1 large)
1 (1-pound) boneless beef shoulder
  roast, trimmed and cut into 2-inch
  cubes
1 (¾-pound) pork blade steak,
  boned, trimmed, and cut into
  2-inch pieces
12 thyme sprigs
10 parsley stems
4 whole cloves
3 bay leaves
2 garlic cloves, halved
1½ cups Riesling or other white wine
1½ teaspoons kosher or sea salt,
  divided
½ teaspoon black pepper
1 pound small red potatoes, quartered
Cooking spray

1. Combine first 5 ingredients in a large nonreactive bowl. Place thyme, parsley, cloves, bay leaves, and garlic on a double layer of cheesecloth. Gather edges of cheesecloth together, and tie securely to form a *bouquet garni*. Add bouquet garni, wine, ½ teaspoon salt, and pepper to bowl. Toss well to coat. Refrigerate mixture 8 to 24 hours, stirring occasionally.
2. Preheat oven to 375°.
3. Place one-third of potatoes in a 3-quart casserole coated with cooking spray. Top with half of meat mixture, and sprinkle with ¼ teaspoon salt. Repeat layers with one-third of potatoes, ¼ teaspoon salt, and remaining meat mixture. Top with remaining potatoes, and sprinkle with ½ teaspoon salt. Pour any remaining marinade (including bouquet garni) over meat mixture. Cover and bake at 375° for 2½ hours. Remove bouquet garni, and discard. Yield: 6 servings (serving size: 1⅓ cups).

WINE NOTE: A dish like this proves that red meats should not be the exclusive territory of red wines. Try a dry and powerful Alsatian Riesling from Domaine Trimbach ($15).

CALORIES 376 (29% from fat); FAT 12.1g (sat 4.4g, mono 5.3g, poly 0.9g); PROTEIN 40g; CARB 25.7g; FIBER 3.9g; CHOL 110mg; IRON 5.3mg; SODIUM 592mg; CALC 61mg

How to Make a *Bouquet Garni*

A bouquet garni is used to season French dishes. Place thyme, parsley, cloves, bay leaves, and garlic on a double layer of cheesecloth. Gather edges of cheesecloth, and secure with a string. Secure tightly; you don't want the bag to break and disperse its contents into the stew. It can also be made with leek leaves as in our Coq au Vin (recipe on page 110).

French Fare Cooking Terms and Techniques

Aïoli: A strongly flavored garlic mayonnaise from the Provence region of southern France.

Beurre blanc: Butter sauce; a reduction of white wine and butter.

Bouquet garni: An assortment of whole herbs and spices secured in a cheesecloth bag and used to flavor soups, stews, and stocks. Typically, it includes fresh thyme, bay leaves, and parsley stems, but it can also include other aromatics like celery and leeks.

Cassoulet: Classic bean dish that includes duck or goose and usually pork.

Deglaze: Adding a small amount of liquid (usually water or wine) to a pan after sautéing food and stirring to loosen the browned bits. This mixture is then used to make a sauce or reduced and served with the food.

Gâteau: Cake.

Gratin (or tian): Any dish topped with cheese and/or breadcrumbs, then heated in the oven or broiler until melted and browned.

Haricots verts: A variety of tender, thin green beans, cousins to pole and bush green beans. The term usually refers to tender, small green beans in general.

Haute cuisine: A style of cooking that emphasizes elaborate meals with many courses. Today, it usually refers to fancy, fussy French fare.

Herbes de Provence: An assortment of dried herbs that usually includes thyme, bay leaves, rosemary, basil, and savory.

Poivre: Pepper. In France, pepper is almost always freshly ground black, but occasionally it's white or pink.

Pommes: Apples.

Pommes frites: French fries.

Potage: Pureed vegetable soup.

Poulet: Chicken.

Roux: A combination of cooked butter and flour that is used to thicken soups and sauces.

Sauté: To cook food quickly in a small amount of fat in a skillet.

Scalloped: Prepared by layering food with cream or a creamy sauce. (Usually applies to potatoes.)

Vinaigrette: One of what the French refer to as the five "mother sauces." Traditionally, a combination of three parts oil to one part vinegar, seasoned with salt and pepper.

Coq au Vin Step-by Steps

1. *Brown chicken in butter to develop rich, caramelized flavors.*

2. *Add liquor, giblets,* **bouquet garni***, broth, wine, and garlic. Simmer 1½ hours. Refrigerate chicken and wine mixture separately overnight.*

3. *Make a* **beurre manié** *with butter and flour. Softened butter and flour are worked together until a paste forms. It is then stirred into wine mixture to thicken it.*

Coq au Vin

This dish hails from Burgundy, where rich wines flow almost like water. It is simultaneously a dish of the farm and of the bourgeoisie—a fine *coq au vin* can go anywhere. Serve with our Baguette (recipe on page 108) to soak up all the flavorful juices. It's also good with the Pommes Anna (recipe on page 107) and a simple green salad. You can use precut chicken quarters—you just won't have the giblets. We've made *bouquet garni* in leek leaves, but you can do it in cheesecloth, if you prefer (see page 109). This dish must be made a day ahead.

- 2 large leeks
- 12 thyme sprigs
- 12 parsley stems
- 4 bay leaves
- 1 (4-pound) roasting chicken
- ¾ teaspoon kosher or sea salt, divided
- ¾ teaspoon black pepper, divided
- 3 tablespoons unsalted butter, divided
- 1 bacon slice, cut into 1-inch pieces
- ½ cup Calvados (apple brandy) or brandy
- 4 cups fat-free, less-sodium chicken broth, divided
- 1 (750-milliliter) bottle hearty dry red wine (Pinot Noir or Burgundy)
- 2 garlic cloves, halved
- 3 (8-ounce) packages mushrooms, stemmed
- 3 tablespoons all-purpose flour

1. To make *bouquet garni*, remove and reserve 8 leek leaves; remove white portion of leek leaves (reserve remaining leaves for another use). Flatten leaves. Place 3 thyme sprigs, 3 parsley sprigs, and 1 bay leaf lengthwise in each of 4 leek leaves. Top each filled leaf with one of remaining leek leaves. Tie leaves with string at 2-inch intervals.

2. Remove giblets and neck from chicken; discard neck. Rinse chicken with cold water; pat dry. Trim excess fat. Remove skin; cut chicken into quarters. Mince giblets; set aside. Sprinkle chicken pieces with ½ teaspoon salt and ½ teaspoon pepper. Heat 1 tablespoon butter in a large Dutch oven over medium heat. Add chicken to pan; cook 10 minutes, browning on all sides. Remove from pan. Add bacon; cook until crisp. Return chicken to pan. Add bouquet garni, giblets, Calvados, 2 cups broth, wine, and garlic; bring to a boil. Cover, reduce heat, and simmer 1½ hours.

3. Remove chicken from wine mixture; cover and refrigerate. Cover and chill wine mixture 8 to 24 hours. Discard bouquet garni. Skim solidified fat from surface; discard.

4. Combine mushrooms and 2 cups broth in a large nonstick skillet; bring to a boil. Partially cover, reduce heat, and simmer 30 minutes. Uncover and cook 10 minutes or until liquid almost evaporates. Sprinkle with ¼ teaspoon salt and ¼ teaspoon pepper. Remove from pan.

5. Add wine mixture to pan; bring to a boil. Reduce heat, and simmer 20 minutes. Combine 2 tablespoons butter and flour in a small bowl; work into a paste with fingers or a fork. Add ¼ cup wine mixture, stirring with a whisk until well blended. Add butter mixture to wine mixture in pan; bring to a boil. Reduce heat, and simmer 10 minutes. Add chicken and mushrooms to pan. Bring to a boil; reduce heat, and simmer 10 minutes or until thoroughly heated. Yield: 4 servings (serving size: 1 chicken quarter and 1 cup broth mixture).

WINE NOTE: The quintessential French comfort food, Coq au Vin is traditionally served with a red Burgundy. An exemplary choice would be a sublime, earthy wine like Domaine de l'Arlot Nuits-St.-Georges Clos des Forêts Premier Cru ($50). But a more hearty Rhône wine such as Domaine Santa Duc Côtes-du-Rhône ($12.99) would be nearly as good, and its price is a little more in keeping with the accessibility of the dish.

CALORIES 470 (32% from fat); FAT 16.5g (sat 7g, mono 4.6g, poly 2.5g); PROTEIN 48g; CARB 36.6g; FIBER 2.5g; CHOL 267mg; IRON 7.8mg; SODIUM 1,109mg; CALC 54mg

Baking with Buttermilk

We have the secret to delicious, old-fashioned flavor in cakes, sweet breads, and more.

Buttermilk is more than just a beverage. Experienced farm cooks and bakers have always known that buttermilk is the secret ingredient for making exceptionally tender and delicious baked goods—from biscuits and pancakes to crumb cakes and layer cakes.

How does buttermilk lend special qualities to baking? When buttermilk, which has acidic qualities, is combined with baking soda, an alkali, in a flour-based batter, bubbles of carbon dioxide gas begin to form. As the batter bakes, steam is created; the bubbles expand, causing the batter to lightly rise while creating a fine texture. The heat of the oven sets the batter and prevents it from collapsing. The result is a delicate but stable crumb. Buttermilk also adds moisture, richness, and a bit of tang.

Old-Fashioned Buttermilk Crumb Cake

CRUMB MIXTURE:
- 2 (1-ounce) slices white bread
- 3 tablespoons chopped walnuts
- 2 tablespoons sugar
- 2 teaspoons butter, melted
- ½ teaspoon ground cinnamon

CAKE:
- 2 cups sifted cake flour
- ½ teaspoon baking powder
- ½ teaspoon baking soda
- ⅛ teaspoon salt
- ¾ cup sugar
- 2 tablespoons vegetable shortening
- 1 teaspoon grated orange rind
- 2 teaspoons vanilla extract
- 1 cup low-fat buttermilk
- Cooking spray

1. Preheat oven to 325°.

2. To prepare crumb mixture, place bread in a food processor; pulse 10 times or until coarse crumbs form to measure ¾ cup. Combine breadcrumbs, walnuts, and next 3 ingredients in a small bowl.

3. To prepare cake, combine flour, baking powder, baking soda, and salt in a medium bowl. Combine ¾ cup sugar, shortening, rind, and vanilla in a large bowl, and beat with a mixer at high speed until well blended. Add flour mixture to shortening mixture alternately with buttermilk, beginning and ending with flour mixture. Spread batter into an 8-inch square baking pan coated with cooking spray. Sprinkle batter with crumb mixture.

4. Bake at 325° for 45 minutes or until cake begins to pull away from sides of pan. Yield: 9 servings.

CALORIES 238 (22% from fat); FAT 5.7g (sat 1.5g, mono 1.7g, poly 2.2g); PROTEIN 4g; CARB 42.7g; FIBER 0.3g; CHOL 2mg; IRON 2.1mg; SODIUM 177mg; CALC 61mg

Buttermilk Layer Cake with Praline Icing

CAKE:
- Cooking spray
- 2 teaspoons all-purpose flour
- 1¼ cups granulated sugar
- ½ cup butter, softened
- 2 large eggs
- 1 large egg white
- 2 teaspoons vanilla extract
- 2 cups all-purpose flour
- ½ teaspoon baking soda
- ½ teaspoon salt
- 1 cup low-fat buttermilk

ICING:
- 1 cup packed dark brown sugar
- 6 tablespoons 1% low-fat milk
- 1 tablespoon dark corn syrup
- 2 teaspoons butter
- Dash of salt
- 2 cups powdered sugar
- 1 teaspoon vanilla extract
- 2 tablespoons chopped pecans, toasted

1. Preheat oven to 350°.

2. To prepare cake, coat 2 (8-inch) round cake pans with cooking spray, and line bottoms with wax paper. Coat wax paper with cooking spray, and dust with 2 teaspoons flour.

3. Combine granulated sugar and ½ cup butter in a large bowl, and beat with a mixer at medium speed until well blended (about 5 minutes). Add eggs and egg white, 1 at a time, beating well after each addition; beat in 2 teaspoons vanilla. Lightly spoon 2 cups flour into dry measuring cups; level with a knife. Combine 2 cups flour, baking soda, and salt; stir well with a whisk. Add flour mixture to sugar mixture alternately with buttermilk, beginning and ending with flour mixture; beat well after each addition.

4. Pour batter into prepared pans. Bake at 350° for 25 minutes or until a wooden pick inserted in center comes out clean. Cool in pans 10 minutes on a wire rack; remove from pans. Carefully peel off wax paper, and cool completely on wire rack.

5. To prepare icing, combine brown sugar and next 4 ingredients in a medium saucepan. Bring to a boil over medium-high heat, stirring constantly. Reduce heat, and simmer until slightly thick (about 5 minutes), stirring occasionally. Pour brown sugar mixture into a large bowl. Add powdered sugar and 1 teaspoon vanilla; beat with a mixer at medium speed until smooth. Cool 2 to 3 minutes (icing will be thin but thickens as it cools).

6. Place 1 cake layer on a plate, and spoon ⅓ cup icing onto cake layer, spreading to cover. Top with remaining cake layer. Spread remaining icing over top and sides of cake. Sprinkle top with pecans. Store cake loosely covered in refrigerator. Yield: 16 servings (serving size: 1 slice).

CALORIES 301 (25% from fat); FAT 8.2g (sat 4.4g, mono 2.6g, poly 0.7g); PROTEIN 3.6g; CARB 53.9g; FIBER 0.5g; CHOL 45mg; IRON 1.1mg; SODIUM 213mg; CALC 42mg

Buttermilk-Apple Coffee Cake

CAKE:

1½ cups thinly sliced peeled Granny Smith apple
3 tablespoons brown sugar
1 tablespoon lemon juice
½ teaspoon ground cinnamon
1 cup all-purpose flour
½ teaspoon baking soda
⅛ teaspoon salt
⅓ cup granulated sugar
2 tablespoons butter, softened
1 large egg
1 teaspoon vanilla extract
½ teaspoon almond extract
½ cup low-fat buttermilk
Cooking spray
2 tablespoons sliced almonds

GLAZE:

¼ cup sifted powdered sugar
1 teaspoon low-fat buttermilk
¼ teaspoon vanilla extract

1. Preheat oven to 350°.
2. To prepare cake, combine first 4 ingredients in a small saucepan over medium-high heat. Cook 5 minutes or until syrupy, stirring frequently; cool.
3. Lightly spoon flour into a dry measuring cup; level with a knife. Combine flour, baking soda, and salt in a small bowl, stirring well with a whisk. Combine granulated sugar and butter in a large bowl; beat with a mixer at medium speed until well blended. Add egg and extracts, beating well. Add flour mixture to sugar mixture alternately with buttermilk, beginning and ending with flour mixture; beat well after each addition.
4. Spoon batter into an 8-inch round cake pan coated with cooking spray.

Arrange apple mixture over cake. Sprinkle with almonds. Bake at 350° for 25 minutes or until cake begins to pull away from sides of pan. Cool in pan on wire rack 10 minutes.
5. To prepare glaze, combine powdered sugar, 1 teaspoon buttermilk, and ¼ teaspoon vanilla in a small bowl; stir with a whisk. Drizzle glaze over cake. Serve warm or at room temperature. Yield: 8 servings (serving size: 1 wedge).

CALORIES 185 (24% from fat); FAT 5g (sat 2.3g, mono 1.7g, poly 0.6g); PROTEIN 3.4g; CARB 31.8g; FIBER 1g; CHOL 35mg; IRON 1mg; SODIUM 162mg; CALC 36mg

Lazy Daisy Cake

CAKE:

2 tablespoons butter, softened
⅔ cup granulated sugar
1 teaspoon vanilla extract
2 large eggs
1 cup all-purpose flour
¼ teaspoon baking soda
¼ teaspoon salt
½ cup low-fat buttermilk
Cooking spray

TOPPING:

⅔ cup low-fat buttermilk
½ cup packed brown sugar
2 teaspoons butter
½ teaspoon ground cinnamon
⅔ cup regular oats
¼ cup shredded sweetened coconut
3 tablespoons coarsely chopped walnuts

1. Preheat oven to 350°.
2. To prepare cake, beat 2 tablespoons butter, granulated sugar, and vanilla in a large bowl with a mixer at medium speed until well blended. Add eggs, 1 at a time, beating well after each addition. Lightly spoon flour into a dry measuring cup; level with a knife. Combine flour, baking soda, and salt in a medium bowl, stirring well with a whisk. Add flour mixture to sugar mixture alternately with ½ cup buttermilk, beginning and ending with flour mixture; beat well after each addition. Pour batter into an 8-inch square baking pan coated with cooking

spray. Bake at 350° for 25 minutes or until a wooden pick inserted in center comes out clean. Cool in pan 10 minutes on a wire rack.
3. Preheat broiler.
4. To prepare topping, combine ⅔ cup buttermilk and next 3 ingredients in a small saucepan over medium heat. Bring to a boil. Stir in oats; cook 1 minute. Remove from heat; stir in coconut and walnuts. Spread topping over cake. Broil 2 minutes or until lightly browned. Yield: 9 servings.

CALORIES 273 (27% from fat); FAT 8.2g (sat 3.8g, mono 2.1g, poly 1.6g); PROTEIN 5.8g; CARB 44.8g; FIBER 1.3g; CHOL 58mg; IRON 1.5mg; SODIUM 178mg; CALC 65mg

Blueberry-Cranberry Orange Muffins

2 cups all-purpose flour
⅔ cup sugar
1½ teaspoons baking powder
½ teaspoon baking soda
¼ teaspoon salt
1¼ cups low-fat buttermilk
¼ cup butter, melted
¼ cup dried blueberries
¼ cup dried cranberries
2 teaspoons grated orange rind
1 teaspoon vanilla extract
1 large egg, lightly beaten
Cooking spray
1 tablespoon sugar

1. Preheat oven to 400°.
2. Lightly spoon flour into dry measuring cups; level with a knife. Combine flour and next 4 ingredients in a large bowl; make a well in center of mixture. Combine buttermilk and next 6 ingredients in a bowl; add to flour mixture. Stir just until moist. Spoon batter into 12 muffin cups coated with cooking spray, and sprinkle evenly with 1 tablespoon sugar.
3. Bake at 400° for 18 minutes or until lightly browned. Remove muffins from pans; cool on a wire rack. Yield: 1 dozen (serving size: 1 muffin).

CALORIES 197 (23% from fat); FAT 5.1g (sat 2.8g, mono 1.5g, poly 0.4g); PROTEIN 3.9g; CARB 34.5g; FIBER 0.8g; CHOL 29mg; IRON 1.2mg; SODIUM 221mg; CALC 75mg

The Gift of Green Tea

The most popular and venerated beverage in East Asia is also one of the most healthy and flavorful ideas for American cooking.

Green tea tempers the spirit, arouses thought, prevents drowsiness, and calms and harmonizes the mind. It also lightens and refreshes the body. Scientists see it as a gift, crediting it with contributing to the prevention of heart disease, cancer, and rheumatoid arthritis.

Green Tea Types

Loose or bagged, green tea comes either pure or flavored with flowers (such as jasmine) or fruit (such as lemon). Use lemon- or ginger-flavored teas for seafood dishes. Fruit- and flower-flavored teas work well in desserts and drinks.

Because availability varies in the United States, we used common commercial types easily found in the tea section of your supermarket. But if you want to look a little more, try some of these other varieties.

Gunpowder: This makes a dark-green tea with a strong, pleasant flavor and a long-lasting aftertaste. One of the first teas exported from China to Europe, it derives its name from its resemblance to the gunpowder used during the 17th century. Each leaf is rolled tightly into a pellet shape, but the leaves unfurl when brewed in hot water.

Dragon Well: A light-green, fresh and mellow tea with a flowery aroma when brewed. The tea leaves are flat, long, and vibrant green. When the highest grades of Dragon Well brew, the leaves open to reveal intact buds within.

New Mist: Not really a tea type, but if you find this on a label, get it. The name refers to the highest-quality grade of any tea; it's based on the time of day the tea is harvested. Only the youngest leaves are used; they're hand-picked before dawn and processed the same day.

Tea-Crusted Tofu over Greens

(pictured on page 95)

VINAIGRETTE:
- ½ cup boiling water
- 2 green tea bags or 2 teaspoons loose green tea
- 2 tablespoons minced green onions
- 2 tablespoons fresh lime juice
- 1 tablespoon honey
- 2 teaspoons fish sauce
- 2 garlic cloves, chopped

SALAD:
- 1 (12.3-ounce) package reduced-fat extra-firm tofu, drained
- 1 tablespoon olive oil
- 2 teaspoons loose green tea or 2 green tea bags, opened
- 1½ teaspoons sesame seeds
- ⅛ teaspoon salt
- 4 cups gourmet salad greens
- 2 cups cubed Asian pear or ripe pear (about 2 pears)
- 1 cup halved cherry tomatoes (about 8 ounces)

1. To prepare vinaigrette, pour boiling water over 2 tea bags in a medium bowl. Steep 3 minutes; discard tea bags or strain tea leaves. Combine tea, onions, and next 4 ingredients; set aside.
2. To prepare salad, cut tofu into 8 slices. Heat olive oil in a large nonstick skillet over medium-high heat. Add 2 teaspoons tea leaves, sesame seeds, and salt; stir-fry 30 seconds or until fragrant. Arrange tofu on tea leaves mixture; sauté 6 minutes or until golden brown, turning after 3 minutes. Place tofu on a paper towel. Combine greens, pear, and tomatoes in a large bowl. Drizzle with vinaigrette; toss well. Arrange 1¼ cups salad on each of 4 plates. Top each serving with 2 tofu slices. Yield: 4 servings.

CALORIES 166 (30% from fat); FAT 5.6g (sat 0.8g, mono 3g, poly 1.4g); PROTEIN 8.6g; CARB 23.7g; FIBER 3.7g; CHOL 0mg; IRON 2.2mg; SODIUM 401mg; CALC 92mg

Asian Chicken Dinner

Green-Tea-and-Orange-Smoked Chicken

Julienne carrots

Rice noodles with sesame seeds

Green-Tea-and-Orange-Smoked Chicken

- 4 (4-ounce) skinless, boneless chicken breast halves
- Tea Sauce for All Occasions (recipe on page 114)
- 3 oranges
- ½ cup loose green tea
- 2 tablespoons sugar
- 1 tablespoon low-sodium teriyaki sauce

1. Make 2 diagonal cuts ¼-inch deep across each chicken breast half. Combine chicken and Tea Sauce for All Occasions in a zip-top plastic bag. Seal and marinate in refrigerator 24 hours, turning bag occasionally. Remove chicken from bag, reserving ⅔ cup marinade.
2. Carefully remove rind from oranges using a vegetable peeler, making sure not to get any of white pithy part of the rind. Cut rind into 2-inch pieces. Line bottom of a Dutch oven with foil. Add orange rind, tea, and sugar to pan. Place a vegetable steamer in pan over rind mixture. Place chicken breast halves in steamer. Cover with foil, and top with lid. Cook over medium-high heat 25 minutes or until done. Remove from heat.

Continued

3. Combine reserved marinade and teriyaki sauce in a small saucepan. Bring to a boil, and cook 1 minute. Strain mixture through a sieve into a bowl; discard solids. Remove chicken from steamer; discard orange rind mixture. Serve teriyaki sauce with chicken. Yield: 4 servings (serving size: 1 chicken breast half and 2 tablespoons sauce).

CALORIES 194 (35% from fat); FAT 7.5g (sat 1.5g, mono 4.4g, poly 1g); PROTEIN 26.9g; CARB 3.1g; FIBER 0.1g; CHOL 72mg; IRON 1mg; SODIUM 258mg; CALC 19mg

Tea Sauce for All Occasions

This sauce is great with a variety of dishes: Brush it on pork loin or salmon before baking, use it as a dipping sauce for dumplings or pot stickers, or try it as a salad dressing. Despite the high fat percentage, the sauce is low in fat grams and calories.

¾ cup boiling water
2 teaspoons loose green tea or 2 green tea bags, opened
3 tablespoons minced fresh chives or green onions
2 tablespoons extra-virgin olive oil
1 tablespoon fresh lemon juice
1 tablespoon low-sodium soy sauce
1½ teaspoons honey
1 teaspoon minced peeled fresh ginger
¼ teaspoon minced seeded hot red chile
⅛ teaspoon salt
3 garlic cloves, minced

1. Combine boiling water and green tea in a bowl; cover and steep 3 minutes. Strain tea mixture through a fine sieve into a bowl, and discard tea leaves. Add chives and remaining ingredients to tea. Cover and chill 30 minutes. Yield: 1 cup (serving size: 2 tablespoons).

CALORIES 38 (81% from fat); FAT 3.4g (sat 0.5g, mono 2.5g, poly 0.3g); PROTEIN 0.3g; CARB 1.9g; FIBER 0.1g; CHOL 0mg; IRON 0.1mg; SODIUM 97mg; CALC 5mg

---

Best Ways to Brew

- We brewed the green tea for these recipes to the boiling point (212° F) using standard tap water. Among some connoisseurs, who may also favor bottled water over tap, the tea (especially for drinking purposes) is considered best when brewed to 160° to 170° F.
- We found it best to brew the tea, either as loose leaves or in bags, for 3 to 5 minutes for cooking purposes. If you are using the leaves, you'll notice them fully unfurl and soften.
- Avoid aluminum or plastic containers for brewing, as they will affect the flavor.

Pan-Fried Udon Noodles with Teriyaki Sauce

1 (12.3-ounce) package extra-firm tofu, drained and cut into 1-inch cubes
2 tablespoons low-sodium teriyaki sauce
1 tablespoon rice vinegar or white wine vinegar
1 tablespoon vegetable oil
2 teaspoons loose green tea or 2 green tea bags, opened
1 tablespoon minced peeled fresh ginger
2 large garlic cloves, minced
1 cup (2-inch) julienne-cut peeled daikon radish or jícama or radish
1 cup thinly sliced leek (about 1 large)
½ cup (2-inch) julienne-cut carrot
3 cups hot cooked udon noodles (thick, round fresh Japanese wheat noodles) or spaghetti (about 9 ounces uncooked)

1. Combine first 3 ingredients in a large zip-top plastic bag; seal and marinate in refrigerator 15 minutes. Remove tofu from bag, reserving marinade.
2. Heat oil in a large nonstick skillet over medium-high heat. Add tea; sauté 30 seconds. Add tofu, ginger, and garlic; sauté 2 minutes. Add daikon, leek, and carrot; sauté 1 minute. Add noodles and reserved marinade; cook 2 minutes or

---

until thoroughly heated. Yield: 4 servings (serving size: 1½ cups).

CALORIES 335 (18% from fat); FAT 6.6g (sat 1.1g, mono 1.6g, poly 3.3g); PROTEIN 12.8g; CARB 56.3g; FIBER 3g; CHOL 0mg; IRON 5.6mg; SODIUM 152mg; CALC 87mg

Spicy Garlic Spinach with Sesame Seeds and Rice

1 tablespoon vegetable oil
2 teaspoons loose green tea or 2 green tea bags, opened
1 teaspoon chopped seeded hot red chile pepper
3 garlic cloves, minced
1 pound fresh spinach
1 tablespoon rice vinegar
2 tablespoons sesame seeds
¼ teaspoon salt
¼ teaspoon freshly ground black pepper
2 cups hot cooked long-grain rice

1. Heat oil in a Dutch oven over medium-high heat. Add tea, and stir-fry about 30 seconds or until fragrant. Add chile pepper and garlic; stir-fry 30 seconds. Add spinach; stir-fry 2 minutes. Stir in vinegar, and cook 1 minute or until spinach wilts. Sprinkle with sesame seeds, salt, and black pepper. Serve over rice. Yield: 4 servings (serving size: ½ cup spinach and ½ cup rice).

CALORIES 198 (28% from fat); FAT 6.1g (sat 1g, mono 1.9g, poly 2.8g); PROTEIN 6.3g; CARB 30.8g; FIBER 5.3g; CHOL 0mg; IRON 4.8mg; SODIUM 239mg; CALC 173mg

Sunrise Smoothie

We tried this smoothie with 2% reduced-fat milk but liked it much better with the soy milk. Any kind of fruit will work—try strawberries and peaches.

4 cubed peeled kiwifruit (about ¾ pound)
2 medium ripe bananas, cut into 1-inch pieces
4 fruit-flavored green tea bags
1½ cups boiling reduced-fat soy milk
1 tablespoon honey

1. Place cubed kiwifruit and banana pieces in a large zip-top plastic bag; seal and place in freezer 30 minutes or until almost firm. Place tea bags in a medium bowl. Pour boiling soy milk over tea bags, and steep 3 minutes. Strain tea mixture through a fine sieve into a bowl, and discard tea bags. Stir in honey, and cool. Combine kiwifruit, bananas, and tea mixture in a blender; process until mixture is smooth. Yield: 5 servings (serving size: ½ cup).

CALORIES 125 (8% from fat); FAT 1.1g (sat 0.1g, mono 0.2g, poly 0.5g); PROTEIN 2.4g; CARB 29.2g; FIBER 4g; CHOL 0mg; IRON 0.7mg; SODIUM 32mg; CALC 28mg

Tea-Marinated Beef-Vegetable Kebabs

Tea is used twice here: in the marinade for the beef and in the Tea Sauce for All Occasions. Do not cut off the root end of the onion. That way, the edges will hold together on the grill.

- 1 (1-pound) beef tenderloin, cut into 24 (1-inch) pieces
- 2 tablespoons low-sodium soy sauce
- 1 tablespoon minced peeled fresh lemongrass or 2 teaspoons grated lemon rind
- 1 tablespoon hot chili oil
- 1 tablespoon lemon juice
- 2 teaspoons loose green tea or 2 green tea bags, opened
- 3 garlic cloves, minced
- 1 serrano chile, seeded and minced
- 1 yellow squash, halved lengthwise and sliced into 8 (1-inch) pieces
- 1 large onion, cut into 8 wedges
- 8 large cherry or grape tomatoes
- Cooking spray
- 4 cups hot cooked long-grain rice
- ½ cup Tea Sauce for All Occasions (recipe on page 114)

1. Combine first 8 ingredients in a large zip-top plastic bag. Seal bag, and marinate in refrigerator 24 hours. Remove beef from bag, and discard marinade.
2. Prepare grill or broiler.
3. Thread 6 tenderloin cubes, 2 squash pieces, 2 onion wedges, and 2 tomatoes onto each of 4 (12-inch) skewers. Place kebabs on grill rack or broiler pan coated with cooking spray; grill 10 minutes or until desired degree of doneness. Serve kebabs over rice with Tea Sauce for All Occasions. Yield: 4 servings (serving size: 1 kebab, 1 cup rice, and 2 tablespoons sauce).

CALORIES 485 (25% from fat); FAT 13.5g (sat 3.9g, mono 6.3g, poly 1.5g); PROTEIN 30g; CARB 59.4g; FIBER 3g; CHOL 71mg; IRON 5.6mg; SODIUM 279mg; CALC 54mg

Shrimp Won Tons with Shiitake Mushroom-Miso Soup

Won ton wrappers and gyoza skins can be found next to the tofu near the produce section of the supermarket.

BROTH:

- 6 cups boiling water
- 1 green tea bag or 1 teaspoon loose green tea
- 3 tablespoons red miso (soybean paste) or tahini
- 1 cup thinly sliced shiitake mushroom caps (about 3 ounces mushrooms)

FILLING:

- ⅓ cup minced green onions
- 1 tablespoon low-sodium soy sauce
- 2 teaspoons rice vinegar
- 2 teaspoons dark sesame oil
- 2 teaspoons grated peeled fresh ginger
- ⅛ teaspoon white pepper
- ½ pound large shrimp, peeled and finely chopped
- ¼ pound lean ground pork
- 2 garlic cloves, minced
- 20 won ton wrappers or gyoza skins
- ¼ cup (1-inch) thinly sliced red bell pepper
- 2 tablespoons (1-inch) sliced green onions

1. To prepare broth, pour boiling water over tea bag in a large saucepan; steep 5 minutes. Remove and reserve tea bag or loose tea. Bring tea mixture to a boil. Add miso, stirring with a whisk until blended.
Add mushrooms; bring to a boil. Reduce heat, and simmer 5 minutes. Remove from heat; cover and set aside.
2. To prepare filling, cut open reserved tea bag, and pour out loose tea; chop, if needed. Combine loose tea, minced onions, and next 8 ingredients in a medium bowl. Working with 1 won ton wrapper at a time (cover remaining wrappers with a damp towel to keep from drying), spoon 1 tablespoon shrimp mixture on half of each wrapper. Moisten edges of wrapper with water; bring 2 opposite corners together. Pinch edges together to seal, forming a triangle.
3. Bring reserved tea mixture to a boil; add won tons, gently stir, and cook 4 minutes or until won tons float to top. Ladle 5 won tons and 1 cup broth into each of 4 bowls. Divide bell pepper and onion slices evenly among bowls. Serve immediately. Yield: 4 servings.
NOTE: Ground turkey may be substituted for ground pork.

CALORIES 277 (23% from fat); FAT 7g (sat 1.7g, mono 2.6g, poly 1.9g); PROTEIN 19.6g; CARB 31.2g; FIBER 0.7g; CHOL 88mg; IRON 3.4mg; SODIUM 888mg; CALC 61mg

---

Getting the Most from Green Tea

- Use the highest-quality green tea for maximum flavor. But when getting started, you'll probably find that standard supermarket brands work just fine.
- Loose or bagged tea can be interchanged in many dishes, but not in all of them, so it's a good idea for you to have both types on hand. One tea bag contains about 1 teaspoon tea leaves.
- Once it's opened, store green tea in a sealed container in a cool, dark place for no more than six months.
- Don't use green tea that is more than six months old for cooking. Most of its flavor will have been lost beyond that point.
- Save used tea leaves, and spread them around the bases of your plants as the Chinese do. Because used tea leaves contain organic matter, they make a good fertilizer.

A Little Side Action

Enliven your relationship with those same old entrées by adding side dishes that sizzle.

The main course doesn't always have to be the main event. Inventive sides can transform mealtime standbys into real standouts.

Caramelized Onion Bruschetta

Serve with an entrée salad, a pasta dish, or a hearty bowl of soup.

  2 teaspoons butter
  ½ cup chopped onion
  ¼ teaspoon sugar
  1 tablespoon chopped fresh or
     1 teaspoon dried basil
  1 (6-inch) piece French bread
     baguette (about 4 ounces)
  2 tablespoons grated fresh Parmesan
     cheese
  ¼ teaspoon freshly ground black
     pepper

1. Preheat broiler.
2. Melt butter in a small skillet over medium heat. Add onion and sugar; cook 14 minutes or until golden brown, stirring frequently. Remove from heat; stir in basil.
3. Cut bread in half horizontally. Place bread, cut sides up, on a baking sheet. Broil bread 2 minutes or until toasted. Spread 1 tablespoon caramelized onion mixture over each bread half. Sprinkle each bread half with 1 tablespoon Parmesan cheese and ⅛ teaspoon black pepper. Broil 1 minute or until cheese melts. Yield: 2 servings (serving size: 1 bread half).

CALORIES 236 (29% from fat); FAT 7.5g (sat 3.9g, mono 2.3g, poly 0.6g); PROTEIN 8.1g; CARB 34.1g; FIBER 2.6g; CHOL 15mg; IRON 1.7mg; SODIUM 499mg; CALC 139mg

Double-Mango Salad
(pictured on page 93)

The fresh, fruity flavors of this salad pair well with a spicy shrimp, chicken, or pork dish. In place of pistachios, you could substitute toasted almonds, pine nuts, macadamia nuts, or hazelnuts.

  1 cup cubed peeled ripe mango,
     divided
  1 tablespoon fresh lime juice
  ½ teaspoon vegetable oil
  ½ teaspoon ground coriander
  ⅛ teaspoon salt
  3 cups gourmet salad greens
  ½ cup sliced strawberries
  1 tablespoon chopped pistachios

1. Place ¾ cup mango in a food processor; process until finely chopped. Add juice, oil, coriander, and salt; process until smooth, scraping sides of bowl once.
2. Combine ¼ cup mango, greens, and strawberries in a large bowl. Divide salad between 2 serving dishes, and sprinkle with nuts. Serve with dressing. Yield: 2 servings (serving size: 1½ cups).

CALORIES 114 (28% from fat); FAT 3.6g (sat 0.5g, mono 1.8g, poly 3.7g); PROTEIN 2.9g; CARB 20.4g; FIBER 4g; CHOL 0mg; IRON 1.5mg; SODIUM 150mg; CALC 52mg

Mushroom-Barley Pilaf with Spinach

The earthy, robust flavors of this pilaf are perfect with a beef tenderloin.

  2 teaspoons butter
  ⅓ cup sliced shallots
  2 cups sliced fresh shiitake
     mushroom caps (about 4 ounces)
  2 garlic cloves, minced
  ½ cup uncooked quick-cooking
     barley
  1 cup fat-free, less-sodium chicken
     broth
  ¼ teaspoon freshly ground black
     pepper
  ⅛ teaspoon salt
  2 cups fresh spinach leaves

1. Melt butter in a medium saucepan over medium-high heat. Add shallots; cook 1 minute, stirring occasionally. Stir in mushrooms and garlic; cook 2 minutes, stirring occasionally. Stir in barley; cook 1 minute, stirring constantly. Stir in broth, pepper, and salt. Bring to a boil; cover, reduce heat, and simmer 15 minutes or until liquid is absorbed. Stir in spinach; cook 1 minute or until spinach wilts. Yield: 2 servings (serving size: 1 cup).

CALORIES 271 (16% from fat); FAT 4.9g (sat 2.6g, mono 1.2g, poly 0.6g); PROTEIN 10.2g; CARB 49.6g; FIBER 11.1g; CHOL 11mg; IRON 3.9mg; SODIUM 481mg; CALC 91mg

Mashed Sweet Potatoes with Pecan Butter

Use your microwave to make this easy side dish for roast chicken, turkey, or pork; you can prepare it while the roast is standing.

  2 medium sweet potatoes (about
     1 pound)
  3 tablespoons 1% low-fat milk
  2 tablespoons brown sugar, divided
  ⅛ teaspoon salt
  1 tablespoon butter, softened
  1 tablespoon chopped pecans,
     toasted
  ⅛ teaspoon ground cinnamon

1. Pierce potatoes with a fork; arrange on paper towels in microwave oven. Microwave potatoes at HIGH 10 minutes, rearranging potatoes after 5 minutes. Wrap potatoes in a towel; let stand 5 minutes. Scoop out pulp; discard skins. Combine pulp, milk, 1 tablespoon brown sugar, and salt in a bowl; mash.
2. Combine 1 tablespoon brown sugar, softened butter, pecans, and cinnamon in a small bowl. Top each serving of potato mixture with pecan mixture. Yield: 2 servings (serving size: ¾ cup potatoes and 1 tablespoon pecan mixture).

CALORIES 299 (27% from fat); FAT 9g (sat 4.1g, mono 3.3g, poly 1.1g); PROTEIN 3.9g; CARB 52g; FIBER 5.4g; CHOL 16mg; IRON 1.4mg; SODIUM 237mg; CALC 78mg

Balsamic-Glazed Oranges

These orange slices, drenched with a richly flavored syrup, are the perfect partner for dark-meat poultry such as duck breast or chicken thighs or drumsticks.

    2 tablespoons packed brown
        sugar
    2 tablespoons balsamic vinegar
    2 oranges, peeled and cut into
        ¼-inch-thick slices
    ½ teaspoon chopped fresh mint
        (optional)

1. Combine sugar and vinegar in a small saucepan. Bring to a boil. Cook mixture until reduced to 2 tablespoons (about 1 minute), stirring constantly; remove mixture from heat. Divide orange slices evenly between 2 salad plates. Drizzle each serving with 1 tablespoon vinegar glaze. Garnish with chopped mint, if desired. Yield: 2 servings.

CALORIES 96 (2% from fat); FAT 0.2g; PROTEIN 1.2g; CARB 24.4g; FIBER 5.8g; CHOL 0mg; IRON 0.4mg; SODIUM 4mg; CALC 60mg

Chipotle Black Beans

You'll love the versatility of this recipe. Match it with highly seasoned dishes such as beef or pork fajitas. You can substitute regular salsa for the chipotle salsa if you prefer.

    2 teaspoons vegetable oil
    ½ cup chopped red bell pepper
    2 garlic cloves, minced
    ¼ cup bottled chipotle salsa (such as
        Jardine's)
    1 (15-ounce) can black beans, rinsed
        and drained
    2 tablespoons chopped fresh cilantro

1. Heat oil in a medium saucepan over medium heat. Add bell pepper and garlic; cook 5 minutes, stirring occasionally. Stir in salsa and beans; simmer 5 minutes. Sprinkle with cilantro. Yield: 2 servings (serving size: ¾ cup).

CALORIES 268 (20% from fat); FAT 5.9g (sat 1.1g, mono 1.4g, poly 2.7g); PROTEIN 14.8g; CARB 42.1g; FIBER 7.9g; CHOL 0mg; IRON 4.4mg; SODIUM 462mg; CALC 67mg

Maple-Glazed Acorn Squash Rings

These attractive rings complement ham, rotisserie chicken, and even sautéed tofu.

    1 medium acorn squash (about
        1½ pounds)
    2 tablespoons maple syrup
    1 tablespoon bourbon
    2 teaspoons butter, melted
    ¼ teaspoon salt
    ⅛ teaspoon ground nutmeg

1. Cut squash crosswise into 4 (1-inch-thick) slices; remove seeds. Place squash slices on a microwave-safe plate. Cover with plastic wrap; vent. Microwave at HIGH 6 minutes or until tender.
2. Preheat broiler.
3. Place squash on a baking sheet. Combine syrup and remaining 4 ingredients. Brush syrup mixture over squash. Broil 3 minutes or until bubbly. Drizzle with remaining syrup mixture. Yield: 2 servings (serving size: 2 squash rings).

CALORIES 239 (16% from fat); FAT 4.3g (sat 2.5g, mono 1.1g, poly 0.3g); PROTEIN 2.8g; CARB 48.8g; FIBER 4.1g; CHOL 10mg; IRON 2.3mg; SODIUM 344mg; CALC 127mg

inspired vegetarian

Fresh Take on Lasagna

With or without ripples, this versatile pasta is good for going meatless.

Lasagna is comforting, rich, and hearty. But can the vegetarian version fit the bill? Sure it can. And it's easy to make. Virtually any kind of meatless fillings can be sandwiched between those sheets of pasta.

If you're a traditionalist who says, "It's not lasagna if it doesn't have rippled pasta," then the new flat, no-boil noodles, recommended in half of the following recipes, might take some getting used to. But go ahead and try them—they have a fresh-pasta taste and work so beautifully that you might not miss the ripples at all.

Spring Vegetable Lasagna

(pictured on page 94)

    Cooking spray
    8 cups torn Swiss chard (about
        ¾ pound)
    2 cups chopped yellow squash
    1½ cups chopped onion
    1 cup chopped red bell pepper
    1 cup shredded carrot
    ½ teaspoon salt
    1 tablespoon butter
    4 garlic cloves, crushed
    2 tablespoons all-purpose flour
    1½ cups fat-free milk
    6 tablespoons (1½ ounces) grated
        fresh Parmesan cheese, divided
    1 cup fat-free ricotta cheese
    1 cup fat-free cottage cheese
    1 cup (4 ounces) grated Asiago
        cheese, divided
    ½ teaspoon dried oregano
    6 no-boil lasagna noodles (such as
        Barilla or Vigo)

1. Preheat oven to 375°.
2. Heat a Dutch oven coated with cooking spray over medium-high heat. Add chard, squash, onion, pepper, carrot, and salt; sauté 10 minutes or until tender.
3. Melt butter in a saucepan over medium heat. Add garlic; sauté 30 seconds. Add flour; cook 1 minute, stirring constantly with a whisk. Gradually add milk, stirring with a whisk until blended. Cook until thick (about 4 minutes). Remove from heat; add ¼ cup Parmesan. Stir until cheese melts.
4. Combine ricotta, cottage cheese, ½ cup Asiago, and oregano in a bowl.
5. Spread 2 tablespoons milk mixture in bottom of an 8-inch square baking dish coated with cooking spray. Arrange 2 noodles over milk mixture; top with half of ricotta mixture, half of vegetable mixture, and ½ cup milk mixture. Repeat layers, ending with noodles. Spread remaining milk mixture over noodles. Sprinkle with ½ cup Asiago cheese and 2 tablespoons Parmesan. Bake at 375° for 45 minutes. Let stand 15 minutes. Yield: 6 servings.

CALORIES 308 (30% from fat); FAT 10.3g (sat 5.9g, mono 2.6g, poly 0.7g); PROTEIN 25.8g; CARB 30.8g; FIBER 3.3g; CHOL 53mg; IRON 2.2mg; SODIUM 865mg; CALC 495mg

Wild Mushroom-and-Spinach Lasagna with Goat-Cheese Sauce

1½ cups boiling water
1 cup dried porcini mushrooms (about 1 ounce)
2 (3½-ounce) packages shiitake mushrooms
Cooking spray
1 (8-ounce) package presliced button mushrooms
½ teaspoon salt, divided
¼ teaspoon dried thyme
¼ teaspoon black pepper, divided
¼ cup dry white wine
1 tablespoon butter
2 tablespoons all-purpose flour
1½ cups fat-free milk
½ cup (2 ounces) crumbled goat cheese
¼ cup (1 ounce) grated fresh Parmesan cheese, divided
6 no-boil lasagna noodles (such as Barilla or Vigo)
1 (10-ounce) package frozen chopped spinach, thawed, drained, and squeezed dry
2 cups chopped plum tomato
¾ cup (3 ounces) shredded part-skim mozzarella cheese

1. Preheat oven to 375°.
2. Combine water and porcini in a medium bowl; cover and let stand 15 minutes. Drain in a sieve over a bowl, reserving 1 cup liquid. Bring liquid to a boil in small saucepan; reduce heat to medium, and cook until reduced to ¼ cup (about 5 minutes). Remove stems from shiitakes; discard stems. Slice caps.
3. Heat a large nonstick skillet coated with cooking spray over medium-high heat. Add porcini, shiitake, and button mushrooms, ¼ teaspoon salt, thyme, and ⅛ teaspoon pepper; sauté 12 minutes or until soft. Add wine, and cook 2 minutes or until liquid almost evaporates.
4. Melt butter in a medium saucepan over medium heat. Add flour, and cook 30 seconds, stirring constantly with a whisk. Gradually add ¼ cup porcini mushroom liquid and milk, stirring with a whisk until blended. Cook until thick (about 4 minutes). Remove from heat. Add goat cheese, 2 tablespoons Parmesan,

¼ teaspoon salt, and ⅛ teaspoon pepper, and stir until cheese melts.
5. Spread ½ cup cheese sauce in bottom of an 8-inch square baking dish coated with cooking spray. Arrange 2 noodles over cheese sauce, and top with half of mushroom mixture, half of spinach, ¾ cup tomato, ½ cup cheese sauce, and ¼ cup mozzarella. Repeat layers, ending with noodles. Spread remaining cheese sauce over noodles. Sprinkle with ¼ cup mozzarella, ½ cup tomato, and 2 tablespoons Parmesan. Cover and bake at 375° for 25 minutes. Uncover and bake an additional 25 minutes. Let stand 5 minutes. Yield: 4 servings.

CALORIES 375 (33% from fat); FAT 13.8g (sat 7.8g, mono 3.3g, poly 1.5g); PROTEIN 22.3g; CARB 44.4g; FIBER 6.1g; CHOL 65mg; IRON 4.6mg; SODIUM 699mg; CALC 479mg

Eggplant Parmesan Lasagna

2 large egg whites
1 large egg
1 (1-pound) eggplant, cut crosswise into ¼-inch-thick slices
3 tablespoons all-purpose flour
1 cup Italian-seasoned breadcrumbs
Cooking spray
2 cups (8 ounces) shredded part-skim mozzarella cheese, divided
5 tablespoons (1¼ ounces) grated fresh Parmesan cheese, divided
1 teaspoon dried oregano
1 teaspoon dried basil
1 (15-ounce) carton part-skim ricotta cheese
1 (12-ounce) carton 1% low-fat cottage cheese
1 large egg white
1 (26-ounce) bottle fat-free tomato-basil pasta sauce
12 cooked lasagna noodles

1. Preheat oven to 450°.
2. Combine 2 egg whites and egg in a small bowl, stirring with a whisk. Dredge each eggplant slice in flour. Dip each in egg mixture, and dredge in breadcrumbs. Place slices in a single layer on a baking sheet coated with cooking spray. Coat tops of slices with

cooking spray. Bake at 450° for 20 minutes, turning eggplant after 10 minutes. Remove from baking sheet; cool. Reduce oven temperature to 375°.
3. Combine 1 cup shredded mozzarella, 3 tablespoons Parmesan, oregano, basil, ricotta, cottage cheese, and 1 egg white in a large bowl.
4. Spread ¼ cup pasta sauce in bottom of a 13 x 9-inch baking dish coated with cooking spray. Arrange 4 lasagna noodles slightly overlapping over pasta sauce; top with half of cheese mixture, half of eggplant slices, and ¾ cup pasta sauce. Repeat layers, ending with noodles. Spread remaining pasta sauce over noodles. Sprinkle with 1 cup mozzarella and 2 tablespoons Parmesan. Cover and bake at 375° for 15 minutes. Uncover and bake an additional 35 minutes or until cheese melts. Let stand 5 minutes. Yield: 9 servings.

CALORIES 432 (23% from fat); FAT 11g (sat 6.2g, mono 3.1g, poly 0.9g); PROTEIN 28.3g; CARB 53.8g; FIBER 3.7g; CHOL 58mg; IRON 3.2mg; SODIUM 976mg; CALC 460mg

Mediterranean Lasagna

Cooking spray
2 cups chopped leek
1½ cups chopped onion
1 teaspoon dried mint flakes
½ teaspoon fennel seeds
3 garlic cloves, minced
1 (14-ounce) can artichoke hearts, drained and coarsely chopped
1 (7-ounce) bottle roasted red bell peppers, drained and chopped
1 cup drained canned cannellini beans
1½ tablespoons butter
2 tablespoons all-purpose flour
1½ cups fat-free milk
1 (4-ounce) package crumbled feta cheese
3 tablespoons grated fresh Parmesan cheese, divided
6 no-boil lasagna noodles (such as Barilla or Vigo)
1 (10-ounce) package frozen chopped spinach, thawed, drained, and squeezed dry
¾ cup (3 ounces) shredded part-skim mozzarella cheese, divided

1. Preheat oven to 375°.

2. Heat a nonstick skillet coated with cooking spray over medium-high heat. Add leek and next 4 ingredients; sauté 5 minutes. Add artichokes and pepper; sauté 3 minutes. Stir in beans; remove from heat.

3. Melt butter in a medium saucepan over medium heat. Add flour, and cook 2 minutes, stirring constantly with a whisk. Gradually add milk, stirring with a whisk until blended, and cook until slightly thick (about 4 minutes). Remove from heat. Add feta and 2 tablespoons Parmesan; stir until cheese melts.

4. Spread ¼ cup cheese sauce in bottom of an 8-inch square baking dish coated with cooking spray. Arrange 2 noodles over cheese sauce; top with half of leek mixture, half of spinach, ¼ cup mozzarella, and ½ cup cheese sauce. Repeat layers, ending with noodles. Pour remaining cheese sauce over noodles, and sprinkle with ¼ cup mozzarella and 1 tablespoon Parmesan.

5. Cover and bake at 375° for 35 minutes. Uncover and bake 15 minutes or until top is golden. Let stand 5 minutes. Yield: 6 servings.

CALORIES 341 (31% from fat); FAT 11.9g (sat 6.9g, mono 2.8g, poly 0.9g); PROTEIN 18.8g; CARB 42.6g; FIBER 4.4g; CHOL 53mg; IRON 4.1mg; SODIUM 548mg; CALC 410mg

Black-Bean Lasagna

    4   jalapeño peppers
    2   cups chopped onion
    1   cup chopped green bell pepper
    1   cup chopped red bell pepper
    4   garlic cloves, minced
    2   cups chopped tomato
 1½   teaspoons ground cumin
    1   teaspoon ground coriander
    2   (15.5-ounce) cans black beans,
        rinsed and drained
    3   tablespoons chopped fresh cilantro
    1   (8-ounce) carton reduced-fat sour
        cream
    1   large egg, lightly beaten
    1   (16-ounce) bottle chunky salsa
        Cooking spray
  12   cooked lasagna noodles
 1½   cups (6 ounces) shredded Monterey
        Jack cheese

1. Preheat broiler.

2. Cut jalapeños in half lengthwise; discard seeds and membranes. Place halves, skin sides up, on a foil-lined baking sheet; flatten with hand. Broil 4 minutes or until blackened. Place in a zip-top plastic bag; seal. Let stand 5 minutes. Peel and chop. Reduce oven temperature to 375°.

3. Heat a large nonstick skillet over medium-high heat. Add onion, bell peppers, and garlic; sauté 6 minutes. Add tomato, cumin, and coriander; cook 3 minutes. Add jalapeño and beans, and cook 3 minutes. Remove from heat; cool 10 minutes. Stir in cilantro, sour cream, and egg.

4. Spread 3 tablespoons salsa in bottom of a 13 x 9-inch baking dish coated with cooking spray. Arrange 4 noodles slightly overlapping over salsa, and top with half of bean mixture, ½ cup cheese, and 3 tablespoons salsa. Repeat layers, ending with noodles. Spread remaining salsa over noodles, and sprinkle with ½ cup cheese. Cover and bake at 375° for 30 minutes. Uncover and bake an additional 15 minutes or until cheese melts. Let stand 5 minutes. Yield: 8 servings.

CALORIES 452 (25% from fat); FAT 12.6g (sat 6.7g, mono 3.4g, poly 1.3g); PROTEIN 21.8g; CARB 65.2g; FIBER 7.5g; CHOL 55mg; IRON 5.4mg; SODIUM 559mg; CALC 262mg

Caramelized-Onion Lasagna with Gorgonzola Sauce

    3   tablespoons butter, divided
    8   cups thinly sliced onion (about
        2 pounds)
  ½   teaspoon dried thyme
  ¼   teaspoon salt
  ¼   teaspoon black pepper
  ½   cup dry white wine
 1½   pounds zucchini, cut lengthwise
        into ¼-inch-thick slices
    2   tablespoons all-purpose flour
    2   (12-ounce) cans evaporated
        fat-free milk
 1¼   cups (5 ounces) crumbled
        Gorgonzola or other blue cheese
  ⅛   teaspoon ground nutmeg
        Cooking spray
  12   cooked lasagna noodles
  ¼   cup (1 ounce) grated fresh Parmesan
        cheese

1. Preheat oven to 375°.

2. Melt 2 teaspoons butter in a large nonstick skillet over medium heat. Add onion, thyme, salt, and pepper; cook 20 minutes, stirring occasionally. Add wine; cook 2 minutes or until wine evaporates. Spoon into a bowl; cool.

3. Melt 1 teaspoon butter in pan over medium-high heat. Add half of zucchini; cook 2 minutes or until crisp-tender. Remove from pan. Add remaining zucchini; cook 2 minutes or until crisp-tender. Set aside.

4. Melt 2 tablespoons butter in a medium saucepan over medium heat. Add flour; cook 1 minute, stirring constantly with a whisk. Gradually add milk, stirring with a whisk. Cook until thick (about 5 minutes), stirring constantly. Remove from heat. Add Gorgonzola and nutmeg; stir until cheese melts.

5. Spread ¼ cup cheese sauce in bottom of a 13 x 9-inch baking dish coated with cooking spray. Arrange 4 noodles slightly overlapping over cheese sauce; top with half of onion mixture, half of zucchini, and 1 cup cheese sauce. Repeat layers, ending with noodles. Spread remaining cheese sauce over noodles. Sprinkle with Parmesan. Cover and bake at 375° for 30 minutes. Uncover and bake an additional 15 minutes. Let stand 5 minutes. Yield: 8 servings.

CALORIES 407 (26% from fat); FAT 11.8g (sat 6.9g, mono 3.1g, poly 0.9g); PROTEIN 19.8g; CARB 56.4g; FIBER 3.6g; CHOL 31mg; IRON 2.8mg; SODIUM 534mg; CALC 440mg

Choose Your Noodle

For a big pan, we suggest using regular lasagna noodles and precooking them before layering. But the no-boil noodles, which are smaller than the traditional noodles, are perfect for a small-family supper. Feel free, though, to use either type interchangeably. Most importantly, be sure to read the package directions carefully before preparation, and resist the urge to precook the no-boil noodles. Treating the no-boil noodles the same as you do the traditional ripply stuff will only turn them to mush.

Matchmaking for the Perfect Picnic

A sweet spot in the country, bankside at the lake, a sheltered glade in the city park—choose your setting. Add a blanket and your desired companion to our perfect picnic picks.

Artichoke-Potato Salad with Toasted Brown Mustard Seeds

The mustard seeds add a bold flavor to this potato salad. All the work for this one-fork side is done the day before.

    3   artichokes (about ¾ pound each)
    ¾   pound small red potatoes
    ½   cup frozen green peas, thawed
    1   tablespoon brown mustard
        seeds
    ¼   cup reduced-calorie salad dressing
        (such as Miracle Whip Light)
    1   tablespoon chopped fresh or
        1 teaspoon dried dill
    3   tablespoons fresh lemon juice
    2   tablespoons Dijon mustard
    ¼   teaspoon salt
    ¼   teaspoon freshly ground black
        pepper
    1   garlic clove, minced

1. Cut off stems of artichokes; remove bottom leaves. Trim about ½ inch from tops of artichokes. Place artichokes, stem ends down, in a large Dutch oven filled two-thirds with water. Bring to a boil. Cover, reduce heat, and simmer 30 minutes or until a leaf near center of each artichoke pulls out easily. Drain and rinse with cold water. Cool. Remove bottom leaves and tough outer leaves, leaving tender hearts and bottoms; reserve leaves for another use. Cut artichokes in half lengthwise. Remove fuzzy thistles from bottoms with a spoon. Coarsely chop artichoke hearts and bottoms. Place chopped artichoke in a large bowl.

2. While artichokes are cooking, place potatoes in a saucepan, and cover with water; bring to a boil. Reduce heat, and simmer 15 minutes or until tender; drain and rinse with cold water. Cool. Cut potatoes into ¼-inch-thick slices. Add potatoes and peas to chopped artichoke in bowl.

3. Cook mustard seeds in a small skillet over medium heat 1 minute or until toasted. Combine mustard seeds, dressing, and next 6 ingredients in a small bowl, and stir well with a whisk. Pour over artichoke mixture, and toss well. Cover and chill. Yield: 4 servings (serving size: 1 cup).

NOTE: Substitute 1 cup of chopped drained canned artichoke hearts or bottoms for fresh artichokes, if desired. If you are unable to find brown mustard seeds, substitute whole-grain mustard for Dijon.

CALORIES 166 (30% from fat); FAT 5.5g (sat 0.7g, mono 1.8g, poly 2.6g); PROTEIN 5.1g; CARB 25.2g; FIBER 1.9g; CHOL 5mg; IRON 2.4mg; SODIUM 522mg; CALC 56mg

Blueberry Turnovers

CRUST:

    ½   cup all-purpose flour
    2   tablespoons sugar
    2   tablespoons (1 ounce) ⅓-less-fat
        cream cheese
    1   tablespoon butter
        Dash of salt
    1   tablespoon ice water

FILLING:

    ⅔   cup blueberries
    1½ tablespoons sugar
    1   teaspoon cornstarch
    1   teaspoon grated lemon rind
    1   teaspoon fresh lemon juice
    1   large egg white, lightly beaten
        Cooking spray
    1   teaspoon sugar, divided

1. To prepare crust, lightly spoon flour into a dry measuring cup; level with a knife. Place flour and next 4 ingredients in a food processor; pulse 5 times or until mixture resembles coarse meal. With processor on, add ice water through food chute, processing just until combined (do not form a ball). Press mixture gently into a 3-inch circle on heavy-duty plastic wrap; cover with additional plastic wrap. Chill 15 minutes.

2. Preheat oven to 400°.

3. Divide dough into 4 equal portions; place each portion between 2 sheets of plastic wrap. Roll each portion into a 5-inch circle. Place dough in freezer 5 minutes or until plastic wrap can be easily removed.

4. To prepare filling, combine blueberries and next 4 ingredients in a bowl. Working with 1 dough portion at a time, remove plastic wrap. Place each circle on a lightly floured surface, and brush with egg white. Spoon about 2 tablespoons blueberry filling onto half of circle. Fold dough over filling, and press edges together with a fork to seal. Place turnovers on a foil-lined baking sheet coated with cooking spray. Lightly coat turnovers with cooking spray, and sprinkle each with ¼ teaspoon sugar. Pierce turnovers with a fork.

5. Bake at 400° for 15 minutes or until lightly browned. Remove from pan, and cool on a wire rack. Yield: 4 servings (serving size: 1 turnover).

NOTE: Expect blueberries to ooze out of crust a little during baking.

CALORIES 177 (29% from fat); FAT 5.8g (sat 3g, mono 1.6g, poly 0.8g); PROTEIN 3.4g; CARB 28.4g; FIBER 1.1g; CHOL 13mg; IRON 0.8mg; SODIUM 108mg; CALC 11mg

---

Menu 2

Herb-Marinated Fresh Mozzarella Wraps

Baked chips

Strawberry-Kiwi Salad with Basil

Cashew-and-Golden Raisin Biscotti

Herb-Marinated Fresh Mozzarella Wraps

¾ cup (3 ounces) diced fresh mozzarella cheese
2 tablespoons chopped fresh basil
2 tablespoons chopped pitted kalamata olives
1 tablespoon chopped fresh chives
1 tablespoon chopped fresh oregano
1 teaspoon olive oil
¼ pound thinly sliced pepper ham
16 asparagus spears, steamed and chilled (about ¼ pound)
4 (8-inch) fat-free flour tortillas

1. Combine first 6 ingredients in a medium bowl. Cover and chill 2 hours.
2. Arrange 1 ounce of ham and 4 asparagus spears on each tortilla. Spoon about ⅓ cup cheese mixture over asparagus on each tortilla, and roll up. Yield: 4 servings (serving size: 1 wrap).
NOTE: These wraps may be assembled up to 4 hours in advance, though tortillas will begin to absorb moisture if prepared too far in advance. Pepper ham is available in the deli section of most supermarkets. If you are unable to find it, substitute regular ham, and add ¼ teaspoon freshly ground black pepper to cheese as it marinates.

CALORIES 230 (30% from fat); FAT 7.7g (sat 3.5g, mono 3.2g, poly 0.5g); PROTEIN 13.4g; CARB 26.7g; FIBER 1.8g; CHOL 30mg; IRON 1.9mg; SODIUM 862mg; CALC 130mg

Strawberry-Kiwi Salad with Basil

The soupy sauce on this salad is irresistible, especially with angel-food cake "dunkers."

¼ cup half-and-half
1 tablespoon sugar
2 tablespoons white balsamic vinegar
¼ teaspoon salt
3 peeled kiwifruit, each cut into 6 wedges
2 cups quartered strawberries (about 1 pint)
2 tablespoons finely chopped fresh basil

1. Combine first 4 ingredients in a bowl. Add kiwifruit and strawberries; toss well. Cover and chill 1 hour. Stir in basil just before serving. Yield: 4 servings (serving size: ¾ cup).

CALORIES 90 (23% from fat); FAT 2.3g (sat 1.1g, mono 0.6g, poly 0.4g); PROTEIN 1.6g; CARB 17.8g; FIBER 3.8g; CHOL 6mg; IRON 0.7mg; SODIUM 157mg; CALC 46mg

Cashew-and-Golden Raisin Biscotti

1⅔ cups all-purpose flour
¾ teaspoon baking powder
½ teaspoon grated whole nutmeg
¼ teaspoon baking soda
¼ teaspoon ground mace
¾ cup sugar
2 teaspoons vanilla extract
2 large eggs
¾ cup chopped dry-roasted cashews
¾ cup golden raisins
Cooking spray

1. Preheat oven to 300°.
2. Lightly spoon flour into dry measuring cups, and level with a knife. Combine flour and next 4 ingredients in a large bowl. Beat sugar, vanilla, and eggs in a large bowl with a mixer at medium speed until thick. Stir in flour mixture, cashews, and raisins. Turn dough out onto a lightly floured surface, and knead lightly 7 or 8 times. Shape dough into a 12-inch roll. Place roll on a baking sheet

coated with cooking spray, and pat to 1-inch thickness. Bake at 300° for 45 minutes. Cool 10 minutes on a wire rack.
3. Cut roll diagonally into 24 (½-inch) slices; stand slices upright on baking sheet. Bake 20 minutes (cookies will be slightly soft in center but will harden as they cool). Remove from baking sheet; cool completely on wire rack. Yield: 2 dozen (serving size: 1 biscotto).

CALORIES 102 (23% from fat); FAT 2.6g (sat 0.6g, mono 1.4g, poly 0.5g); PROTEIN 2.2g; CARB 18g; FIBER 0.7g; CHOL 18mg; IRON 0.8mg; SODIUM 52mg; CALC 14mg

---

Menu 3

Steamed snow peas with commercial peanut dipping sauce

Pork-and-Rice Noodle Salad with Lemon-Coconut Dressing

Marinated asparagus

Cashew-and-Golden Raisin Biscotti

Pork-and-Rice Noodle Salad with Lemon-Coconut Dressing

The texture of rice noodles and pork is impervious to the Thai-inspired dressing. The longer this sits, the better its flavor.

1 (8-ounce) package uncooked rice sticks (rice-flour noodles) or vermicelli
1 (¾-pound) pork tenderloin, trimmed
2 tablespoons grated peeled fresh ginger, divided
1 teaspoon salt, divided
1 garlic clove, minced
1 teaspoon vegetable oil
1½ cups light coconut milk
⅔ cup fresh lemon juice (about 4 lemons)
2 tablespoons sugar
1 jalapeño pepper, minced
¼ cup chopped fresh mint
¼ cup chopped peanuts

Continued

1. Cook rice sticks according to package directions, omitting salt and fat. Drain and rinse with cold water, and drain well. Place cooked noodles in a large bowl.

2. Slice pork lengthwise, cutting to, but not through, other side. Open halves, laying pork flat, and rub with 1 tablespoon ginger, ¼ teaspoon salt, and garlic. Heat oil in a large nonstick skillet over medium-high heat. Add pork; sauté 7 minutes on each side or until done. Cool slightly. Coarsely chop pork; add to noodles in bowl.

3. Combine coconut milk, juice, and sugar in a small saucepan, and bring to a boil. Reduce heat, and simmer until reduced to 1½ cups (about 10 minutes). Stir in 1 tablespoon ginger and ¾ teaspoon salt. Remove from heat; cool.

4. Add coconut dressing, jalapeño, mint, and peanuts to noodle mixture; toss well to combine. Chill until ready to serve. Yield: 4 servings (serving size: 1½ cups).

NOTE: To keep peanuts fresh, toss with salad just before serving. Seed jalapeño for a milder salad.

CALORIES 450 (25% from fat); FAT 12.7g (sat 5.6g, mono 3.7g, poly 2.2g); PROTEIN 25.5g; CARB 60.3g; FIBER 1.1g; CHOL 55mg; IRON 2.3mg; SODIUM 677mg; CALC 60mg

---

Menu 4

Marinated Mushrooms

Barley-Salmon Salad with Arugula Vinaigrette

Ciabatta or sourdough bread

Blueberry Turnovers

Marinated Mushrooms

  3 tablespoons minced shallots
  2 tablespoons white wine vinegar
  1 tablespoon grated orange rind
  ¼ cup fresh orange juice
  2 teaspoons minced fresh or
       ½ teaspoon dried thyme
  2 teaspoons extra-virgin olive oil
  ½ teaspoon salt
  3 cups small mushrooms (about 8
       ounces)
Freshly ground black pepper (optional)

1. Combine first 7 ingredients in a bowl. Add mushrooms; toss well. Cover and chill 1 hour, stirring occasionally. Garnish with pepper, if desired. Yield: 4 servings (serving size: ½ cup).

CALORIES 38 (33% from fat); FAT 1.4g (sat 0.2g, mono 0.8g, poly 0.2g); PROTEIN 1.5g; CARB 6g; FIBER 0.9g; CHOL 0mg; IRON 0.9mg; SODIUM 297mg; CALC 11mg

---

Barley-Salmon Salad with Arugula Vinaigrette

This salad can be tossed ahead. It's a one-fork dish.

  2 cups water
  1 cup uncooked quick-cooking barley
  1 (8-ounce) salmon fillet (about 1
       inch thick)
  ½ teaspoon salt, divided
Cooking spray
  2 cups trimmed arugula
  3 tablespoons white wine vinegar
  2 teaspoons extra-virgin olive oil
  ¼ teaspoon black pepper
  2 garlic cloves, crushed
  ½ cup (2 ounces) crumbled ricotta
       salata or feta cheese

1. Bring water to a boil in a large saucepan. Add barley; cover, reduce heat, and simmer 15 minutes or until tender. Remove from heat; let stand 5 minutes. Spoon barley into a bowl. Cool completely.

2. Sprinkle fillet with ⅛ teaspoon salt. Place fillet in a small nonstick skillet coated with cooking spray over medium heat; cook 6 minutes on each side or until fish flakes easily when tested with a fork. Remove fillet from pan; cool completely. Discard skin. Cut fillet into 1-inch pieces; add to barley in bowl.

3. Place ⅜ teaspoon salt, arugula, and next 4 ingredients in a blender, and process until smooth, scraping down sides of blender. Pour arugula vinaigrette over barley and fish; add cheese. Toss gently to combine. Cover and chill. Yield: 4 servings (serving size: 1¼ cups).

CALORIES 337 (30% from fat); FAT 11.1g (sat 3.4g, mono 4.8g, poly 1.9g); PROTEIN 19.1g; CARB 40.6g; FIBER 8.1g; CHOL 50mg; IRON 1.9mg; SODIUM 489mg; CALC 114mg

---

Menu 5

Salsa with baked tortilla chips

Jícama Salad with Chili-Spiced Chicken

Strawberry-Kiwi Salad with Basil

Jícama Salad with Chili-Spiced Chicken

  4 (6-inch) corn tortillas, cut into
       strips
Cooking spray
  2 teaspoons chili powder
  2 teaspoons ground cumin
  ½ teaspoon salt, divided
  ¼ teaspoon ground red pepper
  1 pound skinless, boneless chicken
       breast halves
  ¼ cup fresh lime juice
  2 tablespoons extra-virgin olive
       oil
  1 tablespoon honey
  3 cups (⅛-inch) julienne-cut peeled
       jícama (about ¾ pound)
  ¼ cup minced fresh cilantro
Lime wedges (optional)

1. Preheat oven at 375°.

2. Arrange tortilla strips in a single layer on a baking sheet; coat strips with cooking spray. Bake at 375° for 8 minutes or until toasted.

3. Combine chili powder, cumin, ¼ teaspoon salt, and pepper in a medium bowl. Add chicken, turning to coat on both sides. Heat a large nonstick skillet coated with cooking spray over medium-high heat. Add chicken, and cook 7 minutes on each side or until done. Cool.

4. Cut chicken diagonally into ¼-inch slices. Combine ¼ teaspoon salt, juice, oil, and honey in a medium bowl. Add jícama, cilantro, and tortilla strips; toss well. Divide salad evenly among 4 plates; top with chicken. Garnish with lime wedges, if desired. Yield: 4 servings (serving size: ⅔ cup salad and 3 ounces chicken).

CALORIES 307 (29% from fat); FAT 9.9g (sat 1.5g, mono 5.8g, poly 1.6g); PROTEIN 28.8g; CARB 26.3g; FIBER 6.2g; CHOL 66mg; IRON 2.8mg; SODIUM 427mg; CALC 87mg

may

The Other Side of the Mediterranean

The tastes of North Africa are as old as the pyramids and as exotic as the red brick walls of Marrakesh.

The northern Mediterranean tastes of tomatoes and eggplants, of pastas and paellas, are as familiar to many of us as fried chicken and baked beans. But to the south, across the Mediterranean Sea, lies a territory of flavors as exotic and complex as the region's history.

To many, the flavors of the southern Mediterranean remain a mystery. But the basic ingredients of this cuisine are as familiar as the names *Casablanca* and *Marrakesh*: poultry and fish, lamb and lentils, carrots and lemons. In North African hands, these common ingredients become extraordinary, transformed into savory salads and long-simmered stews rich with flavor.

Egyptian Greens-and-Chicken Stew

Meloukhia, a leafy green, is traditionally the base of this dish. Because it's sometimes hard to find, we've replaced it with spinach.

- 8 cups water
- 2 cardamom pods
- 1 (2½-pound) chicken, skinned
- 1 large onion, halved
- 1 bay leaf
- 2 (10-ounce) packages fresh spinach
- 1 tablespoon olive oil
- 2 teaspoons ground coriander
- ¾ teaspoon salt
- 10 garlic cloves, crushed
- 3 tablespoons fresh lemon juice
- 2 cups hot cooked rice

1. Combine first 5 ingredients in an 8-quart Dutch oven or stockpot, and bring to a boil. Reduce heat to medium, and cook, uncovered, 1 hour. Remove from heat. Remove chicken from pan, and place in a bowl; cool. Strain chicken broth through a cheesecloth-lined colander or fine sieve into a bowl, reserving onion; discard remaining solids. Return broth to pan. Remove chicken from bones, discarding bones; shred chicken into bite-size pieces. Keep warm.

2. Place onion in a bowl, and mash with a fork or potato masher. Add onion to broth; bring to a boil. Add spinach to broth in batches, cooking until wilted.

3. Heat oil in a small nonstick skillet over medium-high heat. Add coriander, salt, and garlic; sauté 30 seconds or until garlic begins to brown. Add to spinach mixture, and stir in lemon juice. Serve chicken and spinach mixture over rice. Yield: 4 servings (serving size: 3 ounces chicken, 2½ cups spinach mixture, and ½ cup rice).

CALORIES 302 (20% from fat); FAT 6.7g (sat 1.2g, mono 3.2g, poly 1.2g); PROTEIN 25.3g; CARB 36.4g; FIBER 7g; CHOL 60mg; IRON 5.8mg; SODIUM 620mg; CALC 186mg

---

Prized Date

Characterized by its high sugar content and meaty plumpness, the Medjool date was once considered a prized possession of Morocco—so captivating in its flavor that royalty hoarded the fruit, allowing only their families to enjoy its delicate taste. No longer reserved for royalty, the Medjool date has become the most widely chosen date in the world and can be purchased in most large supermarkets or online at www.medjooldates.com.

Algerian Stuffed Dates

- 24 Medjool dates (about 1 pound)
- 2 drops green food coloring (optional)
- ⅔ cup marzipan (almond paste)
- 2 teaspoons powdered sugar

1. Cut a lengthwise slit down center, but not through, each date.
2. Sprinkle food coloring over marzipan, if desired; gently knead 4 or 5 times or until color is incorporated into marzipan. Divide marzipan mixture evenly among dates; stuff into slits. Sprinkle with powdered sugar. Yield: 24 dates (serving size: 1 stuffed date).

CALORIES 50 (17% from fat); FAT 0.9g (sat 0.1g, mono 0.6g, poly 0.2g); PROTEIN 0.6g; CARB 10.8g; FIBER 0.6g; CHOL 0mg; IRON 0.1mg; SODIUM 0mg; CALC 7mg

Moroccan Mint Tea

- 2½ cups boiling water
- 2 teaspoons sugar
- 2 teaspoons loose Chinese gunpowder green tea or green tea
- 6 mint leaves, crushed

1. Combine all ingredients in a medium bowl; cover and steep 5 minutes. Strain tea mixture through a fine sieve into a bowl; discard solids. Yield: 2 servings (serving size: 1 cup).

NOTE: When you get loose tea from tea bags, one regular green tea bag will yield 1 teaspoon loose tea leaves.

CALORIES 17 (0% from fat); FAT 0g; PROTEIN 0g; CARB 4.2g; FIBER 0g; CHOL 0mg; IRON 0.1mg; SODIUM 0mg; CALC 0mg

Orange-and-Radish Salad

- 2 cups orange sections
- 1 cup grated radish
- 1 tablespoon minced fresh cilantro
- 2 tablespoons fresh orange juice
- 1¼ teaspoons orange-flower water (optional)
- 1 teaspoon powdered sugar
- ¼ teaspoon salt

1. Combine all ingredients in a medium bowl; cover and let stand 30 minutes. Serve at room temperature. Yield: 4 servings (serving size: ½ cup).

NOTE: Add an extra teaspoon of powdered sugar to salad if the oranges aren't very sweet.

CALORIES 54 (5% from fat); FAT 0.3g (sat 0.1g, mono 0.1g, poly 0.1g); PROTEIN 1.1g; CARB 13.1g; FIBER 4.2g; CHOL 0mg; IRON 0.2mg; SODIUM 154mg; CALC 44mg

---

Sweet Scent

The Arabs invented the process for distilling orange-flower water. Quite fragrant, the liquid is used to scent salads and desserts. In some households, it's also used to perfume hands after dining. The taste is unmistakable, and there are no substitutes. Orange-flower water (also called orange-blossom water) can be found in some supermarkets on the spice aisle, in Middle Eastern markets, in specialty shops, and online at www.ethnicgrocer.com.

Harira

During the ninth month of their calendar, Muslims observe the ritual fast of Ramadan. This is a variation of the soup that is traditionally eaten to break the fast.

1¼ pounds boneless leg of lamb,
       trimmed and cut into 1-inch cubes
½ teaspoon salt
¼ teaspoon black pepper
1 tablespoon olive oil
1 cup chopped onion
1 tablespoon tomato paste
4 cups water
1 cup drained canned chickpeas
       (garbanzo beans)
½ teaspoon ground cinnamon
¼ teaspoon ground red pepper
2 cups chopped tomato
½ cup dried small red or brown lentils
½ cup chopped red bell pepper
½ cup hot cooked angel hair (about 1
       ounce uncooked pasta)
1 tablespoon minced fresh cilantro
1 tablespoon fresh lemon juice

1. Sprinkle lamb with salt and black pepper. Heat oil in a large Dutch oven over high heat. Add lamb; cook 5 minutes or until browned, stirring occasionally. Add onion; cook 1 minute, stirring frequently. Stir in tomato paste; cook 1 minute, stirring frequently. Stir in water, chickpeas, cinnamon, and ground red pepper. Bring to a boil; reduce heat, and simmer 30 minutes.

2. Stir in tomato, lentils, and bell pepper. Bring to a boil; reduce heat, and simmer 30 minutes or until lentils are tender. Stir in pasta, cilantro, and juice; cook 1 minute or until thoroughly heated. Yield: 4 servings (serving size: 1¼ cups).

CALORIES 359 (23% from fat); FAT 9.2g (sat 2.1g, mono 4.4g, poly 1.5g); PROTEIN 30.4g; CARB 40.6g; FIBER 6.8g; CHOL 55mg; IRON 6.3mg; SODIUM 544mg; CALC 60mg

---

Chicken Tagine with Lemons and Olives

This dish is best served over couscous.

2 chicken breast halves (about
       1½ pounds), skinned
2 chicken leg quarters (about
       1 pound), skinned
¼ teaspoon salt
¼ teaspoon black pepper
1 teaspoon olive oil
1 cup chopped onion
2 garlic cloves, minced
¾ cup fat-free, less-sodium chicken
       broth
¾ cup pitted whole green olives
1 teaspoon ground cinnamon
½ teaspoon ground ginger
1½ teaspoons grated lemon rind
¼ cup fresh lemon juice
1 tablespoon minced fresh cilantro
1 tablespoon minced fresh parsley

1. Sprinkle chicken with salt and pepper. Heat oil in a large Dutch oven over high heat. Add chicken; cook 3 minutes on each side or until browned. Remove chicken from pan. Add onion and garlic to pan; cook 30 seconds, stirring constantly. Add chicken, broth, olives, cinnamon, and ginger; bring to a boil. Cover, reduce heat, and simmer mixture 45 minutes. Turn chicken over; cook, uncovered, 15 minutes.

2. Remove chicken from pan with a slotted spoon; place 1 chicken piece on each of 4 plates. Add lemon rind, juice, cilantro, and parsley to pan; cook 30 seconds, stirring constantly. Spoon sauce over chicken. Yield: 4 servings (serving size: 1 chicken piece and ⅓ cup sauce).

CALORIES 345 (30% from fat); FAT 11.5g (sat 2.5g, mono 5.9g, poly 2.3g); PROTEIN 49.9g; CARB 9.2g; FIBER 2.5g; CHOL 145mg; IRON 3.7mg; SODIUM 769mg; CALC 87mg

---

Course in Couscous

In North Africa, couscous—a traditional accompaniment—is usually steamed (often with a simmering *tagine* or stew) rather than prepared by soaking in hot water. The process is fairly simple, but it demands attention so the final result is fluffy and airy. For a streamlined version of the traditional preparation, try the following technique from Claudia Roden, author of *The New Book of Middle Eastern Food* (Knopf, 2000).

Put the couscous in a wide ovenproof dish to avoid crowding the grains. Gradually add the same amount of salted water (for example, 3 cups water for 3 cups couscous, which will serve 6 to 8), stirring all the time so it's evenly absorbed. Keep fluffing up the couscous with a fork, breaking up any lumps. After 10 to 15 minutes, mix in 3 tablespoons vegetable oil, and rub the couscous between your hands to break up any remaining lumps.

Place the uncovered dish in a preheated 400° oven, and heat for 15 to 20 minutes. Fluff the couscous again with a fork after about 10 minutes. Traditionally, an additional 2 to 3 tablespoons of oil or butter would be worked in before serving, but you may omit this.

Our Test Kitchens staff found this technique easy, yielding a much fluffier result than what is obtained by following the package directions.

Sea Bass Crusted with Moroccan Spices

The coast of the southern Mediterranean yields a rich bounty of fish that's prepared in numerous ways. One constant in Morocco, however, is the use of *chermoula*, a combination marinade and spice rub. It typically contains an acid-based marinade (we used lemon juice) and a spice rub made from black pepper, cumin, coriander, and paprika.

MARINADE:
- ¼ cup fresh lemon juice
- 1 tablespoon minced fresh cilantro
- 1 teaspoon ground cumin
- ¼ teaspoon crushed red pepper
- 3 garlic cloves, crushed
- 4 (6-ounce) sea bass fillets (about 1 inch thick)

SPICE RUB:
- 2 tablespoons ground coriander
- 2 teaspoons freshly ground black pepper
- 1 teaspoon caraway seeds
- 1 teaspoon ground cumin
- 1 teaspoon paprika
- ¼ teaspoon salt

REMAINING INGREDIENTS:
- 1 tablespoon olive oil
- Lemon wedges (optional)
- Cilantro sprigs (optional)

1. To prepare marinade, combine first 5 ingredients in a large zip-top plastic bag; add fillets to bag. Seal and marinate in refrigerator 45 minutes. Remove fillets from bag; discard marinade.

2. To prepare spice rub, combine coriander and next 5 ingredients in a medium bowl. Rub fillets with spice mixture to coat.

3. Heat oil in a large nonstick skillet over medium heat. Add fillets; cook 6 minutes on each side or until fish flakes easily when tested with a fork. If desired, garnish with lemon wedges and cilantro sprigs. Yield: 4 servings.

CALORIES 210 (30% from fat); FAT 7.2g (sat 1.4g, mono 3.4g, poly 1.7g); PROTEIN 32.1g; CARB 3.2g; FIBER 0.7g; CHOL 70mg; IRON 2mg; SODIUM 267mg; CALC 48mg

Local Color

An advocate for community farmers' markets, Ann Yonkers reaps—and relishes—what she sows.

On the Eastern Shore of Maryland's Chesapeake Bay lies Pot Pie Farm, 10 acres that Ann bought with her husband, Charlie, in 1991.

Ann specializes in what she calls "eco-culinary enterprises." The eggs, produce, and herbs raised organically at Pot Pie aren't just Ann's backyard pantry; they're also sold every Saturday from May through October at the nearby farmers' market in St. Michaels, Maryland, which Ann organized and currently manages. She also orchestrates a larger market in downtown Washington, which is open every Sunday from spring through winter.

Managing the two markets is part of Ann's work for the American Farmland Trust, a Washington-based nonprofit organization whose mission is to protect America's farms from urban sprawl.

"People have to realize," Ann says, "that if we want to eat well, we can't get rid of our farms."

Spring Risotto with Peas and Asparagus

- 1½ cups water
- 2 (14½-ounce) cans vegetable broth
- 2 tablespoons olive oil
- ¼ cup finely chopped shallots
- 1 cup uncooked Arborio rice or other short-grain rice
- ⅓ cup dry white wine
- ½ teaspoon salt
- ¼ teaspoon black pepper
- 2 cups shelled green peas (about 1½ pounds unshelled green peas)
- ½ cup asparagus, diagonally cut into thin slices
- 1 teaspoon grated lemon rind
- 1 teaspoon chopped fresh mint

1. Bring water and broth to a simmer in a medium saucepan (do not boil). Keep warm over low heat.

2. Heat oil in a large saucepan over medium heat. Add shallots; cook 1 minute, stirring constantly. Add rice; cook 2 minutes, stirring constantly. Stir in wine, salt, and pepper; cook 1 minute or until liquid is nearly absorbed, stirring constantly. Add broth mixture, ½ cup at a time, stirring constantly until each portion of broth is absorbed before adding next (about 20 minutes total). Stir in peas, asparagus, rind, and mint; cook 5 minutes, stirring constantly. Yield: 6 servings (serving size: 1 cup).

CALORIES 227 (22% from fat); FAT 5.5g (sat 0.7g, mono 3.4g, poly 0.5g); PROTEIN 5.3g; CARB 37g; FIBER 2.4g; CHOL 0mg; IRON 2.4mg; SODIUM 800mg; CALC 20mg

for two

Saved by the Bells

An undisputed supper solution—versatile, stuffable bell peppers.

Looking for a tasty dinner that you can knock out in a hurry? Try bell peppers. You can stuff them with almost any filling, and they provide an easy one-dish dinner in minutes. Prep and cook time can be kept to a minimum by using the microwave.

Meat-and-Potato-Stuffed Peppers

- 2 large green bell peppers
- ¼ pound turkey kielbasa, cut into ½-inch pieces
- 2 cups frozen hash brown potatoes with onions and peppers (such as Ore-Ida Potatoes O'Brien)
- ¼ cup sliced green onions
- ¼ teaspoon hot pepper sauce
- ½ cup (2 ounces) shredded reduced-fat cheddar cheese
- ¼ cup fat-free sour cream

1. Preheat oven to 350°.
2. Cut bell peppers in half lengthwise; discard seeds and membranes. Arrange halves in a 9-inch pie plate. Cover with heavy-duty plastic wrap. Microwave at HIGH 5 minutes or until crisp-tender; drain. Return peppers to pie plate.
3. Heat a medium nonstick skillet over medium heat. Add kielbasa; sauté 2 minutes. Add potatoes; sauté 3 minutes or until thoroughly heated. Stir in onions and pepper sauce. Divide sausage mixture evenly among pepper halves; top each pepper half with 2 tablespoons cheese. Bake at 350° for 10 minutes or until cheese melts. Top each pepper half with 1 tablespoon sour cream. Yield: 2 servings (serving size: 2 pepper halves).

CALORIES 332 (29% from fat); FAT 10.8g (sat 4.5g, mono 1.9g, poly 1.6g); PROTEIN 21.3g; CARB 36.9g; FIBER 2.1g; CHOL 48mg; IRON 8.4mg; SODIUM 859mg; CALC 273mg

Asian Stuffed Peppers

2½ ounces uncooked curly Chinese-style noodles or angel hair pasta, broken into thirds
2 large red bell peppers
1 cup cubed firm tofu (about 6 ounces)
2 tablespoons hoisin sauce
1 tablespoon low-sodium soy sauce
2 teaspoons dark sesame oil
2 garlic cloves, minced
½ cup diagonally sliced snow peas
½ cup (1½-inch) julienne-cut carrot
2 tablespoons chopped fresh cilantro

1. Cook noodles according to package directions, omitting salt and fat; drain.
2. Cut bell peppers in half lengthwise; discard seeds and membranes. Arrange halves in a 9-inch pie plate. Cover with heavy-duty plastic wrap. Microwave at HIGH 5 minutes or until crisp-tender; drain. Return peppers to pie plate.
3. Combine tofu, hoisin sauce, and soy sauce in a small bowl. Heat oil in a nonstick skillet over medium-high heat. Add garlic; sauté 15 seconds. Add peas and carrot; sauté 3 minutes or until vegetables are tender. Add tofu mixture;

sauté 1 minute or until thoroughly heated. Stir in noodles. Divide noodle mixture evenly among pepper halves; sprinkle each pepper half with 1½ teaspoons cilantro. Yield: 2 servings (serving size: 2 pepper halves).

CALORIES 327 (28% from fat); FAT 10.2g (sat 1.5g, mono 3g, poly 5g); PROTEIN 14.5g; CARB 46.4g; FIBER 5.5g; CHOL 0mg; IRON 8.3mg; SODIUM 525mg; CALC 140mg

Moroccan Chickpea-and-Couscous-Stuffed Peppers

2 large red bell peppers
2 teaspoons olive oil
4 garlic cloves, minced
½ teaspoon ground cumin
½ teaspoon ground turmeric
¼ teaspoon ground cinnamon
1⅓ cups drained canned chickpeas (garbanzo beans)
¾ cup vegetable broth
⅓ cup uncooked couscous
½ cup (2 ounces) crumbled feta cheese with garlic and herbs, divided
2 tablespoons chopped fresh mint, divided
2 tablespoons hot mango chutney

1. Cut bell peppers in half lengthwise; discard seeds and membranes. Arrange halves in a 9-inch pie plate. Cover with heavy-duty plastic wrap. Microwave at HIGH 5 minutes or until crisp-tender; drain. Return peppers to pie plate.
2. Heat oil in a large saucepan over medium heat. Add garlic; sauté 2 minutes. Add cumin, turmeric, and cinnamon, and sauté 30 seconds. Stir in chickpeas and broth; bring to a boil. Stir in couscous; remove from heat. Cover and let stand 5 minutes or until liquid is absorbed. Stir in 6 tablespoons cheese and 1 tablespoon mint. Divide couscous mixture evenly among pepper halves. Top each pepper half with 1½ teaspoons cheese, ¾ teaspoon mint, and 1½ teaspoons chutney. Yield: 2 servings (serving size: 2 pepper halves).

CALORIES 460 (28% from fat); FAT 14.4g (sat 5.3g, mono 5.4g, poly 2.2g); PROTEIN 18.4g; CARB 67.7g; FIBER 6.3g; CHOL 25mg; IRON 5.8mg; SODIUM 959mg; CALC 226mg

Cajun Chicken-and-Rice-Stuffed Peppers

2 large red bell peppers
½ pound skinless, boneless chicken breast, cut into ½-inch pieces
1¼ teaspoons Cajun seasoning
2 teaspoons olive oil
½ cup chopped onion
2 garlic cloves, minced
1¼ cups fat-free, less-sodium chicken broth
½ cup uncooked converted rice
¼ teaspoon salt
2 cups baby spinach leaves
5 teaspoons chopped fresh chives

1. Cut bell peppers in half lengthwise; discard seeds and membranes. Arrange halves in a 9-inch pie plate. Cover with heavy-duty plastic wrap. Microwave at HIGH 5 minutes or until crisp-tender; drain. Return peppers to pie plate.
2. Combine chicken and Cajun seasoning in a bowl. Heat oil in a medium saucepan over medium heat. Add chicken; sauté 4 minutes or until done. Remove from pan.
3. Add onion and garlic to pan; sauté 1 minute. Add broth, rice, and salt; bring to a boil. Cover, reduce heat, and simmer 15 minutes. Return chicken to pan; cover and cook 3 minutes or until rice is done. Stir in spinach and chives. Divide rice mixture evenly among pepper halves. Yield: 2 servings (serving size: 2 pepper halves).

CALORIES 403 (16% from fat); FAT 7g (sat 1.2g, mono 3.8g, poly 1.1g); PROTEIN 34.6g; CARB 49.4g; FIBER 5.2g; CHOL 66mg; IRON 5.8mg; SODIUM 833mg; CALC 109mg

Kitchen Tip

Bell peppers shouldn't be overcooked. Once they're done, let them cool; for firmer flesh, place them in the freezer for a minute or two. Then spoon in the filling and perhaps pop them into your oven for brief baking, which helps unite the flavors. For these recipes, we used peppers weighing a half-pound each, but if you can't find peppers that size, adjust the filling portions as needed.

Time for Strudel

We help a reader with a heavy schedule by lightening her favorite chicken recipe.

Carole Lypaczewski, 44, from Aurora, Ontario, Canada, doesn't stop. The mother of two boys, ages 16 and 12, Carole takes yoga and aquatic-fitness classes, skis in winter, plays golf in spring and summer, and volunteers at her church and kids' school. She's also an avid member of a local walking group and is ready for a hike most any day of the week.

While it's obvious that she's up for nearly any challenge, Carole turned to *Cooking Light* to help lighten the recipe she describes as "easy-to-make-yet-bound-to-impress-the-guests Chicken Strudel."

We reduced the number of phyllo sheets, coated them with cooking spray instead of butter, cut down on the Swiss cheese, and added garlic to the chicken-spinach filling to heighten the flavor.

Having found our lightened version even more flavorful than the original, Carole describes it as "great taste without the guilt."

Chicken Strudel

Cooking spray
1 cup chopped onion
1 (10-ounce) package fresh spinach, chopped (about 8 cups)
4 cups chopped cooked chicken breast (about 1¼ pounds)
¾ cup (3 ounces) shredded Swiss cheese
¼ cup egg substitute
2 tablespoons dry white wine
¼ teaspoon salt
⅛ teaspoon black pepper
2 garlic cloves, minced
8 sheets frozen phyllo dough, thawed
½ cup dry breadcrumbs
1 tablespoon butter, melted
¼ teaspoon paprika

1. Heat a large nonstick skillet coated with cooking spray over medium heat. Add onion, and sauté 6 minutes or until tender. Stir in spinach, and cook 2 minutes or until spinach wilts, stirring constantly. Remove from heat. Stir in chicken and next 6 ingredients.

2. Preheat oven to 375°.

3. Lightly coat 1 sheet phyllo dough with cooking spray (cover remaining dough to keep from drying). Sprinkle with 1 tablespoon breadcrumbs. Repeat layers with 3 sheets phyllo, cooking spray, and 3 tablespoons breadcrumbs.

4. Gently press layers together. Place about 2½ cups chicken mixture along 1 long edge of top phyllo sheet, leaving a ½-inch border. Starting at long edge with ½-inch border, roll up jelly-roll fashion. Place, seam side down, on a baking sheet coated with cooking spray. Tuck ends under. Repeat with remaining 4 sheets phyllo, cooking spray, ¼ cup breadcrumbs, and 2½ cups chicken mixture. Brush strudels evenly with melted butter. Sprinkle each with ⅛ teaspoon paprika.

5. Bake strudels at 375° for 20 minutes or until brown. Let stand 5 minutes before slicing. Cut each strudel into 4 slices. Serve immediately. Yield: 2 strudels, 4 servings per strudel (serving size: 1 slice).

CALORIES 248 (30% from fat); FAT 8.2g (sat 3.6g, mono 2.3g, poly 1.5g); PROTEIN 23.8g; CARB 18.8g; FIBER 2g; CHOL 59mg; IRON 2.8mg; SODIUM 345mg; CALC 172mg

BEFORE	AFTER
SERVING SIZE	
1 slice	
CALORIES PER SERVING	
501	248
FAT	
28.2 g	8.2 g
PERCENT OF TOTAL CALORIES	
51%	30%
SODIUM	
569mg	345mg

Barbecue Roasted Salmon

We resolved back in January to eat more fish. If you did the same, then you'll love this unusual Barbecue Roasted Salmon, which debuted in our September 1998 issue.

The flavor is an intriguing blend of sweet, spicy, and tart. Try it with asparagus, or—for a Cinco de Mayo twist—with a side of jícama salad.

Barbecue Roasted Salmon

¼ cup pineapple juice
2 tablespoons fresh lemon juice
4 (6-ounce) salmon fillets
2 tablespoons brown sugar
4 teaspoons chili powder
2 teaspoons grated lemon rind
¾ teaspoon ground cumin
½ teaspoon salt
¼ teaspoon ground cinnamon
Cooking spray
Lemon slices (optional)

1. Combine first 3 ingredients in a zip-top plastic bag; seal and marinate in refrigerator 1 hour, turning occasionally.

2. Preheat oven to 400°.

3. Remove fillets from bag; discard marinade. Combine sugar and next 5 ingredients in a bowl. Rub over fillets; place in an 11 x 7-inch baking dish coated with cooking spray. Bake at 400° for 12 minutes or until fish flakes easily when tested with a fork. Serve with lemon slices, if desired. Yield: 4 servings.

CALORIES 314 (42% from fat); FAT 14.7g (sat 2.5g, mono 6.9g, poly 3.3g); PROTEIN 35.3g; CARB 9g; FIBER 1g; CHOL 111mg; IRON 1.5mg; SODIUM 405mg; CALC 30mg

Chicken with Prosciutto and Tomatoes over Polenta, page 134

Carrot-Ginger Soup, page 152

Strawberry
Parfait,
page 157

French West Indian Grilled Snapper
with Caper Sauce, page 147

Asparagus Melt with Pesto
Spread, page 140

Chickpea-Vegetable Salad with Curried
Yogurt Dressing, page 139

Thigh Masters

Truth be known, we love chicken thighs.

Don't get us wrong—we think chicken breasts definitely have their place. But when it comes to flavor, thighs rule.

It's true that thighs have a slightly higher fat content than the oh-so-lean breast. But dark meat with the skin removed has less total fat than the same amount of beef sirloin or tenderloin, a pork chop, or a portion of salmon.

In the following recipes, we've put both boneless and bone-in thighs through their paces, using the dark meat's depth of flavor as a base on which to build some spectacular successes.

Oven-Fried Chicken Thighs with Buttermilk-Mustard Sauce

Preheating the baking sheet helps to crisp the chicken on the bottom. Serve with mashed potatoes.

  ¼ cup low-fat buttermilk
  4 teaspoons Dijon mustard
  1 tablespoon honey
  ¼ teaspoon salt
  ¼ teaspoon freshly ground black pepper
  ⅛ teaspoon dried rosemary
  ¼ cup dry breadcrumbs
  1½ tablespoons grated fresh Parmesan cheese
  4 (6-ounce) chicken thighs, skinned
Cooking spray

1. Preheat oven to 425°.
2. Combine first 6 ingredients in a small microwave-safe bowl. Spoon 3 tablespoons buttermilk mixture into a shallow bowl; reserve remaining mixture.
3. Combine breadcrumbs and Parmesan cheese in a small bowl. Dip chicken in 3 tablespoons buttermilk mixture; dredge in breadcrumb mixture. Chill 15 minutes. Lightly coat a baking sheet with cooking spray, and place in oven 5 minutes.
4. Place chicken on baking sheet. Bake at 425° for 24 minutes or until a meat thermometer registers 180°, turning chicken after 12 minutes. Microwave reserved buttermilk mixture at HIGH 20 seconds or until warm. Drizzle sauce over chicken. Yield: 2 servings (serving size: 2 thighs and 2 tablespoons sauce).

CALORIES 376 (29% from fat); FAT 12g (sat 3.5g, mono 4g, poly 2.8g); PROTEIN 43.6g; CARB 20.4g; FIBER 0.4g; CHOL 168mg; IRON 3mg; SODIUM 971mg; CALC 152mg

Chicken Thighs with Marsala-Mushroom Cream Sauce over Noodles

Sun-dried tomatoes, shiitake mushrooms, and Marsala wine give this sauce a rich, robust flavor. While the sun-dried tomatoes are rehydrating, prepare the rest of the ingredients.

  ¼ cup sun-dried tomatoes, packed without oil (about 12)
  4 (6-ounce) chicken thighs, skinned
  ½ teaspoon salt, divided
  ¼ teaspoon black pepper, divided
  2 teaspoons olive oil
  2 cups quartered button mushrooms (about 4 ounces)
  1½ cups sliced fresh shiitake mushroom caps (about 3 ounces)
  ½ teaspoon dried thyme
  1 garlic clove, minced
  1 bay leaf
  ⅓ cup fat-free, less-sodium chicken broth
  5 tablespoons Marsala wine, divided
  3 tablespoons half-and-half
  4 teaspoons chopped fresh parsley
  2 cups hot cooked wide egg noodles (about 1½ cups uncooked)

1. Combine boiling water and sun-dried tomatoes in a bowl; let stand 15 minutes. Drain and chop.
2. Sprinkle chicken with ¼ teaspoon salt and ⅛ teaspoon pepper. Heat olive oil in a large nonstick skillet over medium-high heat. Add chicken, and sauté 5 minutes, turning once. Remove chicken from pan.
3. Reduce heat to medium-low. Add ¼ teaspoon salt, ⅛ teaspoon pepper, and mushrooms; sauté 2 minutes. Add thyme, garlic, and bay leaf; sauté 30 seconds. Return chicken to pan. Add sun-dried tomatoes, broth, and ¼ cup wine. Cover, reduce heat, and simmer 25 minutes, turning chicken once.
4. Add 1 tablespoon wine and half-and-half, and bring to a boil. Discard bay leaf. Sprinkle with parsley. Serve over noodles. Yield: 4 servings (serving size: 1 thigh, ¼ cup sauce, and ½ cup noodles).

CALORIES 333 (28% from fat); FAT 10.2g (sat 2.7g, mono 4g, poly 2g); PROTEIN 31.5g; CARB 28.5g; FIBER 3.4g; CHOL 137mg; IRON 4.8mg; SODIUM 583mg; CALC 63mg

Chicken with Paprika and Potatoes

We've seasoned the chicken by rubbing it with a spice paste.

  ½ teaspoon salt, divided
  1½ teaspoons paprika
  1 teaspoon Worcestershire sauce
  ½ teaspoon dried thyme
  ¼ teaspoon freshly ground black pepper
  4 (4-ounce) skinless, boneless chicken thighs
  3 cups thinly sliced red potatoes (about 1 pound)
  ¾ cup chopped green bell pepper
  ½ cup chopped onion
  2 teaspoons olive oil
  1 garlic clove, finely chopped
  ⅓ cup fat-free, less-sodium chicken broth
Thyme sprigs (optional)

1. Combine ¼ teaspoon salt and next 4 ingredients. Rub over chicken.

Continued

2. Combine ¼ teaspoon salt, potatoes, bell pepper, onion, oil, and garlic in a large bowl. Heat a large nonstick skillet over medium-high heat. Add potato mixture, and cook 5 minutes, stirring occasionally. Add broth; cover, reduce heat, and simmer 5 minutes. Uncover; add thighs to pan, nestling them into vegetable mixture. Cover and cook 20 minutes or until vegetables are tender and chicken is done. Garnish with thyme sprigs, if desired. Yield: 2 servings (serving size: 2 thighs and 1 cup vegetables).

CALORIES 525 (24% from fat); FAT 14.3g (sat 3.1g, mono 6.1g, poly 3g); PROTEIN 51.2g; CARB 47.4g; FIBER 6.5g; CHOL 188mg; IRON 8.3mg; SODIUM 906mg; CALC 100mg

Boning a Chicken Thigh Step-by-Step

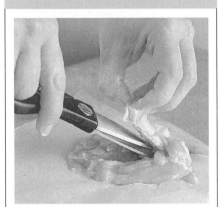

1. *Work from inside of thigh, and cut along both sides of thigh bone, separating from meat.*

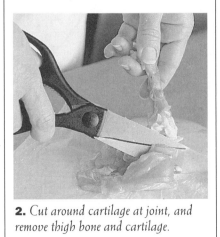

2. *Cut around cartilage at joint, and remove thigh bone and cartilage.*

Stir-Fried Chicken and Broccoli with Black Bean Sauce

While the chicken marinates, prepare the sauce and chop the vegetables. Jarred black bean sauce is in the Asian-food sections of grocery stores or in Asian markets.

CHICKEN:
- 1 tablespoon dry sherry
- ¼ teaspoon salt
- ¾ pound skinless, boneless chicken thighs, cut into ¼-inch-wide strips

SAUCE:
- 2 teaspoons cornstarch
- 2 tablespoons water
- ⅓ cup fat-free, less-sodium chicken broth
- 2 tablespoons dry sherry
- 2 tablespoons low-sodium soy sauce
- 1 tablespoon black bean sauce
- 1 teaspoon dark sesame oil

STIR-FRY:
- 1 tablespoon vegetable oil
- 3 cups broccoli florets
- 1 cup red bell pepper strips
- 1½ teaspoons finely chopped peeled fresh ginger
- 3 tablespoons fat-free, less-sodium chicken broth

REMAINING INGREDIENT:
- 2 cups hot cooked rice

1. To prepare chicken, combine first 3 ingredients in a medium bowl. Cover and marinate in refrigerator 20 minutes.
2. To prepare sauce, combine cornstarch and water in a medium bowl. Stir in ⅓ cup broth and next 4 ingredients.
3. To prepare stir-fry, heat vegetable oil in a large nonstick skillet over medium-high heat. Add chicken mixture; stir-fry 3 minutes or until chicken loses its pink color. Remove from pan. Add broccoli, bell pepper, and ginger; stir-fry 30 seconds. Stir in 3 tablespoons broth, and stir-fry 2 minutes. Stir sauce with a whisk until blended; add sauce and chicken mixture to pan. Bring to a boil; cook 2 minutes or until vegetables are crisp-tender and chicken is done. Serve over rice. Yield: 4 servings (serving size: about 1 cup stir-fry and ½ cup rice).

CALORIES 296 (26% from fat); FAT 8.5g (sat 1.7g, mono 2.6g, poly 3.2g); PROTEIN 21.1g; CARB 32.6g; FIBER 3g; CHOL 71mg; IRON 2.9mg; SODIUM 571mg; CALC 55mg

Chicken with Prosciutto and Tomatoes over Polenta
(pictured on page 129)

While the chicken cooks, prepare the polenta.

- 4 (6-ounce) chicken thighs, skinned
- 1 tablespoon chopped fresh or 1 teaspoon dried rubbed sage
- ¼ teaspoon salt, divided
- ¼ teaspoon freshly ground black pepper
- ½ cup all-purpose flour
- 2 teaspoons olive oil
- ½ cup dry white wine
- ⅔ cup yellow cornmeal
- 2 cups water
- 1 cup chopped seeded peeled tomato
- 1 teaspoon fresh lemon juice
- 2 very thin slices prosciutto or ham, cut into thin strips (about ¼ cup)
- Sage sprigs (optional)

1. Sprinkle chicken with chopped sage, ⅛ teaspoon salt, and pepper. Place flour in a shallow dish. Dredge chicken in flour. Heat oil in a nonstick skillet over medium-high heat. Add chicken; cook 4 minutes on each side. Add wine; cover, reduce heat, and simmer 20 minutes or until a meat thermometer registers 180°.
2. Place cornmeal and ⅛ teaspoon salt in a 1-quart casserole. Gradually add water, stirring until blended. Cover. Microwave at HIGH 12 minutes, stirring every 3 minutes. Let stand, covered, 5 minutes.
3. Remove chicken from pan. Add tomato to pan; cook 1 minute. Stir in juice and prosciutto. Spoon polenta onto plates, and top with chicken. Serve with tomato sauce. Garnish with sage sprigs, if desired. Yield: 2 servings (serving size: 2 thighs, ½ cup polenta, and ½ cup sauce).

CALORIES 482 (30% from fat); FAT 15.8g (sat 3.7g, mono 5g, poly 5.2g); PROTEIN 47.3g; CARB 37.3g; FIBER 5.8g; CHOL 175mg; IRON 4.5mg; SODIUM 753mg; CALC 48mg

Caramelized-Chicken Salad with Chile-Garlic Vinaigrette

Serve this one-dish meal in large, shallow individual bowls.

NOODLES:

4 ounces uncooked rice stick noodles

SAUCE:

6 tablespoons fresh lime juice
¼ cup chopped seeded jalapeño pepper
3 tablespoons sugar
1 tablespoon fish sauce
8 garlic cloves, peeled

CHICKEN:

2 teaspoons vegetable oil
1 pound skinless, boneless chicken thighs, cut into ½-inch-wide strips
½ cup minced shallots
2 tablespoons sugar
1 tablespoon fish sauce
¼ teaspoon black pepper

REMAINING INGREDIENTS:

1 cup (¼-inch) julienne-cut red bell pepper
½ cup (⅛-inch) julienne-cut carrot
¼ cup fresh bean sprouts
¼ cup coarsely chopped fresh basil
¼ cup cilantro sprigs
¼ cup coarsely chopped fresh mint
1 small cucumber (about 6 ounces), peeled, halved lengthwise, seeded, and thinly sliced

1. To prepare noodles, cook noodles in boiling water 1½ minutes; drain. Rinse under cold water. Drain and place in a large bowl.
2. To prepare sauce, place lime juice and next 4 ingredients in a blender, and process until smooth.
3. To prepare chicken, heat oil in a large nonstick skillet over medium-high heat. Add chicken; sauté 3 minutes. Stir in shallots. Cook 1 minute; stir constantly. Add 2 tablespoons sugar; cook 5 minutes, stirring frequently. Remove from heat; stir in 1 tablespoon fish sauce and black pepper.
4. To prepare salad, combine noodles, sauce, chicken mixture, bell pepper, and remaining ingredients in a large bowl, and toss well. Yield: 6 servings (serving size: 1⅔ cups).

CALORIES 248 (17% from fat); FAT 4.7g (sat 1.1g, mono 1.4g, poly 1.6g); PROTEIN 16.6g; CARB 35.3g; FIBER 1.1g; CHOL 58mg; IRON 2mg; SODIUM 539mg; CALC 44mg

Chicken Thighs with Garlic and Lime

After the chicken is baked, it's removed from the pan. The drippings are reduced on the stovetop to a slightly syrupy sauce that is then spooned over the thighs.

1 tablespoon minced garlic
1½ teaspoons ground cumin
½ teaspoon dried oregano
¼ teaspoon salt
⅛ teaspoon black pepper
2 tablespoons fresh lime juice, divided
4 (6-ounce) chicken thighs, skinned
3 tablespoons fat-free, less-sodium chicken broth
1 tablespoon white vinegar
2 teaspoons chopped fresh cilantro
2 lime wedges

1. Preheat oven to 350°.
2. Combine first 5 ingredients in a small bowl; stir in 1 tablespoon juice. Rub garlic mixture over chicken. Place chicken in a medium skillet.
3. Combine 1 tablespoon juice, chicken broth, and vinegar; pour over chicken. Place over medium-high heat; bring to a boil. Remove from heat. Wrap handle of pan with foil. Cover and bake at 350° for 30 minutes or until a meat thermometer registers 180°.
4. Remove chicken from pan; keep warm. Place pan over medium-high heat. Bring sauce to a boil, and cook until reduced to ¼ cup (about 3 minutes). Spoon over chicken. Sprinkle with cilantro, and serve with lime wedges. Yield: 2 servings (serving size: 2 thighs and 2 tablespoons sauce).

CALORIES 326 (29% from fat); FAT 10.4g (sat 2.6g, mono 3.3g, poly 2.6g); PROTEIN 51.1g; CARB 4.8g; FIBER 0.5g; CHOL 212mg; IRON 4mg; SODIUM 517mg; CALC 59mg

Chicken Thighs with Goat Cheese Sauce and Tarragon

If you have an adventurous palate, you'll love this bold pairing of tart goat cheese and anise-flavored tarragon.

¼ cup fat-free, less-sodium chicken broth, divided
1 (3-ounce) package goat cheese, softened
4 (4-ounce) skinless, boneless chicken thighs, halved
¼ teaspoon salt
⅛ teaspoon black pepper
1 teaspoon butter
2 tablespoons finely chopped onion
2 tablespoons finely chopped celery
2 tablespoons finely chopped carrot
2 tablespoons finely chopped red bell pepper
1 garlic clove, minced
1½ teaspoons chopped fresh or ½ teaspoon dried tarragon
2 cups hot cooked rice

1. Combine 1 tablespoon chicken broth and cheese in a small bowl, stirring with a whisk until blended. Sprinkle chicken with salt and pepper.
2. Melt butter in a large nonstick skillet over medium-low heat. Add onion, celery, carrot, bell pepper, and garlic; sauté 3 minutes. Add chicken; cook 2 minutes. Stir in 3 tablespoons broth; cover, reduce heat, and simmer 15 minutes or until chicken is done.
3. Stir in cheese mixture and tarragon until blended. Serve with rice. Yield: 4 servings (serving size: 2 chicken pieces, ¼ cup sauce, and ½ cup rice).

CALORIES 319 (28% from fat); FAT 10g (sat 4.9g, mono 2.6g, poly 1.3g); PROTEIN 27.7g; CARB 27.1g; FIBER 0.8g; CHOL 116mg; IRON 2.3mg; SODIUM 526mg; CALC 133mg

Here's an easy blue-plate weeknight dinner.

Chicken Thighs with Sweet Red Onions and Balsamic Vinegar

Mashed potatoes

Green beans with toasted almonds

Dinner rolls

Chicken Thighs with Sweet Red Onions and Balsamic Vinegar

The chicken is smothered in a thick onion sauce; serve it over mashed potatoes.

- 2 teaspoons olive oil
- 1 pound red onions, cut into (½-inch-thick) slices and separated into rings (about 3 medium)
- ½ teaspoon coarsely ground black pepper, divided
- ¼ teaspoon salt, divided
- 4 (6-ounce) chicken thighs, skinned
- ¼ teaspoon dried oregano
- ¼ teaspoon dried marjoram
- 4 teaspoons balsamic vinegar, divided
- 2 tablespoons chopped fresh flat-leaf parsley
- 4 lemon wedges

1. Heat oil in a large nonstick skillet over medium heat. Add onion, ¼ teaspoon pepper, and ⅛ teaspoon salt; sauté 5 minutes.
2. Add ¼ teaspoon pepper, ⅛ teaspoon salt, chicken, oregano, and marjoram to pan, and sprinkle with 3 teaspoons vinegar. Cover, reduce heat, and simmer 25 minutes or until chicken is done. Uncover, increase heat, and cook 2 minutes or until liquid almost evaporates. Stir in 1 teaspoon vinegar, and sprinkle with parsley. Serve with lemon wedges. Yield: 2 servings (serving size: 2 thighs and 1 cup onion mixture).

CALORIES 371 (31% from fat); FAT 12.8g (sat 2.7g, mono 5.8g, poly 2.5g); PROTEIN 42.1g; CARB 23.3g; FIBER 4.6g; CHOL 165mg; IRON 3.3mg; SODIUM 474mg; CALC 94mg

Spicy Yogurt-Marinated Chicken with Couscous

Since this recipe marinates overnight, all you need to do when you get home from work is preheat the broiler and start cooking the chicken. In the meantime, you can make the couscous.

CHICKEN:
- ¼ cup plain fat-free yogurt
- 2 teaspoons grated lemon rind
- 1½ teaspoons fresh lemon juice
- ½ teaspoon salt
- ¼ teaspoon ground ginger
- ¼ teaspoon ground cumin
- ¼ teaspoon curry powder
- ⅛ teaspoon ground red pepper
- ⅛ teaspoon ground cloves
- ⅛ teaspoon black pepper
- 4 (4-ounce) skinless, boneless chicken thighs
  Cooking spray

COUSCOUS:
- 1 cup fat-free, less-sodium chicken broth
- ¾ cup uncooked couscous
- 2 tablespoons currants
- 1 tablespoon sliced green onion tops
- ¼ teaspoon black pepper

1. To prepare chicken, combine first 11 ingredients in a large zip-top plastic bag. Seal bag, and marinate chicken in refrigerator 24 hours, turning bag occasionally. Remove chicken from bag, and discard marinade.
2. Preheat broiler.
3. Place chicken thighs on a broiler pan coated with cooking spray. Broil 10 minutes or until a meat thermometer registers 180°.
4. To prepare couscous, bring broth to a boil in a medium saucepan, and gradually stir in couscous. Remove from heat; cover and let stand 5 minutes. Fluff with a fork. Stir in currants, onion tops, and ¼ teaspoon black pepper. Yield: 2 servings (serving size: 2 thighs and 1 cup couscous).

CALORIES 490 (19% from fat); FAT 10.5g (sat 2.5g, mono 3.1g, poly 3g); PROTEIN 53.9g; CARB 42.5g; FIBER 2.5g; CHOL 189mg; IRON 3.8mg; SODIUM 746mg; CALC 61mg

sound bites

Deceiving Desserts

Mild-mannered tofu goes incognito in these tempting desserts.

Tofu's noteworthy virtues are its nutrient profile—it's high in isoflavones and protein, and is devoid of cholesterol—and its ability to disguise itself in myriad culinary applications.

Tofu is incredible at masquerading in nearly any dessert. We found out firsthand in our Test Kitchens, where even the tofu skeptics acknowledged defeat.

But tofu's crowning achievement is its role in a chocolate mousse, which our food staff unanimously—and enthusiastically—awarded its highest rating.

So, yes, these desserts are deceitfully healthy. Far more important, however, is that they're shockingly good.

Chocolate Mousse

Even our food staff was surprised when they tasted this sinfully delicious dessert. The best part—it contains two ingredients most women want more of: soy and chocolate!

- ¾ cup semisweet chocolate chips, melted
- 1 (12.3-ounce) package reduced-fat extra-firm silken tofu (such as Mori-Nu)
- ¼ teaspoon salt
- 3 large egg whites
- ½ cup sugar
- ¼ cup water
  Fat-free whipped topping, thawed (optional)
  Grated chocolate (optional)

1. Place melted chocolate chips and tofu in a food processor or blender, and process 2 minutes or until smooth.
2. Place salt and egg whites in a medium bowl, and beat with a mixer at high speed until stiff peaks form. Combine sugar and water in a small saucepan; bring to a boil. Cook, without stirring,

until candy thermometer registers 238°. Pour hot sugar syrup in a thin stream over egg whites, beating at high speed. Gently stir one-fourth of meringue into tofu mixture; gently fold in remaining meringue. Spoon ½ cup mousse into each of 8 (6-ounce) custard cups. Cover and chill at least 4 hours. If desired, garnish with whipped topping and grated chocolate. Yield: 8 servings.

CALORIES 147 (34% from fat); FAT 5.6g (sat 3.3g, mono 1.8g, poly 0.5g); PROTEIN 5.2g; CARB 22.5g; FIBER 0.2g; CHOL 0mg; IRON 0.9mg; SODIUM 134mg; CALC 26mg

Rocky Road Snack Cake

A cross between a snacking cake and a brownie, this chocolaty dessert is best cut and served warm. Use a sharp knife coated with cooking spray to keep the cake from sticking.

  ¾ cup all-purpose flour
  ¼ cup soy flour
  ¾ cup unsweetened cocoa
  ¾ teaspoon baking powder
  ½ teaspoon salt
1¼ cups sugar
  1 cup cubed reduced-fat firm tofu (about 6 ounces)
  ½ cup vanilla-flavored low-fat soy milk
  ¼ cup butter, softened
  1 cup miniature marshmallows, divided
  ⅓ cup chopped walnuts, divided
Cooking spray

1. Preheat oven to 375°.
2. Lightly spoon flours into dry measuring cups, and level with a knife. Combine flours, cocoa, baking powder, and salt in a large bowl.
3. Combine sugar, tofu, soy milk, and butter in a food processor or blender, and process until smooth. Add to flour mixture, stirring just until moist. Stir in ⅔ cup marshmallows and ¼ cup walnuts.
4. Spread batter into a 9-inch square baking pan coated with cooking spray. Sprinkle with ⅓ cup marshmallows and 4 teaspoons walnuts. Bake at 375° for 25 minutes or until a wooden pick inserted in center comes out clean. Cool in pan on a wire rack 5 minutes. Cut into squares. Yield: 12 servings.

NOTE: Soy flour and soy milk are often available in health-food stores and some supermarkets.

CALORIES 218 (30% from fat); FAT 7.4g (sat 3.1g, mono 2g, poly 2g); PROTEIN 5.1g; CARB 34g; FIBER 0.5g; CHOL 11mg; IRON 1.8mg; SODIUM 185mg; CALC 39mg

Brandied Tiramisu

This version of the popular Italian dessert combines a coffee- and brandy-soaked layer of ladyfingers with a puddinglike topping of mascarpone cheese and tofu. Look for ladyfingers in your market's frozen-food or bakery section.

1½ cups strong brewed coffee
  3 tablespoons brandy
36 cake-style ladyfingers (3 [3-ounce] packages), split in half lengthwise
  4 ounces mascarpone cheese (about ½ cup)
  ¼ cup packed brown sugar
  1 (12.3-ounce) package reduced-fat extra-firm tofu, drained
  3 large egg whites
  ½ cup granulated sugar
  ¼ cup water
  1 tablespoon unsweetened cocoa

1. Combine coffee and brandy in a shallow dish. Quickly dip 36 ladyfinger halves, flat sides down, into coffee mixture; arrange, dipped sides down, in bottom of a 13 x 9-inch baking dish. Dip 36 more ladyfinger halves, flat sides down, into coffee mixture; arrange, dipped sides down, on top of first layer. Pour remaining coffee mixture over ladyfingers.
2. Combine cheese, brown sugar, and tofu in a food processor or blender, and process until smooth, scraping sides of bowl occasionally. Place tofu mixture in a large bowl, and set aside.
3. Place egg whites in a large bowl, and beat with a mixer at high speed until stiff peaks form. Combine granulated sugar and water in a saucepan; bring to a boil. Cook, without stirring, until candy thermometer registers 238°. Pour hot sugar syrup in a thin stream over egg whites, beating at high speed. Stir one-third of egg white mixture into tofu mixture; gently fold in remaining egg white mixture. Spread meringue mixture evenly over ladyfingers; sprinkle with cocoa. Cover and chill 2 hours. Yield: 12 servings.

CALORIES 238 (30% from fat); FAT 7.9g (sat 3.6g, mono 2.7g, poly 0.9g); PROTEIN 7.2g; CARB 32.4g; FIBER 0.3g; CHOL 129mg; IRON 1.7mg; SODIUM 107mg; CALC 53mg

Butter-Rum Pudding

We experimented with several types of tofu. Extra-firm held up best and provided a creamy consistency.

  1 cup packed brown sugar
  ⅔ cup spiced rum (such as Captain Morgan's) or white rum
  ½ cup water
  3 tablespoons butter
  ⅛ teaspoon salt
  2 (12.3-ounce) packages reduced-fat extra-firm tofu, drained
  1 teaspoon vanilla extract

1. Combine first 5 ingredients in a medium saucepan. Bring to a boil; reduce heat, and cook until mixture is reduced to 1 cup (about 15 minutes).
2. Place tofu in a food processor or blender; process until smooth, scraping sides of bowl occasionally. With processor on, slowly pour rum mixture and vanilla through food chute; process until well blended. Spoon tofu mixture into a medium bowl. Cover and chill 4 hours. Yield: 8 servings (serving size: ½ cup).

CALORIES 176 (28% from fat); FAT 5.4g (sat 2.9g, mono 1.5g, poly 0.8g); PROTEIN 6.1g; CARB 26.9g; FIBER 0g; CHOL 12mg; IRON 1.1mg; SODIUM 170mg; CALC 55mg

Cookies-and-Cream Ice Cream

1 (12.3-ounce) package reduced-fat firm tofu, drained
½ cup sugar
½ cup half-and-half
1 teaspoon vanilla extract
¼ teaspoon salt
2 cups frozen fat-free whipped topping, thawed
10 cream-filled chocolate sandwich cookies (such as Oreos), crushed
8 cream-filled chocolate sandwich cookies (such as Oreos, optional)

1. Combine first 5 ingredients in a food processor or blender; process until smooth. Place tofu mixture in a large bowl. Fold in whipped topping. Pour mixture into freezer can of an ice-cream freezer; freeze according to manufacturer's instructions. Stir in crushed cookies during last 5 minutes of freezing. Spoon ice cream into a freezer-safe container; cover and freeze 1 hour or until firm. Garnish with whole cookies, if desired. Yield: 8 servings (serving size: ½ cup).

CALORIES 184 (25% from fat); FAT 5.2g (sat 1.8g, mono 1.9g, poly 0.6g); PROTEIN 3.8g; CARB 29.3g; FIBER 0.4g; CHOL 6mg; IRON 0.7mg; SODIUM 307mg; CALC 31mg

---

Sneaky Soy

For the tofu-finicky, here's a great way to add soy to your diet without confronting it head on. Whip it up in a food processor or blender for a creamy-smooth texture and low-key taste. This way, it slips effortlessly into desserts of all kinds without getting in the way of other great flavors. Why bother? Because soybeans contain isoflavones, a potent group of phytochemicals (substances that can reduce the risks of a host of diseases) that are unique to soy. Studies have shown that adding soy to your diet can lower cholesterol and help reduce your risk of heart disease. Soy foods may also help reduce the risks of breast and other cancers.

Date Spice Cake

1½ cups chopped pitted dates
1 cup low-fat vanilla soy milk
1 cup granulated sugar
6 ounces soft tofu, drained (about ¾ cup)
3 tablespoons butter, softened
1½ cups all-purpose flour
1½ teaspoons baking powder
1 teaspoon ground cinnamon
½ teaspoon salt
½ teaspoon baking soda
¼ teaspoon ground nutmeg
¼ teaspoon ground cloves
Cooking spray
1 tablespoon powdered sugar

1. Preheat oven to 350°.
2. Combine dates and milk in a small saucepan; bring to a boil. Cover and remove from heat; let stand 5 minutes or until dates are soft. Place date mixture in a food processor or blender, and process until almost smooth, scraping sides of bowl occasionally. Add granulated sugar, tofu, and butter, and process until smooth. Spoon flour into dry measuring cups, and level with a knife. Combine flour and next 6 ingredients in a large bowl, stirring with a whisk. Stir in date mixture.
3. Spread batter into an 11 x 7-inch baking dish coated with cooking spray. Bake at 350° for 30 minutes or until a wooden pick inserted in center comes out clean. Cool 10 minutes in dish on a wire rack; remove from dish. Cool completely on wire rack. Sprinkle with powdered sugar. Yield: 8 servings.

CALORIES 227 (16% from fat); FAT 4.1g (sat 2g, mono 1.1g, poly 0.7g); PROTEIN 3.5g; CARB 46.5g; FIBER 2.4g; CHOL 8mg; IRON 1.4mg; SODIUM 245mg; CALC 60mg

dinner tonight

Salad for Supper?

You betcha. Paired with superfast homemade breads, these main-dish salads make tasty dinners.

Sizzling Salmon-and-Spinach Salad with Soy Vinaigrette

TOTAL TIME: 37 MINUTES
QUICK TIP: Slide a spatula between cooked fish and skin when removing salmon from pan. Skin will stick to foil.

DRESSING:
3 tablespoons thinly sliced green onions
3 tablespoons rice vinegar
3 tablespoons low-sodium soy sauce
1 tablespoon water
1 teaspoon sesame seeds, toasted
1 teaspoon bottled minced garlic
1 teaspoon dark sesame oil
½ teaspoon chile paste with garlic or ¼ teaspoon crushed red pepper

SALAD:
2 teaspoons dark sesame oil, divided
4 cups thinly sliced shiitake or button mushroom caps (about 8 ounces)
1 cup (1-inch) sliced green onions
1 cup fresh or frozen corn kernels, thawed
4 (6-ounce) salmon fillets (about 1 inch thick)
8 cups baby spinach
1 cup fresh bean sprouts
1 cup red bell pepper strips

1. Preheat broiler.

2. To prepare dressing, combine first 8 ingredients in a small bowl, and stir well with a whisk.

3. To prepare salad, heat 1 teaspoon oil in a large nonstick skillet over medium-high heat. Add mushrooms and 1 cup onions; sauté 8 minutes. Stir in corn; remove from heat.

4. Place fillets on a foil-lined baking sheet; brush evenly with 1 teaspoon oil. Broil 8 minutes or until fish flakes easily when tested with a fork.

5. Place 2 cups spinach on each of 4 plates; top each serving with ¼ cup bean sprouts, ¼ cup red bell pepper, ½ cup mushroom mixture, and 1 fillet. Drizzle about 2 tablespoons dressing over each salad. Yield: 4 servings.

CALORIES 418 (40% from fat); FAT 18.8g (sat 3.2g, mono 8.3g, poly 5.1g); PROTEIN 42.9g; CARB 21.8g; FIBER 7.8g; CHOL 111mg; IRON 6.1mg; SODIUM 549mg; CALC 163mg

Menu 2
serves 6

Chickpea-Vegetable Salad with Curried Yogurt Dressing

Spiced pita wedges*

*Combine 1 tablespoon melted butter and ¼ teaspoon each of coriander, cumin, and turmeric. Brush evenly over rough sides of an 8-inch split pita. Cut each pita half into 6 wedges; place on a baking sheet. Bake at 350° for 12 minutes or until toasted.

Chickpea-Vegetable Salad with Curried Yogurt Dressing

(pictured on page 132)

TOTAL TIME: 28 MINUTES

QUICK TIP: To cut prep time, pick up packages of shredded carrots and torn romaine lettuce in the produce section of your market. In addition, if you are preparing the entire menu suggested in the menu box above, we recommend preparing the dressing and salad ingredients while the pita toasts.

DRESSING:

⅓ cup chopped fresh cilantro
2 tablespoons olive oil
1 tablespoon lemon juice
1½ teaspoons curry powder
¾ teaspoon salt
½ teaspoon bottled minced garlic
¼ teaspoon freshly ground black pepper
1 (8-ounce) carton plain fat-free yogurt

SALAD:

2 cups finely shredded carrot
1½ cups thinly sliced yellow or red bell pepper
1½ cups chopped plum tomato
½ cup golden raisins
¼ cup finely chopped red onion
2 (15½-ounce) cans chickpeas (garbanzo beans), drained
12 cups chopped romaine lettuce

1. To prepare dressing, combine first 8 ingredients in a small bowl; stir mixture with a whisk.

2. To prepare salad, combine carrot and next 5 ingredients in a large bowl. Pour ½ cup dressing over carrot mixture, tossing gently to coat. Place 2 cups lettuce on each of 6 plates, and drizzle each serving with about 1 tablespoon dressing. Top each serving with 1⅓ cups carrot mixture. Yield: 6 servings.

CALORIES 337 (21% from fat); FAT 8g (sat 1.1g, mono 4.1g, poly 2g); PROTEIN 15.4g; CARB 55.4g; FIBER 8.9g; CHOL 1mg; IRON 5.7mg; SODIUM 573mg; CALC 201mg

Menu 3
serves 6

Lemon-Dill Bulgur Salad with Scallops

Greek bread*

*Combine 4 ounces ⅓-less-fat cream cheese, 1 tablespoon low-fat mayonnaise, and 1 teaspoon Greek seasoning. Spread over cut sides of an 8-ounce bread loaf split in half horizontally. Sprinkle with ½ cup crumbled feta cheese, 2 tablespoons chopped kalamata olives, and ¼ cup chopped pepperoncini peppers. Bake at 375° for 10 minutes.

Lemon-Dill Bulgur Salad with Scallops

Watercress is a pungent green with a peppery bite. Generally sold in small bunches, its dark green leaves are small and crisp. Wash and shake it dry just before serving.

TOTAL TIME: 29 MINUTES

QUICK TIP: To seed a cucumber, cut in half lengthwise, and scoop out seeds with a spoon. Then chop as directed. Peeling is optional and based on personal preference.

2 cups water
1 cup uncooked bulgur
Cooking spray
1½ pounds sea scallops
2 cups chopped seeded cucumber
1½ cups chopped plum tomato
1 cup frozen corn kernels, thawed
¼ cup chopped fresh or 1 tablespoon dried dill
¼ cup lemon juice
2 tablespoons olive oil
1½ teaspoons salt
1 teaspoon sugar
1 teaspoon bottled minced garlic
¼ teaspoon freshly ground black pepper
6 cups trimmed watercress (about 2 bunches) or baby spinach

1. Bring 2 cups water to a boil in a medium saucepan. Add bulgur; partially cover, reduce heat, and simmer 5 minutes. Drain; cool.

2. While bulgur cooks, heat a medium nonstick skillet coated with cooking spray over medium-high heat. Add scallops, and cook 3 minutes, turning once. Remove from heat; place scallops in a large bowl.

3. Add bulgur, cucumber, and next 9 ingredients to scallops in bowl; toss well to coat. Place 1 cup watercress on each of 6 plates; top each serving with 1 cup scallop mixture. Yield: 6 servings.

CALORIES 275 (21% from fat); FAT 6.5g (sat 0.8g, mono 3.5g, poly 1g); PROTEIN 24.4g; CARB 32.4g; FIBER 6.9g; CHOL 37mg; IRON 1.7mg; SODIUM 795mg; CALC 103mg

Soba Noodle Salad with Vegetables and Tofu

TOTAL TIME: 25 MINUTES

QUICK TIP: Napa cabbage is traditionally used in Asian-inspired salads, but if you're short on time, substitute bagged sliced cabbage or coleslaw mix.

DRESSING:

- ½ cup low-sodium soy sauce
- ¼ cup packed brown sugar
- 1 tablespoon sesame seeds, toasted
- 2 tablespoons orange juice
- 1 tablespoon bottled minced or minced peeled fresh ginger
- 1 tablespoon rice vinegar
- 2 teaspoons dark sesame oil
- 1 teaspoon bottled minced garlic
- 1 teaspoon chile paste with garlic

SALAD:

- 4 cups hot cooked soba (about 8 ounces uncooked buckwheat noodles) or whole wheat spaghetti
- 3 cups very thinly sliced napa (Chinese) cabbage
- 2 cups fresh bean sprouts
- 1 cup shredded carrot
- ½ cup chopped fresh cilantro
- 1 (12.3-ounce) package firm tofu, drained and cut into 1-inch cubes

1. To prepare dressing, combine first 9 ingredients in a small bowl; stir with a whisk.

2. To prepare salad, combine noodles and remaining 5 ingredients in a large bowl. Drizzle with dressing, tossing well to coat. Yield: 5 servings (serving size: 2 cups).

CALORIES 336 (19% from fat); FAT 7g (sat 1g, mono 1.8g, poly 3g); PROTEIN 15.1g; CARB 53.8g; FIBER 2.8g; CHOL 0mg; IRON 6.6mg; SODIUM 850mg; CALC 169mg

in season

Amazing Asparagus

It requires a lot of TLC to harvest and produce, but this delicate vegetable is worth it.

If you want to grow asparagus yourself, you'll have to be patient. It takes several years. But once it gets started, it grows at an amazing rate.

When selecting asparagus, reach for green instead of white: This variety is higher in vitamins A and C, and in folate. Choose spears with tight, compact tips and a similar diameter so they'll cook at the same rate. As for cooking asparagus, don't overdo it. The slender shoots should turn out crisp and bright in color.

Sesame-Roasted Asparagus

Try this easy side dish with Barbecue Roasted Salmon (recipe on page 128).

- 36 asparagus spears
- 1½ teaspoons dark sesame oil
- 1 teaspoon low-sodium soy sauce
- ⅛ teaspoon black pepper

1. Preheat oven to 450°.

2. Snap off tough ends of asparagus. Combine asparagus and remaining 3 ingredients in a jelly-roll pan, turning asparagus to coat.

3. Bake at 450° for 10 minutes or until asparagus is crisp-tender; turn once. Yield: 4 servings (serving size: 9 asparagus spears).

CALORIES 43 (44% from fat); FAT 2.1g (sat 0.3g, mono 0.7g, poly 0.9g); PROTEIN 3g; CARB 4.9g; FIBER 1.2g; CHOL 0mg; IRON 0.9mg; SODIUM 53mg; CALC 23mg

Vegetable Fried Rice with Pecans and Ginger

- Cooking spray
- 2 cups thinly sliced shiitake mushroom caps (about 3 ounces)
- 2 teaspoons olive oil
- 2 cups hot cooked basmati rice
- 1½ cups (½-inch) diagonally cut asparagus
- 1 teaspoon minced peeled fresh ginger
- ¼ teaspoon salt
- ¼ teaspoon black pepper
- 3 tablespoons chopped pecans, toasted
- 2 tablespoons low-sodium soy sauce

1. Heat a large nonstick skillet coated with cooking spray over medium-high heat. Add mushrooms; sauté 5 minutes or until tender. Remove mushrooms from pan. Heat oil in pan. Add rice, asparagus, ginger, salt, and pepper; cook 5 minutes, stirring frequently. Add mushrooms, pecans, and soy sauce; cook 1 minute or until hot. Yield: 4 servings (serving size: ¾ cup).

CALORIES 194 (30% from fat); FAT 6.4g (sat 0.7g, mono 4g, poly 1.2g); PROTEIN 4.8g; CARB 30.5g; FIBER 2.4g; CHOL 0mg; IRON 2.1mg; SODIUM 391mg; CALC 27mg

Asparagus Melt with Pesto Spread

(pictured on page 131)

- 16 asparagus spears
- 3 tablespoons fat-free mayonnaise
- 1 tablespoon commercial pesto
- 2 (2-ounce) slices sourdough bread, toasted
- 2 (1-ounce) thin slices ham
- 4 (¼-inch-thick) slices tomato
- 2 (1-ounce) slices part-skim mozzarella cheese
- Freshly ground black pepper

1. Snap off tough ends of asparagus. Steam, covered, 2 minutes or until crisp-tender.

2. Preheat broiler.

3. Combine mayonnaise and pesto in a bowl, and stir with a whisk. Spread 2 tablespoons pesto mixture onto 1 side of each bread slice. Layer each slice with 8 asparagus spears, 1 ham slice, 2 tomato slices, and 1 cheese slice. Place on a baking sheet; broil 3 minutes or until cheese melts. Sprinkle with pepper. Yield: 2 servings (serving size: 1 sandwich).

CALORIES 343 (30% from fat); FAT 11.5g (sat 4.3g, mono 4.7g, poly 1.1g); PROTEIN 21.7g; CARB 40.7g; FIBER 2.8g; CHOL 31mg; IRON 3.6mg; SODIUM 1,041mg; CALC 324mg

Patio Supper Menu
serves 4

Spring's warmer weather is reason enough to take this meal outdoors. The coleslaw and roasted-pepper mayonnaise can be made early in the day and refrigerated. Steam the asparagus and warm the tortillas before serving.

Asparagus-Turkey Wraps with Roasted-Pepper Mayonnaise

Cabbage-and-carrot slaw*

Purple grapes

Chocolate cookies

*Combine 2 cups thinly sliced green cabbage, 1 cup julienne-cut carrot, 2 tablespoons cider vinegar, 2 teaspoons olive oil, 2 teaspoons sugar, ¼ teaspoon salt, ⅛ teaspoon celery seeds, and ⅛ teaspoon pepper in a bowl. Cover; chill.

Asparagus-Turkey Wraps with Roasted-Pepper Mayonnaise

To save time, you can use bottled roasted red bell peppers.

24　asparagus spears
　1　red bell pepper
1½　teaspoons honey
　1　teaspoon fresh lemon juice
　⅛　teaspoon salt
　⅛　teaspoon ground red pepper
　¼　cup light mayonnaise
　4　(8-inch) flour tortillas
　4　romaine lettuce leaves
　8　(1-ounce) slices cooked turkey breast
　2　cups alfalfa sprouts

1. Preheat broiler.
2. Snap off tough ends of asparagus. Steam asparagus, covered, 2 minutes or until crisp-tender.
3. Cut bell pepper in half lengthwise; discard seeds and membranes. Place pepper halves, skin sides up, on a foil-lined baking sheet; flatten with hand. Broil 10 minutes or until blackened. Place in a zip-top plastic bag; seal. Let stand 15 minutes; peel. Place bell pepper, honey, juice, salt, and ground red pepper in a blender; process until smooth. Combine pepper mixture and mayonnaise.
4. Warm tortillas according to package directions. Spread 1 tablespoon mayonnaise mixture over each tortilla. Layer each tortilla with 1 romaine leaf, 2 turkey slices, ½ cup sprouts, and 6 asparagus spears; roll up. Serve with remaining mayonnaise mixture. Yield: 4 servings (serving size: 1 wrap and about 1 tablespoon mayonnaise mixture).

CALORIES 307 (24% from fat); FAT 8.2g (sat 1.3g, mono 2.4g, poly 4g); PROTEIN 24.3g; CARB 34.4g; FIBER 3.1g; CHOL 52mg; IRON 3.5mg; SODIUM 445mg; CALC 92mg

Asparagus Salad with Beans and Feta

So the beans and feta don't break up too much, gently toss the mixture with your hands.

　3　cups (1-inch) diagonally cut asparagus
　1　cup canned cannellini beans or other white beans, rinsed and drained
　½　cup thinly sliced radishes
　½　cup (2 ounces) crumbled feta cheese
　2　tablespoons thinly sliced green onions
　2　teaspoons fresh lemon juice
　1　teaspoon chopped fresh mint
　1　teaspoon extra-virgin olive oil
　¼　teaspoon salt
　⅛　teaspoon black pepper

1. Steam asparagus, covered, 2 minutes or until crisp-tender. Rinse asparagus with cold water, and drain. Combine asparagus and next 4 ingredients in a large bowl.

2. Combine juice and remaining 4 ingredients in a bowl; stir well with a whisk. Pour over asparagus mixture; toss gently to coat. Yield: 4 servings (serving size: 1 cup).

CALORIES 150 (28% from fat); FAT 4.7g (sat 2.4g, mono 1.5g, poly 0.4g); PROTEIN 9.3g; CARB 20g; FIBER 5.9g; CHOL 13mg; IRON 2.1mg; SODIUM 531mg; CALC 132mg

Curried Vegetables and Pork with Rice Noodles

　4　teaspoons roasted peanut oil, divided
　1　(1-pound) pork tenderloin, trimmed and cut into thin strips
　1　tablespoon minced peeled fresh ginger
　1　garlic clove, minced
　2　cups coarsely chopped onion
1½　cups (2-inch) sliced asparagus
　1　cup (½-inch) pieces yellow bell pepper
　1　cup sugar snap peas, trimmed
　2　tablespoons red curry paste
　1　teaspoon brown sugar
　1　(14-ounce) can light coconut milk
2½　cups hot cooked rice sticks or vermicelli (about 5 ounces uncooked rice-flour noodles)
　¼　cup chopped fresh basil
　5　lime wedges

1. Heat 2 teaspoons peanut oil in a large nonstick skillet over medium-high heat. Add pork, and stir-fry 3 minutes. Remove pork from pan; keep warm. Add 2 teaspoons peanut oil, ginger, and garlic, and stir-fry 1 minute. Add onion, asparagus, bell pepper, and peas, and stir-fry 5 minutes. Remove from pan; keep warm.
2. Add curry paste, sugar, and coconut milk to pan, and stir well. Bring curry paste mixture to a boil; reduce heat, and simmer 10 minutes. Add pork, asparagus mixture, and rice noodles to pan, and cook 1 minute or until mixture is thoroughly heated. Sprinkle evenly with basil; garnish with lime wedges. Yield: 5 servings (serving size: 1 cup pork mixture and ½ cup noodles).

CALORIES 347 (27% from fat); FAT 10.4g (sat 5.1g, mono 2.9g, poly 1.6g); PROTEIN 22.3g; CARB 39.8g; FIBER 3.8g; CHOL 59mg; IRON 3.3mg; SODIUM 390mg; CALC 52mg

Weekend Brunch Menu

Serve this for Mother's Day or whenever you're in the mood for a special weekend breakfast.

Asparagus-and-Ham Casserole

Corn muffins

Fresh fruit cup

Mimosas

Asparagus-and-Ham Casserole

Because of the delicate flavors in this dish, we preferred using a mild baked ham to a smoked one.

    1   (1-ounce) slice white bread
    3¾ cups uncooked extra-broad egg
        noodles
    2½ cups (1½-inch) sliced asparagus
    ¼   cup all-purpose flour
    ½   teaspoon dried thyme
    ¼   teaspoon salt
    ⅛   teaspoon black pepper
    1   cup whole milk
    1   cup fat-free, less-sodium chicken
        broth
    1   tablespoon butter
    ¾   cup finely chopped onion
    1   tablespoon fresh lemon juice
    1½ cups (½-inch) cubed ham (about
        8 ounces)
    ¼   cup chopped fresh flat-leaf parsley
    2   tablespoons grated fresh Parmesan
        cheese

1. Preheat oven to 450°.
2. Place bread in a food processor, and pulse 10 times or until coarse crumbs form to measure ½ cup.
3. Cook pasta in boiling water 7 minutes, omitting salt and fat. Add asparagus; cook 1 minute. Drain.
4. Lightly spoon flour into a dry measuring cup, and level with a knife. Place flour, thyme, salt, and pepper in a medium bowl; gradually add milk and broth, stirring with a whisk until well blended. Melt butter in a medium

saucepan over medium-high heat. Add onion; sauté 4 minutes. Add milk mixture; cook until thick (about 4 minutes), stirring constantly. Remove from heat, and stir in juice. Combine pasta mixture, milk mixture, ham, and parsley in a large bowl; spoon into a 2-quart casserole. Sprinkle with breadcrumbs and cheese.
5. Bake at 450° for 10 minutes or until filling is bubbly and topping is golden. Yield: 6 servings (serving size: 1 cup).

CALORIES 250 (26% from fat); FAT 7.1g (sat 3.4g, mono 2.4g, poly 0.7g); PROTEIN 16g; CARB 30.9g; FIBER 2.7g; CHOL 52mg; IRON 2.6mg; SODIUM 835mg; CALC 114mg

Chicken Salad with Asparagus and Toasted Almonds

Serve this salad on lettuce leaves with fruit salad and muffins.

    2½ cups (1-inch) diagonally cut
        asparagus
    ¼   cup fat-free mayonnaise
    ¼   cup plain low-fat yogurt
    1   teaspoon curry powder
    1   teaspoon fresh lemon juice
    ¼   teaspoon salt
    ⅛   teaspoon black pepper
    2   cups chopped roasted skinless,
        boneless chicken breast (about
        2 breast halves)
    ⅓   cup chopped red bell pepper
    ¼   cup chopped fresh flat-leaf parsley
    2   tablespoons sliced almonds, toasted

1. Steam asparagus, covered, 2 minutes or until crisp-tender.
2. Combine mayonnaise and next 5 ingredients in a large bowl, stirring well with a whisk. Add asparagus, chicken, bell pepper, parsley, and almonds; toss to coat. Yield: 4 servings (serving size: 1 cup).

CALORIES 188 (25% from fat); FAT 5.3g (sat 1.3g, mono 2.2g, poly 1.1g); PROTEIN 25.4g; CARB 10g; FIBER 2.7g; CHOL 61mg; IRON 2.1mg; SODIUM 415mg; CALC 73mg

inspired vegetarian

A Few Favorite Greens

'Tis the season when spring greens abound.

Spring greens have a pleasant range of flavors, from mellow to pungent, and are the first shoots to come up in the garden when little else is ready to grow. Greens tolerate the cool temperatures of early spring and grow very fast; this means you can harvest the leaves well before even planting most other vegetables.

Dark-green leafy vegetables are nutritional powerhouses. And more often than not, they're interchangeable in recipes, which adds to their appeal. Escarole and spinach are mildest, while kale, Swiss chard, and collards have slightly more pronounced flavors. Broccoli rabe, beet greens, turnip greens, and mustard greens are the most assertive and need to be cooked with care. Arugula, romaine, and the mixture of baby greens known as mesclun are usually eaten raw in salads.

Greek Sandwiches with Feta Vinaigrette

VINAIGRETTE:

    2   tablespoons crumbled feta cheese
    2   tablespoons fresh lemon juice
    1   tablespoon olive oil
    ½   teaspoon sugar
    ½   teaspoon dried oregano
    ⅛   teaspoon salt
    1   garlic clove, minced

SANDWICH:

    ¼   teaspoon salt
    ¼   teaspoon black pepper
    8   (¼-inch-thick) slices tomato
    8   (1-ounce) slices sourdough
        bread
    1   peeled cucumber, diagonally cut
        into ¼-inch-thick slices
    3   cups chopped arugula
    ½   cup vertically sliced red onion
    2   tablespoons chopped pitted
        kalamata olives

1. To prepare vinaigrette, combine first 7 ingredients in a medium bowl, stirring with a whisk.

2. To prepare sandwich, combine ¼ teaspoon salt and pepper in a medium bowl. Place 2 tomato slices on each of 4 bread slices, and sprinkle evenly with half of salt mixture. Arrange cucumber slices over tomato slices; sprinkle evenly with remaining salt mixture. Add arugula, onion, and chopped olives to vinaigrette; toss to coat. Arrange arugula mixture evenly over cucumber slices. Top with bread slices. Yield: 4 servings (serving size: 1 sandwich).

CALORIES 228 (26% from fat); FAT 6.7g (sat 1.5g, mono 3.7g, poly 0.9g); PROTEIN 6.9g; CARB 36.1g; FIBER 2.9g; CHOL 3mg; IRON 2mg; SODIUM 652mg; CALC 115mg

Kale and Mushrooms with Basmati Rice

    3   bunches kale (about 1½ pounds)
    1   cup water
1½   tablespoons red wine vinegar
1½   teaspoons olive oil
    1   cup finely chopped onion
    2   garlic cloves, minced
    1   (8-ounce) package presliced mushrooms
    1   cup uncooked basmati rice
    1   teaspoon dried basil
    1   (14.5-ounce) can vegetable broth
    1   bay leaf
    ½   cup (2 ounces) finely grated fresh Parmesan cheese
    ¼   teaspoon freshly ground black pepper

1. Remove stems from kale; wash leaves thoroughly. Bring 1 cup water to a boil in a large Dutch oven; add kale. Cook 15 minutes or until tender. Drain kale; cool slightly. Chop kale, and sprinkle with vinegar.

2. Heat oil in pan over medium heat. Add onion; sauté 3 minutes. Add garlic and mushrooms; sauté 2 minutes. Add rice; cook 1 minute, stirring frequently. Add basil, broth, and bay leaf. Bring to a boil; cover, reduce heat, and simmer 12 minutes. Spread kale over rice. Cover and cook 5 minutes or until liquid is

absorbed. Discard bay leaf. Sprinkle with cheese and pepper; toss well. Yield: 6 servings (serving size: ¾ cup).

CALORIES 224 (19% from fat); FAT 4.8g (sat 1.9g, mono 1.7g, poly 0.5g); PROTEIN 9.1g; CARB 37.8g; FIBER 2.5g; CHOL 6mg; IRON 3.2mg; SODIUM 519mg; CALC 228mg

Curried Rice Salad with Spinach and Citrus Vinaigrette

The refreshing vinaigrette balances the rice salad's sweetness.

    ⅓   cup plain fat-free yogurt
    ⅓   cup low-fat mayonnaise
    2   teaspoons curry powder
    ¼   teaspoon salt
    3   garlic cloves, minced
    4   cups cold cooked long-grain brown rice
    1   cup finely chopped Granny Smith apple
    ⅓   cup thinly sliced green onions
    ⅓   cup raisins
    ⅓   cup finely chopped carrot
    2   tablespoons fresh lemon juice
    1   tablespoon water
    1   tablespoon olive oil
    1   tablespoon thawed orange juice concentrate
    ¼   teaspoon salt
    ⅛   teaspoon freshly ground black pepper
    1   garlic clove, minced
    8   cups torn spinach

1. Combine first 5 ingredients in a large bowl, and stir well with a whisk. Stir in rice and next 4 ingredients.

2. Combine lemon juice and next 6 ingredients in a large bowl; stir well with a whisk. Add spinach; toss gently. Serve rice mixture over spinach mixture. Yield: 5 servings (serving size: 1 cup rice mixture and about 1½ cups spinach mixture).

CALORIES 312 (17% from fat); FAT 5.8g (sat 0.9g, mono 2.8g, poly 1.5g); PROTEIN 8.4g; CARB 60g; FIBER 8g; CHOL 0mg; IRON 3.8mg; SODIUM 478mg; CALC 157mg

Mesclun Salad with Roasted Tofu

For a light lunch entrée, serve this salad with some crusty French bread and a bowl of minestrone. Use either romaine or mesclun, a mix of gourmet greens.

    1   (12.3-ounce) package reduced-fat firm tofu, drained
    2   teaspoons dry sherry
    2   teaspoons low-sodium soy sauce
    1   teaspoon dark sesame oil
    8   cups gourmet salad greens
    1   cup (¼-inch-thick) slices peeled cucumber
    ¼   cup chopped green onions
    2   tablespoons fresh lemon juice
    1   teaspoon olive oil
    1   teaspoon red wine vinegar
    ¼   teaspoon sugar
    ¼   teaspoon salt
    ¼   teaspoon black pepper
    1   garlic clove, minced

1. Cut tofu lengthwise into 4 slices. Place slices on several layers of paper towels; cover with additional paper towels. Let stand 5 minutes. Cut each slice diagonally into 2 triangles. Place tofu in a shallow baking dish. Combine sherry, soy sauce, and sesame oil in a small bowl. Pour over tofu, and refrigerate 20 minutes.

2. Preheat oven to 450°.

3. Bake tofu at 450° for 25 minutes. Cool to room temperature; chill 30 minutes.

4. Combine greens, cucumber, and onions. Combine juice and remaining 6 ingredients; stir with a whisk. Drizzle juice mixture over greens, and toss well to coat. Place 2 cups salad on each of 4 plates; top each portion with 2 tofu triangles. Yield: 4 servings.

CALORIES 86 (38% from fat); FAT 3.6g (sat 0.6g, mono 1.5g, poly 1.3g); PROTEIN 7.5g; CARB 6.4g; FIBER 2.3g; CHOL 0mg; IRON 2.2mg; SODIUM 311mg; CALC 83mg

Baked Cheese Polenta with Swiss Chard

Parmesan and goat cheeses add a sharp flavor and creamy texture to the polenta. Serve with focaccia and cherry tomatoes tossed in a vinaigrette.

CHARD:
- 2 bunches Swiss chard (about 1½ pounds)
- Cooking spray
- 8 garlic cloves, minced
- 2 tablespoons water

POLENTA:
- 1¾ cups water
- ¼ teaspoon salt
- 1 (14½-ounce) can vegetable broth
- 1 cup yellow cornmeal
- ½ cup (2 ounces) crumbled goat cheese
- 3 tablespoons grated fresh Parmesan cheese
- ¼ cup reduced-fat sour cream

1. Preheat oven to 400°.
2. To prepare chard, remove stems and center ribs. Discard stems and chop ribs; coarsely chop leaves. Heat a large nonstick skillet coated with cooking spray over medium heat. Add garlic; sauté 30 seconds. Add ribs and 2 tablespoons water; cover and cook 5 minutes. Add leaves; cover and cook 5 minutes or until wilted.
3. To prepare polenta, place 1¾ cups water, salt, and broth in a large saucepan. Gradually add cornmeal, stirring constantly with a whisk. Bring to a boil; reduce heat to medium, and cook 8 minutes, stirring constantly. Add cheeses, stirring constantly with a whisk. Spoon half of polenta into a 2-quart baking dish coated with cooking spray, spreading evenly. Top with chard mixture. Spoon sour cream over chard, spreading evenly. Quickly add remaining polenta, spreading evenly.
4. Bake at 400° for 20 minutes. Let stand 5 minutes. Yield: 6 servings (serving size: about 1 cup).

CALORIES 169 (28% from fat); FAT 5.3g (sat 2.9g, mono 1.2g, poly 0.5g); PROTEIN 6.4g; CARB 24.1g; FIBER 1.9g; CHOL 15mg; IRON 2.4mg; SODIUM 647mg; CALC 146mg

---

Italian Vegetarian Menu

Toss sliced tomatoes and red onions with a low-fat balsamic or zesty Italian dressing.

Orecchiette with Broccoli Rabe and Smoked Cheese

Marinated tomato-and-red onion salad

Focaccia

Orange sorbet

Orecchiette with Broccoli Rabe and Smoked Cheese

- 1 teaspoon olive oil
- ¼ teaspoon crushed red pepper
- 4 garlic cloves, minced
- 4 cups chopped broccoli rabe
- ½ cup vegetable broth
- ¼ teaspoon salt
- 4 cups hot cooked orecchiette (about 8 ounces uncooked small ear-shaped pasta)
- ½ cup (2 ounces) shredded smoked mozzarella or smoked gouda cheese

1. Heat oil in a large nonstick skillet over medium heat. Add pepper and garlic; cook 1 minute or until garlic begins to brown. Stir in broccoli rabe; cook 1 minute. Add broth and salt; cover and cook 5 minutes or until tender. Stir in pasta and cheese. Serve immediately. Yield: 4 servings (serving size: 1 cup).

CALORIES 283 (17% from fat); FAT 5.4g (sat 2.2g, mono 1.9g, poly 0.7g); PROTEIN 11.9g; CARB 47.1g; FIBER 3.2g; CHOL 11mg; IRON 2.8mg; SODIUM 344mg; CALC 116mg

---

Arugula, White Bean, and Roasted Red Pepper Salad

SALAD:
- 3 cups torn arugula leaves
- ½ cup chopped bottled roasted red bell peppers
- ⅓ cup vertically sliced red onion
- 1 (16-ounce) can navy beans, rinsed and drained

DRESSING:
- 1½ tablespoons balsamic vinegar
- 1 tablespoon olive oil
- 1 teaspoon honey
- ¼ teaspoon salt
- ¼ teaspoon black pepper
- 1 garlic clove, minced

1. To prepare salad, combine first 4 ingredients in a large bowl.
2. To prepare dressing, combine vinegar and remaining 5 ingredients in a small bowl, stirring with a whisk until blended. Pour over salad; toss to coat. Yield: 4 servings (serving size: 1 cup).

CALORIES 164 (29% from fat); FAT 5.3g (sat 0.7g, mono 2.9g, poly 1.2g); PROTEIN 7.1g; CARB 23.6g; FIBER 2.9g; CHOL 0mg; IRON 2.3mg; SODIUM 500mg; CALC 80mg

---

Clean Greens

Store leafy greens *unwashed* in plastic bags in the refrigerator; any added moisture will cause them to spoil more rapidly. When you're ready to use them, remove unwanted stems and tear leaves into smaller pieces.

Leafy greens harbor sand and other debris, so you'll need to wash them thoroughly. Avoid using a colander for the job, because just running water over the leaves isn't enough to clean them.

Instead, dunk greens in a large bowl, pot, or sink filled with cold water. The dirt will sink to the bottom while the greens float to the top. Remove the leaves by hand and place them in another bowl. Pour out the water and repeat the procedure until the water is free of debris. Dunking and soaking greens is the only method that removes all the grit. Next, spin the greens in a salad spinner if they need to be dry for a salad or other recipe. If your recipe allows, forgo the spinner and cook the greens with the water that clings to them.

How to Cook Caribbean

Cultures and seasonings from around the world collide in this spicy, flavorful island cuisine.

The very thought of the Caribbean summons up visions of fiery barbecue and festive beach parties, of seductive cocktails and tropical desserts. The region is home to some of the world's most explosively flavorful cooking—dishes ranging from Jamaica's jerk pork to Trinidad's curries, from Puerto Rico's crusty *arañitos* (plantain fritters) to Guadeloupe's velvety vegetable soups, from the refreshing conch salads of the Bahamas to Cuba's creamy rice puddings.

Here, then, is a Caribbean sampler that's bursting with flavor, not fat. It's the next best thing to boarding a plane and flying to the islands for dinner.

Rice and Pigeon Peas

Pigeon peas, popular throughout the West Indies, are small, oval beans with a nutty flavor. Look for them in Caribbean markets, or substitute kidney beans or black-eyed peas. We've used canned pigeon peas because they're more readily available than dried.

2 cups water
1½ cups uncooked long-grain parboiled rice (such as Uncle Ben's)
1 teaspoon olive oil
½ teaspoon salt
1 tablespoon olive oil
1 cup chopped onion
¼ cup chopped Canadian bacon (about 3 ounces)
2 garlic cloves, minced
2 tablespoons finely chopped green onions
½ teaspoon ground cumin
½ teaspoon freshly ground black pepper
1 (15-ounce) can green pigeon peas, drained
2 tablespoons chopped fresh flat-leaf parsley
Green onions (optional)

1. Bring water to a boil in a medium saucepan. Add rice, 1 teaspoon oil, and salt; cover, reduce heat, and simmer 20 minutes or until liquid is absorbed.
2. Heat 1 tablespoon oil in a large nonstick skillet over medium heat. Add 1 cup onion, bacon, and garlic; cook 10 minutes or until lightly browned, stirring occasionally. Stir in rice, chopped onions, cumin, pepper, and peas; cook 8 minutes or until thoroughly heated. Stir in parsley. Garnish with green onions, if desired. Yield: 6 servings (serving size: 1 cup).

CALORIES 186 (21% from fat); FAT 4.4g (sat 0.8g, mono 2.7g, poly 0.5g); PROTEIN 8.1g; CARB 29.2g; FIBER 3.2g; CHOL 7mg; IRON 1.5mg; SODIUM 572mg; CALC 50mg

Plantain Chips

Use plantains that are moderately ripe (mottled-looking) for this recipe.

1 tablespoon olive oil
2 medium plantains, peeled and cut into ¼-inch diagonal slices (about 2 cups)
¼ teaspoon salt
⅛ teaspoon ground red pepper

1. Heat oil in a large nonstick skillet over medium heat. Add plantain slices; cook 3 minutes on each side or until browned. Sprinkle salt and pepper over chips. Yield: 4 servings (serving size: ½ cup).

CALORIES 190 (18% from fat); FAT 3.9g (sat 0.5g, mono 2.5g, poly 0.3g); PROTEIN 1.7g; CARB 42g; FIBER 0.7g; CHOL 0mg; IRON 0.8mg; SODIUM 152mg; CALC 4mg

Arroz con Coco
Cuban Coconut Rice Pudding

3 cups water
1 cup short-grain rice (such as Arborio)
4 whole cloves
1 (2-inch) piece vanilla bean, split lengthwise
1 (2-inch) cinnamon stick
1 (14-ounce) can fat-free sweetened condensed milk
½ cup evaporated fat-free milk
½ cup light coconut milk
½ cup golden raisins
1 tablespoon chopped crystallized ginger
1 teaspoon grated lemon rind
Pinch of salt
½ teaspoon ground cinnamon (optional)

1. Place water and rice in a large saucepan. Place cloves, vanilla, and cinnamon stick on a double layer of cheesecloth. Gather edges of cheesecloth together; tie securely. Add to rice mixture. Bring to a simmer over medium heat, stirring frequently. Reduce heat to low; cook 20 minutes or until rice is tender and liquid is almost absorbed.
2. Stir in milks and raisins; cook 10 minutes, stirring frequently. Stir in ginger, rind, and salt; cook 5 minutes, stirring frequently. Remove cheesecloth with spices. Pour rice mixture into a bowl or individual bowls; cover surface of rice mixture with plastic wrap. Chill. Sprinkle pudding with ground cinnamon, if desired. Yield: 8 servings (serving size: ½ cup).

CALORIES 286 (3% from fat); FAT 1g (sat 0.7g, mono 0.1g, poly 0.1g); PROTEIN 7g; CARB 61.9g; FIBER 0.8g; CHOL 7mg; IRON 1.7mg; SODIUM 95mg; CALC 184mg

Jamaican Jerk Pork Tenderloin Step-by-Steps

1. *To butterfly pork, cut it lengthwise with a boning knife, cutting to, but not all the way through, the other side. Open up halves like a book. Cut each half the same way, opening pork so that it lies flat. This increases surface area into which marinade penetrates.*

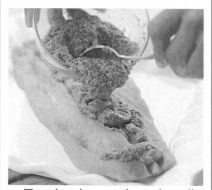

2. *To make jerk marinade, combine all ingredients in a blender or food processor. (Marinade will be thick and pasty.) Pour over pork, and marinate up to 24 hours. The longer you marinate pork, the more flavorful it will be.*

3. *Keep as much marinade on pork as possible, and grill until done. To serve, cut horizontally across grain into thin slices.*

Jamaican Jerk Pork Tenderloin

    2 cups coarsely chopped green
       onions
    ½ cup coarsely chopped onion
    2 tablespoons white vinegar
    1 tablespoon soy sauce
    1 tablespoon vegetable oil
    2 teaspoons kosher salt
    2 teaspoons fresh thyme
    2 teaspoons brown sugar
    2 teaspoons chopped peeled fresh
       ginger
    1 teaspoon ground allspice
    ¼ teaspoon ground nutmeg
    ¼ teaspoon black pepper
    ⅛ teaspoon ground cinnamon
    2 garlic cloves, minced
    1 to 4 Scotch bonnet or habanero
       peppers, seeded and chopped
    1 (1½-pound) pork tenderloin,
       trimmed
       Cooking spray

1. Place first 15 ingredients in a blender or food processor; process until smooth.
2. Slice pork lengthwise, cutting to, but not through, other side. Open halves, laying each side flat. Slice each half lengthwise, cutting to, but not through, other side; open flat. Combine pork and green onion mixture in a dish or large zip-top plastic bag. Cover or seal; marinate in refrigerator 3 to 24 hours. Remove pork from dish or bag; discard marinade.
3. Prepare grill.
4. Place pork on grill rack coated with cooking spray; grill 8 minutes on each side or until meat thermometer registers 160° (slightly pink). Yield: 4 servings (serving size: 3 ounces pork).
WINE NOTE: This intense dish calls for an equally dramatic wine. White-wine lovers should try a dry Gewürztraminer from Alsace, France—Hugel and Trimbach are great producers with wines starting at about $18. Red-wine lovers should try a spicy Côtes-du-Rhône from France, such as one from E. Guigal, Santa Duc, or Château Trignon ($12 to $14).

CALORIES 248 (27% from fat); FAT 7.5g (sat 2g, mono 2.8g, poly 2g); PROTEIN 36.9g; CARB 7.1g; FIBER 1.5g; CHOL 111mg; IRON 3.1mg; SODIUM 1,126mg; CALC 52mg

Fire in the Islands

Caribbean food is anything but mild. Therefore, we've allowed for a range of peppers in some of these dishes—use the lower end of the range for mildly spicy, the upper end for very spicy. Leaving the seeds intact increases the heat. Also, when you're working with hot peppers such as the Scotch bonnet or habanero, it's wise to use gloves. If you don't have gloves, wash your hands immediately after cutting the peppers, and keep your hands away from your face.

Conch Salad

    1 pound uncooked conch or bay
       scallops
    2 teaspoons olive oil
 1½ cups chopped tomato
    1 cup chopped onion
    1 cup chopped green bell pepper
    1 cup chopped celery
    ⅓ cup fresh orange juice
    ⅓ cup fresh lime juice
 1½ teaspoons minced Scotch bonnet
       or habanero pepper
    1 teaspoon kosher salt
    ½ teaspoon freshly ground black pepper

1. Place conch between 2 sheets of heavy-duty plastic wrap; pound to a ½-inch thickness using a meat mallet or rolling pin. Cut conch into ¼-inch-wide strips. (If using scallops, heat oil in a large nonstick skillet over medium-high heat. Add scallops; cook 5 minutes. Drain.)
2. Combine conch or scallops and remaining ingredients in a large bowl; cover and chill at least 1 hour. Yield: 5 servings (serving size: 1 cup).
WINE NOTE: The sweet, tangy flavors of orange and lime call for a white wine with verve. Try a semidry California or Washington state Riesling. From California, look for Chateau St. Jean (about $15); from Washington state, try Columbia Crest (about $6).

CALORIES 157 (17% from fat); FAT 3g (sat 0.4g, mono 1.4g, poly 0.6g); PROTEIN 17.1g; CARB 16.4g; FIBER 2.8g; CHOL 30mg; IRON 1.2mg; SODIUM 560mg; CALC 54mg

Spicy West Indian Pumpkin Soup

1½ tablespoons olive oil
2½ cups chopped peeled calabaza or butternut squash (about 1 pound)
1 cup chopped onion
½ cup chopped celery
1 to 1½ teaspoons minced seeded Scotch bonnet or habanero pepper
2 garlic cloves, minced
1 tablespoon brown sugar
2 teaspoons minced peeled fresh ginger
½ teaspoon dried thyme
¼ teaspoon salt
2 (15.75-ounce) cans fat-free, less-sodium chicken broth
1 bay leaf

1. Heat oil in a saucepan over medium-high heat. Add squash, onion, celery, pepper, and garlic; sauté 5 minutes. Add remaining ingredients; bring to a boil. Cover, reduce heat, and simmer 25 minutes or until tender. Discard bay leaf.
2. Place half of squash mixture in a blender, and process until smooth. Pour pureed mixture into a bowl; repeat procedure with remaining squash mixture. Return pureed mixture to pan; cook over medium heat 3 minutes or until heated. Yield: 5 servings (serving size: 1 cup).

CALORIES 117 (32% from fat); FAT 4.2g (sat 0.6g, mono 3g, poly 0.4g); PROTEIN 3.8g; CARB 17.3g; FIBER 2.1g; CHOL 0mg; IRON 1mg; SODIUM 518mg; CALC 60mg

French West Indian Grilled Snapper with Caper Sauce

(pictured on page 131)

MARINADE:
¼ cup fresh lime juice
1 teaspoon salt
1 teaspoon fresh or ¼ teaspoon dried thyme
1 teaspoon black pepper
3 garlic cloves, chopped
1 to 2 Scotch bonnet or habanero peppers, minced
4 (6-ounce) red snapper or other firm white fish fillets

CAPER SAUCE:
2 tablespoons chopped fresh cilantro
2 tablespoons fresh lime juice
2 tablespoons water
2 tablespoons extra-virgin olive oil
1 tablespoon capers
1 tablespoon red wine vinegar
1½ teaspoons minced Scotch bonnet or habanero pepper
¼ teaspoon salt
¼ teaspoon freshly ground black pepper
1 garlic clove, chopped
1 large shallot, chopped
Cooking spray

1. To prepare marinade, place first 6 ingredients in a blender; process until smooth. Combine marinade and fillets in a large zip-top plastic bag; seal. Marinate in refrigerator 2 to 4 hours, turning bag occasionally.
2. Prepare grill.
3. To prepare caper sauce, place cilantro and next 10 ingredients in a blender or food processor; process until smooth.
4. Remove fillets from marinade; discard marinade. Place fillets on grill rack coated with cooking spray; grill 3 minutes on each side or until fish flakes easily when tested with a fork. Serve with caper sauce. Yield: 4 servings (serving size: 1 fillet and 2 tablespoons sauce).
WINE NOTE: The lime and thyme in this snappy dish hint at the direction the wine should follow—namely jazzy, citrusy, and green. Try the Villa Maria Private Bin Sauvignon Blanc from New Zealand ($13).

CALORIES 246 (35% from fat); FAT 9.6g (sat 1.5g, mono 5.5g, poly 1.6g); PROTEIN 35.4g; CARB 2.8g; FIBER 0.2g; CHOL 63mg; IRON 0.6mg; SODIUM 425mg; CALC 63mg

---

Caribbean Pantry

Allspice Also known as *pimiento* or Jamaican pepper, it's made from the aromatic berries of a Caribbean tree. One of the defining ingredients in Jamaican jerk and French West Indian fish soups, allspice seems to encompass the tastes of cinnamon, nutmeg, and cloves—hence its name. Allspice is used in sweet and savory dishes.

Annatto seed Known as *achiote* in Spanish, this is a rust-colored, earthy-flavored seed. Considered the poor man's saffron by some, it's used in Spanish Caribbean rice dishes and French West Indian stews.

Calabaza This large, round Caribbean pumpkin has a dense, bright-orange flesh. The flavor is similar to butternut squash, a good substitute.

Coconut milk The "cream" of the tropics, produced by blending freshly grated coconut with hot water. Taste of Thai makes a canned "lite" coconut milk that's great to use in healthy Caribbean cooking.

Conch This giant sea snail's delicate, mild, white flesh is used in dishes ranging from salads to stews to steaks. Substitute bay scallops if you can't find conch.

Guava An egg-shaped tropical fruit with a musky, perfumy flavor. Because it contains seeds, it's generally enjoyed as juice or jelly.

Pigeon pea A brown, oval bean originally from Africa; in the Caribbean, also known as the *gunga* (Congo) pea and the *pois d'Angole* (Angola pea). Endowed with a nutty, earthy flavor, the pigeon pea is often paired with rice.

Plantain A jumbo cooking banana that can be eaten at every stage of ripeness. When green, it tastes starchy, like a potato; when ripe, it tastes sweet, like a banana.

Scotch bonnet chile This chile, shaped like a Chinese lantern, is one of the world's hottest—50 times hotter than a jalapeño. Behind all that heat is a complex flavor that's earthy, floral, and apricot-like. If you can't find the Scotch bonnet, substitute its Mexican cousin, the habanero.

Regional Caribbean Dishes

Accras (French West Indies): Spicy salt-cod fritters.

Adobo (Cuba): A mixture of sour-orange juice, cumin, and garlic used to marinate meats and fish. Dishes made with it are often served with *mojo*, a sauce prepared from the same ingredients.

Arroz con leche (Spanish islands): Creamy rice pudding.

Arroz con pollo (Spanish islands): A sort of landlubber's paella made with chicken and annatto.

Asopao (Puerto Rico and Dominican Republic): A soupy seafood-rice stew flavored with annatto.

Blaff de poisson (French islands): Pan-fried fish served in a broth flavored with lime juice, allspice berries, and Scotch bonnet chiles. (The name of the dish is said to echo the sound the fish makes as it hits the frying pan.)

Boka dushi (Dutch islands): "Sweet mouth" in the Papamiento dialect; refers to Indonesian-style chicken satés.

Bolo pretu (Curaçao and other islands): Black fruitcake.

Christophene farcie (French islands): Cheese-and-chile-stuffed chayote squash.

Choka (Trinidad): A grilled-vegetable dip.

Court-bouillon (French islands): A delicate fish stew flavored with lime juice and allspice.

Cutters (Barbados): Sandwiches that are traditionally made with flying fish.

Jerk (Jamaica): Fiery barbecued pork that's smoked over allspice wood.

Keshi yena (Curaçao): Hollowed-out Edam cheese filled with olive- and caper-spiced beef.

Pepperpot (Barbados and other islands): A soulful beef-and-vegetable stew enriched with *callaloo* (spinachlike *malanga* leaves) and *cassareep* (cassava vinegar).

Pika (Dutch islands): Pickled onion-and-chile sauce.

Pindasaus (Dutch islands): Spicy peanut sauce.

Poulet boucane (Guadeloupe): "Buccaneer chicken," seasoned with island spices and smoked over sugarcane.

Rotis (Trinidad and Tobago, and other islands): Flatbreads filled with split peas. Rotis are the tortillas of the southern Caribbean; filled with everything from stewed vegetables to curried goat.

Run down (Jamaica): A stew made with smoked fish and coconut milk.

Salmagundi (Jamaica): Spicy potted fish.

Sauce chien (French islands): "Dog sauce" is the literal translation, but it's really just a fiery vinaigrette.

Souse (Barbados): Pickled pig ears and tails.

Yuca frita (Cuba): Fried yuca (cassava) with garlic sauce.

Boka Dushi Step-by-Steps

1. *Marinate the chicken in a combination of* **kejap manis**, *a sweet soy sauce, and* **sambal ulek**, *a spicy paste made from peppers for 30 minutes.*

2. *Thread chicken onto skewers, and grill.*

Boka Dushi
Dutch West Indian Chicken Kebabs

This is the Dutch West Indian version of the classic Indonesian saté. *Boka* means "mouth" and *dushi* means "sweet" in Papamiento, the musical dialect that blends Dutch, Portuguese, Spanish, and West African languages. *Kejap manis*, the ancestor of modern ketchup, is a thick, sweet soy sauce; you can substitute equal parts soy sauce and molasses. *Sambal ulek* is a fiery paste made of red peppers. Look for both in Asian markets.

¼ cup *kejap manis* or 2 tablespoons soy sauce plus 2 tablespoons molasses
1 tablespoon fresh lime juice
1 teaspoon ground cumin
2 teaspoons grated peeled fresh ginger
1 teaspoon *sambal ulek* or Thai chile paste
½ teaspoon ground turmeric
1½ pounds skinless, boneless chicken breast, cut into ½-inch-wide strips, or 1½ pounds chicken tenders
Cooking spray
Dutch West Indian Peanut Sauce

1. Combine first 7 ingredients in a large zip-top plastic bag; seal and marinate in refrigerator 30 minutes.

2. Prepare grill.

3. Remove chicken from bag, and discard marinade. Thread chicken strips onto 18 (8-inch) skewers.

4. Place kebabs on grill rack coated with cooking spray; grill 2 minutes on each side or until done. Serve with Dutch West Indian Peanut Sauce. Yield: 6 servings (serving size: 3 kebabs and 2 tablespoons Dutch West Indian Peanut Sauce).

WINE NOTE: Because the sweet spiciness of the chicken is underscored by the creaminess of the peanut sauce, you need a contrast when it comes to wine. Go for something super-refreshing and bubbly—a California sparkling wine such as Mumm Napa Valley Brut Prestige (about $16) or Gloria Ferrer Sonoma Brut (about $18).

(Totals include Dutch West Indian Peanut Sauce) CALORIES 212 (26% from fat); FAT 6.1g (sat 1.1g, mono 2.5g, poly 1.8g); PROTEIN 29.5g; CARB 9.5g; FIBER 0.9g; CHOL 66mg; IRON 1.9mg; SODIUM 676mg; CALC 40mg

⅓ cup fat-free, less-sodium chicken broth

3 tablespoons creamy peanut butter

½ cup chopped seeded tomato

2 tablespoons minced green onions

2 tablespoons chopped fresh cilantro

1 tablespoon fish sauce

1 tablespoon fresh lime juice

1 teaspoon grated peeled fresh ginger

1 teaspoon minced seeded Thai chile

1 teaspoon honey

1 garlic clove, crushed

1. Combine broth and peanut butter in a small saucepan; cook over low heat 5 minutes or until smooth, stirring with a whisk. Pour peanut butter mixture into a bowl; stir in remaining ingredients. Serve at room temperature. Yield: ¾ cup (serving size: 2 tablespoons).

CALORIES 60 (63% from fat); FAT 4.2g (sat 0.7g, mono 2g, poly 1.3g); PROTEIN 2.9g; CARB 3.8g; FIBER 0.8g; CHOL 0mg; IRON 0.4mg; SODIUM 301mg; CALC 9mg

Planter's Punch

Planter's punch is a traditional drink of welcome throughout the Caribbean.

1 cup white rum

1 cup fresh orange juice (about 2 oranges)

1 cup pineapple juice

1 cup bottled guava nectar

2 tablespoons sugar

2 tablespoons fresh lime juice

¼ teaspoon Angostura bitters

6 cinnamon sticks

6 fresh pineapple slices

6 orange slices

6 maraschino cherries

¼ teaspoon grated nutmeg (optional)

1. Combine first 7 ingredients in a pitcher. Serve over ice. Garnish each serving with 1 cinnamon stick, 1 pineapple slice, 1 orange slice, and 1 cherry. Sprinkle with nutmeg, if desired. Yield: 6 servings.

CALORIES 213 (1% from fat); FAT 0.1g (sat 0.1g, mono 0g, poly 0g); PROTEIN 0.6g; CARB 23.8g; FIBER 0.6g; CHOL 0mg; IRON 0.3mg; SODIUM 2mg; CALC 15mg

The Extra-Nice Spice

Ginger, like Gilligan's costar, adds a lot of sparkle.

No doubt about it. Ginger definitely gets around. Historical evidence shows that the Chinese have been using ginger for 2,000 years or more, and through the centuries, its influence has spread around the globe.

Cooks from almost every culture use ginger in one form or another, and you will find ginger in many guises. Its fresh form is available in most any grocery's produce department; the gnarled root (or, more correctly, the rhizome) with its papery brown skin can often be found in the specialty-ingredients section. Sushi lovers will recognize pickled ginger, preserved in sweet vinegar, as a side dish as traditional as the daub of fiery wasabi paste. Accomplished bakers and chefs, meanwhile, often use crystallized (or candied) ginger as another way to warm and mellow their creations.

Though its powerful scent and peppery flavor are smoothed in cooking, ginger adds a fresh, herbal liveliness to both sweet and savory dishes. In the following recipes, we've put ginger to work in all its delicious incarnations.

Chicken-and-Pickled Ginger Salad with Curry Dressing

When Chicago reader Beth Ghadimi wrote and asked us to come up with a recipe like the one she once enjoyed in St. Martin, we gave it a try. We're glad we did; Beth says she is, too.

2 cups cubed cooked chicken breast (about 8 ounces)

Curry Dressing

5 cups torn romaine lettuce

½ cup thinly sliced red onion

¼ cup chopped pickled ginger

¼ cup chopped dry-roasted cashews

1 (11-ounce) can mandarin oranges in light syrup, drained

1. Combine chicken and Curry Dressing in a medium bowl. Cover and chill 15 minutes.

2. Combine chicken mixture, lettuce, and remaining 4 ingredients; toss gently to coat. Serve salad immediately. Yield: 4 servings (serving size: 1½ cups).

(Totals include Curry Dressing) CALORIES 283 (31% from fat); FAT 9.6g (sat 2g, mono 4.1g, poly 2.8g); PROTEIN 20.3g; CARB 29.1g; FIBER 2.2g; CHOL 48mg; IRON 2.2mg; SODIUM 319mg; CALC 45mg

1 tablespoon vegetable oil

1 tablespoon honey

1 teaspoon curry powder

1 bay leaf

2 tablespoons fresh lemon juice

½ teaspoon grated orange rind

1 tablespoon fresh orange juice

¼ teaspoon salt

⅛ teaspoon black pepper

1. Combine vegetable oil, honey, curry, and bay leaf in a small saucepan over low heat; cook 2 minutes or until warm. Remove from heat; let stand 15 minutes. Discard bay leaf. Add lemon juice and remaining 4 ingredients, stirring well with a whisk. Yield: 6 tablespoons (serving size: 1½ tablespoons).

CALORIES 53 (59% from fat); FAT 3.5g (sat 0.6g, mono 1.1g, poly 1.7g); PROTEIN 0.2g; CARB 5.9g; FIBER 0.3g; CHOL 0mg; IRON 0.2mg; SODIUM 147mg; CALC 5mg

Grilled Flank Steak with Green Onion-Ginger Chimichurri

Mint, rice vinegar, ginger, and green onions add an Asian twist to a Latin condiment.

- ¾ cup (1-inch) sliced green onions
- ⅓ cup chopped fresh parsley
- ¼ cup fresh mint leaves
- 3 tablespoons rice vinegar
- 2 tablespoons finely chopped peeled fresh ginger
- 2 tablespoons olive oil
- 1 tablespoon water
- ½ teaspoon salt
- ½ teaspoon black pepper
- 2 garlic cloves, peeled
- 1 (1½-pound) flank steak, trimmed
- ½ teaspoon salt
- ½ teaspoon black pepper
- Cooking spray

1. Prepare grill.

2. Place first 10 ingredients in a blender or food processor; process until smooth.

3. Sprinkle steak with ½ teaspoon salt and ½ teaspoon pepper. Place steak on grill rack coated with cooking spray, and grill 8 minutes on each side or until desired degree of doneness. Let stand 5 minutes. Cut steak diagonally across grain into thin slices. Serve with sauce. Yield: 6 servings (serving size: 3 ounces meat and about 2 tablespoons sauce).

CALORIES 218 (54% from fat); FAT 13g (sat 4.2g, mono 6.7g, poly 0.9g); PROTEIN 22.1g; CARB 2g; FIBER 0.6g; CHOL 54mg; IRON 2.6mg; SODIUM 462mg; CALC 24mg

Ginger Pudding

Garnish with a few fresh berries for a contrast in color, texture, and flavor.

- 3 cups 1% low-fat milk, divided
- ⅓ cup finely chopped crystallized ginger
- ⅔ cup sugar
- 3 tablespoons cornstarch
- Dash of salt
- 3 large egg yolks
- 1 tablespoon butter
- 1 teaspoon grated lemon rind
- 1 teaspoon vanilla extract

1. Combine 2½ cups milk and ginger in a medium saucepan; bring to a simmer over medium heat, stirring frequently. Remove from heat; let stand 5 minutes.

2. Combine ½ cup milk, sugar, cornstarch, salt, and egg yolks in a medium bowl, and stir with a whisk until well blended. Gradually stir one-fourth of hot milk mixture into egg mixture; add to remaining milk mixture, stirring constantly. Bring to a boil over medium heat; cook 1 minute or until thick and creamy, stirring constantly. Remove mixture from heat; stir in butter, rind, and vanilla. Pour into a bowl; cover surface of pudding with plastic wrap. Chill. Yield: 6 servings (serving size: ½ cup).

CALORIES 226 (23% from fat); FAT 5.8g (sat 2.8g, mono 1.9g, poly 0.5g); PROTEIN 5.5g; CARB 38.1g; FIBER 0.1g; CHOL 119mg; IRON 1.9mg; SODIUM 114mg; CALC 179mg

Thai-Style Mussels with Pickled Ginger

Serve as an appetizer with an Asian meal, or double the serving size and spoon over hot cooked rice or rice noodles for four entrées.

- 2 teaspoons vegetable oil
- ½ cup minced shallots
- 1 tablespoon chile paste with garlic
- 1 garlic clove, minced
- ½ cup light coconut milk
- ¼ teaspoon lime rind
- ¼ cup fresh lime juice
- ¼ cup minced pickled ginger
- ¼ cup chopped fresh parsley
- 2 pounds mussels, scrubbed and debearded (about 40 mussels)
- Parsley sprigs (optional)

1. Heat oil in a large Dutch oven over medium-high heat. Add shallots, chile paste, and garlic; cook 2 minutes or until tender, stirring constantly. Add coconut milk and next 5 ingredients; bring to a boil. Cover and cook 5 minutes or until shells open. Remove from heat; discard any unopened shells. Garnish with parsley sprigs, if desired. Yield: 8 servings (serving size: about 5 mussels and 2 tablespoons sauce).

CALORIES 80 (32% from fat); FAT 2.8g (sat 0.9g, mono 0.6g, poly 0.8g); PROTEIN 5.3g; CARB 8.1g; FIBER 0.2g; CHOL 12mg; IRON 2mg; SODIUM 184mg; CALC 38mg

Preparing Fresh Ginger Step-by-Steps

1. *Use a vegetable peeler to remove tough skin and reveal yellowish flesh.*

2. *Cut peeled ginger into slices, then stack slices and cut into strips. Line up strips and cut crosswise into small pieces to mince.*

Grilled Pork Tenderloin with Apple-Ginger Sauce

Serve with couscous or rice to soak up the spicy-sweet sauce. Try peach or apricot jelly to vary the flavor of the sauce.

- ¾ cup apple jelly
- 2 tablespoons minced peeled fresh ginger
- 2 tablespoons cider vinegar
- ½ teaspoon salt
- ½ to 1 teaspoon crushed red pepper
- ½ teaspoon black pepper
- 2 garlic cloves, peeled
- 1 (1-pound) pork tenderloin, trimmed

Cooking spray

1. Prepare grill.

2. Place first 7 ingredients in a blender or food processor; process until smooth.

3. Insert a meat thermometer into thickest portion of pork. Place pork on grill rack coated with cooking spray; grill 16 minutes or until thermometer registers 160° (slightly pink), turning pork occasionally. Place pork on a platter, and let stand 5 minutes. Serve pork with sauce. Yield: 4 servings (serving size: 4 ounces pork and ¼ cup sauce).

CALORIES 290 (11% from fat); FAT 3.4g (sat 1g, mono 1.4g, poly 0.6g); PROTEIN 24.2g; CARB 41.5g; FIBER 0.5g; CHOL 74mg; IRON 1.8mg; SODIUM 370mg; CALC 18mg

Baked Salmon with Ginger-Fruit Relish

RELISH:

- 2 cups finely chopped peeled mango
- ½ cup finely chopped red onion
- ½ cup finely chopped red bell pepper
- ½ cup finely chopped seeded peeled cucumber
- 3 tablespoons chopped fresh parsley
- 2 tablespoons cider vinegar
- 2 tablespoons fresh lime juice
- 1½ tablespoons minced peeled fresh ginger
- 1 tablespoon honey
- 2 teaspoons olive oil
- ⅛ teaspoon salt
- ⅛ teaspoon black pepper
- 1 (8-ounce) can crushed pineapple in juice, undrained

SALMON:

- 2 tablespoons Dijon mustard
- 1 tablespoon minced peeled fresh ginger
- 1 tablespoon honey
- 2 teaspoons olive oil
- ⅛ teaspoon black pepper
- 4 (6-ounce) salmon fillets, skinned (about 1 inch thick)

Cooking spray

1. To prepare relish, combine first 13 ingredients in a bowl. Cover and chill 1 hour, stirring mixture occasionally.

2. Preheat oven to 400°.

3. To prepare salmon, combine mustard and next 4 ingredients in a small bowl. Place fillets on a jelly-roll pan coated with cooking spray; brush fillets with mustard mixture. Bake at 400° for 14 minutes or until fish flakes easily when tested with a fork. Serve with relish. Yield: 4 servings (serving size: 1 fillet and 1 cup relish).

CALORIES 470 (38% from fat); FAT 20g (sat 3.2g, mono 10.7g, poly 4.1g); PROTEIN 36.2g; CARB 37.3g; FIBER 2.7g; CHOL 111mg; IRON 1.6mg; SODIUM 283mg; CALC 40mg

Double-Ginger Cookies

Small chunks of crystallized ginger add spark to these cookies, so don't chop the ginger too finely.

- 1½ cups all-purpose flour
- 1 cup whole wheat flour
- ¾ cup chopped crystallized ginger
- 1 teaspoon baking powder
- ½ teaspoon baking soda
- ½ teaspoon salt
- ½ teaspoon ground ginger
- 1¼ cups sugar, divided
- ½ cup applesauce
- ¼ cup vegetable oil
- 1 teaspoon grated lemon rind
- 1 tablespoon lemon juice
- ¼ teaspoon vanilla extract

Cooking spray

1. Lightly spoon flours into dry measuring cups, and level with a knife. Combine flours and next 5 ingredients; stir well with a whisk. Make a well in center of mixture. Combine 1 cup sugar, applesauce, and next 4 ingredients. Add to flour mixture, stirring just until moist; cover and chill dough at least 1 hour.

2. Preheat oven to 350°.

3. Lightly coat hands with flour. Shape dough into 24 balls (about 2 tablespoons each; dough will be sticky). Roll balls in ¼ cup sugar. Place balls 2 inches apart on baking sheets coated with cooking spray. Bake at 350° for 15 minutes or until lightly browned. Cool 1 minute on pan. Remove from pan; cool completely on wire racks. Yield: 2 dozen (serving size: 1 cookie).

NOTE: These freeze well. Place cooled cookies in a heavy-duty zip-top plastic bag; store in freezer for up to 1 month. Thaw at room temperature.

CALORIES 123 (18% from fat); FAT 2.5g (sat 0.5g, mono 0.7g, poly 1.2g); PROTEIN 1.5g; CARB 24.2g; FIBER 0.9g; CHOL 0mg; IRON 1.4mg; SODIUM 98mg; CALC 24mg

Carrot-Ginger Soup

(pictured on page 129)

Ginger juice—squeezed from grated or shredded fresh ginger—provides a subtle hint of flavor without altering the puree's creamy smoothness. The ginger juice is added at the end so the flavor stays strong.

    2   tablespoons coriander seeds
    1   tablespoon black peppercorns
    3   garlic cloves, peeled
    2   star anise
    2   (3-inch) cinnamon sticks
    1   tablespoon olive oil
    3   cups chopped onion
    3   garlic cloves, minced
    2½ cups chopped carrot (about 1
        pound)
    2   cups water
    2   (14½-ounce) cans vegetable broth
    ⅓   cup chopped peeled fresh ginger
    1   tablespoon water
    ½   cup 2% reduced-fat milk
    2   tablespoons honey
        Fresh chives (optional)

1. Place first 5 ingredients on a double layer of cheesecloth. Gather edges of cheesecloth together; tie securely.
2. Heat oil in a Dutch oven over medium-high heat. Add onion; sauté 5 minutes or until tender. Add minced garlic; sauté 1 minute. Add cheesecloth bag, carrot, 2 cups water, and broth; bring to a boil. Cover, reduce heat, and cook 1 hour or until carrot is tender. Discard cheesecloth pouch.
3. Place ginger and 1 tablespoon water in a food processor; process until finely minced, scraping sides of bowl occasionally. Place ginger mixture on a double layer of cheesecloth. Gather edges of cheesecloth together; squeeze to extract juice to equal 2 tablespoons. Add ginger juice, milk, and honey to carrot mixture. Place half of carrot mixture in food processor; process until smooth. Pour pureed mixture into a large bowl. Repeat procedure with remaining mixture. Garnish with chives, if desired. Yield: 6 servings (serving size: 1 cup).

CALORIES 125 (26% from fat); FAT 3.6g (sat 0.6g, mono 1.8g, poly 0.3g); PROTEIN 2.5g; CARB 24.3g; FIBER 4g; CHOL 2mg; IRON 0.6mg; SODIUM 706mg; CALC 65mg

Ginger-Infused Black Beans

Serve with grilled fish and sautéed bok choy.

    1   (6-ounce) bottle pickled ginger
    1   teaspoon olive oil
    ½   cup chopped onion
    2   garlic cloves, minced
    ¼   teaspoon salt
    2   (15-ounce) cans black beans,
        undrained

1. Drain ginger in a colander over a bowl, reserving ¼ cup ginger juice. Reserve pickled ginger for another use.
2. Heat oil in a medium nonstick saucepan over medium heat. Add onion, and sauté 5 minutes. Add garlic; sauté 1 minute. Stir in salt and beans. Bring to a boil; reduce heat, and simmer 15 minutes, stirring occasionally. Stir in ginger juice. Yield: 6 servings (serving size: ½ cup).

CALORIES 219 (7% from fat); FAT 1.8g (sat 0.3g, mono 0.6g, poly 0.4g); PROTEIN 12.7g; CARB 39.7g; FIBER 6.3g; CHOL 0mg; IRON 3.1mg; SODIUM 527mg; CALC 71mg

---

Guide to Gingers

Fresh. Look for it in the produce section of your supermarket. The hearty root will keep for up to three weeks when stored tightly wrapped in plastic wrap in your fridge's vegetable crisper.
Crystallized/candied. This variety is generally found in supermarket spice sections or in produce departments' specialty areas. Before chopping crystallized ginger, coat your knife with cooking spray to keep the ginger from sticking to it.
Pickled. Find this version of ginger preserved in sweet vinegar, in Asian markets or the Asian sections of large supermarkets. Or order a 6-ounce jar for $3.45 from www.localflavor.com.

Waffles Worth the Workout

A weekend family tradition carries on— minus the swim team.

The ritual started when Jennifer McLaughlin was a kid. "Every Sunday morning, Dad would prepare the batter, and Mom would pour the waffles as my brother, sister, and I drifted into the kitchen," she says. But the cozy family routine didn't stay that way for very long. All three McLaughlin kids were on the swim team, and soon their friends and teammates were stopping in as well. "By the time my sister began to swim, the waffles had become so popular that the entire team would come over after Saturday morning practice," Jennifer says. "My parents had to borrow waffle irons from the neighbors so they could appease all those hungry swimmers."

Now residing in Reston, Virginia, Jennifer has long since left her home and swim mates, but she hasn't let go of the waffles.

Weekend Morning Waffles

Soy flour, a finely ground flour made from soybeans, is richer in natural fat and much higher in protein than other flours. Because it doesn't contain gluten, the protein that gives bread its structure, it should be mixed with other flours for baking.

    1½ cups all-purpose flour
    ½   cup soy flour
    1½ tablespoons ground cinnamon
    2½ teaspoons baking powder
    ½   teaspoon salt
    2   cups 1% low-fat milk
    ¼   cup vegetable oil
    2   large egg yolks
    2   large egg whites
        Dash of sugar
        Cooking spray
    1½ cups maple syrup
        Whole strawberries (optional)

1. Lightly spoon flours into dry measuring cups, and level with a knife. Combine flours, cinnamon, baking powder, and salt in a large bowl; stir with a whisk. Combine milk, oil, and egg yolks; add to flour mixture, stirring until smooth.

2. Place egg whites in a large bowl, and beat with a mixer at high speed until foamy. Add sugar, beating until soft peaks form. Fold egg white mixture into batter.

3. Coat a waffle iron with cooking spray; preheat. Spoon about ⅓ cup batter per 4-inch waffle onto hot waffle iron, spreading batter to edges. Cook 5 to 6 minutes or until steaming stops; repeat procedure with remaining batter. Serve with syrup; garnish with strawberries, if desired. Yield: 8 servings (serving size: 2 waffles and 3 tablespoons syrup).

CALORIES 373 (25% from fat); FAT 10.5g (sat 2.3g, mono 3g, poly 4.3g); PROTEIN 7.8g; CARB 63.3g; FIBER 0.7g; CHOL 57mg; IRON 2.6mg; SODIUM 351mg; CALC 225mg

Aloha Salsa

"I'm a new cook, and my wife has been showing me how to have fun in the kitchen. This salsa is a combination of my very favorite things. I use the freshest ingredients I can get my hands on—the quality of the ingredients ensures the success of the recipe—and never skimp on the spices."

—Milton Sweet, Dallas, Texas

    1 cup finely chopped fresh pineapple
    1 cup chopped peeled mango
    1 cup coarsely chopped red bell pepper
    1 cup cubed peeled kiwifruit (about 3 kiwifruit)
    ¾ cup chopped red onion
    ⅓ cup minced fresh cilantro
    2 tablespoons lime juice
    2 teaspoons chopped seeded jalapeño pepper

1. Combine all ingredients in a bowl. Cover and chill 2 hours. Yield: 4 cups (serving size: ¼ cup).

CALORIES 27 (7% from fat); FAT 0.2g (sat 0g, mono 0g, poly 0.1g); PROTEIN 0.5g; CARB 6.5g; FIBER 1.1g; CHOL 0mg; IRON 0.3mg; SODIUM 2mg; CALC 10mg

Grilled Chicken with Hot 'n' Spicy Tequila-Orange Marinade

"I created this dish for a poolside barbecue with a Mexican grill theme, and it went over really well with my friends. I like to serve it with spicy black beans, fruit salsa, and tortillas (although tortilla chips will also work). There are never leftovers!"

—Robin M. Monahan, Fountain Valley, California

MARINADE:

    2 tablespoons olive oil
    2 cups chopped onion
    4 garlic cloves, minced
    4 jalapeño peppers, seeded and chopped
    4 oranges, peeled and sliced
    1 cup orange juice
    1 cup tequila
    2 teaspoons chopped fresh rosemary
    2 teaspoons minced fresh cilantro
    2 teaspoons balsamic vinegar

CHICKEN:

    2 pounds chicken pieces, skinned
    2 teaspoons chili powder
    1 teaspoon salt
    1 teaspoon black pepper
    Cooking spray

1. To prepare marinade, heat oil in a nonstick skillet over medium-high heat. Add onion and garlic; sauté 3 minutes. Add jalapeño peppers and oranges; cook 2 minutes, stirring occasionally. Add juice; cook 2 minutes. Add tequila; cook 3 minutes. Add rosemary, cilantro, and vinegar; cook 1 minute.

2. Place marinade in a blender or food processor; process until smooth. Strain mixture through a sieve into a bowl. Discard solids. Reserve ½ cup marinade. Place remaining marinade in a large zip-top plastic bag.

3. To prepare chicken, pierce chicken pieces with a fork. Add chicken, chili powder, salt, and black pepper to marinade in bag. Seal and marinate in refrigerator 2 hours, turning bag occasionally.

4. Prepare grill.

5. Remove chicken from bag; discard marinade in bag. Place chicken on grill rack coated with cooking spray; cook 12 minutes on each side or until chicken is done, basting frequently with reserved marinade. Yield: 4 servings.

NOTE: For chicken pieces, use a combination of chicken breasts, thighs, and drumsticks. Look for packages labeled "pick of the chick" in the butcher case.

CALORIES 324 (45% from fat); FAT 16.3g (sat 3.7g, mono 7.7g, poly 3.2g); PROTEIN 34.1g; CARB 11.9g; FIBER 2.4g; CHOL 120mg; IRON 0.4mg; SODIUM 324mg; CALC 29mg

Wild Rice-and-Quinoa Garden Salad

"This salad travels well and can be served at room temperature, so it's a great potluck dish. The colorful combination of grains and vegetables makes for a beautiful presentation."

—Michelle Bultman, Lake Elmo, Minnesota

    3 cups water, divided
    ½ cup uncooked wild rice
    1 cup uncooked quinoa
    ½ cup thinly sliced green onions
    ½ cup chopped red bell pepper
    ½ cup chopped seeded peeled cucumber
    2 tablespoons olive oil
    2 tablespoons balsamic vinegar
    1 teaspoon Dijon mustard
    ½ teaspoon salt
    ½ teaspoon dried thyme
    ¼ teaspoon dried rosemary
    ¼ teaspoon freshly ground black pepper
    2 garlic cloves, minced

1. Combine 1 cup water and wild rice in a medium saucepan; bring to a boil. Cover, reduce heat, and simmer 1 hour or until rice is tender and liquid is absorbed.

2. Combine 2 cups water and quinoa in a medium saucepan, and bring to a boil. Cover, reduce heat, and simmer 20 minutes or until liquid is absorbed. Remove from heat; fluff with a fork.

3. Place rice and quinoa in a large bowl. Stir in green onions, bell pepper, and cucumber.

Continued

4. Combine oil and remaining 7 ingredients in a small bowl, stirring with a whisk. Drizzle over quinoa mixture; toss gently to coat. Cover and chill at least 2 hours. Yield: 10 servings (serving size: ½ cup).

CALORIES 122 (29% from fat); FAT 3.9g (sat 0.5g, mono 2.3g, poly 0.7g); PROTEIN 3.7g; CARB 19g; FIBER 3g; CHOL 0mg; IRON 2.1mg; SODIUM 145mg; CALC 20mg

Middle Eastern Chicken Breasts

"We like to take the different flavors from ethnic recipes and incorporate them into our own recipes. This one combines Middle Eastern and Indian flavors, and tastes sweet and tart but not overpowering. This dish should be eaten slowly and savored to enjoy all the different flavors."

—Joe and Becky Terza, Altoona, Pennsylvania

    2 tablespoons balsamic vinegar
    2 teaspoons olive oil, divided
    4 (4-ounce) skinless, boneless
       chicken breast halves
    Cooking spray
 1½ cups chopped red potato
    1 cup chopped Vidalia or other
       sweet onion
    2 teaspoons ground cumin
    2 teaspoons ground coriander
    2 teaspoons chili powder
    2 teaspoons curry powder
    5 garlic cloves, minced
 2½ cups chopped tomato
    ¾ cup frozen green peas, thawed
    2 tablespoons minced fresh
       cilantro
    ½ teaspoon kosher salt
    ½ teaspoon black pepper
    ½ cup balsamic vinegar

1. Prepare grill.
2. Combine 2 tablespoons vinegar and 1 teaspoon oil in a large zip-top plastic bag; add chicken. Seal and marinate in refrigerator 10 minutes. Remove chicken from bag, and discard marinade. Place chicken on grill rack coated with cooking spray, and cook 4 minutes on each side or until chicken is done. Cut into ¼-inch-wide strips.

3. Heat 1 teaspoon oil in a large saucepan over medium heat. Add potato; cook 10 minutes or until tender, stirring constantly. Stir in onion and next 5 ingredients; cook 5 minutes, stirring occasionally. Stir in tomato and next 4 ingredients. Cook 3 minutes; remove from heat.
4. Place ½ cup vinegar in a small saucepan. Bring to a boil; cook until reduced to ¼ cup (about 3 minutes).
5. Spoon 1 cup cooked vegetables onto each of 4 plates. Arrange 1 sliced chicken breast half over vegetables on each plate. Drizzle 1 tablespoon reduced vinegar over each serving. Yield: 4 servings.

CALORIES 277 (14% from fat); FAT 4.2g (sat 0.7g, mono 1.6g, poly 1.1g); PROTEIN 31.6g; CARB 28.9g; FIBER 5.4g; CHOL 66mg; IRON 4.6mg; SODIUM 380mg; CALC 75mg

Mango-Habanero Salsa

"This salsa has a complex aroma, but it remains light and tropical, with a fruity taste and lots of heat. It's excellent with fish and chicken dishes, and benefits from an overnight wait to allow the flavors to mix. Those not accustomed to really spicy food may wish to start with just one—or even a half—habanero pepper, although it's essential to the flavor of the salsa."

—Brett Thomas, Davis, California

    2 cups cubed peeled mango
    ¾ cup chopped onion
    ¼ cup white vinegar
    ¼ cup water
    ¼ cup fresh lime juice
    1 tablespoon vegetable oil
    ¼ teaspoon salt
    3 yellow tomatoes, chopped
       (about 1½ pounds)
    ½ to 3 habanero peppers, seeded

1. Place all ingredients in a food processor; process until almost smooth. Cover and chill 2 hours. Yield: 4 cups (serving size: ¼ cup).

CALORIES 35 (28% from fat); FAT 1.1g (sat 0.2g, mono 0.3g, poly 0.5g); PROTEIN 0.6g; CARB 6.9g; FIBER 1g; CHOL 0mg; IRON 0.3mg; SODIUM 41mg; CALC 6mg

Chocolate-Mint Cookies

"I love to experiment when I cook, mixing recipes and adding my own ingredients. These taste just like mint Girl Scout cookies. They're delicious, but they're low-fat. Don't worry if you don't have time to roll and cut the dough—the recipe works just as well if you drop spoonfuls directly onto the baking sheet."

—Nicole Schnaus, Marietta, Georgia

    1 cup all-purpose flour
    ½ cup unsweetened cocoa
    ¼ teaspoon baking soda
    ½ cup packed brown sugar
    ½ cup granulated sugar
    3 tablespoons butter, softened
    3 tablespoons applesauce
    1 teaspoon vanilla extract
    ¼ teaspoon peppermint extract
    1 large egg white, lightly beaten
    Cooking spray

1. Lightly spoon flour into a dry measuring cup; level with a knife. Combine flour, cocoa, and baking soda in a small bowl, stirring well with a whisk.
2. Combine brown sugar and next 5 ingredients in a medium bowl; beat with a mixer at high speed 2 minutes. Beat in egg white. Add flour mixture; beat at low speed until well blended.
3. Coat hands lightly with cooking spray. Shape dough into a 6-inch log. Wrap log in plastic wrap; freeze 1 hour or until firm.
4. Preheat oven to 350°.
5. Cut log into 24 (¼-inch) slices, and place 1 inch apart on baking sheets lightly coated with cooking spray. Bake at 350° for 10 minutes. Remove from pans; cool on wire racks. Yield: 2 dozen (serving size: 1 cookie).

CALORIES 76 (22% from fat); FAT 1.8g (sat 1.1g, mono 0.5g, poly 0.1g); PROTEIN 1.2g; CARB 13.7g; FIBER 0.2g; CHOL 4mg; IRON 0.7mg; SODIUM 33mg; CALC 8mg

Tastes of the Tropics

Let our fruit-themed desserts transport you to your favorite beach hammock.

These sun-kissed delicacies will conjure memories or dreams of palm trees, beach breezes, and wavelets lapping the sand. Reinforce the imagery with the refreshing tastes of citrus and tropical fruits—lemons, limes, oranges, pineapples, and bananas.

Light and airy, these desserts are ideal for late-spring and summer menus—while keeping you bathing-suit beautiful for the season to come.

Key Lime Sorbet with Gingersnaps

5   cups water
1   cup sugar
3   (⅛-inch-thick) slices peeled fresh ginger
2   teaspoons grated Key lime rind or lime rind
½   cup fresh Key lime juice or lime juice (about 10 Key limes)
    Gingersnaps

1. Combine first 3 ingredients in a large nonaluminum saucepan; bring to a boil. Add lime rind, and cook over low heat 10 minutes, stirring occasionally. Strain mixture through a sieve into a bowl. Discard solids. Cool sugar mixture completely. Stir in lime juice.
2. Pour juice mixture into freezer can of an ice-cream freezer, and freeze according to manufacturer's instructions. Spoon sorbet into a freezer-safe container; cover and freeze 2 hours or until firm. Serve with Gingersnaps. Yield: 12 servings (serving size: ½ cup sorbet and 2 cookies).

(Totals include Gingersnaps) CALORIES 294 (23% from fat); FAT 7.5g (sat 4.4g, mono 2.1g, poly 0.4g); PROTEIN 2.7g; CARB 55.2g; FIBER 0.6g; CHOL 36mg; IRON 1.1mg; SODIUM 311mg; CALC 12mg

GINGERSNAPS:
2   cups all-purpose flour
1   tablespoon ground ginger
2   teaspoons baking soda
½   teaspoon salt
1   cup granulated sugar, divided
7   tablespoons butter, softened
¼   cup packed dark brown sugar
2   tablespoons honey
1   teaspoon vanilla extract
1   large egg
    Cooking spray

1. Lightly spoon flour into dry measuring cups, and level with a knife. Combine flour, ginger, baking soda, and salt in a small bowl. Place ¾ cup granulated sugar, butter, and brown sugar in a large bowl, and beat with a mixer at medium speed until well blended. Add honey, vanilla, and egg; beat well. Add flour mixture, beating at low speed until well blended. Cover dough, and freeze 1 hour or until firm.
2. Preheat oven to 350°.
3. Lightly coat hands with cooking spray; shape dough into 24 (1-inch) balls. Roll balls in ¼ cup granulated sugar; place balls 2 inches apart on baking sheets. Bake at 350° for 12 minutes or until lightly browned. Cool cookies 2 minutes on pans. Remove cookies from pans, and cool on wire racks. Yield: 2 dozen (serving size: 1 cookie).

CALORIES 113 (30% from fat); FAT 3.8g (sat 2.2g, mono 1.1g, poly 0.2g); PROTEIN 1.3g; CARB 18.8g; FIBER 0.3g; CHOL 18mg; IRON 0.5mg; SODIUM 155mg; CALC 5mg

Citrus Slush

To create a jazzy presentation, drizzle a teaspoon of a flavored, colored syrup (such as Knott's Red Raspberry Syrup) over the top of the citrus slush just before serving.

2   cups frozen lemon sorbet
1   cup fresh orange juice (about 3 oranges)
½   cup fresh grapefruit juice
¼   cup honey
8   ice cubes

1. Place first 4 ingredients in a blender; process until smooth. With blender on, add ice cubes, 1 at a time, and process mixture until smooth. Yield: 4 servings (serving size: 1 cup).

CALORIES 244 (0% from fat); FAT 0.1g (sat 0g, mono 0g, poly 0.1g); PROTEIN 0.6g; CARB 60.9g; FIBER 0.2g; CHOL 0mg; IRON 0.2mg; SODIUM 17mg; CALC 9mg

Orange, Banana, and Pineapple Frappé

A frappé is similar to a breakfast smoothie, but it's made mostly with fruits instead of dairy products. It's sweet enough to serve as a light dessert.

2⅓ cups banana chunks (about 3 medium bananas)
¾   cup pineapple juice
½   cup orange sections (about 1 medium orange)
½   cup plain low-fat yogurt
1   tablespoon flaked sweetened coconut
2   tablespoons thawed orange juice concentrate
1   (8-ounce) can pineapple chunks in juice, undrained

1. Combine all ingredients in a blender; cover and process until smooth. Serve immediately. Yield: 4 servings (serving size: 1 cup).

CALORIES 177 (8% from fat); FAT 1.5g (sat 0.9g, mono 0.2g, poly 0.1g); PROTEIN 3.4g; CARB 40.8g; FIBER 3.6g; CHOL 2mg; IRON 0.7mg; SODIUM 27mg; CALC 90mg

Orange Tea Cake

This not-too-sweet cake is also great for breakfast or brunch.

CAKE:

    1   cup granulated sugar
    7   tablespoons butter, softened
    1   large egg
    1⅔ cups sifted cake flour
    1   teaspoon baking powder
    ½   teaspoon salt
    ½   cup 2% reduced-fat milk
    1   tablespoon grated orange rind
    ½   teaspoon almond extract
    2   large egg whites
        Cooking spray

GLAZE:

    1   cup powdered sugar
    1   tablespoon Cointreau
        (orange-flavored liqueur) or
        orange juice
    2   teaspoons orange juice

1. Preheat oven to 350°.

2. To prepare cake, place granulated sugar and butter in a large bowl, and beat with a mixer at high speed until well blended. Add 1 egg, beating well. Combine cake flour, baking powder, and salt in a bowl, stirring well with a whisk. Add flour mixture to sugar mixture alternately with milk, beginning and ending with flour mixture. Stir in rind and extract.

3. Beat egg whites with a mixer at high speed until stiff peaks form, using clean, dry beaters (do not overbeat). Fold egg whites into batter; pour batter into an 8 x 4-inch loaf pan coated with cooking spray. Bake at 350° for 50 minutes or until a wooden pick inserted in center comes out clean. Cool in pan 10 minutes on a wire rack, and remove from pan. Cool completely on wire rack.

4. To prepare glaze, combine powdered sugar, liqueur, and juice in a small bowl. Poke holes in top of cake using a skewer; drizzle glaze over cake. Yield: 10 servings (serving size: 1 [¾-inch] slice).

CALORIES 287 (29% from fat); FAT 9.2g (sat 5.4g, mono 2.7g, poly 0.6g); PROTEIN 3.3g; CARB 47.9g; FIBER 0g; CHOL 45mg; IRON 1.5mg; SODIUM 272mg; CALC 51mg

Lemon Meringue Pie

The glossy, billowy topping is prepared by beating cooked sugar syrup into slightly beaten egg whites, producing what is known as an Italian meringue. Because the sugar syrup is hot, it "cooks" the egg whites to the recommended safe temperature. You'll need a candy thermometer to check the temperature of the sugar syrup.

FILLING:

    ¾   cup sugar
    2   tablespoons cornstarch
    2   tablespoons all-purpose flour
    2   teaspoons grated lemon rind
        Dash of salt
    1   cup water
    2   tablespoons butter
    ⅓   cup fresh lemon juice
    2   large egg yolks
    1   (6-ounce) reduced-fat graham
        cracker crust

MERINGUE:

    3   large egg whites
    ¼   teaspoon cream of tartar
    ⅔   cup sugar
    ¼   cup water

1. To prepare filling, combine first 5 ingredients in a saucepan. Add 1 cup water, stirring constantly with a whisk. Bring to a simmer over medium heat, and cook 5 minutes, stirring frequently. Stir in butter, and remove from heat. Stir in lemon juice. Add egg yolks, 1 at a time, beating well with a mixer after each addition. Place pan over low heat; cook 3 minutes, stirring constantly. Spoon filling into crust. Cool to room temperature.

2. To prepare meringue, place egg whites and cream of tartar in a large bowl; beat with a mixer at high speed until foamy, using clean, dry beaters. Combine ⅔ cup sugar and ¼ cup water in a small saucepan; bring to boil. Cook mixture, without stirring, until candy thermometer registers 238°. Pour hot sugar syrup in a thin stream over egg white mixture, beating at high speed until stiff peaks form. Spread meringue evenly over filling, and seal meringue to edge of crust.

3. Preheat broiler.

4. Broil meringue 1 minute or until lightly browned; cool pie on a wire rack. Chill until set. Yield: 8 servings (serving size: 1 wedge).

CALORIES 292 (24% from fat); FAT 7.7g (sat 2.9g, mono 2.9g, poly 1.6g); PROTEIN 3.3g; CARB 54g; FIBER 0.1g; CHOL 62mg; IRON 0.6mg; SODIUM 172mg; CALC 10mg

Pineapple Fool

Fools are desserts that are traditionally made with gooseberries and custard. Nowadays, whipped cream and virtually any stewed fruit can be blended to create this cloudlike dessert.

    2   cups (1-inch) cubed fresh
        pineapple
    ½   cup water
    1   tablespoon chopped crystallized
        ginger
    ¼   cup packed brown sugar
    2   tablespoons fresh lemon juice
    2   cups frozen reduced-calorie
        whipped topping, thawed

1. Combine first 3 ingredients in a medium saucepan, and bring to a boil. Cover, reduce heat, and simmer 10 minutes or until liquid almost evaporates. Add sugar and lemon juice, and cook over medium-high heat 8 minutes or until slightly syrupy. Place pineapple mixture in a blender; process until smooth. Pour mixture into a bowl; cover and chill.

2. Reserve ¼ cup chilled pineapple mixture. Fold whipped topping into remaining chilled pineapple mixture. Spoon ½ cup pineapple mixture into each of 6 glasses, and chill. Top each serving with 2 teaspoons reserved pineapple mixture before serving. Yield: 6 servings.

CALORIES 114 (24% from fat); FAT 3.1g (sat 2.9g, mono 0g, poly 0.1g); PROTEIN 0.9g; CARB 22.1g; FIBER 0.6g; CHOL 0mg; IRON 0.7mg; SODIUM 21mg; CALC 30mg

Strawberry Fields Forever

When good things come in small packages.

It's best to pick strawberries early in the morning or later in the day, when the fruit is coolest. But if you can't pick your own, the grocery store or farmers' market are great alternatives. When choosing your berries, use a sniff test. If they smell fragrant, take them home.

Spring Strawberry Pie

CRUST:

1⅓ cups graham cracker crumbs
3 tablespoons butter, melted
2 tablespoons sugar
Cooking spray

FILLING:

2 cups sliced strawberries
2 tablespoons balsamic vinegar
¼ cup sugar
2 tablespoons water
2 teaspoons cornstarch
1 tablespoon fresh lemon juice
6 cups small strawberries

TOPPING:

3 tablespoons graham cracker crumbs
1 tablespoon chopped hazelnuts or almonds
1½ teaspoons sugar
1½ teaspoons butter, melted
½ cup frozen reduced-calorie whipped topping, thawed

1. Preheat oven to 350°.
2. Combine first 3 ingredients in a bowl, tossing with a fork until moist. Press into bottom and up sides of a 9-inch pie plate coated with cooking spray. Bake at 350° for 15 minutes; cool on a wire rack.
3. Combine strawberry slices and vinegar in a medium nonstick skillet. Place berry mixture over medium-high heat; cook 3 minutes, stirring occasionally. Stir in ¼ cup sugar. Combine water and cornstarch in a small bowl. Add to pan;

bring to a boil. Cook 1 minute, stirring constantly. Remove from heat; stir in juice. Cool completely. Arrange whole strawberries, stem sides down, in crust. Pour strawberry mixture over whole strawberries. Cover loosely; chill 4 hours.
4. To prepare topping, combine 3 tablespoons cracker crumbs, nuts, 1½ teaspoons sugar, and 1½ teaspoons melted butter in a small bowl. Place crumb mixture in a small skillet over medium heat. Cook 2 minutes or until golden brown; cool. Sprinkle crumb mixture over pie. Top each serving with whipped topping. Yield: 8 servings (serving size: 1 wedge and 1 tablespoon whipped topping).

CALORIES 229 (35% from fat); FAT 8.8g (sat 4.1g, mono 2.8g, poly 1.4g); PROTEIN 2.3g; CARB 37g; FIBER 3.5g; CHOL 14mg; IRON 1.4mg; SODIUM 176mg; CALC 34mg

Strawberry Parfaits
(pictured on page 130)

4 cups sliced strawberries, divided
¼ cup granulated sugar
1 cup fat-free ricotta cheese
½ cup (4 ounces) ⅓-less-fat cream cheese, softened
¼ cup powdered sugar
1 tablespoon water
1 teaspoon vanilla extract
1 cup amaretti cookie crumbs (about 8 cookies)
½ cup frozen reduced-calorie whipped topping, thawed
2 tablespoons slivered almonds, toasted

1. Place 2 cups strawberry slices and granulated sugar in a blender or food processor, and process until smooth. Set strawberry puree aside.
2. Combine ricotta and next 4 ingredients in a medium bowl; stir well with a whisk. Spoon 2 tablespoons cookie crumbs into each of 4 parfait glasses. Top each portion with 2 tablespoons strawberry puree, ¼ cup strawberry slices, and 3 tablespoons ricotta mixture; repeat layers. Drizzle remaining strawberry puree over each serving. Chill 2 hours. Top each parfait with 2 tablespoons whipped topping and 1½ teaspoons almonds. Yield: 4 servings.

CALORIES 347 (30% from fat); FAT 11.6g (sat 5.6g, mono 3.8g, poly 1.1g); PROTEIN 14g; CARB 50.8g; FIBER 3.8g; CHOL 28mg; IRON 0.8mg; SODIUM 160mg; CALC 157mg

Spinach-and-Strawberry Salad

2 cups whole strawberries
⅓ cup champagne vinegar or white wine vinegar
2 tablespoons orange juice
2 teaspoons extra-virgin olive oil
1½ teaspoons chopped fresh or ½ teaspoon dried thyme
1 teaspoon sugar
1 teaspoon Dijon mustard
¼ teaspoon salt
⅛ teaspoon freshly ground black pepper
6 cups torn spinach
¾ cup diced fennel bulb
2 cups quartered strawberries
¼ cup (1 ounce) crumbled feta cheese

1. Place first 9 ingredients in a blender or food processor; process until smooth. Place 2 tablespoons dressing, spinach, and fennel in a large bowl; toss gently to coat. Arrange 1¼ cups spinach mixture on each of 4 plates, and top each serving with ½ cup quartered strawberries and 1 tablespoon feta cheese. Drizzle each serving with 1½ teaspoons dressing. Yield: 4 servings.

CALORIES 120 (36% from fat); FAT 4.8g (sat 1.5g, mono 2.1g, poly 0.6g); PROTEIN 4.9g; CARB 16.8g; FIBER 7g; CHOL 6mg; IRON 3.4mg; SODIUM 334mg; CALC 159mg

Chicken and Strawberries over Mixed Greens

2 cups chopped roasted skinless, boneless chicken breast (about 2 breast halves)
2 cups quartered small strawberries (about 1 pint)
⅓ cup finely chopped celery
⅓ cup finely chopped red onion
2 tablespoons golden raisins
1 tablespoon sesame seeds, toasted
1 tablespoon chopped fresh or 1 teaspoon dried tarragon
1 tablespoon extra-virgin olive oil
1 tablespoon balsamic vinegar
½ teaspoon paprika
⅛ teaspoon salt
⅛ teaspoon black pepper
4 cups gourmet salad greens

1. Combine first 5 ingredients in a large bowl. Combine sesame seeds and next 6 ingredients in a small bowl, stirring well with a whisk. Pour over chicken mixture; toss well to coat. Cover and chill 1 hour. Serve over salad greens. Yield: 4 servings (serving size: 1¼ cups chicken mixture and 1 cup greens).

CALORIES 164 (35% from fat); FAT 6.3g (sat 1.2g, mono 3.4g, poly 1.3g); PROTEIN 15.3g; CARB 13.3g; FIBER 3.5g; CHOL 35mg; IRON 1.7mg; SODIUM 376mg; CALC 78mg

Strawberry Salsa

Serve with grilled fish, pork, or chicken.

1½ cups chopped strawberries
½ cup chopped peeled kiwifruit
½ cup chopped cucumber
½ cup chopped red onion
2 tablespoons chopped seeded jalapeño pepper
1 tablespoon chopped fresh cilantro or mint
1 teaspoon grated lime rind
2 tablespoons fresh lime juice
1 tablespoon orange juice
1 tablespoon honey
¼ teaspoon salt

1. Combine all ingredients in a medium bowl. Cover and chill. Serve salsa with a slotted spoon. Yield: 3 cups (serving size: ½ cup).

NOTE: Store salsa in refrigerator for up to 2 days.

CALORIES 48 (6% from fat); FAT 0.3g (sat 0g, mono 0g, poly 0.2g); PROTEIN 0.8g; CARB 11.9g; FIBER 2.1g; CHOL 0mg; IRON 0.4mg; SODIUM 100mg; CALC 18mg

Lemon Sponge Cake with Strawberry Filling

CAKE:
1 cup all-purpose flour
1¼ teaspoons baking powder
⅛ teaspoon salt
2 large eggs
¾ cup sugar
¼ cup water
1½ teaspoons grated lemon rind
1 tablespoon fresh lemon juice
1 teaspoon vanilla extract
Cooking spray

SAUCE:
1 cup chopped strawberries
⅓ cup water
¼ cup sugar
1½ teaspoons fresh lemon juice

REMAINING INGREDIENTS:
2 cups sliced strawberries
1 cup frozen reduced-calorie whipped topping, thawed

1. Preheat oven to 350°.
2. To prepare cake, lightly spoon flour into a dry measuring cup; level with a knife. Combine flour, baking powder, and salt in a medium bowl, stirring well with a whisk. Beat eggs in a large bowl with a mixer at high speed 2 minutes. Gradually add ¾ cup sugar, beating until thick and pale (about 4 minutes). Add ¼ cup water, rind, 1 tablespoon juice, and vanilla, beating at low speed until blended. Add flour mixture, beating just until blended. Pour batter into a 9-inch round cake pan coated with cooking spray. Bake at 350° for 25 minutes or until a wooden pick inserted in center comes out clean. Cool in pan 10 minutes on a wire rack; remove from pan. Cool completely on wire rack.

3. To prepare sauce, combine chopped strawberries, ⅓ cup water, ¼ cup sugar, and 1½ teaspoons lemon juice in a medium nonaluminum saucepan. Bring to a boil; cook until reduced to ¾ cup (about 15 minutes). Cool.
4. Split cake in half horizontally, using a serrated knife; place bottom cake layer, cut side up, on a plate. Spread with 6 tablespoons sauce. Top with 1 cup sliced strawberries and ½ cup whipped topping. Top with remaining cake layer. Repeat layers with remaining sauce, sliced strawberries, and whipped topping. Cut into 8 slices. Yield: 8 servings (serving size: 1 slice).

CALORIES 213 (13% from fat); FAT 3g (sat 1.5g, mono 0.6g, poly 0.5g); PROTEIN 3.9g; CARB 43.6g; FIBER 1.8g; CHOL 55mg; IRON 1.2mg; SODIUM 135mg; CALC 66mg

Strawberry Soup

3½ cups halved strawberries (about 1 pound)
1¼ cups pineapple juice
2 tablespoons sugar
1 tablespoon fresh lemon juice
⅛ teaspoon ground cinnamon
⅛ teaspoon ground nutmeg
Dash of ground cardamom (optional)
1⅓ cups plain low-fat yogurt
2 teaspoons grated lemon rind

1. Place first 7 ingredients in a blender or food processor; process until smooth. Add yogurt; process just until blended. Chill 3 hours. Sprinkle each serving with rind. Yield: 5 servings (serving size: 1 cup).

CALORIES 124 (10% from fat); FAT 1.4g (sat 0.7g, mono 0.3g, poly 0.2g); PROTEIN 4.2g; CARB 25.1g; FIBER 2.2g; CHOL 4mg; IRON 0.6mg; SODIUM 47mg; CALC 145mg

---

Freezing Berries

To freeze strawberries, place them in a single layer on a cookie sheet, then put them in the freezer for a couple of hours. Once the berries are frozen, transfer them to a heavy-duty zip-top plastic bag or a freezer-safe container. This keeps the strawberries separated.

june

Start with the Best

Choose the right ingredients, and you don't have to do much to make great food.

Some say the secret to preparing great food is to do as little as possible. The idea is this: Start with the very best ingredients you can find, and let simple preparations provide the backdrop for the food to shine.

Quality specialty ingredients—extra-virgin olive oil, Parmigiano-Reggiano cheese, fresh herbs, and aged vinegars like balsamic and sherry—deliver big, bold flavors that elevate a dish from simply good to truly extraordinary. Used sparingly as accents or finishing touches, they bring out the flavors of the whole dish. These premium ingredients don't overwhelm food, yet set it apart.

Pasta with Prosciutto and Peas

(pictured on page 166)

Cooking spray
- 3 ounces very thin slices prosciutto, chopped
- 3 tablespoons extra-virgin olive oil
- 2 garlic cloves, thinly sliced
- 6 cups hot cooked fusilli (about 12 ounces uncooked short twisted spaghetti)
- 1 cup (4 ounces) shaved Parmigiano-Reggiano cheese
- ⅓ cup chopped fresh parsley
- 1 tablespoon fresh lemon juice
- ½ teaspoon kosher salt
- ½ teaspoon freshly ground black pepper
- 1 (10-ounce) package frozen peas, cooked and drained

1. Heat a large nonstick skillet coated with cooking spray over medium heat. Add prosciutto; cook 3 minutes or until lightly browned. Remove from pan. Add oil and garlic to pan; cook 1 minute or until garlic begins to brown. Combine prosciutto, oil mixture, pasta, and remaining ingredients in a large bowl; toss to coat. Yield: 8 servings (serving size: 1 cup).

CALORIES 312 (30% from fat); FAT 10.6g (sat 3.5g, mono 5.4g, poly 1.1g); PROTEIN 14.9g; CARB 37.8g; FIBER 1.2g; CHOL 16mg; IRON 2.7mg; SODIUM 554mg; CALC 189mg

Adobo Flank Steak with Summer Corn-and-Tomato Relish

The sherry vinegar gives the relish lots of flavor, so choose a good one.

STEAK:
- 1 teaspoon black peppercorns
- 1 teaspoon cumin seeds
- 2 whole cloves
- 1 (7-ounce) can chipotle chiles in adobo sauce, undrained
- 2 tablespoons sherry vinegar
- 1 tablespoon fresh thyme leaves
- 2 teaspoons brown sugar
- ¾ teaspoon kosher salt
- 1 garlic clove, peeled
- 1 (1¼-pound) flank steak, trimmed
Cooking spray

RELISH:
- 2 cups fresh corn kernels (about 4 ears)
- 1 cup chopped seeded tomato
- ¼ cup chopped bottled roasted red bell peppers
- 2 tablespoons sherry vinegar
- 1 tablespoon extra-virgin olive oil
- ¾ teaspoon kosher salt
Fresh thyme leaves (optional)

1. To prepare steak, cook first 3 ingredients in a small nonstick skillet over medium heat 45 seconds or until toasted. Place peppercorn mixture in a spice or coffee grinder; process until finely ground.

2. Remove 1 chile from can; reserve remaining chiles and sauce for another use. Place peppercorn mixture, chile, 2 tablespoons vinegar, and next 4 ingredients in a blender; process until smooth, scraping sides occasionally. Combine vinegar mixture and steak in a large zip-top plastic bag; seal and marinate in refrigerator 24 hours. Remove steak from bag; discard marinade.

3. Prepare grill or broiler.

4. Place steak on grill rack or broiler pan coated with cooking spray; cook 6 minutes on each side or until desired degree of doneness. Cut steak diagonally across grain into thin slices.

5. To prepare relish, heat a large nonstick skillet coated with cooking spray over medium-high heat. Add corn; sauté 5 minutes or until lightly browned. Remove from heat; stir in tomato and next 4 ingredients. Garnish with thyme, if desired. Yield: 5 servings (serving size: 3 ounces steak and ½ cup relish).

CALORIES 303 (44% from fat); FAT 14.9g (sat 5.2g, mono 6.7g, poly 1.3g); PROTEIN 25.2g; CARB 16.5g; FIBER 2.7g; CHOL 57mg; IRON 3.2mg; SODIUM 634mg; CALC 20mg

Chicken with Two-Olive Topping

We've used two varieties of olives to make a chunky, salsa-textured topping. Any combination of good olives will work well.

- 1 red bell pepper
- 1 orange bell pepper
- 1 yellow bell pepper
- 6 (4-ounce) skinless, boneless chicken breast halves
- ¾ teaspoon kosher salt
- ¼ teaspoon freshly ground black pepper
- 2 teaspoons olive oil, divided
- 2 teaspoons chopped fresh rosemary
- 2 garlic cloves, minced
- 3 tablespoons chopped pitted kalamata olives
- 3 tablespoons chopped pitted green olives
- 2 teaspoons fresh lemon juice

1. Preheat broiler.

2. Cut bell peppers in half lengthwise; discard seeds and membranes. Place pepper halves, skin sides up, on a foil-lined baking sheet; flatten with hand. Broil 10 minutes or until blackened. Place in a zip-top plastic bag; seal. Let stand 10 minutes. Peel and chop.

3. Sprinkle chicken with salt and black pepper. Heat 1 teaspoon oil in a large nonstick skillet over medium-high heat. Add chicken; cook 5 minutes on each side or until done. Remove from pan; keep warm.

4. Add 1 teaspoon oil, rosemary, and garlic to pan; sauté 30 seconds or until garlic begins to brown. Stir in bell peppers, olives, and lemon juice; cook 1 minute or until thoroughly heated, stirring constantly. Yield: 6 servings (serving size: 1 chicken breast half and ⅓ cup sauce).

CALORIES 159 (22% from fat); FAT 3.9g (sat 0.8g, mono 2g, poly 0.6g); PROTEIN 26.7g; CARB 3.2g; FIBER 1g; CHOL 66mg; IRON 1.7mg; SODIUM 390mg; CALC 30mg

Oven-Roasted Sea Bass with Couscous and Warm Tomato Vinaigrette

(pictured on page 168)

For extra moistness, we used more liquid in our couscous than the package calls for.

```
 1   green onion
 2   tablespoons olive oil
 2   garlic cloves, minced
 1   cup chopped tomato
 3   tablespoons fresh lemon juice,
     divided
 1   tablespoon sherry vinegar
 1   teaspoon kosher salt, divided
1¼   cups fat-free, less-sodium chicken
     broth
 ⅔   cup uncooked couscous
 ¼   cup chopped fresh chives
 4   (6-ounce) sea bass or halibut fillets
     (about 1½ inches thick)
 ¼   teaspoon freshly ground black
     pepper
Cooking spray
 8   (¼-inch-thick) slices lemon,
     halved (about 1 lemon)
Whole chives (optional)
```

1. Preheat oven to 350°.

2. Cut green onion into 3-inch pieces, and cut pieces into julienne strips.

3. Heat oil in a large nonstick skillet over medium-high heat. Add garlic; sauté 30 seconds or until garlic begins to brown. Add tomato and onions; reduce heat to medium, and cook 1 minute. Remove from heat; stir in 2 tablespoons lemon juice, vinegar, and ½ teaspoon salt. Keep warm.

4. Combine 1 tablespoon lemon juice, ¼ teaspoon salt, and broth in a medium saucepan; bring to a boil. Gradually stir in couscous and chopped chives. Remove from heat; cover and let stand 5 minutes. Fluff with a fork. Cover and keep warm.

5. Sprinkle fillets with ¼ teaspoon salt and pepper. Place fillets in an 11 x 7-inch baking dish coated with cooking spray. Place 4 halved lemon slices on each fillet. Bake at 350° for 20 minutes or until fish flakes easily when tested with a fork. Serve over couscous, and top with vinaigrette. Garnish with whole chives, if desired. Yield: 4 servings (serving size: 1 fillet, ½ cup couscous, and ¼ cup vinaigrette).

CALORIES 346 (29% from fat); FAT 11.2g (sat 1.9g, mono 5.8g, poly 2.2g); PROTEIN 36.5g; CARB 25.2g; FIBER 1.9g; CHOL 70mg; IRON 1.6mg; SODIUM 777mg; CALC 49mg

Roasted-Corn-and-Tomato Tart

Fresh basil and flavorful cheeses make this simple tart stand out. If you choose frozen corn in place of fresh, use cooking spray on the skillet to keep it from sticking. Sprinkling a small amount of cheese on the crust helps hold the vegetables in place.

CRUST:
```
 1   cup all-purpose flour
 2   tablespoons yellow cornmeal
 ¾   teaspoon baking powder
 ¼   teaspoon kosher salt
 5   tablespoons water
1½   tablespoons olive oil
Cooking spray
```

FILLING:
```
1½   cups fresh corn kernels (about 3 ears)
 ½   cup (2 ounces) shredded smoked
     mozzarella cheese, divided
 3   tablespoons chopped fresh basil
 ¼   teaspoon kosher salt
 ¼   teaspoon freshly ground black pepper
 1   large tomato, cut into ¼-inch-thick
     slices
 1   tablespoon grated Parmigiano-
     Reggiano cheese
```

1. Preheat oven to 375°.

2. To prepare crust, lightly spoon flour into a dry measuring cup; level with a knife. Combine flour, cornmeal, baking powder, and ¼ teaspoon salt in a large bowl; make a well in center of mixture. Add water and oil; stir until well blended. Turn dough out onto a lightly floured surface; knead 2 minutes.

3. Slightly overlap 2 lengths of plastic wrap on a slightly dampened surface. Gently press dough into a 4-inch circle on plastic wrap. Cover with 2 additional lengths of overlapping plastic wrap. Chill 15 minutes. Roll dough, still covered, into an 11-inch circle. Freeze 5 minutes or until plastic can be easily removed. Remove top sheets of plastic wrap; let stand 1 minute or until pliable. Fit dough, plastic-wrap side up, into a 10-inch round removable-bottom tart pan coated with cooking spray. Remove remaining sheets of plastic wrap. Press dough against bottom and sides of pan. Pierce dough with a fork several times.

4. Bake crust at 375° for 15 minutes or until lightly browned; cool on a wire rack.

5. To prepare filling, heat a large nonstick skillet coated with cooking spray over medium-high heat. Add corn; sauté 5 minutes or until lightly browned.

6. Sprinkle 1 tablespoon mozzarella on crust. Top with corn, basil, ¼ teaspoon salt, and pepper. Sprinkle with ¼ cup mozzarella. Arrange tomato slices in a circular pattern over cheese. Sprinkle with 3 tablespoons mozzarella and Parmigiano-Reggiano. Bake at 375° for 15 minutes or until lightly browned. Yield: 4 servings (serving size: 1 wedge).

CALORIES 279 (30% from fat); FAT 9.4g (sat 2.6g, mono 4.9g, poly 1.3g); PROTEIN 9.8g; CARB 40.4g; FIBER 3.3g; CHOL 9mg; IRON 2.2mg; SODIUM 439mg; CALC 175mg

Quality Specialty Ingredients

Sherry Vinegar

Made in the Andalusian region of Spain, Vinagre de Jerez is produced using the *solera* process, a five-tiered system of oak casks used to make wine. Grape juice is aged first in one cask and then transferred down the line until it has fermented in five casks, where it mixes with older batches of vinegar. Sherry vinegar has a sour-sweet flavor and deep notes of oak. It's a great everyday vinegar for salad dressings and marinades, or for drizzling over cooked vegetables.

Our Picks: Gran Capirete, Columela.

Buying Tips: Read the label to see how long the vinegar has aged; some are aged six years, others for as long as 30 years. The longer the aging, the more complex the flavor.

Storage Tips: Keep tightly capped at room temperature.

Balsamic Vinegar

Balsamic vinegars range in price from a few dollars to a few hundred dollars per bottle. The pricier stuff is the real thing: Trebbiano grape juice aged 12 years in wooden casks according to a time-honored Italian process. Tasted and graded by a consortium of experts, this *tradizionale* balsamic is rich, sweet, and intense. A few drops on strawberries or meat are enough to dramatically change the flavors of a finished dish.

For cooking, the best balsamic vinegars are labeled *condimento balsamico* and are more reasonably priced. These have a slightly more acidic, but no less complex, nature. Aged for shorter periods and by slightly different methods, these vinegars, though not rated by the consortium, are still quite tasty.

Our Picks: Fini Condimento, a balsamic aged in casks of juniper, chestnut, and mulberry; Gaeta Condimento, aged four years in antique barrels; Cavalli Condimento of Reggio Emilia.

Buying Tips: Look for the words *condimento* or *tradizionale* on the label. Though most of the balsamic vinegars you'll find at the supermarket are just a mixture of grape juice, vinegar, and caramel coloring, Alessi's Balsamic Vinegar Aged 20 Years is an exception.

Storage Tips: Keep tightly capped at room temperature.

Real Parmesan

Real Parmesan is a world apart in flavor from the canned stuff—particularly when it's the top-of-the-line Parmigiano-Reggiano, a hard, granular cheese made by hand in the Emilia-Romagna region of Italy. This artisanal cheese is matchless. Aged for at least two years, it's mellow and sweet, with a hint of nuttiness. Sprinkle it on casseroles, gratins, or pizzas for a nicely browned crust. Strew thin slices over a fresh salad. It's costly but a little goes a long way.

Buying Tips: Look for the name "Parmigiano-Reggiano" spelled out repeatedly in red around the rind. Without this rind, it isn't Parmigiano-Reggiano.

Storage Tips: Grate only the cheese you need. The rest, lightly wrapped in plastic, should last for a few months in the refrigerator—but change the plastic wrap frequently.

Fresh Herbs

There really isn't any comparison between dried and fresh herbs. Once you start using fresh, you won't go back.

Buying Tips: Look for herbs with vibrant colors and fragrant aromas.

Storage Tips: Don't wash herbs until you're ready to use them. Instead, wrap the stems in a damp paper towel and store loosely in a zip-top plastic bag. (Or seal the towel-wrapped herbs in a roomy plastic container.) Keep delicate herbs like basil, dill, and cilantro refrigerated, and use as soon as possible. Hardier herbs like rosemary and sage will stay fresh for a week or two.

Prosciutto

This specialty Italian ham is air-cured with salt and seasonings. Pressed into a dense-textured meat, it's typically sliced thin and eaten raw or lightly cooked. In Italy, prosciutto (pro-SHOO-toe) is labeled with the name of the city or region in which it's produced. Prosciutto di Parma is considered the ultimate indulgence, although some Canadian and American companies now make good prosciutto.

Buying Tips: Prosciutto di Parma is typically found in Italian delis or large supermarkets. Buy only what you need and ask for paper-thin slices.

Storage Tips: Keep tightly wrapped in the refrigerator, and use within three to five days.

Premium Oils

No two olive oils are alike. Tastes run the gamut from buttery to fruity to peppery, depending on what type of olive was used and where it was grown. While color isn't always a guide to quality or flavor, the greener oils, made from olives that aren't fully ripe, are generally the most prized. Extra-virgin oils come from the first cold pressing of the olive. Since neither heat nor chemicals are used, the result is a rich, deep olive flavor. Use extra-virgin olive oils to make a vinaigrette, drizzle over bread, or add a finishing touch to just about any dish.

Our Picks: DaVero (California), Capoleuca Labbate (Italy), Nuñez de Prado (Spain), Morea (Greece), Hain (Italy), and DaVinci (Italy). You can find Hain and DaVinci brands in most supermarkets.

Buying Tips: Imported extra-virgin olive oils once were the most highly prized, but many California olive oils—such as DaVero—are winning international awards.

Storage Tips: Store in a cool cabinet away from the stove, and use within six months.

Chicken-and-Brie Sandwich with Roasted Cherry Tomatoes

(pictured on page 165)

A good balsamic vinegar makes all the difference in the roasted tomatoes, whose heat will melt the soft Brie. There's no need to cut the edible rind off the Brie.

  1 teaspoon olive oil
  2 cups halved cherry tomatoes
    (about 1 pound)
  2 tablespoons balsamic vinegar
  1 tablespoon chopped fresh thyme
  ¼ teaspoon kosher salt
  ⅛ teaspoon black pepper
  ¼ cup low-fat mayonnaise
  1 tablespoon whole-grain Dijon
    mustard
  1 garlic clove, minced
  1 (16-ounce) loaf French bread, cut
    in half horizontally
  3 ounces Brie cheese, sliced
  3 cups shredded cooked chicken
    breast (about 1 pound)
  2 teaspoons extra-virgin olive oil
  1 teaspoon balsamic vinegar
  ⅛ teaspoon kosher salt
  2 cups fresh spinach

1. Preheat oven to 300°.
2. Heat 1 teaspoon oil in a large nonstick skillet over medium-high heat. Add tomatoes; cook 4 minutes, stirring once. Remove from heat; stir in 2 tablespoons vinegar. Sprinkle tomatoes with thyme, ¼ teaspoon salt, and pepper. Wrap handle of pan with foil; bake at 300° for 15 minutes. Keep warm.
3. Combine mayonnaise, mustard, and garlic in a small bowl. Spread mayonnaise mixture evenly over top half of bread loaf. Spoon tomatoes evenly over bottom half of loaf. Arrange Brie over tomatoes; top with chicken. Combine 2 teaspoons oil, 1 teaspoon vinegar, and ⅛ teaspoon salt in a medium bowl, stirring with a whisk. Add spinach, tossing gently to coat. Top chicken with spinach mixture; replace top half of bread. Cut loaf into 6 pieces. Yield: 6 servings.

CALORIES 440 (25% from fat); FAT 12.3g (sat 4.2g, mono 4.9g, poly 1.9g); PROTEIN 34.3g; CARB 46.7g; FIBER 3.9g; CHOL 78mg; IRON 3.7mg; SODIUM 826mg; CALC 119mg

Spinach-and-Prosciutto Strata

Day-old or stale bread absorbs liquid best.

  3 cups fat-free milk, divided
  1 cup sliced green onions
  1 (16-ounce) loaf peasant bread, cut
    into 2-inch cubes
  1 (10-ounce) package frozen
    chopped spinach, thawed, drained,
    and squeezed dry
  2 teaspoons olive oil
  3 cups quartered cremini mushrooms
    (about 6 ounces)
  1 cup finely chopped red bell pepper
  ¾ cup chopped prosciutto (about 3
    ounces)
  2 garlic cloves, minced
  3 tablespoons chopped fresh basil,
    divided
  ¼ teaspoon kosher salt, divided
  ¼ teaspoon black pepper, divided
  4 large eggs
  2 large egg whites
    Cooking spray
  ¾ cup (3 ounces) shredded Asiago
    cheese

1. Combine 2 cups milk and onions in a bowl. Add bread; toss gently to coat. Cover and chill 30 minutes. Stir in spinach.
2. Preheat oven to 375°.
3. Heat oil in a large nonstick skillet over medium-high heat. Add mushrooms; sauté 5 minutes. Add bell pepper; sauté 3 minutes. Add prosciutto and garlic; sauté 1 minute. Remove from heat; stir in 1 tablespoon basil, ⅛ teaspoon salt, and ⅛ teaspoon black pepper.
4. Place 1 cup milk, 2 tablespoons basil, ⅛ teaspoon salt, ⅛ teaspoon black pepper, eggs, and egg whites in a large bowl; stir well with a whisk.
5. Place half of bread mixture in an 11 x 7-inch dish coated with cooking spray. Spoon mushroom mixture over bread mixture; sprinkle with half of cheese. Top with remaining bread mixture. Pour egg mixture over bread mixture; sprinkle with remaining cheese. Bake at 375° for 1 hour or until set. Yield: 8 servings.

CALORIES 328 (27% from fat); FAT 10g (sat 3.7g, mono 3.9g, poly 1.4g); PROTEIN 20g; CARB 39.5g; FIBER 3.7g; CHOL 130mg; IRON 3.5mg; SODIUM 816mg; CALC 337mg

Mediterranean Shrimp-and-Pasta Salad

VINAIGRETTE:
  ¼ cup extra-virgin olive oil
  ¼ cup fresh lemon juice
  2 tablespoons sherry vinegar
  1 teaspoon Dijon mustard
  ¾ teaspoon kosher salt
  ½ teaspoon freshly ground black
    pepper

SALAD:
  6 cups water
  2 bay leaves
  1 pound medium shrimp
  ¼ teaspoon kosher salt
  ¼ teaspoon freshly ground black
    pepper
  4 cups uncooked cavatappi or other
    short twisted pasta
  1 cup trimmed arugula
  1 zucchini, halved lengthwise and
    thinly sliced (about 1 cup)
  1 cup yellow bell pepper strips
  ¾ cup (3 ounces) crumbled feta cheese
  ½ cup vertically sliced red onion
  3 tablespoons chopped fresh parsley
  3 tablespoons chopped fresh basil
  1 tablespoon chopped fresh oregano

1. To prepare vinaigrette, combine first 6 ingredients in a small bowl; stir with a whisk. Set aside.
2. To prepare salad, combine water and bay leaves in a large saucepan; bring to a boil. Add shrimp; cook 3 minutes or until done. Drain and rinse with cold water. Discard bay leaves. Peel shrimp; sprinkle with ¼ teaspoon salt and ¼ teaspoon black pepper. Cover and chill.
3. Cook pasta according to package directions, omitting salt and fat; drain and rinse with cold water.
4. Combine shrimp, pasta, arugula, and remaining 7 ingredients in a large bowl. Drizzle vinaigrette over salad, and toss gently to coat. Yield: 5 servings (serving size: 2 cups).

CALORIES 577 (28% from fat); FAT 17.8g (sat 5g, mono 4.4g, poly 6.6g); PROTEIN 32.5g; CARB 69.4g; FIBER 3g; CHOL 153mg; IRON 6.4mg; SODIUM 688mg; CALC 178mg

Cilantro Pesto Pizza Topped with Portobellos and Red Onion

Extra-virgin olive oil, Parmigiano-Reggiano, and fresh cilantro make the pesto that tops this simple-to-make pizza. To save time, use a refrigerated pizza crust.

CRUST:

    1   package dry yeast (about 2¼ teaspoons)
    1   teaspoon sugar
    ½   cup warm water (100° to 110°)
    1½ cups all-purpose flour, divided
    ¼   teaspoon kosher salt
        Cooking spray
    2   teaspoons yellow cornmeal

PESTO:

    2   cups fresh cilantro leaves
    1   tablespoon coarsely chopped walnuts
    1   tablespoon grated Parmigiano-Reggiano cheese
    1½ teaspoons extra-virgin olive oil
    1½ teaspoons water
    ½   teaspoon kosher salt

PIZZA:

    4½ cups coarsely chopped portobello mushrooms (about 10 ounces)
    1   tablespoon balsamic vinegar
    ¼   teaspoon kosher salt
    ¼   teaspoon freshly ground black pepper
    ¾   cup thinly sliced red onion
    ¾   cup (3 ounces) shredded fontina cheese

1. To prepare crust, dissolve yeast and sugar in warm water in a large bowl, and let stand 5 minutes. Lightly spoon flour into dry measuring cups, and level with a knife. Add 1¼ cups flour and ¼ teaspoon salt to yeast mixture; stir until a soft dough forms. Turn dough out onto a floured surface. Knead until smooth and elastic (about 10 minutes); add enough of remaining flour, 1 tablespoon at a time, to prevent dough from sticking to hands (dough will feel tacky).

2. Place dough in a large bowl coated with cooking spray, turning to coat top. Cover and let rise in a warm place (85°), free from drafts, 30 minutes or until doubled in size. (Press two fingers into dough. If indentation remains, dough has risen enough.)

3. Punch dough down; cover and let rest 5 minutes. Roll dough into a 12-inch circle on a floured surface. Place dough on a 12-inch pizza pan or baking sheet sprinkled with cornmeal. Crimp edges of dough with fingers to form a rim. Cover and let rise 10 minutes or until puffy.

4. Preheat oven to 450°.

5. To prepare pesto, place cilantro and next 5 ingredients in a food processor, and process until smooth, scraping sides of bowl occasionally.

6. To prepare pizza, heat a large non-stick skillet coated with cooking spray over medium-high heat. Add mushrooms; cook 5 minutes or until moisture evaporates, stirring constantly. Add vinegar, and cook until liquid evaporates. Sprinkle with ¼ teaspoon salt and ¼ teaspoon pepper. Spoon mushroom mixture onto pizza crust. Drop pesto by teaspoonfuls onto pizza crust. Top with onion, and sprinkle with fontina. Bake at 450° for 15 minutes or until crust is lightly browned. Let stand 5 minutes. Yield: 6 servings (serving size: 1 wedge).

CALORIES 233 (30% from fat); FAT 7.7g (sat 3.3g, mono 2.5g, poly 1.3g); PROTEIN 10.1g; CARB 31.8g; FIBER 3.3g; CHOL 17mg; IRON 3.8mg; SODIUM 354mg; CALC 133mg

back to the best

Blackberry-Lemon Pudding Cake

Try our transitional treat, Blackberry-Lemon Pudding Cake, which first appeared in our January-February 1998 issue.

It's not quite a pudding and not quite a cake, but something in between. As the dessert bakes, a light, spongy cake forms over a delicate bottom layer of custard. Lemon juice and lemon rind provide a double dose of tartness—but the berries keep sweetness in the balance. (Use blueberries or raspberries, if you prefer.)

Blackberry-Lemon Pudding Cake

(pictured on page 165)

    ¼   cup all-purpose flour
    ⅔   cup granulated sugar
    ⅛   teaspoon salt
    ⅛   teaspoon ground nutmeg
    1   cup low-fat buttermilk
    1   teaspoon grated lemon rind
    ¼   cup fresh lemon juice
    2   tablespoons butter, melted
    2   large egg yolks
    3   large egg whites
    ¼   cup granulated sugar
    1½ cups blackberries
        Cooking spray
    ¾   teaspoon powdered sugar

1. Preheat oven to 350°.

2. Lightly spoon flour into a dry measuring cup, and level with a knife. Combine flour, ⅔ cup granulated sugar, salt, and nutmeg in a large bowl; add buttermilk, lemon rind, and next 3 ingredients, stirring with a whisk until mixture is smooth.

3. Beat egg whites with a mixer at high speed until foamy. Add ¼ cup granulated sugar, 1 tablespoon at a time, beating until stiff peaks form. Gently stir one-fourth of egg white mixture into buttermilk mixture; gently fold in remaining egg white mixture. Fold in blackberries.

4. Pour batter into an 8-inch square baking pan coated with cooking spray. Place in a larger baking pan; add hot water to larger pan to depth of 1 inch. Bake at 350° for 35 minutes or until cake springs back when touched lightly in center. Sprinkle cake with powdered sugar. Serve warm. Yield: 5 servings (serving size: 1 cup).

CALORIES 285 (23% from fat); FAT 7.2g (sat 1.7g, mono 2.8g, poly 1.8g); PROTEIN 6g; CARB 51.2g; FIBER 3.3g; CHOL 89mg; IRON 0.8mg; SODIUM 198mg; CALC 86mg

Blackberry-Lemon Pudding
Cake, page 164

Chicken-and-Brie Sandwich with
Roasted Cherry Tomatoes, page 163

Pasta with Prosciutto and Peas, page 160

**Drunken Stir-Fried Beef with
Green Beans, page 177**

Sweet Hoisin Sauce, page 171

Orange-Chipotle Sauce, page 171

Chunky Mango-Ginger Sauce, page 173

Oven-Roasted Sea Bass with Couscous and Warm Tomato Vinaigrette, page 161

Spicy Pork-and-Bell Pepper Tacos, page 169

Pork Pleasers

Pork tenderloin makes these suppers snappy.

Menu 1
serves 6

Spicy Pork-and-Bell Pepper Tacos

Black bean salad*

*Combine 1 (15-ounce) can black beans, drained and rinsed; 2 chopped green onions; 1 chopped plum tomato; and 1 tablespoon each of chopped fresh cilantro, fresh lime juice, and olive oil.

Spicy Pork-and-Bell Pepper Tacos

(pictured on page 168)

TOTAL TIME: 29 MINUTES

QUICK TIP: To save time, use preshredded cheese and a thawed 16-ounce package of frozen pepper stir-fry with yellow, green, and red bell peppers and onions.

1½ pounds pork tenderloin, trimmed and cut into ½-inch strips
1½ teaspoons dried Italian seasoning
½ teaspoon ground red pepper
¼ teaspoon salt
4 teaspoons vegetable oil, divided
Cooking spray
1½ cups red bell pepper strips (about 1 large)
1½ cups green bell pepper strips (about 1 large)
1½ cups yellow bell pepper strips (about 1 large)
1½ teaspoons bottled minced garlic
¼ teaspoon salt
6 (8-inch) fat-free flour tortillas
¾ cup (3 ounces) shredded reduced-fat cheddar cheese
¾ cup bottled salsa
Lime wedges (optional)

1. Combine first 4 ingredients in a medium bowl. Heat 2 teaspoons oil in a large nonstick skillet coated with cooking spray over medium-high heat. Add pork, and cook 8 minutes or until pork loses its pink color. Remove from pan; keep warm.
2. Heat 2 teaspoons oil in pan coated with cooking spray over medium-high heat. Add bell peppers, garlic, and ¼ teaspoon salt, and sauté 5 minutes or until tender. Divide pork evenly among tortillas; top each serving with ½ cup pepper mixture, 2 tablespoons cheese, and 2 tablespoons salsa, and fold. Serve with lime wedges, if desired. Yield: 6 servings.

CALORIES 341 (25% from fat); FAT 9.3g (sat 3.2g, mono 2.2g, poly 2.1g); PROTEIN 32.2g; CARB 31.2g; FIBER 2.9g; CHOL 83mg; IRON 4.3mg; SODIUM 839mg; CALC 148mg

Menu 2
serves 4

Pork au Poivre

Boiled new potatoes tossed with parsley

Creamed spinach*

*Coat a large nonstick skillet with cooking spray; add ½ cup chopped onion. Sauté over medium-high heat 5 minutes or until tender. Stir in 2 (10-ounce) packages thawed frozen chopped spinach; cook 1 minute. Stir in ½ cup spreadable cheese with garlic and herbs (such as Alouette); sprinkle with 2 tablespoons grated fresh Parmesan cheese.

Pork au Poivre

TOTAL TIME: 27 MINUTES

1 pound pork tenderloin, trimmed
1 tablespoon coarsely ground black pepper
2 teaspoons olive oil
Cooking spray
½ cup fat-free, less-sodium chicken broth
½ cup dry red wine
1 teaspoon Dijon mustard
1 teaspoon tomato paste
¼ teaspoon salt

1. Preheat oven to 425°.
2. Cut pork lengthwise, cutting to, but not through, other side. Open halves, laying pork flat. Sprinkle each side of pork with 1½ teaspoons pepper. Heat oil over medium-high heat in a large ovenproof skillet coated with cooking spray. Add pork; cook 2 minutes on each side. Place pan in oven, and bake at 425° for 12 minutes or until meat thermometer registers 160° (slightly pink). Remove pork from pan; keep warm.
3. Add broth and remaining 4 ingredients to pan; stir well with a whisk. Bring to a boil over medium heat; cook until reduced to ½ cup (about 3 minutes). Yield: 4 servings (serving size: 3 ounces pork and 2 tablespoons sauce).

CALORIES 162 (32% from fat); FAT 5.7g (sat 1.3g, mono 2.9g, poly 0.5g); PROTEIN 24.5g; CARB 1.9g; FIBER 0.5g; CHOL 74mg; IRON 2.1mg; SODIUM 303mg; CALC 18mg

Menu 3
serves 4

Tangy Pork with Tomatillos, Tomatoes, and Cilantro

Mango salad*

*Combine ¼ cup white wine vinegar, 2 tablespoons honey, and 1 tablespoon olive oil. Toss with 1 (10-ounce) bag gourmet mixed salad greens and 2 cups cubed mango.

Tangy Pork with Tomatillos, Tomatoes, and Cilantro

TOTAL TIME: 28 MINUTES

1½ teaspoons ground cumin
1 teaspoon chili powder
½ teaspoon salt
¼ teaspoon ground red pepper
1 pound pork tenderloin, trimmed and cut into 1-inch cubes
1 tablespoon olive oil, divided
Cooking spray
1 cup chopped Vidalia or other sweet onion
1 teaspoon bottled minced garlic
2 cups chopped tomatillos (about 8 ounces)
2 cups halved cherry tomatoes (about 8 ounces)
½ cup chopped fresh cilantro
4 cups hot cooked instant rice

Continued

1. Combine first 4 ingredients in a medium bowl. Add pork; toss well. Heat 1½ teaspoons oil in a large nonstick skillet coated with cooking spray. Add pork; sauté 3 minutes. Remove pork from pan; keep warm.

2. Heat 1½ teaspoons oil in pan over medium-high heat. Add onion and garlic; sauté 30 seconds. Add tomatillos; sauté 1 minute. Add pork, and cover and cook 10 minutes or until pork is done. Add tomatoes and cilantro; cover and cook 1 minute. Serve with rice. Yield: 4 servings (serving size: 1 cup pork mixture and 1 cup rice).

CALORIES 375 (18% from fat); FAT 7.7g (sat 1.6g, mono 4.1g, poly 0.9g); PROTEIN 29.4g; CARB 46g; FIBER 4g; CHOL 74mg; IRON 4.3mg; SODIUM 379mg; CALC 62mg

---

Menu 4
serves 4

Pork Medallions with Olive-Caper Sauce

Steamed fresh (or frozen whole) green beans

Vermicelli with garlic and herbs*

*Cook 8 ounces vermicelli according to package directions, omitting salt and fat. Drain and toss with 2 tablespoons each of extra-virgin olive oil, lemon juice, and chopped fresh parsley; 2 teaspoons bottled minced garlic; and 1 teaspoon each of dried basil, salt, and black pepper.

Pork Medallions with Olive-Caper Sauce

TOTAL TIME: 25 MINUTES

    1 pound pork tenderloin, trimmed
    ½ teaspoon salt
    ½ teaspoon black pepper
    ¼ cup all-purpose flour
    1 tablespoon olive oil, divided
    ½ cup dry white wine
    ½ cup fat-free, less-sodium chicken broth
    ½ cup coarsely chopped pitted kalamata olives
    2 tablespoons capers
    2 tablespoons chopped fresh flat-leaf parsley

1. Cut pork crosswise into 8 pieces. Place each pork piece between 2 sheets of heavy-duty plastic wrap, and pound to ¼-inch thickness using a meat mallet or rolling pin. Sprinkle both sides of pork with salt and pepper. Place flour in a shallow bowl. Dredge pork in flour; shake off excess flour. Heat 1½ teaspoons olive oil in a nonstick skillet over medium-high heat. Add half of pork, and cook 2 minutes on each side or until done. Remove pork from pan, and keep warm. Repeat procedure with remaining 1½ teaspoons oil and pork. Return pork to pan. Add wine and broth; bring to a boil. Stir in olives and capers; cook 4 minutes. Sprinkle with parsley. Yield: 4 servings (serving size: 2 medallions and 2 tablespoons sauce).

CALORIES 212 (34% from fat); FAT 8.1g (sat 1.8g, mono 5.1g, poly 0.9g); PROTEIN 25.5g; CARB 8.1g; FIBER 0.9g; CHOL 74mg; IRON 2.7mg; SODIUM 894mg; CALC 30mg

---

cooking light profile

Doctor's Orders: Cook Something

If cooking is therapy, this Chicago psychiatrist is his own best patient.

Twice a year, when the mood strikes him, Howard Alt transforms his Evanston, Illinois, home into Howard's End, a white-tablecloth "restaurant" offering 25 lucky diners—friends, colleagues, neighbors, and family—a multicourse gourmet extravaganza. To feed his cooking passion he also moonlights at area restaurants such as Charlie Trotter's and Frontera Grill.

The most important lesson he's learned is how cooking for someone—whether a five-course dinner or a five-minute snack—can be an exercise in nurturing and creating. Though he stops short of actually prescribing recipes to his patients, he often finds himself talking to them about the therapeutic benefits of "the experience of cooking," about how it's an opportunity to be responsive and loving to others.

Black Bean Dip with Tortilla Chips

Howard Alt's addition of allspice to a fairly traditional Tex-Mex dip gives it a unique flavor. We've included homemade tortilla chips in the recipe, but you can also serve the dip with fresh vegetables.

    1 red bell pepper
    ¾ cup minced fresh cilantro (about 1 bunch)
    3 tablespoons finely chopped green onions
    2 tablespoons lime juice
    2 tablespoons balsamic vinegar
    2 tablespoons hot sauce
    ½ teaspoon ground allspice
    ½ teaspoon ground cumin
    ¼ teaspoon salt
    ¼ teaspoon black pepper
    2 (15-ounce) cans black beans, drained
    1 jalapeño pepper, seeded and diced
    1 garlic clove, minced
    Chopped red bell pepper (optional)
    6 (10-inch) flour tortillas, each cut into 8 wedges
    Cooking spray

1. Preheat broiler.

2. Cut bell pepper in half lengthwise, discarding seeds and membranes. Place bell pepper halves, skin sides up, on a foil-lined baking sheet, and flatten with hand. Broil 5 minutes or until blackened. Place broiled bell pepper in a zip-top plastic bag, and seal. Let stand 5 minutes, and peel. Place peeled bell pepper, cilantro, and next 11 ingredients in a food processor, and process until smooth. Spoon into a bowl, and garnish with chopped bell pepper, if desired.

3. Preheat oven to 400°.

4. Arrange tortilla wedges in a single layer on a baking sheet coated with cooking spray. Bake at 400° for 5 minutes or until golden. Serve dip with chips. Yield: 12 servings (serving size: ¼ cup dip and 4 chips).

CALORIES 189 (14% from fat); FAT 2.9g (sat 0.7g, mono 1.4g, poly 0.5g); PROTEIN 7.7g; CARB 33.3g; FIBER 5.8g; CHOL 0mg; IRON 2.4mg; SODIUM 354mg; CALC 65mg

Saucy Talk

A grilling pro serves up six of his best sauces with lessons for great grilling.

The backyard barbecue is the place to be in the summertime. So for some grilling pointers, we consulted one of grilling's reigning gurus, Chris Schlesinger, chef/owner of the East Coast Grill in Cambridge, Massachusetts, and the Back Eddy in nearby Westport. In addition to running two restaurants known for their grilled seafood, he's also written six books that emphasize using bold flavors.

Schlesinger believes the solution for bolstering flavor when grilling is layering. By using dry rubs and pastes you get a crisp, highly flavored outer coating and a completely different texture and flavor on the inside. As for sauces, Schlesinger prefers serving his flavorful sauces on the side or using them as glazes rather than basting. These rubs and sauces are for novices and seasoned grillers alike, and they'll impart flavors unmatched by anything from a bottle.

Grilled Shrimp-and-Plum Skewers with Sweet Hoisin Sauce

The ginger gives these kebabs a spicy, peppery bite that's mellowed by the sweet sauce.

12 jumbo shrimp, peeled and
    deveined (about 1 pound)
3   plums, quartered
2   tablespoons minced peeled fresh
    ginger
1   tablespoon olive oil
½   teaspoon kosher salt
½   teaspoon white or black pepper
Cooking spray
Sweet Hoisin Sauce, divided
¼   cup (1½-inch) julienne-cut green
    onions (optional)
1   lime, quartered (optional)

1. Prepare grill.
2. Place first 6 ingredients in a large bowl, and toss. Thread 3 shrimp and 3 plum sections alternately onto each of 4 (10-inch) skewers.
3. Place kebabs on a grill rack coated with cooking spray; cook 4 minutes. Turn kebabs; brush with about ¼ cup Sweet Hoisin Sauce. Cook 4 minutes. Turn kebabs; brush with about ¼ cup sauce. Cook 2 minutes, turning once.

Serve remaining sauce as a dipping sauce. Garnish with onions and lime, if desired. Yield: 4 servings (serving size: 1 kebab and about 2 tablespoons sauce).

(Totals include Sweet Hoisin Sauce) CALORIES 220 (26% from fat); FAT 6.4g (sat 0.9g, mono 3.2g, poly 1.6g); PROTEIN 18.6g; CARB 21.5g; FIBER 1.5g; CHOL 130mg; IRON 2.6mg; SODIUM 800mg; CALC 60mg

SWEET HOISIN SAUCE:

(pictured on page 167)

Hoisin is a blend of soybeans, garlic, chile peppers, and spices; it serves as the base for this Chinese-inspired barbecue sauce. Five-spice powder, also used extensively in Chinese cooking, is a pungent mixture of ground cinnamon, cloves, fennel, star anise, and peppercorns.

⅓   cup bottled hoisin sauce
¼   cup rice vinegar
2   tablespoons sherry
2   tablespoons ketchup
1   tablespoon brown sugar
½   teaspoon five-spice powder

1. Combine all ingredients in a small bowl. Yield: about 1 cup (serving size: 1 tablespoon).

CALORIES 17 (11% from fat); FAT 0.2g (sat 0g, mono 0.1g, poly 0.1g); PROTEIN 0.2g; CARB 3.5g; FIBER 0.2g; CHOL 0mg; IRON 0.1mg; SODIUM 108mg; CALC 3mg

Spicy Cumin-Crusted Chicken with Orange-Chipotle Sauce

Slather on this smoky, citrus-infused sauce during the last half of the cooking time to avoid charring.

⅓   cup cumin seeds
½   teaspoon kosher salt
¼   teaspoon black pepper
4   (4-ounce) skinless, boneless
    chicken breast halves
Cooking spray
Orange-Chipotle Sauce

1. Prepare grill.
2. Combine first 3 ingredients in a small bowl. Rub both sides of chicken with spice mixture. Place chicken on grill rack coated with cooking spray; cover and grill 6 minutes.
3. Uncover chicken, and brush with ½ cup Orange-Chipotle Sauce; cook 6 minutes or until done, turning once. Serve with remaining sauce. Yield: 4 servings (serving size: 3 ounces chicken and about ⅓ cup sauce).

(Totals include Orange-Chipotle Sauce) CALORIES 448 (23% from fat); FAT 11.2g (sat 1.6g, mono 6.7g, poly 1.7g); PROTEIN 30.5g; CARB 61.2g; FIBER 3.4g; CHOL 66mg; IRON 8.5mg; SODIUM 891mg; CALC 189mg

ORANGE-CHIPOTLE SAUCE:

(pictured on page 167)

2   tablespoons olive oil
1   cup chopped onion
1   cup chopped tomato
2   tablespoons minced garlic
    (about 6 cloves)
2   tablespoons chopped drained
    canned chipotle chile in adobo
    sauce
2   cups fresh orange juice (about 4
    oranges)
1   cup white vinegar
½   cup ketchup
¼   cup packed brown sugar
¼   cup molasses
¼   teaspoon kosher salt
¼   teaspoon black pepper
¼   cup fresh lime juice
½   cup chopped fresh cilantro

Continued

1. Heat oil in a large nonstick skillet over medium-high heat. Add onion; sauté 10 minutes or until browned. Add tomato, garlic, and chile; cook 3 minutes. Add orange juice and vinegar; bring to a boil. Reduce heat; simmer until reduced to 1⅓ cups (about 30 minutes). Stir in ketchup, sugar, molasses, salt, and pepper; cook 5 minutes. Place mixture in a food processor; process until smooth. Stir in lime juice and cilantro. Yield: 2 cups (serving size: 1 tablespoon).

CALORIES 36 (23% from fat); FAT 0.9g (sat 0.1g, mono 0.6g, poly 0.1g); PROTEIN 0.4g; CARB 7.2g; FIBER 0.3g; CHOL 0mg; IRON 0.3mg; SODIUM 71mg; CALC 13mg

Grilled Pork Chops with Sweet Peach Sauce

Serve the sweet, citrusy sauce on the side to complement the fragrant spices rubbed on the pork; the combo also works well as an accompaniment to grilled chicken or fish. Store the remaining spice mixture in an airtight container.

3 tablespoons ground coriander
3 tablespoons paprika
3 tablespoons cracked black pepper
2 tablespoons kosher salt
2 tablespoons ground cumin
1 tablespoon brown sugar
4 (6-ounce) bone-in center-cut pork chops (about ¼-inch thick)
Cooking spray
1 cup Sweet Peach Sauce

1. Prepare grill.
2. Combine first 6 ingredients in a bowl. Rub pork chops with ¼ cup spice mixture, and reserve remaining spice mixture for another use. Place pork chops on a grill rack coated with cooking spray. Cook pork chops 4 minutes on each side or until done. Serve with Sweet Peach Sauce. Yield: 4 servings (servings size: 1 chop and ¼ cup sauce).

(Totals include Sweet Peach Sauce) CALORIES 266 (35% from fat); FAT 10.3g (sat 3.3g, mono 4.8g, poly 1.3g); PROTEIN 26.5g; CARB 17g; FIBER 2.5g; CHOL 72mg; IRON 3.1mg; SODIUM 1,083mg; CALC 44mg

SWEET PEACH SAUCE:
1 tablespoon olive oil
2 cups sliced red onion
3 cups chopped peeled peaches
2 cups chopped tomato
2 tablespoons minced peeled fresh ginger
½ cup cider vinegar
½ cup fresh orange juice (about 1 orange)
⅓ cup packed brown sugar
1 teaspoon ground allspice
¼ teaspoon kosher salt
¼ teaspoon black pepper

1. Heat olive oil in a large nonstick skillet over medium-high heat. Add onion, and sauté 10 minutes. Add peaches, tomato, and ginger, and cook 2 minutes. Add vinegar and remaining ingredients, and bring to a boil. Reduce heat, and simmer 20 minutes. Place peach mixture in a food processor, and process until smooth. Yield: 3 cups (serving size: 1 tablespoon).

CALORIES 16 (17% from fat); FAT 0.3g (sat 0.1g, mono 0.2g, poly 0g); PROTEIN 0.2g; CARB 3.4g; FIBER 0.4g; CHOL 0mg; IRON 0.1mg; SODIUM 11mg; CALC 3mg

Parsley- and Garlic-Rubbed Flank Steak with Sweet-and-Sour Red Onion-Vinegar Sauce

⅓ cup chopped fresh parsley
3 tablespoons minced garlic (about 6 large cloves)
1 tablespoon crushed red pepper
1 tablespoon olive oil
½ teaspoon kosher salt
¼ teaspoon cracked black pepper
1 (2½-pound) flank steak, trimmed
Sweet-and-Sour Red Onion-Vinegar Sauce

1. Prepare grill.
2. Combine first 6 ingredients. Rub both sides of steak with mixture. Place steak on grill rack; grill 8 minutes on each side or until desired degree of doneness. Cut steak diagonally across grain into thin slices. Serve with Sweet-and-Sour Red Onion-Vinegar Sauce. Yield: 10 servings (serving size: 3 ounces beef and about ¼ cup sauce).

(Totals include Sweet-and-Sour Red Onion-Vinegar Sauce) CALORIES 248 (50% from fat); FAT 13.7g (sat 5g, mono 6.5g, poly 0.7g); PROTEIN 23.4g; CARB 7.6g; FIBER 1.3g; CHOL 57mg; IRON 2.8mg; SODIUM 206mg; CALC 30mg

SWEET-AND-SOUR RED ONION-VINEGAR SAUCE:
3 cups thinly sliced red onion
1 cup red wine vinegar
3 tablespoons sugar
¼ teaspoon kosher salt
¼ teaspoon cracked black pepper
½ cup white vinegar
3 tablespoons coriander seeds, crushed
1 tablespoon olive oil

1. Combine first 5 ingredients; cover and refrigerate 3 hours. Drain onion; place in a bowl. Stir in white vinegar, coriander, and oil. Yield: 3 cups (serving size: 1 tablespoon).

CALORIES 8 (34% from fat); FAT 0.3g (sat 0g, mono 0.3g, poly 0g); PROTEIN 0.1g; CARB 1.4g; FIBER 0.2g; CHOL 0mg; IRON 0.1mg; SODIUM 5mg; CALC 4mg

Grilled Striped Bass with Chunky Mango-Ginger Sauce

4 (6-ounce) striped bass or other firm white fish fillets (such as amberjack or grouper)
1 tablespoon olive oil
½ teaspoon kosher salt
¼ teaspoon black pepper
1 cup Chunky Mango-Ginger Sauce

1. Prepare grill.
2. Brush fillets with oil; sprinkle with salt and pepper. Grill fillets 4 minutes on each side or until fish flakes easily when tested with a fork. Serve with Chunky Mango-Ginger Sauce. Yield: 4 servings (serving size: 1 fillet and ¼ cup sauce).

(Totals include Chunky Mango-Ginger Sauce) CALORIES 296 (34% from fat); FAT 11.3g (sat 2.2g, mono 6.1g, poly 2.1g); PROTEIN 32.9g; CARB 15.3g; FIBER 1.2g; CHOL 116mg; IRON 3mg; SODIUM 363mg; CALC 157mg

CHUNKY MANGO-GINGER SAUCE:

(pictured on page 167)

- 1 tablespoon olive oil
- 2 cups finely chopped red onion
- 2 cups cubed peeled ripe mango
- 1 cup chopped tomato
- 3 tablespoons minced peeled fresh ginger
- 2 tablespoons minced garlic (about 6 cloves)
- ½ cup fresh lime juice (about 2 limes)
- ¼ cup orange juice
- ¼ cup dry sherry
- 3 tablespoons brown sugar
- 3 tablespoons white vinegar

1. Heat oil in a large nonstick skillet over medium-high heat. Add onion; sauté 7 minutes. Add mango, tomato, ginger, and garlic; cook 5 minutes. Stir in remaining ingredients; bring to a boil. Reduce heat; simmer 20 minutes. Yield: 2½ cups (serving size: 1 tablespoon).

CALORIES 18 (20% from fat); FAT 0.4g (sat 0.1g, mono 0.3g, poly 0g); PROTEIN 0.2g; CARB 3.8g; FIBER 0.3g; CHOL 0mg; IRON 0.1mg; SODIUM 1mg; CALC 5mg

---

Curry- and Ginger-Rubbed Lamb Chops with Apricot-Lime Sauce

The sauce and paste make a versatile combination that's equally suited to grilled beef or pork.

- 2½ tablespoons curry powder
- 1½ tablespoons minced peeled fresh ginger
- 1½ teaspoons olive oil
- ¼ teaspoon kosher salt
- ⅛ teaspoon black pepper
- 8 (6-ounce) lamb shoulder chops, trimmed
- ½ cup Apricot-Lime Sauce, divided

1. Prepare grill.
2. Combine first 5 ingredients; rub paste evenly over lamb.
3. Place lamb on grill rack, and cook 4 minutes. Turn lamb; brush with ¼ cup Apricot-Lime Sauce. Cook 4 minutes. Turn lamb, and brush with ¼ cup sauce.

Cook 2 minutes, turning once. Yield: 8 servings (serving size: 1 chop).

(Totals include Apricot-Lime Sauce) CALORIES 241 (45% from fat); FAT 12.1g (sat 4.1g, mono 5.2g, poly 1.1g); PROTEIN 24.1g; CARB 8.2g; FIBER 0.9g; CHOL 77mg; IRON 2.6mg; SODIUM 195mg; CALC 28mg

APRICOT-LIME SAUCE:

- ⅔ cup apricot preserves
- ½ cup fresh lime juice (about 2 limes)
- ⅓ cup golden raisins
- ⅓ cup chopped fresh mint
- ¼ cup balsamic vinegar
- ¼ cup ketchup
- ¼ cup Worcestershire sauce
- 1 tablespoon hot sauce
- ¼ teaspoon kosher salt
- ¼ teaspoon black pepper

1. Melt preserves in a saucepan over medium-low heat. Stir in remaining ingredients. Remove from heat. Yield: 2 cups (serving size: 1 tablespoon).

CALORIES 26 (0% from fat); FAT 0g; PROTEIN 0.2g; CARB 6.9g; FIBER 0.2g; CHOL 0mg; IRON 0.1mg; SODIUM 61mg; CALC 5mg

---

in season

Green Without Envy

Don't let the color fool you. Green tomatoes have a culinary charm all their own.

Green tomatoes are ideal for the grill or in soups, sauces, or desserts. Although they are unmistakably Southern, fresh green tomatoes are frequently used in Mediterranean and Indian cuisines, too.

As soon as you pick green tomatoes, use them. After a day or so, they will begin to turn red. As the green color disappears, so does the distinctive tartness. If you can't use them immediately, keep them in your refrigerator's vegetable drawer for a couple of days to slow down the ripening process (we don't recommend this for ripe red tomatoes, however). Bring them to room temperature before you cook them so they'll be more like they are when you first bring them in from the garden.

Unfried Green Tomatoes with Fresh Tomato Gravy

We found a way to get the flavor of a fried tomato without all the oil. To make sure the pan is hot enough to yield a crispy crust, preheat it while you're preparing the green tomatoes.

GREEN TOMATOES:

- ¼ cup all-purpose flour
- ¼ cup yellow cornmeal
- ¼ teaspoon salt
- ¼ teaspoon black pepper
- Dash of sugar
- 16 (½-inch-thick) slices green tomatoes (about 3 green tomatoes)
- ⅓ cup fat-free milk
- Cooking spray

GRAVY:

- 1 tablespoon butter
- 1 cup chopped mushrooms
- ½ cup finely chopped onion
- 2 cups finely chopped peeled red tomato
- ¼ teaspoon salt
- ¼ teaspoon black pepper

1. Preheat oven to 400°.
2. To prepare green tomatoes, combine first 5 ingredients in a shallow dish. Dip tomato slices in milk; dredge in flour mixture. Lightly coat both sides of tomato slices with cooking spray.
3. Place a baking sheet in oven; heat at 400° for 5 minutes. Remove from oven; immediately coat with cooking spray. Place tomato slices on preheated baking sheet. Bake at 400° for 25 minutes, turning after 15 minutes.
4. To prepare gravy, melt butter in a medium nonstick saucepan over medium heat. Add mushrooms and onion, and cook 4 minutes or until tender, stirring frequently. Add chopped red tomato; bring to a boil, and cook 10 minutes or until liquid almost evaporates. Stir in ¼ teaspoon salt and ¼ teaspoon pepper. Spoon gravy over tomato slices. Yield: 4 servings (serving size: 4 tomato slices and about ⅓ cup gravy).

CALORIES 142 (27% from fat); FAT 4.2g (sat 1.9g, mono 1g, poly 0.5g); PROTEIN 4.2g; CARB 23.5g; FIBER 3g; CHOL 8mg; IRON 1.7mg; SODIUM 348mg; CALC 41mg

Grilled Eggplant-and-Green-Tomato Sandwiches with Dijon-Rosemary Spread

Grilling the tomatoes softens their texture a bit but doesn't take away any of their tang.

```
 1   large eggplant (about 1¼ pounds),
       cut crosswise into 8 slices
 ¼   teaspoon salt
 ½   cup low-fat mayonnaise
 5   tablespoons fat-free milk
 2   tablespoons Dijon mustard
 2   teaspoons chopped fresh or
       ½ teaspoon dried rosemary
 1   teaspoon fresh lemon juice
 2   garlic cloves, minced
 2   cups trimmed arugula
Cooking spray
 2   green tomatoes, each cut into
       4 slices
 8   (1-ounce) slices sourdough bread
 ¼   cup (1 ounce) crumbled goat cheese
```

1. Prepare grill.
2. Sprinkle both sides of each eggplant slice with salt. Place eggplant slices on paper towels; let stand 20 minutes. Blot dry with paper towels.
3. Combine mayonnaise and next 5 ingredients in a medium bowl. Remove ¼ cup mayonnaise mixture; set aside. Add arugula to mayonnaise mixture in bowl; toss gently.
4. Coat both sides of eggplant slices with cooking spray. Place on grill rack, and grill 5 minutes on each side or until lightly browned. Transfer eggplant to a plate. Coat both sides of tomato slices with cooking spray. Place tomato slices and bread slices on grill rack; grill 2 minutes on each side or until tomato is tender and bread is lightly browned.
5. Place 1 bread slice on each of 4 plates. Top each slice with ⅓ cup arugula mixture, 2 eggplant slices, 2 tomato slices, and 1 tablespoon goat cheese. Drizzle 1 tablespoon reserved mayonnaise mixture over each serving. Top with remaining bread slices. Yield: 4 servings (serving size: 1 sandwich).

CALORIES 295 (21% from fat); FAT 6.8g (sat 1.9g, mono 1.7g, poly 2g); PROTEIN 8.8g; CARB 50.6g; FIBER 5.8g; CHOL 7mg; IRON 2.2mg; SODIUM 926mg; CALC 145mg

Indian-Style Green Tomatoes and Vegetables over Rice

This side dish is a spicy counterpoint for grilled chicken. The black mustard seeds add a contrasting color to the mixture, which is yellow from the turmeric. Look for black mustard seeds at Asian markets.

```
 1    tablespoon vegetable oil
 1    teaspoon black mustard seeds
 1    cup chopped baking potato
 1    cup chopped cauliflower
 1    cup chopped green tomato
 1½  teaspoons ground coriander
 1    teaspoon ground cumin
 ½   teaspoon salt
 ½   teaspoon ground turmeric
 ⅛   teaspoon ground red pepper
 1    cup water
 2    cups hot cooked basmati rice
```

1. Heat oil in a large nonstick skillet over medium-high heat. Add mustard seeds; cook 1 minute. Add potato and next 7 ingredients, stirring until blended. Add water; bring to a boil. Cover, reduce heat, and simmer 20 minutes or until tender. Uncover and cook 4 minutes or until liquid evaporates, stirring frequently. Serve over rice. Yield: 4 servings (serving size: ½ cup vegetables and ½ cup rice).

CALORIES 195 (19% from fat); FAT 4.2g (sat 0.8g, mono 1.3g, poly 1.8g); PROTEIN 4.1g; CARB 35.8g; FIBER 2.4g; CHOL 0mg; IRON 2.1mg; SODIUM 308mg; CALC 34mg

Sweet-and-Sour Green-Tomato Salsa

Serve this down-home version of tomatillo salsa with tortilla chips.

```
 1    red bell pepper
 2½  cups chopped green tomato
 1    tablespoon balsamic vinegar
 1    teaspoon brown sugar
 ½   teaspoon salt
 ⅓   cup finely chopped sweet
        onion
 1    garlic clove, minced
```

1. Preheat broiler.

2. Cut bell pepper in half lengthwise, discarding seeds and membranes. Place pepper halves, skin sides up, on a foil-lined baking sheet; flatten with hand. Broil 10 minutes or until blackened. Place in a zip-top plastic bag; seal. Let stand 10 minutes. Peel and finely chop.
3. Place chopped green tomato, vinegar, sugar, and salt in a blender or food processor, and process until smooth.
4. Place tomato mixture in a small saucepan; cook over medium-high heat 5 minutes or until liquid almost evaporates. Place in a small bowl; cool to room temperature. Add roasted pepper, onion, and garlic to tomato mixture; toss well. Yield: ¾ cup (serving size: ¼ cup).

CALORIES 13 (14% from fat); FAT 0.2g (sat 0g, mono 0g, poly 0.1g); PROTEIN 0.4g; CARB 2.9g; FIBER 0.6g; CHOL 0mg; IRON 0.3mg; SODIUM 102mg; CALC 4mg

Green-Tomato-and-Raspberry Cobbler

Green tomatoes make a surprise appearance in this dessert. In the winter, you can substitute cranberries for the raspberries.

```
 3    cups fresh raspberries
 1    tablespoon all-purpose flour
 6    cups chopped green tomato (about
        1¾ pounds)
 1    cup granulated sugar
 ¼   cup water
Cooking spray
 1    cup all-purpose flour
 ⅓   cup granulated sugar
 ⅓   cup packed brown sugar
 ½   teaspoon baking powder
 ½   teaspoon baking soda
 ¼   cup chilled butter, cut into small
        pieces
 ½   cup low-fat buttermilk
```

1. Preheat oven to 350°.
2. Combine raspberries and 1 tablespoon flour in a medium bowl; toss well.
3. Bring tomato, 1 cup granulated sugar, and water to a boil in a medium saucepan; cook 4 minutes. Remove from heat; stir in raspberry mixture. Pour mixture into a 13 x 9-inch baking pan coated with cooking spray.

4. Lightly spoon 1 cup flour into a dry measuring cup, and level with a knife. Combine 1 cup flour, ⅓ cup granulated sugar, brown sugar, baking powder, and baking soda in a bowl, stirring with a whisk. Cut in butter with a pastry blender or 2 knives until mixture resembles coarse meal. Add buttermilk, stirring just until moist. Drop dough by heaping tablespoons onto fruit mixture. Bake at 350° for 50 minutes or until filling is bubbly and crust is browned. Yield: 9 servings.

CALORIES 298 (19% from fat); FAT 6.3g (sat 3.3g, mono 1.6g, poly 0.7g); PROTEIN 3.5g; CARB 59.7g; FIBER 4.5g; CHOL 14mg; IRON 1.7mg; SODIUM 171mg; CALC 58mg

taste of america

Salad Made Macho

Mix a summer staple with a Tex-Mex favorite. The result? Muy delicioso.

Salad may be a staple of the summer dinner table, but it's hardly known as a supper of substance. Top it off with a little something extra to nibble on—such as quesadillas—and you can create a main dish that will satisfy even the heartiest appetites.

Dijon-Lemon Vinaigrette

This is the base for our other vinaigrettes, but it also tastes great on its own. Refrigerated, the vinaigrette keeps for about a week.

- 3 tablespoons vegetable broth or water
- 2 tablespoons fresh lemon juice
- 2 tablespoons extra-virgin olive oil
- 1½ tablespoons red wine vinegar
- 1 tablespoon Dijon mustard
- 2 teaspoons minced garlic
- 2 teaspoons Worcestershire sauce
- ½ teaspoon black pepper
- ¼ teaspoon salt

1. Combine all ingredients in a jar; cover tightly, and shake vigorously. Store in refrigerator. Yield: ⅔ cup (serving size: 1 tablespoon).

CALORIES 25 (86% from fat); FAT 2.4g (sat 0.3g, mono 1.7g, poly 0.2g); PROTEIN 0.1g; CARB 1g; FIBER 0g; CHOL 0mg; IRON 0.1mg; SODIUM 93mg; CALC 3mg

Lemon-Rosemary Chicken Quesadilla Salad with Shallot-Mustard Vinaigrette

VINAIGRETTE:
- 3 tablespoons Dijon-Lemon Vinaigrette
- 2 teaspoons minced shallots
- 1 teaspoon Dijon mustard
- 1 teaspoon extra-virgin olive oil
- ½ teaspoon grated lemon rind
- ¼ teaspoon freshly ground black pepper

QUESADILLAS:
- ¼ cup (2 ounces) goat cheese, softened
- 2 tablespoons fat-free cottage cheese
- 1 tablespoon fresh lemon juice
- 1 teaspoon Dijon mustard
- ½ teaspoon chopped fresh or ⅛ teaspoon dried rosemary
- ¼ teaspoon freshly ground black pepper
- 4 (8-inch) fat-free flour tortillas
- 2 cups chopped roasted skinless, boneless chicken breasts (about 2 breasts)
Cooking spray

REMAINING INGREDIENT:
- 8 cups gourmet salad greens

1. To prepare vinaigrette, combine first 6 ingredients; stir with a whisk. Set aside.
2. To prepare quesadillas, combine goat cheese and next 5 ingredients in a small bowl. Spread 2 tablespoons goat cheese mixture over each tortilla. Arrange 1 cup chopped chicken over goat cheese mixture on each of 2 tortillas, and top with remaining tortillas cheese side down.
3. Heat a large nonstick skillet coated with cooking spray over medium heat.

Cook quesadillas 4 minutes on each side or until golden brown. Remove quesadillas from skillet, and cut each quesadilla into 8 wedges. Combine vinaigrette with salad greens, and toss well. Arrange 2 cups salad on each of 4 plates, and top each serving with 4 quesadilla wedges. Yield: 4 servings.

CALORIES 271 (26% from fat); FAT 7.8g (sat 3.1g, mono 3.3g, poly 0.9g); PROTEIN 21g; CARB 29.2g; FIBER 3g; CHOL 48mg; IRON 2.6mg; SODIUM 830mg; CALC 129mg

Cheddar-Jalapeño Quesadilla Salad with Cilantro-Lime Vinaigrette

This fresh take on the traditional taco salad works well as a vegetarian main course.

VINAIGRETTE:
- ¼ cup Dijon-Lemon Vinaigrette
- 2 tablespoons minced fresh cilantro
- 1 tablespoon lime juice

QUESADILLAS:
- 1 (15-ounce) can black beans, undrained
- 8 (6-inch) corn tortillas
- 1 cup (4 ounces) shredded reduced-fat sharp cheddar cheese
- 3 to 4 tablespoons chopped pickled jalapeño peppers
Cooking spray

REMAINING INGREDIENTS:
- 6 cups chopped iceberg lettuce
- 2 cups chopped tomato
- 1 cup bottled salsa
- ½ cup chopped onion
- ¼ cup low-fat sour cream

1. To prepare vinaigrette, combine first 3 ingredients; stir with a whisk. Set aside.
2. To prepare quesadillas, drain beans through a sieve over a bowl, reserving 1 tablespoon bean liquid; discard remaining liquid. Combine ½ cup beans and 1 tablespoon reserved bean liquid in a small bowl; mash with a fork. Reserve remaining beans. Spread bean mixture evenly over 4 tortillas. Sprinkle each with
Continued

¼ cup cheese and about 1 tablespoon jalapeño; top with remaining tortillas.

3. Heat a large nonstick skillet coated with cooking spray over medium heat. Cook quesadillas 4 minutes on each side or until golden brown. Remove quesadillas from pan, and cut each into 4 wedges. Combine vinaigrette and lettuce; toss well. Arrange 1½ cups lettuce mixture on each of 4 plates. For each serving, spoon 3 tablespoons reserved beans over lettuce mixture, and place ½ cup tomato over beans. Top each serving with ¼ cup salsa, 2 tablespoons chopped onion, and 1 tablespoon sour cream. Serve each with 4 quesadilla wedges. Yield: 4 servings.

CALORIES 389 (29% from fat); FAT 12.4g (sat 4.9g, mono 4.2g, poly 1.5g); PROTEIN 20.2g; CARB 53.9g; FIBER 8.5g; CHOL 25mg; IRON 3.9mg; SODIUM 985mg; CALC 424mg

Seared Tuna Salad with Lemon-Caper Vinaigrette and Feta Quesadillas

VINAIGRETTE:

2 tablespoons low-fat mayonnaise
2 tablespoons Dijon-Lemon Vinaigrette (recipe on page 175)
2 teaspoons grated lemon rind
1½ tablespoons fresh lemon juice
1½ teaspoons capers, drained
⅛ teaspoon freshly ground black pepper

QUESADILLAS:

1 (15-ounce) can cannellini beans or other white beans, undrained
½ teaspoon dried oregano
4 (8-inch) fat-free flour tortillas
½ cup (2 ounces) crumbled feta cheese

REMAINING INGREDIENTS:

1 (8-ounce) tuna steak (about ¾ inch thick)
½ teaspoon freshly ground black pepper
½ teaspoon olive oil
Cooking spray
8 cups gourmet salad greens
2 cups chopped tomato
¼ cup chopped pitted kalamata olives

1. To prepare vinaigrette, combine first 6 ingredients; stir with a whisk. Set aside.

2. To prepare quesadillas, drain beans through a sieve over a bowl, reserving 1 tablespoon bean liquid, and discard remaining liquid. Combine ½ cup beans, 1 tablespoon reserved liquid, and oregano in a small bowl, and mash with a fork. Spread bean mixture evenly over 2 tortillas. Sprinkle cheese evenly over bean mixture; top with remaining tortillas, and set aside.

3. Sprinkle fish with ½ teaspoon pepper. Heat oil in a large nonstick skillet over medium-high heat. Add fish; cook 2 minutes on each side or until fish is medium-rare or desired degree of doneness. Remove fish from pan; coarsely chop fish.

4. Heat pan coated with cooking spray over medium heat. Cook quesadillas 4 minutes on each side or until golden brown. Remove quesadillas from pan; cut each into 8 wedges. Combine vinaigrette, remaining beans, greens, tomato, and olives; toss well. Arrange 2 cups salad on each of 4 plates; divide fish evenly among salads. Top each serving with 4 quesadilla wedges. Yield: 4 servings.

CALORIES 395 (24% from fat); FAT 10.5g (sat 3.5g, mono 3.8g, poly 2.3g); PROTEIN 24.6g; CARB 51.5g; FIBER 8.9g; CHOL 34mg; IRON 4.9mg; SODIUM 914mg; CALC 157mg

Flank Steak-and-Blue Cheese Quesadilla Salad

Because they're filled with steak, these quesadillas are somewhat tricky to cut. To make matters easier, let the quesadillas stand a minute or so after cooking, then cut them with kitchen shears.

VINAIGRETTE:

3 tablespoons Dijon-Lemon Vinaigrette (recipe on page 175)
1½ tablespoons sugar
1½ tablespoons red wine vinegar
¼ teaspoon freshly ground black pepper
¼ teaspoon chopped fresh thyme (optional)

QUESADILLAS:

½ pound flank steak
¼ teaspoon salt
¼ teaspoon freshly ground black pepper
Cooking spray
½ cup (2 ounces) crumbled blue cheese
4 (8-inch) fat-free flour tortillas

REMAINING INGREDIENTS:

10 cups torn red leaf lettuce
1 cup vertically sliced red onion
2 large tomatoes, each cut into 8 wedges

1. Prepare grill.

2. To prepare vinaigrette, combine first 5 ingredients; set aside.

3. To prepare quesadillas, sprinkle steak with salt and ¼ teaspoon pepper. Place steak on grill rack coated with cooking spray, and cook 4 minutes on each side or until done. Let stand 5 minutes. Cut steak diagonally across grain into thin slices. Sprinkle ¼ cup cheese evenly over each of 2 tortillas. Divide steak evenly over cheese; top with remaining tortillas.

4. Heat a large nonstick skillet coated with cooking spray over medium heat. Cook quesadillas 4 minutes on each side or until golden brown. Remove quesadillas from pan, and cut each into 8 wedges. Combine vinaigrette, lettuce, onion, and tomato in a large bowl; toss well. Divide salad evenly among 4 plates; top each serving with 4 quesadilla wedges. Yield: 4 servings.

CALORIES 338 (29% from fat); FAT 10.9g (sat 4.8g, mono 4.2g, poly 0.8g); PROTEIN 20.9g; CARB 39.5g; FIBER 4.8g; CHOL 11mg; IRON 4.3mg; SODIUM 809mg; CALC 142mg

It's a Wrap

For an extra kick, try making quesadillas with flavored flour tortillas. Léona's de Chimayó, a family-owned restaurant in New Mexico, sells six-inch flour tortillas by mail order in a variety of flavors. To order, call 800-453-6627. Unlike the tortillas we used, however, these contain fat—if you choose them, keep in mind that they add three to four grams of fat per serving.

World-Class Thai

Fresh herbs, pungent spices, caramel flavors, and smoky aromas mingle in this cuisine that engages all the senses.

1. *Place a mortar on top of a damp towel. Add salt and garlic to mortar, and blend together by holding pestle securely in center of palm of one hand. Pound straight up and down into center of mortar, anchoring it with other hand.*

In recent years, not only has the popularity of Thai cooking burgeoned, but Thais are also rediscovering the traditional food preparation methods of their ancestors.

Thai food gets its distinct flavors from four basic seasonings: salt, garlic, cilantro, and Thai or white peppercorn. These, in turn, are supported by a cast of chiles and fish sauce.

The following recipes are fairly simple to prepare, and they represent the most well-known and diverse varieties of Thai regional cooking. Most of these dishes taste best when accompanied by long-grain Thai jasmine rice.

2. *Add chile, galangal, lemongrass, and lime leaves, one at a time, pounding until each ingredient is incorporated into the paste.*

Drunken Stir-Fried Beef with Green Beans

(pictured on page 166)

Most Thai dishes are named after the main ingredients or cooking techniques. But occasionally, a dish has a playful or poetic name, such as this one. Serve over jasmine rice.

DRUNKEN PASTE:

- ½ teaspoon kosher salt
- 7 garlic cloves, minced
- 1¼ teaspoons minced bird chile or 2½ teaspoons minced serrano chile
- 2 teaspoons coarsely chopped galangal or peeled fresh ginger
- 1 tablespoon chopped peeled fresh lemongrass
- 2 kaffir lime leaves, thinly sliced, or 1 teaspoon grated lime rind

STIR-FRY:

- Cooking spray
- 1 (1-pound) flank steak, trimmed and cut into ¼-inch strips
- 2 cups (1-inch) diagonally cut green beans
- 1 cup quartered cherry tomatoes
- 1 tablespoon sugar
- 3 tablespoons Thai fish sauce
- 1 teaspoon cider vinegar
- 1 cup Thai basil leaves

1. To prepare paste, combine salt and minced garlic in a mortar and pestle, and pound to form a paste. Add chile, galangal, lemongrass, and lime leaves, one at a time, pounding until each ingredient is incorporated into paste before adding the next.

2. To prepare stir-fry, heat a wok or large nonstick skillet coated with cooking spray over medium-high heat. Add paste, and stir-fry 30 seconds (fumes may cause eyes and throat to burn slightly). Add beef; stir-fry 3 minutes. Add beans; stir-fry 1 minute. Add tomatoes, sugar, fish sauce, and vinegar; stir-fry 1 minute or until beef reaches desired degree of doneness. Stir in basil. Yield: 5 servings (serving size: ¾ cup).

WINE NOTE: Here's a great example of a beef dish laced with lots of green flavors—in this case, lemongrass, lime, and basil. A Sauvignon Blanc, itself sporting green notes, would pair wonderfully with this dish. Try Jepson Sauvignon Blanc 1999 (Mendocino County, California; $11.)

CALORIES 202 (41% from fat); FAT 9.2g (sat 3.7g, mono 3.5g, poly 0.5g); PROTEIN 20.2g; CARB 10g; FIBER 1.4g; CHOL 45mg; IRON 2.7mg; SODIUM 1,100mg; CALC 50mg

Mortar and Pestle

Thai food is renowned for its complex and surprising flavors—often a result of the simple but precise process of pounding dried and fresh herbs and spices into a seasoning paste. Using a mortar and pestle not only bruises the ingredients to release natural oils, but also combines and purees. While traditional Thai mortars are made from stone, we successfully used a standard 1½-cup-capacity marble version. (If you don't have a mortar and pestle, we recommend using a food processor.)

Thai Grilled Chicken

2 tablespoons white peppercorns
1 tablespoon coriander seeds
1 cup minced fresh cilantro stems (optional)
3 tablespoons low-sodium soy sauce
2 tablespoons vegetable oil
1 teaspoon kosher or sea salt
10 garlic cloves, minced
2 chicken breast halves (about 1½ pounds)
2 chicken leg quarters (about 1½ pounds)
Cooking spray

1. Prepare grill.
2. Place peppercorns and coriander seeds in a large skillet over medium-high heat; cook 1 minute or until toasted. Place peppercorns and coriander seeds in a spice or coffee grinder; process until finely ground.
3. Combine pepper mixture, cilantro (if desired), and next 4 ingredients. Loosen skin from chicken breasts and thighs by inserting fingers, gently pushing between skin and meat. Rub seasoning mixture under loosened chicken skin. Place chicken in a large zip-top plastic bag. Seal and marinate in refrigerator 3 to 8 hours. Remove chicken from bag; discard marinade. Place chicken on grill rack coated with cooking spray; grill 8 minutes on each side or until chicken is done. Discard skin. Yield: 4 servings (serving size: 1 piece of chicken).

WINE NOTE: Lots of coriander, soy sauce, and garlic, plus the char from grilling, mean this chicken will need a boldly fruity, densely textured wine partner. A great bet: Dry Creek Vineyard Old Vines Zinfandel 1998 (Sonoma County, California; $19).

CALORIES 315 (29% from fat); FAT 10.3g (sat 2.3g, mono 3g, poly 3.2g); PROTEIN 49.6g; CARB 3.6g; FIBER 1g; CHOL 141mg; IRON 3mg; SODIUM 577mg; CALC 52mg

---

Glass-Noodle Salad with Chicken and Shrimp

DRESSING:
½ cup sugar
¼ cup Thai fish sauce
3 tablespoons palm sugar or light brown sugar
2 tablespoons cider vinegar
½ cup fresh lime juice
1 tablespoon minced fresh cilantro stems
1 teaspoon minced bird chile or 2 teaspoons minced serrano chile
1 garlic clove, minced

SALAD:
2 ounces uncooked bean threads (cellophane noodles)
2 cups chopped, cooked, peeled shrimp (about ½ pound)
6 ounces cooked chicken breast, cut into ¼-inch strips
2 cups torn romaine lettuce
1 cup chopped tomato
½ cup thinly sliced onion
⅓ cup thinly sliced celery
2 tablespoons chopped dry-roasted peanuts
2 tablespoons minced fresh cilantro stems
2 teaspoons minced bird chile or 4 teaspoons minced serrano chile

1. To prepare dressing, combine first 4 ingredients in a small saucepan. Bring to a boil, and cook 2 minutes or until sugar dissolves. Cool; stir in lime juice, 1 tablespoon cilantro, 1 teaspoon chile, and garlic.

2. To prepare salad, cook noodles in boiling water 1½ minutes; drain. Rinse with cold water. Drain. Coarsely chop noodles. Combine noodles, shrimp, and next 5 ingredients in a large bowl. Drizzle dressing over salad; toss gently to coat. Sprinkle with peanuts, 2 tablespoons cilantro, and 2 teaspoons chile. Yield: 5 servings (serving size: 1 cup).

CALORIES 249 (13% from fat); FAT 3.6g (sat 0.7g, mono 1.4g, poly 1.1g); PROTEIN 21.1g; CARB 34.5g; FIBER 1.6g; CHOL 113mg; IRON 2.7mg; SODIUM 1,250mg; CALC 60mg

---

Thai-Style Broiled Shrimp

This dish is typically served with the shells on the shrimp. But since it's tricky to devein jumbo shrimp and leave the shells intact, we removed them.

1 tablespoon white peppercorns
1 tablespoon minced fresh cilantro stems
1 tablespoon Thai fish sauce
1 teaspoon sugar
½ teaspoon minced bird chile or 1 teaspoon minced serrano chile
¼ teaspoon kosher or sea salt
12 jumbo shrimp (about 1 pound)
12 garlic cloves, minced
Cooking spray
3 tablespoons vegetable oil

1. Place peppercorns in a small skillet over medium-high heat; cook 1 minute or until toasted. Place peppercorns in a spice or coffee grinder, and process until finely ground.
2. Combine ground pepper, cilantro, and next 6 ingredients in a large zip-top plastic bag. Seal and marinate in refrigerator 30 minutes.
3. Preheat broiler.
4. Remove shrimp from bag, shaking off excess marinade; reserve marinade. Place shrimp on a broiler pan coated with cooking spray; broil 5 minutes on each side or until shrimp are done. Keep warm.
5. Heat oil in a large nonstick skillet over medium-high heat. Add marinade; sauté 1 minute or until garlic is golden. Remove from heat; stir in shrimp. Yield: 6 servings (serving size: 2 shrimp).

These superpeppery, super-garlicky shrimp need a counterpoint. A boldly fruity Riesling with just a touch of sweetness would make a great partner. Try Columbia Winery Cellarmasters Reserve Riesling 2000 (Columbia Valley, Washington state; $8).

CALORIES 136 (39% from fat); FAT 5.9g (sat 1.1g, mono 1.6g, poly 2.7g); PROTEIN 16g; CARB 4.2g; FIBER 0.4g; CHOL 115mg; IRON 2.3mg; SODIUM 426mg; CALC 57mg

Stir-Fried Tofu, Shiitake Mushrooms, and Chinese Peas

In this recipe, fresh ginger is combined with salt then sits for five minutes. The salt draws out some of the ginger juice, making it drier, which is better for stir-frying; it also decreases the ginger's pungency.

 1 tablespoon julienne-cut peeled
    fresh ginger
 ½ teaspoon kosher or sea salt
 1 teaspoon cornstarch
 1 tablespoon vegetable oil
 2 cups thinly sliced shiitake
    mushroom caps
 1 cup snow peas, trimmed
 ½ teaspoon minced bird chile or
    1 teaspoon minced serrano chile
 1 (12.3-ounce) package reduced-fat
    firm tofu, drained and cubed
 ½ cup (1-inch) sliced green onions
 3 tablespoons low-sodium soy sauce

1. Combine ginger and ½ teaspoon salt in a small bowl; let stand 5 minutes. Rinse ginger with cold water; pat dry. Combine ginger and cornstarch in bowl.
2. Heat oil in a wok or large nonstick skillet over medium-high heat. Add mushrooms, and stir-fry 2 minutes or until tender. Add ginger mixture, snow peas, and chile, and stir-fry 2 minutes. Add tofu; stir-fry 1 minute. Add onions and soy sauce; stir-fry 2 minutes. Yield: 2 servings (serving size: 1¾ cups).

CALORIES 208 (41% from fat); FAT 9.4g (sat 2g, mono 2.5g, poly 4g); PROTEIN 15.4g; CARB 16.2g; FIBER 3.4g; CHOL 0mg; IRON 4.7mg; SODIUM 775mg; CALC 120mg

Sour and Spicy Shrimp Soup

The key to the recipe is the flavorful broth, made by combining canned chicken broth, shrimp shells, chiles, and seasonings. After the mixture cooks for 30 minutes, it's strained and the seasonings are discarded. Look for dried japones chiles in your supermarket or through produce companies such as Melissa's (800-588-0151 or www.melissas.com).

 1½ pounds medium shrimp
  2 tablespoons vegetable oil
  6 dried japones or arbol chiles
  3 (15.75-ounce) cans fat-free,
     less-sodium chicken broth
 10 thinly sliced peeled fresh galangal
     pieces or 7 slices peeled fresh
     ginger, lightly crushed
  6 kaffir lime leaves or 2½ teaspoons
     grated lime rind
  4 bird chiles or serrano chiles,
     lightly crushed
  4 cilantro stems, lightly crushed
  2 stalks chopped peeled fresh lemon-
     grass, lightly crushed
  2 large shallots, peeled and halved
  3 tablespoons Thai fish sauce
  3 tablespoons fresh lime juice
 ½ cup cilantro leaves

1. Peel shrimp, reserving 6 shells; set shrimp aside. Heat oil in a large Dutch oven over medium-high heat. Add japones chiles and shrimp shells; sauté 3 minutes or until chiles are blackened. Add broth, and bring to a boil. Add galangal and next 5 ingredients. Cover, reduce heat to medium-low, and simmer 30 minutes.
2. Strain soup through a sieve into a bowl; discard solids. Return soup to pan. Increase heat to medium-high. Add shrimp and fish sauce; cook 2 minutes or until shrimp are done. Remove from heat; stir in lime juice. Sprinkle with cilantro leaves. Serve immediately. Yield: 7 servings (serving size: 1 cup).

CALORIES 135 (35% from fat); FAT 5.2g (sat 1g, mono 1.4g, poly 2.4g); PROTEIN 17.9g; CARB 6.6g; FIBER 0.2g; CHOL 111mg; IRON 2.1mg; SODIUM 1,118mg; CALC 48mg

Lemongrass Tips

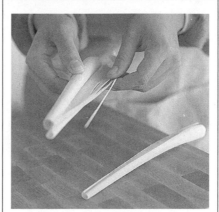

1. *Look for stalks that have thick, firm, heavy bulbs and tightly bound green leaves. You should smell the characteristic citrus scent when you press your fingernail into the bulb. Remove outer woody leaves to expose white inner core.*

2. *Thinly chop or slice core.*

3. *Crush slices with back of a knife to release aroma and oils.*

13 Key Ingredients in Thai Cooking

Turmeric Related to ginger, it gives food a golden color and a slightly pungent flavor. In Thai cuisine, turmeric root is grated or pounded to release its color and aroma. Since raw turmeric is not widely available in the United States, we've used the ground variety.

Bird chiles Although bird chiles are often identified with Thai cooking, they're actually from South America and have been embraced by Thai cooks only recently. Bird, or chiltepín, chiles are small, red or green, and very hot. Thai chiles, which look similar but are a bit larger, are just as hot and can be used in the same capacity. In the accompanying recipes, we call for milder serranos rather than Thai chiles as a substitute, though, because they're easier to find. In general, two bird chiles yield one teaspoon minced.

Garlic Most recipes incorporate garlic, a seasoning familiar to Thai cooking since ancient times.

Fresh mint Mint is used often in combination with cilantro to flavor and garnish salads. Thais tear mint by hand instead of slicing it. Once bruised, the leaves release a potent and refreshing aroma.

Shallots Thais love shallots for their mildly peppery taste and earthy scent. Thinly sliced fresh shallots are added to salads; minced shallots (which exude a liquid that helps blend other ingredients when pounded) are used for seasoning pastes.

Coriander Thais use every part of this aromatic herb for seasoning. The root is pounded with other ingredients into seasoning pastes; the seeds are ground and used to impart their grassy, peppery flavor to soups and curries. The stems and leaves, known as cilantro, are used as garnishes and in stir-fries, soups, and stews. While coriander root is important for Thai seasoning, it's not readily available, so we've substituted cilantro stems instead.

Thai white peppercorn An indigenous spice, Thai white peppercorn was used to add heat long before Westerners introduced chiles. You can use white peppercorn, commonly available in supermarkets, in place of the spicier Thai variety.

Kaffir lime leaves Along with lemongrass, kaffir lime leaf is closely identified with Thai cooking for its distinct citrusy aroma. Fresh leaves are hard to come by, but you can purchase them frozen in small bags at most Asian markets. If you can't find them, substitute lime zest.

Lemongrass Thai cooking has brought fame to this tart herb. Its white bulb is pulverized for seasoning pastes or added to perfume soups and stews, while the tender green stalk is thinly sliced for salads. Steeped in hot water, lemongrass also makes a refreshing tea. Look for it in the produce section of your supermarket or in Asian markets.

Galangal Also called Laos ginger, galangal is that distinctive Thai flavor most Americans can't identify. We found galangal, which you can buy in Asian markets, to be stronger, more astringent, and spicier than ginger, but you can substitute the latter.

Ginger The Chinese introduced this aromatic and pungent rhizome to the Thais. Its unmistakable peppery flavor adds a layer of spiciness.

Thai fish sauce Today, this ingredient is a must in Thai cooking, but like chiles, fish sauce is a latecomer to the cuisine. This condiment has gained favor over the use of fermented fish in many parts of Thailand and in the United States, because of its versatility and less intense taste and scent. It's still plenty potent, though—just a small spoonful makes a world of difference in Thai dishes.

Thai basil Thais use many varieties of basil, which taste more like licorice than the Italian kind. To retain Thai basil's fresh flavor, add it to stir-fries, soups, or stews at the last minute.

Laab
Northern Thai Spicy Beef Salad

The rice powder is a traditional component of this dish, but you can omit it, if you prefer.

RICE POWDER:
- ½ cup water
- 2 tablespoons uncooked long-grain Thai sticky rice

MARINADE:
- 1 teaspoon white peppercorns
- 1 teaspoon kosher or sea salt
- 6 garlic cloves, minced
- 1 (6-ounce) can pineapple juice
- 1½ pounds boneless sirloin steak, trimmed
- Cooking spray

REMAINING INGREDIENTS:
- 3 tablespoons fresh lime juice
- 1 cup torn fresh mint
- ⅓ cup coarsely chopped fresh cilantro leaves
- ¼ cup minced shallots
- 3 tablespoons thinly sliced green onions
- 2 tablespoons Thai fish sauce
- 1 tablespoon crushed red pepper
- 1 tablespoon thinly sliced kaffir lime leaves (about 8 leaves) or 1 tablespoon grated lime rind
- 1 teaspoon minced bird chile or 2 teaspoons minced serrano chile
- ½ teaspoon kosher or sea salt
- 12 tender napa (Chinese) cabbage leaves or any sturdy lettuce leaves

1. To prepare rice powder, combine water and rice in a bowl. Let stand 1 hour. Drain and rinse rice with cold water; pat dry. Cook rice in a small nonstick skillet over medium-high heat 7 minutes, stirring constantly until lightly browned. Cool completely. Place rice in a spice or coffee grinder; process until rice resembles cornmeal. Set aside.

2. To prepare marinade, place peppercorns in pan over medium-high heat, and cook 3 minutes, or until toasted, stirring constantly. Place peppercorns in spice or coffee grinder; process until ground. Combine ground pepper, 1 teaspoon salt, garlic, pineapple juice, and steak in a large zip-top plastic bag; seal and marinate in refrigerator 30 minutes.

3. Preheat broiler.

4. Remove steak from bag, reserving marinade. Place steak on a broiler pan coated with cooking spray. Broil 16 minutes or until desired degree of doneness, turning and basting with reserved marinade after 8 minutes. Cut steak diagonally across grain into thin slices. Cut slices crosswise into thin slivers. Combine steak and lime juice in a large bowl. Add rice powder, mint, and next 8 ingredients, and toss well. Spoon ⅓ cup steak mixture into each cabbage leaf. Yield: 6 servings (serving size: 2 filled leaves).

CALORIES 209 (27% from fat); FAT 6.3g (sat 2.2g, mono 2.4g, poly 0.4g); PROTEIN 25.7g; CARB 11.7g; FIBER 0.9g; CHOL 69mg; IRON 4.1mg; SODIUM 1,022mg; CALC 51mg

Coconut Soup with Chicken

4 cups water
1 (14-ounce) can coconut milk
½ cup sliced peeled fresh lemongrass, slightly crushed
20 pieces thinly sliced peeled galangal or 15 pieces thinly sliced peeled fresh ginger, slightly crushed
5 bird chiles or 4 serrano chiles, slightly crushed
5 kaffir lime leaves, slightly torn, or 1½ teaspoons grated lime rind
2 chicken breast quarters (about 1¾ pounds), skinned
2 chicken thigh quarters (about ¾ pound), skinned
¼ cup Thai fish sauce
3 tablespoons fresh lime juice
6 tablespoons chopped fresh cilantro

1. Combine water and coconut milk in a Dutch oven; bring to a boil over medium heat. Stir in lemongrass, galangal, chiles, and lime leaves; bring to a boil. Add chicken; cover, reduce heat, and simmer 50 minutes or until chicken is done.

2. Remove chicken from broth. Place chicken in a bowl; chill 15 minutes. Strain broth through a colander into a bowl; discard solids. Return broth to pan.

3. Remove chicken from bones, and cut meat into bite-size pieces. Discard bones. Return chicken to pan. Stir in fish sauce, and cook 1 minute over medium heat. Stir in lime juice. Remove soup from heat. Garnish with cilantro. Yield: 6 servings (serving size: 1 cup).

CALORIES 298 (51% from fat); FAT 17g (sat 13.3g, mono 1.4g, poly 0.9g); PROTEIN 33.3g; CARB 3.2g; FIBER 0.2g; CHOL 93mg; IRON 3.7mg; SODIUM 1,038mg; CALC 38mg

Thai-Style Pork Saté with Peanut Sauce

SAUCE:

5 dried japones or arbol chiles
½ teaspoon coriander seeds
½ teaspoon cumin seeds
½ teaspoon kosher or sea salt
1 garlic clove, minced
1 tablespoon minced peeled lemongrass
1 tablespoon minced peeled fresh ginger
1 tablespoon minced shallots
¾ cup light coconut milk
2 tablespoons creamy peanut butter
2 tablespoons palm sugar or light brown sugar
2 tablespoons fresh lime juice
1 tablespoon Thai fish sauce

MARINADE:

1 cup light coconut milk
1 tablespoon granulated sugar
3 tablespoons minced shallots
2 tablespoons low-sodium soy sauce
1 tablespoon minced peeled fresh ginger
1 teaspoon ground turmeric
1½ pounds pork tenderloin, trimmed and cut diagonally into thin slices
Cooking spray

1. To prepare sauce, place chiles in a bowl; cover with hot water. Let stand 30 minutes. Drain; finely chop chiles.

2. Place coriander and cumin seeds in a small skillet over medium-high heat; cook 1 minute or until toasted. Combine salt and garlic in a mortar and pestle; crush to form a paste. Add chiles, toasted seeds, lemongrass, 1 tablespoon

ginger, and 1 tablespoon shallots, one at a time, pounding until each ingredient is incorporated into paste before adding the next. Heat ¾ cup coconut milk in a small saucepan over medium heat. Add paste mixture, and cook 1 minute. Stir in peanut butter until smooth. Add sugar, juice, and fish sauce; cook 1 minute. Remove from heat; cool.

3. To prepare marinade, combine 1 cup coconut milk and next 5 ingredients in a large zip-top plastic bag. Add pork to bag. Seal and marinate in refrigerator 45 minutes. Remove pork from bag; discard marinade. Thread pork slices evenly onto 12 (6-inch) skewers.

4. Prepare grill.

5. Place skewers on grill rack coated with cooking spray, and grill 5 minutes on each side or until done. Serve with sauce. Yield: 6 servings (serving size: 2 skewers and 2 tablespoons sauce).

CALORIES 247 (35% from fat); FAT 9.5g (sat 4.6g, mono 2.8g, poly 1.2g); PROTEIN 26.2g; CARB 13.7g; FIBER 0.6g; CHOL 74mg; IRON 2.8mg; SODIUM 665mg; CALC 25mg

---

Adapting Thai Flavors to an American Kitchen

Peppers These recipes represent real Thai cooking and, as a result, are very spicy. If you don't like hot food, decrease the chiles and peppercorns.

Coconut milk To see just how much trouble extracting fresh coconut milk is, we tried it in our Test Kitchens. Although it's not hard, it's time-consuming. We tasted the fresh milk side by side with diluted canned coconut milk and found the two almost identical in taste.

Palm sugar Palm sugar is made from the sap of the sugar palm tree. In Thai markets, it's displayed in large mounds, scraped up with a paddle, and smeared onto the fresh banana leaves used to transport it. In Asian markets in the United States, it's sold in small, round crystallized blocks. Light brown sugar is an acceptable substitute.

Pie Worth Pursuing

The reader's gone missing, but this savory pie is destined to stay found.

We tried our best, but we couldn't find the reader who sent us this recipe. With deadlines approaching, we decided to go ahead and publish a lightened success story too good not to share.

When the recipe for Buttercrust Corn Pie with Fresh Tomato Salsa—hand written on an index card that looked like it came straight from a box on the reader's kitchen counter—arrived in our Test Kitchens, we couldn't wait to try it; it seemed just right for summer.

With a name like "buttercrust," you can guess where most of our challenges lay. The pie was a natural for all the fat-cutting tricks we've learned over the years.

We trimmed the butter, and added an egg white to hold the crust together. By substituting two egg whites for one of the whole eggs in the filling we cut even more fat. Snipping some Parmesan cheese and olives let us reduce fat even further without reducing the flavor. When we realized we could increase the corn and tomatoes at practically no cost to the calorie content, that's exactly what we did. With the two recipes side-by-side we agree the lightened version is a winner.

BEFORE		AFTER
SERVING SIZE		
1 wedge and ½ cup salsa		
CALORIES PER SERVING		
383		277
FAT		
24g		9.6g
PERCENT OF TOTAL CALORIES		
54%		30%
SODIUM		
930mg		758mg

Buttercrust Corn Pie with Fresh Tomato Salsa

Serve the salsa with a slotted spoon.

SALSA:

2½ cups chopped tomato
½ cup thinly sliced green onions
2 tablespoons chopped seeded jalapeño pepper
2 tablespoons fresh lemon juice
½ teaspoon salt
½ teaspoon dried oregano
⅛ teaspoon black pepper

PIE:

1¼ cups crushed fat-free saltine crackers (about 35 crackers)
3 tablespoons grated fresh Parmesan cheese
3 tablespoons butter, melted
1 large egg white, lightly beaten
Cooking spray
1¼ cups fat-free milk, divided
2¾ cups fresh corn kernels (about 5 ears)
1 teaspoon sugar
½ teaspoon onion salt
2 tablespoons all-purpose flour
½ cup thinly sliced green onions
3 tablespoons chopped ripe olives
2 large egg whites, lightly beaten
1 large egg, lightly beaten
⅛ teaspoon paprika

1. Preheat oven to 400°.
2. To prepare salsa, combine first 7 ingredients in a medium bowl.
3. To prepare pie, combine crackers, cheese, butter, and 1 egg white in a medium bowl. Toss with a fork until moist; reserve 2 tablespoons. Press remaining cracker mixture into bottom and up sides of a 9-inch pie plate coated with cooking spray. Bake at 400° for 5 minutes; cool on a wire rack.
4. Combine 1 cup milk, corn, sugar, and onion salt in a medium saucepan. Bring to a boil over medium heat; reduce heat, and simmer 3 minutes. Combine ¼ cup milk and flour in a small bowl; gradually add to corn mixture. Cook until thick (about 1 minute); remove from heat. Stir in ½ cup onions and olives. Combine 2 egg whites and egg in a small bowl; gradually add to corn mixture. Pour into prepared crust, and sprinkle with 2 tablespoons cracker mixture and paprika.
5. Bake at 400° for 20 minutes or until center is set. Yield: 6 servings (serving size: 1 wedge and ½ cup salsa).

CALORIES 277 (30% from fat); FAT 9.6g (sat 4.8g, mono 3g, poly 0.9g); PROTEIN 11.1g; CARB 40.2g; FIBER 3.9g; CHOL 54mg; IRON 2.3mg; SODIUM 758mg; CALC 140mg

A New Flame

Grill these hearty veggie dishes at your next cookout, and make even the most dedicated meat eaters envious.

Barbecued Tempeh Sandwiches Smothered with Peppers and Onions

Tempeh is a soybean cake with a slightly nutty flavor that pairs well with the sweet and spicy barbecue sauce. You can prepare the sauce and slice the vegetables and tempeh ahead of time.

⅓ cup ketchup
1 tablespoon brown sugar
1½ teaspoons vegetable oil
1½ teaspoons cider vinegar
1 teaspoon Dijon mustard
¼ teaspoon chili powder
¼ teaspoon low-sodium soy sauce
¼ teaspoon hot sauce
1 garlic clove, minced
1 (8-ounce) package tempeh
1 red bell pepper, cut in half
1 yellow bell pepper, cut in half
1 red onion, cut into ½-inch-thick slices
Cooking spray
4 (1½-ounce) hamburger buns

1. Prepare grill.
2. Combine first 9 ingredients in a small bowl, stirring with a whisk.
3. Cut tempeh in half lengthwise; cut slices in half. Brush tempeh slices, bell

peppers, and onion with ketchup mixture. Place on grill rack coated with cooking spray; grill 4 minutes on each side or until tempeh is thoroughly heated. Remove tempeh, bell peppers, and onion from grill. Cut bell peppers into ½-inch-wide strips; separate onions into rings.

4. Place 1 tempeh slice on bottom half of each bun. Top each tempeh slice with one-fourth of bell peppers, one-fourth of onion, and top half of bun. Yield: 4 servings (serving size: 1 sandwich).

CALORIES 309 (25% from fat); FAT 8.7g (sat 1.5g, mono 1.9g, poly 4.5g); PROTEIN 15.6g; CARB 45.2g; FIBER 3g; CHOL 0mg; IRON 3.6mg; SODIUM 531mg; CALC 130mg

---

Get Ready to Grill

All grilling—whether vegetables or meat—can be easy and hassle-free with a little indoor preparation to set the stage. Take time to organize so that once the grilling begins, all that remains to be done is a quick assembly for the final presentation. For these recipes, the soba salad should be ready for topping the grilled vegetables, the relish standing by to be matched with the burgers, and all sauces prepared before the grill is hot.

Black Bean Burgers with Spicy Cucumber and Red Pepper Relish

The cucumber releases some liquid while chilling, so serve the relish with a slotted spoon. Shape the patties, and wrap them in wax paper to transport them from the kitchen to the patio grill. Serve with baked potato chips and dill pickle spears.

RELISH:
⅔ cup finely chopped peeled
    cucumber
½ cup finely chopped red bell pepper
¼ cup finely chopped red onion
1 tablespoon fresh lime juice
1 tablespoon honey
1 teaspoon finely chopped dill
⅛ teaspoon salt
Dash of ground red pepper

BURGERS:
1 (15-ounce) can black beans, rinsed
    and drained
½ cup dry breadcrumbs
¼ cup minced red onion
½ teaspoon dried oregano
¼ teaspoon ground cumin
⅛ teaspoon black pepper
1 large egg
Cooking spray
¼ cup light mayonnaise
4 (1½-ounce) hamburger buns
Dill sprigs (optional)

1. To prepare relish, combine first 8 ingredients in a medium bowl. Cover and chill 2 hours.

2. To prepare burgers, place beans in a large bowl; partially mash with a fork. Stir in breadcrumbs and next 5 ingredients. Divide bean mixture into 4 equal portions, shaping each into a ½-inch-thick patty.

3. Prepare grill.

4. Place patties on grill rack coated with cooking spray; grill 5 minutes on each side or until thoroughly heated. Spread 1 tablespoon mayonnaise on bottom half of each bun; top each with a patty, ¼ cup relish, and top half of bun. Garnish with dill sprigs, if desired. Yield: 4 servings (serving size: 1 burger).

CALORIES 375 (23% from fat); FAT 9.5g (sat 1.9g, mono 2.4g, poly 3.7g); PROTEIN 14.6g; CARB 59.2g; FIBER 5.7g; CHOL 60mg; IRON 4.7mg; SODIUM 767mg; CALC 136mg

---

Invite the Neighbors Menu
serves 4

Grilled Stuffed Portobello Mushrooms

Grilled salmon fillets*

Spinach salad with sliced strawberries, feta cheese, and balsamic vinaigrette

Corn muffins

*Sprinkle 4 (6-ounce) salmon fillets evenly with ¼ teaspoon each of salt, pepper, and thyme. Top each fillet with a thin slice of lemon. Grill, skin side down, 10 minutes or until fish flakes easily when tested with a fork.

Grilled Stuffed Portobello Mushrooms

Since the garlic isn't really cooked, the mushrooms, which work as an appetizer or side, have a strong garlic flavor. Grill the mushrooms stem sides down first, so that when they're turned they'll be in the right position to be filled. If you want to plan ahead, remove the gills and stems from the mushrooms and combine the filling, then cover and chill until ready to grill.

⅔ cup chopped plum tomato
¼ cup (1 ounce) shredded part-skim
    mozzarella cheese
1 teaspoon olive oil, divided
½ teaspoon finely chopped fresh or
⅛ teaspoon dried rosemary
⅛ teaspoon coarsely ground black
    pepper
1 garlic clove, crushed
4 (5-inch) portobello mushroom caps
2 tablespoons fresh lemon juice
2 teaspoons low-sodium soy sauce
Cooking spray
2 teaspoons minced fresh parsley

1. Prepare grill.

2. Combine tomato, cheese, ½ teaspoon oil, rosemary, pepper, and garlic in a small bowl.

3. Remove brown gills from undersides of mushroom caps using a spoon, and discard gills. Remove stems; discard. Combine ½ teaspoon oil, juice, and soy sauce in a small bowl; brush over both sides of mushroom caps. Place mushroom caps, stem sides down, on grill rack coated with cooking spray, and grill 5 minutes on each side or until soft.

4. Spoon ¼ cup tomato mixture into each mushroom cap. Cover and grill 3 minutes or until cheese is melted. Sprinkle with parsley. Yield: 4 servings (serving size: 1 mushroom).

CALORIES 83 (38% from fat); FAT 3.5g (sat 1g, mono 1.2g, poly 0.4g); PROTEIN 5.4g; CARB 10.1g; FIBER 2.5g; CHOL 4mg; IRON 2.2mg; SODIUM 123mg; CALC 60mg

Tofu Pita with Peanut Sauce

Use the leftover coconut milk, which adds a subtle coconut flavor, to cook rice or couscous. You can prepare the sauce, cut the vegetables and pitas, and drain the tofu ahead of time so that all you have left to do is grill the tofu slices.

SAUCE:
- ¼ cup canned light coconut milk
- 2 tablespoons natural-style peanut butter (such as Smucker's)
- 1 tablespoon water
- 2 teaspoons brown sugar
- 2 teaspoons fresh lime juice
- 1 teaspoon low-sodium soy sauce
- ½ teaspoon curry powder
- ¼ teaspoon salt
- ¼ teaspoon crushed red pepper
- 1 garlic clove, minced

TOFU:
- 1 pound firm or extra-firm tofu, drained
- 1 tablespoon low-sodium soy sauce
- 1 teaspoon sesame oil
- ¼ teaspoon salt
- 1 red bell pepper, cut into 1-inch strips
- Cooking spray
- 3 cups trimmed watercress (about 2 bunches)
- 1 large cucumber, halved lengthwise, seeded, and chopped
- 3 (6-inch) pitas, cut in half

1. Prepare grill.

2. To prepare sauce, combine first 10 ingredients in a small bowl, stirring with a whisk.

3. To prepare tofu, cut tofu lengthwise into 3 slices. Cut tofu slices in half vertically. Place tofu slices on several layers of heavy-duty paper towels; cover with additional paper towels. Let stand 30 minutes, pressing down occasionally.

4. Combine 1 tablespoon soy sauce, oil, and ¼ teaspoon salt in a small bowl. Brush tofu slices with soy sauce mixture. Place tofu slices and bell pepper on grill rack coated with cooking spray, and grill 4 minutes on each side or until tofu is golden.

5. Combine sauce, bell pepper, watercress, and cucumber in a large bowl, tossing gently to coat. Fill each pita half with about ½ cup watercress mixture and 1 tofu slice. Yield: 6 servings (serving size: 1 filled pita half).

CALORIES 204 (36% from fat); FAT 8.1g (sat 1.5g, mono 2.5g, poly 3.4g); PROTEIN 11.2g; CARB 23.2g; FIBER 2.7g; CHOL 0mg; IRON 5.5mg; SODIUM 503mg; CALC 136mg

Soba Salad with Grilled Sweet Potato, Eggplant, and Red Pepper

To streamline the preparation, cook the noodles ahead of time, and have the vegetables already marinating in a bag. Another quick tip: Remove the potato slices from the simmering water using a slotted spoon, then return the water to a boil, and use the same pot to cook the soba. Use a spatula to carefully turn the potatoes on the grill so they won't stick.

- 12 (½-inch-thick) slices sweet potato (about 2 medium)
- ⅓ cup orange juice
- 2½ tablespoons molasses
- 1 tablespoon water
- 2 teaspoons vegetable oil
- 1½ teaspoons Dijon mustard
- 1 garlic clove, crushed
- 8 (½-inch-thick) slices eggplant (about 1 medium)
- 1 red bell pepper, cut into 4 wedges
- Cooking spray
- ⅓ cup thinly sliced green onions
- 1½ tablespoons low-sodium soy sauce
- 1 tablespoon sherry
- 1 tablespoon dark sesame oil
- 2 teaspoons brown sugar
- 1 teaspoon minced peeled fresh ginger
- 4 cups cooked soba (about 8 ounces uncooked buckwheat noodles)

1. Place potato slices in a saucepan, and cover with water; bring to a boil. Reduce heat, and simmer 5 minutes or until crisp-tender; drain. Rinse with cold water; drain well.

2. Combine juice and next 5 ingredients in a large zip-top plastic bag. Add potato slices, eggplant, and bell pepper to bag; seal and marinate in refrigerator 1 hour, turning bag occasionally. Remove vegetables from bag, reserving marinade.

3. Prepare grill.

4. Place vegetables on grill rack coated with cooking spray, and grill 4 minutes on each side or until done, basting frequently with ½ cup reserved marinade. Place vegetables on a platter; drizzle with remaining marinade.

5. Combine onions and next 5 ingredients. Place soba in a large bowl, and drizzle with dressing. Serve with vegetables. Yield: 4 servings (serving size: 1¼ cups soba mixture, 3 slices sweet potato, 2 slices eggplant, and 1 bell pepper wedge).

CALORIES 439 (15% from fat); FAT 7.3g (sat 1.1g, mono 2.2g, poly 2.9g); PROTEIN 10.1g; CARB 80.9g; FIBER 5.4g; CHOL 0mg; IRON 2.8mg; SODIUM 259mg; CALC 64mg

---

Playing with Fire

Whether you're cooking with gas, wood, or charcoal, make sure your grill is properly heated before you put food on it. The hand test is a reliable measure of the grill's readiness: Place your hand about two inches above the grate; if you can keep it there for only two to three seconds, then the grill is sufficiently heated. Once you place your items on the grate to begin cooking, don't move them around until they've had time to sear. This will prevent them from sticking and help create the "crust" that is so desirable with grilled food.

Soul Food

What do you get when you garden? Fresh vegetables, sure, but more than that, a solace to the spirit.

It's no secret that gardening is one of America's favorite activities, with some surveys suggesting that one in four people keeps some kind of garden. Born of a nation of farmers, Americans still seem to yearn for an abiding connection with the soil. A garden reconnects you with nature, nurtures you by bestowing food, and reminds you that some of life's most important pleasures can't be rushed.

Almost every garden yields far more than its steward needs. Having enough to share is a blessing acknowledged in all cultures. Yet a garden doesn't need to be big to reap benefits. If you've got a sunny step, you've got a place to tuck a tomato.

Whether you grow the season's delicacies yourself or someone else grows them for you, in the end they all add up to one thing...soul food. These recipes will help you put summer's riches to good use.

Tomato-and-Mango Salad with Curry-Orange Vinaigrette

This recipe is also delicious with peaches or nectarines in place of the mangoes.

    2   cups fresh orange juice (about 6
        oranges)
    1   tablespoon vegetable oil
    1   teaspoon curry powder
    ⅛   teaspoon salt
    3   medium tomatoes (about 1½
        pounds), cored and cut into
        ¾-inch-thick wedges
    2   medium mangoes (about 2
        pounds), peeled, pitted, and cut
        into ½-inch-thick strips
    1   tablespoon thinly sliced mint leaves

1. Bring orange juice to a boil in a medium saucepan. Reduce heat to medium, and cook until reduced to ½ cup (about 25 minutes). Remove from heat. Stir in oil, curry powder, and salt. Cool to room temperature.
2. Divide tomato wedges and mango strips evenly among 6 salad plates. Drizzle evenly with dressing; sprinkle with mint. Yield: 6 servings.

CALORIES 181 (16% from fat); FAT 3.2g (sat 0.6g, mono 0.9g, poly 1.3g); PROTEIN 2.3g; CARB 40.1g; FIBER 3.8g; CHOL 0mg; IRON 0.9mg; SODIUM 61mg; CALC 30mg

Roasted Red Pepper-and-Corn Salsa

To keep the corn from drying out on the grill, soak the ears in water first. You can grill the corn and bell peppers at the same time, but check the peppers earlier, since they cook faster. The salsa is great as an appetizer or as a topping for grilled meats, fish, or poultry.

    2   ears corn with husks (about 1¼
        pounds)
    2   red bell peppers
    2   tablespoons minced fresh parsley
    2   tablespoons fresh lemon juice
    1½ teaspoons minced seeded jalapeño
        pepper
    ¼   teaspoon salt

1. Cover corn with water; let stand 30 minutes. Drain. Remove husks from corn; discard husks. Scrub silks from corn; set corn aside.
2. Prepare grill.
3. Place corn on grill rack; cook 25 minutes or until corn is lightly browned, turning every 5 minutes. Cool. Cut kernels from ears of corn to measure 2 cups. Set kernels aside; discard cobs.
4. Cut bell peppers in half lengthwise; discard seeds and membranes. Flatten with hand; place bell pepper halves, skin sides down, on grill rack. Cook 20 minutes or until blackened. Place in a zip-top plastic bag; seal. Let stand 15 minutes. Peel and finely chop to measure ¾ cup.
5. Combine corn, bell peppers, and remaining ingredients in a medium bowl. Cover and chill. Yield: 5 servings (serving size: ½ cup).

CALORIES 42 (11% from fat); FAT 0.5g (sat 0.1g, mono 0.1g, poly 0.3g); PROTEIN 1.3g; CARB 9.8g; FIBER 1.7g; CHOL 0mg; IRON 0.7mg; SODIUM 124mg; CALC 5mg

Brown-Bag Lunch Menu

Prepare this meal the night before and dole out servings in zip-top plastic bags or plastic containers to carry to work. To make pita chips, bake pita wedges at 350° for 20 minutes.

Pasta with Corn, Beans, and Tomatoes

Pita chips

Fruit salad

Pasta with Corn, Beans, and Tomatoes

    8   ounces uncooked medium seashell
        pasta
    1   cup (1-inch) cut green beans
        (about ¼ pound)
    1   tablespoon olive oil
    3   cups fresh corn kernels (about 6
        ears)
    1½ cups finely chopped red bell
        pepper
    ¾   cup chopped green onions
    1   cup chopped seeded plum tomato
    6   tablespoons chopped fresh
        parsley, divided
    2   tablespoons chopped fresh mint
    1   tablespoon chopped fresh dill
    ½   teaspoon salt
    ¼   teaspoon black pepper
    1   cup (4 ounces) crumbled feta
        cheese
    6   lime wedges

1. Cook pasta in boiling water 10 minutes. Add green beans; cook 3 minutes. Drain well.

Continued

2. Heat oil in a large nonstick skillet over medium heat. Add corn, bell pepper, and onions; sauté 8 minutes. Add tomato, ¼ cup parsley, mint, dill, salt, and black pepper. Remove from heat. Stir in pasta mixture and cheese, and sprinkle with 2 tablespoons parsley. Serve with a lime wedge. Yield: 6 servings (serving size: 1½ cups).

CALORIES 304 (24% from fat); FAT 8.1g (sat 3.4g, mono 2.9g, poly 1.1g); PROTEIN 11.3g; CARB 49.7g; FIBER 5.2g; CHOL 17mg; IRON 3.3mg; SODIUM 430mg; CALC 130mg

Open-Faced Smoked Bell Pepper and Basil Sandwich with Goat Cheese Sauce

Buy a wide loaf of bakery bread for the base of this sandwich. Cutting the bread diagonally yields a surface area large enough for the topping.

BELL PEPPERS:
  2 cups hickory wood chips
  4 medium red bell peppers
Cooking spray
  ¼ cup thinly sliced fresh basil
  ¼ teaspoon salt
  ¼ teaspoon freshly ground black pepper

CROSTINI:
  4 (1-ounce) slices diagonally cut French bread (about ½ inch thick)
  1 large garlic clove

SAUCE:
  ¼ cup (2 ounces) goat cheese
  2½ tablespoons half-and-half
  ⅛ teaspoon salt

1. Prepare grill.
2. To prepare bell peppers, wrap wood chips in a double layer of foil; pierce foil packet several times. Place foil packet on grill rack; grill 10 minutes. Place bell peppers on grill rack coated with cooking spray; cover and grill 15 minutes or until blackened, turning occasionally. Place in a zip-top plastic bag; seal. Let stand 15 minutes. Peel and cut into

strips. Combine bell peppers, basil, ¼ teaspoon salt, and black pepper.
3. To prepare crostini, coat both sides of bread with cooking spray. Place on grill rack; grill 30 seconds on each side or until lightly browned. Remove from grill; rub each bread slice with garlic clove.
4. To prepare sauce, combine cheese, half-and-half, and ⅛ teaspoon salt in a small microwave-safe bowl. Microwave at HIGH 25 seconds; stir well with a whisk.
5. Top each crostino with about ⅓ cup bell peppers; drizzle each with about 1 tablespoon sauce. Yield: 4 servings.

CALORIES 134 (29% from fat); FAT 4.3g (sat 2g, mono 1g, poly 0.5g); PROTEIN 4.5g; CARB 19.8g; FIBER 2.1g; CHOL 10mg; IRON 1.7mg; SODIUM 475mg; CALC 77mg

Summer Tomato-and-Carrot Soup

  2½ teaspoons olive oil
  1 cup chopped onion
  ½ cup chopped carrot
  6 cups chopped seeded peeled tomato (about 3½ pounds)
  ¼ teaspoon black pepper
  1 (14½-ounce) can vegetable broth
  6 tablespoons plain fat-free yogurt
  1 tablespoon minced fresh tarragon

1. Heat oil in a large saucepan over medium heat. Add onion and carrot; sauté 5 minutes or until tender. Add tomato; cook 10 minutes. Stir in pepper and broth; cook 10 minutes. Pour half of tomato mixture into blender; process until smooth. Pour soup into a large bowl. Repeat procedure with remaining tomato mixture. Ladle 1 cup soup into each of 6 serving bowls; top each serving with 1 tablespoon yogurt and ½ teaspoon tarragon. Yield: 6 servings.

CALORIES 84 (31% from fat); FAT 2.9g (sat 0.4g, mono 1.5g, poly 0.4g); PROTEIN 2.8g; CARB 13.9g; FIBER 2.8g; CHOL 0mg; IRON 1.1mg; SODIUM 331mg; CALC 49mg

Grilled Flank Steak with Roasted-Poblano Relish

Poblanos are large, dark-green chiles that are surprisingly mild. They can be roasted, peeled, and seeded much like a bell pepper can.

  6 poblano chiles (about 1 pound)
  2 tablespoons chopped fresh cilantro
  1 tablespoon fresh lime juice
  ½ teaspoon salt, divided
  ¼ teaspoon black pepper, divided
  1 (1-pound) flank steak, trimmed

1. Prepare grill.
2. Cut poblanos in half lengthwise; discard seeds and membranes. Place poblanos, skin sides down, on grill rack. Grill 15 minutes or until blackened. Place in a zip-top plastic bag; seal. Let stand 15 minutes. Peel and dice. Place in a small bowl. Stir in cilantro, juice, ¼ teaspoon salt, and ⅛ teaspoon black pepper.
3. Sprinkle steak with ¼ teaspoon salt and ⅛ teaspoon black pepper. Place on grill rack; grill 8 minutes on each side or until meat thermometer registers 145° (medium-rare) or until desired degree of doneness. Remove from grill; let stand 5 minutes. Cut steak diagonally across grain into thin slices. Serve with relish. Yield: 4 servings (serving size: 3 ounces steak and about ⅓ cup relish).

CALORIES 239 (41% from fat); FAT 10.9g (sat 4.6g, mono 4.3g, poly 0.6g); PROTEIN 24.9g; CARB 11.2g; FIBER 2.1g; CHOL 57mg; IRON 3.8mg; SODIUM 384mg; CALC 28mg

Spicy Cucumber Salad with Peanuts

Try this Thai-inspired salad with chicken or fish. The sugar in the dressing balances the heat of the red pepper. Salting the cucumber slices draws out some of the moisture, so they're especially crisp in the salad.

1½   pounds cucumber, peeled, halved lengthwise, and thinly sliced (about 4 cups)
2   teaspoons kosher salt
½   cup rice vinegar
½   cup water
3   tablespoons sugar
¼   teaspoon crushed red pepper
2   tablespoons minced red onion
1   tablespoon chopped dry-roasted peanuts

1. Place cucumber slices in a colander; sprinkle with salt. Toss well. Drain 1 hour. Place cucumber slices on several layers of paper towels; cover with additional paper towels. Let stand 5 minutes, pressing down occasionally. Rinse and pat dry.
2. Combine vinegar, water, sugar, and pepper in a small saucepan. Bring to a boil. Reduce heat; cook until reduced to ⅓ cup (about 10 minutes). Remove vinegar reduction from heat; cool. Stir in onion. Combine cucumbers and vinegar reduction in a medium bowl; toss well. Sprinkle with peanuts. Yield: 4 servings (serving size: ¾ cup).

CALORIES 76 (17% from fat); FAT 1.4g (sat 0.2g, mono 0.6g, poly 0.5g); PROTEIN 1.6g; CARB 14.6g; FIBER 1.5g; CHOL 0mg; IRON 0.3mg; SODIUM 247mg; CALC 27mg

Green and Yellow Bean Salad with Chunky Tomato Dressing and Feta Cheese

Yellow wax beans in the salad complement a traditional green bean salad nicely. If wax beans are unavailable, use extra green beans in their place.

¾   pound wax beans, trimmed
¾   pound green beans, trimmed
2   cups chopped tomato
1   tablespoon sherry vinegar
2   teaspoons extra-virgin olive oil
½   teaspoon salt
¼   teaspoon freshly ground black pepper
½   cup thinly sliced fresh basil
½   cup (2 ounces) crumbled feta cheese

1. Cook beans in boiling water 5 minutes or until crisp-tender. Drain and rinse with cold water.
2. Combine tomato and next 4 ingredients in a bowl. Divide beans evenly among 8 plates. Spoon ¼ cup tomato mixture over each serving. Sprinkle each serving with 1 tablespoon sliced basil and 1 tablespoon cheese. Yield: 8 servings.

CALORIES 67 (39% from fat); FAT 2.9g (sat 1.3g, mono 1.2g, poly 0.3g), PROTEIN 3g; CARB 8.7g; FIBER 2.3g; CHOL 6mg; IRON 1.1mg; SODIUM 246mg; CALC 73mg

---

Favorite Vegetable Varieties and Tips from the Pros

CORN Brad Hunter of Appleton, Maine, is a sail maker and a farm manager for Appleton Creamery, a goat dairy he operates with his wife, Caitlan, a cheese maker. **Favorite corn varieties:** Early Choice and Kandy Korn. **Top tip:** "Plant corn in blocks, not rows; grow an early and a later variety to stagger harvest."

CUCUMBERS Jamie MacMillan is a carpenter and gardener from Islesboro, Maine. **Favorite cucumber varieties:** The Japanese varieties, especially Suyo: "They're sweet and prolific." **Top tip:** "Watering is very important. Pick cukes young, before they get pithy."

GREEN BEANS Terri Wuori from Islesboro, Maine, is a carpenter and gardener. **Favorite bean varieties:** Provider (bush, early) "for good flavor, and it freezes well"; Fortex (pole) and Kentucky Wonder (pole), "because you can harvest them over the whole summer." **Top tip:** "Prepare the soil well, and cultivate or mulch to preserve moisture."

PEPPERS Amy LeBlanc, a small-market gardener and heirloom-vegetable specialist, lives in East Wilton, Maine. **Favorite pepper varieties:** Gypsy and Hungarian Hot Wax. **Top tip:** "Even people with just a front step can successfully grow most peppers in containers. Start with a good potting soil, and don't ever fertilize, but water every single day. Find that sunny spot, and put your pot there. And you can take it inside in the winter."

TOMATOES Kristie Scott, a cookbook author and caterer, lives in Lincolnville Beach, Maine. **Favorite tomato varieties:** Heirloom and old standard varieties, like Black Russian, "which is unusual looking and very sweet"; both Yellow and Red Romas "for making paste and pastas, as well as for the table." **Top tip:** "Lay tomato plants in a trench, burying the stems almost all the way up to the bottom set of leaves when you plant. And mulch the plants to conserve water, but only after they're established."

Starting from Scratch

A health-minded Montana reader skips shortcuts to go the culinary distance.

Karen Rose of Three Forks, Montana, insists on making virtually every family meal from scratch. "I've always cooked that way because it's so much healthier for my family," she explains. "If you read the labels on precooked, prepackaged foods, all you see is fat, sodium, and sugar. Besides, I think my dinners taste better!"

True to form, Karen didn't run to the bakery to pick up dessert for a going-away party she threw a few years back. Instead, she went to work punching up the flavor of a light chocolate-amaretto cheesecake recipe a friend had given her. The result looked and tasted so much like its full-fat version that several guests asked for the recipe.

Creamy Chocolate-Amaretto Cheesecake

Karen likes to top this cheesecake with crushed chocolate wafers, chocolate chips, or slivered almonds. For our testing purposes we used semisweet chocolate minichips.

    6 chocolate wafers (about 1½ ounces)
    Cooking spray
    1 cup sugar
    1 cup 1% low-fat cottage cheese
    ½ cup (4 ounces) block-style fat-free
       cream cheese
    6 tablespoons unsweetened cocoa
    ¼ cup all-purpose flour
    ¼ cup amaretto (almond-flavored
       liqueur)
    1 teaspoon vanilla extract
    ¼ teaspoon salt
    1 (8-ounce) block ⅓-less-fat cream
       cheese
    1 large egg
    2 tablespoons semisweet chocolate
       minichips

1. Preheat oven to 300°.
2. Place wafers in a food processor, and pulse until coarsely ground. Sprinkle crumbs into bottom of an 8-inch springform pan coated with cooking spray.
3. Place sugar and next 8 ingredients in a food processor, and process until smooth. Add egg; process until blended. Pour cheese mixture into prepared pan, and sprinkle with minichips. Bake at 300° for 55 minutes or until center barely moves when pan is touched. Remove cheesecake from oven, and run a knife around outside edge. Cool to room temperature. Cover and chill at least 8 hours. Yield: 8 servings (serving size: 1 wedge).

CALORIES 292 (30% from fat); FAT 9.7g (sat 5.7g, mono 2.5g, poly 0.4g); PROTEIN 10.9g; CARB 40.2g; FIBER 0.4g; CHOL 52mg; IRON 1.2mg; SODIUM 418mg; CALC 76mg

Quick Salsa

"The best thing about this salsa is that everything can be thrown into the blender with very little chopping—you can even leave some stems on the cilantro. It takes no more than five minutes from start to finish. I frequently make it for dinner parties and other gatherings, and it's so popular that I end up giving away several copies of the recipe every time."

—Kristy Ossege, Tempe, Arizona

    ¾ cup chopped red onion
    ½ cup minced fresh cilantro
    1 (10-ounce) can diced tomatoes and
       green chiles, undrained (such as
       Rotel)
    1 (10-ounce) can diced tomatoes
       with lime juice and cilantro,
       undrained (such as Rotel)
    1 garlic clove

1. Place all ingredients in a blender, and process until smooth. Serve salsa with low-fat tortilla chips. Yield: 3 cups (serving size: ¼ cup).

CALORIES 17 (0% from fat); FAT 0g; PROTEIN 0.2g; CARB 2.8g; FIBER 0.3g; CHOL 0mg; IRON 0.2mg; SODIUM 200mg; CALC 6mg

Black-Bean Quesadillas with Goat Cheese

"Before he tried these quesadillas, my boyfriend wouldn't eat beans. Now, he can't get enough of them! All of my health-conscious friends love this creamy, flavorful dish. The key ingredient is the cumin: It brings everything together."

—Danushka Lysek, New York, New York

    2 teaspoons olive oil, divided
    1 cup chopped onion
    2 garlic cloves, minced
    ½ cup salsa
    ¼ teaspoon ground cumin
    1 (19-ounce) can black beans,
       undrained
    ⅓ cup minced fresh cilantro
    1 (4-ounce) package goat cheese,
       crumbled
    8 (8-inch) flour tortillas
    ½ cup fat-free sour cream
    ½ cup salsa

1. Heat 1 teaspoon olive oil in a large nonstick skillet over medium-high heat. Add onion and garlic, and sauté 3 minutes. Stir in ½ cup salsa, cumin, and beans, and bring to a boil. Reduce heat, and simmer 5 minutes or until thick. Mash bean mixture slightly with a potato masher. Remove from heat; stir in cilantro and goat cheese.
2. Spread bean mixture evenly over 4 tortillas; top each with 1 tortilla, pressing gently.
3. Heat ¼ teaspoon olive oil in pan over medium-high heat. Add 1 quesadilla, and cook 2 minutes on each side. Repeat procedure with remaining olive oil and quesadillas. Cut each quesadilla into 6 wedges. Serve with fat-free sour cream and ½ cup salsa. Yield: 8 servings (serving size: 3 quesadilla wedges, 1 tablespoon sour cream, and 1 tablespoon salsa).

CALORIES 279 (24% from fat); FAT 7.3g (sat 2.8g, mono 2.6g, poly 1.4g); PROTEIN 12.8g; CARB 41.3g; FIBER 5g; CHOL 13mg; IRON 3.2mg; SODIUM 662mg; CALC 152mg

Low-Fat Italian-Style Bread

"I sometimes include a touch of oregano to add some 'herbiness' to the bread. It fills the kitchen with a wonderful aroma while it bakes, and because the recipe makes two loaves, I usually keep one and give the other to a friend. I like to serve this bread with salad, soup, chili, or stew."

—Anne M. Ausderau,
Albuquerque, New Mexico

1 package dry yeast (about 2¼ teaspoons)
1 tablespoon sugar
2 cups warm water (100° to 110°)
6 cups all-purpose flour, divided
2 teaspoons salt
Cooking spray
2 tablespoons cornmeal
2 tablespoons cold water

1. Dissolve yeast and sugar in warm water in a large bowl; let stand 5 minutes. Lightly spoon flour into dry measuring cups, and level with a knife. Add 5¾ cups flour and salt to yeast mixture, and beat with a mixer at medium speed until smooth. Turn dough out onto a floured surface. Knead until smooth and elastic (about 10 minutes); add enough of remaining flour, 1 tablespoon at a time, to prevent dough from sticking to hands (dough will feel tacky).
2. Place dough in a large bowl coated with cooking spray, turning to coat top. Cover and let rise in a warm place (85°), free from drafts, 45 minutes or until doubled in size. (Press two fingers into dough. If indentation remains, dough has risen enough.) Punch dough down; cover and let rest 5 minutes. Divide in half. Working with one portion at a time (cover remaining dough to keep from drying), shape each portion into a 12-inch loaf on a floured surface. Place loaves on a large baking sheet coated with cooking spray and sprinkled with cornmeal. Cover and let rise 15 minutes.
3. Uncover dough. Brush loaves with cold water; make 5 diagonal cuts ¼ inch deep across top of each loaf using a sharp knife. Place baking sheet in cold oven, and set to 400°. Bake for 40 minutes or until loaves are browned on bottom and sound hollow when tapped. Remove from baking sheet, and cool on wire racks. Yield: 2 loaves, 12 servings per loaf (serving size: 1 slice).

CALORIES 120 (3% from fat); FAT 0.4g (sat 0.1g, mono 0g, poly 0.1g); PROTEIN 3.4g; CARB 25g; FIBER 1g; CHOL 0mg; IRON 1.5mg; SODIUM 196mg; CALC 5mg

Shrimp on the Barbie for Two Menu
serves 2

While the grill is heating and the shrimp are marinating, prepare the jícama salad. Don't forget the baguette—it's great for sopping up the sauce.

Tequila-Cane Shrimp

Jícama salad*

Baguette

Vanilla frozen yogurt with fat-free caramel sauce

*Combine 1 cup julienne-cut peeled jícama, 1 cup orange sections, 2 tablespoons chopped green onions, and 1 tablespoon bottled low-fat vinaigrette. Cover and chill.

Tequila-Cane Shrimp

"Since we're originally from the Southwest, chiles, cumin, and other spicy foods are always in our pantry. The sweetness of the cane syrup in this dish balances the heat from the chipotles—a great combination."

—Joshua Wilkinson, Beaverton, Oregon

1 to 2 tablespoons chopped drained canned chipotle chiles in adobo sauce
¼ cup tequila
¼ cup cane or maple syrup
½ teaspoon ground cumin
¼ teaspoon salt
¼ teaspoon black pepper
1 garlic clove, minced
24 medium shrimp, peeled and deveined (about ¾ pound)
Cooking spray

1. Prepare grill.
2. Place chipotle chiles in a zip-top plastic bag. Add tequila and next 5 ingredients to bag, and stir well. Add shrimp; seal and marinate in refrigerator 20 minutes. Remove shrimp from bag, reserving marinade. Place reserved marinade in a small saucepan; bring to a boil, and cook 2 minutes. Remove from heat.
3. Thread shrimp onto 6 (6-inch) skewers. Place shrimp on a grill rack coated with cooking spray, and grill 2 minutes on each side or until shrimp are done. Serve with sauce. Yield: 2 servings (serving size: 3 kebabs and about 3 tablespoons sauce).
NOTE: Place remaining chiles in adobo sauce in an airtight container; freeze or refrigerate for another use. Look for cane syrup with other syrups at the grocery store.

CALORIES 353 (9% from fat); FAT 3.7g (sat 0.6g, mono 0.7g, poly 1.4g); PROTEIN 35g; CARB 44.1g; FIBER 0.4g; CHOL 259mg; IRON 6.1mg; SODIUM 680mg; CALC 131mg

Bread Pudding with Rum Sauce

"This pudding is even better when the bread is a bit dried out. It can be assembled ahead of time, then popped into the oven about 45 minutes before serving. The sauce can also be made ahead of time, then warmed up over low heat. It smells as good as it tastes, too. The cinnamon scent permeates the house."

—Connie Sarros, Cuyahoga Falls, Ohio

PUDDING:

1 cup 1% low-fat milk
½ cup raisins
½ cup packed light brown sugar
⅓ cup granulated sugar
1¼ teaspoons vanilla extract
½ teaspoon ground cinnamon
1 (12-ounce) can evaporated fat-free milk
3 large egg whites
1 large egg
10 cups (½-inch) cubed white bread (about 14 [½-ounce] slices)
Cooking spray

Continued

SAUCE:

- 1 cup 1% low-fat milk
- 1 tablespoon cornstarch
- ½ cup granulated sugar
- 2 tablespoons butter
- 3 tablespoons white rum

1. To prepare pudding, combine first 9 ingredients in a large bowl, and stir well with a whisk. Add bread cubes, and toss gently. Cover and chill 1 hour.

2. Preheat oven to 350°.

3. Spoon bread mixture into an 11 x 7-inch baking dish coated with cooking spray. Bake bread mixture at 350° for 45 minutes or until set.

4. To prepare sauce, combine 1 cup low-fat milk and cornstarch in a bowl. Combine ½ cup granulated sugar and butter in a medium saucepan over medium heat. Add low-fat milk mixture; bring to a boil. Cook mixture until thick (about 4 minutes), stirring constantly. Remove from heat; stir in rum. Yield: 10 servings (serving size: 1 piece bread pudding and 2 tablespoons rum sauce).

CALORIES 268 (15% from fat); FAT 4.5g (sat 2.2g, mono 1.4g, poly 0.4g); PROTEIN 7.9g; CARB 49.7g; FIBER 0.8g; CHOL 32mg; IRON 1.2mg; SODIUM 236mg; CALC 198mg

Horseradish Beets

"This recipe was passed down to me from my mother. It's very simple to make with canned beets, although you can use fresh beets if you don't mind the work. I like to serve it with leg of lamb, along with carrots, potatoes, and hot rolls. It keeps well in the fridge, too."

—Nancy Moran, Sarasota, Florida

- 1 (15-ounce) can sliced beets, undrained
- 3 tablespoons sugar
- 2 tablespoons prepared horseradish
- 1½ tablespoons cider vinegar
- 1 tablespoon cornstarch
- 1 tablespoon butter
- ⅛ teaspoon salt

1. Preheat oven to 350°.

2. Drain beets in a colander over a bowl, reserving juice. Combine beet

juice, sugar, and next 5 ingredients in a small saucepan; bring to a boil. Reduce heat; simmer until thick (about 2 minutes). Stir in beets. Place beet mixture in a 1-quart baking dish. Cover and bake at 350° for 35 minutes. Yield: 4 servings (serving size: ½ cup).

CALORIES 104 (26% from fat); FAT 3g (sat 1.8g, mono 0.9g, poly 0.2g); PROTEIN 1g; CARB 19.4g; FIBER 1.5g; CHOL 8mg; IRON 0.8mg; SODIUM 394mg; CALC 20mg

Mini-Spanakopitas
Greek Spinach Pies

"I like to make individual bundles and serve them as appetizers or as an accompaniment to a fish or meat dish for dinner. They taste best with fresh spinach. You can prepare the filling well ahead of time and keep it in the fridge."

—Jan McFarlane, Scottsdale, Arizona

FILLING:

- 1 (10-ounce) package fresh spinach, coarsely chopped
- ⅓ cup (about 1½ ounces) feta cheese, crumbled
- ¼ cup 1% low-fat cottage cheese
- 2 tablespoons grated Parmesan cheese
- 2 teaspoons olive oil
- 1½ cups chopped green onions
- 1½ tablespoons chopped fresh or 1½ teaspoons dried dill
- 1 tablespoon fresh lemon juice
- ¼ teaspoon salt
- ¼ teaspoon black pepper
- 2 large egg whites, lightly beaten

REMAINING INGREDIENTS:

- 1 tablespoon olive oil
- ¼ teaspoon salt
- 1 large egg white
- 5 sheets frozen phyllo dough, thawed

1. Preheat oven to 350°.

2. To prepare filling, place spinach in a large skillet or Dutch oven. Place over medium heat; cook until spinach wilts. Place spinach in a colander, pressing until barely moist. Combine spinach and cheeses in a bowl; set aside.

3. Heat 2 teaspoons olive oil in a non-stick skillet over medium-high heat. Add green onions; sauté 2 minutes or until soft. Stir green onions, dill, and next 4 ingredients into spinach mixture.

4. Combine 1 tablespoon olive oil, ¼ teaspoon salt, and 1 egg white in a small bowl, stirring with a whisk. Working with 1 phyllo sheet at a time, (cover remaining phyllo dough to keep it from drying) cut each sheet lengthwise into 4 (3½-inch-wide) strips; lightly brush phyllo sheet with egg mixture. Spoon about 1 tablespoon spinach mixture onto one end of each strip. Fold one corner of strip over mixture, forming a triangle; keep folding back and forth into a triangle to end of strip.

5. Place triangles, seam sides down, on a baking sheet. Bake at 350° for 20 minutes or until golden. Yield: 20 appetizers (serving size: 1 triangle).

CALORIES 43 (44% from fat); FAT 2.1g (sat 0.6g, mono 1.1g, poly 0.3g); PROTEIN 2.3g; CARB 4g; FIBER 0.8g; CHOL 2mg; IRON 0.8mg; SODIUM 147mg; CALC 44mg

july

Lobster Comes Home

The best locale to eat a lobster dinner is on the Maine coast. The second best? Your place.

Forget the restaurant scenario—bib, shellfish fork, white linen tablecloth. As those from New England have always known, lobster is best served outdoors, informally, and preferably with a view of the water. Mainers pull the sweet white meat from the shell to savor right away, mix it with mayonnaise for a chilled salad, or add it to a thick chowder. But if you can't make it to the coast there's no need to worry. With lobster now so widely available, you can enjoy a shore dinner wherever you are.

Boiled Lobster

3 gallons water
¾ cup salt
4 (1½-pound) live Maine lobsters

1. Bring water and salt to a boil in a 5-gallon stockpot. Add lobsters. Cover and cook 12 minutes or until shells are bright orange-red and tails are curled. Yield: 4 servings (serving size: 1 lobster).

CALORIES 111 (6% from fat); FAT 0.7g (sat 0.1g, mono 0.2g, poly 0.1g); PROTEIN 23.2g; CARB 1.5g; FIBER 0g; CHOL 82mg; IRON 0.5mg; SODIUM 2,189mg; CALC 70mg

Lobster Roll

This salad is also great over greens for a main dish.

4 cups cooked lobster meat, cut into bite-size pieces
½ cup low-fat mayonnaise
¼ cup chopped green onions
1 tablespoon chopped celery
1 tablespoon fresh lemon juice
½ teaspoon salt
Dash hot sauce
4 hot dog buns

1. Combine first 7 ingredients. Spoon ¾ cup lobster salad into each bun. Yield: 4 servings.

CALORIES 352 (13% from fat); FAT 5.2g (sat 0.7g, mono 0.6g, poly 2.2g); PROTEIN 42.1g; CARB 31.2g; FIBER 1.2g; CHOL 136mg; IRON 2.1mg; SODIUM 1,516mg; CALC 175mg

Lobster Chowder

If you're using store-bought lobster meat, you can substitute equal parts clam juice and chicken broth for the lobster stock, which is made from the lobster shells. The chowder also works with two pounds of shrimp, substituting shrimp shells for lobster shells. This soup tastes best after it's spent an hour or two in the refrigerator, but you can serve it immediately, if you prefer.

2 (1½-pound) live Maine lobsters or 2½ cups chopped cooked lobster meat
3 gallons water
¾ cup salt
8 cups water
2 bay leaves
2 bacon slices, chopped
1 cup chopped green onions
1 teaspoon Hungarian sweet paprika
½ teaspoon ground cumin
2 cups diced peeled baking potato
1 cup half-and-half
2 teaspoons sugar
½ teaspoon salt
¼ teaspoon white pepper
2 cups fresh corn kernels (about 4 ears)
Chopped fresh chives (optional)

1. Bring 3 gallons of water and ¾ cup salt to a boil in a 5-gallon stockpot. Add lobsters. Cover and cook 10 minutes or until shells are bright orange-red and tails are curled. Remove from pan; cool. Remove meat from shells. Coarsely chop meat; refrigerate.

2. Combine lobster shells, 8 cups water, and bay leaves in stockpot. Bring to a boil, reduce heat, and simmer 1 hour. Strain lobster stock through a colander into a large bowl; discard shells. Reserve 4 cups.

3. Cook bacon in a large Dutch oven over medium-high heat until crisp. Add onions; sauté 2 minutes. Stir in paprika and cumin. Add reserved 4 cups stock and potato; bring to a boil. Cook 15 minutes or until potato is tender. Remove from heat. Stir in lobster meat, half-and-half, sugar, ½ teaspoon salt, and pepper. Cover pan, and refrigerate 1 hour, if desired.

4. Return pan to low heat. Add corn; cook 5 minutes. Garnish with chives, if desired. Yield: 8 servings (serving size: 1 cup).

CALORIES 204 (35% from fat); FAT 7.9g (sat 3.7g, mono 2.8g, poly 0.8g); PROTEIN 13.2g; CARB 21g; FIBER 2.2g; CHOL 49mg; IRON 0.9mg; SODIUM 385mg; CALC 71mg

---

Lobster Know-How

Buy only live lobsters. The more active they are—legs, claws, and tails moving—the better. Once you get the lobsters home, it's best to cook them immediately. (If you're sensitive about dropping live lobsters into boiling water, consider that they're invertebrates; with a simple nervous system and no brain, they're incapable of feeling pain. If you're still concerned, the University of Maine's Lobster Institute has determined that 10 minutes in the freezer before cooking helps minimize movement after the lobster is dropped into the water—a reflex commonly mistaken for an indication of pain.) If you can't cook them immediately, you can refrigerate lobsters with hard shells, covered with a damp cloth or seaweed, for up to 24 hours. Cooked lobster meat can be refrigerated for two to three days.

Stuffed Lobster

4 (1¼-pound) lobsters, cooked
2 cups crushed reduced-fat round buttery crackers (such as Ritz)
¼ cup chopped fresh parsley
3 tablespoons fresh Parmesan cheese
2½ tablespoons butter, melted
2 tablespoons fresh lemon juice
2 tablespoons Worcestershire sauce
4 lemon wedges

1. Preheat broiler.
2. Remove meat from cooked lobster tail and claws, and chop meat. Set lobster tail shells aside. Combine lobster, crackers, and next 5 ingredients in a large bowl. Divide lobster mixture evenly among tail shells. Broil stuffed lobster tails 8 minutes or until golden brown. Serve with lemon wedges. Yield: 4 servings (serving size: 1 stuffed lobster tail and 1 lemon wedge).
NOTE: You can also use 6 frozen lobster tails, cooked, for this recipe, reserving just 4 of the tails to stuff.

CALORIES 379 (37% from fat); FAT 15.5g (sat 7.6g, mono 5.5g, poly 1.7g); PROTEIN 25.9g; CARB 30.7g; FIBER 0.1g; CHOL 95mg; IRON 2.1mg; SODIUM 990mg; CALC 243mg

Lobster Hash

This traditional New England dish is perfect for breakfast or dinner.

4 cups coarsely chopped cooked lobster meat (about 2¼ pounds lobster)
4 cups chopped cooked peeled red potato
1 cup finely chopped green onions
½ cup chopped red bell pepper
1 teaspoon dried thyme
¾ teaspoon salt
¼ teaspoon black pepper
2 tablespoons butter
1 tablespoon fresh lemon juice

1. Combine first 7 ingredients in a large bowl; cover and chill 1 hour.
2. Heat butter in a large nonstick skillet over medium heat. Add lobster mixture to pan, spreading evenly. Cook lobster

mixture 10 minutes on each side or until lightly browned. Sprinkle with lemon juice. Yield: 4 servings (serving size: about 1⅓ cups).

CALORIES 393 (16% from fat); FAT 7.2g (sat 3.9g, mono 2g, poly 0.5g); PROTEIN 43g; CARB 38.3g; FIBER 3.8g; CHOL 151mg; IRON 3.3mg; SODIUM 1,229mg; CALC 153mg

---

How to Get It

Here's the simplest way to get the meat from a lobster. First, twist the tail from the body. Cut the tail lengthwise on the top with scissors to split it open, and remove the meat. Then twist off the claws. Pull the pincers apart, and remove the lower pincer. Use a lobster cracker to break the claw shell. Break the legs in half with your hands, and push the meat out with a cocktail or shellfish fork.

What You Get

Four 1½-pound lobsters yield about four cups of cooked lobster meat. Most of the lobsters we used were between 1¼ pounds and 1½ pounds. If you can't get or don't want to use live lobsters, use frozen tails, as we did in many of these recipes. Six six-ounce tails, which you should steam for eight minutes, yield about two cups cooked meat.

Pasta Salad with Lobster and Corn-Citrus Vinaigrette

4 cups cooked farfalle (about 3 cups uncooked bow tie pasta) or other short pasta
3 cups coarsely chopped cooked lobster meat
2 cups fresh corn kernels (about 4 ears)
½ cup chopped bottled roasted red bell peppers
½ cup chopped green onions
2 tablespoons chopped fresh mint
2 teaspoons grated orange rind
½ cup fresh orange juice
3 tablespoons olive oil
¾ teaspoon salt
¼ teaspoon black pepper

1. Combine first 6 ingredients in a large bowl. Combine orange rind and remaining 4 ingredients in a small bowl, stirring well with a whisk. Pour juice mixture over lobster mixture; toss well. Cover and chill. Yield: 8 servings (serving size: 1 cup).

CALORIES 238 (24% from fat); FAT 6.3g (sat 0.9g, mono 4g, poly 0.9g); PROTEIN 18.4g; CARB 27g; FIBER 2.2g; CHOL 51mg; IRON 1.6mg; SODIUM 547mg; CALC 54mg

---

Shore Dinner
Steamed Lobster with Thai Hot Sauce

Spicy Grilled Corn

Fresh tomatoes

Rolls

Iced tea and beer

Steamed Lobster

(pictured on page 202)

4 cups water
2 tablespoons salt
4 (1½-pound) live Maine lobsters

1. Bring water and salt to a boil in a 5-gallon stockpot. Place a vegetable steamer or rack in bottom of pan. Add lobsters; steam, covered, 14 minutes or until done. Yield: 4 servings (serving size: 1 lobster).

CALORIES 111 (5% from fat); FAT 0.7g (sat 0.1g, mono 0.2g, poly 0.1g); PROTEIN 23.2g; CARB 1.5g; FIBER 0g; CHOL 82mg; IRON 0.4mg; SODIUM 504mg; CALC 69mg

Thai Hot Sauce

This sauce is a complement to sweet, buttery lobster meat. The recipe uses the entire pepper—seeds and all. For a milder sauce, halve the jalapeños, then remove and discard the seeds and membranes.

¼ cup water
¼ cup fresh lime juice
1 teaspoon salt
10 red or green jalapeño peppers
10 garlic cloves, peeled

Continued

1. Place all ingredients in a blender, and process until smooth. Yield: 1 cup (serving size: 2 tablespoons).

NOTE: Store extra sauce in an airtight container for 1 week in refrigerator.

CALORIES 13 (7% from fat); FAT 0.1g (sat 0g, mono 0g, poly 0.1g); PROTEIN 0.5g; CARB 3.1g; FIBER 0.3g; CHOL 0mg; IRON 0.2mg; SODIUM 295mg; CALC 10mg

---

Cooking Up Lobster

Boiling: Boiling is probably the most familiar way to cook lobster (and it's our preferred method), but it presents the risk of overcooking, so you'll need to pay attention to time. Boiling makes removing the meat easier, since the intense, immediate heat causes it to shrink from the shell as the boiling water cooks the lobster from the outside in. Pick a five-gallon pot (if you use a smaller one, you may need to cook the lobsters in batches). You'll need about three gallons of water to cook four 1½-pound lobsters. Use fresh seawater or salted tap water, adding about a quarter-cup of salt for each gallon of water. Bring the water to a rolling boil. Add the live lobsters head first, cover the pot, reduce heat, and cook about 12 minutes or until the shells are bright orange-red, the tails are curled, and the antennae can be removed easily. If you plan to cook the lobster meat again in another recipe, boil the lobsters for only about 10 minutes.

Steaming: Since steaming cooks whole lobsters more slowly than boiling, it reduces the chance of overcooking. Place a vegetable steamer in the bottom of the pot, or rig it with a metal colander turned upside down. If you don't have anything in your kitchen that will work as a steamer, you can do without. Pour in enough water so that it reaches a depth of two inches, and add two tablespoons of salt. Place the live lobsters, head first, into the steamer rack or directly into the water in the bottom of the pot. Cover and steam about 14 minutes.

Spicy Grilled Corn

(pictured on page 202)

- 4 ears corn with husks
- 2 tablespoons Thai Hot Sauce (recipe on page 193)
- 1 cup hickory wood chips (optional)

1. Prepare grill.
2. Pull husks back from corn, and scrub silks. Brush sauce over corn. Pull husks back over corn to cover. Tie a string around top of husks to secure. Repeat procedure with remaining corn.
3. If using wood chips, wrap wood chips in a double layer of foil; pierce foil packet several times. Place foil packet on grill rack for 5 minutes. Place corn on grill rack; grill covered, 15 minutes or until done, turning occasionally. Yield: 4 servings (serving size: 1 ear of corn).

CALORIES 68 (11% from fat); FAT 0.8g (sat 0.1g, mono 0.2g, poly 0.4g); PROTEIN 2.1g; CARB 15.8g; FIBER 2.3g; CHOL 0mg; IRON 0.4mg; SODIUM 87mg; CALC 4mg

---

lighten up

Grams' Cracker Pie

We revamp a Pittsburgh family's beloved Graham Cracker Pie. Now it's ready to be handed down.

Lisa Grandstaff, 37, recently ran across one of her family favorites—Graham Cracker Pie. It was handed down by Lisa's grandmother, Gram. One glance at the handwritten recipe and Lisa was forced to turn to *Cooking Light* for help.

To fine-tune the calories and fat, we substituted fat-free milk for the whole milk and cut down on the eggs. We upgraded from butter-flavored shortening to real butter. And although we cut down on the amount of fat we used, the crust was even more flavorful than before. In the end, we trimmed almost 80 grams of fat and more than 600 calories from the entire recipe and ended up with a dessert that our Test Kitchens staff could hardly distinguish from the original.

Graham Cracker Pie

Pair with fresh seasonal berries.

CRUST:
- 1½ cups graham cracker crumbs
- 3 tablespoons sugar
- 1 tablespoon all-purpose flour
- ¼ cup butter, melted
- Cooking spray

FILLING:
- ½ cup sugar
- ¼ cup cornstarch
- ¼ teaspoon salt
- 2 cups fat-free milk
- 2 large eggs, lightly beaten
- ¼ teaspoon vanilla extract

MERINGUE:
- 3 large egg whites
- ½ teaspoon cream of tartar
- ½ teaspoon vanilla extract
- ⅓ cup sugar

1. Preheat oven to 350°.
2. To prepare crust, combine first 3 ingredients, and stir well with a whisk. Add melted butter; toss until moist. Reserve 2 tablespoons crumb mixture; set aside. Press remaining mixture into bottom and up sides of a 9-inch pie plate coated with cooking spray, and lightly coat crust with cooking spray. Bake at 350° for 15 minutes, and remove from oven. Reduce oven temperature to 350°.
3. To prepare filling, combine ½ cup sugar, cornstarch, and salt in a saucepan; stir in milk. Bring mixture to a boil over medium heat. Cook 1 minute, stirring constantly. Gradually add hot milk mixture to eggs, stirring constantly with a whisk. Return mixture to pan. Cook over medium heat until thick (about 2 minutes), stirring constantly. Remove from heat, and stir in ¼ teaspoon vanilla. Pour hot filling into prepared crust.
4. To prepare meringue, place egg whites and cream of tartar in a large bowl; beat with a mixer at high speed until foamy. Add ½ teaspoon vanilla; beat well. Gradually add ⅓ cup sugar, 1 tablespoon at a time, beating until stiff peaks form. Spread meringue evenly over hot filling, sealing to edge of crust. Sprinkle with

reserved crumb mixture. Bake at 350° for 15 minutes or until meringue is golden. Cool 1 hour on a wire rack. Chill at least 2 hours. Yield: 8 servings (serving size: 1 slice).

CALORIES 298 (28% from fat); FAT 9.3g (sat 4.4g, mono 3g, poly 1.2g); PROTEIN 6.2g; CARB 47.3g; FIBER 0.1g; CHOL 72mg; IRON 1mg; SODIUM 319mg; CALC 91mg

BEFORE	AFTER
SERVING SIZE	
1 slice	
CALORIES PER SERVING	
375	298
FAT	
19.1g	*9.3g*
PERCENT OF TOTAL CALORIES	
46%	28%

inspired vegetarian

Salad as the Main Event

These main-dish salads are hearty enough to satisfy big appetites.

Entrée salads can be light *and* substantial. To add heft, include beans or a starch. If you want to expand the menu, include sandwiches, crusty bread, olives, crostini, cold fruit soup, or marinated vegetables.

Summer Vegetable Salad with Grilled Bread

Toss in the bread cubes and sprinkle with cheese just before serving.

DRESSING:

    2   tablespoons red wine vinegar
    1   tablespoon extra-virgin olive oil
    1   tablespoon honey
    1   teaspoon salt
    ⅛   teaspoon black pepper
    1   garlic clove, minced

SALAD:

    1½ teaspoons extra-virgin olive oil
    1   garlic clove, minced
    4   (1-ounce) slices diagonally cut day-old French bread (about 1 inch thick)
    ⅛   teaspoon black pepper
    2   large tomatoes, cored, cut in half crosswise, and seeded
    1   red bell pepper, quartered
    1   yellow bell pepper, quartered
    1   red onion, cut into ½-inch-thick wedges
    Cooking spray
    3   cups (¼-inch) sliced zucchini (about 1 pound)
    3   cups (¼-inch) sliced yellow squash (about 1 pound)
    1   cup canned cannellini beans or other white beans, rinsed and drained
    1   tablespoon chopped fresh or 1 teaspoon dried basil
    1   tablespoon chopped fresh or 1 teaspoon dried thyme
    ½   cup (2 ounces) crumbled feta cheese

1. To prepare dressing, combine first 6 ingredients in a small jar; cover tightly, and shake vigorously.
2. Prepare grill.
3. To prepare salad, combine 1½ teaspoons oil and 1 garlic clove in a small bowl. Brush one side of each bread slice with garlic mixture; sprinkle with ⅛ teaspoon black pepper. Grill bread 4 minutes on each side or until golden brown. Cool; cut toast into ½-inch cubes.
4. Place tomato, bell peppers, and onion in a wire grilling basket coated with cooking spray. Place grilling basket on grill rack; grill 6 minutes on each side or until tender. Remove vegetables from basket. Place zucchini and yellow squash in basket. Place basket on grill rack; grill 6 minutes on each side or until tender. Combine grilled vegetables; cool.
5. Coarsely chop vegetables; place in a large bowl. Add dressing, toasted bread cubes, beans, basil, and thyme; toss to coat. Divide salad evenly among 6 plates; sprinkle with cheese. Serve immediately. Yield: 6 servings (serving size: 1⅔ cups salad and 4 teaspoons cheese).

CALORIES 240 (30% from fat); FAT 7.9g (sat 2.3g, mono 3.6g, poly 1.4g); PROTEIN 9.3g; CARB 35.9g; FIBER 5g; CHOL 8mg; IRON 3mg; SODIUM 685mg; CALC 118mg

Orzo Salad with Corn, Tomatoes, and Basil

The tiny pasta soaks up the vinaigrette as it stands. Ditalini or small shells also work well.

DRESSING:

    2   tablespoons fresh lemon juice
    1   tablespoon olive oil
    1   teaspoon red wine vinegar
    ½   teaspoon salt
    ¼   teaspoon black pepper
    3   garlic cloves, crushed

SALAD:

    1   cup uncooked orzo (rice-shaped pasta)
    2   cups fresh yellow corn kernels (about 4 ears)
    2   cups chopped tomato
    ½   cup vertically sliced red onion
    ¼   cup finely chopped fresh basil

1. To prepare dressing, combine first 6 ingredients in a jar; cover tightly, and shake vigorously.
2. To prepare salad, cook pasta according to package directions, omitting salt and fat. Drain and place in a large bowl. Spoon half of dressing over pasta; toss to coat. Cool to room temperature. Add remaining dressing, corn, tomato, onion, and basil to pasta mixture; toss to coat. Let stand 30 minutes. Yield: 4 servings (serving size: about 1½ cups).

CALORIES 312 (16% from fat); FAT 5.4g (sat 0.8g, mono 3g, poly 1.2g); PROTEIN 10.1g; CARB 59g; FIBER 5.1g; CHOL 0mg; IRON 2.9mg; SODIUM 318mg; CALC 27mg

Penne, Crispy Tofu, and Green Bean Salad

(pictured on page 201)

SALAD:

- 1 (15-ounce) package extra-firm tofu, drained and cut into 1-inch cubes
- 1 teaspoon olive oil
- 2 cups uncooked penne pasta (8 ounces tube-shaped pasta)
- 2 cups (2-inch) cut green beans (about 8 ounces)
- 2 cups halved cherry tomatoes
- 1 tablespoon chopped fresh or 1 teaspoon dried dill

DRESSING:

- 2 tablespoons red wine vinegar
- 1 tablespoon fresh lemon juice
- 1 tablespoon olive oil
- 1 teaspoon low-sodium soy sauce
- ¼ teaspoon sugar
- ¼ teaspoon salt
- ¼ teaspoon black pepper
- 3 garlic cloves, crushed

1. To prepare salad, pat tofu dry with a paper towel. Heat 1 teaspoon oil in a non-stick skillet over medium-high heat. Add tofu; sauté 5 minutes, browning on all sides. Remove from pan; chill 30 minutes.
2. Cook pasta in boiling water 5 minutes. Add beans; cook 5 minutes. Drain. Rinse with cold water; drain. Combine tofu, pasta mixture, tomatoes, and dill in a bowl.
3. Combine vinegar and next 7 ingredients in a jar; cover tightly, and shake vigorously. Pour over salad; toss well to coat. Cover and refrigerate 30 minutes. Yield: 8 servings (serving size: 1½ cups).

CALORIES 187 (26% from fat); FAT 5.4g (sat 0.7g, mono 2.2g, poly 2g); PROTEIN 8.9g; CARB 27.1g; FIBER 2.4g; CHOL 0mg; IRON 4.5mg; SODIUM 101mg; CALC 78mg

White Bean, Tomato, and Spinach Salad

DRESSING:

- 2 tablespoons red wine vinegar
- 1½ tablespoons olive oil
- ½ teaspoon black pepper
- ¼ teaspoon salt
- 2 garlic cloves, crushed

SALAD:

- 4 cups chopped spinach
- 2 cups chopped tomato (about 1 pound)
- 2 cups chopped yellow tomato (about 1 pound)
- ½ cup chopped red onion
- 1 teaspoon chopped fresh or ¼ teaspoon dried rosemary
- 2 (15.5-ounce) cans cannellini beans or other white beans, rinsed and drained

1. To prepare dressing, combine first 5 ingredients in a jar; cover tightly, and shake vigorously.
2. To prepare salad, combine spinach and next 5 ingredients in a bowl. Pour dressing over salad, tossing to coat. Yield: 4 servings (serving size: 2 cups).

CALORIES 207 (28% from fat); FAT 6.4g (sat 0.8g, mono 3.8g, poly 0.8g); PROTEIN 9.1g; CARB 29.9g; FIBER 11.5g; CHOL 0mg; IRON 4.3mg; SODIUM 489mg; CALC 89mg

Sesame Noodle Salad with Red Bell Pepper and Peanuts

DRESSING:

- ¼ cup fresh lime juice
- 3 tablespoons low-sodium soy sauce
- 1 tablespoon brown sugar
- 1 tablespoon tomato paste
- 1 tablespoon water
- 1 tablespoon sesame oil
- 1 teaspoon grated peeled fresh ginger
- 1 teaspoon vegetable oil
- ¼ teaspoon crushed red pepper
- 2 garlic cloves, crushed

SALAD:

- ½ pound uncooked spaghettini
- 1½ cups fresh bean sprouts
- ¾ cup (2 x ¼-inch) julienne-cut red bell pepper
- ¼ cup thinly sliced green onions
- 2 tablespoons chopped fresh mint
- 2 tablespoons chopped fresh basil
- 1 tablespoon chopped fresh cilantro
- 2 tablespoons finely chopped dry-roasted peanuts

1. To prepare dressing, combine first 10 ingredients in a jar; cover tightly, and shake vigorously.
2. To prepare salad, cook pasta according to package directions, omitting salt and fat. Drain and rinse with cold water. Combine pasta, bean sprouts, and next 5 ingredients in a large bowl. Pour dressing over salad; toss gently to coat. Let stand 30 minutes. Sprinkle with peanuts. Yield: 4 servings (serving size 1¼ cups salad and 1½ teaspoons peanuts).

CALORIES 320 (22% from fat); FAT 7.9g (sat 1.2g, mono 2.9g, poly 3.2g); PROTEIN 10.8g; CARB 52.7g; FIBER 2.8g; CHOL 0mg; IRON 3.4mg; SODIUM 410mg; CALC 35mg

Curried Couscous Salad with Dried Cranberries

The flavors of this salad meld as it chills. It makes a great portable lunch.

SALAD:

- 1½ cups uncooked couscous (about 1 [10-ounce] box)
- 1 cup dried cranberries (about 4 ounces)
- 1 cup frozen green peas, thawed
- ½ teaspoon curry powder
- 2 cups boiling water
- ¼ cup thinly sliced green onions
- ¼ cup finely chopped fresh basil
- 1 (15½-ounce) can chickpeas (garbanzo beans), rinsed and drained

DRESSING:

- ⅓ cup fresh lemon juice
- 1 tablespoon grated orange rind
- 2 tablespoons water
- 1½ tablespoons olive oil
- 1 tablespoon thawed orange juice concentrate
- ½ teaspoon salt
- ¼ teaspoon black pepper
- 4 garlic cloves, crushed

1. To prepare salad, combine first 4 ingredients in a large bowl. Pour 2 cups boiling water over couscous mixture; cover and let stand 5 minutes. Fluff with a fork; cool. Stir in onions, basil, and chickpeas.

2. To prepare dressing, combine lemon juice and next 7 ingredients in a jar; cover tightly, and shake vigorously. Pour over couscous mixture, and toss well to combine. Cover and chill 1 hour. Yield: 8 servings (serving size: 1 cup).

CALORIES 257 (13% from fat); FAT 3.8g (sat 0.5g, mono 2.1g, poly 0.7g); PROTEIN 8.7g; CARB 47.9g; FIBER 4.1g; CHOL 0mg; IRON 2.1mg; SODIUM 243mg; CALC 31mg

dinner tonight

Cool Summer Entrées

Turkey-Vegetable Wraps

TOTAL TIME: 15 MINUTES

QUICK TIP: Using bagged salad greens cuts down on preparation time.

- 2 cups coarsely chopped smoked turkey breast (about 8 ounces)
- 2 cups gourmet salad greens
- ½ cup fresh corn kernels (about 1 ear)
- ½ cup chopped red bell pepper
- ¼ cup thinly sliced green onions
- 3 tablespoons light ranch dressing
- 4 (8-inch) flour tortillas

1. Combine first 6 ingredients in a large bowl, tossing well to coat. Warm tortillas according to package directions. Top each tortilla with 1 cup turkey mixture;

roll up. Cut each wrap in half diagonally. Yield: 4 servings (serving size: 1 wrap).

CALORIES 252 (26% from fat); FAT 7.2g (sat 1.2g, mono 2.3g, poly 3.3g); PROTEIN 18.2g; CARB 29.8g; FIBER 3g; CHOL 32mg; IRON 2.4mg; SODIUM 741mg; CALC 76mg

Roast-Chicken-and-Cranberry Sandwiches

TOTAL TIME: 20 MINUTES
We prefer cranberry chutney, but any variety will do.

- ¼ cup (2 ounces) ⅓-less-fat cream cheese
- ¼ cup bottled cranberry chutney (such as Crosse & Blackwell)
- 8 (1-ounce) slices multigrain bread
- ½ cup thinly sliced radishes
- ½ cup trimmed arugula or spinach
- 2 cups chopped roasted skinless, boneless chicken breast (about 2 breast halves)

1. Combine cream cheese and cranberry chutney in a small bowl. Spread 1 tablespoon cream cheese mixture over each bread slice. Arrange one-fourth of radishes, arugula, and chicken on each

of 4 bread slices. Top with remaining bread slices. Yield: 4 servings (serving size: 1 sandwich).

CALORIES 361 (23% from fat); FAT 9.1g (sat 3.6g, mono 3.2g, poly 1.2g); PROTEIN 30.3g; CARB 39.7g; FIBER 3.2g; CHOL 76mg; IRON 2.7mg; SODIUM 459mg; CALC 63mg

Asian Beef-Noodle Salad

TOTAL TIME: 25 MINUTES

QUICK TIP: Bottled fresh ground ginger is a speedy way to invigorate this salad; look for it in the produce sections of larger supermarkets. You may also substitute an equal amount of grated fresh ginger.

- 1 (3.75-ounce) package bean threads (cellophane noodles)
- 8 ounces sliced deli roast beef, cut lengthwise into thin strips
- 1 cup snow peas, trimmed and cut lengthwise into thin strips
- ½ cup julienne-cut carrot
- ½ cup low-sodium teriyaki sauce
- 2 tablespoons lime juice
- 2 teaspoons dark sesame oil
- 2 teaspoons chile paste with garlic
- ½ teaspoon bottled fresh ground ginger (such as Spice World)
- 6 cups torn spinach
- ¼ cup chopped fresh cilantro

1. Cover noodles with boiling water in a bowl. Let stand 15 minutes or until tender; drain.
2. Combine beef, snow peas, and carrot in a microwave-safe bowl. Combine teriyaki sauce and next 4 ingredients, and pour over beef mixture. Microwave

Continued

at HIGH 2 minutes or until thoroughly heated. Add noodles; toss well. Serve over spinach. Sprinkle with cilantro. Yield: 6 servings (serving size: 1 cup beef mixture and 1 cup spinach).

CALORIES 173 (26% from fat); FAT 5g (sat 1g, mono 1.5g, poly 0.8g); PROTEIN 10g; CARB 22.8g; FIBER 2.8g; CHOL 32mg; IRON 2.9mg; SODIUM 653mg; CALC 58mg

---

Menu 4

serves 4

Couscous Salad with Chicken, Tomato, and Basil

Cucumber-dill soup*

*Combine 1¾ cups chopped seeded peeled cucumber and ½ cup sliced green onions in a food processor; process until minced. Add 2 tablespoons chopped fresh or 2 teaspoons dried dill, ¾ teaspoon salt, ¾ teaspoon sugar, ¼ teaspoon white pepper, and 1 (16-ounce) carton plain low-fat yogurt; process until smooth. Ladle ¾ cup soup into each of 4 bowls. Top each serving with ½ teaspoon fresh dill and ½ teaspoon low-fat sour cream.

Toasted pita triangles

Couscous Salad with Chicken, Tomato, and Basil

TOTAL TIME: 29 MINUTES

QUICK TIP: We used packaged roasted chicken; it's available in the meat department of your supermarket.

- 2 tablespoons extra-virgin olive oil, divided
- 2 garlic cloves, minced
- 1 (15.75-ounce) can fat-free, less-sodium chicken broth
- 1½ cups uncooked couscous
- 2 cups chopped tomato (about 1¼ pounds)
- 2 cups chopped roasted skinless, boneless chicken breast (about 2 breast halves)
- ⅓ cup thinly sliced fresh basil
- 2 tablespoons balsamic vinegar
- ½ teaspoon salt
- ¼ teaspoon black pepper
- ¼ cup (1-ounce) crumbled feta cheese

1. Combine 1 tablespoon olive oil and garlic in a large microwave-safe bowl, and microwave at HIGH 45 seconds. Add broth; microwave at HIGH 4 minutes or until mixture simmers. Gradually stir in couscous; cover and let stand 5 minutes. Fluff with a fork. Stir in tomato, chicken, basil, vinegar, salt, and pepper. Drizzle with 1 tablespoon oil, and sprinkle with cheese. Yield: 4 servings (serving size: 1½ cups).

CALORIES 487 (23% from fat); FAT 12.7g (sat 3g, mono 6.5g, poly 1.5g); PROTEIN 34.7g; CARB 57.5g; FIBER 3.7g; CHOL 71mg; IRON 2.8mg; SODIUM 718mg; CALC 60mg

---

back to the best

Peach Cobbler

Thoreau said, "Simplify, simplify." What's that got to do with peach cobbler? A lot.

This is the premier dessert of peach season and our June 1995 issue. When the peaches are at the apex of ripeness, the cobbler virtually makes itself. Brown sugar and almonds show their affinity for the fruits of the season. Rather than fussing with the dough, you just fold the crust over the filling. What could be more simple—or satisfying?

Peach Cobbler

- 2 cups all-purpose flour
- 1 tablespoon granulated sugar
- ¼ teaspoon salt
- 6 tablespoons chilled butter, cut into 6 pieces
- 6 tablespoons ice water
- Cooking spray
- 6 cups sliced peeled peaches (about 3¾ pounds)
- ¾ cup packed brown sugar, divided
- 2½ tablespoons all-purpose flour
- 1 tablespoon vanilla extract
- 1 teaspoon ground cinnamon
- ¼ cup slivered almonds
- 1 large egg
- 1 teaspoon water
- 1 tablespoon granulated sugar

1. Preheat oven to 375°.

2. Lightly spoon 2 cups flour into dry measuring cups; level with a knife. Place flour, 1 tablespoon granulated sugar, and salt in a food processor; pulse 2 or 3 times. Add butter pieces; pulse 10 times or until mixture resembles coarse meal. With processor on, slowly add ice water through food chute, processing just until combined (do not form a ball).

3. Gently press dough into a 4-inch circle. Slightly overlap 2 lengths of plastic wrap on a slightly damp surface. Place dough on plastic wrap; cover with 2 additional lengths of overlapping plastic wrap. Roll dough, still covered, into a 15 x 13-inch rectangle. Place in freezer 5 minutes or until plastic wrap can be easily removed; remove top sheets. Fit dough, uncovered side down, into a 2-quart baking dish coated with cooking spray, allowing dough to extend over edges; remove remaining plastic wrap.

4. Combine peaches, ½ cup brown sugar, 2½ tablespoons flour, vanilla, and cinnamon in a large bowl; toss gently. Spoon into prepared dish; fold edges of dough over peach mixture. Sprinkle ¼ cup brown sugar over mixture; sprinkle with almonds.

5. Combine egg and water in a small bowl. Brush egg mixture over dough; sprinkle with 1 tablespoon granulated sugar. Bake at 375° for 45 minutes or until filling is bubbly and crust is lightly browned. Let stand 30 minutes before serving. Yield: 10 servings.

CALORIES 302 (27% from fat); FAT 9.2g (sat 1.6g, mono 4.3g, poly 2.7g); PROTEIN 4.5g; CARB 51.5g; FIBER 2.8g; CHOL 11mg; IRON 1.9mg; SODIUM 149mg; CALC 39mg

La Dolce Vita

The first sweet taste will convince you why Italians are so passionate about gelato.

Any of your friends who have traveled to Italy will confirm that everybody has a memory or story about gelato. This distant cousin of American ice cream is gloriously glopped into cups and cones in *gelaterias* and street cars all over Italy. The best ones are, of course, handmade with ripe seasonal fruits like raspberries and mangoes. Most gelato is low in fat, and fruit juice-based gelato is fat-free, which means you have no excuse not to experiment with the recipes that follow.

Wild Blueberry Gelato

Blueberries give this cool, frozen treat a vibrant color. For best results and flavor, cook the blueberry mixture in a nonaluminum pan.

    2   cups fresh or frozen blueberries
    ¼   cup blueberry jam
    ¼   cup water
    ¼   teaspoon salt
    ⅔   cup sugar
    3   large egg yolks
    2   cups 2% reduced-fat milk
    2   tablespoons fresh lemon juice

1. Combine first 4 ingredients in a medium saucepan, and bring to a boil. Reduce heat to medium; cook 10 minutes. Place mixture in a blender, and process until smooth.
2. Beat sugar and egg yolks in a large bowl with a whisk until thick and pale (about 5 minutes). Heat milk over medium-high heat in a small, heavy saucepan to 180° or until tiny bubbles form around edge of pan, stirring frequently (do not boil). Add one-third of hot milk to sugar mixture, stirring with a whisk. Gradually add to remaining hot milk, stirring constantly with a whisk. Cook over medium-low heat until mixture coats back of a spoon (about 4 minutes). Remove from heat. Stir in blueberry mixture, and cool completely. Stir in juice.
3. Pour mixture into freezer can of an ice-cream freezer; freeze according to manufacturer's instructions. Yield: 3 cups (serving size: ½ cup).

CALORIES 213 (22% from fat); FAT 4.4g (sat 1.8g, mono 1.5g, poly 0.5g); PROTEIN 4.5g; CARB 38.4g; FIBER 1.3g; CHOL 115mg; IRON 0.5mg; SODIUM 145mg; CALC 114mg

Lemon-Ginger Sorbetto

(pictured on page 201)

    3   cups water
    1   cup sugar
    6   tablespoons honey
    1   (2-inch) piece peeled fresh ginger
    1   cup fresh lemon juice (about 8 lemons)
    Lemon slices (optional)

1. Combine water and sugar in a saucepan; bring to a boil, stirring until sugar dissolves. Remove from heat; stir in honey. Cool completely.
2. Grate ginger; place ginger on several layers of damp cheesecloth. Gather edges of cheesecloth together; squeeze cheesecloth bag over a small bowl to measure 1 tablespoon ginger juice. Combine sugar mixture, ginger juice, and lemon juice in a large bowl.
3. Pour mixture into freezer can of an ice-cream freezer; freeze according to manufacturer's instructions. Spoon sorbetto into a freezer-safe container; cover and freeze 1 hour or until firm. Garnish with lemon slices, if desired. Yield: 4 cups (serving size: ½ cup).

CALORIES 153 (0% from fat); FAT 0g; PROTEIN 0.2g; CARB 40.7g; FIBER 0.1g; CHOL 0mg; IRON 0.1mg; SODIUM 1mg; CALC 4mg

Chambord Granita

(pictured on page 201)

Don't use a substitute for the Chambord, a liqueur made with black raspberries, honey, and herbs; it's essential to the flavor.

    3   cups water, divided
    1   cup sugar
    4   cups fresh raspberries (about
        1½ pounds)
    1   cup Chambord (raspberry-flavored
        liqueur)

1. Combine 1 cup water and sugar in a saucepan, and bring to a boil, stirring until sugar dissolves. Remove from heat, and cool completely.
2. Place raspberries in a blender; process until smooth. Press raspberry puree through a sieve into a medium bowl, and discard seeds. Stir in sugar syrup, 2 cups water, and liqueur. Pour mixture into an 11 x 7-inch baking dish. Cover and freeze 8 hours or until firm. Remove mixture from freezer; let stand 10 minutes. Scrape entire mixture with a fork until fluffy. Yield: 8 cups (serving size: ½ cup).

CALORIES 105 (2% from fat); FAT 0.2g (sat 0g, mono 0g, poly 0.1g); PROTEIN 0.3g; CARB 21.3g; FIBER 0g; CHOL 0mg; IRON 0.2mg; SODIUM 0mg; CALC 7mg

Earl Grey Gelato

The tea mixture may appear curdled after you add the milk. But don't be alarmed; you'll be rewarded with a smooth, luxurious gelato when the mixture comes out of the ice-cream freezer.

    3   cups water
    1½   cups sugar
    5   Earl Grey tea bags
    2   tablespoons fresh lemon juice
    1½   cups whole milk

1. Combine water and sugar in a large saucepan; bring to a boil, stirring until sugar dissolves. Remove from heat, and add tea bags. Cover and steep 5 minutes; discard tea bags. Stir in juice; cool completely. Stir in milk.

Continued

2. Pour tea mixture into freezer can of an ice-cream freezer; freeze according to manufacturer's instructions. Yield: 5 cups (serving size: ½ cup).

CALORIES 140 (8% from fat); FAT 1.2g (sat 0.8g, mono 0.4g, poly 0.4g); PROTEIN 1.2g; CARB 32.1g; FIBER 0g; CHOL 5mg; IRON 0mg; SODIUM 20mg; CALC 44mg

Strawberry-Buttermilk Gelato

(pictured on page 201)

Pureed strawberries flavor this gelato.

  2 cups sugar
  2 cups water
  5 cups quartered strawberries
      (about 4 pints)
  2 cups low-fat buttermilk

1. Combine sugar and water in a large saucepan; bring to a boil, stirring until sugar dissolves. Pour into a large bowl; cool completely.
2. Place strawberries in a blender, and process until smooth. Add strawberry puree and buttermilk to sugar syrup; stir to combine.
3. Pour strawberry mixture into freezer can of an ice-cream freezer, and freeze according to manufacturer's instructions. Yield: 8 cups (serving size: ½ cup).

CALORIES 134 (5% from fat); FAT 0.8g (sat 0.3g, mono 0.2g, poly 0.1g); PROTEIN 1.6g; CARB 31.7g; FIBER 1.7g; CHOL 1mg; IRON 0.3mg; SODIUM 17mg; CALC 48mg

Pineapple-Coconut Gelato

Try this gelato in a cone with shredded coconut sprinkled on top.

  1½ cups sugar
  1½ cups water
    1 (15¼-ounce) can crushed
        pineapple in juice, undrained
   ⅔ cup coconut milk

1. Combine sugar and water in a large saucepan; bring to a boil, stirring until sugar dissolves. Remove from heat; cool completely.

2. Combine pineapple and milk in a large bowl; stir in sugar syrup.
3. Pour mixture into freezer can of an ice-cream freezer, and freeze according to manufacturer's instructions. Spoon gelato into a freezer-safe container; cover and freeze 1 hour or until firm. Yield: 4 cups (serving size: ½ cup).

CALORIES 215 (17% from fat); FAT 4.1g (sat 3.6g, mono 0.2g, poly 0.2g); PROTEIN 0.6g; CARB 46.5g; FIBER 0.4g; CHOL 0mg; IRON 0.8mg; SODIUM 3mg; CALC 11mg

Mimosa Granita

  1 cup sugar
  1 cup water
  3 cups fresh orange juice (about 10
      oranges)
  2 cups Champagne or sparkling
      wine
  2 tablespoons fresh lime juice
Lime wedges (optional)

1. Combine sugar and water in a large saucepan, and bring to a boil, stirring until sugar dissolves. Remove from heat, and cool completely. Stir in orange juice, Champagne, and lime juice; pour into an 11 x 7-inch baking dish. Cover and freeze 8 hours or until firm. Remove mixture from freezer; let stand 10 minutes. Scrape entire mixture with a fork until fluffy, and garnish with lime wedges, if desired. Yield: 8 cups (serving size: ½ cup).

CALORIES 92 (0% from fat); FAT 0g; PROTEIN 0.4g; CARB 18g; FIBER 0.1g; CHOL 0mg; IRON 0.2mg; SODIUM 2mg; CALC 5mg

Mango-Passion Fruit Gelato

You'll find passion fruit nectar, which has a flavor that's both sweet and tart, in large supermarkets.

  1 cup sugar
  1 cup water
  3 cups chopped peeled mango
      (about 2 mangoes)
  2 cups passion fruit nectar
  1½ cups half-and-half

1. Combine sugar and water in a medium saucepan, and bring to a boil, stirring until sugar dissolves. Place sugar mixture and mango in a blender; process until smooth. Pour into a large bowl; cool completely. Stir in nectar and half-and-half.
2. Pour mango mixture into freezer can of an ice-cream freezer; freeze according to manufacturer's instructions. Yield: 7 cups (serving size ½ cup).

CALORIES 130 (21% from fat); FAT 3.1g (sat 1.9g, mono 0.9g, poly 0.1g); PROTEIN 1g; CARB 26g; FIBER 0.6g; CHOL 10mg; IRON 0.1mg; SODIUM 12mg; CALC 32mg

All in the Gelato Family

GELATO (jeh-LAH-toh)—which comes from *gelare*, the Italian word for "to freeze"—is the umbrella term for any frozen Italian dessert. With these recipes, you can make three varieties of gelato:

- **Gelato**—in addition to its more general definition, it also refers to a milk-based concoction with a dense, buttery consistency similar to that of American ice cream. You can serve it in an ice-cream cone.

- **Sorbetto** (sor-BAY-toh)—a fruit-based gelato that contains no dairy products. You may know it better as sorbet.

- **Granita** (GRAH-nee-tah)—another fruit-based gelato, it has a decidedly different texture from that of sorbetto or gelato. Because it's frozen and then scraped to form coarse ice granules, granita is slushy.

Penne, Crispy Tofu, and Green Bean Salad,
page 196

Chambord Granita, page 199, Strawberry-Buttermilk
Gelato, page 200, and Lemon-Ginger Sorbetto,
page 199

Steamed Lobster, page 193, and
Spicy Grilled Corn, page 194

Kaleidoscope Tomato Salad with
Balsamic-Olive Vinaigrette, page 211

Oven-Fried Catfish, page 217, Chile-Vinegar Turnip
Greens, page 217, Jalapeño Corn Bread, page 218,
and Chipotle-Maple Sweet Potatoes, page 218

Split Pea-Garlic Dip,
page 210

Rosemary-Rubbed Duck Breast with
Caramelized Apricots, page 214

How to Cook Greek

Humble, ingenious cooking from a land blessed with olive oil, greens, and grains.

Greek dishes are based on humble but delicious regional produce: seasonal vegetables; leafy greens, wild or cultivated; grains, mainly in the form of homemade bread; fruity olive oil; home-cured olives; beans and other legumes; local cheeses; yogurt; occasionally fresh or cured fish; and sometimes meat. And the true ingenious Greek cook creates an interesting and delicious dish from these humble ingredients on a daily basis. Now you can, too.

How to Prepare Eggplant and Yogurt

1. Roast eggplant until dark brown and tender. This gives it a smoky flavor and softens the pulp, making it easy to peel. Coarsely chop eggplant.

2. Draining yogurt on a paper towel gives it more body and a consistency similar to Greek yogurt, which is much thicker and creamier than American yogurt.

Eggplant Spread with Yogurt and Parsley
Melintzanosalata

Every Greek cook has a version of this spread. It is a fresh-tasting condiment that's great with pita chips or as a topping for steamed potatoes.

- 3 eggplants (about 2 pounds)
- 3 tablespoons extra-virgin olive oil, divided
- 2 cups fresh parsley leaves, divided
- 2/3 cup coarsely chopped green onions
- 2 tablespoons red wine vinegar
- 2 garlic cloves, quartered
- 1 bottled pepperoncini pepper
- 2 tablespoons capers
- 1/2 teaspoon salt
- 1/4 teaspoon freshly ground black pepper
- 1 (8-ounce) carton plain low-fat yogurt

1. Preheat broiler.

2. Cut eggplants in half lengthwise. Place on a jelly-roll pan, cut sides up; brush cut sides with 1 tablespoon oil. Broil 15 minutes or until tender and browned. Remove from oven; cool on pan 10 minutes. Peel eggplants; chop pulp. Place pulp in a bowl.

3. Finely chop 1 cup parsley; set aside. Combine remaining parsley, 2 tablespoons oil, onions, vinegar, garlic, and pepperoncini pepper in a food processor.

Process until smooth, scraping sides of bowl occasionally; add to eggplant. Stir in reserved chopped parsley, capers, salt, and black pepper. Cover and chill 2 hours.

4. Spoon yogurt onto several layers of heavy-duty paper towels, and spread to 1/2-inch thickness. Cover with additional paper towels; let stand 5 minutes. Scrape yogurt from paper towel into eggplant mixture; stir gently. Yield: 3 cups (serving size: 1 tablespoon).

CALORIES 16 (56% from fat); FAT 1g (sat 0.2g, mono 0.6g, poly 0.1g); PROTEIN 0.5g; CARB 1.6g; FIBER 0.5g; CHOL 0mg; IRON 0.1mg; SODIUM 60mg; CALC 13mg

Moussaka with Eggplant and Peppers and Yogurt Béchamel

This is an ideal dish for entertaining. Assemble it up to four hours ahead, then pop it in the oven when your guests arrive. Serve with a salad of mixed greens.

- 1 (1½-pound) eggplant, cut crosswise into 1/4-inch-thick slices
- 1¾ teaspoons kosher salt, divided
- 1 (32-ounce) carton plain low-fat yogurt
- Cooking spray
- 3 large green bell peppers
- 1 pound peeled baking potato, cut into 1/4-inch-thick slices
- 1 pound lean ground lamb or beef
- 1½ cups chopped onion
- 2 cups chopped peeled tomato (about 1 pound)
- 1/3 cup dry red wine
- 1/2 cup dried currants
- 2 teaspoons Aleppo pepper or dash of crushed red pepper
- 1/4 teaspoon ground nutmeg
- 1 (3-inch) cinnamon stick
- 1/4 teaspoon black pepper, divided
- 1/4 cup all-purpose flour
- 3 tablespoons olive oil
- 1½ cups 1% low-fat milk
- 3/4 cup (3 ounces) grated extra-sharp cheddar cheese or Romano cheese
- Dash of nutmeg
- 2 large egg yolks

Continued

1. Place eggplant in a large bowl; sprinkle with 1 teaspoon salt. Let stand 30 minutes. Rinse and drain; pat dry with paper towels.

2. Spoon yogurt onto several layers of heavy-duty paper towels; spread to ½-inch thickness. Cover with additional paper towels; let stand 10 minutes. Scrape into a bowl using a rubber spatula; cover and refrigerate.

3. Preheat broiler.

4. Place half of eggplant slices on a broiler pan coated with cooking spray, and broil 6 minutes on each side or until lightly browned. Repeat procedure with remaining eggplant.

5. Cut bell peppers in half lengthwise; discard seeds and membranes. Place pepper halves, skin sides up, on a broiler pan; flatten with hand. Broil 15 minutes or until blackened. Place in a zip-top plastic bag; seal. Let stand 15 minutes; peel.

6. Place potato slices on a broiler pan coated with cooking spray; broil 7 minutes on each side or until golden on both sides.

7. Arrange potato slices in bottom of a 13 x 9-inch baking dish coated with cooking spray. Top with eggplant slices. Arrange bell pepper halves over eggplant.

8. Heat a large nonstick skillet over medium-high heat. Add lamb; sauté 5 minutes or until browned, stirring to crumble. Drain well; return to pan. Add onion; sauté 5 minutes. Stir in tomato and next 5 ingredients; bring to a boil. Reduce heat, and simmer 8 minutes. Sprinkle with ½ teaspoon salt and ⅛ teaspoon black pepper; discard cinnamon stick. Spoon lamb mixture over bell pepper halves.

9. Preheat oven to 400°.

10. Lightly spoon flour into a dry measuring cup, and level with a knife. Combine olive oil and flour in a large saucepan over medium heat, stirring with a whisk. Cook 3 minutes, stirring frequently. Combine drained yogurt and milk. Add yogurt mixture to flour mixture, stirring constantly; cook until thick (do not boil). Remove from heat; stir in ¼ teaspoon salt, ⅛ teaspoon black pepper, cheese, nutmeg, and egg yolks.

11. Spoon sauce over lamb mixture, spreading carefully; run a knife around outside edge to allow sauce to run into dish (dish will be very full). Place on a foil-lined baking sheet. Bake at 400° for 45 minutes or until golden brown and bubbly. Let stand 20 minutes. Yield: 8 servings.

WINE NOTE: With its intriguing balance of slightly bitter flavors (eggplant) juxtaposed against sweet flavors (currants), this dish calls for a wine that's dark and earthy. A lot of Italian reds would fit the bill perfectly. Two great bets: Allegrini Valpolicella Classico Superiore 1999 (about $11) and Renato Ratti Dolcetto d'Alba (about $12).

CALORIES 434 (36% from fat); FAT 17.4g (sat 6.4g, mono 7.7g, poly 1.4g); PROTEIN 27.4g; CARB 43.8g; FIBER 4.9g; CHOL 115mg; IRON 2.9mg; SODIUM 514mg; CALC 384mg

Greens-and-Cheese Pie
Hortopita

Greens and herbs are the secret to a successful and fragrant *hortopita*.

    1   tablespoon olive oil
    2   cups thinly sliced green onions
 1½   cups minced fennel (about 1 large
        bulb)
  10   cups packaged fresh spinach
        (about 5 ounces)
    8   cups thinly sliced mustard greens
        (about 8 ounces)
 1¼   cups (5 ounces) feta cheese
   ¼   cup chopped fresh parsley
   ¼   cup chopped fresh or 1 tablespoon
        dried dill
    1   teaspoon dried Greek oregano
   ½   teaspoon salt
   ½   teaspoon black pepper
    8   sheets frozen phyllo dough,
        thawed
  Cooking spray
  Flat-leaf parsley sprigs (optional)

1. Preheat oven to 375°.

2. Heat oil in a large nonstick skillet over medium-high heat. Add onions; sauté 4 minutes. Add fennel; sauté 3 minutes. Remove onion mixture from pan; cool. Add spinach to pan; sauté 30 seconds or until spinach wilts. Place spinach in a colander, pressing until barely moist. Add greens to pan; sauté 30 seconds or until greens wilt. Place greens in a colander, pressing until barely moist. Combine onion mixture, spinach, mustard greens, feta, and next 5 ingredients in a large bowl.

3. Working with 1 phyllo sheet at a time (cover remaining dough to keep from drying), place 2 sheets in a 13 x 9-inch baking pan coated with cooking spray. Gently press sheets into bottom and up sides of pan, allowing ends to extend over edges of pan. Coat top sheet with cooking spray. Fold 1 sheet of phyllo in half crosswise; place on sheets in bottom of pan, and coat with cooking spray. Top with 1 sheet of phyllo, gently pressing sheet into bottom and up sides of pan; coat with cooking spray. Spread greens mixture evenly over top of phyllo. Fold 1 sheet of phyllo in half; gently press on top of greens mixture, and coat with cooking spray. Top with remaining 3 sheets of phyllo, coating each with cooking spray. Trim ends extending over pan. Fold edges of phyllo to form a rim; flatten rim with a fork. Cut 4 slits in top of phyllo using a sharp knife. Bake at 375° for 50 minutes. Cool 30 minutes. Garnish with parsley sprigs, if desired. Yield: 6 servings.

WINE NOTE: This dish's green flavors deserve an herbal wine. Some of the world's freshest, green wines are New Zealand Sauvignon Blancs; try Villa Maria Private Bin (about $12).

CALORIES 194 (44% from fat); FAT 9.4g (sat 4.1g, mono 3.2g, poly 1.3g); PROTEIN 8.1g; CARB 20.8g; FIBER 2g; CHOL 21mg; IRON 3.6mg; SODIUM 622mg; CALC 234mg

Weeknight Greek Supper

The lemony sauce is also great for spooning over the potatoes.

Garlic Tuna Steaks in Lemon Sauce

Grilled eggplant slices

Steamed new-potato wedges

Mixed greens salad

Vanilla low-fat ice cream with honey and sliced almonds

Garlic Tuna Steaks in Lemon Sauce

This recipe is adapted from a cookbook by Michalis Magoulas called *The Cuisine of Ithaca*. The original recipe calls for bonito steaks, but since they're hard to find, we've used tuna instead. Serve with steamed potatoes and a mixed-green salad.

> 4 (6-ounce) tuna steaks (about 1 inch thick)
> 2 teaspoons dried Greek oregano, divided
> ½ teaspoon sea or kosher salt
> 4 garlic cloves, peeled and quartered
> Cooking spray
> ½ cup fresh lemon juice (about 4 lemons)
> 1 tablespoon extra-virgin olive oil
> ⅛ teaspoon freshly ground black pepper
> 4 oregano sprigs (optional)

1. Sprinkle tuna steaks with 1 teaspoon oregano and salt; place in a shallow dish. Marinate in refrigerator 2 hours, turning occasionally.
2. Prepare grill.
3. Cut 2 slits into each steak. Insert 2 garlic quarters into each slit. Place steaks on a grill rack coated with cooking spray. Grill 4 minutes on each side until fish is medium-rare or until desired degree of doneness.
4. Combine 1 teaspoon oregano and juice in a medium bowl. Dip grilled steaks into juice mixture; place on a plate. Add oil to remaining juice mixture; stir well with a whisk. Spoon juice mixture over steaks; sprinkle with pepper. Garnish with oregano sprigs, if desired. Yield: 4 servings (serving size: 1 steak and 2½ tablespoons sauce).

WINE NOTE: There's a lot of lemon in this dish; be sure to choose a white wine with a bit of citrus zing. (Avoid red wines; they clash badly with lemon.) Many fresh, light whites from around the Mediterranean would be ideal. Try, for example, Bodegas Morgadío Albariño, one of Spain's most exciting whites (about $19).

CALORIES 283 (37% from fat); FAT 11.7g (sat 2g, mono 5.5g, poly 2g); PROTEIN 39g; CARB 4.2g; FIBER 0.3g; CHOL 63mg; IRON 2.1mg; SODIUM 358mg; CALC 20mg

Veal-and-Artichoke Stew with Avgolemono

Meat cooked with artichokes takes on a sweetness that contrasts with the lemon juice. This dish is usually served on its own, but it's equally delicious with rice, orzo, or egg noodles mixed into the sauce.

STEW:
> 4 cups water, divided
> ⅔ cup fresh lemon juice (about 4 lemons), divided
> 8 medium artichokes (about 10 ounces each)
> 4 lemons, cut in half
> 2½ pounds veal round, trimmed and cut into 2-inch cubes
> 1½ cups coarsely chopped onion
> ½ cup dry white wine
> 2 (15.75-ounce) cans fat-free, less-sodium chicken broth, divided
> ½ cup chopped fresh dill
> ½ teaspoon sea salt
> ½ teaspoon freshly ground black pepper

AVGOLEMONO:
> 1 large egg
> 5 tablespoons water, divided
> 2 tablespoons fresh lemon juice
> 1½ teaspoons cornstarch
> ¼ cup chopped fresh dill
> Lemon wedges (optional)

1. To prepare stew, combine 3 cups water and ⅓ cup lemon juice in a large bowl. Working with 1 artichoke at a time, cut off stem to within 1 inch of base, and peel stem. Remove bottom leaves and tough outer leaves, and trim about 2 inches from top of artichoke. Cut artichoke in half vertically. Remove fuzzy thistle from bottom with a spoon. Trim any remaining leaves and dark green layer from base. Rub edges with a lemon half, and place artichoke halves in lemon water. Repeat procedure with remaining artichokes.
2. Heat a Dutch oven over medium-high heat, and add veal, browning on all sides. Add onion, and cook 5 minutes. Add wine and 1 can of broth; bring to a boil. Cover, reduce heat, and simmer 45 minutes.

3. Drain artichoke halves. Add artichoke halves, 1 cup water, ⅓ cup lemon juice, ½ cup dill, 1 can of broth, salt, and pepper to pan; cover and simmer 30 minutes or until artichokes are tender. Remove veal and artichoke halves with a slotted spoon. Keep warm.
4. To prepare avgolemono, combine egg, 3 tablespoons water, and 2 tablespoons lemon juice in a medium bowl. Combine 2 tablespoons water and cornstarch in a small bowl; add to egg mixture. Add egg mixture to juices in pan. Bring to a boil, and cook 5 minutes, stirring constantly with a whisk. Serve sauce over veal and artichokes, and sprinkle with ¼ cup dill. Garnish with lemon wedges, if desired. Yield: 8 servings (serving size: 4 ounces meat, 2 artichoke halves, ¼ cup sauce, and 1½ teaspoons dill).

CALORIES 294 (17% from fat); FAT 5.4g (sat 2g, mono 0.6g, poly 0.6g); PROTEIN 36g; CARB 26.9g; FIBER 9.6g; CHOL 137mg; IRON 4.9mg; SODIUM 573mg; CALC 128mg

---

Avgolemono Sauce

Avgolemono (egg-and-lemon sauce) is a classic Greek sauce. It's made by thickening the cooking juices of meat, fish, or vegetable dishes with egg. The egg is beaten together with freshly squeezed lemon juice before they're combined with a cornstarch slurry. This mixture is then poured back into the food's juices and slowly heated until it's thick. Chopped dill or fennel tops are the herbs most commonly used in classic avgolemono dishes.

Get to Know the Greek Table

Aleppo peppers: These dried crushed red peppers from the Middle East are milder and more flavorful than Mexican chile peppers. Their taste is closer to that of indigenous Greek hot peppers. You may substitute a smaller amount of crushed red pepper.

Feta cheese: Probably the most familiar Greek cheese, feta is a slightly pungent, crumbly cheese that has taken the entire Greek market by storm. Originally from the northern mainland, authentic feta is made primarily from sheep's milk, with the addition of goat's milk. Greek feta packed in brine is stronger-tasting than that wrapped in plastic. Either kind will work well in these recipes.

Cinnamon: On the islands, in the Peloponnese, and in other parts of Greece, most tomato-flavored sauces for vegetables, as well as for meat dishes, are spiced with cinnamon sticks.

Horta: Various sweet, bitter, sour, and fragrant greens are gathered from the hills and fields after the first rains of fall and throughout the winter; some greens are also cultivated. Horta are used in myriad combinations—different in each part of the country—to make *hortopites* (greens pies), stews, and, more often, salads. A delicious mixture of different wild greens (either boiled, blanched, or sometimes raw), horta used to be the center of poor peasants' meals. The greens, simply dressed with olive oil and freshly squeezed lemon juice, were complemented with olives, home-baked bread, and maybe some cheese, cured pork, or salted fish. Many city folks dream of this frugal meal and drive many miles on weekends to get it.

Kalamata olives: These are probably the best known and most loved olives in the world. Kalamata olives take their name from a city in the southern Peloponnese and are the most flavorful olives from that region. Almond-shaped with a pointed tip, black and firm yet juicy, authentic kalamata olives are cured in brine, which contains high-quality local red wine vinegar.

Lemon: Freshly squeezed lemon juice is the most commonly used flavoring in savory and many sweet dishes. Lemon vinaigrette stars in most boiled or raw salads, and in grilled or barbecued meat or fish.

Olive oil: Greek olive oils are a great bargain in American markets. Many small olive groves, mainly on Crete and in the Peloponnese, now produce excellent organic olive oils.

Oregano: Typically, dried oregano is used in traditional Greek cooking. It's gathered in the summer from various mountains and hills, where it grows wild. Densely fragrant, imported Greek oregano is often mixed with domestic varieties when packaged in the United States, because it's considered too potent for unaccustomed users. We used Spice Hunter's Greek oregano, which is available in the spice sections of some supermarkets.

Phyllo: These paper-thin sheets of pastry dough—usually made with flour and water, some olive oil, and maybe a little lemon juice or vinegar—wrap all sorts of fillings: greens or vegetables with or without cheese; meat, fish, or seafood with rice; or bulgur, herbs, and spices. Phyllo is also used in many sweets, like baklava and *galatomboureko*, a luscious milk custard. *Kataifi*, used in our baklava recipe, is shredded phyllo pastry that comes frozen in one-pound packages.

Yogurt: Greeks love sweet, creamy yogurt made from sheep's milk. Unfortunately, it's not available in most American markets. For that reason, we used drained plain low-fat yogurt in all of these recipes.

How to Make Rolled Baklava

1. Kataifi *resembles shredded wheat. After phyllo is brushed with lemon oil and almonds, kataifi is sprinkled over it.*

2. *Tightly roll up phyllo jelly-roll fashion.*

3. *Slice with a serrated bread knife into 1½-inch pieces.*

Rolled Baklava

This baklava is rolled jelly-roll fashion and cut into rolls instead of being assembled in flat layers and cut into triangles. Let the rolls stand for 11 hours; they'll soak up more flavor. Find shredded phyllo called *kataifi* (ka-ta-EE-fee) in Middle Eastern markets.

ROLLS:

- 2 tablespoons olive oil
- 2 tablespoons vegetable oil
- 2 lemon wedges
- ¾ cup whole almonds (5 ounces), toasted
- 1½ tablespoons sugar
- ½ teaspoon ground cinnamon
- ¼ teaspoon ground nutmeg
- 12 sheets frozen phyllo dough, thawed
- 8 ounces frozen shredded phyllo dough (*kataifi*), thawed
- Cooking spray

SYRUP:

- 1⅓ cups sugar
- 1⅓ cups water
- 1⅓ cups honey
- 4 lemon wedges
- 1 (3-inch) cinnamon stick

1. Preheat oven to 350°.

2. To prepare rolls, combine first 3 ingredients in a small saucepan. Cook over medium-low heat 5 minutes. Cool; discard lemon. Place almonds, 1½ tablespoons sugar, ground cinnamon, and nutmeg in a food processor; process until coarsely chopped.

3. Place 2 phyllo sheets on a large cutting board or work surface (cover remaining dough to keep from drying); lightly brush with 1½ teaspoons oil mixture. Top with 2 phyllo sheets, and lightly brush with 1½ teaspoons oil mixture. Sprinkle about 2½ tablespoons almond mixture evenly over phyllo stack, leaving a 1½-inch border on 1 short edge. Crumble one-third of shredded phyllo over almond mixture; top with 2½ tablespoons almond mixture.

4. Starting at short edge without border, tightly roll up phyllo stack jelly-roll fashion. Lightly brush border and outside of roll with 1½ teaspoons oil mixture. Cut roll into 10 equal pieces.

Repeat procedure twice with remaining phyllo sheets, oil mixture, almond mixture, and shredded phyllo. Place all 30 rolls on a jelly-roll pan or baking sheet coated with cooking spray. Bake at 350° for 30 minutes.

5. To prepare syrup, combine 1⅓ cups sugar and remaining 4 ingredients in a large saucepan. Cook over medium heat 5 minutes or until sugar dissolves; discard lemon and cinnamon stick.

6. Carefully place baked baklava rolls, cut sides up, in a 13 x 9-inch baking pan coated with cooking spray (rolls will fit snugly). Pour syrup over rolls; let stand at room temperature 3 hours. Carefully turn rolls; cover and let stand 8 hours. Yield: 15 servings (serving size: 2 rolls).

CALORIES 343 (27% from fat); FAT 10g (sat 1.3g, mono 5.7g, poly 2.6g); PROTEIN 4.2g; CARB 61.8g; FIBER 1.8g; CHOL 0mg; IRON 1.5mg; SODIUM 147mg; CALC 29mg

Meat, Bulgur, and Rice Dolmades

Dolmades make great appetizers. Look for grape leaves in the Mediterranean section of your supermarket.

- 1 cup coarsely chopped fennel (about 1 bulb)
- ½ cup coarsely chopped onion
- ¼ cup coarsely chopped green onions
- ½ pound ground round
- 2 tablespoons uncooked medium-grain rice
- 2 tablespoons uncooked bulgur
- 1½ teaspoons olive oil
- 1 large tomato, cored and cut in half crosswise (about 1 pound)
- ½ teaspoon Aleppo pepper or dash of crushed red pepper
- ¼ teaspoon salt
- 30 bottled large grape leaves
- Cooking spray
- 1 (15.75-ounce) can fat-free, less-sodium chicken broth
- ¼ cup fresh lemon juice
- 1 tablespoon cornstarch
- 1 tablespoon water
- 3 tablespoons chopped fresh or 1 tablespoon dried dill
- Lemon wedges (optional)

1. Combine first 3 ingredients in a food processor, and process until minced. Combine fennel mixture, beef, rice, bulgur, and oil. Grate tomato halves over mixture; discard skin. Sprinkle beef mixture with pepper and salt; stir to combine.

2. Rinse grape leaves with cold water; drain and pat dry with paper towels. Remove stems, and discard. Spoon 1 rounded tablespoon of beef mixture onto center of each grape leaf. Fold 2 opposite sides of leaves over filling. Beginning at 1 short side, roll up each leaf tightly, jelly-roll fashion.

3. Place stuffed grape leaves close together, seam sides down, in a Dutch oven coated with cooking spray. Add broth and juice; bring to a boil. Cover, reduce heat, and simmer 30 minutes. Carefully remove dolmades from pan. Combine cornstarch and water. Stir cornstarch mixture into broth mixture; bring to a boil, and cook 1 minute. Stir in dill. Serve with dolmades. Garnish with lemon wedges, if desired. Yield: 6 servings (serving size: 5 dolmades and ¼ cup lemon broth).

CALORIES 132 (23% from fat); FAT 3.3g (sat 0.8g, mono 1.5g, poly 0.4g); PROTEIN 11.2g; CARB 14.3g; FIBER 3g; CHOL 22mg; IRON 2.1mg; SODIUM 255mg; CALC 81mg

Grater Technique

Greek cooks don't peel or seed tomatoes. Instead, they cut the tomatoes in half and grate them. While it seemed a bit odd to us, it's really quite clever. It's much quicker than a water bath and peeling. If the tomato is ripe, the skin will just fall away, leaving the pulp. We used the largest holes on a box grater to do this in Meat, Bulgur, and Rice Dolmades (recipe at left), and it worked like a charm.

Split Pea-Garlic Dip

Skordalia

(pictured on page 204)

This is an island variation on a much-loved *mezze* (appetizer); instead of the typical potatoes and soaked bread, pureed peas form its base. (Garbanzo beans or white beans can also be used.) Serve with baked pita wedges and assorted raw vegetables. Add vegetable stock or white wine to make the dip into a sauce, which is delicious over steamed vegetables and grilled fish or chicken.

- ½ cup green split peas
- ½ cup yellow split peas
- 2 cups water
- 1 tablespoon dried oregano
- 2 bay leaves
- ½ teaspoon salt, divided
- 1½ tablespoons red wine vinegar
- 1½ tablespoons olive oil
- ¼ teaspoon freshly ground black pepper
- 2 garlic cloves, peeled
- 3 tablespoons chopped pitted kalamata olives
- ¼ cup chopped fresh cilantro (optional)
- ¼ cup chopped arugula (optional)

1. Sort and wash peas. Combine peas, water, oregano, and bay leaves in a medium saucepan. Bring to a boil; cover, reduce heat, and simmer 25 minutes. Stir in ¼ teaspoon salt; cook 15 minutes or until tender. Drain; discard bay leaves.
2. Combine pea mixture, ¼ teaspoon salt, vinegar, oil, pepper, and garlic in a food processor; process until smooth, scraping sides of bowl occasionally. Stir in olives. Cover and chill 2 hours. Sprinkle with cilantro and arugula, if desired. Yield: 2¼ cups (serving size: 1 tablespoon).

CALORIES 27 (27% from fat); FAT 0.8g (sat 0.1g, mono 0.5g, poly 0.1g); PROTEIN 1.4g; CARB 3.6g; FIBER 0.4g; CHOL 0mg; IRON 0.4mg; SODIUM 45mg; CALC 7mg

How the Tomato Saved Our Farmers' Markets

Could it be that the search for great-tasting tomatoes is the reason for the resurgence of farmers' markets?

Since the early 1970s, fresh tomato use has risen about 33 percent while farmers' markets have evolved from several hundred to nearly 3,000 today. In just the last five years, the number of farmers' markets across the nation has grown dramatically, by more than 60 percent. And while farmers meet the more sophisticated tastes and demands of consumers, they are also changing the way America eats—by leading us to rediscover naturally fresh foods...such as the tomato. More important, perhaps, is that our love of tomatoes has led us back to our roots as a nation founded on agriculture.

Freezing Tomatoes

You can freeze tomatoes if you're going to use them in a sauce or soup (for other uses, they'll be too mushy). Rinse, cut out the stems and any bad spots, quarter, and toss tomatoes into freezer bags. Then just simmer the frozen tomatoes into a sauce months later to bring back memories of summer.

Eats for Eight

serves 8

Fresh Tomato-Pesto Pizza

Marinated mushroom salad*

Melon balls tossed with chopped mint

*Combine an 8-ounce package of button mushrooms, quartered, and an 8-ounce package of cremini mushrooms, quartered, in a large bowl. Whisk together 2 teaspoons grated lemon rind, ¼ cup fresh lemon juice, 1 tablespoon olive oil, ½ teaspoon dried oregano, ½ teaspoon salt, ¼ teaspoon pepper, and 2 minced garlic cloves; pour mixture over mushrooms. Cover and chill at least 1 hour. Add 2 cups gourmet salad greens just before serving; toss well.

Fresh Tomato-Pesto Pizza

PESTO:

- 4 cups basil leaves
- 2 garlic cloves
- ¼ cup fat-free, less-sodium chicken broth
- 1 tablespoon grated fresh Parmesan cheese
- 1 tablespoon olive oil

PIZZA:

- 1 (1-pound) Italian cheese-flavored pizza crust (such as Boboli)
- 3 cups chopped seeded tomato (about 2 pounds)
- 3 garlic cloves, thinly sliced
- 1 cup (4 ounces) shredded provolone cheese
- ¼ cup thinly sliced basil leaves

1. Preheat oven to 475°.
2. To prepare pesto, place 4 cups basil leaves and 2 garlic cloves in a food processor, and pulse 5 times or until coarsely chopped. With processor on, add broth, Parmesan, and oil through food chute; process until well blended.
3. To prepare pizza, place pizza crust on a baking sheet. Spread pesto over crust, leaving a ½-inch border; top with tomato, garlic slices, and provolone. Bake at 475° for 12 minutes or until cheese

melts. Sprinkle with ¼ cup basil. Cut pizza into 8 wedges. Yield: 8 servings.

CALORIES 242 (33% from fat); FAT 9g (sat 3.8g, mono 3.7g, poly 1g); PROTEIN 11g; CARB 29.1g; FIBER 1.7g; CHOL 10mg; IRON 2.5mg; SODIUM 458mg; CALC 307mg

Gazpacho

To garnish this cold soup, top each serving with an ice cube.

3   large ripe tomatoes, quartered
      (about 1½ pounds)
2   cups chopped cucumber
1   cup chopped onion
1   cup chopped green bell pepper
2   tablespoons red wine vinegar
2   teaspoons olive oil
½   teaspoon salt
¼   teaspoon black pepper
1   garlic clove, minced
1   cup water

1. Combine first 9 ingredients in a food processor; pulse 4 or 5 times or to desired consistency. Pour into a bowl; stir in water. Cover and chill at least 1 hour. Yield: 6 servings (serving size: 1 cup).

CALORIES 58 (31% from fat); FAT 2g (sat 0.3g, mono 1.2g, poly 0.4g); PROTEIN 1.7g; CARB 9.9g; FIBER 2.4g; CHOL 0mg; IRON 1mg; SODIUM 207mg; CALC 19mg

Seafood Salad

1   pound medium shrimp, peeled and
      deveined
½   pound sea scallops
½   pound lump crabmeat, shell pieces
      removed
1½ cups diced seeded tomato
      (about 1 pound)
¼   cup minced fresh cilantro
3   tablespoons minced shallots or
      green onions
3   tablespoons fresh lime juice
1   tablespoon minced seeded
      jalapeño pepper
6   cups gourmet salad greens

1. Steam shrimp and scallops, covered, 6 minutes or until done; cool. Cut shrimp

and scallops into quarters. Combine shrimp, scallops, crabmeat, and next 5 ingredients in a bowl. Serve over salad greens. Yield: 6 servings (serving size: 1 cup seafood mixture and 1 cup salad greens).

CALORIES 158 (13% from fat); FAT 2.2g (sat 0.4g, mono 0.3g, poly 0.9g); PROTEIN 27g; CARB 6.7g; FIBER 1.6g; CHOL 136mg; IRON 2.9mg; SODIUM 261mg; CALC 107mg

Raid-the-Garden Dinner
serves 4

**Baked Snapper with
Tomato-Orange Sauce**

Couscous

Steamed sugar snap peas

Marinated strawberries*

*Combine 4 cups halved strawberries, 1 tablespoon brown sugar, and 1 tablespoon balsamic vinegar. Cover and let stand 30 minutes. Toss well before serving.

Baked Snapper with Tomato-Orange Sauce

Serve this dish with a side of couscous to capture the sauce.

3   cups chopped red tomato
      (about 2 pounds)
2   cups chopped yellow tomato
      (about 1½ pounds)
½   cup chopped onion
¼   cup dry white wine
1   teaspoon grated orange rind
¼   cup fresh orange juice
⅛   teaspoon ground turmeric
2   garlic cloves, minced
4   (6-ounce) red snapper, grouper, or
      other firm white fish fillets
1   teaspoon olive oil
¼   teaspoon salt
⅛   teaspoon black pepper

1. Preheat oven to 400°.
2. Combine first 8 ingredients in an 11 x 7-inch baking dish. Bake at 400° for 20 minutes. Arrange fillets on top of tomato mixture. Drizzle with oil; sprinkle with salt and pepper. Cover with foil; bake 20

minutes or until fish flakes easily when tested with a fork. Yield: 4 servings (serving size: 1 fillet and 1 cup sauce).

CALORIES 246 (15% from fat); FAT 4.2g (sat 0.7g, mono 1.4g, poly 1.2g); PROTEIN 37.3g; CARB 14.9g; FIBER 2.9g; CHOL 63mg; IRON 1.5mg; SODIUM 278mg; CALC 77mg

Kaleidoscope Tomato Salad with Balsamic-Olive Vinaigrette
(pictured on page 203)

Any combination of tomatoes will work in this salad. Olive pâté comes in tubes or jars and can be found with the condiments or in the ethnic-foods section of your supermarket.

VINAIGRETTE:
3   tablespoons balsamic vinegar
2   tablespoons water
1   tablespoon extra-virgin olive oil
1   tablespoon olive pâté (such as
      Alessi)
¼   teaspoon salt
⅛   teaspoon black pepper
1   garlic clove, crushed

SALAD:
6   cups gourmet salad greens
½   cup chopped red onion
¼   cup chopped fresh basil
12 (¼-inch-thick) slices green
      tomato, halved
12 (¼-inch-thick) slices yellow
      tomato, halved
12 (¼-inch-thick) slices red tomato,
      halved

1. To prepare vinaigrette, combine first 7 ingredients in a small bowl; stir well with a whisk.
2. To prepare salad, place greens on a platter. Sprinkle half of onion and half of basil evenly over greens. Arrange tomato slice halves over basil. Top with remaining onion and basil. Drizzle evenly with vinaigrette. Yield: 6 servings (serving size: 1 cup greens, 12 tomato slice halves, and about 1½ tablespoons vinaigrette).

CALORIES 62 (51% from fat); FAT 3.5g (sat 0.5g, mono 2.3g, poly 0.5g); PROTEIN 1.9g; CARB 7.1g; FIBER 2.3g; CHOL 0mg; IRON 1.2mg; SODIUM 119mg; CALC 32mg

Grilled Tomato, Smoked Turkey, and Muenster Sandwiches

1 tablespoon minced red onion
3 tablespoons fat-free sour cream
1 tablespoon Dijon mustard
1 teaspoon chopped fresh or
   ¼ teaspoon dried thyme
4 teaspoons butter, softened
4 (1½-ounce) slices sourdough bread
6 (1-ounce) slices fat-free,
   honey-roasted smoked turkey
   breast
4 (½-inch-thick) slices tomato
2 (½-ounce) slices Muenster cheese

1. Combine first 4 ingredients in a bowl. Spread 1 teaspoon butter on one side of each bread slice. Spread 2 tablespoons mustard mixture over unbuttered side of each of 2 bread slices; top each with 3 turkey slices, 2 tomato slices, 1 cheese slice, and 1 bread slice (with buttered side out).
2. Heat a large nonstick skillet over medium heat until hot. Add sandwiches; cover and cook 3 minutes on each side or until golden brown. Yield: 2 sandwiches (serving size: 1 sandwich).

CALORIES 451 (28% from fat); FAT 14.2g (sat 8g, mono 4.5g, poly 0.9g); PROTEIN 27.9g; CARB 48.7g; FIBER 1.8g; CHOL 65mg; IRON 2.4mg; SODIUM 913mg; CALC 238mg

---

To Seed or Not to Seed?

Ever wonder why some recipes call for seeded tomatoes and others don't? Basically, you should seed when you don't want too much juice, since seeding causes you to lose most of it. We call for seeding in recipes requiring just the pulp, such as Fresh Tomato-Pesto Pizza (recipe on page 210). In recipes that need to be saucy or juicy, such as Baked Snapper with Tomato-Orange Sauce (recipe on page 211), we leave the seeds.

To seed a tomato, core it, then cut it in half crosswise. Use your thumbs to push the seeds out of the tomato halves.

Tropical Yellow Tomato Salsa

This is great with grilled fish or chicken. You can use red tomatoes in place of yellow.

1½ cups diced yellow tomato (about
   1 pound)
½ cup diced peeled mango
½ cup diced peeled papaya
½ cup diced red onion
½ cup diced yellow bell pepper
2 tablespoons minced fresh basil
2 tablespoons minced fresh cilantro
2 tablespoons fresh lime juice
¼ teaspoon salt

1. Combine all ingredients in a bowl; toss well. Let salsa stand at room temperature 2 hours. Yield: 3 cups (serving size: ½ cup).

CALORIES 33 (8% from fat); FAT 0.3g (sat 0.1g, mono 0.1g, poly 0.1g); PROTEIN 0.9g; CARB 8g; FIBER 1.4g; CHOL 0mg; IRON 0.5mg; SODIUM 104mg; CALC 13mg

---

reader recipes

Fishing for Compliments

A Canadian reader reels in praise for an easy chowder that's good year-round.

Seafood lover Linda Petty of Pickering, Ontario, melded the flavors of two of her favorite places: creamed corn and fish over rice from Toronto's Chinatown, and the hearty seafood chowders of her family's vacation spot, Cape Hatteras, North Carolina.

In the process, she netted a standout: a creamy chowder that mingles the sweetness of corn with smoky bacon. Her husband, Mark, and four-year-old son, Vernon, delighted in the dish. But it was only after she received ecstatic compliments from a friend that Linda decided to share the recipe with a larger audience.

Corn-Fish Chowder

This dish works especially well at the height of sweet corn season. Yet it's almost as good complemented by a hearty bread and salad during Canadian winters. Because this soup freezes well, it's an easy weeknight meal.

2 bacon slices
½ cup chopped onion
1½ teaspoons ground thyme
2 (15.75-ounce) cans fat-free,
   less-sodium chicken broth
1 pound peeled baking potato, cut
   into ¼-inch-thick slices
2 cups fresh or frozen whole-kernel
   corn
¼ teaspoon salt
¼ teaspoon black pepper
2 (8¼-ounce) cans cream-style
   corn
1 (12-ounce) can evaporated fat-free
   milk
1 pound orange roughy or catfish
   fillets, cubed
½ cup instant potato flakes (not
   granules)
Coarsely ground black pepper (optional)

1. Cook bacon in a Dutch oven over medium heat until crisp. Remove bacon from pan; crumble. Add onion to drippings in pan; sauté 5 minutes. Stir in thyme, broth, and baking potato; bring to a boil. Reduce heat; simmer 10 minutes.
2. Add whole-kernel corn and next 4 ingredients; bring to a simmer. Stir in fish; cook 9 minutes or until fish flakes easily when tested with a fork. Add potato flakes, and cook until thick (about 1 minute), stirring constantly. Sprinkle bacon evenly over servings. Garnish with coarsely ground pepper, if desired. Yield: 8 servings (serving size: 1½ cups soup and about 1 teaspoon bacon).

CALORIES 261 (14% from fat); FAT 4.2g (sat 1.3g, mono 1.8g, poly 0.7g); PROTEIN 16g; CARB 40.1g; FIBER 2.6g; CHOL 17mg; IRON 1.3mg; SODIUM 527mg; CALC 144mg

Peppered Cauliflower

"This dish is a sort of Indian stir-fry, adapted from the Chinese. Enjoy the delicate flavor of the dish—it's not too spicy."

—Veenu Chopra, M.D., New Delhi, India

    1   tablespoon vegetable oil
    1   cup chopped onion
    2   garlic cloves, minced
    1   cup chopped tomato
    ¼   teaspoon salt
    ¼   to ½ teaspoon black pepper
    ¼   teaspoon ground red pepper
    2   cups cauliflower florets

1. Heat oil in a medium nonstick skillet over medium-high heat. Add onion and garlic; sauté 5 minutes or until lightly browned. Add tomato, salt, and peppers; sauté 2 minutes. Add cauliflower. Cover, reduce heat, and simmer 12 minutes or until tender. Yield: 5 servings (serving size: ½ cup).

CALORIES 57 (47% from fat); FAT 3g (sat 0.7g, mono 0.8g, poly 1.4g); PROTEIN 1.6g; CARB 7.2g; FIBER 2.1g; CHOL 0mg; IRON 0.5mg; SODIUM 134mg; CALC 20mg

Light Honey-Mustard Chicken Salad

—Terren Otis, Sante Fe, New Mexico

    4   cups water
    1   cup chopped onion
    4   garlic cloves, chopped
    3   rosemary sprigs
    1   pound skinless, boneless chicken
        breast
    3   tablespoons egg substitute
    3   tablespoons honey
    2   tablespoons olive oil
    1   tablespoon rice vinegar
    2   teaspoons country-style Dijon
        mustard
    ¼   teaspoon freshly ground black
        pepper
    2   garlic cloves, minced
    6   cups gourmet salad greens
    12 (¼-inch-thick) slices cucumber
    1   medium tomato, cut into 8 wedges
    1   (11-ounce) can mandarin oranges
        in light syrup, drained

1. Combine first 5 ingredients in a Dutch oven over medium-high heat. Bring to a boil; cover, reduce heat, and simmer 12 minutes or until chicken is done. Remove chicken from pan, discarding liquid and solids, and cool chicken slightly. Shred meat with 2 forks to measure 3 cups.
2. Combine egg substitute and next 6 ingredients in a food processor, and process until smooth. Place chicken and honey mixture in a medium bowl; toss to coat.
3. Line plates with salad greens, and top evenly with chicken salad, cucumber, tomato wedges, and oranges. Yield: 4 servings (serving size: 1½ cups greens, ¾ cup chicken salad, 3 cucumber slices, 2 tomato wedges, and about 2 tablespoons mandarin oranges).

CALORIES 328 (24% from fat); FAT 8.7g (sat 1.4g, mono 5.5g, poly 1.1g); PROTEIN 29.9g; CARB 32.7g; FIBER 2.8g; CHOL 66mg; IRON 2.6mg; SODIUM 182mg; CALC 68mg

Mexican Bean Dip

"Just one thing to remember with this dish: Don't forget the napkins!"

—Kristin Zina, Somerville, Massachusetts

    1   (8-ounce) block ⅓-less-fat cream
        cheese
    1   cup (4 ounces) shredded Monterey
        Jack cheese with jalapeño peppers,
        divided
    ½   cup chopped onion
    1   (15-ounce) can vegetarian chili
        with beans
    1   (4.5-ounce) can chopped green
        chiles, undrained

1. Preheat oven to 350°.
2. Spread cream cheese evenly over bottom of a 9-inch pie plate. Combine ½ cup Monterey Jack cheese, onion, chili, and green chiles in a small bowl. Spread chili mixture over cream cheese. Sprinkle with ½ cup Monterey Jack cheese. Bake at 350° for 20 minutes. Yield: 4 cups (serving size: 2 tablespoons).

CALORIES 46 (55% from fat); FAT 2.7g (sat 1.8g, mono 0.8g, poly 0.1g); PROTEIN 2.4g; CARB 3g; FIBER 0.6g; CHOL 8mg; IRON 0.2mg; SODIUM 138mg; CALC 36mg

Beef-Taco Rice with Refried Beans

"My wife and I like this dish even more a day or two after it's made. Dress up the top with grated cheese after it's been reheated."

—Ken Sissney, Aubrey, Texas

    4   cups water
    1   cup chopped onion
    1   cup chopped green bell pepper
    ¼   teaspoon salt
    ¼   teaspoon black pepper
    1   (1.25-ounce) package taco
        seasoning, divided
    4   cups uncooked instant rice
    2   (8-ounce) cans no-salt-added
        tomato sauce
    1   pound ground round
    Cooking spray
    1   (16-ounce) can fat-free refried
        beans
    1   (8-ounce) package preshredded
        reduced-fat Mexican blend or
        cheddar cheese

1. Preheat oven to 350°.
2. Combine first 5 ingredients in a large saucepan; add half of taco seasoning. Bring to a boil. Remove from heat. Stir in rice; cover and let stand 5 minutes. Stir in tomato sauce.
3. Cook meat in a large nonstick skillet over medium-high heat until browned, stirring to crumble. Drain; return meat to pan. Stir in remaining taco seasoning.
4. Spread half of rice mixture in bottom of a 13 x 9-inch baking dish coated with cooking spray. Spread beans evenly over rice mixture; top with beef mixture and half of cheese. Spread remaining rice mixture over cheese; top with remaining cheese. Bake at 350° for 10 minutes or until cheese melts. Yield: 10 servings (serving size: about 1¼ cups).

CALORIES 371 (18% from fat); FAT 7.5g (sat 3.6g, mono 2.5g, poly 0.4g); PROTEIN 23.7g; CARB 51.2g; FIBER 3.8g; CHOL 42mg; IRON 4.4mg; SODIUM 696mg; CALC 221mg

Spicy Turkey Chili

"Other veggies may be substituted—cabbage and mushrooms are both good."
—Marianne Garrett, Washington, D.C.

1¼ cups green bell pepper strips
1 cup sliced onion
½ cup (¼-inch-thick) sliced carrot
½ cup (¼-inch-thick) sliced zucchini
1 pound ground turkey
¼ cup chili powder
1½ teaspoons sugar
¾ teaspoon dried oregano
¼ teaspoon salt
¼ teaspoon black pepper
2 (14.5-ounce) cans no-salt-added stewed tomatoes, undrained
1 (16-ounce) can kidney beans, drained
1 (15-ounce) can black beans, drained
1 (8-ounce) can no-salt-added tomato sauce
½ cup (2 ounces) shredded Monterey Jack cheese
¼ cup chopped onion

1. Heat a large Dutch oven over medium heat. Add first 5 ingredients; cook 5 minutes or until turkey is browned, stirring to crumble. Stir in chili powder and next 8 ingredients, and bring to a boil. Cover, reduce heat, and simmer 1 hour, stirring occasionally. Sprinkle with cheese and chopped onion. Yield: 8 servings (serving size: 1 cup chili, 1 tablespoon cheese, and 1½ teaspoons chopped onion).

CALORIES 272 (26% from fat); FAT 8g (sat 2.9g, mono 2.6g, poly 1.8g); PROTEIN 20.3g; CARB 32.2g; FIBER 6.2g; CHOL 51mg; IRON 4.3mg; SODIUM 398mg; CALC 136mg

in season

Velvety, Gold Apricots

Almost heavenly in appearance, the down-to-earth apricot is versatile and at its peak in July.

Apricot and Cherry Salad with Lime-Poppy Seed Vinaigrette

VINAIGRETTE:
⅓ cup sugar
3 tablespoons water
3 tablespoons fresh lime juice
1 teaspoon salt
1 teaspoon dry mustard
2 tablespoons vegetable oil
1 tablespoon poppy seeds

SALAD:
6 cups trimmed watercress
4 cups sliced apricots (about 12 medium)
3 cups halved pitted cherries

1. To prepare vinaigrette, place first 5 ingredients in a blender; process until blended. Add oil and seeds, and process until blended.
2. To prepare salad, place 1 cup watercress on each of 6 plates. Top each serving with ⅔ cup apricot slices and ½ cup cherries. Drizzle 2 tablespoons vinaigrette over each salad. Yield: 6 servings.

CALORIES 184 (30% from fat); FAT 6.2g (sat 1.1g, mono 1.7g, poly 2.9g); PROTEIN 3g; CARB 32.4g; FIBER 4.2g; CHOL 0mg; IRON 0.9mg; SODIUM 406mg; CALC 85mg

Spiced Pork Skewers with Apricots

Soak wooden skewers in water for 15 minutes so they won't burn. Make the marinade one day ahead and refrigerate it.

½ cup honey
½ cup thawed orange juice concentrate, undiluted
½ teaspoon salt
½ teaspoon ground cinnamon
¼ teaspoon ground allspice
¼ teaspoon black pepper
2 garlic cloves, minced
1½ pounds pork tenderloin, trimmed and cut into 36 pieces
12 apricots, halved and pitted
3 small red onions, each cut into 8 wedges
Cooking spray

1. Combine first 7 ingredients in a small bowl. Reserve half of honey mixture, and set aside. Combine pork and remaining honey mixture in a shallow dish. Cover and marinate in refrigerator 2 hours.
2. Prepare grill.
3. Remove pork from dish; discard marinade. Thread 6 pork pieces onto each of 6 (12-inch) skewers. Combine reserved honey mixture and apricots in a bowl, tossing to coat. Thread 4 apricot halves and 4 onion wedges alternately onto each of 6 (12-inch) skewers.
4. Place pork kebabs on grill rack coated with cooking spray, and grill 4 minutes on each side or until slightly pink. Remove pork kebabs from grill rack. Place apricot kebabs on grill rack; grill 2 minutes on each side or until apricots are tender. Yield: 6 servings (serving size: 1 pork kebab and 1 apricot kebab).

CALORIES 247 (16% from fat); FAT 4.5g (sat 1.4g, mono 2g, poly 0.6g); PROTEIN 26g; CARB 26.2g; FIBER 2.1g; CHOL 79mg; IRON 1.9mg; SODIUM 158mg; CALC 30mg

Rosemary-Rubbed Duck Breast with Caramelized Apricots

(pictured on page 204)

Serve this entrée with couscous or rice to soak up the sauce. If you're not a duck fan, you can also make the recipe with chicken breasts.

3 tablespoons chopped fresh rosemary
2 tablespoons brown sugar
1 tablespoon freshly ground black pepper
2 teaspoons salt
2 (¾-pound) duck breasts, skinned and halved
1 tablespoon olive oil
½ cup granulated sugar
½ cup champagne vinegar or white wine vinegar
5 apricots, quartered

1. Combine first 4 ingredients. Rub rosemary mixture over duck. Cover and chill 2 hours. Rinse duck with cold water; pat dry.

2. Heat oil in a large nonstick skillet over medium-high heat. Add duck, and cook 5 minutes on each side or until done. Remove from pan; let stand 10 minutes.

3. Combine granulated sugar and vinegar in a small saucepan, and bring to a boil. Cook until thick and amber-colored (about 5 minutes). Add apricots; reduce heat, and cook 1 minute or until apricots begin to soften. Cut duck diagonally across grain into slices. Serve with caramelized apricots. Yield: 4 servings (serving size: 3 ounces duck, 5 apricot quarters, and 3 tablespoons sauce).

CALORIES 374 (26% from fat); FAT 10.9g (sat 2.8g, mono 4.6g, poly 1.3g); PROTEIN 34.5g; CARB 33.2g; FIBER 1.5g; CHOL 0mg; IRON 8.4mg; SODIUM 688mg; CALC 23mg

Try New Things Menu

Teriyaki-Glazed Chicken with Tangy Apricot Ketchup

Mashed potatoes

Broccoli florets sautéed with garlic

Teriyaki-Glazed Chicken with Tangy Apricot Ketchup

1 (7-ounce) can chipotle chiles in adobo sauce
½ cup low-sodium teriyaki sauce
8 chicken thighs (about 2½ pounds), skinned
3 teaspoons minced garlic cloves, divided
1 tablespoon olive oil
1 cup chopped onion
2 cups chopped apricots (about ¾ pound)
¼ cup apricot preserves
1 tablespoon fresh lime juice
¾ teaspoon salt, divided
Cooking spray
¼ cup chopped fresh cilantro

1. Remove 1 chile from can, and mince. Place 1 teaspoon minced chile in a large zip-top plastic bag. Reserve ½ teaspoon minced chile, and set aside. Reserve remaining chiles and sauce for another use.

Add teriyaki sauce, chicken, and 2 teaspoons garlic to bag; seal and marinate in refrigerator 3 to 12 hours.

2. Heat oil in a medium nonstick skillet over medium heat. Add 1 teaspoon garlic and onion, and cook 5 minutes or until tender, stirring frequently. Add reserved ½ teaspoon minced chile, chopped apricots, preserves, lime juice, and ½ teaspoon salt; cook mixture over medium-high heat 5 minutes or until apricots are very tender. Remove from heat; cool slightly. Place apricot mixture in a blender; process until smooth. Cool to room temperature. Remove ½ cup apricot mixture.

3. Prepare grill.

4. Remove chicken from bag, and discard marinade. Sprinkle chicken with ¼ teaspoon salt. Place chicken on grill rack coated with cooking spray, and grill 10 minutes on each side, basting frequently with reserved ½ cup apricot mixture during last 5 minutes. Serve chicken with remaining apricot mixture. Sprinkle each serving with cilantro. Yield: 4 servings (serving size: 2 thighs, ¼ cup apricot ketchup, and 1 tablespoon cilantro).

CALORIES 317 (26% from fat); FAT 9.1g (sat 1.9g, mono 4.3g, poly 1.7g); PROTEIN 29.5g; CARB 30.1g; FIBER 3.1g; CHOL 113mg; IRON 2.4mg; SODIUM 824mg; CALC 52mg

Coconut Tapioca Custard with Glazed Apricots

CUSTARD:
2¼ cups whole milk
1 cup sugar
⅔ cup uncooked quick-cooking tapioca
1 teaspoon salt
2 (14-ounce) cans light coconut milk
2 large eggs, lightly beaten
2 tablespoons white rum
1 teaspoon vanilla extract
⅛ teaspoon coconut extract

APRICOTS:
¾ cup apricot preserves
2 tablespoons white rum
1 tablespoon water
¼ teaspoon salt
10 apricots, each cut into 4 wedges

1. To prepare custard, combine first 6 ingredients in a medium saucepan, stirring with a whisk. Let stand 5 minutes. Bring mixture to a boil over medium heat, stirring constantly. Cook 30 seconds, stirring constantly. Remove mixture from heat. Stir in 2 tablespoons rum and extracts, and pour mixture into a large bowl. Cover and chill 2 hours.

2. To prepare apricots, combine preserves and remaining 4 ingredients in a medium skillet; bring to a boil. Reduce heat, and simmer 5 minutes or until apricots are soft, stirring occasionally. Serve over custard. Yield: 10 servings (serving size: about ¾ cup custard and about ¼ cup apricots).

CALORIES 289 (22% from fat); FAT 7g (sat 4g, mono 1.2g, poly 0.3g); PROTEIN 4.7g; CARB 53.3g; FIBER 1g; CHOL 50mg; IRON 0.8mg; SODIUM 363mg; CALC 81mg

Deep Dish Apricot-Apple Betty

FILLING:
4 cups thinly sliced peeled Braeburn or Fuji apple (about 1½ pounds)
4 cups quartered apricots (about 12 medium)
1 cup granulated sugar
2 tablespoons all-purpose flour
1 tablespoon fresh lemon juice
¾ teaspoon ground cinnamon
½ teaspoon ground allspice
½ teaspoon almond extract
¼ teaspoon salt

TOPPING:
2 tablespoons butter
⅓ cup all-purpose flour
⅓ cup packed brown sugar
¼ cup finely chopped almonds
¼ teaspoon salt

1. Preheat oven to 350°.

2. To prepare filling, combine first 9 ingredients in a medium bowl. Spoon apple mixture into an 8-inch square baking dish.

3. To prepare topping, melt butter in a small saucepan over medium heat. Lightly spoon ⅓ cup flour into a dry

Continued

measuring cup, and level with a knife. Add flour and remaining 3 ingredients to butter; stir well. Sprinkle topping evenly over apple mixture. Bake at 350° for 45 minutes or until bubbly and golden brown. Yield: 8 servings (serving size: ¾ cup).

CALORIES 260 (17% from fat); FAT 4.9g (sat 2g, mono 2g, poly 0.6g); PROTEIN 2.2g; CARB 54.7g; FIBER 2.5g; CHOL 8mg; IRON 1.1mg; SODIUM 181mg; CALC 33mg

Sauternes-Poached Apricots with Fresh Berries and Vanilla Crème Fraîche

Poaching infuses apricots with sweet wine and softens the fruit. You can use sour cream in place of crème fraîche, if desired.

APRICOTS:
2 cups sugar
1¾ cups Sauternes or other sweet white wine
1¼ cups water
⅛ teaspoon salt
2 (6-inch) vanilla beans, split lengthwise
12 apricots

CRÈME FRAÎCHE:
½ cup commercial crème fraîche
1 tablespoon sugar
½ teaspoon vanilla extract
Dash of salt

REMAINING INGREDIENTS:
1½ cups fresh blueberries
1½ cups fresh raspberries

1. To prepare apricots, combine first 4 ingredients in a large saucepan. Scrape seeds from vanilla beans; add seeds and beans to wine mixture. Bring to a boil; add apricots. Reduce heat, and simmer 2 minutes. Remove apricots with a slotted spoon. Bring wine mixture to a boil; cook until reduced to 2¼ cups (about 20 minutes). Cool mixture to room temperature. Cut apricots in half, and remove pits. Combine wine mixture and apricot halves in a shallow dish, and discard vanilla beans. Cover and chill 8 hours.

2. To prepare crème fraîche, combine commercial crème fraîche, 1 tablespoon sugar, vanilla extract, and dash of salt.
3. Arrange 3 apricot halves, 3 tablespoons blueberries, and 3 tablespoons raspberries on each of 8 dessert plates. Drizzle each serving with about 2 tablespoons wine mixture; top each with 1 tablespoon crème fraîche. Yield: 8 servings.

CALORIES 288 (11% from fat); FAT 3.5g (sat 1.9g, mono 1g, poly 0.3g); PROTEIN 1.8g; CARB 65.7g; FIBER 3.7g; CHOL 6mg; IRON 0.7mg; SODIUM 69mg; CALC 36mg

---

Preparing Apricots

After rinsing apricots, pitting is all you need to do to prepare them for eating, cooking, or freezing. The pit slides right out when the fruit is split. Freeze split and pitted apricot halves on baking sheets until firm, then transfer to airtight plastic bags.

---

cooking light profile

Family Style

An aspiring physician indulges her inclination to take care of people by cooking for family and friends.

For Jasmine Nguyen, a 26-year-old medical student at the University of California-San Francisco, food and security—food and happiness—are too closely intertwined for her to separate. That's why, when she has free time, you may find this Vietnamese native wandering down Clement Street, drinking a tapioca shake and seeking the perfect young coconut. Or maybe you'll find her browsing the produce stand. Perhaps you may even find her in the kitchen treating family or her classmates and friends to authentic Vietnamese dinners.

The meals started off with just a few close friends, but before long, word got around, and she was fielding calls from weary students craving a home-cooked meal. She knows from her family experiences that there's no such thing as too many people at the table.

Sugar-Snap-Pea Salad with Sweet Ginger-Soy Dressing

Jasmine's friends love this dish, especially the Asian-style sauce. Preparation is quick and easy.

DRESSING:
2 teaspoons dark sesame oil
1 tablespoon minced peeled fresh ginger
1 tablespoon minced fresh garlic
¼ teaspoon crushed red pepper
1 tablespoon oyster sauce
1 tablespoon low-sodium soy sauce
1 tablespoon sugar
⅛ teaspoon salt

SALAD:
1 pound sugar snap peas, trimmed
½ cup julienne-cut carrot
½ cup drained, sliced water chestnuts
½ cup sliced mushrooms
½ cup julienne-cut red bell pepper
2 teaspoons sesame seeds, toasted

1. To prepare dressing, heat oil in a small saucepan over medium heat. Add ginger; sauté 2 minutes. Add garlic and crushed red pepper; cook 1 minute. Stir in oyster sauce, soy sauce, sugar, and salt; bring to a simmer. Remove from heat; cool.
2. To prepare salad, cook peas in boiling water 30 seconds. Drain and rinse with cold water. Combine peas, carrot, and next 3 ingredients. Drizzle dressing over salad; toss well. Sprinkle with sesame seeds. Yield: 5 servings (serving size: 1 cup).

CALORIES 107 (18% from fat); FAT 2.3g (sat 0.3g, mono 0.9g, poly 1g); PROTEIN 4g; CARB 18.9g; FIBER 4.3g; CHOL 0mg; IRON 1.1mg; SODIUM 289mg; CALC 77mg

Catfish, Reconsidered

A down-home classic goes uptown.

Once a staple of Southern cuisine, catfish is now available across the country and is farm-raised, guaranteeing a consistent year-round supply. It's relatively inexpensive, too. And because it has somewhat more fat than other fish, catfish takes well to bold seasonings and marinades.

Mix-and-Match Catfish Dinner

Oven-Fried Catfish
or
Poached Cajun Catfish

Black-Eyed Pea Salad with Sour Cream Dressing
or
Chile-Vinegar Turnip Greens

Chipotle-Maple Sweet Potatoes
or
Grilled Bacon-and-Herb Grit Cakes

Jalapeño Corn Bread

Apples Baked in Phyllo with Pear-and-Pecan Filling

Oven-Fried Catfish

(pictured on page 203)

½ cup light beer
½ cup hot sauce
4 (6-ounce) farm-raised catfish fillets
½ cup yellow cornmeal
2 tablespoons cornstarch
⅛ teaspoon salt
⅛ teaspoon black pepper
Cooking spray

1. Combine first 3 ingredients in a large zip-top plastic bag; seal and marinate in refrigerator 30 minutes. Remove fillets from bag; pat dry with paper towels. Discard marinade.
2. Preheat oven to 450°.
3. Combine cornmeal, cornstarch, salt, and pepper in a shallow dish. Dredge fillets in cornmeal mixture.
4. Lightly coat fillets with cooking spray. Place fillets on a baking sheet coated with cooking spray, and bake at 450° for 15 minutes or until fish flakes easily when tested with a fork. Yield: 4 servings (serving size: 1 fillet).

CALORIES 296 (27% from fat); FAT 8.8g (sat 1.9g, mono 3.1g, poly 2.5g); PROTEIN 32.8g; CARB 17.7g; FIBER 1.1g; CHOL 99mg; IRON 2.8mg; SODIUM 361mg; CALC 74mg

Poached Cajun Catfish

4 (6-ounce) farm-raised catfish fillets
1 teaspoon Creole seasoning (such as Tony Chachere's)
1 teaspoon butter
Cooking spray
½ cup finely chopped shallots
4 garlic cloves, crushed
1½ cups Riesling or other slightly sweet white wine

1. Sprinkle fillets with seasoning.
2. Melt butter in a large nonstick skillet coated with cooking spray over medium-high heat. Add shallots and garlic; sauté 3 minutes. Add wine; bring to a boil. Add fillets; cover, reduce heat, and simmer 16 minutes or until fish flakes easily when tested with a fork. Remove fillets with a spatula; place 1 fillet on each of 4 plates. Bring poaching liquid to a boil; cook until reduced to ½ cup (about 2 minutes). Strain poaching liquid through a sieve into a bowl; discard solids. Spoon 2 tablespoons poaching liquid over each fillet. Yield: 4 servings.

CALORIES 234 (33% from fat); FAT 8.7g (sat 2.3g, mono 3g, poly 1.8g); PROTEIN 31.8g; CARB 5.5g; FIBER 0.2g; CHOL 101mg; IRON 2.3mg; SODIUM 707mg; CALC 89mg

Black-Eyed Pea Salad with Sour Cream Dressing

½ cup fat-free sour cream
⅓ cup white wine vinegar
2 tablespoons sugar
½ teaspoon salt
¼ teaspoon black pepper
1 cup thinly sliced Vidalia or other sweet onion
1 cup thinly sliced cucumber
1 cup julienne-cut red bell pepper
1 (15.8-ounce) can black-eyed peas, rinsed and drained

1. Combine first 5 ingredients in a medium bowl; stir with a whisk.
2. Add remaining ingredients, tossing to coat. Cover and chill 3 hours. Yield: 4 servings (serving size: 1 cup).

CALORIES 115 (4% from fat); FAT 0.5g (sat 0.1g, mono 0.1g, poly 0.2g); PROTEIN 6.3g; CARB 20.6g; FIBER 1.9g; CHOL 0mg; IRON 1mg; SODIUM 377mg; CALC 63mg

Chile-Vinegar Turnip Greens

(pictured on page 203)

1½ teaspoons olive oil
2 garlic cloves, minced
1 (1-pound) bag turnip greens, chopped
1 cup fat-free, less-sodium chicken broth
¼ cup rice vinegar
2 teaspoons chile paste with garlic
½ teaspoon freshly ground black pepper

1. Heat oil in a stockpot over medium-high heat. Add garlic, and sauté 30 seconds or until lightly browned. Add greens, and sauté 5 minutes or until wilted. Add remaining ingredients. Bring to a boil; cover, reduce heat, and cook 45 minutes. Yield: 4 servings (serving size: 1 cup).

CALORIES 56 (32% from fat); FAT 2g (sat 0.3g, mono 1.3g, poly 0.3g); PROTEIN 2g; CARB 7.4g; FIBER 2.8g; CHOL 0mg; IRON 1.4mg; SODIUM 202mg; CALC 219mg

Chipotle-Maple Sweet Potatoes

(pictured on page 203)

Chipotle chile peppers come packed in adobo sauce and are available in seven-ounce cans. Because we use such a small amount in this recipe, you can freeze what's left over in a heavy-duty freezer bag for another use.

1 pound coarsely chopped peeled sweet potato
2 tablespoons maple syrup
2 tablespoons fat-free milk
1 tablespoon butter
1½ teaspoons adobo sauce
¼ teaspoon salt
⅛ teaspoon black pepper
½ drained canned chipotle chile in adobo sauce, minced

1. Place potato in a saucepan, and cover with water; bring to a boil. Reduce heat, and simmer 15 minutes or until tender; drain. Return potato to pan. Add syrup and remaining ingredients; beat with a mixer at medium speed until smooth. Yield: 4 servings (serving size: ½ cup).

CALORIES 177 (17% from fat); FAT 3.4g (sat 1.9g, mono 0.9g, poly 0.3g); PROTEIN 2.1g; CARB 35.2g; FIBER 3.4g; CHOL 8mg; IRON 0.8mg; SODIUM 195mg; CALC 42mg

Grilled Bacon-and-Herb Grit Cakes

Chilling the grits helps them hold their shape when they're cut and grilled.

4 cups hot cooked instant grits
½ cup (2 ounces) shredded white cheddar cheese
1 tablespoon minced fresh or 1 teaspoon dried thyme
2 teaspoons chopped fresh parsley
½ teaspoon garlic powder
½ teaspoon black pepper
3 bacon slices, cooked and crumbled
Cooking spray

1. Combine first 7 ingredients in a large bowl; stir well. Pour grits into a 10-inch square baking dish coated with cooking spray, spreading evenly. Cover and chill 1 hour or until completely cool.
2. Prepare grill.
3. Invert grits onto a cutting board; cut into 4 squares. Cut each square diagonally into 2 triangles.
4. Place grits triangles on grill rack coated with cooking spray; grill 5 minutes on each side or until lightly browned and thoroughly heated. Yield: 4 servings (serving size: 2 triangles).

CALORIES 255 (30% from fat); FAT 8.5g (sat 4g, mono 2.7g, poly 0.5g); PROTEIN 9.3g; CARB 38.8g; FIBER 2.4g; CHOL 20mg; IRON 15.2mg; SODIUM 695mg; CALC 123mg

Jalapeño Corn Bread

(pictured on page 203)

With sour cream and cream-style corn, this is a moist corn bread uncharacteristic of most Southern-style versions. The sour cream also balances the heat from the jalapeño peppers.

1½ cups cornmeal
1 cup fat-free sour cream
¼ cup chopped seeded jalapeño pepper
2 tablespoons vegetable oil
2 tablespoons dark molasses
¾ teaspoon baking powder
¾ teaspoon baking soda
½ teaspoon salt
2 large egg whites, lightly beaten
1 large egg, lightly beaten
1 (14¾-ounce) can cream-style corn
Cooking spray

1. Preheat oven to 400°.
2. Combine all ingredients except cooking spray in a large bowl. Pour mixture into a 9-inch cast-iron skillet coated with cooking spray. Bake at 400° for 40 minutes or until a wooden pick inserted in center of corn bread comes out clean. Cool in pan 10 minutes on a wire rack, and remove from pan. Cool completely on wire rack. Yield: 12 servings (serving size: 1 wedge).

CALORIES 144 (21% from fat); FAT 3.3g (sat 0.6g, mono 1g, poly 1.4g); PROTEIN 4.7g; CARB 23.6g; FIBER 1.2g; CHOL 18mg; IRON 1.2mg; SODIUM 337mg; CALC 55mg

Apples Baked in Phyllo with Pear-and-Pecan Filling

1 tablespoon butter
2 cups chopped peeled Bartlett or Anjou pear
3 tablespoons chopped pecans
2 tablespoons bourbon or water
1 tablespoon maple syrup
½ teaspoon ground cinnamon, divided
4 Granny Smith apples, peeled
4 sheets frozen phyllo dough, thawed
Cooking spray
2 tablespoons sugar
1 cup frozen fat-free whipped topping, thawed
Mint sprigs (optional)

1. Preheat oven to 375°.
2. Cover a baking sheet with parchment paper; secure to sheet with masking tape.
3. Melt butter in a medium nonstick skillet over medium heat. Add pear and pecans; sauté 2 minutes. Add bourbon, syrup, and ¼ teaspoon cinnamon; reduce heat, and simmer 5 minutes. Cool.
4. Cut about ½ inch from tops and bottoms of apples, and discard. Core apples three-fourths way through from top using a melon baller. (Do not cut through bottom.) Fill each apple with 1 tablespoon pear mixture. Set aside remaining pear mixture.
5. Place 1 phyllo sheet on a large cutting board or work surface (cover remaining dough to keep from drying); lightly coat with cooking spray. Place 1 apple in center of phyllo; overlap diagonal corners on top of apple. Place on prepared pan; coat phyllo with cooking spray. Repeat procedure with remaining apples and phyllo.
6. Combine ¼ teaspoon cinnamon and sugar in a small bowl, and sprinkle over wrapped apples. Bake at 375° for 30 minutes or until phyllo is golden brown. Place apples in individual serving dishes. Spoon ¼ cup remaining pear mixture around each apple; top each serving with ¼ cup whipped topping. Garnish with mint sprigs, if desired. Yield: 4 servings.

CALORIES 314 (26% from fat); FAT 9g (sat 2.4g, mono 3.6g, poly 2.2g); PROTEIN 2.3g; CARB 58.5g; FIBER 4.9g; CHOL 8mg; IRON 1.3mg; SODIUM 132mg; CALC 28mg

august

Pick Up Sticks

Supper's simple when skewers steal the show.

Colorful and festive, kebabs are a step up from everyday meat and veggies—and since they're great on the grill, they're ideal for outdoor entertaining. If your crowd is adventurous, set out marinated meats and vegetable pieces, and let guests assemble their own skewers. If your crowd is more sedate, you do the skewering.

Why kebabs instead of burgers or steaks? Because they cook so fast that you won't be left slaving over a hot grill while your guests are left to amuse themselves (all the skewer options we have for you cook in 15 minutes or less). And kebabs are as easy to serve as they are to prepare.

You'll find kebabs inspired by American, Asian, European, and Mediterranean regional cuisines among our offerings. And they're so simple that you could serve both North African Lamb and Potato Kebabs and Cajun-Spiced Catfish Kebabs in the same meal.

Mediterranean Chicken and Vegetable Kebabs

Serve these kebabs over couscous tossed with a bit of salt, cherry tomatoes, and chopped fresh mint.

- ¼ cup fresh lemon juice
- 2 tablespoons fresh chopped or 2 teaspoons dried oregano
- 2 tablespoons olive oil
- 1½ pounds skinless, boneless chicken breast, cut into 24 strips
- 18 (½-inch-thick) slices zucchini
- 1 fennel bulb, cut into 12 wedges
- 12 garlic cloves, peeled
- ½ teaspoon salt
- ¼ teaspoon black pepper
- Cooking spray

1. Combine first 6 ingredients in a zip-top plastic bag; seal and shake well. Marinate in refrigerator 20 minutes. Remove chicken and vegetables from bag; discard marinade.
2. Prepare grill.
3. Cook garlic cloves in boiling water 3 minutes; drain and cool.
4. Thread 4 chicken strips, 3 zucchini slices, 2 fennel wedges, and 2 garlic cloves alternately onto each of 6 (12-inch) skewers. Sprinkle with salt and pepper. Place kebabs on grill rack coated with cooking spray. Grill, turning once, 8 minutes or until chicken is done. Yield: 6 servings (serving size: 1 kebab).

CALORIES 194 (29% from fat); FAT 6.2g (sat 1g, mono 3.7g, poly 0.8g); PROTEIN 28g; CARB 6.4g; FIBER 0.7g; CHOL 66mg; IRON 2mg; SODIUM 274mg; CALC 63mg

Rum-Glazed Pineapple, Mango, and Chicken Kebabs

Serve with hot cooked white rice tossed with toasted coconut.

- ¾ cup pineapple juice
- ¼ cup sugar
- ¼ cup dark rum
- 2 tablespoons finely chopped seeded jalapeño pepper
- 1 tablespoon cider vinegar
- 2 teaspoons cornstarch
- 2 tablespoons chopped fresh cilantro
- 1½ teaspoons grated lime rind
- 1½ pounds skinless, boneless chicken breast, cut into 30 cubes
- 2 mangoes, peeled and each cut into 9 (1-inch) cubes
- 18 (1-inch) cubes fresh pineapple
- 1½ tablespoons vegetable oil
- 1 teaspoon salt
- Cooking spray

1. Prepare grill.
2. Combine first 4 ingredients in a medium saucepan; bring to a boil. Reduce heat; simmer 5 minutes. Combine vinegar and cornstarch in a small bowl. Add cornstarch mixture to pan; bring to a boil. Cook 1 minute, stirring constantly. Let stand 5 minutes. Stir in cilantro and rind.
3. Thread 5 chicken cubes, 3 mango cubes, and 3 pineapple cubes alternately onto each of 6 (12-inch) skewers. Brush kebabs with oil, and sprinkle with salt. Place kebabs on grill rack coated with cooking spray; grill 4 minutes. Turn kebabs; brush with half of glaze. Grill 4 minutes. Turn kebabs; brush with remaining glaze. Grill 2 minutes, turning once. Yield: 6 servings (serving size: 1 kebab).

CALORIES 313 (30% from fat); FAT 10.4g (sat 2.4g, mono 3.5g, poly 3.5g); PROTEIN 26g; CARB 30g; FIBER 1.8g; CHOL 71mg; IRON 1.3mg; SODIUM 450mg; CALC 28mg

---

When a Kebab is a *Kebap*

For centuries, people around the world have been talking about skewers. Here's what they've been saying.

- Go continental and call them *brochettes*, as the French do. The French think of a skewer as a sort of pin (*broche*, or "brooch," plus *-ette*, or "little") that holds food for cooking.
- English cooks used the word *skewer* as early as the 1670s, though its origins are uncertain.
- Or call them *kebap*, as the Turks do—although when they say that, they mean roasted meat only.
- Farther East, the Indonesians indulge in *saté*: grilled strips of meat, fish, or poultry, usually fired with a spicy peanut sauce.
- Around Buffalo, New York, there's a local delicacy of a thinly sliced marinated beef or chicken kebab called a "spiedi" (pronounced "speedy"). That's short for *spiedini*, which is Italian for "skewer" (*spiedo*, or kitchen spit, and *-ini*, or little). The name fits—spiedis grill in moments.

Jamaican Jerk Beef Kebabs

(pictured on page 238)

Jerk is a Jamaican seasoning blend used on beef, pork, chicken, lamb, and fish. Traditionally, jerk is a dry rub, but you can mix it with liquid to form a paste or marinade. Choose yellow plantains with black spots to ensure that they're ripe.

- ½ cup chopped green onions
- 1 tablespoon ground allspice
- 2 tablespoons red wine vinegar
- 1 teaspoon salt
- 1 teaspoon chopped fresh or ¼ teaspoon dried thyme
- 2 teaspoons low-sodium soy sauce
- ½ teaspoon ground cinnamon
- ⅛ teaspoon ground nutmeg
- 2 habanero or serrano peppers, seeded
- 1½ pounds boneless sirloin, trimmed and cut into 30 cubes
- 1 red bell pepper, cut into 18 pieces
- 2 black-ripe plantains, peeled and each cut into 9 pieces
- Cooking spray
- Diagonally cut green onions (optional)
- Lime wedges (optional)

1. Prepare grill.
2. Combine first 9 ingredients in a food processor or blender; process until smooth. Place onion mixture, beef, and bell pepper pieces in a large zip-top plastic bag; seal. Marinate in refrigerator 20 minutes.
3. Remove beef and bell pepper pieces from bag; discard marinade. Place beef, bell pepper pieces, and plantain pieces in a large bowl; toss well to coat.
4. Thread 5 beef cubes, 3 red bell pepper pieces, and 3 plantain pieces alternately onto each of 6 (12-inch) skewers. Lightly coat kebabs with cooking spray. Place kebabs on grill rack coated with cooking spray. Grill 4 minutes on each side for medium-rare or until desired degree of doneness. Garnish with green onion pieces and serve with lime wedges, if desired. Yield: 6 servings (serving size: 1 kebab).

CALORIES 260 (25% from fat); FAT 7.1g (sat 2.7g, mono 2.9g, poly 0.3g); PROTEIN 26.9g; CARB 21.3g; FIBER 2.4g; CHOL 76mg; IRON 3.4mg; SODIUM 358mg; CALC 20mg

North African Lamb and Potato Kebabs

We parboiled the potatoes so they'd be done at the same time as the lamb cubes.

- 12 small red potatoes, halved
- 1 tablespoon ground cumin
- 1 teaspoon salt
- 1 teaspoon ground ginger
- 1 teaspoon dried oregano
- 1 teaspoon ground turmeric
- 2 teaspoons olive oil
- ½ teaspoon ground cinnamon
- ⅛ teaspoon ground cloves
- 3 garlic cloves, minced
- 1 (2-pound) boneless leg of lamb, trimmed and cut into 48 cubes
- 2 large onions, each cut into 12 wedges
- Cooking spray

1. Prepare grill.
2. Place potato halves in a large saucepan, and cover with water; bring to a boil. Reduce heat; simmer 12 minutes or until tender. Drain and set aside.
3. Combine cumin and next 8 ingredients; add lamb, tossing to coat. Cover and refrigerate 20 minutes.
4. Thread 4 lamb pieces, 2 potato halves, and 2 onion pieces alternately onto each of 12 (12-inch) skewers. Place kebabs on grill rack coated with cooking spray; grill 4 minutes on each side or until lamb reaches desired degree of doneness. Yield: 8 servings (serving size: 1½ kebabs).

CALORIES 353 (35% from fat); FAT 13.7g (sat 5.2g, mono 6g, poly 1g); PROTEIN 25.8g; CARB 31g; FIBER 3.9g; CHOL 78mg; IRON 3.7mg; SODIUM 360mg; CALC 46mg

Pinchos Morunos

These spicy pork skewers are commonly found in the tapas bars of Spain. Serve this as an appetizer, or double the serving size for an entrée.

- ¼ cup chopped fresh parsley
- 1 tablespoon paprika
- 1 tablespoon olive oil
- 1 teaspoon dried oregano
- 1 teaspoon ground cumin
- 1 teaspoon ground coriander
- ¾ teaspoon salt
- ¼ teaspoon saffron threads, crushed
- ¼ teaspoon ground red pepper
- 2 garlic cloves, minced
- 1 (1-pound) pork tenderloin, trimmed and cut into 18 cubes
- 2 small red onions, each cut into 6 wedges
- 2 red bell peppers, each cut into 6 wedges
- 2 yellow bell peppers, each cut into 6 wedges
- Cooking spray

1. Prepare grill.
2. Combine first 10 ingredients in a large bowl; add pork, tossing to coat.
3. Thread 3 pork pieces, 2 onion pieces, 2 red bell pepper pieces, and 2 yellow bell pepper pieces alternately onto each of 6 (12-inch) skewers. Place kebabs on grill rack coated with cooking spray; grill 6 minutes on each side or until pork is done. Yield: 6 servings (serving size: 1 kebab).

CALORIES 143 (30% from fat); FAT 4.7g (sat 1g, mono 2.6g, poly 0.7g); PROTEIN 17.2g; CARB 8.2g; FIBER 4.7g; CHOL 49mg; IRON 2.5mg; SODIUM 336mg; CALC 34mg

---

Skewer Savvy

- Soak wooden skewers in water for 15 to 30 minutes so they won't burn on the grill.
- Shrimp, scallops, and other wobbly bits benefit from the double-skewer technique: Thread the pieces on a skewer, then run another one through the pieces parallel to the first, about a half-inch away.
- Expecting vegetarians? Cook the meat and vegetables on separate skewers, so guests who don't want meat can pick up a stick of vegetables. If your guests will assemble their own skewers, place meat and vegetables in separate bowls.
- If you have to move the party inside, you can broil these kebabs; it doesn't take any longer than grilling.

Cajun-Spiced Catfish Kebabs

The creamy mayonnaise-horseradish sauce works wonderfully with the spicy catfish. Serve with rolls, lettuce, and tomato slices if you want to turn these kebabs into easy po'boys.

- 2 teaspoons paprika
- 1 teaspoon garlic powder
- 1 teaspoon dried oregano
- 1 teaspoon dried thyme
- ½ teaspoon salt
- ½ teaspoon ground red pepper
- 4 (6-ounce) catfish fillets, cut into 24 (1-inch) pieces
- ½ cup fat-free mayonnaise
- 1 tablespoon fresh lemon juice
- 2 teaspoons capers, chopped
- 2 teaspoons prepared horseradish
- 2 ears corn, each cut crosswise into 8 pieces
- 3 green bell peppers, each cut into 8 wedges
- Cooking spray

1. Combine first 6 ingredients in a medium bowl; add fish, tossing to coat. Cover and refrigerate 20 minutes.
2. Combine mayonnaise, juice, capers, and horseradish in a small bowl; stir with a whisk. Cover and refrigerate.
3. Prepare grill.
4. Cook corn in boiling water 3 minutes, and drain.
5. Thread 3 fish pieces, 2 corn pieces, and 3 bell pepper pieces alternately onto each of 8 (12-inch) skewers. Place kebabs on grill rack coated with cooking spray; grill 4 minutes on each side or until fish flakes easily when tested with a fork. Serve with sauce. Yield: 4 servings (serving size: 2 kebabs and 2½ tablespoons sauce).

CALORIES 290 (26% from fat); FAT 8.3g (sat 1.8g, mono 2.9g, poly 2.3g); PROTEIN 33.2g; CARB 21.3g; FIBER 2.8g; CHOL 99mg; IRON 3.2mg; SODIUM 645mg; CALC 85mg

Teriyaki Shrimp and Scallop Kebabs

The simple glaze (which also goes well with chicken, pork, or beef) is easy to make the night before—just chill until you're ready to use it. Serve these kebabs over chilled soba noodles tossed with some orange juice, sesame oil, a touch of soy sauce, and chopped green onions.

- ¼ cup low-sodium soy sauce
- 3 tablespoons dark brown sugar
- 1½ tablespoons rice wine vinegar
- 1 tablespoon minced peeled fresh ginger
- ¼ teaspoon crushed red pepper
- 1 garlic clove, minced
- 1½ teaspoons cornstarch
- 1½ teaspoons water
- 16 jumbo shrimp, peeled and deveined (about 12 ounces)
- 16 sea scallops (about 12 ounces)
- 16 mushrooms, halved
- 24 (1½-inch) pieces green onions
- 1 tablespoon vegetable oil
- Cooking spray

1. Prepare grill.
2. Combine first 6 ingredients in a small saucepan over medium-high heat. Bring to a boil, and cook 2 minutes. Combine cornstarch and water. Stir cornstarch mixture into soy sauce mixture. Bring to a boil; cook 1 minute.
3. Thread 2 shrimp, 2 scallops, 4 mushroom halves, and 3 green onion pieces alternately onto each of 8 (12-inch) skewers. Brush kebabs with oil, and place on grill rack coated with cooking spray; grill 3 minutes. Turn kebabs, and brush with half of soy sauce glaze; grill 1 minute. Turn kebabs. Brush with remaining glaze; grill 1 minute or until seafood is done. Yield: 4 servings (serving size: 2 kebabs).

CALORIES 248 (19% from fat); FAT 4.9g (sat 0.7g, mono 0.9g, poly 2.3g); PROTEIN 33.4g; CARB 14.8g; FIBER 1.8g; CHOL 166mg; IRON 3mg; SODIUM 881mg; CALC 50mg

dinner tonight

Fire Up the Grill

Fire up the grill for quick, hearty menus sizzling with flavor.

Menu 1
serves 4

Grilled Tenderloin with Warm Vegetable Salad

Steamed new potato wedges

Garlic-herb French bread*

*Cut a baguette into ½-inch-thick slices. Place bread slices on a baking sheet. Coat bread with olive oil-flavored cooking spray; sprinkle with garlic powder and Italian seasoning. Bake at 350° for 5 minutes or until crisp.

Grilled Tenderloin with Warm Vegetable Salad
(pictured on page 237)

TOTAL TIME: 36 MINUTES

QUICK TIP: Bottled minced garlic is a smart timesaver. For each garlic clove in a recipe, substitute ½ teaspoon bottled minced garlic.

- 4 (4-ounce) beef tenderloin steaks, trimmed (about 1 inch thick)
- ½ teaspoon salt, divided
- ½ teaspoon black pepper, divided
- 2 tablespoons red wine vinegar
- 2 teaspoons bottled minced garlic
- 2 small zucchini, halved lengthwise
- 2 small yellow squash, halved lengthwise
- 2 plum tomatoes, halved lengthwise
- 2 green onions
- Cooking spray
- 1 tablespoon commercial pesto
- Oregano sprigs (optional)

1. Prepare grill or broiler.
2. Sprinkle steaks with ¼ teaspoon salt and ¼ teaspoon pepper.
3. Combine ¼ teaspoon salt, ¼ teaspoon pepper, vinegar, and next 5 ingredients

in a large zip-top plastic bag. Seal bag, and shake to coat.

4. Place tenderloin steaks on grill rack or broiler pan coated with cooking spray; cook 4 minutes on each side or until desired degree of doneness. Place zucchini and yellow squash on grill rack or broiler pan coated with cooking spray; cook 3 minutes on each side or until tender. Place tomato and onions on grill rack or broiler pan; cook 2 minutes or just until tender.

5. Coarsely chop vegetables, and place in a bowl. Add pesto; stir gently. Serve with steaks. Garnish with oregano, if desired. Yield: 4 servings (serving size: 1 steak and ½ cup vegetable mixture).

CALORIES 245 (39% from fat); FAT 10.5g (sat 3.7g, mono 4.3g, poly 0.6g); PROTEIN 27.2g; CARB 10.4g; FIBER 4.1g; CHOL 72mg; IRON 4.4mg; SODIUM 385mg; CALC 85mg

---

Menu 2
serves 4

Greek Salad with Grilled Chicken

Oregano breadsticks*

*Brush refrigerated breadstick dough with 1 tablespoon olive oil; sprinkle with 1 teaspoon dried oregano. Separate dough into individual breadsticks. Place dough sticks on a baking sheet coated with cooking spray. Bake at 375° for 13 minutes or until lightly browned.

Lime sherbet

Greek Salad with Grilled Chicken

(pictured on page 240)

TOTAL TIME: 35 MINUTES

QUICK TIP: Prepare the dressing up to a week in advance; cover and store it in the refrigerator. Try making a double or triple batch to have on hand for quick, throw-together salads or to use as a marinade.

¼ cup fat-free, less-sodium chicken broth
2 tablespoons red wine vinegar
2 teaspoons olive oil

1 teaspoon sugar
1 teaspoon dried oregano
½ teaspoon salt
½ teaspoon freshly ground black pepper
1 garlic clove, minced
4 (4-ounce) skinless, boneless chicken breast halves
Cooking spray
8 cups torn romaine lettuce
1 cup sliced cucumber (about 1 small)
8 pitted kalamata olives, halved
4 plum tomatoes, quartered lengthwise
2 (¼-inch-thick) slices red onion, separated into rings
¼ cup (1 ounce) crumbled feta cheese

1. Prepare grill or broiler.
2. Combine first 8 ingredients in a small bowl. Brush chicken with 2 tablespoons dressing; set remaining dressing aside.
3. Place chicken on grill rack or broiler pan coated with cooking spray; cook 5 minutes on each side or until chicken is done. Cut into ¼-inch-thick slices.
4. Combine romaine lettuce and next 4 ingredients in a large bowl; toss with remaining salad dressing. Divide salad evenly among 4 plates; top each serving with sliced chicken, and sprinkle with feta cheese. Yield: 4 servings (serving size: 2 cups salad, 3 ounces chicken, and 1 tablespoon feta cheese).

CALORIES 231 (30% from fat); FAT 7.7g (sat 2.1g, mono 3.9g, poly 1g); PROTEIN 30.3g; CARB 10.3g; FIBER 3.4g; CHOL 72mg; IRON 2.9mg; SODIUM 613mg; CALC 110mg

---

Menu 3
serves 4

Tex-Mex Flank Steak and Vegetables

Chipotle refried beans*

*Combine 1 (16-ounce) can fat-free refried beans, 2 tablespoons chipotle salsa, and 2 tablespoons chopped fresh cilantro. Microwave at HIGH 1½ minutes or until thoroughly heated.

Sliced ripe papaya and fresh lime wedges

Tex-Mex Flank Steak and Vegetables

TOTAL TIME: 34 MINUTES (MARINATING EXCLUDED)

QUICK TIP: Because the steak has to marinate at least four hours, you'll need to start this recipe ahead of time. Marinating in a zip-top plastic bag eliminates cleanup—you can just throw the bag away.

½ cup bottled chipotle salsa (such as Pace)
2 tablespoons fresh lime juice
4 (¼-inch-thick) slices red onion (about 1 large)
2 garlic cloves, minced
1 red bell pepper, quartered and seeded
1 yellow bell pepper, quartered and seeded
1 (1-pound) flank steak, trimmed
Cooking spray
8 (7-inch) flour tortillas
¼ cup bottled chipotle salsa
2 tablespoons minced fresh cilantro

1. Combine first 7 ingredients in a large zip-top plastic bag. Seal and marinate in refrigerator 4 hours or overnight, turning occasionally.
2. Prepare grill or broiler.
3. Remove steak and vegetables from bag; discard marinade. Place steak and vegetables on grill rack or broiler pan coated with cooking spray; cook 7 minutes on each side or until desired degree of doneness. Cut steak diagonally across grain into thin slices. Cut peppers into thin strips. Cut onion slices in half.
4. Warm tortillas according to package directions. Divide steak, bell peppers, and onion evenly among tortillas; roll up. Top each serving with 1 tablespoon chipotle salsa and 1½ teaspoons cilantro. Serve immediately. Yield: 4 servings.

CALORIES 547 (26% from fat); FAT 16.1g (sat 5.6g, mono 7.3g, poly 1.5g); PROTEIN 33.9g; CARB 65.5g; FIBER 5.5g; CHOL 59mg; IRON 6.3mg; SODIUM 685mg; CALC 73mg

Sure to Please, Meat-and-Three

It's a meal and an institution, a taste of some of the best in home-style cooking and company.

The southern United States is blessed with many home-style eateries traditionally known as a meat-and-three restaurant. The menu: one meat and three vegetables, accompanied by hot rolls or corn bread and sweaty tumblers of iced tea. It's no wonder the meat-and-three has become an institution. The meals are usually a good value—a good-sized, home-style lunch that's nourishing and tasty for not much money. It's the kind of food most everyone loves, especially when it's updated and lightened, as it is here.

Veracruz-Style Red Snapper

(pictured on page 239)

TOTAL TIME: 25 MINUTES

QUICK TIP: To chop cilantro quickly, wash and dry the entire bunch while it's still bound together. Starting at the top of the bunch, chop only the amount of cilantro leaves you need. (Don't worry about including the stems; they won't affect the flavor.) This method also works for parsley.

  4 (6-ounce) red snapper or tilapia fillets
     Cooking spray
  ½ teaspoon ground cumin
  ¼ teaspoon salt
  ¼ teaspoon ground red pepper
  ¼ cup chopped fresh cilantro
  ¼ cup chopped pitted green olives
  ¼ cup bottled salsa
  1 (16-ounce) can pinto beans, drained
  1 (14.5-ounce) can diced tomatoes, drained
  4 lime wedges (optional)

1. Prepare grill or broiler.
2. Coat both sides of fillets with cooking spray; sprinkle with cumin, salt, and pepper. Place fillets on grill rack or broiler pan coated with cooking spray; cook 5 minutes on each side or until fish flakes easily when tested with a fork.
3. Combine cilantro and next 4 ingredients. Serve fillets with salsa mixture and, if desired, lime wedges. Yield: 4 servings (serving size: 1 fish fillet, ½ cup salsa, and 1 lime wedge).

CALORIES 202 (14% from fat); FAT 3.2g (sat 0.5g, mono 1g, poly 1.2g); PROTEIN 28.2g; CARB 14.6g; FIBER 5.2g; CHOL 42mg; IRON 1.9mg; SODIUM 571mg; CALC 94mg

Crisp-Crusted Catfish

Hands down, this is the best darned catfish we've ever eaten.

  2 tablespoons light ranch dressing
  2 large egg whites
  6 tablespoons yellow cornmeal
  ¼ cup (1 ounce) grated fresh Parmesan cheese
  2 tablespoons all-purpose flour
  ¼ teaspoon ground red pepper
  ⅛ teaspoon salt
  4 (6-ounce) farm-raised catfish fillets
     Cooking spray
  4 lemon wedges

1. Preheat oven to 425°.
2. Combine dressing and egg whites in a small bowl, and stir well with a whisk. Combine cornmeal, cheese, flour, pepper, and salt in a shallow dish. Dip fillets in egg white mixture; dredge in cornmeal mixture.
3. Place fillets on a baking sheet coated with cooking spray; bake at 425° for 12 minutes on each side or until lightly browned and fish flakes easily when tested with a fork. Serve with lemon wedges. Yield: 4 servings.

CALORIES 313 (26% from fat); FAT 9.1g (sat 2.8g, mono 3.6g, poly 3.3g); PROTEIN 32.9g; CARB 14.3g; FIBER 1.1g; CHOL 87mg; IRON 1.2mg; SODIUM 348mg; CALC 101mg

Baked Lemon-Garlic Chicken with Bell Peppers

SAUCE:

  ¾ cup fresh lemon juice (about 6 lemons)
  ¾ cup fat-free Italian dressing
  ½ teaspoon freshly ground black pepper
  3 garlic cloves, minced

CHICKEN:

  2 cups (¼-inch) red bell pepper strips
  1 cup (¼-inch) green bell pepper strips
  1 cup (¼-inch) yellow bell pepper strips
  3 chicken breast halves (about 1½ pounds)
  3 chicken leg quarters (about 1½ pounds)
 12 (⅛-inch-thick) slices lemon (about 1 lemon)
     Cooking spray

1. To prepare sauce, combine first 4 ingredients in a medium bowl, stirring with a whisk. Cover and chill ½ cup sauce.
2. To prepare chicken, combine remaining 1 cup sauce, bell peppers, and chicken in a large bowl, and toss to coat.

Cover chicken mixture, and refrigerate 4 hours or overnight.

3. Preheat oven to 400°.

4. Remove chicken and bell peppers from bowl, and discard sauce. Loosen skin from breast halves and leg quarters by inserting fingers, gently pushing between skin and meat. Insert 2 lemon slices under loosened skin of each chicken piece. Place chicken pieces, loosened skin sides up, on a broiler pan coated with cooking spray. Spread bell pepper strips on broiler pan around chicken. Bake at 400° for 50 minutes or until chicken is done. Remove skin from chicken. Arrange chicken and bell peppers on a platter, and keep warm.

5. Place ½ cup chilled sauce in a small saucepan, and cook over medium heat 3 minutes or until warm. Pour warm sauce over baked chicken and bell peppers. Yield: 6 servings (serving size: 1 chicken piece, ⅓ cup bell peppers, and about 1 tablespoon sauce).

CALORIES 216 (28% from fat); FAT 6.7g (sat 1.8g, mono 2.4g, poly 1.6g); PROTEIN 30.2g; CARB 9g; FIBER 1.7g; CHOL 91mg; IRON 1.7mg; SODIUM 385mg; CALC 28mg

Creamy Two-Cheese Macaroni

In meat-and-three restaurants, this side is commonly considered a vegetable.

    ¼ cup all-purpose flour
    2½ cups 1% low-fat milk
    1 cup (4 ounces) shredded extra-
       sharp cheddar cheese, divided
    6 ounces light processed cheese,
       cubed (such as Velveeta Light)
    6 cups hot cooked elbow macaroni
       (about 3 cups uncooked)
    ¼ teaspoon salt
       Cooking spray

1. Preheat oven to 375°.

2. Lightly spoon flour into a dry measuring cup, and level with a knife. Heat a large saucepan over medium heat; add flour. Gradually add milk, stirring with a whisk until blended. Cook until thick (about 8 minutes), stirring frequently. Stir in ⅔ cup cheddar cheese and processed cheese; cook 3 minutes or until cheese melts, stirring frequently. Remove from heat; stir in macaroni and salt.

3. Spoon mixture into a 2-quart casserole dish coated with cooking spray. Sprinkle with ⅓ cup cheddar cheese. Bake at 375° for 25 minutes or until bubbly. Yield: 9 servings (serving size: ⅔ cup).

CALORIES 260 (26% from fat); FAT 7.5g (sat 4.5g, mono 1.5g, poly 0.4g); PROTEIN 13.7g; CARB 33.7g; FIBER 1.3g; CHOL 24mg; IRON 1.6mg; SODIUM 478mg; CALC 290mg

Black-Eyed Peas with Ham and Pickled Onions

Black-eyed peas are omnipresent at meat-and-threes. Add a little more broth and some rice, and you have another Southern classic: hoppin' John. The pickled onions are best after several days' refrigeration, but overnight works fine, too.

PICKLED ONIONS:

    1½ tablespoons cider vinegar
    1 teaspoon sugar
       Dash of ground red pepper
    ½ cup finely chopped onion

PEAS:

    1 teaspoon vegetable oil
    1 cup finely chopped onion
    2 garlic cloves, minced
    3 cups frozen black-eyed peas (about
       1 pound)
    ½ teaspoon salt
    ½ teaspoon dried thyme
    ½ teaspoon black pepper
    ⅛ teaspoon ground red pepper
    1 (15.75-ounce) can fat-free,
       less-sodium chicken broth
    ½ pound diced ham (about ¼ inch
       thick)

1. To prepare onions, combine first 3 ingredients in a microwave-safe bowl. Microwave at HIGH 25 seconds; stir until sugar dissolves. Stir in ½ cup onion; cover and refrigerate overnight.

2. To prepare peas, heat oil in a medium saucepan over medium-high heat. Add 1 cup onion and garlic; cook 2 minutes, stirring frequently. Stir in peas and remaining 6 ingredients, and bring to a boil. Cover, reduce heat, and simmer 20 minutes. Partially mash peas with a potato masher; cook, uncovered, 5 minutes. Serve topped with pickled onions. Yield: 8 servings (serving size: ½ cup peas and 1 tablespoon pickled onions).

CALORIES 141 (17% from fat); FAT 2.6g (sat 0.7g, mono 0.9g, poly 0.7g); PROTEIN 11.9g; CARB 17.6g; FIBER 4.3g; CHOL 15mg; IRON 1.8mg; SODIUM 603mg; CALC 24mg

Fried Green Tomatoes

To lighten this classic, we added a fried crust to just one side.

    8 (½-inch-thick) slices green
       tomato (about 4 tomatoes)
    ½ teaspoon salt
    ¼ teaspoon black pepper
    ½ cup yellow cornmeal
    1 tablespoon vegetable oil

1. Sprinkle 1 side of tomato slices evenly with salt and pepper. Dredge seasoned sides in cornmeal.

2. Heat oil in a large skillet over medium-high heat. Add tomato slices, coated sides down; cook 6 minutes, turning after 3 minutes. Serve immediately. Yield: 4 servings (serving size: 2 slices).

CALORIES 123 (29% from fat); FAT 3.9g (sat 0.6g, mono 0.9g, poly 2.2g); PROTEIN 3g; CARB 19.8g; FIBER 2.7g; CHOL 0mg; IRON 0.9mg; SODIUM 310mg; CALC 18mg

Meat-and-Three

The term is most frequently used in the South, but the concept is universal, for what is a meat-and-three but a modern-day take on the traditional midday meal? When mothers of generations past sent their sons and daughters off into the world admonishing them to eat well, this is what they had in mind. It's food that good country cooks from Iowa to New Jersey can claim as their own, whether it's called a plate lunch in Mississippi, a blue-plate special in Michigan, or a meat-and-three in Tennessee.

Turnip Greens

To preserve their texture, we cooked these greens less than most Southerners do.

>   1   pound trimmed turnip greens or
>   collard greens
>   2   cups water
>   1   teaspoon sugar
>   1   (4-ounce) piece salt pork, cut into
>   4 pieces
>   1   dried red chile
>   ¼   teaspoon salt

1. Wash greens; pat dry. Coarsely chop.
2. Combine water, sugar, pork, and chile in a large Dutch oven. Bring to a boil; cover, reduce heat, and simmer 20 minutes. Discard chile. Stir in greens and salt; cover and cook over medium heat 10 minutes or until tender, stirring occasionally. Discard pork. Yield: 6 servings (serving size: ½ cup).

CALORIES 53 (68% from fat); FAT 4g (sat 1.4g, mono 1.8g, poly 0.5g); PROTEIN 1.1g; CARB 3.8g; FIBER 1.7g; CHOL 4mg; IRON 0.6mg; SODIUM 189mg; CALC 105mg

Stewed Okra and Tomatoes

>   1   teaspoon vegetable oil
>   ½   cup chopped onion
>   4   cups okra pods, trimmed
>   (about 1 pound)
>   ½   cup water
>   ½   teaspoon sugar
>   ½   teaspoon salt
>   ¼   teaspoon black pepper
>   1   (14.5-ounce) can no-salt-added
>   diced tomatoes, undrained

1. Heat oil in a medium saucepan over medium heat. Add onion; sauté 2 minutes. Add okra and remaining ingredients; bring to a boil. Cover, reduce heat, and simmer 20 minutes. Yield: 4 servings (serving size: 1 cup).

CALORIES 72 (18% from fat); FAT 1.4g (sat 0.2g, mono 0.3g, poly 0.8g); PROTEIN 3.2g; CARB 14.3g; FIBER 4.6g; CHOL 0mg; IRON 1.5mg; SODIUM 313mg; CALC 117mg

Yellow Squash Casserole

Meat-and-three casseroles are usually laden with mayo, cream, butter, cheese, or any combination of the four. Here's our lightened rendition of a traditional favorite.

>   8   cups sliced yellow squash
>   (about 2 pounds)
>   1   tablespoon water
>   6   ounces hot turkey Italian sausage
>   (about 2 links)
>   ½   cup chopped onion
>   2   garlic cloves, minced
>   2   (1-ounce) slices day-old white
>   bread
>   ½   cup fat-free sour cream
>   ⅓   cup (1½ ounces) diced provolone
>   cheese
>   ¼   teaspoon salt
>   ¼   teaspoon black pepper
>   1   (10¾-ounce) can condensed
>   reduced-fat, reduced-sodium cream
>   of mushroom soup, undiluted
>   Cooking spray

1. Preheat oven to 350°.
2. Combine squash and water in a large microwave-safe bowl. Cover with plastic wrap; vent. Microwave at HIGH 6 minutes or until tender. Drain well.
3. Remove casings from sausage. Cook sausage, onion, and garlic in a large nonstick skillet over medium-high heat until browned, stirring to crumble. Drain.
4. Place bread in a food processor, and pulse 10 times or until coarse crumbs form to measure 1 cup. Combine squash, sausage mixture, ½ cup breadcrumbs, sour cream, cheese, salt, pepper, and soup. Spoon squash mixture into a 2-quart casserole coated with cooking spray. Top with remaining ½ cup breadcrumbs. Spray breadcrumbs with cooking spray. Bake at 350° for 30 minutes. Yield: 12 servings (serving size: ⅔ cup).

CALORIES 85 (31% from fat); FAT 2.9g (sat 1.2g, mono 0.5g, poly 0.6g); PROTEIN 4.8g; CARB 10.3g; FIBER 1.8g; CHOL 12mg; IRON 0.7mg; SODIUM 279mg; CALC 91mg

Peach Cobbler with a Cinnamon Crust

(pictured on page 237)

Some people think the crust is the best part. This recipe has plenty of it. It's baked separately and laid on top of the peaches—unorthodox, but crispy and flavorful nonetheless.

>   ¼   cup all-purpose flour
>   1   cup sugar
>   ¾   teaspoon ground cinnamon,
>   divided
>   6   cups sliced peeled fresh ripe
>   peaches or 2 (16-ounce) packages
>   frozen sliced peaches
>   Cooking spray
>   2   tablespoons sugar
>   1   (15-ounce) package refrigerated
>   pie dough (such as Pillsbury)
>   1   large egg white, lightly beaten

1. Preheat oven to 350°.
2. Lightly spoon flour into a dry measuring cup; level with a knife. Combine flour, 1 cup sugar, and ½ teaspoon cinnamon in a small bowl. Place peaches in an 11 x 7-inch baking dish coated with cooking spray. Sprinkle with sugar mixture; let stand 30 minutes.
3. Combine ¼ teaspoon cinnamon and 2 tablespoons sugar in a small bowl. Unfold 1 pie dough, reserving remaining dough for another use. Brush with egg white; sprinkle with cinnamon and sugar mixture. Cut dough into 16 wedges. Place dough wedges, coated sides up, on a baking sheet coated with cooking spray. Bake at 350° for 15 minutes or until golden brown; set aside.
4. Bake peaches at 350° for 30 minutes or until bubbly. Arrange crust over peaches. Serve warm. Yield: 10 servings.

CALORIES 236 (22% from fat); FAT 5.7g (sat 2.4g, mono 0.1g, poly 0.1g); PROTEIN 2.1g; CARB 45.5g; FIBER 2g; CHOL 4mg; IRON 0.3mg; SODIUM 86mg; CALC 8mg

inspired vegetarian

Pizza Party

*There's bound to be something to please
everyone when pizza's on the menu.*

Pizza Dough

1   teaspoon sugar
1   package dry yeast (about 2¼
    teaspoons)
1¼ cups warm water (100° to 110°)
3   cups all-purpose flour, divided
1   tablespoon olive oil
1   teaspoon salt
Cooking spray

1. Dissolve sugar and yeast in warm
water in a large bowl; let stand 5 minutes. Lightly spoon flour into dry measuring cups, and level with a knife. Add
2¾ cups flour, oil, and salt to yeast mixture; stir until blended. Turn dough out
onto a floured surface. Knead until
smooth and elastic (about 10 minutes);
add enough of remaining flour, 1 tablespoon at a time, to prevent dough from
sticking to hands (dough will feel tacky).
2. Place dough in a large bowl coated
with cooking spray, turning to coat top.
Cover and let rise in a warm place (85°),
free from drafts, 1 hour or until doubled
in size. (Press two fingers into dough. If
indentation remains, dough has risen
enough.) Punch dough down; cover and
let rest 5 minutes. Divide dough in half.
Shape dough according to recipe directions. Yield: 2 (12-inch) crusts.

CALORIES 761 (11% from fat); FAT 8.8g (sat 1.2g, mono 5.2g,
poly 1.3g); PROTEIN 20.7g; CARB 146.5g; FIBER 5.8g; CHOL 0mg;
IRON 9.3mg; SODIUM 1,179mg; CALC 32mg

Shiitake Mushroom and Gorgonzola Pizza

Gorgonzola has a pronounced flavor, but
any blue cheese will work nicely.

½   recipe Pizza Dough (recipe at left)
Cooking spray
1   tablespoon cornmeal
1   teaspoon olive oil
1½ cups thinly sliced button
    mushrooms
1⅓ cups thinly sliced shiitake
    mushrooms
1   cup vertically sliced red onion
⅛   teaspoon salt
⅛   teaspoon black pepper
3   tablespoons low-fat sour cream
½   cup (3 ounces) crumbled
    Gorgonzola or other blue
    cheese

1. Preheat oven to 450°.
2. Roll dough into a 12-inch circle
on a lightly floured surface. Place
dough on a 12-inch pizza pan or a baking sheet coated with cooking spray
and sprinkled with cornmeal. Crimp
edges of dough with your fingers to
form a rim.
3. Heat oil in a large nonstick skillet
over medium heat. Add mushrooms and
onion; sauté 5 minutes. Cover, reduce heat to medium-low, and cook 3
minutes or until onion is very tender. Stir
in salt and pepper.
4. Spread sour cream over pizza crust,
leaving a 1-inch border. Top with mushroom mixture; sprinkle with cheese. Bake
at 450° for 15 minutes or until lightly
browned. Cut into 8 wedges. Yield: 4
servings (serving size: 2 wedges).

CALORIES 296 (26% from fat); FAT 8.7g (sat 3.8g, mono 3.4g,
poly 0.8g); PROTEIN 10.3g; CARB 44.4g; FIBER 2.7g; CHOL 16mg;
IRON 3.1mg; SODIUM 382mg; CALC 118mg

Doughy Issues

- To make the dough in a food processor, process the flour and salt just
  until mixed. With the machine on,
  pour the yeast mixture and olive oil
  through the chute. Process 2 minutes
  or until a ball forms and the dough is
  smooth and elastic.
- The pizza dough recipe (at left)
  makes two thin crusts. Roll the dough
  into two 12-inch disks. If it resists
  being stretched, let it relax for a few
  minutes.
- If you want to freeze pizza dough for
  future use, let it rise once, punch it
  down, and shape it into a ball. Place
  the dough in a heavy-duty zip-top
  plastic bag coated with cooking spray,
  remove excess air, and seal. Dough
  can be frozen for up to two months,
  then thawed in the refrigerator for 12
  hours or overnight. When ready to
  use, cut away the plastic bag with
  scissors, and shape dough according
  to recipe directions.
- If you'd like to shape your pizza dough
  before freezing, place the rolled dough
  on a baking sheet, preferably one
  without sides. Freeze until firm (about
  30 minutes), remove the dough with a
  spatula, and wrap in heavy-duty
  plastic wrap.
- To thaw the dough, place it on a
  baking sheet coated with cooking
  spray and dusted with cornmeal.
- Let the dough thaw for about 30
  minutes (otherwise the toppings
  and crust will cook at different rates),
  then add the toppings.
- Bake according to the recipe.

Tomato Pizza with Garlic and Smoked Gouda

With its juicy tomatoes and smoked cheese, this pizza has a flavor that's reminiscent of a BLT. Plum tomatoes work best because of their firmness, but any variety will do. We prebaked the crust a few minutes to prevent the tomatoes from making it soggy.

½ recipe Pizza Dough (recipe on page 227)
Cooking spray
  1 tablespoon cornmeal
½ cup (2 ounces) shredded smoked Gouda cheese
1½ cups sliced plum tomato (about 4)
  2 teaspoons olive oil
  2 garlic cloves, minced
½ teaspoon freshly ground black pepper
  2 tablespoons thinly sliced fresh basil

1. Preheat oven to 450°.
2. Roll dough into a 12-inch circle on a lightly floured surface. Place dough on a 12-inch pizza pan or baking sheet coated with cooking spray and sprinkled with cornmeal. Crimp edges of dough with fingers to form a rim. Bake at 450° for 5 minutes.
3. Sprinkle cheese over pizza crust, leaving a 1-inch border. Arrange tomato slices over cheese. Combine oil and garlic; sprinkle over tomato. Sprinkle with pepper.
4. Bake at 450° for 15 minutes or until lightly browned. Top with basil. Cut into 8 wedges. Yield: 4 servings (serving size: 2 wedges).

CALORIES 291 (29% from fat); FAT 9.3g (sat 3.7g, mono 3g, poly 0.6g); PROTEIN 9.6g; CARB 42.4g; FIBER 2.5g; CHOL 13mg; IRON 2.9mg; SODIUM 382mg; CALC 119mg

Leek, Ricotta, and Walnut Pizza

Leeks and ricotta share a natural sweetness that contrasts with the richness of toasted walnuts. You can always use pine nuts or pecans.

½ recipe Pizza Dough (recipe on page 227)
Cooking spray
  1 tablespoon cornmeal
  1 teaspoon olive oil
  4 cups thinly sliced leek (about 3 large)
½ cup part-skim ricotta cheese
¼ cup (1 ounce) grated fresh Parmesan cheese
¼ teaspoon salt
¼ teaspoon black pepper
  1 garlic clove, minced
  2 tablespoons coarsely chopped walnuts

1. Preheat oven to 450°.
2. Roll dough into a 12-inch circle on a lightly floured surface. Place dough on a 12-inch pizza pan or baking sheet coated with cooking spray and sprinkled with cornmeal. Crimp edges of dough with fingers to form a rim.
3. Heat oil in a large nonstick skillet over medium heat. Add leek; sauté 10 minutes. Cool to room temperature.
4. Combine cheeses, salt, pepper, and garlic in a bowl. Spread cheese mixture over pizza crust, leaving a 1-inch border. Top with leek, and sprinkle with walnuts. Bake at 450° for 15 minutes or until lightly browned. Cut into 8 wedges. Yield: 4 servings (serving size: 2 wedges).

CALORIES 359 (26% from fat); FAT 10.3g (sat 3.4g, mono 3.7g, poly 2.5g); PROTEIN 13.4g; CARB 53.6g; FIBER 3.5g; CHOL 14mg; IRON 4.6mg; SODIUM 611mg; CALC 234mg

Olive-Potato Pizza

Potatoes readily soak up the flavors of the garlicky, herb-spiked tomato sauce that coats them. Because of the waxy texture of red-skinned potatoes, the slices remain perfectly intact. Try to slice the potatoes so that they're a consistent thickness; doing so will ensure they cook evenly.

  2 cups sliced small red potato (about ¾ pound)
½ recipe Pizza Dough (recipe on page 227)
Cooking spray
  1 tablespoon cornmeal
¼ cup tomato sauce
½ teaspoon minced fresh rosemary
¼ teaspoon salt
¼ teaspoon crushed red pepper
  1 garlic clove, crushed
¾ cup (3 ounces) shredded part-skim mozzarella cheese
½ cup chopped pitted kalamata olives

1. Preheat oven to 450°.
2. Place potato slices in a saucepan; cover with water. Bring to a boil; cook 7 minutes or until tender. Drain.
3. Roll dough into a 12-inch circle on a lightly floured surface. Place dough on a 12-inch pizza pan or baking sheet coated with cooking spray and sprinkled with cornmeal. Crimp edges of dough with fingers to form a rim.
4. Combine potato slices, tomato sauce, rosemary, salt, pepper, and garlic. Spread over pizza crust, leaving a 1-inch border. Sprinkle pizza with cheese and olives.
5. Bake at 450° for 15 minutes or until lightly browned. Cut into 8 wedges. Yield: 4 servings (serving size: 2 wedges).

CALORIES 367 (24% from fat); FAT 9.7g (sat 3.1g, mono 5.2g, poly 0.9g); PROTEIN 13.1g; CARB 56.4g; FIBER 3.4g; CHOL 11mg; IRON 2.9mg; SODIUM 851mg; CALC 176mg

How to Cook Spanish

A land of spectacular scenery and diverse climates, Spain offers a dazzling variety of foods cooked with simple techniques.

Spanish cooking may be the last great undiscovered cuisine for Americans, although it's not likely to remain that way for long. The foods of Spain are linked to such robust Mediterranean ingredients as olive oil, garlic, dried legumes, grains, tomatoes, and peppers. But what gives Spanish food its complexity is the country's different regions. In a land with both snowcapped peaks and vast plains, there are also forests, valleys, deserts, and marshlands. Together, Spain's regions create optimum conditions for producing a great diversity of foods.

Seafood Paella
(pictured on page 239)

Paellas are as varied as the cooks who make them. The constants are good broth, short-grain rice, Spanish smoked paprika, and a paella pan—although a 13-inch skillet will work, too. Although saffron is traditional in paella, it's not crucial.

½ cup dry white wine
¼ teaspoon saffron threads, crushed (optional)
3 (8-ounce) bottles clam juice
¼ pound large shrimp, peeled and deveined
½ pound grouper or other white fish fillets, cut into 1-inch pieces
½ pound cleaned skinless squid, cut into ½-inch-thick slices
¼ teaspoon kosher salt
3 tablespoons olive oil, divided
½ cup chopped green bell pepper
½ cup chopped red bell pepper
½ cup chopped onion
4 garlic cloves, minced
2½ teaspoons Spanish smoked paprika or regular paprika
1 cup chopped tomato
1½ cups uncooked short-grain rice (such as Calasparra or Arborio)
1 pound small mussels, scrubbed and debearded

1. Preheat oven to 400°.
2. Bring first 3 ingredients to a simmer in a small saucepan (do not boil). Keep warm over low heat.
3. Combine shrimp, fish, and squid in a bowl; sprinkle with salt, and let stand 5 minutes. Heat 1 tablespoon oil in a 13-inch paella pan or large skillet over medium-high heat. Add fish mixture, and sauté 1 minute (mixture will not be completely done). Place fish mixture and any liquid from pan in a bowl.
4. Heat 2 tablespoons oil in pan over medium-high heat. Add bell peppers, onion, garlic, and paprika; sauté 3 minutes. Stir in tomato; cook 2 minutes. Stir in rice, and coat well. Add clam juice mixture; bring to a boil, and cook 3 minutes. Add reserved fish mixture; cook 2 minutes. Add mussels to pan, nestling them into rice mixture.
5. Bake at 400° for 15 minutes or until shells open; discard any unopened shells. Remove from oven; cover and let stand 10 minutes. Yield: 8 servings (serving size: 1 cup).

CALORIES 179 (32% from fat); FAT 6.3g (sat 0.9g, mono 3.9g, poly 0.9g); PROTEIN 15g; CARB 15g; FIBER 1.3g; CHOL 97mg; IRON 2.1mg; SODIUM 322mg; CALC 44mg

How to Make Paella

1. *Dissolve saffron in wine and clam juice, and keep warm. It's important to keep the broth warm since cold broth can keep rice from cooking completely.*

2. *Sauté aromatics—bell peppers, onion, garlic, and paprika—to bring out their flavors. Add rice, and stir to coat with oil. This "seals" rice, preventing it from releasing its starch and keeping it firm.*

3. *Stir in clam juice mixture, and bring to a boil. Add reserved seafood and mussels. Bake at 400° for 15 minutes or until shells open and rice is slightly underdone. It should be firm in center, similar to Italian risotto. Let paella stand 10 minutes, covered with a dish towel. This lets it continue cooking.*

Regional Cooking

Each of Spain's regions offers particular culinary pleasures.

Galicia—This region is known for savory empanadas made with meat and fish; hearty *caldo gallego* (Galician soup) made with greens, beans, and meats; wonderfully moist country breads; and bountiful seafood, including scallops still attached to their shells.

Asturias—The cuisine of this land of spectacularly abrupt green mountains and rugged coastlines features *fabada* bean stew, Cabrales blue cheese aged in mountain caves, salmon, trout, and hard apple cider.

Basque Country—Food is preeminent in Basque culture, where traditional male-only gourmet clubs still flourish. Dishes made with the freshest fish coexist with classic preparations based on the traditional salt cod.

Aragón—The highest peaks of the Spanish Pyrenees offer a dramatic backdrop for this region. Navarra is renowned for its trout streams and the legendary running of the bulls; La Rioja is celebrated for its wines. Both border the fertile valley of the Ebro River. The peppers that grow here are essential to such regional dishes as *chilindrón* stews of lamb or chicken and traditional vegetable medleys. Delicate fire-roasted *piquillo* peppers, sautéed or stuffed, have recently captured the attention of the wider culinary world for their versatility and flavor.

Cataluña—This privileged region encompasses the Pyrenees and its valleys, the agricultural lands of La Cerdanya and L'Empordà, the stunning Costa Brava, and Barcelona, where fine eating is a way of life. Catalan cooks are fond of sweet and savory combinations, and of sauces flavored and thickened with almonds, pine nuts, and hazelnuts (like the sauce in the fish medley *romesco de pescado*).

Valencia—The orange groves of this region alternate with vast, swampy rice fields. *Paella valenciana,* the classic rice dish, was created here.

Andalucía—Hillsides in this region are lined with the olive trees responsible for the exceptional oils essential to Spanish cooking. Andalusians still accent their cooking with Eastern spices inherited from the Moors. Chilled gazpachos, both red and white, are wonderfully refreshing in Andalucía's warm sunny climate; so, too, are shellfish vinaigrettes drizzled with the region's superb sherry vinegar. Iberian ham is revered for its singular texture and nutty flavor. Devotees will recognize the name *Jabugo*, the town where hams by the hundreds of thousands cure in cool mountain caves.

Castilla—Although Madrid is at the center of landlocked Castilla (comprising Castilla y León to the north and Castilla La Mancha to the south), the freshest seafood is rushed overnight from every coast to satisfy the locals' demanding palates. Other gastronomic pleasures from the region: chorizo, Spain's typical sausage spiced with garlic and paprika; *manchego*, sheep's milk cheese; garlic soups and bean stews; and suckling pig and baby lamb, roasted in wood-burning, brick-vaulted ovens.

Editor's Note

Spanish cooks tend to have a lavish hand with olive oil. While we decreased the oil considerably, some of these recipes still contain more than 30 percent fat. We hesitated to trim more because we wanted to preserve the authenticity and flavor of the cuisine. Also, most of the fat is the heart-healthy monounsaturated variety.

Garlic-Lovers' Menu

Be sure to serve plenty of bread to mop up every drop of the sauce.

Chicken in Garlic Sauce

Crusty bread

Green salad

Raspberry sorbet

Chicken in Garlic Sauce

This dish is traditionally—and most simply—prepared by quickly frying the chicken, cut into small pieces, in olive oil with garlic cloves. The seasoned oil is served as a sauce. The dish has infinite variations. This version uses less oil; includes wine, saffron, and a chile pepper; and is slow-cooked for extra succulence.

- 2 chicken breast halves, skinned (about 1 pound)
- 2 chicken drumsticks, skinned (about ¾ pound)
- 2 chicken thighs, skinned (about ¾ pound)
- ½ teaspoon kosher salt
- 1 tablespoon olive oil
- 10 garlic cloves, crushed
- 1 dried hot red chile
- ¼ cup fat-free, less-sodium chicken broth
- 2 tablespoons dry white wine
- ¼ teaspoon saffron threads, crushed
- 1 bay leaf
- 2 tablespoons minced fresh parsley

1. Sprinkle chicken with salt. Heat oil in a large nonstick skillet over medium-high heat. Add chicken, and cook 5 minutes or until golden brown. Turn chicken over. Add garlic and chile, and cook 5 minutes, stirring frequently.
2. Stir in broth, wine, saffron, and bay leaf. Bring to a boil; cover, reduce heat, and simmer 30 minutes or until chicken is done. Discard chile and bay leaf. Sprinkle with parsley. Yield: 4 servings (serving size: 3 ounces chicken and 3 tablespoons sauce).

CALORIES 238 (30% from fat); FAT 7.8g (sat 1.6g, mono 3.8g, poly 1.4g); PROTEIN 37g; CARB 3g; FIBER 0.2g; CHOL 120mg; IRON 1.7mg; SODIUM 397mg; CALC 34mg

Sopa de Ajo Castellana
Castilian Garlic Soup

Originally, garlic soup was a peasant's dish made with the most basic ingredients: garlic, bread, and water. Traditional additions of broth, spices, ham, and poached eggs make a much tastier soup. The cooked egg whites give the soup a cloudy appearance.

SOUP:
- 1½ teaspoons extra-virgin olive oil
- 4 garlic cloves, crushed
- 1½ ounces Spanish serrano ham or prosciutto, diced
- 1 teaspoon Spanish smoked paprika or sweet paprika
- ¼ teaspoon ground cumin
- ¼ teaspoon freshly ground black pepper
- ⅛ teaspoon crumbled saffron threads
- 3 (15.75-ounce) cans fat-free, less-sodium chicken broth

CROUTONS:
- 1½ teaspoons extra-virgin olive oil
- 1 garlic clove, crushed
- 3 cups (1-inch) cubed hearty country bread (about 4¾ ounces)
- ½ teaspoon Spanish smoked paprika or sweet paprika

REMAINING INGREDIENT:
- 4 large eggs

1. To prepare soup, heat 1½ teaspoons oil in a large saucepan over medium heat. Add 4 crushed garlic cloves; sauté 1 minute. Add ham and 1 teaspoon paprika; sauté 30 seconds. Stir in cumin, pepper, saffron, and broth; bring to a boil. Cover, reduce heat, and simmer 20 minutes.

2. Preheat oven to 350°.

3. To prepare croutons, combine 1½ teaspoons oil and 1 crushed garlic clove in a large bowl. Add bread cubes, tossing to coat. Place bread cubes in a single layer on a baking sheet. Bake at 350° for 12 minutes or until toasted. Sprinkle bread cubes with ½ teaspoon paprika; toss well.

4. Increase oven temperature to 450°.

5. Break 1 egg into each of 4 ovenproof bowls. Divide broth mixture evenly among bowls. Place bowls on a baking sheet. Bake at 450° for 15 minutes or until eggs are set. Top each serving with croutons. Yield: 4 servings (1¼ cups soup and ½ cup croutons).

CALORIES 238 (38% from fat); FAT 10g (sat 2.2g, mono 4.7g, poly 1.1g); PROTEIN 16g; CARB 20g; FIBER 2.2g; CHOL 218mg; IRON 1.8mg; SODIUM 1,058mg; CALC 53mg

Tortilla Española
Spanish Potato Omelet

Tortilla Española (its relation to Mexican tortillas comes solely from its round shape) is among the most popular dishes in Spain. Although its ingredients couldn't be more basic—potatoes, eggs, onions, and oil—they're combined and cooked in a way that makes this dish irresistible and versatile. The potatoes are normally fried, but we've roasted them with excellent results. Unlike American omelets, this one's best made several hours ahead then served at room temperature.

- 6 cups thinly sliced peeled baking potato (about 3 pounds)
- 2 cups thinly sliced sweet onion
- Cooking spray
- 2 tablespoons olive oil, divided
- ¾ teaspoon kosher salt, divided
- 4 large eggs
- Oregano sprigs (optional)

1. Preheat oven to 350°.

2. Place potato and onion in a roasting pan coated with cooking spray. Drizzle with 1 tablespoon plus 2 teaspoons oil, and sprinkle with ½ teaspoon salt. Toss well. Bake at 350° for 1 hour or until potato is tender, stirring occasionally with a metal spatula to prevent sticking.

3. Combine eggs and ¼ teaspoon salt in a large bowl. Stir in potato mixture; let stand 10 minutes. Heat 1 teaspoon oil in an 8-inch nonstick skillet over medium heat. Pour potato mixture into pan (pan will be very full). Cook 7 minutes or until almost set, gently shaking pan frequently. Place a plate upside down on top of omelet; invert onto plate. Carefully slide omelet cooked side up into pan; cook 3 minutes or until set, gently shaking pan occasionally. Carefully loosen omelet with a spatula; gently slide omelet onto a plate. Cool. Cut into wedges. Garnish with oregano, if desired. Yield: 6 servings (serving size: 1 wedge).

CALORIES 315 (23% from fat); FAT 8g (sat 1.7g, mono 4.6g, poly 1g); PROTEIN 9g; CARB 52.6g; FIBER 4g; CHOL 142mg; IRON 1.4mg; SODIUM 345mg; CALC 36mg

How to Make a Spanish Potato Omelet

1. *Roast potatoes before adding them to eggs for omelet.*

2. *Combine potatoes and eggs, and let stand 10 minutes. This allows potatoes to absorb eggs. Pour mixture into a nonstick pan. When set, invert onto a plate, sliding omelet back into pan to cook other side.*

Empanada Gallega
Galician Pork and Pepper Pie

A large two-crusted savory pie from Galicia, the Spanish empanada is typically filled with fish or meat, red or green peppers, and lots of onion. Substitute pizza dough if you're pressed for time, though the pastry crust is easy to make. Empanadas are best at room temperature; serve with a mixed salad for dinner.

PORK:

- 2 tablespoons minced fresh parsley
- 1 tablespoon Spanish smoked paprika or hot paprika
- 1 tablespoon extra-virgin olive oil
- 1 teaspoon dried oregano
- 3 garlic cloves, minced
- 1 pound pork tenderloin, trimmed and cut into ½-inch-wide strips

DOUGH:

- 2¾ cups all-purpose flour
- 1 tablespoon baking powder
- 1½ teaspoons salt
- ½ cup water
- ¼ cup olive oil
- 1 large egg, lightly beaten

FILLING:

- Cooking spray
- ¼ teaspoon salt
- 2 cups thinly sliced sweet onion
- 2 cups red bell pepper strips
- 1 cup chopped tomato
- ¼ cup chopped Spanish serrano ham or prosciutto (about 1½ ounces)
- 2 tablespoons dry white wine
- Dash of crumbled saffron threads

REMAINING INGREDIENT:

- 1 large egg, lightly beaten

1. To prepare pork, combine first 5 ingredients in a large zip-top plastic bag, and add pork to bag. Seal and marinate in refrigerator 2 hours, turning bag occasionally.

2. To prepare dough, lightly spoon flour into dry measuring cups; level with a knife. Combine flour, baking powder, and 1½ teaspoons salt in a large bowl, stirring with a whisk. Combine water, ¼ cup oil, and 1 egg in a medium bowl.

Gradually add oil mixture to flour mixture, stirring just until moist. Turn dough out onto a lightly floured surface; knead lightly until smooth. Divide dough in half. Cover with plastic wrap; let rest about 30 minutes.

3. To prepare filling, heat a large nonstick skillet coated with cooking spray over medium heat. Add pork mixture; sprinkle with ¼ teaspoon salt. Cook 5 minutes or until pork loses its pink color. Add onion and bell pepper; cook 5 minutes. Cover, reduce heat, and simmer 20 minutes or until vegetables are tender. Stir in tomato, ham, wine, and saffron; cook 5 minutes.

4. Preheat oven to 350°.

5. Working with 1 portion of dough at a time (cover remaining dough to keep from drying), roll each portion into a 13-inch circle on a floured surface. Place 1 portion of dough on a large baking sheet coated with cooking spray. Spoon filling onto dough using a slotted spoon, leaving a 1-inch border around edge. Place remaining portion of dough over filling. Pinch edges to seal. Cut several slits in top of dough to allow steam to escape. Brush with 1 egg. Bake at 350° for 30 minutes or until golden brown; cool. Cut into wedges. Yield: 8 servings (serving size: 1 wedge).

CALORIES 366 (33% from fat); FAT 13.5g (sat 2.7g, mono 8g, poly 1.5g); PROTEIN 21g; CARB 39.5g; FIBER 3g; CHOL 96mg; IRON 3.7mg; SODIUM 814mg; CALC 134mg

Chorizo a la Llama
Flamed Chorizo

- ½ pound soft-cured sweet chorizo
- ¾ cup dry white wine
- 1 tablespoon brandy
- 1 small whole jarred pimiento, cut into thin strips (such as Goya)
- 16 (½-inch-thick) slices diagonally cut French bread baguette
- Parsley sprigs (optional)

1. Remove sausage from casing. Place in a small skillet; add wine, and bring to a boil. Reduce heat, and simmer 20 minutes or until wine almost evaporates. Add brandy. Ignite brandy with a long match, and let flames die down. Continue cooking 2 minutes or until liquid evaporates and sausage is lightly browned.

2. Remove sausage from pan, and cool slightly. Carefully cut sausage crosswise into 16 slices. Place 1 sausage slice and 1 pimiento strip onto each bread slice; secure each with a wooden pick. Garnish with parsley, if desired. Yield: 16 servings (serving size: 1 appetizer).

CALORIES 127 (43% from fat); FAT 6g (sat 2.1g, mono 2.9g, poly 0.7g); PROTEIN 5.4g; CARB 12g; FIBER 0.7g; CHOL 13mg; IRON 0.9mg; SODIUM 313mg; CALC 18mg

Sangría

3 tablespoons sugar
3 tablespoons white rum
3 tablespoons Cointreau (orange-flavored liqueur)
3 tablespoons brandy
6 orange slices
6 lemon slices
1 peach, cut into 6 wedges
1 cinnamon stick
1 (750-milliliter) bottle Rioja or other fruity red wine (such as Beaujolais or Zinfandel)
1 cup sparkling water, chilled

1. Combine all ingredients except sparkling water in a large pitcher. Chill 8 hours. Stir in water immediately before serving. Yield: 6 servings.

CALORIES 189 (0% from fat); FAT 0g; PROTEIN 0.6g; CARB 15.8g; FIBER 1g; CHOL 0mg; IRON 0.6mg; SODIUM 7mg; CALC 25mg

Where to Find Ingredients

We thought these recipes tasted best with authentic Spanish ingredients such as smoked paprika, chorizo, and serrano ham, but they tasted good with our substitutes, too. You can order smoked paprika, chorizo, serrano ham (*jamón*), Calasparra rice (*arroz*), and paella pans from the Spanish Table (206-682-2827 or www.tablespan.com) or Tienda (888-472-1022 or www.tienda.com).

A Healthy Cuisine

Adopting wholesome, nutritious foods and eating patterns has never been an issue in Spain. It would be difficult to improve on a diet that places Spaniards in the enviable position of enjoying the world's third-highest life expectancy.

Fast foods and other processed foods are merely novelties and snacking is negligible. Meals typically end with fresh fruits; sweets, although occasionally enjoyed, are not daily necessities. Old-fashioned, home-cooked food remains the standard rather than the exception in Spanish life.

Gazpacho Andaluz

Gazpacho is a refreshing start to a meal.

1½ pounds ripe tomatoes, each cut into quarters
1 cup coarsely chopped peeled cucumber
½ cup coarsely chopped Vidalia or other sweet onion
½ cup coarsely chopped red bell pepper
½ cup coarsely chopped green bell pepper
3 tablespoons sherry vinegar
2 tablespoons extra-virgin olive oil
½ teaspoon salt
¼ teaspoon sugar
¼ teaspoon ground cumin
5 garlic cloves, coarsely chopped

1. Combine all ingredients in a food processor; process until smooth. Press tomato mixture through a sieve over a bowl, pressing solids through with back of a spoon; discard any remaining solids. Cover and chill. Yield: 6 servings (serving size: ½ cup).

CALORIES 80 (51% from fat); FAT 5g (sat 0.7g, mono 3.4g, poly 0.6g); PROTEIN 1.5g; CARB 9g; FIBER 2g; CHOL 0mg; IRON 0.8mg; SODIUM 207mg; CALC 18mg

back to the best

Polenta with Roasted Red Peppers and Fontina Cheese

Sometimes the simplest ingredients can create winning dishes.

That's the case with Polenta with Roasted Red Peppers and Fontina Cheese. It first appeared in our pages in May 1997, when it captured runner-up honors in that year's *Cooking Light* with Wisconsin Cheese Recipe Contest.

The meatless main dish features just four ingredients. Though it uses convenience items like prepared polenta and canned tomatoes, it does so in a food-savvy way—to provide speed without sacrificing quality. Hands-on preparation time is less than 15 minutes.

Polenta with Roasted Red Peppers and Fontina Cheese

3 large red bell peppers
1 (14.5-ounce) can whole tomatoes, undrained and chopped
Cooking spray
1 (16-ounce) tube polenta, cut crosswise into 12 slices
1¼ cups (5 ounces) shredded fontina cheese
Fresh basil (optional)

1. Preheat broiler.
2. Cut peppers in half lengthwise; discard seeds and membranes. Place pepper halves, skin sides up, on a foil-lined baking sheet; flatten with hand. Broil 10 minutes or until blackened. Place in a zip-top plastic bag; seal. Let stand 15 minutes. Peel and cut into strips.
3. Preheat oven to 350°.
4. Drain tomatoes in a sieve over a bowl; reserve liquid. Heat a large skillet
Continued

over medium-low heat; add tomatoes. Cook 1 minute. Gradually add tomato liquid; simmer 1 minute. Add bell pepper strips, and simmer 5 minutes. Remove mixture from heat.

5. Spread ¼ cup pepper sauce in bottom of a 13 x 9-inch baking dish coated with cooking spray. Arrange polenta slices over pepper sauce; spread remaining pepper sauce over polenta. Sprinkle with cheese. Bake at 350° for 25 minutes. Garnish with fresh basil, if desired. Yield: 6 servings.

CALORIES 187 (38% from fat); FAT 7.8g (sat 4.6g, mono 2.1g, poly 0.6g); PROTEIN 9.2g; CARB 20.2g; FIBER 3.4g; CHOL 27mg; IRON 2.4mg; SODIUM 622mg; CALC 151mg

reader recipes

Young Doctors in Love

A Texas medical student woos his wife with a colorful corn and black bean salad.

Aaron and Stephanie Segal, both third-year medical students at the University of Texas Health Science Center in San Antonio, are lately hard-pressed to squeeze in a dinner date. But when they do, you can be sure Grilled Corn and Black Bean Salad is on the menu.

Grilled Corn and Black Bean Salad

Serve this juicy salad with a slotted spoon over chips or chicken.

    3 ears shucked corn
    ½ cup fresh lime juice (about 2 limes)
    ⅓ cup minced red onion
    ⅓ cup minced fresh cilantro
    3 tablespoons white vinegar
    2 teaspoons sugar
    2 teaspoons ground cumin
    2 teaspoons chili powder
    1 (15-ounce) can black beans,
       drained
Lime wedges (optional)

1. Prepare grill.

2. Place corn on a grill rack; grill 20 minutes or until corn is lightly browned, turning every 5 minutes. Cool. Cut kernels from corn; place in a bowl. Add juice and remaining ingredients except lime wedges; stir gently. Cover salad, and chill 1 hour. Garnish with lime wedges, if desired. Yield: 6 servings (serving size: ½ cup).

CALORIES 98 (8% from fat); FAT 0.8g (sat 0.1g, mono 0.2g, poly 0.3g); PROTEIN 4.7g; CARB 22.9; FIBER 5.4g; CHOL 0mg; IRON 1.6mg; SODIUM 238mg; CALC 36mg

Meyer Lemon Sorbet

"I came up with this recipe years ago, when I had several dozen lemons from my parents' Meyer lemon tree. I had already made lemon bars and lemon pie, and I was looking for something different. This recipe is the perfect ending to a spicy meal. It's low in calories, tasty, and can be made ahead. I love the refreshing flavor on a hot summer day."

—Theresa Liu, Alameda, California

    2 cups water
    1⅓ cups sugar
    2 tablespoons grated lemon rind
    ⅔ cup fresh lemon juice (about 3
       lemons)
    ½ cup fresh lime juice (about 2 limes)
Mint sprigs (optional)
Lemon rind strips (optional)

1. Combine first 5 ingredients in a medium bowl, stirring until sugar dissolves.

2. Pour mixture into freezer can of an ice-cream freezer, and freeze according to manufacturer's instructions. Spoon sorbet into a freezer-safe container; cover and freeze 1 hour or until firm. Garnish with mint sprigs and lemon rind strips, if desired. Yield: 8 servings (serving size: ½ cup).

NOTE: Meyer lemons are sweeter and more intense than regular lemons. But because they're also hard to find, we tested the sorbet with regular lemons.

CALORIES 138 (0% from fat); FAT 0g; PROTEIN 0.2g; CARB 36.6g; FIBER 0.1g; CHOL 0mg; IRON 0mg; SODIUM 1mg; CALC 5mg

Lemon-Ginger Chicken Stir-Fry

"I probably make this dish once a week for family, friends, and clients. I'm a personal chef and from experience can say that this is a crowd pleaser. It's simple enough to prepare for dinner any night, or you can jazz it up with steamed dumplings and a salad for a dinner party."

—Kay Chung, Durham, North Carolina

    1 pound skinless, boneless chicken
       breast, cut into 1-inch strips
    ¼ teaspoon freshly ground black
       pepper
    1 teaspoon canola oil
    ¾ cup thinly sliced onion
    2 tablespoons minced peeled fresh
       ginger, divided
    1 teaspoon dark sesame oil
    2 cups julienne-cut yellow squash
    1 cup red bell pepper strips
    1 tablespoon grated lemon rind
    1 tablespoon minced fresh garlic
    3 tablespoons honey
    3 tablespoons low-sodium soy sauce
    3 tablespoons fresh lemon juice
    2 tablespoons water
    2 teaspoons cornstarch
    3 cups hot cooked jasmine rice

1. Sprinkle chicken with black pepper. Heat canola oil in a large nonstick skillet over medium-high heat. Add chicken, onion, and 1 tablespoon ginger, and stir-fry 4 minutes. Remove from pan, and keep warm.

2. Heat sesame oil in pan over medium-high heat. Add squash and bell pepper, and stir-fry 3 minutes. Combine 1 tablespoon minced ginger, lemon rind, and next 6 ingredients in a small bowl. Add chicken and honey mixture to pan, and stir-fry 4 minutes or until chicken is done. Serve with rice. Yield: 4 servings (serving size: 1 cup chicken mixture and ¾ cup rice).

CALORIES 395 (10% from fat); FAT 4.3g (sat 0.8g, mono 1.6g, poly 1.3g); PROTEIN 31.4g; CARB 57g; FIBER 3g; CHOL 66mg; IRON 3.1mg; SODIUM 479mg; CALC 55mg

Indonesian Chicken

"This recipe is one of my favorites because it's simple to make, tastes delicious, and is healthy. I have yet to find anyone who doesn't like it. I like to double this recipe and enjoy the leftovers. I prefer spicy food so sometimes I'll add extra garlic, crushed red pepper, and a dash of hot sauce. For friends who don't like spicy food, I just stick to the recipe. To get the best flavor, poke the chicken with a fork so it can really absorb the marinade."

—Tiffany Amazon, Cincinnati, Ohio

1 teaspoon crushed red pepper
1 tablespoon grated peeled fresh ginger
2 tablespoons fresh lime juice
2 tablespoons hoisin sauce
1 tablespoon low-sodium soy sauce
3 garlic cloves, minced
4 (4-ounce) skinless, boneless chicken breast halves
Cooking spray

1. Prepare grill.
2. Combine first 6 ingredients in a large zip-top plastic bag; add chicken to bag. Seal and marinate in refrigerator 30 minutes. Remove chicken from bag; discard marinade.

3. Place chicken on grill rack coated with cooking spray, and grill 5 minutes on each side or until chicken is done. Yield: 4 servings (serving size: 1 chicken breast half).

CALORIES 158 (19% from fat); FAT 3.3g (sat 0.9g, mono 1.1g, poly 0.8g); PROTEIN 26.9g; CARB 3.8g; FIBER 0.3g; CHOL 73mg; IRON 1mg; SODIUM 238mg; CALC 19mg

Crunchy Shrimp-Pasta Salad

"This delicious shrimp salad recipe was given to me by my mother-in-law, who's made it for many years. To lighten it, I substituted cottage cheese and olive oil for the mayonnaise, and I added cilantro to enhance the flavor. The salad tastes fresh, and the cauliflower and other crunchy veggies give it a wonderful texture."

—Susan Runkle, Walton, Kentucky

½ cup fat-free cottage cheese
1 tablespoon fresh lemon juice
1 tablespoon olive oil
1 tablespoon light mayonnaise
½ teaspoon salt
¼ to ½ teaspoon black pepper
⅛ teaspoon hot sauce
1½ cups chopped cooked shrimp
3 cups cooked elbow macaroni (about 1½ cups uncooked)
1 cup chopped cauliflower florets
⅓ cup sliced pimiento-stuffed olives
⅓ cup finely chopped red bell pepper
⅓ cup finely chopped green bell pepper
⅓ cup chopped onion
1 tablespoon chopped fresh cilantro

1. Place cottage cheese in a food processor; process until smooth. Combine cheese, juice, and next 5 ingredients, stirring well with a whisk. Add shrimp; toss well. Add pasta and remaining ingredients; toss well. Cover and chill completely. Yield: 7 servings (serving size: 1 cup).

CALORIES 162 (21% from fat); FAT 3.8g (sat 0.6g, mono 2g, poly 0.8g); PROTEIN 12.1g; CARB 20.1g; FIBER 2g; CHOL 61mg; IRON 2.3mg; SODIUM 380mg; CALC 39mg

Stuffed Shells Florentine

"I invented a few new recipes when my boyfriend discovered he had high cholesterol. This one tastes outstanding. The mixture of spinach and cheese adds so much flavor, and it looks so pretty. It's a no-guilt food that's gotten raves from family and friends."

—Pat Sarratt, Fallston, Maryland

2 cups (8 ounces) shredded part-skim mozzarella cheese, divided
½ cup (2 ounces) grated fresh Parmesan cheese
½ cup egg substitute
¼ cup chopped fresh parsley
2 teaspoons dried basil
2 teaspoons dried oregano
¼ teaspoon salt
2 garlic cloves, minced
2 (10-ounce) packages frozen chopped spinach, thawed, drained, and squeezed dry
1 (15-ounce) carton fat-free ricotta cheese
24 cooked jumbo pasta shells (about 8 ounces)
Cooking spray
1 (26-ounce) bottle fat-free marinara sauce (such as Muir Glen)

1. Preheat oven to 350°.
2. Combine 1 cup mozzarella cheese, Parmesan cheese, and next 8 ingredients in a large bowl. Spoon cheese mixture evenly into cooked shells. Arrange stuffed shells in a 13 x 9-inch baking dish coated with cooking spray. Pour marinara sauce over stuffed shells, and sprinkle with 1 cup mozzarella cheese. Bake at 350° for 30 minutes. Yield: 6 servings (serving size: 4 shells).

CALORIES 331 (27% from fat); FAT 9.8g (sat 5.8g, mono 2.8g, poly 0.9g); PROTEIN 30.2g; CARB 30.7g; FIBER 6g; CHOL 51mg; IRON 4.0mg; SODIUM 627mg; CALC 793mg

Chicken Piccata

"My mom always made chicken piccata, but I never thought it had enough sauce. I love my version because the chicken absorbs the juice from the artichokes and capers, so it's never dry. My friends ask me to cook this dish for them, and I always make it the first time I cook for a date."

—Amy Gulino, Boston, Massachusetts

    1   (14-ounce) can quartered artichoke
        hearts, undrained
    ½   cup fat-free, less-sodium chicken
        broth
    ⅓   cup fresh lemon juice
    ¼   cup dry white wine
    4   (4-ounce) skinless, boneless
        chicken breast halves
    Cooking spray
    1   cup chopped onion
    1   garlic clove, minced
    3   tablespoons capers
    ¼   teaspoon black pepper
    2   cups cooked wild rice

1. Drain artichokes in a colander over a bowl, reserving 3 tablespoons liquid; set artichokes aside.
2. Combine reserved artichoke liquid, broth, juice, and wine in a shallow dish. Add chicken; cover and marinate in refrigerator 30 minutes.
3. Heat a large nonstick skillet coated with cooking spray over medium-high heat. Add onion and garlic; sauté 4 minutes or until tender. Remove chicken from dish, reserving marinade. Add chicken to pan; sauté 1 minute. Add reserved marinade, and cook 12 minutes or until chicken is done. Add artichokes, capers, and pepper to pan; reduce heat, and simmer 5 minutes. Serve over rice. Yield: 4 servings (serving size: 1 chicken breast half, ½ cup sauce, and ½ cup rice).

CALORIES 288 (6% from fat); FAT 2.0g (sat 0.5g, mono 0.4g, poly 0.5g); PROTEIN 34.1g; CARB 34.1g; FIBER 6.1g; CHOL 66mg; IRON 1.5mg; SODIUM 686mg; CALC 31mg

lighten up

Enchilada Emergency

We nurse a favorite south-of-the-border recipe back to health.

Jane Gausch, a nurse manager at Washington University School of Medicine in St. Louis, turned to *Cooking Light* to lighten her family's favorite Enchiladas de Pollo.

By substituting reduced-fat extra sharp cheddar for some of the milder Jack, we were able to get away with less cheese and still keep the flavor. By replacing the whipping cream with 2% milk, we cut 63 grams of fat and 529 calories. Instead of frying the tortillas in oil, we softened them in simmering water—slashing an additional 27 grams of fat and 241 calories. Fat-free sour cream worked like a charm and further lowered the fat by 46 grams. In all, we reduced the total fat by 185 grams and the calories by an impressive 1,586—without sacrificing creaminess or flavor.

Enchiladas de Pollo
Chicken Enchiladas

FILLING:

    3   cups water
    ¼   teaspoon salt
    8   black peppercorns
    1   onion, quartered
    1   bay leaf
    1   pound skinless chicken breast halves
    ¾   cup (3 ounces) shredded Monterey
        Jack cheese, divided
    ¾   cup (3 ounces) shredded reduced-fat
        extra-sharp cheddar cheese, divided
    ½   cup chopped onion

SAUCE:

    ⅔   cup 2% reduced-fat milk
    ¼   cup chopped fresh cilantro
    ¼   cup egg substitute
    ⅛   teaspoon salt
    1   (11-ounce) can tomatillos, drained
    1   (4.5-ounce) can chopped green
        chiles, undrained

REMAINING INGREDIENTS:

    8   (6-inch) corn tortillas
    ⅔   cup fat-free sour cream

1. To prepare filling, place first 6 ingredients in a Dutch oven; bring to a boil. Cover, reduce heat, and simmer 45 minutes. Remove chicken from cooking liquid; cool. Remove chicken from bones; shred with 2 forks. Discard bones. Reserve broth for another use.
2. Preheat oven to 375°.
3. Combine chicken, ½ cup each Monterey Jack and cheddar cheeses, and ½ cup onion in a bowl; set aside.
4. To prepare sauce, place milk and next 5 ingredients in a food processor; process until smooth.
5. To prepare tortillas, fill a medium skillet with 1 inch of water; bring to a simmer. Dip 1 tortilla in water using tongs. Spoon ½ cup filling in center of tortilla; roll tightly, and place in an 11 x 7-inch baking dish. Repeat procedure with remaining tortillas and filling.
6. Pour sauce over enchiladas. Cover and bake at 375° for 20 minutes. Uncover; sprinkle with ¼ cup each Monterey Jack and cheddar cheeses. Bake an additional 5 minutes or until cheeses melt. Top with sour cream. Yield: 4 servings (serving size: 2 enchiladas and about 2½ tablespoons sour cream).

CALORIES 502 (30% from fat); FAT 16.6g (sat 8.4g, mono 3.7g, poly 2g); PROTEIN 47.6g; CARB 40g; FIBER 4.6g; CHOL 114mg; IRON 3mg; SODIUM 725mg; CALC 598mg

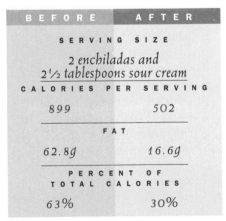

BEFORE	AFTER
SERVING SIZE	
2 enchiladas and 2½ tablespoons sour cream	
CALORIES PER SERVING	
899	502
FAT	
62.8g	16.6g
PERCENT OF TOTAL CALORIES	
63%	30%

Peach Cobbler with a
Cinnamon Crust,
page 226

Grilled Tenderloin with Warm Vegetable
Salad, page 222

Jamaican Jerk Beef Kebabs,
page 221

Veracruz-Style Red Snapper, page 224

Seafood Paella, page 229

Greek Salad with Grilled
Chicken, page 223

Pineapple Upside-Down Cake,
page 242

Peachy Keen

These desserts showcase peaches in all their splendor—if you can resist the urge to eat them out of hand.

Peach Upside-Down Cake

The sugar and fruit juice tossed with the peaches create a caramelized glaze as the cake bakes.

- 3 cups thinly sliced peeled peaches (about 1½ pounds)
- 1 tablespoon sugar
- 1 teaspoon cornstarch
- 1 teaspoon lemon juice
- Cooking spray
- ⅔ cup sugar
- ¼ cup butter, softened
- 2 teaspoons grated lemon rind
- 1 teaspoon vanilla extract
- 1 large egg
- 1¼ cups all-purpose flour
- 1 teaspoon baking powder
- ½ teaspoon baking soda
- ⅛ teaspoon salt
- ¾ cup low-fat buttermilk
- 2¼ cups vanilla fat-free frozen yogurt
- 6 tablespoons fat-free caramel sundae syrup, warmed

1. Preheat oven to 350°.
2. Combine first 4 ingredients in a bowl. Spoon into a 9-inch round cake pan coated with cooking spray.
3. Place ⅔ cup sugar and next 4 ingredients in a large bowl; beat with a mixer at medium speed until well blended (about 5 minutes). Lightly spoon flour into dry measuring cups; level with a knife. Combine flour, baking powder, baking soda, and salt, stirring well with a whisk. Add flour mixture to sugar mixture alternately with buttermilk, beginning and ending with flour mixture; mix after each addition.
4. Spoon batter over peach mixture in pan. Bake at 350° for 45 minutes or until a wooden pick inserted in center comes out clean. Cool 10 minutes in pan on a wire rack. Place a plate upside down on top of cake, and invert onto plate. Serve warm with frozen yogurt and caramel syrup. Yield: 9 servings (serving size: 1 cake piece, ¼ cup frozen yogurt, and 2 teaspoons caramel syrup).

CALORIES 307 (18% from fat); FAT 6.2g (sat 3.6g, mono 1.8g, poly 0.4g); PROTEIN 6.1g; CARB 57.3g; FIBER 1.7g; CHOL 39mg; IRON 1.1mg; SODIUM 307mg; CALC 153mg

Peach Marmalade Betty

A betty is a dessert that usually features layers of sugared, spiced fruit covered with a layer of buttered breadcrumbs. We added oatmeal cookie crumbs for a spicier topping; to get crumbs, pulse the cookies in a food processor, or run them over the large holes of a box grater.

- 5 cups thinly sliced peeled peaches (about 2½ pounds)
- ½ cup sugar
- ¼ cup orange marmalade
- 3 tablespoons orange juice
- 5 soft oatmeal cookies (such as Archway Homestyle)
- 1 (1½-ounce) slice white bread
- 2 tablespoons butter, melted
- Cooking spray

1. Preheat oven to 350°.
2. Combine first 4 ingredients in a large bowl.
3. Place cookies and bread in a food processor; pulse 10 times or until coarse crumbs form to measure 1½ cups. Combine cookie crumb mixture and butter; toss well. Sprinkle ½ cup crumb mixture in bottom of a 2-quart casserole coated with cooking spray. Add peach mixture, and sprinkle with remaining crumb mixture. Cover and bake at 350° for 25 minutes; uncover and bake 15 minutes or until bubbly. Yield: 8 servings (serving size: ½ cup).

CALORIES 191 (19% from fat); FAT 4.2g (sat 2.1g, mono 1.3g, poly 0.2g); PROTEIN 1.8g; CARB 38.7g; FIBER 2.3g; CHOL 9mg; IRON 0.5mg; SODIUM 98mg; CALC 19mg

Peach-Ginger Crisp

- ½ cup all-purpose flour
- ¼ cup granulated sugar
- ¼ cup packed brown sugar
- 3 tablespoons chilled butter, cut into small pieces
- 2 tablespoons sliced almonds, toasted
- 6 cups sliced peeled peaches (about 3 pounds)
- 1 tablespoon granulated sugar
- 2 teaspoons cornstarch
- 2 teaspoons lemon juice
- ¾ teaspoon minced peeled fresh ginger

1. Preheat oven to 375°.
2. Lightly spoon flour into a dry measuring cup, and level with a knife. Combine flour, ¼ cup granulated sugar, and brown sugar in a bowl. Cut in butter with a pastry blender or 2 knives until crumbly. Stir in almonds.
3. Combine peaches and next 4 ingredients in a bowl. Spoon peach mixture into an 8-inch square baking dish. Sprinkle with flour mixture. Bake mixture at 375° for 45 minutes or until lightly browned and bubbly. Yield: 5 servings (serving size: 1 cup).

CALORIES 300 (26% from fat); FAT 8.6g (sat 4.5g, mono 3g, poly 0.7g); PROTEIN 3.3g; CARB 56g; FIBER 4.6g; CHOL 19mg; IRON 1.2mg; SODIUM 76mg; CALC 30mg

Peach Compote with Rum

Serve this with grilled chicken or pork, or over ice cream. You can use fresh strawberries in place of the raspberries.

- ½ cup water
- ¼ cup sugar
- 3 tablespoons white rum
- ½ teaspoon grated lime rind
- 1 tablespoon fresh lime juice
- 3 cups sliced peeled peaches (about 1½ pounds)
- 1 cup seedless red grapes, halved
- 1 cup fresh raspberries
- Mint sprigs (optional)

1. Combine water and sugar in a small saucepan. Bring to a boil, and cook 30
Continued

seconds or until sugar dissolves, stirring constantly. Remove from heat, and stir in rum, lime rind, and lime juice. Cool to room temperature.

2. Combine peaches, grapes, and raspberries in a large bowl. Add rum mixture, tossing to coat. Garnish with mint sprigs, if desired. Yield: 6 servings (serving size: ⅔ cup).

CALORIES 116 (3% from fat); FAT 0.4g (sat 0.1g, mono 0.1g, poly 0.2g); PROTEIN 1g; CARB 24.9g; FIBER 3.5g; CHOL 0mg; IRON 0.3mg; SODIUM 1mg; CALC 13mg

Peach Ice Cream

Ripe peaches at peak season are key to this creamy, refreshing ice cream. It's best eaten the same day it's prepared.

    3 cups sliced peeled peaches
       (about 1½ pounds)
    1 cup half-and-half
    ½ cup sugar
    ½ cup whole milk
    1 teaspoon vanilla extract

1. Place peaches in a blender or food processor; process until finely chopped. Combine peaches and remaining ingredients in a large bowl. Pour peach mixture into freezer can of an ice-cream freezer; freeze according to manufacturer's instructions. Spoon ice cream into a freezer-safe container; cover and freeze 2 hours or until firm. Yield: 8 servings (serving size: ½ cup).

CALORIES 125 (29% from fat); FAT 4g (sat 2.5g, mono 1.2g, poly 0.2g); PROTEIN 1.8g; CARB 21.3g; FIBER 1.2g; CHOL 13mg; IRON 0.1mg; SODIUM 20mg; CALC 53mg

Peeling a Peach

The peel lends the peach its appetizing rosy glow, but some folks simply don't like the feel; others are allergic to it. Peeling a peach is as simple as boiling water: Plunge the peach into the bubbling water for 30 seconds, remove, and plunge into iced water for a few seconds more. The peel should slide off easily.

One Bowl. One Whisk. One Cake.

A simplified technique yields great cakes fast.

Want a made-from-scratch cake ready to go in the oven in less than 10 minutes with only a small mess to clean up? Here's what you do. Melt the butter in the microwave in a large bowl, then whisk in the sugar to cool the butter so the eggs won't scramble. Add the eggs to the bowl, and whisk them just until they're well combined. At this point, if you want to incorporate some air into the batter, whisk it a while longer and a bit more vigorously. Next, add flavorings and spices along with the baking powder and baking soda, stirring them in with the whisk until dissolved. Then stir in the liquid. Stir in the flour gently with the whisk only until the mixture is smooth. Don't beat the batter once the flour is added, or the flour's gluten will be activated and toughen the cake's texture. If the recipe calls for fruits or nuts, stir them in just before pouring the batter into the pan. Nothing could be simpler.

Black-and-White Cake

    Cooking spray
    2 teaspoons all-purpose flour
    6 tablespoons butter
    1 cup sugar
 1½ teaspoons vanilla extract
    4 large egg whites
    ¾ cup low-fat buttermilk
    ½ teaspoon salt
    ½ teaspoon baking soda
 1½ cups all-purpose flour
    3 tablespoons unsweetened cocoa
    ¼ teaspoon almond extract

1. Preheat oven to 350°.
2. Coat an 8-inch square baking pan with cooking spray, and dust with 2 teaspoons flour.
3. Place butter in a large microwave-safe bowl. Cover and microwave at HIGH 1 minute or until butter melts. Add sugar, stirring with a whisk. Add vanilla and egg whites; stir well. Stir in buttermilk, salt, and baking soda. Lightly spoon 1½ cups flour into dry measuring cups; level with a knife. Add flour to bowl, stirring just until blended (do not overstir). Spread half of batter into prepared pan. Add cocoa and almond extract to remaining batter; stir well with a whisk.

Slowly pour chocolate batter over batter in pan.
4. Bake at 350° for 30 minutes or until a wooden pick inserted in center comes out clean. Cool 10 minutes in pan on a wire rack. Cut into squares. Yield: 9 servings (serving size: 1 cake square).

CALORIES 255 (29% from fat); FAT 8.3g (sat 5.1g, mono 2.4g, poly 0.4g); PROTEIN 5g; CARB 40.9g; FIBER 1.2g; CHOL 22mg; IRON 1.3mg; SODIUM 324mg; CALC 32mg

Pineapple Upside-Down Cake

(pictured on page 240)

    1 (20-ounce) can pineapple slices in
       juice, drained
    Cooking spray
    ⅓ cup fat-free caramel topping
    9 maraschino cherries, drained
    5 tablespoons butter
    ⅔ cup sugar
    2 large eggs
    ½ cup low-fat buttermilk
    1 teaspoon baking powder
    1 teaspoon vanilla extract
    ¼ teaspoon salt
    ¼ teaspoon baking soda
 1¼ cups all-purpose flour

1. Preheat oven to 350°.

2. Press 9 pineapple slices between paper towels until barely moist; set aside. Reserve remaining pineapple for another use.

3. Coat a 9-inch square baking pan with cooking spray; drizzle caramel topping over bottom of pan. Arrange prepared pineapple slices in a single layer over caramel; place 1 cherry in center of each slice.

4. Place butter in a large microwave-safe bowl. Cover and microwave at HIGH 1 minute or until butter melts. Add sugar, stirring with a whisk. Add eggs, and stir well. Stir in low-fat buttermilk and next 4 ingredients. Lightly spoon 1¼ cups flour into dry measuring cups, and level with a knife. Add flour to bowl, stirring just until blended (do not overstir). Pour batter into prepared pan.

5. Bake at 350° for 30 minutes or until a wooden pick inserted in center comes out clean. Cool 1 minute in pan on a wire rack. Place a plate upside down on top of cake, and invert cake onto plate. Cool completely. Cut cake into squares. Yield: 9 servings (serving size: 1 cake square).

CALORIES 264 (27% from fat); FAT 7.9g (sat 4.5g, mono 2.4g, poly 0.5g); PROTEIN 4g; CARB 45.1g; FIBER 0.9g; CHOL 65mg; IRON 1.2mg; SODIUM 280mg; CALC 68mg

Blueberry-Pecan Cake

This tender cake is packed with sweet berries and crunchy nuts.

Cooking spray
  2 teaspoons all-purpose flour
  5 tablespoons butter
  ¾ cup granulated sugar
  2 large eggs
  ⅔ cup low-fat buttermilk
  2 teaspoons grated orange rind
  1 teaspoon baking powder
  ½ teaspoon salt
1½ teaspoons vanilla extract
  ½ teaspoon almond extract
  ¼ teaspoon baking soda
1½ cups all-purpose flour
  2 cups fresh or frozen blueberries
  ⅓ cup finely chopped pecans
  2 tablespoons sifted powdered sugar

1. Preheat oven to 350°.

2. Coat a 9-inch round springform pan with cooking spray, and dust pan with 2 teaspoons flour.

3. Place butter in a large microwave-safe bowl. Cover and microwave at HIGH 1 minute or until butter melts. Add granulated sugar, stirring with a whisk. Add eggs; stir well. Stir in buttermilk and next 6 ingredients; stir well. Lightly spoon 1½ cups flour into dry measuring cups; level with a knife. Add flour to bowl, stirring just until blended (do not overstir). Stir in blueberries and pecans. Spoon batter into prepared pan, spreading evenly.

4. Bake at 350° for 45 minutes or until lightly browned and a pick inserted in center comes out clean. Cool 10 minutes in pan on a wire rack. Sprinkle with powdered sugar. Cut into wedges. Yield: 10 servings (serving size: 1 wedge).

CALORIES 253 (36% from fat); FAT 10.1g (sat 4.3g, mono 3.8g, poly 1.3g); PROTEIN 4.5g; CARB 36.9g; FIBER 1.7g; CHOL 59mg; IRON 1.3mg; SODIUM 287mg; CALC 60mg

Espresso-Walnut Cake

This cake was screaming for a streusel topping, so we actually used two bowls.

Cooking spray
  2 teaspoons all-purpose flour
  ¼ cup packed brown sugar
  3 tablespoons finely chopped walnuts
  1 teaspoon ground cinnamon
  1 tablespoon instant espresso or 2 tablespoons instant coffee granules, divided
  5 tablespoons butter
  1 cup granulated sugar
  2 large eggs
  ⅔ cup plain fat-free yogurt
  2 teaspoons vanilla extract
  ½ teaspoon baking soda
  ¼ teaspoon salt
1⅓ cups all-purpose flour

1. Preheat oven to 350°.

2. Coat an 8-inch square baking pan with cooking spray, and dust with 2 teaspoons flour.

3. Combine brown sugar, walnuts, cinnamon, and 1 teaspoon espresso granules in a small bowl.

4. Place butter in a large microwave-safe bowl. Cover and microwave at HIGH 1 minute or until butter melts. Add granulated sugar, stirring with a whisk. Add eggs; stir well. Stir in yogurt, vanilla, baking soda, and salt. Lightly spoon 1⅓ cups flour into dry measuring cups; level with a knife. Add flour and 2 teaspoons espresso powder to yogurt mixture, stirring just until blended (do not overstir).

5. Spread half of batter into prepared pan, and sprinkle with half of brown sugar mixture. Carefully spread remaining batter over brown sugar mixture, and sprinkle with remaining brown sugar mixture.

6. Bake at 350° for 25 minutes or until a wooden pick inserted in center comes out clean. Cool 10 minutes in pan on a wire rack. Cut into squares. Yield: 9 servings (serving size: 1 cake square).

CALORIES 284 (30% from fat); FAT 9.4g (sat 4.5g, mono 2.6g, poly 1.7g); PROTEIN 5g; CARB 45.4g; FIBER 0.8g; CHOL 65mg; IRON 1.4mg; SODIUM 231mg; CALC 58mg

Spicy Molasses Cake

Aromatic spices give this moist cake an assertive flavor. It's great served warm or at room temperature.

Cooking spray
  2 teaspoons all-purpose flour
  5 tablespoons butter
  ⅓ cup packed brown sugar
  ⅔ cup molasses
  2 large eggs
  2 teaspoons ground ginger
1½ teaspoons pumpkin pie spice
  ½ teaspoon baking soda
  ½ teaspoon dry mustard
  ¼ teaspoon salt
  ½ cup fat-free milk
1½ teaspoons grated orange rind
1½ cups all-purpose flour
  ½ cup frozen fat-free whipped topping, thawed

Continued

1. Preheat oven to 350°.
2. Coat an 8-inch square baking pan with cooking spray, and dust bottom of pan with 2 teaspoons flour.
3. Place butter in a large microwave-safe bowl. Cover and microwave at HIGH 1 minute or until butter melts. Add sugar, stirring with a whisk. Add molasses and eggs; stir with a whisk until smooth. Add ginger, pie spice, baking soda, mustard, and salt; stir well with a whisk. Add milk and orange rind; stir well with a whisk. Lightly spoon 1½ cups flour into dry measuring cups; level with a knife. Add flour to bowl, stirring just until blended (do not overstir). Pour batter into pan.
4. Bake at 350° for 30 minutes or until a wooden pick inserted in center comes out clean. Cool in pan 10 minutes on a wire rack. Cut into squares. Serve with whipped topping. Yield: 9 servings (serving size: 1 cake square and about 1 tablespoon whipped topping).

CALORIES 262 (27% from fat); FAT 7.9g (sat 4.4g, mono 2.4g, poly 0.5g); PROTEIN 4.3g; CARB 43.8g; FIBER 0.7g; CHOL 65mg; IRON 2.6mg; SODIUM 236mg; CALC 88mg

Devil's Food Cake

Stir the espresso granules into the same measuring cup you use for the hot water and you won't have to use more than one bowl.

Cooking spray
    2 teaspoons all-purpose flour
    5 tablespoons butter
    ½ cup Dutch process cocoa
    1 cup packed dark brown sugar
    2 large eggs
    ½ teaspoon baking soda
 1½ teaspoons vanilla extract
    ¼ teaspoon salt
    ¾ cup all-purpose flour
    ½ cup hot water
    1 teaspoon instant espresso granules
        or 2 teaspoons instant coffee
        granules
    1 tablespoon powdered sugar

1. Preheat oven to 350°.
2. Coat an 8-inch square baking pan with cooking spray, and dust pan with 2 teaspoons flour.

3. Place butter in a large microwave-safe bowl. Cover and microwave at HIGH 1 minute or until butter melts. Add cocoa, stirring well with a whisk. Add brown sugar, stirring well until mixture pulls away from sides of bowl. Add eggs, 1 at a time, stirring with a whisk until smooth. Stir in baking soda, vanilla, and salt. Lightly spoon ¾ cup flour into dry measuring cups; level with a knife. Gradually add flour to bowl, stirring just until blended (do not overstir). Combine hot water and espresso. Add to flour mixture, stirring just until blended.
4. Pour batter into prepared pan. Bake at 350° for 25 minutes or until a wooden pick inserted in center comes out clean. Cool 10 minutes on a wire rack. Sprinkle with powdered sugar. Cut into squares; serve warm or at room temperature. Yield: 9 servings (serving size: 1 cake square).

CALORIES 221 (33% from fat); FAT 8.2g (sat 4.7g, mono 2.5g, poly 0.5g); PROTEIN 3.5g; CARB 36g; FIBER 1.7g; CHOL 65mg; IRON 1.9mg; SODIUM 225mg; CALC 36mg

Rum-Raisin Applesauce Cake

Cooking spray
    2 teaspoons all-purpose flour
    6 tablespoons butter
    1 cup granulated sugar
    2 large eggs
    1 cup applesauce
    3 tablespoons dark rum
    1 teaspoon ground cinnamon
    2 teaspoons vanilla extract
    ½ teaspoon ground nutmeg
    ½ teaspoon baking soda
    ¼ teaspoon salt
 1½ cups all-purpose flour
    1 cup golden raisins
    1 tablespoon powdered sugar

1. Preheat oven to 350°.
2. Coat an 8-inch square baking pan with cooking spray, and dust pan with 2 teaspoons flour.
3. Place butter in a large microwave-safe bowl. Cover and microwave at HIGH 1 minute or until butter melts. Add granulated sugar, stirring with a whisk. Add

eggs, and stir well. Stir in applesauce and next 6 ingredients. Lightly spoon 1½ cups flour into dry measuring cups, and level with a knife. Add flour to bowl, stirring just until blended (do not overstir). Stir in raisins. Pour batter into prepared pan.
4. Bake at 350° for 30 minutes or until a wooden pick inserted in center comes out clean. Cool 10 minutes in pan on a wire rack. Sprinkle with powdered sugar. Cut into squares. Yield: 9 servings (serving size: 1 cake square).

CALORIES 323 (25% from fat); FAT 9.1g (sat 5.2g, mono 2.7g, poly 0.6g); PROTEIN 4.4g; CARB 58g; FIBER 1.8g; CHOL 68mg; IRON 1.6mg; SODIUM 230mg; CALC 24mg

Tips for One-Bowl Success

- This one might sound like a no-brainer, but make sure your bowl is microwave-safe, fits in the microwave, and is big enough to accommodate all the ingredients.
- We like bowls with spouts (also called batter bowls) because they make pouring the batter easier.
- We tested most of these recipes in eight-inch square shiny metal baking pans, but they'll also work in glass baking dishes or dark baking pans. Decrease the temperature by 25 degrees since glass and dark pans conduct heat better than shiny metal.
- Be careful not to overbake your cake. Low-fat cakes are sensitive to overcooking; because ovens vary widely, an oven thermometer is a must. And it's best to start checking for doneness 10 minutes before the recommended baking time.
- You can store these cakes at room temperature, covered in their baking pans, for up to three days.
- All of these cakes are good candidates for the freezer. They'll keep for up to a month if you wrap them tightly in plastic wrap then overwrap in foil.

Simple, Fresh, Inspired, Natural

. . . and ready in just about 20 minutes.

Our new monthly column, Superfast, features recipes that can be made in about 20 minutes. We start with short lists of fresh, high-quality ingredients, then put them together with minimal fuss. And we do it with little reliance on processed foods.

Barley "Tabbouleh" with Chicken

Serve with a mixed greens salad or broccoli.

    2 cups water
    1 cup uncooked quick-cooking
       barley
    2 cups fresh parsley leaves
    ½ cup mint sprigs
    ¼ cup fresh lemon juice
    3 tablespoons olive oil, divided
    1 teaspoon salt, divided
    2 cups chopped tomato (about
       1 pound)
    1 pound skinless, boneless chicken
       breast, cut into ¼-inch strips
    1 teaspoon ground cumin
    ⅛ teaspoon black pepper

1. Bring water to a boil in a medium saucepan. Add barley; cover, reduce heat, and simmer 15 minutes. Remove from heat; cover and let stand 5 minutes. Spoon barley into a bowl.
2. While barley cooks, place parsley, mint, juice, 2½ tablespoons oil, and ½ teaspoon salt in a food processor; process until herbs are finely chopped. Add tomato; pulse until finely chopped.
3. Place chicken in a medium bowl; sprinkle with ½ teaspoon salt, cumin, and black pepper. Toss well. Heat 1½ teaspoons oil in a large nonstick skillet over medium-high heat. Add chicken; cook 3 minutes on each side or until done. Add chicken and tomato mixture

to barley, and toss well. Yield: 4 servings (serving size: 1¼ cups).

CALORIES 438 (29% from fat); FAT 14.3g (sat 2.4g, mono 8.8g, poly 1.9g); PROTEIN 32.8g; CARB 46g; FIBER 9.8g; CHOL 73mg; IRON 4.1mg; SODIUM 675mg; CALC 66mg

Tortellini and Spinach in Broth

The pasta will quickly soak up the broth, so it's important that you serve this soup immediately.

    1   tablespoon olive oil
    5   garlic cloves, thinly sliced
    ½   cup dry white wine
    3   (15.75-ounce) cans fat-free,
        less-sodium chicken broth
    2   (9-ounce) packages fresh
        three-cheese tortellini
    1¼ cups chopped tomato
    1   (6-ounce) bag baby spinach
    1   tablespoon butter

1. Heat olive oil in a Dutch oven over medium-high heat. Add garlic; cook 30 seconds, stirring constantly. Stir in wine and broth. Bring to a boil; cook 2 minutes. Add tortellini; cook 6 minutes. Stir in tomato and spinach; cook 2 minutes or until spinach wilts. Add butter, and cook until butter melts. Serve soup immediately. Yield: 4 servings (serving size: 2 cups).

CALORIES 481 (24% from fat); FAT 13g (sat 5.4g, mono 5.6g, poly 1.0g); PROTEIN 23.5g; CARB 69.2g; FIBER 6.4g; CHOL 46mg; IRON 3.8mg; SODIUM 1,394mg; CALC 269mg

Chicken Thighs with Honey-Ginger Glaze

    ¼ cup honey
    1 tablespoon fresh lemon juice
    1 tablespoon low-sodium soy sauce
    2 teaspoons grated peeled fresh
       ginger
    1 teaspoon Worcestershire sauce
    Dash of hot sauce
    1 teaspoon vegetable oil
    4 skinless, boneless chicken thighs
       (about ¾ pound)

1. Combine first 6 ingredients in a small bowl. Heat oil in a medium nonstick skillet over medium-high heat. Add chicken; cook 5 minutes on each side or until browned. Add sauce; cover, reduce heat, and simmer 10 minutes or until done. Yield: 2 servings (serving size: 2 chicken thighs and 2 tablespoons sauce).

CALORIES 360 (23% from fat); FAT 9g (sat 2.0g, mono 2.6g, poly 3.0g); PROTEIN 34g; CARB 37g; FIBER 0.2g; CHOL 142mg; IRON 2.2mg; SODIUM 444mg; CALC 24mg

Saucy Sirloin Steak

Serve with mashed potatoes.

    ½ teaspoon salt
    ½ teaspoon garlic powder
    ¼ teaspoon black pepper
    1 pound boneless sirloin steak,
       trimmed
    Cooking spray
    1 teaspoon olive oil
    2 garlic cloves, minced
    ½ cup beef broth
    ¼ cup hoisin sauce
    3 teaspoons red wine vinegar
    2 teaspoons Dijon mustard
    1 teaspoon tomato paste

1. Preheat broiler.
2. Combine first 3 ingredients in a small bowl; sprinkle over steak. Place steak on a broiler pan coated with cooking spray. Broil 6 minutes on each side or until desired degree of doneness. Let stand 5 minutes.
3. While steak is standing, heat olive oil in a small saucepan over medium heat. Add garlic, and cook 30 seconds, stirring constantly. Add broth and remaining 4 ingredients. Bring to a boil; reduce heat, and simmer 5 minutes or until thick, stirring with a whisk. Cut steak diagonally across grain into thin slices, and serve with sauce. Yield: 4 servings (serving size: 3 ounces steak and 3 tablespoons sauce).

CALORIES 227 (35% from fat); FAT 8.8g (sat 2.9g, mono 4g, poly 0.7g); PROTEIN 27.1g; CARB 8.5g; FIBER 0.7g; CHOL 76mg; IRON 3.2mg; SODIUM 765mg; CALC 24mg

Citrus-Roasted Salmon

    1 teaspoon grated lemon rind
    2 tablespoons fresh lemon juice
    2 tablespoons honey
    4 teaspoons chili powder
    1 teaspoon ground cumin
    ½ teaspoon salt
    ½ teaspoon ground coriander seeds
    ¼ teaspoon ground red pepper
    1 (6-ounce) can thawed orange juice concentrate
    4 (6-ounce) salmon fillets, skinned (1 inch thick)
       Cooking spray
       Orange wedges (optional)
       Flat-leaf parsley sprigs (optional)

1. Preheat oven to 400°.
2. Combine first 9 ingredients in a bowl; brush both sides of fillets with orange mixture. Reserve remaining orange mixture. Place fillets on a broiler pan coated with cooking spray. Bake at 400° for 15 minutes or until fish flakes easily when tested with a fork.
3. Place remaining orange mixture in a small saucepan; bring to a boil, and cook until reduced to ½ cup (about 2 minutes). Serve with fish, and garnish with orange wedges and parsley, if desired. Yield: 4 servings (serving size: 1 fillet and 2 tablespoons orange sauce).

CALORIES 366 (33% from fat); FAT 13.5g (sat 2.3g, mono 6.3g, poly 3g); PROTEIN 33.5g; CARB 27g; FIBER 1.6g; CHOL 102mg; IRON 1.4mg; SODIUM 399mg; CALC 37mg

Grilled Chicken Breasts with Plum Salsa

Peaches, nectarines, or pineapple can be used in place of the plums.

CHICKEN:

    2 teaspoons brown sugar
    ½ teaspoon salt
    ½ teaspoon ground cumin
    ¼ teaspoon garlic powder
    4 (4-ounce) skinless, boneless chicken breast halves
    2 teaspoons vegetable oil

PLUM SALSA:

    1 cup chopped ripe plum (about 2 plums)
    2 tablespoons chopped fresh or 1 teaspoon dried cilantro
    2 tablespoons chopped red onion
    2 teaspoons cider vinegar
    ¼ teaspoon hot sauce
    ⅛ teaspoon salt

1. To prepare chicken, combine first 4 ingredients. Rub chicken with mixture.
2. Heat oil in a grill pan or nonstick skillet over medium heat. Add chicken; cook 6 minutes on each side or until done.
3. While chicken is cooking, combine plum and remaining 5 ingredients in a bowl. Serve with chicken. Yield: 4 servings (serving size: 1 chicken breast half and ¼ cup salsa).

CALORIES 203 (26% from fat); FAT 5.8g (sat 1.2g, mono 1.8g, poly 2.1g); PROTEIN 27.1g; CARB 9.8g; FIBER 1g; CHOL 72mg; IRON 1.3mg; SODIUM 431mg; CALC 24mg

Broiled Sea Bass with Pineapple-Chili-Basil Glaze

    3 tablespoons pineapple preserves
    2 tablespoons rice vinegar
    1 teaspoon chopped fresh or ¼ teaspoon dried basil
    ⅛ teaspoon crushed red pepper
    1 garlic clove, minced
    ¾ teaspoon salt, divided
    4 (6-ounce) sea bass or other firm white fish fillets (about 1 inch thick)
    ¼ teaspoon black pepper
       Cooking spray

1. Preheat broiler.
2. Combine first 5 ingredients and ¼ teaspoon salt in a small bowl.
3. Sprinkle fillets with ½ teaspoon salt and black pepper. Place fillets on a broiler pan coated with cooking spray, and broil 5 minutes. Remove from oven; brush fillets evenly with glaze. Return to oven; broil 5 minutes or until fish flakes easily when tested with a fork. Yield: 4 servings (serving size: 1 fillet).

CALORIES 208 (15% from fat); FAT 3.4g (sat 0.9g, mono 0.7g, poly 1.3g); PROTEIN 31.4g; CARB 10.7g; FIBER 0.2g; CHOL 70mg; IRON 0.6mg; SODIUM 487mg; CALC 23mg

taste of america

Take Sides at Family Reunions

Celebrate the gathering of your kin with these great side dishes.

Chipotle, Tomato, and Roasted Vegetable Salad

Serve with tortilla chips or grilled chicken.

SALAD:

    1½ cups coarsely chopped onion
    1⅓ cups coarsely chopped green bell pepper
    1⅓ cups coarsely chopped yellow bell pepper
        Cooking spray
    1⅓ cups chopped seeded tomato
    ¼   cup minced fresh cilantro

1 (7-ounce) can chipotle chiles in
    adobo sauce
2 tablespoons cider vinegar
2 teaspoons extra-virgin olive oil
½ teaspoon salt

1. Preheat broiler.
2. To prepare salad, place first 3 ingredients on a large baking sheet coated with cooking spray. Lightly coat onion mixture with cooking spray; broil 8 minutes or until onion and bell peppers begin to blacken, stirring once. Place onion mixture in a bowl; cool. Add tomato and cilantro to onion mixture.
3. To prepare dressing, remove 1 chile from can, and chop to measure 1½ teaspoons. Reserve remaining chiles and sauce for another use. Combine chile, vinegar, oil, and salt, and stir with a whisk. Drizzle over onion mixture; toss gently to coat. Yield: 12 servings (serving size: ⅓ cup).

CALORIES 28 (37% from fat); FAT 1.1g (sat 0.1g, mono 0.6g, poly 0.2g); PROTEIN 0.7g; CARB 4.5g; FIBER 1.1g; CHOL 0mg; IRON 0.6mg; SODIUM 106mg; CALC 8mg

German-Style Potato Salad

2 pounds red potatoes, cut into
    ⅛-inch-thick slices (about 5 cups)
8 bacon slices, cut into ½-inch pieces
⅓ cup cider vinegar
2½ teaspoons sugar
¾ teaspoon salt
¼ teaspoon black pepper
½ cup finely chopped onion
¼ cup finely chopped red bell pepper
¼ cup finely chopped fresh parsley

1. Steam potato, covered, 10 minutes or until tender.
2. Cook bacon in a nonstick skillet over medium heat until crisp. Remove from pan, reserving 2 teaspoons drippings.
3. Combine drippings, vinegar, sugar, salt, and black pepper in a large bowl; stir well with a whisk. Add potato, onion, and bell pepper; toss gently to coat. Cover and let stand 1 hour, stirring occasionally. Add bacon and parsley;

toss gently. Yield: 11 servings (serving size: ½ cup).

CALORIES 108 (30% from fat); FAT 3.6g (sat 1.3g, mono 1.6g, poly 0.5g); PROTEIN 3.6g; CARB 15.9g; FIBER 1.7g; CHOL 5mg; IRON 1.3mg; SODIUM 253mg; CALC 14mg

Barley "Pasta" Salad

2 cups water
½ cup uncooked pearl barley
2 tablespoons fresh lemon juice
1 tablespoon olive oil
½ teaspoon salt
2 cups finely chopped seeded tomato
1 cup thinly sliced spinach
½ cup finely chopped green bell pepper
½ cup chopped seeded peeled
    cucumber
½ cup (2 ounces) diced part-skim
    mozzarella cheese
¼ cup finely chopped pepperoncini
    peppers
2 teaspoons dry oregano

1. Bring 2 cups water to a boil in a large saucepan. Add barley; cover, reduce heat, and simmer 45 minutes. Drain and rinse with cold water; drain.
2. Combine juice, oil, and salt in large bowl; stir well with a whisk. Add barley, tomato, and remaining ingredients; toss gently to coat. Yield: 5 servings (serving size: about 1 cup).

CALORIES 153 (31% from fat); FAT 5.2g (sat 1.6g, mono 2.6g, poly 0.6g); PROTEIN 6g; CARB 22.4g; FIBER 5g; CHOL 7mg; IRON 1.8mg; SODIUM 436mg; CALC 107mg

Fresh-from-the-Garden Vegetable Salad

4 quarts water
¾ pound green beans, trimmed
¾ pound carrots, cut into
    3½ x ¼-inch sticks
1 tablespoon sugar
2 tablespoons cider vinegar
2 tablespoons Dijon mustard
1 tablespoon vegetable oil
¾ teaspoon salt
1 cup yellow bell pepper strips
¼ cup finely chopped onion

1. Bring water to a boil in an 8-quart stockpot. Add beans; cook 1 minute. Add carrot; cook mixture 2 minutes or until crisp-tender. Drain; place vegetables in ice water. Let stand 1 minute or until cool; drain.
2. Combine sugar, vinegar, mustard, oil, and salt in a large bowl; stir well with a whisk. Add beans, carrots, bell pepper, and onion; toss gently to coat. Yield: 6 servings (serving size: 1 cup).

CALORIES 84 (31% from fat); FAT 2.9g (sat 0.5g, mono 0.7g, poly 1.2g); PROTEIN 1.8g; CARB 14g; FIBER 3.4g; CHOL 0mg; IRON 1.1mg; SODIUM 466mg; CALC 39mg

Try New Things Menu
serves 8
Crunchy Bok Choy Salad
Asian burgers*

*Combine ½ cup hoisin sauce, 1 teaspoon garlic powder, ¼ teaspoon ground ginger, and 2 pounds ground turkey. Divide turkey mixture into 8 equal portions, shaping each into a ¾-inch-thick patty. Grill or broil 5 minutes on each side or until done. Serve with hamburger buns, lettuce leaves, and tomato slices.

Crunchy Bok Choy Salad

Bok choy is a mild cabbage that resembles wide-stalked celery with full leaves. Raw ramen noodles add a pleasing crunch to the salad.

DRESSING:
2 tablespoons sugar
3 tablespoons cider vinegar
3 tablespoons low-sodium soy sauce
2 teaspoons peanut butter
½ teaspoon curry powder
¼ teaspoon crushed red pepper

SALAD:
1 (3-ounce) package ramen noodles
¼ cup unsalted dry-roasted peanuts
3 cups thinly sliced bok choy
1 cup very thin red bell pepper strips
½ cup shredded carrot
¼ cup diagonally cut green onions

Continued

1. To prepare dressing, combine first 6 ingredients in a large bowl; stir well with a whisk.

2. To prepare salad, crumble noodles, and discard seasoning packet. Heat a nonstick skillet over medium-high heat. Add peanuts; sauté 4 minutes or until browned. Remove from heat. Combine crumbled noodles, peanuts, bok choy, and remaining 3 ingredients in a large bowl. Drizzle dressing over salad; toss gently to coat. Serve immediately. Yield: 10 servings (serving size: ½ cup).

CALORIES 86 (39% from fat); FAT 3.7g (sat 1.9g, mono 1g, poly 0.7g); PROTEIN 2.6g; CARB 11.7g; FIBER 1.4g; CHOL 0mg; IRON 0.8mg; SODIUM 178mg; CALC 28mg

Deviled Eggs

Make-ahead tip: Prepare the eggs up to 24 hours in advance. Then, be sure to store the eggs, covered, either in the refrigerator or in a cooler until you're ready to serve them. Keeping the eggs cool is essential.

```
12   large eggs
 ⅓   cup plain fat-free yogurt
 3   tablespoons low-fat mayonnaise
 1   tablespoon Dijon mustard
 1   to 2 teaspoons hot pepper
       sauce
 ⅛   teaspoon salt
 ⅛   teaspoon paprika
 ⅛   teaspoon black pepper
 2   tablespoons chopped green
       onions (optional)
```

1. Place eggs in a large saucepan. Cover with water to 1 inch above eggs; bring just to a boil. Remove from heat; cover and let stand 15 minutes. Drain and rinse with cold running water until cool. Slice eggs in half lengthwise, and remove yolks. Discard 3 yolks.

2. Combine yogurt and next 4 ingredients in a medium bowl. Add remaining yolks; beat with a mixer at high speed until smooth. Spoon about 1 tablespoon yolk mixture into each egg white half. Cover and chill 1 hour. Sprinkle with paprika and black pepper. Garnish with green onions, if desired. Yield: 24 servings (serving size: 1 egg half).

CALORIES 38 (50% from fat); FAT 2.1g (sat 0.6g, mono 0.7g, poly 0.3g); PROTEIN 3.1g; CARB 1.3g; FIBER 0g; CHOL 80mg; IRON 0.3mg; SODIUM 82mg; CALC 21mg

cooking light profile

Snapshot of an Adventurous Life

National Geographic *Editor in Chief Bill Allen maintains his healthy habits while traveling the world.*

In 1989 this veteran National Geographic photographer and writer's life changed forever. His routine six-mile jogs became too exhausting to complete. After consulting a cardiologist, Bill learned that he needed immediate bypass surgery.

Bill was shocked. He was always diligent about exercising and paying attention to his cholesterol and fat intake. "The only thing I did wrong," he says now, "was have the wrong grandparents."

After surgery, the doctors gave Bill strict orders regarding diet and exercise. Because his wife is an excellent cook who was already attuned to healthy living, Bill knew that complying with these orders wasn't going to be a problem. Carol threw herself into studying food labels and seeking out low-fat, low-cholesterol recipes. Hearty Italian dishes (pasta primavera is a favorite) make up the bulk of her repertoire, and a grateful Bill swears, "She's made such a science of it that I can hardly tell I'm eating health food."

There's no sign that the 1989 bypass surgery has in any way dampened his adventurous fire. "I have to be more realistic about my physical capabilities now," Bill says as he turns over a machete from the Republic of the Congo, examining the weapon. "But I've always wanted to see more and do more than I possibly could, and that hasn't changed at all."

Stuffed Portobellinis

Carol Allen serves these as an appetizer or a side dish with one of Bill's other Italian favorites.

```
1¼   cups fat-free, less-sodium chicken
       broth, divided
 ½   cup balsamic vinegar
 1   garlic clove, minced
 6   (3-inch) portobellini or portobello
       mushrooms
 1   (1½-ounce) slice French bread or
       other firm white bread
 1   teaspoon olive oil
 1   tablespoon chopped fresh chives
 1   tablespoon chopped fresh sage
 ¼   teaspoon salt
 ⅛   teaspoon black pepper
     Cooking spray
     Sage leaves (optional)
```

1. Preheat oven to 350°.

2. Combine ¾ cup broth, vinegar, and garlic in a small bowl; let stand 15 minutes. Strain through a sieve over a small saucepan; reserve garlic. Bring vinegar mixture to a boil, and cook until reduced to 6 tablespoons (about 6 minutes). Keep warm.

3. Remove brown gills from undersides of mushrooms using a spoon; discard gills. Remove stems from mushrooms; finely chop stems, and set aside. Place bread in a food processor, and pulse 10 times or until fine crumbs form to measure 1 cup. Heat oil in a large nonstick skillet over medium-high heat. Add breadcrumbs; cook 4 minutes or until lightly browned, stirring frequently. Stir in reserved garlic, chopped mushroom stems, chives, chopped sage, salt, and pepper; cook 2 minutes. Remove from heat; stir in ½ cup broth. Keep warm.

4. Place mushroom caps, stem sides up, on a baking sheet coated with cooking spray. Bake at 350° for 10 minutes or until tender. Divide breadcrumb mixture evenly among mushroom caps, and drizzle 1 tablespoon vinegar mixture over each serving. Garnish with sage leaves, if desired. Yield: 6 servings.

CALORIES 66 (15% from fat); FAT 1.2g (sat 0.2g, mono 0.6g, poly 0.2g); PROTEIN 3.7g; CARB 11.4g; FIBER 1.6g; CHOL 0mg; IRON 0.9mg; SODIUM 238mg; CALC 22mg

september

The Cooking of South America

From *anticuchos* to *sopa paraguaya*, South American foods reflect a rich and diverse culinary landscape.

South America is a continent of explosive flavors and culinary sophistication, yet most North Americans know next to nothing about its cooking. That's starting to change, thanks to the arrival in the United States of Peruvian seviche bars, Argentinean steak houses, and Brazilian *churrascarias*. But most of us would be hard pressed to name a single culinary specialty of Chile, Bolivia, or Paraguay. It's high time to discover the lands that gave us *chimichurri, caipirinhas,* and *pisco* sours.

Brazilian Fish Stew
Moqueca de Peixe

Moqueca de peixe (moo-KAY-ka duh PAY-shuh) is a fragrant fish stew from the state of Bahia in northern Brazil.

- ⅓ cup fresh lime juice
- ½ teaspoon salt
- ½ teaspoon freshly ground black pepper
- 2 garlic cloves, minced
- 1 (1½-pound) sea bass or halibut fillet, cut into ½-inch-wide strips
- 1½ pounds large shrimp, peeled and deveined
- 2 tablespoons olive oil
- 2 cups finely chopped onion
- 1 cup finely chopped green bell pepper
- 1 cup finely chopped red bell pepper
- ¾ cup minced green onions (about 1 bunch)
- 5 garlic cloves, minced
- 1 bay leaf
- 2 cups chopped tomato (about 2 large)
- ½ cup minced fresh cilantro, divided
- 2 (8-ounce) bottles clam juice
- 1 (14½-ounce) can fat-free, less-sodium chicken broth
- 1 cup light coconut milk
- ¼ teaspoon ground red pepper

1. Combine first 6 ingredients in a large bowl; toss to coat. Marinate in refrigerator 30 minutes.

2. Heat oil in a large Dutch oven over medium heat. Add onion, bell peppers, green onions, garlic, and bay leaf; cook 6 minutes, stirring occasionally. Increase heat to medium-high; add tomato, and cook 2 minutes. Add ¼ cup cilantro, clam juice, and broth. Bring to a boil; reduce heat, and simmer 10 minutes. Discard bay leaf. Remove vegetable mixture from pan.

3. Place one-third of vegetable mixture in a blender, and puree until smooth. Pour pureed vegetable mixture into pan. Repeat procedure with remaining vegetable mixture. Add coconut milk and ground red pepper to pureed vegetable mixture. Bring to a boil over medium-high heat; cook 3 minutes. Add fish mixture; cook 3 minutes or until fish is done. Sprinkle with ¼ cup cilantro. Yield: 6 servings (serving size: 1½ cups).

CALORIES 309 (24% from fat); FAT 8.4g (sat 2.6g, mono 2.5g, poly 1.8g); PROTEIN 41.5g; CARB 15.9g; FIBER 3g; CHOL 178mg; IRON 3.8mg; SODIUM 733mg; CALC 102mg

Sofrito

South Americans use prodigious amounts of onions, garlic, and bell peppers—the ingredients of a flavoring called *sofrito* in Spanish-speaking countries and *refogado* in Brazil. Sautéed in olive oil or lard until soft and fragrant, the sofrito is the foundation of hundreds of South American dishes. It's often the first aroma you notice when you enter a South American home.

How to Make Brazilian Fish Stew

1. *To make sofrito, a flavorful base for the soup, sauté onion, peppers, and garlic. Add remaining ingredients, and simmer 10 minutes.*

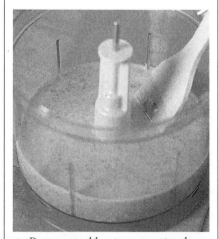

2. *Puree vegetable mixture to give the soup body.*

Uruguayan Bean Salad

(pictured on page 257)

In Uruguay and Argentina, this salad belongs to a roster of side dishes that accompany cocktails and steaks. It's traditionally made with *poroto*, a small, dark, rectangular bean with an earthy flavor. Fava beans come closest in flavor, but you can also use kidney or pinto beans.

    3   cups canned fava or kidney beans,
        drained and rinsed
    1   cup chopped seeded tomato
    ¾   cup finely chopped onion
    ¼   cup chopped fresh flat-leaf parsley
    3   tablespoons red wine vinegar
    2   tablespoons extra-virgin olive oil
    1   teaspoon dried oregano
    ½   teaspoon crushed red pepper
    ½   teaspoon freshly ground black
        pepper
    ¼   teaspoon salt

1. Combine all ingredients in a bowl, and toss gently. Yield: 6 servings (serving size: ⅔ cup).

CALORIES 167 (28% from fat); FAT 5.2g (sat 0.6g, mono 3.3g, poly 0.5g); PROTEIN 6.7g; CARB 23.7g; FIBER 6g; CHOL 0mg; IRON 2mg; SODIUM 353mg; CALC 34mg

Grilled Flank Steak with Chimichurri

Steak with chimichurri is one of Argentina's national dishes. The steak is flavored with a rub modeled on "dry" chimichurri, popular among Argentina's gauchos (cowboys).

    1   tablespoon olive oil
    2   teaspoons dried oregano
    1   teaspoon dried basil
    1   teaspoon paprika
    1   teaspoon crushed red pepper
    ½   teaspoon salt
    ½   teaspoon freshly ground black
        pepper
    2   garlic cloves, minced
    1   (1½-pound) flank or skirt steak,
        trimmed
    Cooking spray
    1½ cups Chimichurri (recipe at right)

1. Prepare grill.
2. Combine first 8 ingredients in a small bowl; rub steak with spice mixture. Marinate in refrigerator 30 minutes.
3. Place steak on grill rack coated with cooking spray; grill 6 minutes on each side or until desired degree of doneness. Serve with Chimichurri. Yield: 6 servings (serving size: 3 ounces steak and 2 tablespoons Chimichurri).

(Totals include Chimichurri) CALORIES 218 (50% from fat); FAT 12.1g (sat 4.1g, mono 6g, poly 1g); PROTEIN 23.5g; CARB 3g; FIBER 0.7g; CHOL 57mg; IRON 2.8mg; SODIUM 314mg; CALC 26mg

Paraguayan Corn Bread
Sopa Paraguaya
(pictured on page 257)

Because it's so moist, this bread resembles spoon bread or corn pudding much more than it does traditional American corn bread.

    Cooking spray
    2   tablespoons grated fresh Parmesan
        cheese
    1   tablespoon butter
    1   tablespoon vegetable oil
    1   cup chopped onion
    ⅓   cup chopped green bell pepper
    2   cups fresh corn kernels (about
        4 ears), divided
    ½   cup 1% low-fat cottage cheese
    1½ cups yellow cornmeal
    ¾   cup (3 ounces) shredded Muenster
        or sharp cheddar cheese
    ½   cup fat-free milk
    1   teaspoon salt
    ½   teaspoon black pepper
    4   large egg whites
    ½   teaspoon cream of tartar

1. Preheat oven to 400°.
2. Coat a 9-inch round cake pan with cooking spray. Sprinkle with Parmesan cheese, and set aside.
3. Heat butter and oil in a medium skillet over medium heat. Add onion and bell pepper; cook 5 minutes or until soft. Place onion mixture in a food processor. Add 1½ cups corn and cottage cheese; process until almost smooth, scraping sides of bowl occasionally. Place pureed mixture in a large bowl. Stir in remaining ½ cup corn, cornmeal, Muenster cheese, milk, salt, and black pepper.
4. Place egg whites and cream of tartar in a large bowl; beat with a mixer at high speed until stiff peaks form. Gently stir one-fourth of egg white mixture into batter; gently fold in remaining egg white mixture. Spoon batter into prepared pan.
5. Bake at 400° for 30 minutes or until a wooden pick inserted in center comes out clean (cover loosely with foil if it becomes too brown). Cool in pan 10 minutes on a wire rack. Place a plate upside down on top of bread; invert onto plate. Cut into wedges. Yield: 8 servings (serving size: 1 wedge).

CALORIES 235 (30% from fat); FAT 7.9g (sat 3.7g, mono 2.2g, poly 1.5g); PROTEIN 10.9g; CARB 31g; FIBER 3.4g; CHOL 16mg; IRON 0.7mg; SODIUM 503mg; CALC 133mg

Chimichurri

Considered the barbecue sauce of Argentina, this emerald-colored condiment is built on garlic and parsley, and is a pungent cross between vinaigrette and pesto.

    2   cups coarsely chopped fresh
        flat-leaf parsley (about 2 bunches)
    1   cup coarsely chopped onion
    ⅔   cup coarsely chopped carrot
    ¼   cup coarsely chopped garlic
    ½   cup vegetable broth
    ⅓   cup white vinegar
    2   tablespoons extra-virgin olive oil
    1   teaspoon dried oregano
    ½   teaspoon crushed red pepper
    ¼   teaspoon salt
    ¼   teaspoon black pepper

1. Combine first 4 ingredients in a food processor; pulse until mixture is finely chopped.
2. Combine broth and remaining 6 ingredients. With processor on, slowly pour broth mixture through food chute; process until well blended. Yield: 1½ cups (serving size: 2 tablespoons).

CALORIES 32 (68% from fat); FAT 2.4g (sat 0.3g, mono 1.7g, poly 0.2g); PROTEIN 0.5; CARB 2.5g; FIBER 0.5g; CHOL 0mg; IRON 0.4mg; SODIUM 94mg; CALC 15mg

Beef Empanadas Step-by-Steps

1. *For flavorful empanada filling, cook potatoes, onions, beef, and spices together. Finely chop cooked ingredients on a cutting board.*

2. *Place filling in center of each won ton wrapper; moisten edges of wrapper, then fold to form a triangle.*

Popular South American Dishes

Ajiaco colombiano: Colombian chicken and vegetable stew

Anticuchos: Peruvian beef kebabs

Arepas: Cornmeal flat cakes popular in Colombia

Arroz chaufa de mariscos: Peruvian fried rice with seafood

Arroz con camarones: Colombian rice pilaf with shrimp

Asado: Argentinean grilled beef, lamb, or pork roasted gaucho-style, in front of a campfire

Caldillo de congrio: Chilean fish stew made with conger eel

Cau-cau de mariscos: Peruvian seafood stew

Chimichurri: Argentinean garlic-parsley-vinegar sauce served with grilled beef

Chupe de camarones: Ecuadoran shrimp soup

Churrasco: A smorgasbord of grilled meats from Brazil, served on skewers and carved directly onto your plate

Couve mineira: Garlicky Brazilian-style collard greens

Empanadas: Chicken, meat, fish, or cheese turnovers, popular throughout South America

Ensalada de palmitos: Brazilian hearts of palm salad

Guasacaca: Venezuelan avocado sauce

Hallacas venezolanas: Venezuelan tamales

Humitas bolivianas: Bolivian corn tamales

Mariscada: Venezuelan seafood stew

Matambre: Literally, "hunger killer": a stuffed, rolled, grilled flank steak from Argentina and Uruguay

Moqueca de peixe: Brazilian seafood stew flavored with peppers and coconut milk

Pamplona de pollo: A colorful stuffed, rolled, grilled chicken breast from Uruguay

Parrillada: Argentinean grilled steak

Patacón: Colombian fried plantains

Pebre: A pickled onion relish served as a table condiment in Chile

Saltenas: Bolivian meat turnovers

Seviche: Uncooked seafood marinated with lime juice and chiles (popular in Ecuador and Peru)

So'o-losopy: Paraguay's ground beef soup

Sopa paraguaya: Paraguayan corn bread

Tira de asado: A crosscut short rib steak from Argentina

Baked Beef Empanadas

These meat pies are popular throughout Latin America. This recipe uses won ton wrappers instead of pastry for the crust, and the empanadas are baked instead of fried. Placing the uncooked empanadas on preheated baking sheets helps make them crisp. Try them with Roasted Yellow Pepper Sauce (recipe on page 253).

```
 1  cup finely chopped red potato
 1  cup finely chopped onion
 1  cup beef broth
 1  tablespoon finely chopped cilantro
¼  teaspoon salt
¼  teaspoon ground cumin
¼  teaspoon ground allspice
¼  teaspoon black pepper
½  pound boneless beef top sirloin,
    trimmed and diced
 1  garlic clove, minced
 1  tablespoon cornstarch
 1  tablespoon cold water
36  won ton wrappers
Cooking spray
Fresh cilantro sprigs (optional)
```

1. Combine first 10 ingredients in a saucepan. Bring to a boil over medium heat, stirring occasionally. Reduce heat; simmer 8 minutes or until potato is done, stirring occasionally. Remove from heat. Cool.

2. Preheat oven to 400°. Place 2 baking sheets in oven about 10 minutes.

3. Drain meat mixture in a colander over a bowl. Discard liquid. Finely chop meat mixture with a knife, or place in a food processor, and pulse 2 times or until finely chopped. Combine cornstarch and water, stirring with a whisk.

4. Working with one won ton wrapper at a time (cover remaining wrappers with a damp towel to keep from drying), spoon 1 tablespoon beef mixture into center of wrapper. Moisten edges of wrapper with cornstarch mixture. Bring 2 opposite corners together. Pinch points to seal, forming a triangle. Place filled wrapper on a wire rack. Repeat procedure with remaining beef mixture, wrappers, and cornstarch mixture.

5. Remove baking sheets from oven; coat baking sheets with cooking spray.

Arrange empanadas in a single layer on baking sheets. Coat empanadas with cooking spray. Bake empanadas at 400° for 8 minutes or until golden, turning once. Garnish with cilantro sprigs, if desired. Yield: 12 servings (serving size: 3 empanadas).

CALORIES 113 (9% from fat); FAT 1.1g (sat 0.3g, mono 0.3g, poly 0.2g); PROTEIN 7.4g; CARB 17.8g; FIBER 0.9g; CHOL 14mg; IRON 1.4mg; SODIUM 202mg; CALC 17mg

---

Try New Things Menu

Anticuchos
Peruvian Beef Kebabs

Grilled bell peppers, zucchini, and eggplant

Yellow rice

Anticuchos
Peruvian Beef Kebabs

These spicy kebabs are found in Peruvian restaurants and with street vendors. If you live near a Peruvian community, you may be able to buy whole or ground aji amarillo. If not, use hot paprika in its place. We also tried Spanish smoked paprika, which you can find at www.tienda.com.

BEEF:

1½ pounds boneless sirloin steak, trimmed and cut into ½-inch pieces
3 tablespoons red wine vinegar
2 teaspoons ground aji amarillo or hot paprika
1 teaspoon salt
1 teaspoon freshly ground black pepper
½ teaspoon ground cumin
½ teaspoon ground turmeric

FIERY RUB:

1 teaspoon ground aji amarillo or hot paprika
1 teaspoon salt
½ teaspoon freshly ground black pepper
¼ teaspoon ground turmeric
3 tablespoons chopped fresh flat-leaf parsley

REMAINING INGREDIENTS:

Cooking spray
Roasted Yellow Pepper Sauce

1. To prepare beef, combine first 7 ingredients in a large bowl; toss well. Cover and chill 3 hours.
2. To prepare fiery rub, combine 1 teaspoon paprika, 1 teaspoon salt, ½ teaspoon pepper, ¼ teaspoon turmeric, and parsley.
3. Prepare grill.
4. Remove beef from bowl, discarding marinade. Thread beef onto 6 (10-inch) skewers. Press fiery rub onto beef. Place kebabs on grill rack coated with cooking spray; grill 6 minutes or until desired degree of doneness, turning once. Serve with Roasted Yellow Pepper Sauce. Yield: 6 servings (serving size: 3 ounces meat and about 2½ tablespoons sauce).

(Totals include Roasted Yellow Pepper Sauce) CALORIES 188 (34% from fat); FAT 7g (sat 2.7g, mono 3g, poly 0.3g); PROTEIN 26.3g; CARB 3.4g; FIBER 0.8g; CHOL 76mg; IRON 3.6mg; SODIUM 809mg; CALC 23mg

ROASTED YELLOW PEPPER SAUCE:

This sauce is also good with Baked Beef Empanadas (recipe on page 252).

1 large yellow bell pepper (about 10 ounces)
¼ cup finely chopped green onions
2 tablespoons white vinegar
1 tablespoon water
1 tablespoon olive oil
1 tablespoon fresh lemon juice
1 teaspoon ground cumin
1 teaspoon ground aji amarillo or hot paprika
½ teaspoon ground turmeric
¼ teaspoon salt
¼ teaspoon black pepper
1 garlic clove, minced

1. Prepare broiler.
2. Cut bell pepper in half lengthwise, discarding seeds and membranes. Place pepper halves, skin sides up, on a foil-lined baking sheet; flatten with hand. Broil 15 minutes or until blackened. Place in a zip-top plastic bag; seal. Let stand 15 minutes. Peel and coarsely chop. Place bell pepper and remaining ingredients in a blender, and process until smooth. Yield: 1 cup (serving size: 2 tablespoons).

CALORIES 41 (40% from fat); FAT 1.8g (sat 0.2g, mono 1.3g, poly 0.2g); PROTEIN 0.5g; CARB 6.1g; FIBER 0.6g; CHOL 0mg; IRON 0.4mg; SODIUM 152mg; CALC 9mg

---

dinner tonight

Meat Meets Flavor

When affordable cuts of meat meet robust flavors, you get savory dinners in a flash.

Menu 1
serves 4

Gingered Flank Steak

Rice noodle salad*

*Combine 3 cups cooked rice noodles with 1 cup sliced cucumber. Combine 2 tablespoons low-sodium soy sauce, 1 tablespoon rice vinegar, 1 teaspoon sugar, and ¼ teaspoon crushed red pepper in a small bowl. Pour dressing over noodle mixture; toss well. Serve chilled or at room temperature.

Sautéed snow peas

Gingered Flank Steak
(pictured on page 257)

TOTAL TIME: 45 MINUTES

1 (1-pound) flank steak, trimmed
¼ cup low-sodium soy sauce
3 tablespoons sugar
3 tablespoons ketchup
2 tablespoons low-sodium soy sauce
1 tablespoon bottled ground fresh ginger (such as Spice World)
1 tablespoon cider vinegar
¼ teaspoon ground red pepper
Cooking spray

1. Combine steak and ¼ cup soy sauce in a large zip-top plastic bag; seal and marinate in refrigerator 30 minutes or *Continued*

up to 2 hours. Remove steak from bag, discarding marinade.

2. Prepare grill or broiler.

3. Combine sugar and next 5 ingredients in a bowl. Place steak on grill rack or broiler pan coated with cooking spray; cook 5 minutes on each side or until desired degree of doneness, basting frequently with ¼ cup ketchup mixture. Let steak stand 5 minutes. Cut steak diagonally across grain into thin slices. Drizzle steak with remaining mixture. Yield: 4 servings (serving size: 3 ounces steak and about 1 tablespoon ketchup mixture).

CALORIES 240 (33% from fat); FAT 8.9g (sat 3.8g, mono 3.6g, poly 0.4g); PROTEIN 24.7g; CARB 14.4g; FIBER 0.3g; CHOL 59mg; IRON 2.7mg; SODIUM 742mg; CALC 12mg

1. Combine ¼ teaspoon curry, paprika, and salt. Sprinkle pork with mixture.

2. Combine ½ teaspoon curry, marmalade, horseradish, vinegar, and pepper.

3. Heat a large nonstick skillet coated with cooking spray over medium-high heat. Add pork; cook 3 minutes on each side or until pork loses its pink color. Remove from pan. Add marmalade mixture to pan; cook 15 seconds, scraping pan to loosen browned bits. Spoon sauce over pork chops. Yield: 4 servings (serving size: 1 pork chop and 1 tablespoon sauce).

CALORIES 254 (31% from fat); FAT 8.7g (sat 3.1g, mono 3.9g, poly 0.6g); PROTEIN 25.3g; CARB 18.5g; FIBER 0.3g; CHOL 69mg; IRON 0.9mg; SODIUM 224mg; CALC 41mg

1. Cook ground round in a large Dutch oven coated with cooking spray over medium-high heat 4 minutes or until beef is browned, stirring occasionally. Stir in water and remaining ingredients, and bring to a boil. Reduce heat, and simmer 25 minutes, stirring occasionally. Yield: 6 servings (serving size: about 1 cup).

CALORIES 254 (28% from fat); FAT 8g (sat 2.8g, mono 2.4g, poly 0.6g); PROTEIN 18g; CARB 30.5g; FIBER 7.2g; CHOL 24mg; IRON 3.9mg; SODIUM 649mg; CALC 96mg

---

Menu 2

serves 4

Pork with Curried Orange Sauce

Herbed basmati pilaf*

*Heat 2 teaspoons olive oil in a medium saucepan over medium heat. Add 1 teaspoon bottled minced garlic; sauté 1 minute. Add 1 cup basmati rice; sauté 2 minutes. Stir in 2 cups fat-free, less-sodium chicken broth; bring to a boil. Cover, reduce heat, and simmer 20 minutes or until liquid is absorbed. Remove from heat; stir in ¼ cup chopped green onions and ½ teaspoon dried thyme.

Steamed broccoli spears

Menu 3

serves 6

Nonstop, No-Chop Chili

Colby-Jack chiles*

*Cut a lengthwise slit down center of each of 6 (4-inch-long) Anaheim chiles; discard seeds and membranes. Arrange chiles in a 9-inch pie plate. Cover with heavy-duty plastic wrap. Microwave at HIGH 3 minutes or until crisp-tender; drain. Return chiles to pie plate. Split 3 Colby-Jack cheese sticks (such as Sargento) in half lengthwise. Stuff each chile with 1 piece of cheese. Microwave at HIGH 30 seconds or until cheese melts.

Corn bread twists (such as Pillsbury)

Menu 4

serves 4

Lemony Spanish Pepper Chicken

Roasted green beans*

*Combine 1¼ pounds trimmed green beans, 2 teaspoons olive oil, ½ teaspoon salt, ¼ teaspoon garlic powder, and ¼ teaspoon black pepper in a jelly roll pan. Bake at 450° for 10 minutes or until beans are tender and lightly browned, stirring occasionally.

Egg noodles tossed with parsley

Lemony Spanish Pepper Chicken

TOTAL TIME: 40 MINUTES

QUICK TIP: To seed a bell pepper, set the pepper on your cutting board, stem side up. Slice off the four "sides," which will fall away to leave the stem, membranes, and seeds standing. Discard stem, membranes, and seeds, and cut the pepper pieces into strips.

Pork with Curried Orange Sauce

TOTAL TIME: 10 MINUTES

- ¾ teaspoon curry powder, divided
- ¼ teaspoon paprika
- ¼ teaspoon salt
- 4 (4-ounce) boneless center-cut loin pork chops, trimmed (about ½ inch thick)
- ⅓ cup orange marmalade
- 1½ teaspoons prepared horseradish
- 1½ teaspoons balsamic vinegar
- ⅛ teaspoon crushed red pepper
- Cooking spray

Nonstop, No-Chop Chili

TOTAL TIME: 45 MINUTES

- ¾ pound ground round
- Cooking spray
- 2 cups water
- 1½ cups frozen whole-kernel corn
- 1 cup bottled salsa
- 2 tablespoons chili powder
- 1 tablespoon sugar
- 2½ teaspoons ground cumin
- 1½ teaspoons dried oregano
- ¼ teaspoon salt
- 1 (16-ounce) can chili beans, undrained
- 1 (14.5-ounce) can no-salt-added diced tomatoes, undrained

- 8 (6-ounce) chicken thighs, skinned
- 1½ teaspoons dried oregano
- ½ teaspoon salt
- ¼ teaspoon black pepper
- ¼ teaspoon paprika
- Cooking spray
- 1½ cups red bell pepper strips
- 1½ cups green bell pepper strips
- 1 tablespoon grated lemon rind
- ¼ cup fresh lemon juice
- ½ cup fat-free, less-sodium chicken broth
- 2 tablespoons ketchup

1. Sprinkle chicken with oregano, salt, black pepper, and paprika. Heat a large nonstick skillet coated with cooking spray over medium-high heat. Add chicken, and sauté 3 minutes or until lightly browned. Turn chicken over; top with bell peppers, rind, and juice. Cover, reduce heat, and simmer 30 minutes or until chicken is done. Remove chicken from pan. Combine broth and ketchup in a small bowl. Stir ketchup mixture into pepper mixture in pan; bring to a boil. Serve pepper mixture with chicken. Yield: 4 servings (serving size: 2 chicken thighs and ½ cup pepper mixture).

CALORIES 267 (26% from fat); FAT 7.8g (sat 2g, mono 2.4g, poly 2g); PROTEIN 39.4g; CARB 8.7g; FIBER 1.9g; CHOL 161mg; IRON 2.8mg; SODIUM 609mg; CALC 40mg

superfast

Dinner in Just About 20 Minutes

Blackstrap Pork Chops

Serve with garlic mashed potatoes and sautéed spinach.

⅓ cup molasses
3 tablespoons steak sauce (such as A.1.)
1½ tablespoons cider vinegar
¼ teaspoon ground allspice
⅛ teaspoon ground red pepper
4 (6-ounce) bone-in center-cut pork chops (about ½ inch thick)
¼ teaspoon salt
¼ teaspoon black pepper
Cooking spray

1. Combine first 5 ingredients in a small bowl. Set aside.
2. Sprinkle pork with salt and black pepper. Heat a large nonstick skillet coated with cooking spray over medium-high heat. Add pork; cook 2 minutes on each side. Pour molasses mixture over pork; cook 2 minutes. Yield: 4 servings

(serving size: 1 pork chop and 1½ tablespoons sauce).

CALORIES 220 (23% from fat); FAT 5.7g (sat 2.1g, mono 2.6g, poly 0.4g); PROTEIN 21.4g; CARB 19.4g; FIBER 0.1g; CHOL 58mg; IRON 5.5mg; SODIUM 414mg; CALC 259mg

Grilled Cuban Sandwiches

Serve with baked chips.

2 tablespoons Dijon mustard
1 (8-ounce) loaf French bread, cut in half horizontally
6 ounces reduced-fat Swiss cheese, thinly sliced (such as Alpine Lace)
6 ounces deli-sliced ham (such as Hillshire Farms)
8 sandwich-sliced dill pickles
Cooking spray

1. Spread mustard evenly over cut sides of bread. Arrange half of cheese and half of ham on bottom half of loaf; top with pickle slices. Repeat layer with remaining cheese and ham; cover with top half of loaf. Cut into quarters.
2. Heat a large, heavy skillet coated with cooking spray over medium-high heat. Add sandwiches; press with a heavy skillet (such as cast iron). Cook 2 minutes on each side. Yield: 4 servings (serving size: 1 sandwich).

CALORIES 335 (30% from fat); FAT 11g (sat 5.3g, mono 2.1g, poly 0.9g); PROTEIN 23.1g; CARB 36g; FIBER 3g; CHOL 43mg; IRON 2.8mg; SODIUM 1,301mg; CALC 318mg

Chinese-Style Glazed Chicken Breasts

Serve with asparagus and rice.

¼ cup fat-free, less-sodium chicken broth
2 tablespoons hoisin sauce
1 tablespoon apricot preserves or fruit spread
4 (4-ounce) skinless, boneless chicken breast halves
½ teaspoon salt
⅛ teaspoon black pepper
1 tablespoon vegetable oil

1. Combine first 3 ingredients; set aside.
2. Place each chicken breast half between 2 sheets of heavy-duty plastic wrap; pound to ¼-inch thickness using a meat mallet or rolling pin. Sprinkle chicken with salt and pepper.
3. Heat oil in a large skillet over medium-high heat. Add chicken, and sauté 3 minutes on each side. Remove chicken from pan. Reduce heat; carefully stir in broth mixture. Return chicken to pan; cook 3 minutes or until done, turning to coat. Yield: 4 servings (serving size: 1 chicken breast half and 1 tablespoon sauce).

CALORIES 186 (25% from fat); FAT 5.1g (sat 0.9g, mono 1.3g, poly 2.5g); PROTEIN 26.7g; CARB 6.9g; FIBER 0.3g; CHOL 66mg; IRON 0.9mg; SODIUM 526mg; CALC 17mg

Zippy Black-Bean Burritos

2 teaspoons olive oil
¾ cup chopped green bell pepper
1 teaspoon ground cumin
1 teaspoon dried oregano
2 garlic cloves, crushed
1 tablespoon red wine vinegar
1 (10-ounce) can diced tomatoes and green chiles, undrained
1 (15-ounce) can black beans, rinsed and drained
4 (10-inch) flour tortillas
1 cup (4 ounces) reduced-fat shredded cheddar cheese
Fresh cilantro leaves (optional)

1. Heat oil in a large saucepan over medium-high heat. Add bell pepper, cumin, oregano, and garlic; cook 3 minutes, stirring frequently. Stir in vinegar and tomatoes and chilis; reduce heat to medium, and cook 10 minutes. Stir in beans; cook 5 minutes or until thoroughly heated.
2. Warm tortillas according to package directions. Spoon about ½ cup bean mixture down center of each tortilla using a slotted spoon. Sprinkle each serving with ¼ cup cheese, and roll up. Garnish with fresh cilantro, if desired. Yield: 4 servings: (serving size: 1 burrito).

CALORIES 283 (25% from fat); FAT 8g (sat 2.6g, mono 2.3g, poly 0.3g); PROTEIN 15.1g; CARB 41.6g; FIBER 7.4g; CHOL 6mg; IRON 3.5mg; SODIUM 1,100mg; CALC 241mg

Tuna Soft Tacos with Horseradish Sauce

¾ pound fresh tuna (about 1 inch thick)
¾ teaspoon salt, divided
½ teaspoon ground cumin
Cooking spray
½ cup low-fat sour cream
¼ cup finely chopped red onion
1 tablespoon fat-free milk
2 teaspoons fresh lemon juice
2 teaspoons prepared horseradish
2 cups trimmed watercress
   (about 1 bunch) or spinach
4 (8-inch) flour tortillas
½ cup canned mandarin oranges in
   light syrup, drained

1. Sprinkle fish with ½ teaspoon salt and cumin. Heat a nonstick grill pan or skillet coated with cooking spray over medium-high heat. Add fish; cook 3 minutes on each side until fish is medium-rare or desired degree of doneness. Cut fish into ¼-inch strips.
2. While fish is cooking, combine ¼ teaspoon salt, sour cream, onion, milk, juice, and horseradish in a small bowl.
3. Place ½ cup watercress over each tortilla. Divide fish evenly among tortillas; top each serving with 2 tablespoons oranges and 2 tablespoons sauce; fold in half. Yield: 2 servings (serving size: 2 tacos).

CALORIES 621 (22% from fat); FAT 15.5g (sat 6.5g, mono 3.1g, poly 1.5g); PROTEIN 53.6g; CARB 65.9g; FIBER 2.1g; CHOL 108mg; IRON 3.9mg; SODIUM 1,520mg; CALC 400mg

Balsamic Chicken with Grapes and Almonds

Serve with wilted spinach and couscous.

4 (4-ounce) skinless, boneless
   chicken breast halves
½ teaspoon salt
⅛ teaspoon black pepper
2 teaspoons olive oil
1 cup seedless red grapes, halved
½ cup fat-free, less-sodium chicken
   broth
2 tablespoons balsamic vinegar
1 tablespoon brown sugar
¼ cup sliced almonds

1. Sprinkle chicken with salt and pepper. Heat oil in a large nonstick skillet over medium-high heat. Add chicken; sauté 3 minutes on each side or until golden brown. Remove chicken from pan. Reduce heat; stir grapes, broth, vinegar, and sugar into pan drippings. Bring mixture to a boil; cook until reduced to 1 cup (about 6 minutes). Return chicken to pan; cook 3 minutes or until done, turning to coat. Sprinkle with almonds immediately before serving. Yield: 4 servings (serving size: 1 chicken breast half and ¼ cup sauce).

CALORIES 229 (28% from fat); FAT 7.1g (sat 1.1g, mono 3.9g, poly 1.3g); PROTEIN 28.1g; CARB 13.0g; FIBER 1.1g; CHOL 66mg; IRON 1.3mg; SODIUM 385mg; CALC 39mg

lighten up

Cassoulet, More and Less

Pork Cassoulet
(pictured on page 258)

1 pound dried Great Northern beans
2 bacon slices, cut into 1-inch pieces
3 pounds boneless pork loin, cut
   into 1-inch cubes
1 pound turkey kielbasa, cut into
   ½-inch pieces
2½ cups chopped onion
1 cup sliced celery
1 cup (¼-inch) sliced carrot
4 garlic cloves, minced
2 teaspoons dried thyme
¼ cup water
2 tablespoons tomato paste
1 (14½-ounce) can fat-free,
   less-sodium chicken broth
1 (14.5-ounce) can no-salt-added
   diced tomatoes, undrained
½ cup dry white wine
½ teaspoon salt
¼ teaspoon black pepper
1 cup (¼-inch-thick) red bell
   pepper rings
1½ cups (1-inch) cubed French bread
⅓ cup (about 1½ ounces) grated
   fresh Parmesan cheese

1. Sort and wash beans, and place in a large Dutch oven. Cover with water to 2 inches above beans; bring to a boil, and cook 2 minutes. Remove from heat; cover and let stand 1 hour. Drain; return beans to pan. Cover beans with water; bring to a boil. Cover, reduce heat, and simmer 20 minutes; drain and set aside.
2. Preheat oven to 300°.
3. Add bacon to pan; cook over medium heat until crisp. Remove bacon with a slotted spoon. Increase heat to medium-high. Add pork to drippings in pan; cook 5 minutes or until browned, stirring occasionally. Remove pork with a slotted spoon. Add kielbasa to pan; cook 5 minutes or until browned, stirring occasionally. Remove kielbasa with a slotted spoon. Add onion, celery, carrot, garlic, and thyme to pan; sauté 4 minutes or until tender. Stir in ¼ cup water, tomato paste, broth, and tomatoes.
4. Return beans, bacon, pork, and kielbasa to pan; bring to a boil. Cover and bake at 300° for 1 hour. Remove 1 cup of beans and vegetables with a slotted spoon. Place in a blender or food processor; process until smooth. Return to pan. Stir in wine, salt, and black pepper. Arrange bell pepper rings over top.
5. Place bread in a food processor; pulse 10 times or until coarse crumbs form to measure 1½ cups. Combine with cheese. Sprinkle cassoulet with breadcrumb mixture. Return cassoulet to oven; bake, uncovered, an additional 45 minutes. Yield: 10 servings (serving size: about 1½ cups).

CALORIES 526 (30% from fat); FAT 17.6g (sat 6.5g, mono 7.3g, poly 2.5g); PROTEIN 50.7g; CARB 40.8g; FIBER 11.5g; CHOL 117mg; IRON 5.1mg; SODIUM 808mg; CALC 193mg

BEFORE	AFTER
SERVING SIZE	
about 1½ cups	
CALORIES PER SERVING	
703	526
FAT	
36.6g	17.6g
PERCENT OF TOTAL CALORIES	
47%	30%

Gingered Flank Steak, page 253

Paraguayan Corn Bread, page 251,
and Uruguayan Bean Salad, page 251

Pork Cassoulet, page 256

Blueberry-Peach Galettes, page 267

Black-Bottom Banana Cream Pie, page 272

Pistachio-Encrusted Rack of Lamb,
page 263

Braised Zucchini and Leeks,
page 264

Creamy Polenta with
Warm Tomato Compote,
page 264

Citrus Chicken Tagine, Roasted Asparagus with Balsamic Browned Butter, and Green-Onion Pancakes, page 262

Club Fed

Across America, *Cooking Light* supper clubs flourish, and friendships
and great food naturally follow.

S ince the summer of 1999 *Cooking Light* supper clubs have blossomed in more than 150 cities in the United States and Canada. And there are almost as many ways to have a supper club as there are actual clubs themselves. Some groups prefer potlucks while others base their meals on themes. Still others prefer to set a menu ahead of time, but prepare it together at the host's home.

No matter your kitchen size, cooking skill level, or time constraints, there is a supper club format for everyone. Supper clubs offer a great opportunity to broaden your palate, improve your techniques, and cultivate some wonderful friendships. In honor of this flourishing phenomenon, we've created four dinner menus designed expressly for supper club entertaining (although you'll find they work just as well for general entertaining, too).

On the Edge

This fusion menu combines the far-flung flavors of Morocco, Thailand, and France for a decidedly adventurous supper club experience.

On the Edge Menu
serves 8

Spice-Crusted Shrimp with Rémoulade Sauce

Thai Bell Pepper, Cucumber, and Peanut Salad

Citrus Chicken Tagine

Roasted Asparagus with Balsamic Browned Butter

Green-Onion Pancakes

Star Anise Bread Pudding

Wine Suggestions

For the Spice-Crusted Shrimp with Rémoulade Sauce, serve an Australian Chardonnay such as Kim Crawford ($18) or Rosemount Estate Diamond Label ($10). Alongside this, pour a manzanilla sherry. Try one called La Gitana ("The Gypsy") from Hidalgo ($12).

For the Citrus Chicken Tagine try Grgich Hills Fumé Blanc ($18) and/or Trefethen Dry Riesling ($15).

Spice-Crusted Shrimp with Rémoulade Sauce

Eat this cold, at room temperature, or warm.

SAUCE:
- ¼ cup low-fat mayonnaise
- ¼ cup plain fat-free yogurt
- 1½ tablespoons fresh lime juice
- 1 teaspoon grated lime rind
- 1 teaspoon capers, chopped

Dash of ground red pepper

SHRIMP:
- 2 teaspoons ground cumin
- 2 teaspoons paprika
- 1 teaspoon ground coriander
- ½ teaspoon garlic powder
- ¼ teaspoon salt
- ⅛ teaspoon black pepper
- 48 large shrimp, peeled and deveined (about 1½ pounds)
- 1 tablespoon olive oil, divided

Cilantro sprigs (optional)

1. To prepare sauce, combine first 6 ingredients in a bowl; stir with a whisk.
2. To prepare shrimp, combine cumin and next 5 ingredients. Add shrimp; toss well. Heat 1½ teaspoons oil in a large nonstick skillet over medium-high heat; add half of shrimp. Cook 3 minutes on each side or until done. Remove shrimp; keep warm. Repeat procedure with remaining oil and shrimp. Serve shrimp with sauce. Garnish with cilantro, if desired. Yield: 8 servings (serving size: 6 shrimp and about 1 tablespoon sauce).

CALORIES 100 (28% from fat); FAT 3.1g (sat 0.4g, mono 1.4g, poly 0.5g); PROTEIN 13.7g; CARB 3.7g; FIBER 0.5g; CHOL 121mg; IRON 2.3mg; SODIUM 300mg; CALC 48mg

Thai Bell Pepper, Cucumber, and Peanut Salad

DRESSING:
- 1 tablespoon sugar
- 3 tablespoons fresh lime juice
- 1 tablespoon Thai fish sauce
- ¼ teaspoon crushed red pepper

SALAD:
- 2 cups sliced peeled cucumber
- 2 cups red bell pepper strips
- ¾ cup julienne-cut carrot
- ½ cup vertically sliced red onion
- 2 tablespoons chopped fresh mint
- 2 tablespoons finely chopped peanuts

1. To prepare dressing, combine first 4 ingredients in a small bowl; stir with a whisk.
2. To prepare salad, combine cucumber, bell pepper, carrot, onion, and mint. Drizzle dressing over cucumber mixture, tossing gently to coat. Sprinkle salad with peanuts. Yield: 8 servings (serving size: ¾ cup).

CALORIES 36 (23% from fat); FAT 0.9g (sat 0.1g, mono 0.4g, poly 0.3g); PROTEIN 1.1g; CARB 6.6g; FIBER 1.3g; CHOL 0mg; IRON 0.3mg; SODIUM 180mg; CALC 13mg

Citrus Chicken Tagine

(pictured on page 260)

1 tablespoon olive oil
2 pounds skinless, boneless chicken thighs, coarsely chopped
2 cups chopped onion
1 cup chopped red bell pepper
½ teaspoon ground ginger
½ teaspoon ground cinnamon
¼ teaspoon saffron threads, crushed
4 garlic cloves, minced
1 cup fat-free, less-sodium chicken broth
1 cup orange juice
¾ teaspoon salt
¼ teaspoon black pepper
1½ cups chopped orange sections (about 2 oranges)
⅓ cup chopped fresh parsley
⅓ cup chopped fresh cilantro
¼ cup sliced pitted kalamata olives
3 tablespoons chopped lemon sections (about 1 lemon)
5 cups hot cooked couscous
Flat-leaf parsley sprigs (optional)

1. Heat oil in a Dutch oven over medium heat. Add chicken and next 6 ingredients, and cook 12 minutes. Stir in broth, juice, salt, and black pepper. Bring to a boil; cover, reduce heat, and simmer 30 minutes. (Can be prepared ahead up to this point.) Remove from heat, and stir in next 5 ingredients. Serve chicken mixture over couscous, and garnish with parsley sprigs, if desired. Yield: 8 servings (serving size: about 1 cup chicken mixture and ⅔ cup couscous).

CALORIES 331 (21% from fat); FAT 7.8g (sat 1.6g, mono 3.6g, poly 1.5g); PROTEIN 27.9g; CARB 36.5g; FIBER 3.8g; CHOL 94mg; IRON 2.2mg; SODIUM 459mg; CALC 58mg

Roasted Asparagus with Balsamic Browned Butter

(pictured on page 260)

Finish the asparagus just before serving dinner. Cooking the butter until it's slightly brown gives the dish a nutty flavor; watch carefully, though, since it can burn easily.

40 asparagus spears, trimmed (about 2 pounds)
Cooking spray
¼ teaspoon kosher salt
⅛ teaspoon black pepper
2 tablespoons butter
2 teaspoons low-sodium soy sauce
1 teaspoon balsamic vinegar

1. Preheat oven to 400°.
2. Arrange asparagus in a single layer on a baking sheet; coat with cooking spray. Sprinkle with salt and pepper. Bake at 400° for 12 minutes or until tender.
3. Melt butter in a small skillet over medium heat; cook 3 minutes or until lightly browned, shaking pan occasionally. Remove from heat; stir in soy sauce and vinegar. Drizzle over asparagus, tossing well to coat. Serve immediately. Yield: 8 servings (serving size: 5 spears).

CALORIES 45 (60% from fat); FAT 3g (sat 1.8g, mono 0.9g, poly 0.2g); PROTEIN 1.9g; CARB 3.9g; FIBER 1.7g; CHOL 8mg; IRON 0.7mg; SODIUM 134mg; CALC 18mg

Green-Onion Pancakes

(pictured on page 260)

Although these pancakes taste best straight from the skillet, they can be made ahead, stored in the refrigerator or freezer, and reheated like tortillas (by placing between damp paper towels and microwaving for 30 seconds).

3¼ cups all-purpose flour, divided
1½ teaspoons salt
1 cup cold water
2 teaspoons dark sesame oil
¾ cup chopped green onions
8 teaspoons peanut oil, divided

1. Lightly spoon flour into dry measuring cups; level with a knife. Combine 3 cups flour and salt in a small bowl. Add water; stir until soft dough forms. Turn dough out onto a lightly floured surface, and knead until smooth and elastic (about 6 minutes); add enough of remaining flour, 1 tablespoon at a time, to prevent dough from sticking to hands. Place dough in a large bowl, and cover with a damp towel. Let stand 25 minutes.
2. Roll dough into a 20 x 15-inch rectangle. Brush sesame oil over dough, and sprinkle with onions. Roll up dough lengthwise. Cut dough roll crosswise into 8 pieces. Roll each dough portion, cut side up, into a 6-inch circle on a lightly floured surface.
3. Heat 1 teaspoon peanut oil in a large nonstick skillet over medium heat. Add 1 pancake; cook 2 minutes on each side. Repeat procedure with remaining peanut oil and pancakes. Yield: 8 servings (serving size: 1 pancake).

CALORIES 238 (23% from fat); FAT 6.1g (sat 1g, mono 2.6g, poly 2.1g); PROTEIN 5.3g; CARB 39.5g; FIBER 1.8g; CHOL 0mg; IRON 2.4mg; SODIUM 443mg; CALC 8mg

Get Ahead Guide

One month ahead:
• Make pancakes, wrap in plastic wrap, and freeze. Microwave just before serving.

Two days ahead:
• Make rémoulade sauce for shrimp.

One day ahead:
• Prepare vegetables for salad; refrigerate in zip-top plastic bag.
• Make salad dressing; refrigerate in a jar.
• Make egg mixture for dessert.
• Make base of tagine; add citrus, herbs, and olives just before serving.

Last minute:
• Prepare shrimp just before your guests arrive. Keep warm or serve at room temperature.
• Reheat tagine; stir in last-minute ingredients.
• Prepare couscous.
• Prepare asparagus.
• Toss salad and dressing.
• Combine dessert ingredients, and bake while eating dinner.

Star Anise Bread Pudding

This bread pudding is great served warm, but it's good at room temperature, too. We cut each piece into four squares, then stacked them for a dramatic presentation.

2 cups whole milk
6 star anise
½ cup sugar
2 tablespoons chopped crystallized ginger
¼ teaspoon ground cinnamon
4 large eggs, lightly beaten
12 (1-ounce) slices cinnamon-raisin bread, cut into 1-inch pieces
Cooking spray
1 tablespoon sugar
2¼ cups vanilla reduced-fat ice cream (such as Healthy Choice)

1. Combine milk and star anise in a small, heavy saucepan. Heat to 180° or until tiny bubbles form around edge of pan, stirring frequently (do not boil). Remove from heat; cover and steep 20 minutes. Strain milk mixture through a fine sieve into a large bowl; discard star anise. Add ½ cup sugar, ginger, cinnamon, and eggs; stir with a whisk. Gently stir in bread. Let stand 10 minutes, stirring occasionally.
2. Preheat oven to 350°.
3. Pour bread mixture into an 8-inch square baking dish coated with cooking spray. Sprinkle mixture evenly with 1 tablespoon sugar. Bake at 350° for 35 minutes or until a knife inserted in center comes out clean. Serve each piece warm with ¼ cup ice cream. Yield: 9 servings.

CALORIES 284 (23% from fat); FAT 7.1g (sat 2.3g, mono 2g, poly 0.4g); PROTEIN 10.1g; CARB 45.3g; FIBER 1.9g; CHOL 104mg; IRON 2.9mg; SODIUM 220mg; CALC 129mg

Continental Class

An elegant menu ideal for a sophisticated supper.

Here's a meal for the supper club that prefers martinis to beer.

Continental Menu
serves 8

Bagna Cauda

Pistachio-Encrusted Rack of Lamb

Creamy Polenta with Warm Tomato Compote

Braised Zucchini and Leeks

Fresh Berry Pavlovas

Wine Suggestions

Start off with Champagne. You can find one from any of the following wineries for around $30 a bottle: Taittinger, Ayala, Billecart-Salmon, Nicolas Feuillatte, or Deutz. If you'd rather buy domestic, you'll find top California sparklers from Domaine Carneros, Iron Horse, and Gloria Ferrer, all for under $26.

With the Bagna Cauda, serve Pio Cesare's Gavi ($20). Or try a refreshing California Sauvignon Blanc, such as Honig ($14) or Frog's Leap ($16).

For the Pistachio-Encrusted Rack of Lamb, try an elegant red, such as Lynch-Bages Bordeaux ($37) or Sequoia Grove's Cabernet Sauvignon ($29).

Bagna Cauda

Bagna cauda (BAHN-yah KOW-dah) is a warm sauce. Serve with bread and raw vegetables, such as bell peppers and zucchini, for dipping.

6 sun-dried tomato halves
3 tablespoons olive oil, divided
⅔ cup finely chopped red bell pepper
½ cup minced fresh onion
2 garlic cloves, minced
2 canned anchovy fillets, finely chopped (about 1 teaspoon)
2 tablespoons capers, finely chopped
1 cup fat-free, less-sodium chicken broth
2 tablespoons Dijon mustard
¼ teaspoon salt
¼ cup finely chopped green onions
1 tablespoon white wine vinegar

1. Combine boiling water and sun-dried tomatoes in a bowl; let stand 30 minutes or until soft. Drain and mince; set aside.
2. Heat 1 teaspoon oil in a medium saucepan over medium heat. Add bell pepper, minced onion, and garlic; sauté 5 minutes or until tender. Add anchovies; cook 1 minute, stirring frequently. Add sun-dried tomatoes and capers; cook 1 minute. Stir in broth, mustard, and salt. Bring to a boil; reduce heat, and simmer 2 minutes. Stir in 8 teaspoons oil, and remove from heat. Add green onions and vinegar. Serve warm. Yield: 1½ cups (serving size: 1 tablespoon).

CALORIES 23 (74% from fat); FAT 1.9g (sat 0.3g, mono 1.3g, poly 0.2g); PROTEIN 0.5g; CARB 1.2g; FIBER 0.3g; CHOL 0mg; IRON 0.2mg; SODIUM 97mg; CALC 5mg

Pistachio-Encrusted Rack of Lamb

(pictured on page 259)

This striking yet simple entrée will win you applause. You can prepare the mustard mixture earlier in the day. The breadcrumb mixture (minus the lemon juice) can also be prepared ahead; just remember to add the juice before patting the pistachio crust onto the lamb.

3 (1-ounce) slices day-old white bread
⅓ cup finely chopped pistachios
1¼ teaspoons grated lemon rind
2½ tablespoons finely chopped fresh parsley
¼ cup lemon juice
¾ teaspoon salt, divided
¼ cup finely chopped fresh chives
¼ cup finely chopped fresh mint
2½ tablespoons Dijon mustard
2 garlic cloves, minced
2 (1½-pound) French-cut racks of lamb (8 ribs each), trimmed
Cooking spray
Mint sprigs (optional)

1. Preheat oven to 425°.
2. Place bread in a food processor; pulse 10 times or until coarse crumbs form to measure about 1¼ cups.

Continued

3. Combine breadcrumbs, nuts, rind, parsley, juice, and ½ teaspoon salt in a small bowl.

4. Combine chives, mint, mustard, and garlic in a small bowl.

5. Sprinkle lamb with ¼ teaspoon salt. Heat a large nonstick skillet coated with cooking spray over medium-high heat. Add lamb racks; cook 2 minutes on each side or until browned. Spread mustard mixture evenly over meaty portion of lamb racks. Carefully pat breadcrumb mixture into mustard mixture.

6. Place lamb on a broiler pan coated with cooking spray. Bake at 425° for 35 minutes or until meat thermometer registers 140° (medium-rare) to 155° (medium). Place lamb on a platter; cover with foil. Let stand 10 minutes before serving (temperature will increase 5° upon standing). Cut each rack into 4 pieces (2 ribs per piece). Garnish with mint sprigs, if desired. Yield: 8 servings (serving size: 1 piece, 2 ribs).

CALORIES 206 (47% from fat); FAT 10.8g (sat 3.1g, mono 4.6g, poly 1.5g); PROTEIN 18.5g; CARB 8.5g; FIBER 0.9g; CHOL 52mg; IRON 2.1mg; SODIUM 472mg; CALC 37mg

Creamy Polenta with Warm Tomato Compote

(pictured on page 259)

You can keep the polenta warm over very low heat for up to 30 minutes; stir in a little water or milk if it gets too thick. Have a guest serve the polenta while you're carving the lamb.

      6 cups cherry tomatoes (about
        2 pounds)
    Cooking spray
      1 tablespoon olive oil
     ¼ cup sliced shallots (about
        3 medium)
   1½ tablespoons sugar
     ¾ cup dry white wine
   1½ teaspoons salt, divided
     ¼ teaspoon black pepper
      2 cups 1% low-fat milk
      2 cups water
      1 cup dry polenta
     ½ cup (2 ounces) shaved fresh
        Parmesan cheese

1. Preheat oven to 425°.

2. Cut several slits in bottom of each tomato; place, stem sides down, in a shallow roasting pan coated with cooking spray. Bake at 425° for 20 minutes. Reduce oven temperature to 375° (do not remove tomatoes from oven); bake 45 minutes or until browned. Cover and let stand 10 minutes.

3. Heat oil in a large nonstick skillet over medium-high heat. Add shallots; sauté 5 minutes or until browned. Add sugar; sauté 5 minutes. Add wine; reduce heat, and simmer 5 minutes. Add ½ teaspoon salt and pepper. Remove from heat; stir in tomatoes. Cover; set aside.

4. Combine milk and water in a large saucepan; bring to a boil. Remove from heat, and gradually add polenta, stirring constantly with a whisk. Cover and cook over medium-low heat 2 minutes. Add 1 teaspoon salt; cover and let stand 5 minutes or until thick, stirring occasionally. Top polenta with tomato compote and Parmesan cheese. Yield: 8 servings (serving size: ½ cup polenta, ⅓ cup tomato compote, and 1 tablespoon Parmesan cheese).

CALORIES 153 (28% from fat); FAT 4.8g (sat 1.9g, mono 2g, poly 0.4g); PROTEIN 6.8g; CARB 21.6g; FIBER 1.7g; CHOL 7mg; IRON 0.9mg; SODIUM 597mg; CALC 169mg

Braised Zucchini and Leeks

(pictured on page 259)

There's enough moisture in the zucchini to braise this simple side dish. Although it needs to be cooked at the last minute, you can chop the leek and zucchini up to a day ahead; refrigerate the vegetables in separate zip-top plastic bags.

      1 tablespoon butter
      2 cups finely chopped leek
        (about 2 large)
      6 cups finely chopped zucchini
        (about 5 small)
      1 teaspoon salt
      2 garlic cloves, minced

1. Melt butter in a large nonstick skillet over medium heat. Add leek; sauté 2 minutes. Add zucchini, salt, and garlic. Cover; reduce heat to medium-low, and cook 20 minutes, stirring occasionally. Uncover and cook over medium-high heat 10 minutes or until most of liquid evaporates. Serve immediately. Yield: 8 servings (serving size: about ⅔ cup).

CALORIES 52 (26% from fat); FAT 1.5g (sat 0.9g, mono 0.4g, poly 0.1g); PROTEIN 1.7g; CARB 8.4g; FIBER 2.9g; CHOL 4mg; IRON 0.9mg; SODIUM 313mg; CALC 40mg

Get Ahead Guide

One month ahead:
• Make and freeze meringues for pavlovas.

One day ahead:
• Prepare dippers for Bagna Cauda and chop zucchini and leeks; refrigerate in separate zip-top plastic bags.
• Make Bagna Cauda (up to adding green onions and vinegar). Reheat over low heat just before serving; stir in green onions and vinegar.

A few hours ahead:
• Prepare mustard and breadcrumb mixtures for lamb (up to adding lemon juice).
• Make yogurt mixture for pavlovas; cover and refrigerate.

Two hours ahead:
• Start tomato compote for polenta: Roast tomatoes; cover and set aside. Finish sauce by stirring in tomatoes with wine to reheat.
• Sear lamb.

Last minute:
• Finish preparing lamb; put in oven shortly after guests arrive.
• Braise zucchini and leeks while lamb cooks.
• Finish tomato sauce for polenta, and cook polenta just before serving (while lamb stands).
• Assemble pavlovas after dinner.

Fresh Berry Pavlovas

Crème fraîche is cultured cream that has a texture and consistency similar to sour cream, which you could substitute in a pinch. Look for cartons of crème fraîche in your supermarket's dairy case. You can make and freeze the meringues up to a month ahead; just remove them from the freezer before you start putting the pavlovas together—no further thawing or reheating is required.

- 4 large egg whites
- ¼ teaspoon cream of tartar
- 1¼ cups sugar, divided
- 1 (8-ounce) carton plain fat-free yogurt
- ¾ cup commercial crème fraîche
- 1 cup sliced strawberries
- 1 cup blackberries
- 1 cup blueberries

1. Preheat oven to 250°.
2. Cover a baking sheet with parchment paper. Draw 8 (3-inch) circles on paper. Turn paper over; secure with masking tape. Beat egg whites and cream of tartar with a mixer at high speed until soft peaks form. Gradually add ¾ cup sugar, 1 tablespoon at a time, beating until stiff peaks form (do not underbeat). Divide egg white mixture evenly among 8 drawn circles on baking sheet. Shape meringues into nests with 1-inch sides using back of a spoon. Bake at 250° for 1 hour. Turn oven off; cool meringues in closed oven at least 2 hours or until completely dry. Carefully remove meringues from paper.
3. Spoon yogurt onto several layers of heavy-duty paper towels, and spread to ½-inch thickness. Cover with additional paper towels; let stand 5 minutes. Scrape into a bowl using a rubber spatula. Combine ½ cup sugar, drained yogurt, and crème fraîche. Spoon yogurt mixture evenly into meringues. Top each serving with 2 tablespoons each of strawberries, blackberries, and blueberries. Yield: 8 servings.

CALORIES 249 (29% from fat); FAT 8.1g (sat 5g, mono 2.3g, poly 0.4g); PROTEIN 4.5g; CARB 40.7g; FIBER 1.9g; CHOL 18mg; IRON 0.3mg; SODIUM 65mg; CALC 110mg

Tried and True

These classics will please any crowd.

This menu is a cozy choice for first-time supper clubbers or those more comfortable with familiar foods.

Tried and True Menu
serves 8

Layered Bean Dip

Romaine Salad with Sun-Dried Tomato Vinaigrette

Jack Cheese Breadsticks

Bourbon-Glazed Salmon

Wild Mushroom Risotto

Blueberry-Peach Galettes

Wine Suggestions

The Wild Mushroom Risotto is a dish that cries out for a sensuous, earthy wine. Try Pinot Noir or Étude ($40). For more affordable Spanish Riojas, try Muga ($17) or Marqués de Riscal ($13 to $16).

For the Bourbon-Glazed Salmon, an excellent choice is a white like Viognier. Try Calera ($36), Alban Central Coast ($20), or Pepperwood Grove ($7).

Layered Bean Dip

Serve with pita chips or baked tortilla chips.

- 1 (16-ounce) can fat-free refried beans
- 1 (15-ounce) can black beans, rinsed and drained
- ½ cup reduced-fat sour cream
- 1 cup bottled salsa
- 1 cup (4 ounces) preshredded reduced-fat Mexican blend or cheddar cheese
- Chopped cilantro (optional)

1. Preheat oven to 375°.
2. Combine beans; spread in an 8-inch square baking dish. Spread sour cream over beans; top with salsa and cheese. Cover; bake at 375° for 20 minutes. Uncover; bake 10 minutes or until bubbly. Garnish with cilantro, if desired. Yield: about 2½ cups dip (serving size: ¼ cup).
NOTE: To make pita chips, cut 5 (6-inch) onion-flavored or regular pitas into 8 wedges each. Arrange on a baking sheet coated with cooking spray. Lightly coat tops of wedges with cooking spray, and sprinkle with ½ teaspoon garlic powder and ¼ teaspoon salt. Bake at 375° for 8 minutes or until lightly browned.

CALORIES 107 (19% from fat); FAT 2.3g (sat 1.4g, mono 0.2g, poly 0g); PROTEIN 8.8g; CARB 15.8g; FIBER 5.8g; CHOL 8.6mg; IRON 1.6mg; SODIUM 497mg; CALC 111mg

Romaine Salad with Sun-Dried Tomato Vinaigrette

This recipe yields twice as much dressing as you'll need for the menu; the remaining dressing will keep for up to a week in the refrigerator. Shake it well before using.

- 1⅓ cups chopped seeded tomato
- ½ cup sun-dried tomatoes, packed without oil (about 1 ounce)
- 2 tablespoons balsamic vinegar
- 1 tablespoon olive oil
- ¼ teaspoon salt
- ¼ teaspoon black pepper
- 2 garlic cloves, peeled
- ¾ cup water
- 16 cups torn romaine lettuce
- 1 cucumber, peeled and sliced
- 8 (¼-inch-thick) slices red onion

1. Combine first 7 ingredients in a blender; process until well blended. Gradually add water; process until smooth. Arrange 2 cups lettuce on each of 8 individual plates; top lettuce with cucumber and onion slices. Spoon 2 tablespoons dressing over each serving. Reserve remaining dressing for another use. Yield: 8 servings.

CALORIES 37 (27% from fat); FAT 1.1g (sat 0.2g, mono 0.7g, poly 0.2g); PROTEIN 2.2g; CARB 5.8g; FIBER 2.3g; CHOL 0mg; IRON 1.3mg; SODIUM 82mg; CALC 43mg

Jack Cheese Breadsticks

Refrigerated breadstick dough keeps preparation time to a minimum.

¼ cup (1 ounce) finely shredded Monterey Jack cheese with jalapeño peppers
½ teaspoon ground cumin
1 (11-ounce) can refrigerated breadstick dough (such as Pillsbury)
Cooking spray

1. Preheat oven to 375°.
2. Combine cheese and cumin. Cut dough along perforations to form 12 breadsticks; sprinkle cheese mixture over dough, gently pressing into dough. Twist each breadstick, and place on a baking sheet coated with cooking spray.
3. Bake at 375° for 13 minutes or until lightly browned. Yield: 12 servings (serving size: 1 breadstick).

CALORIES 83 (23% from fat); FAT 2.1g (sat 0.5g, mono 0.5g, poly 0.6g); PROTEIN 2.6g; CARB 12.7g; FIBER 0g; CHOL 3mg; IRON 0.8mg; SODIUM 209mg; CALC 18mg

Bourbon-Glazed Salmon

The marinade in this recipe is also good on pork tenderloin or boneless chicken breasts.

1 cup packed brown sugar
¼ cup low-sodium soy sauce
6 tablespoons bourbon
2 tablespoons fresh lime juice
2 teaspoons grated peeled fresh ginger
½ teaspoon salt
¼ teaspoon freshly ground black pepper
2 garlic cloves, crushed
8 (6-ounce) salmon fillets (about 1 inch thick)
Cooking spray
4 teaspoons sesame seeds
½ cup thinly sliced green onions

1. Combine first 8 ingredients in a large zip-top plastic bag; add salmon fillets. Seal bag, and marinate in refrigerator

30 minutes, turning bag once. Remove fillets from bag; discard marinade.
2. Preheat broiler.
3. Place fillets on broiler pan coated with cooking spray. Broil 11 minutes or until fish flakes easily when tested with a fork. Sprinkle each fillet with ½ teaspoon sesame seeds and 1 tablespoon onions. Yield: 8 servings (serving size: 1 fillet).

CALORIES 307 (34% from fat); FAT 11.6g (sat 1.8g, mono 3.9g, poly 4.7g); PROTEIN 34.4g; CARB 14.9g; FIBER 0.4g; CHOL 94mg; IRON 2mg; SODIUM 288mg; CALC 53mg

Get Ahead Guide

Two days ahead:
- Make vinaigrette; cover and refrigerate.
- Restaurant chefs have a great tip for preparing risotto ahead (see recipe note at right).

One day ahead:
- Assemble dip; cover and refrigerate.
- Wash and tear lettuce; refrigerate in a zip-top plastic bag.
- Slice green onions for salmon; cover and refrigerate.
- Make marinade for salmon the night before; refrigerate in a zip-top plastic bag.

Two hours ahead:
- Assemble and bake dessert.

Last minute:
- Bake breadsticks; cover with foil.
- Place salmon in zip-top plastic bag to marinate before beginning risotto; cook salmon about 15 minutes before eating.
- Reheat risotto about 10 to 15 minutes before serving dinner. It will require constant attention, so have guests tackle other duties.
- If you want to serve dessert warm, pop it into an oven heated to 200° before serving the main course.

Wild Mushroom Risotto

½ cup dried porcini mushrooms (about ½ ounce)
½ cup boiling water
1½ cups water
2 (14½-ounce) cans vegetable broth
2 teaspoons olive oil
2 garlic cloves, minced
2½ cups sliced shiitake mushroom caps (about 6 ounces)
2 teaspoons dried thyme
½ teaspoon salt
¼ teaspoon black pepper
1 pound uncooked Arborio rice or other short-grain rice (about 2½ cups)
½ cup dry sherry

1. Combine porcini mushrooms and ½ cup boiling water in a bowl. Cover and let stand 15 minutes or until tender. Drain in a colander over a bowl, reserving liquid.
2. Combine reserved liquid, 1½ cups water, and broth in a medium saucepan. (Reserve 1 cup of broth mixture if making ahead.) Bring remaining broth mixture to a simmer (do not boil). Keep warm over low heat.
3. Heat oil in a large saucepan over medium-high heat. Add garlic; sauté 1 minute. Add shiitake mushrooms, and sauté 2 minutes or until tender. Stir in porcini mushrooms, thyme, salt, and pepper. Add rice; cook 1 minute, stirring constantly.
4. Add broth mixture, ½ cup at a time, stirring constantly until each portion of mixture is absorbed before adding next (about 20 minutes total). (Stop here if making ahead.) Stir in sherry, and cook 2 minutes or until liquid is nearly absorbed, stirring constantly. Serve immediately. Yield: 8 servings (serving size: ¾ cup).
NOTE: Risotto requires long stirring and constant attention. Chefs, however, use a make-ahead method: Reserve 1 cup of broth mixture; prepare risotto with remaining broth mixture. Remove risotto from heat; cool and spread in an even layer on a jelly roll pan, cover, and refrigerate for up to 2 days. Just before serving, bring reserved broth mixture to a simmer in a large saucepan; stir in

partially cooked risotto. Cook until liquid is nearly absorbed, stirring constantly. Add sherry during last 2 minutes; serve.

CALORIES 255 (6% from fat); FAT 1.7g (sat 0.2g, mono 0.9g, poly 0.1g); PROTEIN 6g; CARB 48.9g; FIBER 1.8g; CHOL 0mg; IRON 1.4mg; SODIUM 593mg; CALC 29mg

Blueberry-Peach Galettes
(pictured on page 258)

The recipe makes two galettes, so guests can have a piece for dessert and one to take home. If you use fresh peaches, a lot of juice will ooze out, but it won't ruin your crust.

1 (15-ounce) package refrigerated pie dough (such as Pillsbury)
6 cups fresh or frozen peeled and sliced peaches, thawed
1 cup fresh or frozen blueberries, thawed
¼ cup sugar
2 tablespoons apricot preserves, melted and divided
1 tablespoon turbinado or granulated sugar

1. Preheat oven to 425°.
2. Line a baking sheet with foil or parchment paper. Roll 1 dough portion into a 12-inch circle; place on foil. Combine peaches, blueberries, and ¼ cup sugar. Arrange half of peach mixture in center of dough, leaving a 3-inch border. Fold edges of dough toward center, pressing gently to seal (dough will only partially cover peach mixture). Brush half of melted preserves over peach mixture and edges of dough.
3. Bake at 425° for 10 minutes. Reduce oven temperature to 350° (do not remove galette from oven); bake an additional 20 minutes or until lightly browned. Repeat procedure with remaining dough, peach mixture, and preserves. Sprinkle each galette with 1½ teaspoons of sugar. Serve warm or at room temperature. Cut each galette into 8 wedges. Yield: 2 galettes, 16 servings (serving size: 1 wedge).

CALORIES 232 (29% from fat); FAT 7.6g (sat 1.9g, mono 3.3g, poly 2g); PROTEIN 2.1g; CARB 40.6g; FIBER 2.8g; CHOL 0mg; IRON 1mg; SODIUM 124mg; CALC 6mg

Vegetarian Country French

Robust dishes everyone will enjoy.

If your supper club likes to stretch a meal over an entire evening, here's a menu you can serve as a buffet that will last and last.

Vegetarian Country French Menu
serves 8

Olive and Onion Tapenade

Endive Stuffed with Goat Cheese and Walnuts

Chickpea-Artichoke Stew with Rouille

Tomatoes Provençale

Caramelized Onion and Roasted Red-Pepper Tart

Honey-Roasted Pears with Sweet Yogurt Cream

Wine Suggestions

Sancerre would be great with the Endive Stuffed with Goat Cheese and Walnuts. Made from the Sauvignon Blanc grape, Sancerre is tangy and crisp. Try Henri Bourgeois ($15).

Any table with a Caramelized Onion and Roasted Red-Pepper Tart on it must also have a Pinot Gris from Alsace. Try the one from Trimbach ($16).

The Olive and Onion Tapenade, Tomatoes Provençale, and Chickpea-Artichoke Stew with Rouille all exude the flavors of Provence and would be terrific with an earthy Châteauneuf-du-Pape. Vieux Télégraphe, Beaucastel, and La Nerthe are all wonderful producers—count on spending $35 to $61 for these sensational wines.

Olive and Onion Tapenade

Serve this spread with baguette slices and crudités: fennel slices, radishes, celery, carrot sticks; red and yellow bell pepper pieces.

1 tablespoon olive oil
1 cup chopped onion
2 teaspoons chopped fresh or ½ teaspoon dried thyme
4 garlic cloves, finely chopped
¼ cup dry white wine
2 tablespoons white wine vinegar
1⅔ cups chopped pitted green olives
⅓ cup pitted picholine olives (about 15 olives)
¼ teaspoon freshly ground black pepper

1. Heat oil in a saucepan over medium heat. Add onion; cook 8 minutes or until soft, stirring frequently. Stir in thyme and garlic; cook 2 minutes, stirring frequently. Stir in wine and vinegar. Bring to a boil; reduce heat, and cook 8 minutes or until most of liquid evaporates, stirring occasionally.
2. Place onion mixture in a food processor. Add olives and black pepper, and process until smooth, scraping down sides of bowl. Yield: 1¾ cups (serving size: 1 tablespoon).

CALORIES 19 (81% from fat); FAT 1.7g (sat 0.1g, mono 0.8g, poly 0.2g); PROTEIN 0.2g; CARB 1.1g; FIBER 0.2g; CHOL 0mg; IRON 0.1mg; SODIUM 101mg; CALC 7mg

Endive Stuffed with Goat Cheese and Walnuts

⅓ cup coarsely chopped walnuts
2 tablespoons honey, divided
Cooking spray
¼ cup balsamic vinegar
3 tablespoons orange juice
16 Belgian endive leaves (about 2 heads)
16 small orange sections (about 2 navel oranges)
⅓ cup (1½ ounces) crumbled goat cheese or blue cheese
1 tablespoon minced fresh chives
¼ teaspoon cracked black pepper
Continued

1. Preheat oven to 350°.

2. Combine walnuts and 1 tablespoon honey; spread on a baking sheet coated with cooking spray. Bake at 350° for 10 minutes, stirring after 5 minutes.

3. Combine 1 tablespoon honey, vinegar, and orange juice in a small saucepan. Bring mixture to a boil over high heat, and cook until reduced to 3 tablespoons (about 5 minutes).

4. Fill each endive leaf with 1 orange section. Top each section with 1 teaspoon cheese and 1 teaspoon walnuts; arrange on a plate. Drizzle vinegar mixture evenly over leaves, and sprinkle evenly with chives and pepper. Yield: 8 servings (serving size: 2 stuffed leaves).

CALORIES 92 (44% from fat); FAT 4.5g (sat 1.1g, mono 0.7g, poly 2.4g); PROTEIN 2.5g; CARB 11.9g; FIBER 2g; CHOL 3mg; IRON 0.6mg; SODIUM 29mg; CALC 43mg

Chickpea-Artichoke Stew with Rouille

You can complete the stew just before your guests arrive. *Rouille* (roo-EE), French for "rust," is a spicy sauce that adds a burst of flavor to soups and stews.

    2   leeks (about 1 pound)
    1   (8-ounce) fennel bulb with stalks
    5   cups water
    ½   cup dry white wine
    2   teaspoons fennel seeds
    2   quarts water
    2   tablespoons fresh lemon juice
    3   small artichokes (about 8
        ounces each)
 1 ½   tablespoons olive oil
    1   teaspoon salt
    ½   teaspoon black pepper
    3   garlic cloves, minced
    2   cups diced peeled baking potato
    1   (15½-ounce) can chickpeas
        (garbanzo beans), drained
    1   (14.5-ounce) can diced tomatoes,
        undrained
    ¼   teaspoon saffron threads
        Rouille

1. Remove roots, outer leaves, and tops from leeks, leaving 1½ to 2 inches of dark leaves. Slice leeks in half lengthwise; rinse with cold water. Drain. Remove dark leaves; chop dark leaves to measure 1½ cups; set aside. Chop bulb ends to measure 2 cups; set aside.

2. Remove stalks from fennel bulb. Chop stalks to measure 1½ cups; set aside. Chop fennel bulb to measure 2 cups; set aside.

3. Combine chopped leek leaves, chopped fennel stalks, 5 cups water, wine, and fennel seeds in a large Dutch oven; bring to a boil. Reduce heat; simmer 25 minutes. Strain leek mixture through a sieve over a bowl, reserving stock; discard solids.

4. While vegetable mixture simmers, combine 2 quarts water and lemon juice. Working with 1 artichoke at a time, cut off stem to within 1 inch of base; peel stem. Remove bottom leaves and tough outer leaves, leaving tender heart and bottom. Cut artichoke in half lengthwise. Remove fuzzy thistle from bottom with a spoon. Cut artichoke lengthwise into quarters; place in lemon water. Repeat procedure with remaining artichokes.

5. Drain artichokes; discard lemon water. Heat oil in pan over medium heat. Add chopped leek bulbs, salt, and pepper; sauté 5 minutes. Add garlic; sauté 2 minutes. Stir in chopped fennel bulb, artichoke quarters, reserved stock, potato, chickpeas, tomatoes, and saffron; bring to a boil. Cover, reduce heat, and simmer 35 minutes or until vegetables are tender. Serve with Rouille. Yield: 8 servings (serving size: about 1⅓ cups stew and 2 tablespoons Rouille).

(Totals include Rouille) CALORIES 226 (28% from fat); FAT 7.1g (sat 1g, mono 4.6g, poly 1g); PROTEIN 6.3g; CARB 37.2g; FIBER 7.3g; CHOL 0mg; IRON 3.2mg; SODIUM 802mg; CALC 113mg

ROUILLE:

    1   (1-ounce) slice sourdough bread,
        cubed
    1   cup water
    2   tablespoons water
    2   tablespoons olive oil
    1   teaspoon fresh lemon juice
    ½   teaspoon salt
    ¼   to ½ teaspoon ground red pepper
    2   garlic cloves, chopped
    1   (7-ounce) bottle roasted red bell
        peppers, drained

1. Soak bread in 1 cup water 10 minutes; squeeze moisture from bread.

2. Place bread, 2 tablespoons water, oil, and remaining ingredients in a food processor, and process 2 minutes or until smooth, scraping sides of bowl once. Yield: 8 servings (serving size: 2 tablespoons).

CALORIES 49 (66% from fat); FAT 3.6g (sat 0.5g, mono 2.5g, poly 0.4g); PROTEIN 0.7g; CARB 3.4g; FIBER 0.3g; CHOL 0mg; IRON 0.3mg; SODIUM 256mg; CALC 8mg

Tomatoes Provençale

    8   tomatoes (about 8 ounces each)
    ½   teaspoon salt, divided
    1   (½-ounce) slice sourdough bread
    6   tablespoons chopped fresh parsley
    ¼   cup (1 ounce) grated fresh
        Parmesan cheese
    2   garlic cloves, minced
    2   teaspoons extra-virgin olive oil
        Cooking spray
    ¼   teaspoon black pepper
        Thyme leaves (optional)

1. Preheat oven to 400°.

2. Cut tops off tomatoes; discard. Carefully seed tomatoes, leaving shells intact. Sprinkle cut sides of tomatoes with ¼ teaspoon salt. Place tomatoes, cut sides down, on several layers of paper towels; drain 15 minutes.

3. Place bread in a food processor; pulse 10 times or until coarse crumbs form to measure ½ cup. Combine breadcrumbs, parsley, cheese, and garlic in a bowl.

4. Heat oil in a large nonstick skillet over medium-high heat. Place tomatoes, cut sides down, in pan, and sauté 5 minutes. Remove pan from heat; turn tomatoes over. Spoon about 2 tablespoons breadcrumb mixture over each tomato. Spray breadcrumb mixture with cooking spray, and sprinkle with ¼ teaspoon salt and pepper. Wrap handle of pan with foil. Bake at 400° for 30 minutes or until breadcrumb mixture browns. Garnish with thyme leaves, if desired. Yield: 8 servings (serving size: 1 tomato).

CALORIES 73 (35% from fat); FAT 2.8g (sat 0.8g, mono 1.2g, poly 0.4g); PROTEIN 3.3g; CARB 10.8g; FIBER 2.4g; CHOL 2mg; IRON 1.2mg; SODIUM 234mg; CALC 60mg

Caramelized Onion and Roasted Red-Pepper Tart

CRUST:

1 package dry yeast (about
    2¼ teaspoons)
1 teaspoon honey
¾ cup warm water (100° to 110°)
1½ cups bread flour, divided
¼ cup whole wheat flour
1 tablespoon olive oil
1 teaspoon sea salt
Cooking spray

TOPPING:

1 tablespoon olive oil
6 cups vertically sliced onion
1 teaspoon sea salt
3 thyme sprigs
3 garlic cloves, minced
2 bay leaves
3 large red bell peppers
¼ teaspoon freshly ground black
    pepper
1 tablespoon chopped fresh thyme
Thyme sprigs (optional)

1. To prepare crust, dissolve yeast and honey in warm water in a large bowl; let stand 5 minutes. Lightly spoon flours into dry measuring cups, and level with a knife. Stir 1 cup bread flour and 1 tablespoon oil into yeast mixture. Cover and let rise in a warm place (85°), free from drafts, 1½ hours or until bubbly. Stir in ½ cup bread flour, whole wheat flour, and 1 teaspoon salt.

2. Turn dough out onto a floured surface. Knead until smooth and elastic (about 10 minutes); dough will feel tacky. Place dough in a large bowl coated with cooking spray, turning to coat top. Cover and let rise in a warm place (85°), free from drafts, 1 hour or until doubled in size. (Press two fingers into dough. If indentation remains, dough has risen enough.) Punch dough down; cover and let rest 10 minutes.

3. To prepare topping, heat 1 tablespoon oil in a 12-inch nonstick skillet coated with cooking spray over medium-high heat. Add onion, and cook 5 minutes, stirring frequently. Stir in 1 teaspoon salt, 3 thyme sprigs, garlic, and bay leaves; cook 15 minutes or until deep golden brown, stirring frequently. Remove from heat. Discard thyme sprigs and bay leaves.

4. Prepare broiler.

5. While onion is cooking, cut bell peppers in half lengthwise, discarding seeds and membranes. Place pepper halves, skin sides up, on a foil-lined baking sheet; flatten with hand. Broil 15 minutes or until blackened. Place in a zip-top plastic bag, and seal. Let stand 15 minutes. Peel and coarsely chop.

6. Preheat oven to 425°.

7. Roll dough into a 12 x 8-inch rectangle. Place dough on a baking sheet coated with cooking spray. Top with onion mixture and chopped bell pepper. Sprinkle with black pepper. Bake at 425° for 25 minutes or until crust is golden brown. Cool slightly. Sprinkle with chopped thyme. Cut into 8 pieces, and cut each piece in half diagonally. Garnish with thyme sprigs, if desired. Yield: 8 servings.

CALORIES 192 (20% from fat); FAT 4.2g (sat 0.6g, mono 2.6g, poly 0.6g); PROTEIN 5.6g; CARB 34.3g; FIBER 4.1g; CHOL 0mg; IRON 2mg; SODIUM 581mg; CALC 32mg

Honey-Roasted Pears with Sweet Yogurt Cream

Pears for roasting are best if they're a little on the firm side. Because the skins take on a beautiful deep-amber glaze when roasted, we left them on.

8 firm Bosc pears, each cored and
    quartered
Cooking spray
3 tablespoons chilled butter, cut into
    small pieces
¾ cup apple cider
½ cup honey
1 tablespoon fresh lemon juice
2 teaspoons vanilla extract
Sweet Yogurt Cream

1. Preheat oven to 400°.

2. Place pears in a 13 x 9-inch baking dish coated with cooking spray; dot with butter.

3. Combine cider, honey, juice, and vanilla in a small saucepan. Bring to a boil, and pour over pear mixture. Cover and bake mixture at 400° for 20 minutes. Uncover and bake an additional 30 minutes or until pears are tender, basting occasionally. Remove from oven, and let stand 10 minutes. Serve warm with
Continued

Get Ahead Guide

Two days ahead:
- Make tapenade; store in refrigerator. Allow it to come to room temperature before serving.
- Prepare walnuts for endive; store in an airtight container.
- Drain yogurt.

One day ahead:
- Make and chill Rouille.
- Make onion topping and roast bell peppers for tart; store separately in refrigerator.
- Make Sweet Yogurt Cream.

Hours ahead:
- Prepare crudités and baguette slices for tapenade; store in separate zip-top plastic bags.

- Make sauce for endive; allow it to cool.
- Make stew; reheat over low heat.
- Prepare breadcrumb mixture for tomatoes.
- Complete onion tart up to an hour before guests arrive; serve it at room temperature.

Last minute:
- Place tomatoes in oven shortly after guests arrive.
- Assemble stuffed endive just before serving.
- Roast pears while eating dinner.

Sweet Yogurt Cream. Yield: 8 servings (serving size: 4 pear quarters, 2 tablespoons basting liquid, and 2 tablespoons Sweet Yogurt Cream).

(Totals include Sweet Yogurt Cream) CALORIES 263 (20% from fat); FAT 5.9g (sat 3.3g, mono 1.7g, poly 0.4g); PROTEIN 3.8g; CARB 52.8g; FIBER 4.1g; CHOL 15mg; IRON 0.7mg; SODIUM 86mg; CALC 127mg

SWEET YOGURT CREAM:

    1 (16-ounce) container plain
       low-fat yogurt
 4½ teaspoons honey
  ¼ teaspoon vanilla extract

1. Place a colander in a 2-quart glass measure or medium bowl. Line colander with 4 layers of cheesecloth, allowing cheesecloth to extend over outside edges. Spoon yogurt into colander. Cover loosely with plastic wrap; refrigerate 24 hours. Spoon yogurt cheese into a bowl; discard liquid. Stir in honey and vanilla. Yield: 1 cup (serving size: 2 tablespoons).

CALORIES 48 (17% from fat); FAT 0.9g (sat 0.6g, mono 0.2g, poly 0g); PROTEIN 3g; CARB 7.3g; FIBER 0g; CHOL 4mg; IRON 0.1mg; SODIUM 40mg; CALC 104mg

reader recipes

Soup That Knows No Boundaries

Flavorful soup from Australia, with love.

What do koalas, kangaroos, INXS, boomerangs, and Bree's lentil soup have in common? They are all things from Down Under.

Bree's Lentil-Tomato Soup is the hearty, full-of-flavor blended-vegetable concoction that *Cooking Light* reader Amanda Wonson discovered when her Australian pen pal came to visit her a few years ago.

The soup is quite versatile. It makes a big batch, freezes well, and according to Amanda "has enough of a kick to make it interesting"—just what this busy graduate student at Boston University needs.

Bree's Lentil-Tomato Soup

    1 tablespoon olive oil
    2 cups chopped onion
    1 teaspoon ground turmeric
    1 teaspoon ground cumin
    1 teaspoon chili powder
    1 teaspoon ground red pepper
  ¼ teaspoon salt
  ¼ teaspoon black pepper
    2 garlic cloves, minced
 3⅓ cups water
 2⅓ cups dried lentils
  ⅓ cup chopped fresh cilantro
    3 (14½-ounce) cans fat-free,
       less-sodium chicken broth
    1 (28-ounce) can diced tomatoes,
       undrained
Chopped fresh tomato (optional)
Cilantro sprig (optional)

1. Heat oil in a large Dutch oven over medium-high heat. Add onion; sauté 3 minutes or until tender. Add turmeric and next 6 ingredients; sauté 1 minute. Add water and next 4 ingredients; bring to a boil. Reduce heat; simmer 1 hour.
2. Reserve 2 cups lentil mixture. Place half of remaining mixture in a blender; process until smooth. Pour pureed soup into a large bowl. Repeat procedure with other half of remaining mixture. Stir in reserved 2 cups lentil mixture. Garnish with chopped tomato and a cilantro sprig, if desired. Yield: 11 servings (serving size: 1 cup).

CALORIES 186 (9% from fat); FAT 1.9g (sat 0.3g, mono 1.0g, poly 0.4g); PROTEIN 14.1g; CARB 29.8g; FIBER 13.9g; CHOL 0mg; IRON 4.4mg; SODIUM 412mg; CALC 54mg

---

Curried Squash-Apple Soup

—Ann Webber, Belmont, Massachusetts

 1½ teaspoons olive oil
  ½ cup chopped onion
 3¾ cups (½-inch) cubed peeled
       butternut squash
 3¾ cups chopped Golden Delicious
       apple (about 1½ pounds)
 2¾ cups water
  ¼ cup coarsely chopped celery
 2¼ teaspoons curry powder
  ¾ teaspoon chopped peeled fresh
       ginger
    1 serrano chile, seeded and chopped
    1 vegetable-flavored bouillon cube

1. Heat oil in large saucepan over medium-high heat. Add onion; cook 5 minutes or until soft. Add squash and remaining ingredients; cover and simmer 30 minutes or until squash is tender.
2. Place half of squash mixture in a blender, and process until smooth. Pour pureed soup into a large bowl; repeat procedure with remaining squash mixture. Yield: 4 servings (serving size: 1½ cups).

CALORIES 141 (15% from fat); FAT 2.4g (sat 0.3g, mono 1.3g, poly 0.4g); PROTEIN 2.1g; CARB 32g; FIBER 7.8g; CHOL 0mg; IRON 1.7mg; SODIUM 26mg; CALC 87mg

---

Roasted-Chipotle Salsa

—Brett Thomas, Davis, California

 1½ cups chopped onion
    3 medium tomatoes
    6 garlic cloves, unpeeled
  ¼ cup balsamic vinegar
  ¼ cup lime juice
  ¼ cup water
    1 tablespoon vegetable oil
    1 teaspoon dried oregano
    1 teaspoon black pepper
  ¼ teaspoon salt
  ⅓ cup canned chipotle chiles in
       adobo sauce, undrained

1. Preheat broiler.
2. Place first 3 ingredients on a baking sheet; broil 20 minutes or until blackened,

stirring often. Remove and discard tomato skins. Remove garlic cloves; squeeze to extract garlic pulp. Discard skins.

3. Place onion, tomatoes, and garlic in a food processor; add remaining ingredients, and process until smooth. Serve warm or at room temperature with baked tortilla chips. Yield: 3½ cups salsa (serving size: ¼ cup).

CALORIES 27 (35% from fat); FAT 1.1g (sat 0.2g, mono 0.3g, poly 0.6g); PROTEIN 0.6g; CARB 4.3g; FIBER 0.7g; CHOL 0mg; IRON 0.3mg; SODIUM 46mg; CALC 11mg

Grits "Polenta" with Artichoke and Caper Sauce

—Ruth Ward, Arlington Heights, Illinois

    4 cups boiling water
 1⅓ cups regular grits
   ½ teaspoon salt
Cooking spray
    1 (15-ounce) can no-salt-added
         tomato sauce
    1 teaspoon olive oil
 1½ cups chopped onion
    1 garlic clove, minced
   ¾ cup chopped green bell pepper
   ¾ cup chopped red bell pepper
    1 tablespoon capers
    1 (14-ounce) can artichoke hearts,
         drained and halved
    1 teaspoon chopped fresh or
   ¼ teaspoon dried thyme
    1 teaspoon chopped fresh or
   ¼ teaspoon dried oregano
   ⅛ teaspoon salt
   ⅛ teaspoon black pepper
 1½ cups (6 ounces) shredded
         part-skim mozzarella cheese
   ¼ cup (1 ounce) grated fresh
         Parmesan cheese

1. Combine first 3 ingredients in a large bowl. Microwave at HIGH 10 minutes or until thick, stirring 3 times. Pour into an 8-inch square pan coated with cooking spray. Press plastic wrap onto surface of grits, and chill 1 hour or until firm. Cut into bite-size pieces; set aside.

2. While grits cook and cool, bring tomato sauce to a boil in a small saucepan over medium-high heat.

Reduce heat, and simmer until thick (about 15 minutes). Remove from heat.

3. Preheat oven to 375°.

4. Heat oil in a large nonstick skillet over medium-high heat. Add onion and garlic; sauté 3 minutes. Add bell peppers, capers, and artichokes; sauté 3 minutes. Stir in tomato sauce, thyme, and oregano; cook 4 minutes. Sprinkle with ⅛ teaspoon salt and black pepper.

5. Spoon 1 cup artichoke mixture into bottom of a 13 x 9-inch baking dish coated with cooking spray. Arrange grits pieces in a single layer over artichoke mixture, and sprinkle with mozzarella cheese. Top with remaining artichoke mixture; sprinkle with Parmesan cheese. Bake at 375° for 30 minutes. Yield: 6 servings.

CALORIES 318 (21% from fat); FAT 7.4g (sat 4g, mono 2.3g, poly 0.3g); PROTEIN 14.8g; CARB 47.6g; FIBER 2.9g; CHOL 19mg; IRON 2.7mg; SODIUM 642mg; CALC 280mg

Fish-and-Grits Menu

Herb-Grilled Trout

Gouda grits

Steamed spinach

Ice-cream sandwiches

Herb-Grilled Trout

—Mary Bayramian, Laguna Beach, California

   ¼ cup dry white wine
    1 tablespoon olive oil
    4 (8-ounce) dressed rainbow trout
   ¼ teaspoon salt
   ⅛ teaspoon black pepper
   ½ cup thinly sliced green onions
    2 tablespoons chopped fresh tarragon
    2 tablespoons chopped fresh basil
    1 tablespoon chopped fresh dill
Cooking spray
    4 lemon wedges

1. Prepare grill or broiler.

2. Combine wine and oil; brush inside and outside of fish. Sprinkle insides evenly with salt, pepper, onions, and fresh herbs.

3. Place fish, skin side down, on grill rack or broiler pan coated with cooking spray, and cook 5 minutes or until fish flakes easily when tested with a fork. Serve with lemon wedges. Yield: 4 servings (serving size: 1 fish).

CALORIES 352 (40% from fat); FAT 15.7g (sat 4g, mono 6g, poly 4.4g); PROTEIN 47.5g; CARB 2g; FIBER 0.6g; CHOL 134mg; IRON 0.7mg; SODIUM 229mg; CALC 160mg

Smothered Chicken

—Erika Cross MacDonald,
Nashua, New Hampshire

Cooking spray
    4 (4-ounce) skinless, boneless
         chicken breast halves
   ½ teaspoon salt
   ¼ teaspoon coarsely ground black
         pepper
    1 tablespoon vegetable oil
    2 cups (½-inch) diagonally sliced
         carrot
    1 cup (¼-inch-thick) slices
         onion
    1 garlic clove, minced
    2 (8-ounce) packages presliced
         mushrooms
   ¼ cup all-purpose flour
    1 (14½-ounce) can fat-free,
         less-sodium chicken broth
    1 tablespoon chopped fresh or
         1 teaspoon dried thyme
Chopped fresh chives (optional)

1. Heat a large nonstick skillet coated with cooking spray over medium-high heat. Add chicken, and sprinkle with salt and pepper. Cook 4 minutes on each side or until lightly browned. Remove from pan.

2. Heat oil in pan over medium-high heat. Add carrot, onion, and garlic; cook 2 minutes. Add mushrooms; cook 5 minutes or until vegetables are tender. Sprinkle with flour; cook 2 minutes, stirring constantly.

3. Add broth and thyme; bring to a boil, and cook until slightly thick, stirring frequently. Return chicken to pan; cover, reduce heat, and simmer 10 minutes or

Continued

until chicken is done. Garnish with chives, if desired. Yield: 4 servings (serving size: 1 cup vegetables and 1 chicken breast half).

CALORIES 273 (18% from fat); FAT 5.5g (sat 1.0g, mono 1.2g, poly 2.6g); PROTEIN 33.2g; CARB 23g; FIBER 4.6g; CHOL 66mg; IRON 2.9mg; SODIUM 615mg; CALC 57mg

Date Bread

—Denise Kleine, Pembroke Pines, Florida

    2 cups chopped pitted dates
    2 cups boiling water
    2 teaspoons baking soda
 Cooking spray
    4 teaspoons all-purpose flour
    1 cup sugar
    1 tablespoon butter, melted
    1 teaspoon vanilla extract
    1 large egg, lightly beaten
 2¼ cups all-purpose flour
    ½ teaspoon salt

1. Combine first 3 ingredients in a large bowl; cover and let stand 24 hours.
2. Preheat oven to 325°.
3. Coat 2 (8 x 4-inch) loaf pans with cooking spray, and dust each pan with 2 teaspoons flour. Add sugar, butter, vanilla, and egg to date mixture. Lightly spoon 2¼ cups flour into dry measuring cups, and level with a knife. Add flour and salt to date mixture, stirring just until blended. Divide batter evenly between prepared pans.

4. Bake at 325° for 45 minutes or until a wooden pick inserted in center comes out clean. Cool loaves 10 minutes in pans on a wire rack. Remove loaves from pans, and cool completely on wire rack. Yield: 2 loaves, 16 servings per loaf (serving size: 1 slice).

CALORIES 94 (7% from fat); FAT 0.7g (sat 0.3g, mono 0.2g, poly 0.1g); PROTEIN 1.4g; CARB 21.4g; FIBER 1.1g; CHOL 8mg; IRON 0.6mg; SODIUM 122mg; CALC 6mg

back to the best

Black-Bottom Banana Cream Pie

This delicious pie first appeared in our November 1998 issue.

Black-Bottom Banana Cream Pie

(pictured on page 259)

    1 (9-inch) Pastry Crust
    3 tablespoons cornstarch, divided
    2 tablespoons sugar
    2 tablespoons unsweetened cocoa
 Dash of salt
 1⅓ cups 1% low-fat milk, divided
    1 ounce semisweet chocolate, chopped
    ½ cup sugar
    ¼ teaspoon salt
    2 large eggs
    1 tablespoon butter
    2 teaspoons vanilla extract
    ¼ cup (2 ounces) block-style fat-free cream cheese, softened
    2 cups sliced ripe banana (about 2 large bananas)
 1½ cups frozen fat-free whipped topping, thawed
 Chocolate curls (optional)

1. Prepare and bake Pastry Crust.
2. Combine 1 tablespoon cornstarch, 2 tablespoons sugar, cocoa, and dash of salt in a small, heavy saucepan; gradually add ⅓ cup milk, stirring with a whisk. Cook 2 minutes over medium-low heat. Stir in chocolate; bring to a boil over medium heat. Reduce heat to low; cook 1 minute, stirring constantly. Spread chocolate mixture into bottom of prepared crust.

3. Combine 2 tablespoons cornstarch, 1 cup milk, ½ cup sugar, ¼ teaspoon salt, eggs, and butter in a heavy saucepan over medium heat, stirring constantly with a whisk. Bring to a boil. Reduce heat to low; cook 30 seconds or until thick. Remove from heat. Add vanilla. Beat cream cheese with a mixer at medium speed until light (about 30 seconds). Add ¼ cup hot custard to cream cheese; beat just until blended. Stir in remaining custard.

4. Arrange banana slices on top of chocolate layer; spoon custard over bananas. Press plastic wrap onto surface of custard; chill 4 hours. Remove plastic wrap. Spread whipped topping over custard. Garnish with chocolate curls, if desired. Chill until ready to serve. Yield: 8 servings (serving size: 1 wedge).

(Totals include Pastry Crust) CALORIES 315 (29% from fat); FAT 10.1g (sat 4.8g, mono 3.4g, poly 2.4g); PROTEIN 6.9g; CARB 49.6g; FIBER 1.6g; CHOL 58mg; IRON 1.4mg; SODIUM 253mg; CALC 94mg

PASTRY CRUST:

A slurry is a mixture of flour and liquid (water and vinegar in this recipe); it's the key to this tender low-fat crust. Look for pie weights in gourmet kitchen shops, or substitute uncooked dried beans (reuse them only as weights since they'll be too hard for cooking).

    1 cup all-purpose flour, divided
    3 tablespoons ice water
    ½ teaspoon cider vinegar
    1 tablespoon powdered sugar
    ¼ teaspoon salt
    ¼ cup vegetable shortening

1. Preheat oven to 400°.
2. Lightly spoon flour into a dry measuring cup; level with a knife. Combine ¼ cup flour, ice water, and vinegar, stirring with a whisk until well blended.
3. Combine ¾ cup flour, sugar, and salt in a bowl; cut in shortening with a pastry

blender or 2 knives until mixture resembles coarse meal. Add slurry; toss with a fork until flour mixture is moist. Gently press mixture into a 4-inch circle on 2 lengths of overlapping heavy-duty plastic wrap; cover with additional overlapping plastic wrap. Roll dough, still covered, into a 12-inch circle; freeze 10 minutes or until plastic wrap can be easily removed. Remove 2 lengths of plastic wrap; let stand 1 minute or until pliable. Fit dough, plastic wrap side up, into a 9-inch pie plate. Remove remaining plastic wrap. Press dough against bottom and sides of pan. Fold edges under, or flute decoratively. Line bottom of dough with a piece of foil; arrange pie weights on foil. Bake at 400° for 20 minutes or until edge is lightly browned. Remove pie weights and foil; cool on a wire rack. Yield: 1 (9-inch) crust.

in season

Pine Nuts

Pine nuts are not nuts at all, but the pearly seeds borne on the cones of certain pine trees.

Sweet Pepper and Onion Relish with Pine Nuts

Spread goat cheese on sourdough bread, then slather with relish. The relish is also good on ham sandwiches or grilled chicken.

  1 teaspoon olive oil
     Cooking spray
  8 cups vertically sliced Vidalia or other sweet onion (about 1¾ pounds)
1½ cups red bell pepper strips
 ¾ teaspoon dried thyme
  2 tablespoons pine nuts, toasted
1½ tablespoons rice vinegar
  1 tablespoon honey
 ¼ teaspoon salt
 ⅛ teaspoon coarsely ground black pepper

1. Heat oil in a large nonstick skillet coated with cooking spray over medium heat. Add onion, bell pepper, and thyme; cook 25 minutes or until golden brown, stirring frequently. Remove from heat. Add pine nuts and remaining ingredients, and stir well. Serve at room temperature. Yield: 2 cups (serving size: ¼ cup).

CALORIES 74 (23% from fat); FAT 1.9g (sat 0.3g, mono 0.9g, poly 0.6g); PROTEIN 2g; CARB 13.6g; FIBER 2.6g; CHOL 0mg; IRON 0.6mg; SODIUM 78mg; CALC 27mg

Risotto Cakes with Pine Nuts

Creamy risotto inside a crisp coating makes a great side dish to accompany duck or chicken. Cook the risotto a bit longer than usual, and make sure the last batch of broth is fully absorbed so the patties will be easy to shape.

1¼ cups water
  2 (14½-ounce) cans fat-free, less-sodium chicken broth
     Cooking spray
  2 cups sliced mushrooms
1½ cups chopped onion
1¼ cups Arborio rice or other short-grain rice
  2 tablespoons chopped fresh flat-leaf parsley
  2 tablespoons pine nuts, toasted
 ½ teaspoon salt
 ¼ teaspoon black pepper
 ⅓ cup white cornmeal
  2 tablespoons olive oil, divided

1. Bring water and broth to a simmer in a medium saucepan (do not boil). Keep warm over low heat.
2. Heat a large nonstick skillet coated with cooking spray over medium-high heat. Add mushrooms and chopped onion, and sauté 5 minutes. Add rice, and cook 1 minute, stirring constantly. Stir in ½ cup broth mixture, and cook until liquid is nearly absorbed, stirring constantly. Add remaining broth mixture, ½ cup at a time, stirring constantly until each portion of broth is absorbed before adding next (about 20 minutes total). Remove rice mixture from heat, and stir in parsley, pine nuts, salt, and pepper.
3. Spread rice mixture onto a baking sheet, and chill 20 minutes. Divide mixture into 8 equal portions, shaping each into a ½-inch-thick patty. Dredge patties in cornmeal.
4. Heat 1 tablespoon oil in a large nonstick skillet over medium-high heat. Add 4 patties, and cook 4 minutes. Carefully turn patties over; cook 4 minutes or until thoroughly heated. Repeat procedure with 1 tablespoon oil and 4 patties. Yield: 8 servings (serving size: 1 risotto cake).

CALORIES 229 (22% from fat); FAT 5.6g (sat 1.1g, mono 2.9g, poly 0.8g); PROTEIN 6.2g; CARB 37.2g; FIBER 1.9g; CHOL 2mg; IRON 1mg; SODIUM 214mg; CALC 32mg

Orzo with Chicken, Broccoli, and Pesto

  2 cups small broccoli florets
  2 tablespoons pine nuts, toasted
  1 garlic clove, peeled
  1 cup fresh flat-leaf parsley leaves
 ¼ cup fresh mint leaves
 ¼ cup (1 ounce) grated fresh Parmesan cheese
  1 tablespoon extra-virgin olive oil
  1 tablespoon fresh lemon juice
  1 tablespoon water
 ½ teaspoon salt
 ⅛ teaspoon coarsely ground black pepper
  2 cups hot cooked orzo (about 1 cup uncooked rice-shaped pasta)
1½ cups shredded cooked chicken breast (about 6 ounces)

1. Steam broccoli, covered, 2 minutes or until crisp-tender. Rinse broccoli with cold water. Drain; place in a large bowl.
2. Drop pine nuts and garlic through food chute with food processor on, and process until minced. Add parsley, mint, and cheese; process until finely minced. With processor on, slowly pour oil, lemon juice, water, salt, and pepper through food chute, and process until well blended.

Continued

3. Add parsley mixture, orzo, and chicken to broccoli; stir well. Yield: 5 servings (serving size: 1 cup).

CALORIES 258 (29% from fat); FAT 8.2g (sat 2.1g, mono 3.9g, poly 1.6g); PROTEIN 21g; CARB 25g; FIBER 2.4g; CHOL 40mg; IRON 3.4mg; SODIUM 377mg; CALC 122mg

---

Old-Fashioned Sunday Dinner
serves 8

Butternut Squash, Apple, and Leek Gratin

Lemon-pepper roasted chicken*

Steamed Brussels sprouts tossed with lemon rind

Brown-and-serve rolls

*Remove and discard giblets and neck from 1 (5- to 6-pound) roasting chicken. Rinse with cold water; pat dry. Trim excess fat. Starting at neck cavity, loosen skin from breast and drumsticks by inserting fingers, gently pushing between skin and meat. Combine 1 tablespoon grated lemon rind, 1 teaspoon cracked black pepper, ½ teaspoon garlic powder, and ½ teaspoon salt. Rub lemon mixture under and over the loosened skin. Bake chicken at 400° for 1 hour and 15 minutes or until thermometer registers 180°.

Butternut Squash, Apple, and Leek Gratin

Try this dish with pork, chicken, or turkey.

   5 cups (½-inch) cubed peeled butternut squash
   1 teaspoon olive oil
1½ cups thinly sliced leek (about 2 large)
   2 cups (½-inch) cubed peeled Braeburn apple (about 1 pound)
1½ tablespoons brown sugar
  ½ teaspoon salt
  ⅛ teaspoon ground nutmeg
  ⅛ teaspoon coarsely ground black pepper
Cooking spray
  ½ cup apple cider or juice
   2 (1-ounce) slices white bread
   3 tablespoons pine nuts, toasted
   1 tablespoon butter, melted

1. Preheat oven to 400°.
2. Steam squash, covered, 9 minutes or until tender.
3. Heat oil in a large nonstick skillet over medium heat. Add leek; sauté 5 minutes or until lightly browned.
4. Combine squash, leek, apple, sugar, salt, nutmeg, and pepper in a large bowl; toss gently to coat. Spoon into a 2-quart casserole coated with cooking spray; pour cider over squash mixture. Cover and bake at 400° for 20 minutes.
5. Place bread in a food processor; pulse 10 times or until coarse crumbs form to measure 1 cup. Combine breadcrumbs, pine nuts, and butter. Uncover casserole; sprinkle with breadcrumb mixture. Bake, uncovered, an additional 15 minutes or until golden brown. Yield: 8 servings (serving size: ¾ cup).

CALORIES 151 (25% from fat); FAT 4.2g (sat 1.4g, mono 1.5g, poly 0.9g); PROTEIN 2.5g; CARB 28.6g; FIBER 4.6g; CHOL 4mg; IRON 1.5mg; SODIUM 202mg; CALC 63mg

Pear Cake with Pine Nuts

1¼ cups all-purpose flour
  ¾ cup sugar
  ⅛ teaspoon salt
  ¼ cup chilled butter, cut into small pieces
   2 tablespoons pine nuts, toasted
  ¼ teaspoon ground cinnamon
  ⅓ cup fat-free sour cream
  ¼ cup 1% low-fat milk
   1 teaspoon grated lemon rind
   1 teaspoon vanilla extract
  ½ teaspoon baking powder
  ¼ teaspoon baking soda
   1 large egg
Cooking spray
   2 cups thinly sliced peeled pear

1. Preheat oven to 350°.
2. Lightly spoon flour into dry measuring cups, and level with a knife. Combine flour, sugar, and salt in a large bowl; stir well with a whisk. Cut in butter with a pastry blender or 2 knives until mixture resembles coarse meal. Remove ⅓ cup flour mixture; place in a small bowl. Stir in pine nuts and cinnamon; set aside.
3. Combine remaining flour mixture, sour cream, and next 6 ingredients in a large bowl. Beat with a mixer at medium speed until well blended. Pour batter into a 9-inch round cake pan coated with cooking spray. Arrange pear slices evenly over batter. Sprinkle with pine nut mixture. Bake at 350° for 45 minutes or until a wooden pick inserted in center comes out clean; cool completely on a wire rack. Yield: 8 servings (serving size: 1 wedge).

CALORIES 252 (28% from fat); FAT 7.9g (sat 4g, mono 2.4g, poly 0.9g); PROTEIN 4.2g; CARB 41.9g; FIBER 1.7g; CHOL 43mg; IRON 1.4mg; SODIUM 191mg; CALC 53mg

october

The Dish on Pots & Pans

From Dutch ovens to soufflé dishes, here's how to spring for the right pan.

Whether you're a kid or a culinary wizard, selecting the right utensil for the right job can be very confusing. To alleviate such confusion *Cooking Light* Test Kitchens Director Vanessa Johnson and former Director Becky Pate give you the low-down on what we mean when we call for a specific dish (info on page 277).

Orange-Glazed Cheesecake with Gingersnap Crust

(pictured on page 294)

CRUST:

- 1 cup gingersnap crumbs (about 20 cookies, finely crushed)
- 2 tablespoons sugar
- 1 tablespoon butter, melted
  Cooking spray

FILLING:

- 2 (8-ounce) blocks fat-free cream cheese, softened
- 2 (8-ounce) blocks ⅓-less-fat cream cheese, softened
- 1 (8-ounce) carton reduced-fat sour cream
- ¼ cup all-purpose flour
- 1½ cups sugar
- ¼ cup thawed orange juice concentrate, undiluted
- 1 tablespoon Grand Marnier (orange-flavored liqueur) or orange juice
- 2 teaspoons vanilla extract
- 3 large eggs
- 2 large egg whites

TOPPING:

- ½ cup orange marmalade
- 1 tablespoon Grand Marnier (orange-flavored liqueur) or orange juice
- 1 orange, peeled and sliced

1. Preheat oven to 325°.

2. To prepare crust, combine first 3 ingredients; toss with a fork until moist. Press into bottom of a 9-inch springform pan coated with cooking spray. Bake at 325° for 5 minutes.

3. To prepare filling, beat cheeses and sour cream in a large bowl with a mixer at high speed until smooth. Lightly spoon flour into a dry measuring cup; level with a knife. Add flour, 1½ cups sugar, and next 3 ingredients to cheese mixture, and beat well. Add eggs and egg whites, 1 at a time, beating well after each addition.

4. Pour cheese mixture into prepared pan; bake at 325° for 1 hour and 10 minutes or until almost set. Cheesecake is done when center barely moves when pan is touched. Remove cheesecake from oven, and run a knife around outside edge. Cool to room temperature. Remove sides.

5. To prepare topping, combine marmalade and 1 tablespoon liqueur. Spread half of mixture over top of cheesecake. Cut orange slices in half, and arrange over cheesecake. Spread with remaining marmalade mixture. Cover and chill at least 8 hours. Yield: 16 servings (serving size: 1 wedge).

CALORIES 310 (33% from fat); FAT 11.3g (sat 6.5g, mono 3.1g, poly 0.5g); PROTEIN 10.1g; CARB 42.4g; FIBER 0.6g; CHOL 73mg; IRON 1mg; SODIUM 365mg; CALC 119mg

Chili and Cheddar Bow Tie Casserole

If you don't have farfalle, substitute ziti, rigatoni, or even macaroni.

- 1 (7-ounce) can chipotle chiles in adobo sauce
- 1 tablespoon butter
- 1 cup chopped red bell pepper
- ½ cup diced Canadian bacon (about 2 ounces)
- 1 cup thinly sliced green onions
- 2 tablespoons all-purpose flour
- 1 teaspoon chili powder
- ½ teaspoon salt
- ½ teaspoon ground cumin
- 2¼ cups 2% reduced-fat milk
- 2 cups (8 ounces) shredded reduced-fat sharp cheddar cheese, divided
- 2 tablespoons chopped fresh cilantro
- 8 cups hot cooked farfalle (bow tie pasta) or other short pasta
  Cooking spray

1. Preheat oven to 400°.

2. Remove 1 teaspoon adobo sauce and 1 chile from canned chiles; mince chile. Place remaining sauce and chiles in a zip-top plastic bag; freeze for another use.

3. Melt butter in a large Dutch oven over medium-high heat. Add bell pepper and bacon; sauté 4 minutes. Add onions; sauté 1 minute. Stir in adobo sauce, minced chile, flour, chili powder, salt, and cumin; cook 1 minute. Gradually add milk; cook until thick and bubbly (about 4 minutes), stirring constantly with a whisk. Remove from heat. Gradually add 1½ cups cheese and cilantro, stirring until cheese melts. Add pasta to pan; toss well.

4. Spoon pasta mixture into an 11 x 7-inch baking dish coated with cooking spray. Sprinkle ½ cup cheese over pasta mixture. Bake at 400° for 15 minutes or until browned. Yield: 6 servings (serving size: 1⅓ cups).

CALORIES 369 (30% from fat); FAT 12.4g (sat 7.4g, mono 1.6g, poly 1g); PROTEIN 23.2g; CARB 43g; FIBER 3.1g; CHOL 44mg; IRON 1.6mg; SODIUM 758mg; CALC 472mg

Spring for the Right Pan

Pans and Dishes

Baking pans are made of metal; baking dishes are made of glass or ceramic materials. Glass conducts heat better than metal, so if you use a baking dish in a recipe that calls for a pan, you'll need to decrease the oven temperature by 25 degrees.

Springform Pan

A springform pan is a round, deep pan with tall, removable sides; it's most often used for baking cheesecakes, such as our Orange-Glazed Cheesecake with Gingersnap Crust (recipe on page 276). Springform pans with glass bottoms conduct heat better and decrease baking time, and those with extended edges around the base keep the batter from leaking. Nine-inch pans are most popular—if your springform pan isn't the size called for in the recipe, substitute. If yours is smaller, your cake will be thicker and will need to bake longer. Conversely, if you substitute a larger pan, your product will be thinner and may require less baking time.

Shallow Baking Dish

With sides only a couple of inches high, a shallow baking dish allows foods to cook quickly and brown evenly. These dishes come in ovals and rounds as well as squares and rectangles. You probably have at least one, but you might not call it that: An 11 x 7-inch baking dish is a commonly used 2-quart shallow baking dish.

Skillet

For light cooking, a nonstick skillet is essential, since it requires little added fat. But there are times when food needs to stick. If you want to leave browned bits behind for deglazing or achieve a dark-brown surface on meats, use a heavy skillet without a nonstick coating, such as copper, cast iron, or stainless steel.

Jelly Roll Pan

A jelly roll pan is a 15 x 10 x 1-inch pan that's used to make thin cakes, such as sponge cakes and jelly rolls. Some people call them baking or cookie sheets, but technically, a baking sheet has a rim on just one or two sides. Jelly roll pans come in shiny and dark finishes, and may have nonstick surfaces.

Tube Pan

The 10-inch tube pan, also called an angel food cake pan, is a classic tall-sided, round cake pan with a tube in the center. Sometimes it has a removable center; sometimes it doesn't. Some types have small metal feet so you can turn the pan upside down for cooling. If your pan doesn't have feet, and your recipe tells you to "hang" the cake upside down to cool, as many angel food cake recipes do, you can invert it on a bottle with a long neck.

Soufflé Dish

A soufflé dish is round and has tall, straight sides (5 to 7 inches high) so your egg mixture will climb the sides and rise high. And because they were designed to go from oven to table, soufflé dishes are usually attractive enough to use as a casserole or serving dish.

Roasting Pan

Roasting pans are designed for cooking large cuts of meat, such as a pork loin or Thanksgiving turkey. These heavy pans come in large rectangular or oval shapes with 2- to 4-inch vertical sides, which keep the pan juices from overflowing in the oven. They sometimes come with racks to keep the meat raised above the drippings as it roasts; if your pan doesn't have a rack, you can elevate the meat with vegetables (such as whole carrots and ribs of celery) or a wire rack that fits the pan, unless the roast has to cook for several hours (in which case the drippings help the meat stay moist). A good substitute is a broiling pan with a removable rack.

Dutch Oven

A Dutch oven is neither Dutch nor an oven, but a deep pot with a tight-fitting lid that can go from cooktop to oven—most cookware sets include a pot that fits this description. It usually holds 3 to 6 quarts. Some versions come with a long handle, like a skillet. If you choose one with a handle, make sure there's also a "helper handle" on the other side, since a hot Dutch oven full of food can be quite heavy.

Root Vegetable and Cranberry Bake

Covering the vegetables first allows them to steam and soften. Then, uncovered, they roast, which caramelizes natural sugars, concentrates flavors, and browns the dish.

2 cups thinly sliced peeled Yukon gold potato (about ¾ pound)
2 cups thinly sliced peeled sweet potato (about ¾ pound)
1½ cups thinly sliced parsnip (about ½ pound)
1 cup thinly sliced onion
⅓ cup dried cranberries
½ teaspoon salt
½ teaspoon freshly ground black pepper
Cooking spray
1¼ cups fat-free, less-sodium chicken broth
¼ cup maple syrup
1 tablespoon chopped fresh or 1 teaspoon dried thyme
3 tablespoons bourbon
1½ tablespoons fresh lemon juice
1 tablespoon butter

1. Preheat oven to 375°.
2. Combine first 7 ingredients in an 11 x 7-inch baking dish coated with cooking spray.
3. Combine broth and remaining 5 ingredients in a medium saucepan; bring to a boil. Remove from heat, and pour over vegetables. Cover; bake at 375° for 20 minutes. Uncover and bake an additional 50 minutes. Yield: 6 servings (serving size: about 1 cup).

CALORIES 205 (10% from fat); FAT 2.2g (sat 1.3g, mono 0.6g, poly 0.2g); PROTEIN 3.1g; CARB 42.7g; FIBER 4.5g; CHOL 5mg; IRON 0.9mg; SODIUM 320mg; CALC 41mg

Fall Menu for Eight

This hearty meal is well suited for a chilly fall evening. Broccolini is a cross between broccoli and Chinese kale. It looks like a slimmer version of broccoli, with a small head of buds and slender, sweet, edible stalks.

Garlic and Herb Bread Pudding

Roasted pork tenderloin*

Sautéed broccolini

Apple and pear slices with fat-free caramel sundae syrup

*Combine 3 tablespoons Dijon mustard; 2 tablespoons maple syrup; 2 teaspoons chopped fresh rosemary; and 2 garlic cloves, minced, in a small bowl. Brush mustard mixture over 2 (1-pound) pork tenderloins. Bake at 350° for 50 minutes or until a meat thermometer registers 160° (the meat will be slightly pink).

Garlic and Herb Bread Pudding

Bread puddings are usually reserved for dessert, but this savory version can be a meal in itself or a hearty side for main course soups or grilled meat. Be sure to use good bread—even better if it's a day old. Try rosemary focaccia or sourdough.

⅓ cup sun-dried tomatoes, packed without oil
2 teaspoons olive oil
2 tablespoons minced garlic
2 cups fat-free milk
3 large eggs
⅔ cup (about 2½ ounces) shredded part-skim mozzarella cheese, divided
2 tablespoons grated fresh Parmesan cheese, divided
2 tablespoons chopped fresh or 2 teaspoons dried basil
½ teaspoon salt
½ teaspoon black pepper
6 cups (1-inch) cubed Italian bread (about 8 ounces)
Cooking spray

1. Preheat oven to 350°.
2. Place boiling water and tomatoes in a bowl. Cover and let stand 10 minutes or until tender. Drain well; finely chop.
3. Heat oil in a small nonstick skillet over medium-low heat. Add garlic; cook 1 minute, stirring constantly. Combine milk and eggs in a bowl, stirring with a whisk. Stir in tomatoes, garlic, ½ cup mozzarella, 1 tablespoon Parmesan, basil, salt, and pepper.
4. Place bread in a shallow 1½-quart casserole coated with cooking spray. Pour milk mixture over bread, gently stirring to coat. Let mixture stand 15 minutes. Sprinkle with 8 teaspoons mozzarella and 1 tablespoon Parmesan. Bake at 350° for 45 minutes or until golden brown. Yield: 8 servings.

CALORIES 178 (31% from fat); FAT 6.2g (sat 2.3g, mono 2.4g, poly 0.8g); PROTEIN 10.5g; CARB 19.8g; FIBER 1.2g; CHOL 87mg; IRON 1.5mg; SODIUM 490mg; CALC 201mg

Pork Piccata

This variation on veal piccata features a sauce made by deglazing the pan with lemon juice and chicken broth.

⅓ cup Italian-seasoned breadcrumbs
4 (4-ounce) boneless center-cut loin pork chops, trimmed (about ½ inch thick)
1 tablespoon olive oil
¼ cup chopped shallots
1 cup fat-free, less-sodium chicken broth
1 tablespoon fresh lemon juice
3 tablespoons chopped fresh parsley, divided
2 teaspoons capers
1 teaspoon grated lemon rind
⅛ teaspoon black pepper

1. Place breadcrumbs in a shallow dish. Dredge pork in breadcrumbs. Heat olive oil in a large skillet over medium-high heat. Cook pork 2 minutes on each side or until golden brown. Remove pork from pan. Reduce heat to medium.
2. Add shallots to pan; cook 30 seconds. Stir in broth and juice, scraping pan to loosen browned bits. Stir in 1½

tablespoons parsley, capers, rind, and pepper; simmer 1 minute. Return pork to pan; cook 3 minutes or until thoroughly heated. Sprinkle pork with 1½ tablespoons parsley. Yield: 4 servings (serving size: 1 pork chop and 2 tablespoons sauce).

CALORIES 276 (46% from fat); FAT 14g (sat 4.1g, mono 8g, poly 1.1g); PROTEIN 26.3g; CARB 9.7g; FIBER 0.7g; CHOL 61mg; IRON 1.5mg; SODIUM 458mg; CALC 24mg

Raspberry Jelly Roll with Apricot Coulis

You can experiment with many varieties of fillings, flavors, and sauces. Try peach jam and strawberry sauce, or lemon curd and orange sauce. While the cake is still warm and flexible, roll it up in a towel and let it cool so it won't resist being rolled a second time.

CAKE:
Cooking spray
⅔ cup all-purpose flour
1 teaspoon baking powder
⅛ teaspoon salt
4 large eggs
¾ cup granulated sugar
1½ teaspoons vanilla extract
½ teaspoon grated lemon rind
¼ teaspoon almond extract
¼ cup powdered sugar, divided
1 (10-ounce) bottle seedless raspberry jam

COULIS:
1 (15-ounce) can apricot halves in light syrup, undrained
1 tablespoon honey
1 tablespoon amaretto (almond-flavored liqueur)
2 cups fresh raspberries

1. Preheat oven to 400°.
2. To prepare cake, coat a 15 x 10-inch jelly roll pan with cooking spray, and line with wax paper. Coat paper with cooking spray; set aside.
3. Lightly spoon flour into dry measuring cups, and level with a knife. Combine flour, baking powder, and salt, stirring with a whisk. Beat eggs in a large

bowl with a mixer at high speed until pale and fluffy (about 4 minutes). Gradually add granulated sugar, vanilla, rind, and almond extract, beating until thick (about 4 minutes). Sift half of flour mixture over egg mixture; fold in. Repeat procedure with remaining flour mixture. Spoon batter into prepared pan; spread evenly.
4. Bake at 400° for 10 minutes or until cake springs back when touched lightly in center. Loosen cake from sides of pan; turn out onto a dish towel dusted with 2 tablespoons powdered sugar. Carefully peel off wax paper; cool 1 minute. Starting at narrow end, roll up cake and towel together. Place, seam side down, on a wire rack; cool completely (about 1 hour). Unroll carefully; remove towel. Spread jam over cake, leaving a ½-inch border. Reroll cake, and place, seam side down, on a platter. Sprinkle with 2 tablespoons powdered sugar. Cut into 8 slices.
5. To prepare coulis, drain apricots in a colander over a bowl, reserving 1 tablespoon juice. Place apricots, 1 tablespoon reserved juice, honey, and amaretto in a blender; process until smooth. Serve with cake. Garnish with berries. Yield: 8 servings (serving size: 1 cake slice, about 2 tablespoons coulis, and ¼ cup raspberries).

CALORIES 320 (8% from fat); FAT 2.8g (sat 0.8g, mono 1g, poly 0.5g); PROTEIN 4.6g; CARB 68.9g; FIBER 3.2g; CHOL 106mg; IRON 1.4mg; SODIUM 146mg; CALC 62mg

Dutch-Chocolate Angel Cake

The secret to a perfect angel food cake lies in beating the egg whites and then stabilizing them with cream of tartar. Dutch-process cocoa has nothing to do with the Netherlands but refers to a process in which the cocoa is "dutched," or alkalized, resulting in a more mellow and full-bodied cocoa. Though the regular variety can be used, dutch-process cocoa gives the sauce a subtle richness. Use an ungreased tube pan so the egg whites in the batter will cling to the sides and "climb" as the cake bakes.

1 cup sifted cake flour
1½ cups sugar, divided
¼ cup dutch-process cocoa
¼ teaspoon ground cinnamon
12 large egg whites
1 teaspoon cream of tartar
¼ teaspoon salt
2 teaspoons vanilla extract
1½ teaspoons fresh lemon juice
½ teaspoon almond extract
Dark Cocoa Sauce

1. Preheat oven to 325°.
2. Combine flour, ¾ cup sugar, cocoa, and cinnamon in a small bowl, stirring with a whisk. Beat egg whites in a large bowl with a mixer at high speed until foamy. Add cream of tartar and salt; beat until soft peaks form. Add ¾ cup sugar, 2 tablespoons at a time, beating until stiff peaks form. Sift flour mixture over egg white mixture, ¼ cup at a time, folding in each portion. Fold in vanilla, juice, and almond extract. Spoon batter into an ungreased nonstick 10-inch tube pan, spreading evenly. Break air pockets by cutting through batter with a knife.
3. Bake at 325° for 50 minutes or until cake springs back when lightly touched. Invert pan, and cool completely. Loosen cake from sides of pan using a narrow metal spatula. Invert cake onto plate. Cut into 12 slices using a serrated knife. Serve with Dark Cocoa Sauce. Yield: 12 servings (serving size: 1 cake slice and about 1½ tablespoons sauce).

(Totals include Dark Cocoa Sauce) CALORIES 227 (8% from fat); FAT 2g (sat 1.2g, mono 0.4g, poly 0.1g); PROTEIN 5.9g; CARB 48.7g; FIBER 2g; CHOL 0mg; IRON 1.5mg; SODIUM 113mg; CALC 27mg

DARK COCOA SAUCE:
⅔ cup sugar
⅔ cup fat-free milk
½ cup dutch-process cocoa
1½ ounces bittersweet chocolate, chopped
1 teaspoon vanilla extract

1. To prepare sauce, combine first 3 ingredients in a medium saucepan over medium heat, stirring until smooth. Bring to a boil; cook 3 minutes, stirring constantly. Remove from heat. Stir in

Continued

chocolate and vanilla; let stand 1 minute. Stir until smooth; cool. Yield: about 1¼ cups (serving size: about 1½ tablespoons).

CALORIES 77 (20% from fat); FAT 1.7g (sat 1g, mono 0.3g, poly 0g); PROTEIN 1.4g; CARB 15.8g; FIBER 1.3g; CHOL 0mg; IRON 0.6mg; SODIUM 8mg; CALC 21mg

Greens and Cheese Soufflé

This may be an updated rendition of a spinach soufflé, but it follows the same old rule: Serve it quickly—it will fall.

    1   (10-ounce) package frozen collard
        greens, thawed, drained, and
        squeezed dry
    2   teaspoons butter
    1   cup finely chopped onion
    2   garlic cloves, minced
    3   tablespoons all-purpose flour
    ½   teaspoon salt
    ½   teaspoon hot sauce
    ¼   teaspoon freshly ground black
        pepper
    1   cup fat-free milk
    2   large egg yolks
    ¼   cup (1 ounce) grated fresh
        Parmesan cheese, divided
    6   large egg whites
    ¼   teaspoon cream of tartar
        Cooking spray
    2   tablespoons dry breadcrumbs

1. Place greens in a food processor, and process until finely chopped.
2. Melt butter in a medium saucepan over medium heat. Add onion and garlic; cook 6 minutes or until onion is soft, stirring frequently. Add flour, salt, hot sauce, and pepper; cook 1 minute, stirring constantly. Gradually add milk, and cook until thick and bubbly (about 4 minutes), stirring constantly with a whisk.
3. Place egg yolks in a bowl. Gradually add ½ cup hot milk mixture to egg yolks, stirring constantly with a whisk. Add remaining hot milk mixture, stirring constantly with a whisk. Add yolk mixture to pan; cook over medium-low heat 1 minute. Stir in greens and 3 tablespoons cheese. Pour into a large bowl; cool slightly.
4. Preheat oven to 400°.

5. Place egg whites and cream of tartar in a medium bowl; beat with a mixer at high speed until stiff peaks form. Gently stir one-fourth of egg whites into greens mixture; gently fold in remaining egg whites. Coat a 1½-quart soufflé dish with cooking spray; sprinkle with breadcrumbs. Spoon egg mixture into prepared dish; sprinkle with 1 tablespoon cheese.
6. Place dish in oven. Reduce oven temperature to 375° (do not remove soufflé from oven). Bake for 40 minutes or until puffy and set. Serve immediately. Yield: 6 servings (serving size: 1 cup).

CALORIES 124 (35% from fat); FAT 4.8g (sat 2.4g, mono 1.1g, poly 0.4g); PROTEIN 9.9g; CARB 11.2g; FIBER 1.8g; CHOL 80mg; IRON 1mg; SODIUM 396mg; CALC 217mg

Roasted Pork and Autumn Vegetables

We used baby carrots with tops attached, but bagged baby carrots work fine.

    2   fennel bulbs (about 1½ pounds)
    2   small onions
    1   tablespoon olive oil, divided
    4   cups (1-inch) cubed peeled rutabaga
   16   baby carrots (about ¾ pound)
    1   (2¼-pound) boneless pork loin
        roast, trimmed
        Cooking spray
    2   tablespoons chopped fresh sage
    ¾   teaspoon kosher salt, divided
    ¾   teaspoon freshly ground black
        pepper, divided
    ¾   cup fat-free, less-sodium chicken
        broth
    ½   cup dry white wine
    2   teaspoons Dijon mustard

1. Preheat oven to 400°.
2. Trim stalks from fennel; discard. Cut each fennel bulb into 8 wedges. Peel onions, leaving root intact; cut each onion into 8 wedges.
3. Heat 1½ teaspoons oil in a nonstick skillet over medium-high heat. Add fennel and onion; sauté 8 minutes or until lightly browned, stirring frequently. Remove from pan. Add 1½ teaspoons oil, rutabaga, and carrots to pan; sauté 5 minutes or until lightly browned, stirring frequently.

4. Place pork on a rack coated with cooking spray; place rack in a shallow roasting pan. Sprinkle pork with sage, ½ teaspoon salt, and ½ teaspoon pepper. Arrange vegetables around pork; sprinkle with ¼ teaspoon salt and ¼ teaspoon pepper.
5. Bake at 400° for 50 minutes or until thermometer registers 160° (slightly pink). Remove pork and vegetables from pan; cover loosely with foil. Remove rack. Place pan over medium heat; stir in broth, wine, and mustard, scraping pan to loosen browned bits. Bring to a boil; reduce heat, and simmer 4 minutes, stirring occasionally. Serve with pork and vegetables. Yield: 8 servings (serving size: 3 ounces pork, about ⅔ cup vegetables, and 2 tablespoons sauce).

CALORIES 282 (37% from fat); FAT 11.5g (sat 3.6g, mono 5.5g, poly 1g); PROTEIN 29.9g; CARB 14.6g; FIBER 4.5g; CHOL 78mg; IRON 2.2mg; SODIUM 359mg; CALC 96mg

East African Braised Chicken

Serve this dish with a bowl of plain low-fat yogurt and flatbreads or couscous.

    2   chicken breast halves (about
        ¾ pound), skinned
    2   chicken thighs (about ½ pound),
        skinned
    2   chicken drumsticks (about
        ½ pound), skinned
    ½   teaspoon salt
    ½   teaspoon black pepper
    1   tablespoon olive oil
    3   cups vertically sliced onion
    1   tablespoon chopped peeled fresh
        ginger
    1   teaspoon curry powder
    ½   teaspoon ground cinnamon
    ½   teaspoon ground cardamom
    ¼   teaspoon ground red pepper
    2   large garlic cloves, thinly
        sliced
    ½   cup fat-free, less-sodium chicken
        broth
    ½   cup dry white wine
    3   tablespoons chopped pitted
        dates
    3   tablespoons golden raisins

1. Preheat oven to 350°.
2. Sprinkle chicken with salt and black pepper. Heat oil in a Dutch oven over medium-high heat. Add chicken; cook 4 minutes on each side or until golden brown. Remove chicken from pan.
3. Add onion to pan; reduce heat to medium-low, and cook 10 minutes, stirring frequently. Add ginger and next 5 ingredients; cook 1 minute. Stir in chicken, broth, and remaining ingredients, and bring to a boil. Cover and bake at 350° for 1 hour. Yield: 4 servings (serving size: 3 ounces chicken and about ¼ cup sauce).

CALORIES 279 (29% from fat); FAT 8.9g (sat 2g, mono 4.4g, poly 1.6g); PROTEIN 28.1g; CARB 21.9g; FIBER 3g; CHOL 79mg; IRON 2mg; SODIUM 423mg; CALC 48mg

dinner tonight

Meatless Menus

Minutes in the making, these meatless menus creatively marry fresh ingredients.

Creamy Spinach-Mushroom Skillet Enchiladas

TOTAL TIME: 30 MINUTES

QUICK TIP: Flavored cream cheese delivers the taste of green onions and chives without all the chopping.

- 2 teaspoons olive oil
- 1 teaspoon bottled minced garlic
- ½ teaspoon chili powder
- ½ teaspoon ground cumin
- 1 (8-ounce) package presliced mushrooms
- 1 (6-ounce) package fresh baby spinach (about 6 cups)
- ¼ teaspoon salt
- 2 tablespoons light cream cheese with onions and chives
- 1 (16-ounce) bottle green salsa, divided
- 8 (6-inch) corn tortillas
- ⅓ cup (1½ ounces) shredded Monterey Jack cheese
- ¼ cup fat-free sour cream
- Cilantro sprigs (optional)

1. Preheat broiler.
2. Heat olive oil in a large skillet over medium-high heat. Add garlic, chili powder, cumin, and mushrooms; sauté 5 minutes. Add spinach and salt, and cook 1 minute or until spinach wilts, stirring frequently. Drain; return mushroom mixture to pan. Add cream cheese; cook 2 minutes or until cream cheese melts, stirring frequently. Place mushroom mixture in a bowl; set aside.
3. Heat 1 cup salsa in a saucepan over low heat. Dredge both sides of each tortilla in warm salsa using tongs; stack tortillas on a plate. Spoon 1 heaping tablespoon mushroom mixture into center of each tortilla; fold in half, and arrange in skillet, overlapping slightly. Top with remaining salsa; sprinkle with shredded cheese. Wrap handle of skillet with foil, and broil enchiladas 4 minutes or until cheese melts. Top with sour cream, and garnish with cilantro sprigs, if desired. Yield: 4 servings (serving size: 2 enchiladas and 1 tablespoon sour cream).

CALORIES 273 (29% from fat); FAT 8.7g (sat 3.6g, mono 2.9g, poly 1g); PROTEIN 10.1g; CARB 39.4g; FIBER 6.7g; CHOL 15mg; IRON 2.7mg; SODIUM 806mg; CALC 330mg

Pasta with Roasted Butternut Squash and Shallots

TOTAL TIME: 40 MINUTES

QUICK TIP: Use a sharp vegetable peeler to peel the butternut squash. It's easier to handle and less time consuming than using a knife.

- 3 cups (1-inch) cubed peeled butternut squash
- 1 tablespoon dark brown sugar
- 1½ tablespoons olive oil, divided
- 1 teaspoon salt
- ½ teaspoon black pepper
- 8 shallots, peeled and halved lengthwise (about ½ pound)
- 1 tablespoon chopped fresh or 1 teaspoon dried rubbed sage
- 4 ounces uncooked pappardelle (wide ribbon pasta) or fettuccine
- ¼ cup (1 ounce) grated fresh Parmesan cheese

1. Preheat oven to 475°.
2. Combine squash, sugar, 2½ teaspoons oil, salt, pepper, and shallots in a jelly roll pan; toss well. Bake at 475° for 20 minutes or until tender, stirring occasionally. Stir in sage.
3. While squash mixture bakes, cook pasta according to package directions, omitting salt and fat. Drain. Place cooked pasta in a bowl. Add 2 teaspoons oil; toss well. Serve squash mixture over pasta. Sprinkle with cheese. Yield: 4 servings (serving size: ¾ cup pasta,
Continued

¾ cup squash mixture, and 1 tablespoon cheese).

CALORIES 248 (29% from fat); FAT 7.9g (sat 2g, mono 4.5g, poly 0.8g); PROTEIN 7.1g; CARB 39.4g; FIBER 5.2g; CHOL 5mg; IRON 1.4mg; SODIUM 713mg; CALC 137mg

Menu 3
serves 4

Polenta with Tomato-Shiitake Sauce

Italian broccoli*

*Steam 1 pound broccoli spears, covered, 5 minutes or until crisp-tender. Toss with 3 tablespoons fat-free Italian dressing; sprinkle with 2 tablespoons grated Parmesan cheese.

Rosemary focaccia

Polenta with Tomato-Shiitake Sauce

TOTAL TIME: 40 MINUTES

QUICK TIP: Slice three or four stacked shiitake mushroom caps at a time.

2   teaspoons olive oil
⅓   cup sliced shallots
3   cups thinly sliced shiitake mushroom caps (about ½ pound)
2   teaspoons dried basil
1   teaspoon dried oregano
1   teaspoon bottled minced roasted garlic
¼   teaspoon crushed red pepper
¼   teaspoon sugar
2   (14.5-ounce) cans diced tomatoes, drained
2   cups vegetable broth
1   cup water
¾   cup instant dry polenta
½   cup grated Parmesan cheese

1. Heat oil in a large skillet over medium-high heat. Add shallots; sauté 2 minutes. Add mushrooms; sauté 3 minutes or until tender. Stir in basil and next 5 ingredients; cook 3 minutes or until thoroughly heated. Keep warm.
2. Combine vegetable broth and water in a large saucepan, and bring to a boil. Stir in polenta. Reduce heat, and simmer

until thick (about 5 minutes), stirring frequently. Stir in cheese. Serve tomato mixture over polenta. Yield: 4 servings (serving size: about ⅔ cup polenta and 1 cup tomato mixture).

CALORIES 221 (29% from fat); FAT 7g (sat 2.7g, mono 2.8g, poly 0.3g); PROTEIN 10.8g; CARB 29.4g; FIBER 3.8g; CHOL 10mg; IRON 2.2mg; SODIUM 876mg; CALC 217mg

Menu 4
serves 6

Caramelized Onion and Goat Cheese Pizza

Red-pepper pasta*

*Cook 8 ounces dry spaghetti according to package directions, omitting salt and fat. While pasta cooks, combine 1½ tablespoons olive oil, 2 teaspoons bottled minced garlic, and ¼ teaspoon crushed red pepper in a microwave-safe bowl; cover and microwave at HIGH 1 minute. Toss drained cooked pasta with olive oil mixture and ½ cup vegetable broth. Sprinkle with 3 tablespoons grated Parmesan cheese.

Mixed greens salad with cherry tomatoes and red onion slices

Caramelized Onion and Goat Cheese Pizza

TOTAL TIME: 32 MINUTES

QUICK TIP: Microwaving garlic and crushed red pepper in olive oil quickly infuses the oil with flavor.

2   teaspoons olive oil
2   cups thinly sliced onion, separated into rings (about 1 onion)
1   (1-pound) Italian cheese-flavored pizza crust (such as Boboli)
½   cup bottled pizza sauce (such as Contadina)
¼   cup chopped drained oil-packed sun-dried tomato halves
⅔   cup (3 ounces) crumbled goat cheese
¼   cup chopped fresh basil

1. Preheat oven to 450°.
2. Heat olive oil in a large nonstick skillet over medium-high heat. Add onion;

cover and cook 3 minutes. Uncover and cook 11 minutes or until golden brown, stirring frequently.
3. Place pizza crust on a baking sheet. Combine sauce and tomatoes. Spread sauce mixture over pizza crust. Top with onion and cheese. Bake at 450° for 10 minutes or until crust is golden brown. Sprinkle with basil. Cut into 6 wedges. Yield: 6 servings (serving size: 1 wedge).

CALORIES 285 (29% from fat); FAT 9.2g (sat 3.8g, mono 4g, poly 1g); PROTEIN 11.6g; CARB 38.4g; FIBER 1.4g; CHOL 7mg; IRON 2.6mg; SODIUM 577mg; CALC 238mg

inspired vegetarian

Dynamic Duos

Hearty soups team with fruity salads in a fresh twist on dinner.

Menu 1

Fennel and Apple Salad with Lemon-Shallot Dressing

Vegetable Soup with Corn Dumplings

Fennel and Apple Salad with Lemon-Shallot Dressing

Any lettuce will do, but we liked Boston.

½   cup minced shallots (about 3)
¼   cup fresh lemon juice
2   tablespoons water
2   tablespoons olive oil
2   teaspoons red wine vinegar
1   teaspoon sugar
½   teaspoon salt
½   teaspoon black pepper
2   cups chopped Braeburn or Gala apple (about 1 pound)
2   cups thinly sliced fennel bulb (about 2 small bulbs)
16   cups torn Boston lettuce (about 8 small heads)

1. Combine first 8 ingredients in a small bowl, stirring with a whisk.

2. Place apple and fennel in a large bowl. Spoon 1 tablespoon dressing over apple mixture, tossing to coat. Add remaining dressing and lettuce, tossing to coat. Yield: 8 servings (serving size: 2 cups).

CALORIES 91 (37% from fat); FAT 3.7g (sat 0.5g, mono 2.5g, poly 0.4g); PROTEIN 2g; CARB 14.9g; FIBER 3.8g; CHOL 0mg; IRON 0.8mg; SODIUM 165mg; CALC 51mg

Vegetable Soup with Corn Dumplings

If you plan to serve only a portion of this soup, refrigerate part of the dumpling batter for up to 24 hours to make fresh dumplings for the reheated soup.

SOUP:

- 1 tablespoon olive oil
- 4 cups finely chopped onion
- ⅛ teaspoon ground cloves
- 4 garlic cloves, minced
- 2 bay leaves
- 3 cups water
- 3 (14½-ounce) cans vegetable broth
- 1 (14½-ounce) can diced tomatoes, undrained
- 1½ cups (¼-inch) diced peeled sweet potato
- 1 (15-ounce) can navy beans, rinsed and drained
- 2 cups frozen whole-kernel corn, thawed
- 2 cups sliced zucchini (about 1 medium)
- ¼ cup chopped fresh parsley
- ⅛ teaspoon ground red pepper

DUMPLINGS:

- ¾ cup all-purpose flour
- 1 tablespoon cornmeal
- 1½ teaspoons baking powder
- 1 teaspoon sugar
- ½ teaspoon salt
- 1 tablespoon butter
- ½ cup fat-free milk
- ⅓ cup frozen whole-kernel corn, thawed

1. To prepare soup, heat oil in a large Dutch oven over medium heat. Add onion, cloves, garlic, and bay leaves; cook 10 minutes. Add water, broth, and tomatoes; bring to a boil. Add sweet potato and beans; cook 10 minutes. Stir in 2 cups corn, zucchini, parsley, and red pepper; bring to a boil. Reduce heat, and simmer 5 minutes. Discard bay leaves.

2. To prepare dumplings, lightly spoon flour into dry measuring cups; level with a knife. Combine flour and next 4 ingredients in a bowl; cut in butter with a pastry blender or 2 knives until mixture resembles coarse meal. Add milk and ⅓ cup corn; stir just until moist.

3. Bring soup to a boil. Drop dumpling dough by rounded tablespoonfuls into soup to form 8 dumplings. Cover, reduce heat, and cook over medium-low heat 10 minutes or until dumplings are done (do not boil). Yield: 8 servings (serving size: 1½ cups soup and 1 dumpling).

CALORIES 271 (16% from fat); FAT 4.9g (sat 1.3g, mono 1.9g, poly 0.7g); PROTEIN 11g; CARB 50.9g; FIBER 7.5g; CHOL 4mg; IRON 2.8mg; SODIUM 767mg; CALC 148mg

---

Menu 2
Spinach and Pear Salad
Cauliflower and Red-Pepper Chowder

Spinach and Pear Salad

Flat-leaf or baby spinach works best in this salad, but you can also use red-leaf.

- 2 tablespoons water
- 1½ tablespoons red-wine vinegar
- 1 tablespoon olive oil
- 1 tablespoon honey
- 2 teaspoons Dijon mustard
- ¼ teaspoon black pepper
- 1 Bosc or Anjou pear, cut lengthwise into 15 slices
- 8 cups torn spinach
- ¼ cup thinly sliced red onion

1. Combine first 6 ingredients in a small bowl, stirring with a whisk.
2. Place pear slices in a large bowl. Spoon 1 tablespoon dressing over pear; toss to coat. Add remaining dressing, spinach, and onion; toss to coat. Yield: 5 servings (serving size: about 1½ cups).

CALORIES 72 (41% from fat); FAT 3.3g (sat 0.4g, mono 2.1g, poly 0.4g); PROTEIN 1.8g; CARB 11g; FIBER 2.3g; CHOL 0mg; IRON 1.4mg; SODIUM 89mg; CALC 56mg

Cauliflower and Red-Pepper Chowder

This tastes better after it's chilled for a few hours and the flavors have had a chance to meld. Leaving a portion of the soup chunky gives the finished product a hearty consistency. Serve with baguettes or breadsticks.

- 1 tablespoon butter
- ⅔ cup minced shallots (about 4 large)
- ½ cup sliced celery
- 2 (14½-ounce) cans vegetable broth
- 1½ cups water
- 6 cups finely chopped cauliflower florets (about 1 head)
- 2 cups finely chopped red bell pepper (about 2 medium)
- 1 cup finely chopped peeled red potato
- 1 bay leaf
- 1 cup 2% reduced-fat milk
- ½ teaspoon black pepper
- 3 tablespoons minced fresh or 1 tablespoon dried basil
- 5 tablespoons fat-free sour cream

1. Melt butter in a Dutch oven over medium heat. Add shallots and celery; cook 5 minutes, stirring constantly. Add broth and water; bring to a boil. Add cauliflower, bell pepper, potato, and bay leaf; return to a boil. Reduce heat, and simmer 20 minutes or until potato is tender. Stir in milk and black pepper. Cool slightly; discard bay leaf.
2. Place 1½ cups soup in a blender or food processor; process until smooth. Pour pureed soup into a large bowl. Repeat procedure with 1½ cups soup. Return pureed soup to pan, and stir in basil. Bring to a boil over medium-high heat, stirring frequently. Remove from heat. Spoon 2 cups soup into each of 5 bowls; top each serving with 1 tablespoon sour cream. Yield: 5 servings.

CALORIES 168 (31% from fat); FAT 5.7g (sat 3.1g, mono 1g, poly 0.3g); PROTEIN 8.6g; CARB 24.8g; FIBER 5.3g; CHOL 15mg; IRON 1.5mg; SODIUM 809mg; CALC 130mg

Tuscan Chickpea Soup

Garlic, rosemary, balsamic vinegar, and Parmesan cheese deliver authentic Mediterranean flavors.

- 2 tablespoons olive oil
- 2 cups finely chopped onion
- 8 garlic cloves, minced
- 4 cups water
- 1 teaspoon minced fresh or ¼ teaspoon dried rosemary
- ¾ teaspoon salt
- ¼ teaspoon black pepper
- 3 (15½-ounce) cans chickpeas (garbanzo beans), rinsed and drained
- 1 (14½-ounce) can diced tomatoes, undrained
- 1 to 2 tablespoons balsamic vinegar
- 6 tablespoons (1½ ounces) grated fresh Parmesan cheese

1. Heat olive oil in a Dutch oven over medium heat. Add onion and garlic, and cook 10 minutes, stirring frequently. Stir in water and next 5 ingredients, and bring to a boil. Reduce heat, and simmer 20 minutes.
2. Place 2 cups soup in a blender or food processor, and process until smooth. Pour pureed soup into a bowl. Repeat procedure with 2 cups soup. Return pureed soup to pan. Stir in vinegar, and bring to a boil. Remove from heat. Spoon 1½ cups soup into each of 6 bowls; sprinkle each serving with 1 tablespoon cheese. Yield: 6 servings.

CALORIES 373 (22% from fat); FAT 9.1g (sat 2.1g, mono 4.5g, poly 1.6g); PROTEIN 15g; CARB 59.7g; FIBER 11.4g; CHOL 5mg; IRON 3.7mg; SODIUM 955mg; CALC 197mg

Orange and Arugula Salad

The honey in the vinaigrette balances the salad's peppery, citrusy flavors.

- 3 tablespoons fresh lemon juice
- 1 tablespoon olive oil
- ¾ teaspoon honey
- 2 garlic cloves, crushed
- 6 navel oranges
- 3 cups trimmed arugula
- 6 tablespoons (1½ ounces) crumbled feta cheese

1. Combine first 4 ingredients in a small bowl, stirring with a whisk.
2. Peel oranges, and cut each crosswise into 6 slices. Arrange 6 orange slices on each of 6 arugula-lined plates. Sprinkle 1 tablespoon feta over each salad, and drizzle each with 1 tablespoon dressing. Yield: 6 servings.

CALORIES 118 (34% from fat); FAT 4.4g (sat 1.7g, mono 2.1g, poly 0.3g); PROTEIN 3.1g; CARB 18.8g; FIBER 3.6g; CHOL 8mg; IRON 0.4mg; SODIUM 109mg; CALC 121mg

cooking light profile

Laugh Track

For funny lady Myra J., healthy living is no joke.

Keeping her hectic life in balance is a challenge for Myra J., one of the on-air personalities of ABC Radio Networks' nationally syndicated *Tom Joyner Morning Show.* But Myra manages with good nutrition, exercise, and loads of laughter.

Comedy is indeed Myra's passion. But she also has a love affair with food—especially fresh produce. She loves spicy dishes and Asian cuisine, particularly Thai, and is known for whipping up a mean stir-fry of peppers, onions, cabbage, eggplant, zucchini, soft tofu, and chiles. Now she shares this recipe, Tangy Stir-Fried Vegetables, with *Cooking Light.*

Tangy Stir-Fried Vegetables

Myra likes this dish because it's fresh, quick, and easy—all necessities with her busy travel schedule. Serve with brown rice.

- 1 cup cubed reduced-fat extra-firm tofu (about 4 ounces)
- ¼ cup low-sodium soy sauce
- 2 tablespoons honey
- 1 teaspoon bottled ground fresh ginger (such as Spice World)
- 4 garlic cloves, sliced
- 3 serrano chiles, seeded and sliced
- 1 teaspoon dark sesame oil
- 1½ cups vertically sliced yellow onion
- 1 cup (3 x ⅛-inch) julienne-cut red bell pepper
- 1 cup (3 x ⅛-inch) julienne-cut yellow bell pepper
- ⅓ cup (⅛-inch) diagonally cut carrot
- 6 cups sliced napa (Chinese) cabbage (about 1 small head)
- 2 cups broccoli florets
- ¼ cup chopped green onions

1. Combine first 6 ingredients in a small bowl; marinate 20 minutes. Heat oil in a large skillet over medium-high heat. Add onion, bell peppers, and carrot; sauté 5 minutes or until crisp-tender, stirring frequently. Add tofu mixture, cabbage, broccoli, and onions; cook 5 minutes or until broccoli is crisp-tender, stirring occasionally. Yield: 5 servings (serving size: 1¼ cups).

CALORIES 128 (11% from fat); FAT 1.5g (sat 0.2g, mono 0.4g, poly 0.7g); PROTEIN 6.4g; CARB 26g; FIBER 5.7g; CHOL 0mg; IRON 1.6mg; SODIUM 487mg; CALC 83mg

Bellissimo!

These five pasta sauces are simple and authentic— and worth making from scratch.

In an Italian kitchen, the process of cooking and saucing pasta is an act of improvisation based on what's fresh and readily available. Whatever the sauce, it's most often cooked quickly while the noodles boil, then tossed with—rather than dolloped on top of—the hot cooked pasta to coat each piece or strand.

Americans who are accustomed to bottled sauces will be pleased by the speed and ease of classic Italian pasta preparations, which may include a sauce as simple as sautéed aromatic vegetables, fresh herbs, and perhaps some wine or broth. These recipes were developed to capture the spirit of five classic pasta sauces—follow them to the letter, or consider them an inspiration for your own improvisation.

Pesto

Pesto is a puree of fresh basil, garlic, olive oil, pine nuts, and Parmesan and Romano cheeses. It's typically tossed with hot *trenette* (wide, flat pasta similar to linguine) or cooked potatoes. The word *pesto* means "pounded" and refers to using a mortar and pestle.

"Pesto originated in the port of Genoa as a quick meal for sailors," explains Sally Maraventano, author of *Festa del Giardino: A Harvest of Recipes and Family Memories.* "They could keep the pesto under a layer of olive oil in a cool spot. All they had to do for a meal on the ship was boil the pasta and toss it with the pesto."

But Maraventano attributes the popularity of the dish to its flavor and ease of preparation, not its shelf life. "It's a quick meal for busy people," she says. Plus, it's a great source of "the fresh garden taste of basil that you can enjoy all year long."

Pesto

Avoid packing the basil leaves when you measure them so you won't use too much.

    4 cups fresh basil leaves
    2 tablespoons pine nuts
    2 tablespoons extra-virgin olive
       oil
    ¼ teaspoon salt
    2 garlic cloves, peeled
    ½ cup (2 ounces) grated fresh
       Parmesan cheese
    2 tablespoons grated fresh Romano
       cheese
    2 teaspoons butter, softened
    2 cups uncooked penne (about 8
       ounces)

1. Combine first 5 ingredients in a food processor; process until finely minced. Place in a large bowl. Stir in cheeses and butter until blended.
2. Cook pasta according to package directions, omitting salt and fat. Drain in a colander over a bowl, reserving 3 tablespoons cooking liquid. Add pasta and reserved cooking liquid to pesto, tossing to coat. Yield: 4 servings (serving size: about 1 cup pasta).

CALORIES 390 (39% from fat); FAT 17g (sat 5.4g, mono 6.5g, poly 2.1g); PROTEIN 14.5g; CARB 45.3g; FIBER 3.2g; CHOL 18mg; IRON 4mg; SODIUM 352mg; CALC 281mg

Salsa dei Mollusci

Italy's many miles of seacoast inspire countless regional variations on pasta with clams. Most of the sauces are made by simply tossing tiny clams in their shells with hot olive oil and chopped garlic, then moistening them with wine or broth.

"Italian clams, particularly the common small, round ones from the Adriatic, are very savory, and little or nothing needs to be done to build up their flavor," writes Marcella Hazan in *Essentials of Classic Italian Cooking.* Perhaps national pride overcomes her objectivity, though. Hazan continues, "Clams from other seas are blander, and you must look for help from external sources to approximate the natural spiciness of a clam sauce you'd be likely to experience in Italy." We rely on tomatoes and basil to boost the flavor in our Clam Sauce.

Clam Sauce

    3   (6½-ounce) cans minced clams,
        undrained
    1   tablespoon olive oil
    2   garlic cloves, minced
 1⅓   cups chopped tomato
    2   tablespoons minced fresh parsley
    1   teaspoon crushed red pepper
    ½   cup dry white wine
    4   cups hot cooked fettuccine (about
        8 ounces uncooked pasta)
    2   tablespoons chopped fresh basil

1. Drain clams in a colander over a bowl, reserving liquid.
2. Heat oil in a large nonstick skillet over medium heat. Add garlic; cook 30 seconds, stirring constantly. Add tomato, parsley, and pepper; cook 1 minute. Add wine; cook 30 seconds. Add reserved clam liquid and pasta, tossing to coat; cook 3 minutes or until liquid almost evaporates, stirring frequently. Stir in clams and basil. Serve immediately. Yield: 4 servings (serving size: 1 cup).

CALORIES 289 (20% from fat); FAT 6.3g (sat 1.1g, mono 3.3g, poly 1.1g); PROTEIN 9.8g; CARB 48.5g; FIBER 2.8g; CHOL 64mg; IRON 3.7mg; SODIUM 316mg; CALC 49mg

Marinara

As basic as it is, no one seems to have the true story on marinara. If you look it up in a dozen Italian cookbooks, you're likely to find as many different explanations of what marinara is and how it's made. Two basic concepts predominate, however.

Some say that marinara is a very simple fresh tomato sauce with garlic and olive oil. *Alla marinara* means made in a quick and simple way, with just the few ingredients easily available to fishermen, writes Giuliano Bugialli in *Bugialli on Pasta.* He continues, "Some people mistakenly think the phrase means 'with seafood.'"

Other authorities, like Arthur Schwartz in *Naples at Table,* say the association of marinara with seafood is no mistake. The name, they contend, is derived from the Italian word *mare,* which means sea. According to Schwartz, "*Marinara* in Campania is most often a tomato-based sauce with Gaeta olives, capers, anchovies, garlic, and sometimes preserved (canned or jarred) tuna."

In America, to add to the confusion, the word *marinara* is used to refer to any tomato sauce made without meat. Perhaps Italian cooking authority Marcella Hazan takes the wisest approach to the issue: In an extensive section about tomato sauces in her definitive cookbook, *Essentials of Classic Italian Cooking,* she never once mentions the term.

Marinara Sauce

If fresh tomatoes aren't available, you can substitute a 28-ounce can of whole tomatoes, undrained and chopped, plus a 28-ounce can of diced tomatoes, undrained. To balance the flavor and thicken the sauce, add 3 tablespoons of tomato paste and 1 teaspoon of sugar to the canned tomatoes.

  1 tablespoon olive oil
1½ tablespoons minced garlic
  6 pounds coarsely chopped peeled tomato (about 6 cups)
 ¾ teaspoon salt
 ½ teaspoon black pepper
 ¼ cup chopped fresh basil
 ¼ cup chopped fresh parsley
  8 cups hot cooked spaghetti (about 1 pound uncooked pasta)

1. Heat oil in a large saucepan over medium heat. Add garlic; cook 2 minutes, stirring frequently. Add tomato, salt, and pepper; bring to a boil. Reduce heat; simmer 25 minutes, stirring occasionally. Stir in basil and parsley, and cook 1 minute. Serve over pasta. Yield: 6 servings (serving size: 1 cup sauce and 1⅓ cups pasta).

CALORIES 384 (12% from fat); FAT 5.1g (sat 0.7g, mono 2g, poly 1.3g); PROTEIN 13.1g; CARB 75.1g; FIBER 8.4g; CHOL 0mg; IRON 5mg; SODIUM 338mg; CALC 48mg

Mushroom Sauce

1½ cups dried porcini mushrooms (about 1½ ounces)
  2 teaspoons olive oil
 ½ cup finely chopped prosciutto (about 2 ounces)
 ½ cup finely chopped onion
  4 cups sliced cremini or button mushrooms (about 8 ounces)
 ½ teaspoon grated lemon rind
 ½ teaspoon salt
 ¼ teaspoon black pepper
  2 garlic cloves, minced
  1 cup fat-free, less-sodium chicken broth
 ¾ cup dry red wine
  1 tablespoon cornstarch
  1 tablespoon water
  4 cups hot cooked cavatappi (about 2 cups uncooked pasta)

1. Combine boiling water and porcini mushrooms in a bowl; cover and let stand 30 minutes. Drain. Rinse and coarsely chop porcini mushrooms.
2. Heat oil in a medium skillet over medium-high heat. Add prosciutto, and sauté 1 minute. Add onion; sauté 3 minutes or until tender. Stir in porcini mushrooms, cremini mushrooms, and next 4 ingredients; cook 4 minutes or until browned, stirring frequently. Stir in broth and wine, scraping pan to loosen browned bits. Bring to a boil; cook 3 minutes. Combine cornstarch and 1 tablespoon water in a small bowl. Add cornstarch mixture to pan; bring to a boil. Cook 1 minute, stirring constantly. Add pasta, tossing to coat. Yield: 4 servings (serving size: about 1½ cups pasta).

CALORIES 304 (15% from fat); FAT 5.1g (sat 1g, mono 2.6g, poly 1g); PROTEIN 15.4g; CARB 48.9g; FIBER 4.6g; CHOL 8mg; IRON 4.9mg; SODIUM 627mg; CALC 24mg

Salsa di Funghi

In the spring and autumn throughout Italy, markets are flush with morels, honey mushrooms, oyster mushrooms, porcini, and many other specimens. Dedicated foragers make a cottage industry of picking and selling mushrooms, or *funghi,* to Italian cooks who are crazy for them. Many of these mushrooms find themselves paired with pasta.

"The ideal mushroom sauce for pasta in Emilia-Romagna is made in spring and autumn with fresh porcini or other fresh wild mushrooms," explains Mary Beth Clark, owner of the International Cooking School of Italian Food and Wine in Bologna, Italy. The porcini are frequently prepared *al trifolato:* sautéed in olive oil with garlic and fresh flat-leaf parsley before white wine and stock are added. Since fresh porcini are hard to come by in the United States, we've combined dried porcini with supermarket cremini (baby portobellos) to create our flavorful Mushroom Sauce.

Alfredo

Fettuccine all'Alfredo might have languished as an indulgence in a Roman restaurant if it weren't for the star-making power of Hollywood. John Mariani relates the story in *The Dictionary of Italian Food and Drink:* Restaurateur Alfred Di Lelio tossed hot, fresh egg noodles with melted butter and the soft, sweet core of Parmigiano-Reggiano cheese to create the simple, luxurious dish that Mary Pickford and Douglas Fairbanks Jr. fell in love with on their 1927 honeymoon. Back in Hollywood, the movie stars spread the word about Di Lelio's creation. American chefs began making it, shortening the name to fettuccine Alfredo. Along the way, heavy cream was added to the sauce, and the dish evolved into an international favorite.

Alfredo Sauce

(pictured on page 296)

We used half-and-half instead of whipping cream and decreased the amount of butter and cheese ever so slightly to lower the fat by about 10 grams per serving.

 1 pound uncooked fettuccine
 1 tablespoon butter
1¼ cups half-and-half
 ¾ cup (3 ounces) grated fresh
   Parmesan cheese
 ½ teaspoon salt
 ¼ teaspoon black pepper

1. Cook pasta according to package directions, omitting salt and fat.
2. Melt butter in a large skillet over medium heat. Add half-and-half, cheese, salt, and pepper; cook 1 minute, stirring constantly. Reduce heat; add pasta, tossing gently to coat. Yield: 6 servings (serving size: 1½ cups).

CALORIES 427 (31% from fat); FAT 14.6g (sat 7.8g, mono 4.2g, poly 1.3g); PROTEIN 17.2g; CARB 56.5g; FIBER 2.1g; CHOL 105mg; IRON 3.6mg; SODIUM 479mg; CALC 245mg

How to Cook Middle Eastern

The mystical yet simple cuisine of the Middle East contrasts exotic tastes with comforting foods.

From Morocco to Iran, Middle Eastern cuisine is sensuous, full of rich flavors and aromas. The similarities in food among Middle Eastern countries reflect the unifying influences of the Arab conquests. However, geographic and cultural distinctions have resulted in four major culinary styles.

Four Middle Eastern Culinary Styles

Iran: The most exquisite and refined dishes are prepared in Iran. The cuisine is based on long-grain rice, which is mixed with meats, vegetables, fruits, and nuts, or served plain and accompanied by sauces. Iranians use a variety of gentle spices, especially cinnamon, allspice, and saffron; meat dishes are often served with raisins and fruits such as dates, quinces, cherries, apples, and peaches. Iranians also like sweet and sour flavors, combining vinegar or lemon juice with sugar. Fresh herbs and yogurt are almost always on the table. Dried limes provide a distinctive flavor in stews and soups; another comes from dried sumac, a dark, wine-colored berry.

Syria, Lebanon, Jordan, and Egypt: Cooking is similar in these countries (with the exception of local specialties), City cooking is based on rice, while the country staple is cracked wheat. A variety of *kibbeh*—pies with shells made from cracked wheat and lamb pounded to a paste, and fillings of fried onion, ground meat, and pine nuts—are Syrian and Lebanese specialties. Pomegranate syrup and tamarind lend a delicate sweet-and-sour taste to certain dishes; lemon juice and sumac add sharpness. Mint and flat-leaf parsley are favorite herbs. The distinctive flavor of Egypt is crushed coriander seed, which is fried with garlic or mixed with cumin. Cardamom and turmeric also add flavor.

Turkey: Turkey is famous for its kebabs, pilafs, stuffed vegetables, yogurt dishes, nut sauces, and extraordinary variety of *boreks* (savory pies) filled with cheese, spinach, minced meat, or mashed pumpkin. Favorite spices for meat are cinnamon and allspice; dill, mint, and flat-leaf parsley are favorite herbs; toasted pine nuts and dribbles of red paprika mixed with oil are common garnishes.

North Africa: The fourth distinctive cooking style is found in North Africa. Cumin and chiles are used to flavor cold vegetable appetizers as well as fish dishes. An extraordinary blend of flavors—which include cinnamon, ginger, saffron, mint, and cilantro—is a feature of the high cuisine, which may be very delicate or peppery hot, and where savory may be married with sweet. *Harissa,* a paste of garlic and chile peppers that makes most Tunisian dishes fiery, is added in Morocco with a light hand. Olives and preserved lemons are also used; meat is partnered with vegetables or with such fruit as prunes or quinces. In addition, North Africa is famous for its paper-thin pancakes, its savory stews called tagines, and its steamed dishes.

Burghul bi Jibn wal Batinjan
Bulgur with Cheese and Eggplant

Combining bulgur with eggplant and *halumi* cheese, this Syrian favorite (pronounced boor-GHOUL bee jeebn wal bet-in-JAN) makes a lovely vegetarian entrée. Coarse- or medium-ground bulgur works best. Halumi is a firm, chewy, rather salty cheese. To reduce its saltiness, soak the cheese in a bowl of fresh water for half an hour. You can also substitute mozzarella.

- 1½ cups (6 ounces) diced halumi cheese
- 6 cups (1-inch) cubed eggplant (about 1 pound)
- ¾ teaspoon salt, divided
- 4 teaspoons olive oil, divided
- 4 cups vertically sliced onion
- 2 cups uncooked coarse-ground bulgur
- 3¼ cups boiling water
- ¼ teaspoon black pepper

1. Soak cheese in a bowl of water 30 minutes. Drain.

2. Place eggplant in a colander; sprinkle with ½ teaspoon salt. Toss well. Drain 30 minutes. Rinse and pat dry with paper towels.

3. Heat 1 teaspoon oil in a large nonstick skillet over medium-high heat. Add onion; sauté 15 minutes or until golden brown, stirring frequently. Add ¼ teaspoon salt, bulgur, boiling water, and pepper; bring to a boil. Cover, reduce heat to medium-low, and simmer 15 minutes or until liquid is absorbed.

4. Heat 1 teaspoon oil in a large nonstick skillet over medium-high heat. Add eggplant; sauté 10 minutes or until browned. Combine cheese, bulgur mixture, eggplant, and 2 teaspoons oil in a Dutch oven. Toss well to coat; place over medium heat 5 minutes or until cheese is soft. Serve hot. Yield: 6 servings (serving size: 1½ cups).

CALORIES 325 (30% from fat); FAT 11g (sat 4.8g, mono 2.3g, poly 0.6g); PROTEIN 13.5g; CARB 47.1g; FIBER 12g; CHOL 21mg; IRON 1.6mg; SODIUM 622mg; CALC 306mg

How to Make Bulgur with Cheese and Eggplant

1. *Sprinkle eggplant with salt, let stand 30 minutes, and drain. This removes some of the moisture and bitterness from the eggplant.*

2. *Use just a small amount of oil for browning the eggplant. This requires a nonstick skillet.*

Batrik
Bulgur Salad with Nuts

Bulgur—wheat that has been steamed, dried, and ground—is the basis of many salads in the Middle East. You might have encountered it in *tabbouleh*, the mint and parsley salad made famous by Lebanese restaurants. In this nutty Turkish salad (pronounced bah-TREEK), the bulgur is not cooked but becomes soft as it absorbs fresh tomato juice.

- 1 pound coarsely chopped plum tomato
- ¾ cup uncooked bulgur
- 1 teaspoon tomato paste
- 1 tablespoon olive oil
- ¼ teaspoon salt
- Dash of crushed red pepper
- ½ cup finely chopped green onions
- ⅓ cup finely chopped walnuts

1. Place tomato in a food processor; process until smooth. Combine tomato, bulgur, and tomato paste in a large bowl. Cover and let stand 1 hour. Stir in oil, salt, and pepper. Stir in onions and nuts immediately before serving. Yield: 4 servings (serving size: ¾ cup).

CALORIES 218 (44% from fat); FAT 10.7g (sat 1.2g, mono 3.5g, poly 5.3g); PROTEIN 6g; CARB 28.6g; FIBER 7.1g; CHOL 0mg; IRON 1.5mg; SODIUM 163mg; CALC 29mg

Khoshaf bil Mishmish
Macerated Apricots and Nuts

Throughout the Middle East, the usual conclusion to a family meal is fresh fruit, and dried fruit and nuts or fruit preserves are offered with coffee. This simple, fragrant dessert (pronounced kho-SHAF beel mish-MISH), with macerated—rather than cooked—dried fruit, is a Syrian specialty of the Muslim month of Ramadan, when it's eaten to break the daily fast. Rose water is the distilled essence of rose petals, a distinguishing flavor of Middle Eastern puddings and pastries (as is orange blossom water).

- 3 cups boiling water
- 2½ cups dried apricots
- 2 tablespoons sugar
- ¼ cup raisins
- ¼ cup slivered almonds, toasted
- 2 tablespoons pine nuts, toasted
- 2 tablespoons chopped pistachios, toasted
- 1 teaspoon rose water (optional)

1. Combine boiling water and apricots in a medium bowl; soak 5 minutes. Strain apricots in a colander over a bowl, reserving liquid. Place reserved liquid, ½ cup apricots, and sugar in a blender; process until smooth. Pour pureed mixture into bowl. Stir in remaining apricots, raisins, and remaining ingredients. Serve chilled or at room temperature. Yield: 8 servings (serving size: ½ cup).

CALORIES 190 (18% from fat); FAT 3.9g (sat 0.4g, mono 2.1g, poly 1.2g); PROTEIN 3.6g; CARB 39.8g; FIBER 5.5g; CHOL 0mg; IRON 2.9mg; SODIUM 9mg; CALC 37mg

Megadarra
Brown Lentils and Rice with Caramelized Onions

Megadarra (me-ga-DAR-ra) is immensely popular in Egypt—as it is in the rest of the Arab world. (Elsewhere, the dish is pronounced *mu-jah*-DRA.) It's served either warm or at room temperature as a *mezze*, or appetizer, often accompanied by yogurt. Large quantities of dark caramelized onions are the best part.

¼ cup extra-virgin olive oil, divided
7 cups vertically sliced onion
4½ cups water
1¼ cups dried brown lentils
1¼ cups long-grain rice
1 teaspoon salt
¼ teaspoon black pepper

1. Heat 3 tablespoons oil in a large skillet over medium-low heat. Add onion; cover and cook 15 minutes or until soft, stirring occasionally. Uncover and increase heat to medium; cook 25 minutes or until golden brown, stirring occasionally. Keep warm.
2. While onion cooks, bring 4½ cups water to a boil in a large saucepan. Add lentils; cook 20 minutes or until tender. Stir in ½ cup caramelized onion, rice, salt, and pepper. Cover and cook 25 minutes or until lentils and rice are tender. Spoon lentil mixture into a shallow dish; top with remaining onion. Drizzle 1 tablespoon oil over lentils. Yield: 11 servings (serving size: ½ cup).

CALORIES 222 (22% from fat); FAT 5.4g (sat 0.8g, mono 3.7g, poly 0.6g); PROTEIN 8.5g; CARB 35.6g; FIBER 8.3g; CHOL 0mg; IRON 3.1mg; SODIUM 222mg; CALC 34mg

How to Caramelize Onions

Browned onions play an important role in Middle Eastern cooking. But the extent of browning varies depending on the dish.

To cut an onion vertically, slice it in half from root to stem. Turn cut side down, and cut into slivers.

For the **Megadarra**, *the onions are caramelized. To do this, cook the onions covered for 15 minutes. This allows them to soften. Then cook them uncovered for 25 minutes, which allows them to brown. Once caramelized, onions will be brown and very soft.*

For the **Burghul bi Jibn wal Batinjan** *(recipe on page 288), sauté the onions in oil 15 minutes or until golden. With this procedure, onions will be slightly browned but will retain their shape and texture.*

Tagine Kefta Mkawra
Tagine of Meatballs in Tomato Sauce with Eggs

This Moroccan dish (pronounced tah-JEEN KEF-ta em-KAR-rah) is beautiful and delicious. You can cook the meatballs in their sauce in advance, reheat, and add the eggs just before serving. In Morocco, the cooking is finished in a wide earthenware pot, also called a tagine, which goes on top of the fire. Serve the entrée with plenty of warm bread. The traditional meat is lamb, but ground beef works, too.

MEATBALLS:
1½ pounds ground round or lamb
2 cups finely chopped onion
3 tablespoons finely chopped fresh flat-leaf parsley
1 teaspoon ground cumin
1 teaspoon ground cinnamon
¾ teaspoon salt
½ teaspoon ground ginger
¼ teaspoon black pepper
¼ teaspoon ground red pepper
Cooking spray

SAUCE:
3 cups chopped onion
4 cups chopped tomato (about 1½ pounds)
1 teaspoon sugar
½ teaspoon salt
2 garlic cloves, minced
1 jalapeño pepper, seeded and finely chopped
3 tablespoons chopped fresh flat-leaf parsley
3 tablespoons minced fresh cilantro
3 large eggs
Fresh cilantro sprigs (optional)

1. Preheat oven to 400°.
2. To prepare meatballs, combine first 9 ingredients in a medium bowl. Shape mixture into 1-inch meatballs; place on a broiler pan coated with cooking spray. Bake meatballs at 400° for 12 minutes or until done.
3. To prepare sauce, heat a large Dutch oven coated with cooking spray over medium-high heat. Add 3 cups onion; cook 3 minutes, stirring occasionally.
Continued

Stir in tomato and next 4 ingredients; bring to a simmer over medium-high heat. Reduce heat to medium; cook 20 minutes, stirring occasionally. Add meatballs, cover and cook 5 minutes. Stir in 3 tablespoons parsley and minced cilantro. Gently break eggs over simmering liquid; cover and cook 10 minutes or until eggs are set. Garnish with cilantro sprigs, if desired. Yield: 6 servings (serving size: 1 cup meatball mixture and ½ egg).

CALORIES 268 (37% from fat); FAT 11g (sat 3.9g, mono 4.4g, poly 0.9g); PROTEIN 23.5g; CARB 19.7g; FIBER 4.3g; CHOL 137mg; IRON 3.6mg; SODIUM 600mg; CALC 67mg

Ferakh bel Hummus
Chicken with Chickpeas

This Egyptian dish (pronounced fi-ra-KAH bel hoo-MUS) can be served with plain rice. The mix of turmeric, garlic, and lemon yields a special flavor characteristic of the area. Chickpeas are a staple of the Middle East.

    1 tablespoon vegetable oil
    1 cup finely chopped onion
    ¾ teaspoon ground turmeric
    2 chicken drumsticks (about ½ pound), skinned
    2 chicken thighs (about ½ pound), skinned
    2 chicken breast halves (about 1 pound), skinned
   2½ cups water
    2 tablespoons fresh lemon juice
    ½ teaspoon salt
    ¼ teaspoon black pepper
    3 garlic cloves, crushed
    2 (15½-ounce) cans chickpeas (garbanzo beans), drained

1. Heat oil in a large Dutch oven over medium heat. Add onion, and cook 12 minutes or until onion is golden, stirring frequently. Stir in turmeric. Add chicken to pan, turning to coat. Add water and next 4 ingredients; bring to a boil. Cover, reduce heat, and simmer 1 hour or until chicken is tender. Remove from heat.
2. Remove chicken from broth. Remove chicken from bones, and cut meat into bite-size pieces. Discard bones. Return

chicken to pan, and add chickpeas. Cook 5 minutes or until chickpeas are thoroughly heated. Yield: 6 servings (serving size: 1 cup).

CALORIES 275 (25% from fat); FAT 7.5g (sat 1g, mono 2.4g, poly 3.6g); PROTEIN 25.7g; CARB 26.1g; FIBER 6.3g; CHOL 59mg; IRON 3.1mg; SODIUM 499mg; CALC 68mg

Ajlouk Qura'a
Mashed-Zucchini Salad

In this Tunisian salad (pronounced aj-LUKE coo-rah-AH), served as an appetizer with bread, the rich flavoring lifts the blandness of zucchini. Harissa, a spicy North African sauce made with chile peppers and garlic, is available in specialty markets. You can use a good pinch of ground chile pepper instead. (Begin with a small dash—you can always add more.) Serve with pita bread.

   1¼ pounds zucchini, cut into 1-inch-thick slices
    1 tablespoon fresh lemon juice
    1 tablespoon extra-virgin olive oil
    ½ teaspoon salt
    ½ teaspoon caraway seeds
    ½ teaspoon ground coriander
    ½ teaspoon harissa
    1 garlic clove, crushed
    ¼ cup (2 ounces) crumbled feta cheese

1. Place zucchini in a large saucepan; cover with water to 1 inch above zucchini. Bring to a boil, and cook 20 minutes or until zucchini is very tender. Drain. While zucchini is still in colander, coarsely mash zucchini with a fork; drain.
2. Combine juice and next 6 ingredients in a bowl; stir with a whisk. Add zucchini; toss well. Sprinkle with cheese. Yield: 8 servings (serving size: ¼ cup zucchini and 1½ teaspoons cheese).

CALORIES 39 (65% from fat); FAT 2.8g (sat 1g, mono 1.5g, poly 0.2g); PROTEIN 1.6g; CARB 2.7g; FIBER 1g; CHOL 4mg; IRON 0.4mg; SODIUM 201mg; CALC 37mg

Try New Things Menu
serves 6

Cornish hens make a nice change from chicken. Bulgur consists of wheat kernels that have been steamed, dried, and crushed—they create a hearty pilaflike side. Look for olive bottled tapenade near the gourmet cheeses.

Cornish Hens with Bulgur, Raisins, and Pine Nuts

Green salad

Olive tapenade with pita bread

Hamam Mahshi bi Burghul
Cornish Hens with Bulgur, Raisins, and Pine Nuts

Usually made with pigeons instead of Cornish hens, this dish (pronounced ha-MAM mah-SHE bee boor-GHOUL) is one of the delicacies of Egypt, where villagers along the Nile River raise pigeons. The stuffing is baked separately and served alongside the hens.

CORNISH HENS:

    3 (1½-pound) Cornish hens, skinned
    ½ teaspoon salt
    ¼ teaspoon black pepper
    2 cups coarsely chopped onion
    3 tablespoons fresh lemon juice
    2 tablespoons vegetable oil
   1½ teaspoons ground cardamom
   1½ teaspoons ground cinnamon
    ¾ teaspoon ground allspice
   Cooking spray

BULGUR:

    ¾ cup currants
   3⅓ cups fat-free, less-sodium chicken broth
    2 cups uncooked bulgur
   1½ teaspoons ground cinnamon
    ½ teaspoon salt
    ¼ teaspoon black pepper
    ⅓ cup pine nuts, toasted
    3 tablespoons butter, cut into small pieces

1. To prepare hens, sprinkle with ½ teaspoon salt and ¼ teaspoon pepper. Place onion and next 5 ingredients in a food processor; process until smooth. Combine hens and onion mixture in a large zip-top plastic bag. Seal bag; marinate in refrigerator 1 hour, turning bag occasionally. Remove hens from bag; discard marinade.

2. Preheat oven to 400°.

3. Place hens on a broiler pan coated with cooking spray; bake at 400° for 35 minutes or until thermometer registers 180°.

4. To prepare bulgur, soak currants in a bowl of water 15 minutes. Drain; set aside. Bring broth to a boil in a medium saucepan. Add bulgur and next 3 ingredients; cover, reduce heat, and simmer 15 minutes or until liquid is absorbed. Stir in currants, pine nuts, and butter. Yield: 6 servings (serving size: ½ Cornish hen and 1½ cups bulgur mixture).

CALORIES 506 (29% from fat); FAT 16.4g (sat 5.1g, mono 4.8g, poly 4.6g); PROTEIN 39.5g; CARB 54.4g; FIBER 11.2g; CHOL 144mg; IRON 3.9mg; SODIUM 579mg; CALC 79mg

Samak Tarator
Poached Fish with Pine Nut Sauce

Tarator (tara-TOR) is the name used in different countries for a sauce made with a variety of nuts. This sharp, garlicky version with pine nuts belongs to Syria and Lebanon. In Egypt, the sauce is served over whole fish at grand buffet parties.

FISH:

    2   cups water
    ¼   teaspoon salt
    6   (6-ounce) salmon fillets (about
        1 inch thick)

SAUCE:

    1   cup water
    2   (1-ounce) slices white bread, crusts
        removed
    ½   cup pine nuts
    3   tablespoons fresh lemon juice
    ¼   teaspoon salt
    ⅛   teaspoon white pepper
    1   garlic clove, crushed
    3   tablespoons clam juice

1. To prepare fish, bring 2 cups water to a boil in a large skillet. Add ¼ teaspoon salt and fish. Return to a boil; reduce heat, and simmer 8 minutes or until fish flakes easily when tested with a fork. Remove fish from pan. Cover and refrigerate fish until chilled.

2. To prepare sauce, place 1 cup water in a shallow dish. Dip bread into water, and remove; squeeze bread to remove excess moisture. Combine bread, pine nuts, and next 4 ingredients in a food processor. With processor on, slowly pour clam juice through food chute, and process until smooth. Serve over chilled fish. Yield: 6 servings (serving size: 1 fillet and 2 tablespoons sauce).

CALORIES 321 (47% from fat); FAT 16.7g (sat 3.5g, mono 6.9g, poly 4.9g); PROTEIN 34.7g; CARB 7.3g; FIBER 0.7g; CHOL 81mg; IRON 1.9mg; SODIUM 335mg; CALC 31mg

lighten up

Great Gratin

We transformed a favorite common-ground recipe into a healthy dish that pleases all.

Greg Lundstrom of Oak Forest, Illinois, is a vegetarian. His wife, Denise, is not. So it's important that they try to find common ground when it comes to dinner. When Denise first came across the recipe for Potato Gratin with Goat Cheese and Garlic she knew it would be a big hit. She could have it as a side with chicken or fish, and Greg could have a heftier serving as a main dish with a salad and vegetable.

With 15.4 grams of fat per serving, this ultrarich gratin—with layers of Yukon gold potatoes smothered in a sauce of goat cheese, whole milk, and whipping cream—might have been meatless, but it wasn't exactly healthy.

By substituting half-and-half for the whipping cream, we eliminated 64 grams of fat. Allowing 1% milk to stand in for whole milk, slightly reducing the cheese, and spraying our pan with cooking spray instead of buttering it brought the total down by another 23 grams of fat. We added a little flour to the sauce and ended up with the same rich texture of the original—with less than half of the fat.

Potato Gratin with Goat Cheese and Garlic

    1   cup half-and-half, divided
    1   tablespoon all-purpose flour
    1   cup (4 ounces) crumbled goat
        cheese
    1   cup 1% low-fat milk
    1   teaspoon salt
    ¾   teaspoon black pepper
    ⅛   teaspoon ground nutmeg
    1   garlic clove, minced
    5   cups thinly sliced peeled Yukon
        gold potato (about 2½ pounds)
Cooking spray

1. Preheat oven to 400°.

2. Combine 2 tablespoons half-and-half and flour in a large bowl, stirring with a whisk. Add remaining half-and-half, cheese, and next 5 ingredients, stirring with a whisk. Arrange half of potato slices in a single layer in an 11 x 7-inch baking dish coated with cooking spray. Pour half of milk mixture over potato slices, stirring milk mixture immediately before adding. Repeat procedure with remaining potato slices and milk mixture. Bake at 400° for 1 hour and 10 minutes or until potatoes are tender and golden brown. Yield: 9 servings (serving size: ⅔ cup).

CALORIES 193 (27% from fat); FAT 5.8g (sat 3.8g, mono 1.6g, poly 0.1g); PROTEIN 6.4g; CARB 28.4g; FIBER 2.4g; CHOL 20mg; IRON 0.7mg; SODIUM 341mg; CALC 90mg

BEFORE	AFTER
SERVING SIZE	
⅔ cup	
CALORIES PER SERVING	
239	193
FAT	
15.4g	5.8g
PERCENT OF TOTAL CALORIES	
58%	27%

Stars in Bars

Bar cookies and snack cakes are the easiest of home-baked treats.

Monkey Bars

(pictured on page 293)

This moist snacking cake might remind you of banana bread.

½ cup raisins
1½ tablespoons dark rum or apple juice
1 cup all-purpose flour
½ teaspoon baking powder
½ teaspoon baking soda
¼ teaspoon salt
¾ cup packed brown sugar
¼ cup butter, softened
½ cup mashed ripe banana
3 tablespoons low-fat buttermilk
1 teaspoon vanilla extract
2 large egg whites
⅓ cup chopped walnuts
Cooking spray
1 tablespoon powdered sugar

1. Preheat oven to 350°.
2. Combine raisins and rum in a microwave-safe bowl. Microwave at HIGH 1 minute, and set aside. Lightly spoon flour into a dry measuring cup; level with a knife. Combine flour and next 3 ingredients in a bowl, stirring well with a whisk. Set aside.
3. Combine brown sugar and butter in a large bowl; beat with a mixer at medium speed until well blended. Add banana and next 3 ingredients, beating well. Add flour mixture, beating just until combined. Stir in raisin mixture and walnuts.
4. Spread batter into an 8-inch square baking pan coated with cooking spray. Bake at 350° for 30 minutes or until golden. Cool bars completely on a wire rack. Sprinkle with powdered sugar. Yield: 16 servings (serving size: 1 bar).

CALORIES 135 (31% from fat); FAT 4.7g (sat 2g, mono 1.1g, poly 1.3g); PROTEIN 2g; CARB 21.8g; FIBER 0.9g; CHOL 8mg; IRON 0.8mg; SODIUM 136mg; CALC 27mg

Raspberry-Chocolate Bars

If you prefer, try different types of preserves.

1 cup all-purpose flour
1 cup quick-cooking oats
½ teaspoon baking soda
½ teaspoon salt
¾ cup packed brown sugar
5 tablespoons butter, softened
½ cup semisweet chocolate chips
1 (10-ounce) jar seedless raspberry jam

1. Preheat oven to 375°.
2. Lightly spoon flour into a dry measuring cup; level with a knife. Combine flour, oats, baking soda, and salt in a small bowl, stirring well with a whisk. Set aside.
3. Combine sugar and butter in a medium bowl; beat with a mixer at medium speed until smooth. Add flour mixture to butter mixture, and stir until well blended (mixture will be crumbly). Remove ¾ cup of dough; toss with chocolate chips. Set aside. Press remaining dough into an 8-inch square baking pan, and spread evenly with jam. Sprinkle with chocolate chip mixture.
4. Bake at 375° for 30 minutes or until golden brown. Cool completely on a wire rack. Yield: 16 servings (serving size: 1 bar).

CALORIES 175 (30% from fat); FAT 5.9g (sat 3.4g, mono 1.8g, poly 0.3g); PROTEIN 2g; CARB 30.4g; FIBER 1g; CHOL 10mg; IRON 0.9mg; SODIUM 160mg; CALC 16mg

Scotch Bars

½ cup all-purpose flour
1 cup graham cracker crumbs (about 5 cookie sheets)
⅔ cup packed brown sugar
⅓ cup quick-cooking oats
⅓ cup butterscotch morsels
1 teaspoon baking powder
1 tablespoon vegetable oil
1½ teaspoons vanilla extract
2 large egg whites
Cooking spray
1 tablespoon powdered sugar

1. Preheat oven to 350°.
2. Lightly spoon flour into a dry measuring cup, and level with a knife.

Combine flour and next 5 ingredients, stirring with a whisk. Set aside.
3. Combine oil, vanilla, and egg whites; add to flour mixture. Stir just until blended. Lightly coat hands with cooking spray.
4. Press batter evenly into an 8-inch square baking pan coated with cooking spray. Bake at 350° for 18 minutes or until a wooden pick inserted in center comes out clean. Cool in pan on a wire rack. Sift powdered sugar over top. Yield: 16 servings (serving size: 1 bar).

CALORIES 118 (21% from fat); FAT 2.8g (sat 1.1g, mono 0.6g, poly 0.9g); PROTEIN 1.7g; CARB 21.8g; FIBER 0.5g; CHOL 0mg; IRON 0.8mg; SODIUM 90mg; CALC 29mg

Pecan-Chocolate Chip Snack Cake

You can substitute chopped walnuts, almonds, or cashews for the pecans.

½ cup all-purpose flour
¼ teaspoon baking soda
¼ teaspoon salt
¾ cup packed brown sugar
1 teaspoon vanilla extract
2 large egg whites
⅓ cup chopped pecans
¼ cup semisweet chocolate chips
Cooking spray
2 teaspoons powdered sugar

1. Preheat oven to 350°.
2. Lightly spoon flour into a dry measuring cup, and level with a knife. Combine flour, baking soda, and salt in a small bowl, stirring well with a whisk. Set aside.
3. Combine brown sugar, vanilla, and egg whites in a large bowl; beat with a mixer at high speed 1 minute. Add flour mixture, beating just until combined. Stir in pecans and chocolate chips.
4. Spread batter into an 8-inch square baking pan coated with cooking spray. Bake at 350° for 18 minutes or until golden and crusty on top. Cool in pan 10 minutes. Sprinkle with powdered sugar. Yield: 16 servings (serving size: 1 bar).

CALORIES 87 (27% from fat); FAT 2.6g (sat 0.6g, mono 1.3g, poly 0.6g); PROTEIN 1.2g; CARB 15.4g; FIBER 0.5g; CHOL 0mg; IRON 0.5mg; SODIUM 68mg; CALC 12mg

Spicy Beef Salad, page 301

Monkey Bars, page 292

Orange-Glazed Cheesecake with
Gingersnap Crust, page 276

Fried-Chicken Salad,
page 305

Pear and Roquefort Strata,
page 304

Pork Stew with Pumpkin,
page 297

Alfredo Sauce over fettuccine,
page 287

Pumpkin Circumstance

Bring both the color and flavor of fall to your table with fresh pumpkin.

Pumpkin is a most versatile squash. Clever cooks turn plump fresh pumpkins into soups, ragoûts, casseroles, entrées, and sides. Fresh pumpkin has a more delicate, nuanced flavor than canned, and it renders any dish the golden orange of autumn. In addition to tantalizing taste and inviting color, pumpkin brings a host of nutrients to the table, particularly beta-carotene, vitamin C, and potassium.

Pumpkin, Pear, and Cranberry Gratin

    4   cups (½-inch) cubed peeled fresh
        pumpkin
    2   cups finely chopped peeled pear
    1   teaspoon grated orange rind
    ½   cup fresh orange juice (about
        2 oranges)
    3   tablespoons sweetened dried
        cranberries
    2   tablespoons brown sugar
    1   teaspoon grated peeled fresh ginger
    ¼   teaspoon salt
    ⅛   teaspoon black pepper
    Cooking spray
    2   (1-ounce) slices white bread
    ½   cup (2 ounces) shredded
        reduced-fat sharp cheddar cheese
    1   tablespoon butter, melted

1. Preheat oven to 400°.
2. Steam pumpkin, covered, 10 minutes or until tender. Drain.
3. Place pumpkin, pear, and next 7 ingredients in a large bowl, tossing gently to coat. Spoon into an 11 x 7-inch baking dish coated with cooking spray. Cover and bake at 400° for 20 minutes.
4. Place bread in a food processor; pulse 10 times or until coarse crumbs form to measure 1 cup. Combine breadcrumbs, cheese, and butter. Uncover gratin; top with breadcrumb mixture. Bake an additional 10 minutes or until golden brown. Yield: 6 servings (serving size: 1 cup).

CALORIES 147 (20% from fat); FAT 3.3g (sat 1.8g, mono 0.9g, poly 0.2g); PROTEIN 4.2g; CARB 27g; FIBER 2.2g; CHOL 7mg; IRON 1.2mg; SODIUM 221mg; CALC 76mg

Pork Stew with Pumpkin

(pictured on page 296)

You can also use butternut or acorn squash when pumpkin is out of season.

    1   tablespoon olive oil
    1½   pounds boneless pork loin, trimmed
         and cut into ½-inch pieces
    1   cup finely chopped onion
    1   cup finely chopped red bell pepper
    ¾   cup finely chopped celery
    2   teaspoons dried rubbed sage
    1   teaspoon salt
    ½   teaspoon freshly ground black pepper
    1   (28-ounce) can diced tomatoes,
         undrained
    1   (14.5-ounce) can fat-free,
         less-sodium chicken broth
    4   cups (½-inch) cubed peeled fresh
         pumpkin
    1   (10-ounce) package frozen
         whole-kernel corn
    2   teaspoons grated orange rind
    4½   cups cooked egg noodles (about
         3 cups uncooked)
    6   tablespoons chopped fresh flat-leaf
         parsley

1. Heat oil in a large Dutch oven over high heat. Add pork; cook 4 minutes or until browned, stirring occasionally. Add onion, bell pepper, and celery; cook 2 minutes, stirring occasionally. Stir in sage, salt, black pepper, tomatoes, and broth; bring to a boil. Cover, reduce heat, and simmer 30 minutes. Stir in pumpkin and corn; bring to a boil. Cover, reduce heat, and simmer 1 hour or until pumpkin is tender. Stir in rind. Serve over noodles; sprinkle with parsley. Yield: 6 servings (serving size: 2 cups stew, ¾ cup noodles, and 1 tablespoon parsley).

CALORIES 463 (23% from fat); FAT 11.8g (sat 3.4g, mono 5.3g, poly 1.7g); PROTEIN 35.4g; CARB 56.2g; FIBER 5.7g; CHOL 108mg; IRON 5mg; SODIUM 715mg; CALC 122mg

Pumpkin Waffles

Top with maple syrup and chopped walnuts for a breakfast treat that tastes like pumpkin bread.

    1   cup all-purpose flour
    2   teaspoons baking powder
    ¾   teaspoon ground cinnamon
    ⅛   teaspoon salt
    ⅛   teaspoon ground cloves
    1   cup 1% low-fat milk
    ½   cup Pumpkin Puree (recipe below)
    ¼   cup packed dark brown sugar
    1   tablespoon vegetable oil
    1   large egg, lightly beaten
    Cooking spray

1. Lightly spoon flour into a dry measuring cup; level with a knife. Combine flour and next 4 ingredients in a large bowl; make a well in center of mixture. Combine milk and next 4 ingredients; add to flour mixture. Stir just until moist.
2. Coat a waffle iron with cooking spray; preheat. Spoon about ¼ cup of batter per waffle onto hot waffle iron, spreading batter to edges. Cook 5 to 7 minutes or until steaming stops; repeat procedure with remaining batter. Yield: 8 waffles (serving size: 2 waffles).

CALORIES 255 (20% from fat); FAT 5.7g (sat 1.3g, mono 1.5g, poly 2.3g); PROTEIN 7.4g; CARB 44.1g; FIBER 2g; CHOL 57mg; IRON 2.6mg; SODIUM 372mg; CALC 237mg

Pumpkin Puree

Here's an easy puree recipe for the Pumpkin Waffles (recipe above) and Pumpkin-Cinnamon Streusel Buns (recipe on page 298).

    1   (2-pound) pumpkin

1. Cut pumpkin in half lengthwise, discarding seeds and membranes. Place pumpkin halves, cut sides down, in a baking dish, and add ¼ cup water to dish. Cover with heavy-duty plastic wrap, and vent. Microwave at HIGH 10 minutes (about 5 minutes per pound) or until pumpkin is tender when pierced
Continued

with a fork. Cool slightly; scoop out pulp. Place pulp in a food processor; process until smooth. Yield: about 2½ cups pumpkin puree.

CALORIES 165 (3% from fat); FAT 0.6g (sat 0.3g, mono 0.1g, poly 0g); PROTEIN 6.4g; CARB 41.3g; FIBER 3.2g; CHOL 0mg; IRON 5.1mg; SODIUM 6mg; CALC 133mg

Pumpkin-Cinnamon Streusel Buns

To make these year-round, substitute canned pumpkin puree and add an extra cup of all-purpose flour.

BUNS:
- 1 package dry yeast (about 2¼ teaspoons)
- ¼ cup warm water (100° to 110°)
- 2¾ cups all-purpose flour, divided
- ½ cup Pumpkin Puree (recipe on page 297)
- ½ cup 1% low-fat milk
- ¼ cup butter, melted
- 1 tablespoon granulated sugar
- 1¼ teaspoons salt
- ¼ teaspoon ground nutmeg
- Cooking spray
- 3 tablespoons granulated sugar
- 3 tablespoons brown sugar
- 2 tablespoons all-purpose flour
- 1½ teaspoons ground cinnamon
- 2 tablespoons chilled butter, cut into small pieces

GLAZE:
- ¾ cup sifted powdered sugar
- 1 tablespoon hot water
- ¼ teaspoon vanilla extract

1. To prepare buns, dissolve yeast in warm water in a large bowl; let stand 5 minutes. Lightly spoon 2¾ cups flour into dry measuring cups, and level with a knife. Add 2 cups flour, pumpkin puree, and next 5 ingredients to yeast mixture; beat with a mixer at medium speed until smooth. Turn dough out onto a floured surface. Knead until smooth and elastic (about 10 minutes); add enough of remaining ¾ cup flour, 1 tablespoon at a time, to prevent dough from sticking to hands (dough will feel tacky).

2. Place dough in a large bowl coated with cooking spray, turning to coat top. Cover and let rise in a warm place (85°), free from drafts, 45 minutes or until doubled in size. (Press two fingers into dough. If indentation remains, dough has risen enough.)

3. Combine 3 tablespoons granulated sugar, brown sugar, 2 tablespoons flour, and cinnamon in a small bowl. Cut in chilled butter with a pastry blender or 2 knives until mixture resembles coarse meal.

4. Punch dough down; cover and let rest 5 minutes. Roll dough into a 12 x 10-inch rectangle on a floured surface. Sprinkle with brown sugar mixture. Roll up rectangle tightly, starting with a long edge, pressing firmly to eliminate air pockets; pinch seam and ends to seal. Cut roll into 12 (1-inch) slices. Place slices in a 9-inch square baking pan coated with cooking spray. Cover and let rise 25 minutes or until doubled in size.

5. Preheat oven to 375°.

6. Bake rolls at 375° for 20 minutes or until golden brown. Cool 15 minutes in pan on a wire rack.

7. To prepare glaze, combine powdered sugar, 1 tablespoon water, and vanilla extract in a small bowl, stirring with a whisk until smooth. Drizzle glaze over buns. Serve warm. Yield: 12 servings (serving size: 1 bun).

CALORIES 219 (25% from fat); FAT 6.2g (sat 3.7g, mono 1.8g, poly 0.3g); PROTEIN 3.8g; CARB 36.9g; FIBER 1.2g; CHOL 16mg; IRON 1.6mg; SODIUM 311mg; CALC 24mg

Sugar-Roasted Pumpkin

When the pumpkin comes out of the oven, there will be a small pool of syrup in each wedge, but it's absorbed by the pumpkin almost immediately.

- 1 small pumpkin (about 2½ pounds)
- Cooking spray
- 2 teaspoons butter
- 2 tablespoons dark brown sugar

1. Preheat oven to 425°.

2. Cut pumpkin into 4 wedges, discarding seeds and membrane. Place pumpkin wedges, cut sides up, in an 11 x 7-inch baking dish coated with cooking spray. Place ½ teaspoon butter on each wedge, and sprinkle each wedge with 1½ teaspoons sugar. Bake at 425° for 35 minutes or until tender. Yield: 4 servings (serving size: 1 wedge).

CALORIES 94 (20% from fat); FAT 2.1g (sat 1.3g, mono 0.6g, poly 0.1g); PROTEIN 2g; CARB 19.6g; FIBER 1g; CHOL 5mg; IRON 1.7mg; SODIUM 24mg; CALC 48mg

Pumpkin Crumb Cake with Apples

A fine choice for a fall Sunday brunch, this crumb cake is spiced with cinnamon, cloves, and nutmeg.

CRUMBS:
- 3 tablespoons all-purpose flour
- 3 tablespoons brown sugar
- 1½ tablespoons chilled butter, cut into small pieces

CAKE:
- ¾ cup granulated sugar
- ½ cup fresh pumpkin puree
- 3 tablespoons butter, softened
- 1 teaspoon ground cinnamon
- ¼ teaspoon ground nutmeg
- ⅛ teaspoon ground cloves
- 1 large egg
- 1 large egg white
- 1¼ cups all-purpose flour
- 1 teaspoon baking powder
- ¼ teaspoon baking soda
- ⅛ teaspoon salt
- ½ cup low-fat buttermilk
- Cooking spray
- 2 cups thinly sliced Rome apple (about ¾ pound)

1. Preheat oven to 350°.

2. To prepare crumbs, combine 3 tablespoons flour and brown sugar in a medium bowl; cut in 1½ tablespoons butter with a pastry blender or 2 knives until mixture resembles coarse meal. Set aside.

3. To prepare cake, beat granulated sugar and next 7 ingredients with a mixer at medium speed until well blended. Lightly spoon 1¼ cups flour into dry measuring cups, and level with a knife. Combine 1¼ cups flour, baking powder, soda, and salt in medium bowl, stirring with a whisk. Add flour mixture and buttermilk alternately to sugar mixture, beginning and ending with flour mixture; mix after each addition.

4. Pour batter into a 9-inch round cake pan coated with cooking spray. Arrange apple spokelike on top of batter. Sprinkle with crumb mixture. Bake at 350° for 55 minutes or until a wooden pick inserted in center comes out clean. Cool in pan 10 minutes on a wire rack. Yield: 8 servings (serving size: 1 piece).

CALORIES 274 (25% from fat); FAT 7.5g (sat 4.4g, mono 2.2g, poly 0.4g); PROTEIN 4.3g; CARB 48.5g; FIBER 2.2g; CHOL 45mg; IRON 1.5mg; SODIUM 237mg; CALC 69mg

---

superfast

...And Ready in Just About 20 Minutes.

Great food starts with simple ingredients.

Pork Tenderloin with Mustard Sauce

Serve with steamed asparagus or broccoli.

    2 cups uncooked medium egg noodles
    1 tablespoon olive oil
    1 (1-pound) pork tenderloin, trimmed and cut crosswise into 12 (1-inch-thick) slices
    ½ teaspoon black pepper
    ¼ teaspoon salt
    1 cup dry white wine
    3 tablespoons whole-grain Dijon mustard
    2 tablespoons water
    2 teaspoons cornstarch

1. Cook noodles according to package directions, omitting salt and fat; drain.
2. While noodles cook, heat oil in a large nonstick skillet over medium-high heat. Sprinkle pork with pepper and salt. Place pork in pan; cook 5 minutes, turning once.
3. Combine wine and mustard; pour into pan. Cover, reduce heat, and simmer 10 minutes. Remove pork from pan; keep warm.
4. Combine water and cornstarch in a small bowl. Stir cornstarch mixture into pan; bring to a boil, and cook 1 minute or until thick. Serve pork with sauce and noodles. Yield: 4 servings (serving size: 3 pork slices, about 3 tablespoons sauce, and about ½ cup noodles).

CALORIES 242 (30% from fat); FAT 8g (sat 1.9g, mono 4.4g, poly 0.9g); PROTEIN 26.5g; CARB 14g; FIBER 1.3g; CHOL 89mg; IRON 2mg; SODIUM 298mg; CALC 22mg

Shrimp, Asparagus, and Penne Pasta

Serve with salad and focaccia wedges.

    1 cup uncooked penne (tube-shaped pasta)
    1 tablespoon olive oil
    2 cups (1-inch) sliced asparagus (about ¾ pound)
    ½ cup chopped onion
    1 teaspoon bottled minced garlic
    ½ pound peeled and deveined medium shrimp
    ½ teaspoon dried oregano
    ¼ teaspoon crushed red pepper
    1 (14.5-ounce) can diced tomatoes with basil, garlic, and oregano, undrained
    ¼ cup (1 ounce) preshredded fresh Parmesan cheese

1. Cook pasta according to package directions, omitting salt and fat; drain.
2. While pasta cooks, heat oil in a large skillet over medium-high heat. Add asparagus, onion, garlic, and shrimp; sauté 5 minutes. Add oregano, pepper, and tomatoes; cook over medium-low heat 5 minutes or until thoroughly heated. Stir in cooked pasta; sprinkle with cheese. Yield: 4 servings (serving size: 1¼ cups).

CALORIES 292 (22% from fat); FAT 7g (sat 2g, mono 3.3g, poly 1g); PROTEIN 21.6g; CARB 36.3g; FIBER 4.1g; CHOL 91mg; IRON 4.8mg; SODIUM 738mg; CALC 215mg

Herbed Linguine with Shrimp

Serve with a baguette and gourmet greens.

    4 ounces fresh linguine
    ½ cup half-and-half
    3 tablespoons chopped fresh basil
    2 tablespoons chopped fresh parsley
    2 tablespoons preshredded fresh Parmesan cheese
    ¼ teaspoon salt
    ½ pound cooked and peeled medium shrimp
    ¼ cup fat-free sour cream

1. Cook pasta according to package directions, omitting salt and fat; drain.
2. Combine linguine, half-and-half, and next 4 ingredients in a large nonstick skillet. Cook over medium heat 5 minutes. Stir in shrimp; cook 1 minute or until thoroughly heated. Remove from heat, and stir in sour cream. Yield: 2 servings (serving size: 2 cups).

CALORIES 370 (28% from fat); FAT 11.3g (sat 6.1g, mono 2.9g, poly 1.2g); PROTEIN 26.9g; CARB 39.1g; FIBER 2.5g; CHOL 206mg; IRON 4.5mg; SODIUM 626mg; CALC 240mg

Stir-Fried Moo Shu Vegetable Wraps

    1 tablespoon low-sodium soy sauce
    8 ounces reduced-fat firm tofu, drained and cut into ¾-inch cubes
    2 cups sliced shiitake mushroom caps (about 8 ounces mushrooms)
    2 cups packaged broccoli coleslaw (such as River Ranch)
    1 cup (¼-inch-wide) red bell pepper strips
    ½ cup (½-inch) diagonally cut green onions
    1 tablespoon bottled minced garlic
    1 teaspoon bottled ground fresh ginger (such as Spice World)
    2 teaspoons dark sesame oil
    2 tablespoons hoisin sauce
    ¼ teaspoon crushed red pepper
    8 (7-inch) flour tortillas
    ¼ cup plum sauce

Continued

1. Combine soy sauce and tofu in a small bowl. Combine mushrooms and next 5 ingredients in a medium bowl.

2. Heat oil in a large nonstick skillet over medium-high heat. Add vegetables; stir-fry 3 minutes. Add tofu; stir-fry 1 minute. Stir in hoisin sauce and crushed red pepper; stir-fry 1 minute or until vegetables are crisp-tender.

3. Stack tortillas; wrap in damp paper towels, and microwave at HIGH 25 seconds. Spread 1½ teaspoons plum sauce over each tortilla. Top each tortilla with about ⅓ cup tofu mixture; roll up. Yield: 4 servings (serving size: 2 tortillas).

CALORIES 455 (21% from fat); FAT 10.4g (sat 2.2g, mono 4.8g, poly 2.6g); PROTEIN 16g; CARB 73.7g; FIBER 7.1g; CHOL 0mg; IRON 5.6mg; SODIUM 877mg; CALC 97mg

Brown-Bag Lunch Menu
serves 4

Pack your pita bread and lettuce together in a zip-top plastic bag, and store the chicken mixture separately so the pita won't get soggy. Stir feta cheese, tomatoes, and cucumber into cooked couscous for the salad.

Chicken Curry Pitas

Couscous salad

Fig cookies

Chicken Curry Pitas

Serve with a salad of mixed fresh fruit.

- 3 cups chopped roasted skinless, boneless chicken breast (about 12 ounces)
- ⅓ cup chopped celery
- ¼ cup low-fat mayonnaise
- 2 tablespoons raisins
- 1 tablespoon chopped green onions
- 2 tablespoons hot mango chutney
- 1 teaspoon curry powder
- 2 teaspoons fresh lemon juice
- 4 (6-inch) pitas, cut in half
- 8 red leaf lettuce leaves

1. Combine first 8 ingredients in a medium bowl. Line each pita half with a lettuce leaf. Spoon ½ cup chicken mixture into each pita half. Yield: 4 servings (serving size: 2 pita halves).

CALORIES 363 (11% from fat); FAT 4.6g (sat 1.2g, mono 1.1g, poly 1g); PROTEIN 33.8g; CARB 47g; FIBER 2.5g; CHOL 75mg; IRON 2.1mg; SODIUM 1,096mg; CALC 90mg

Tex-Mex Menu
serves 4

This easy menu lets you get more creative with quesadilla fillings—you don't have to stick with the standard beans and cheese. The fresh, fruity flavor of the salad is in welcome contrast to the more robust food of the season.

Zucchini, Olive, and Cheese Quesadillas

Grapefruit and avocado salad*

Refried beans

Lemon sorbet with fresh orange sections

*Combine 4 cups torn romaine lettuce, 2 cups grapefruit sections, and 1 cup sliced peeled avocado in a large bowl. Combine 2 tablespoons honey, 2 tablespoons white balsamic vinegar, 2 teaspoons Dijon mustard, and 2 teaspoons olive oil in a small bowl; drizzle over salad, and toss well.

Zucchini, Olive, and Cheese Quesadillas

- 1 teaspoon olive oil
- Cooking spray
- ⅓ cup finely chopped onion
- ½ teaspoon bottled minced garlic
- 1¼ cups shredded zucchini
- ¼ teaspoon dried oregano
- ⅛ teaspoon salt
- ⅛ teaspoon black pepper
- 4 (8-inch) fat-free flour tortillas
- ½ cup (2 ounces) preshredded part-skim mozzarella cheese
- ½ cup diced tomato
- ¼ cup chopped pitted kalamata olives
- ¼ cup (1 ounce) crumbled feta cheese

1. Heat olive oil in a large nonstick skillet coated with cooking spray over medium-high heat. Add onion and garlic; sauté 1 minute. Add zucchini; sauté 2 minutes or until lightly browned. Remove from heat; stir in oregano, salt, and pepper.

2. Wipe pan clean with paper towels, and coat with cooking spray. Heat pan over medium heat. Add 1 tortilla to pan, and sprinkle with ¼ cup mozzarella. Top with half of zucchini mixture, ¼ cup tomato, 2 tablespoons olives, 2 tablespoons feta, and 1 tortilla. Cook 3 minutes or until lightly browned on bottom. Carefully turn quesadilla; cook 2 minutes or until lightly browned. Place quesadilla on a cutting board; cut in half using a serrated knife. Repeat procedure with remaining tortillas, mozzarella, zucchini mixture, tomato, olives, and feta. Serve warm. Yield: 4 servings.

CALORIES 235 (30% from fat); FAT 7.9g (sat 3.6g, mono 3.1g, poly 0.5g); PROTEIN 8.7g; CARB 23.7g; FIBER 3.8g; CHOL 14mg; IRON 0.7mg; SODIUM 632mg; CALC 160mg

Chicken-Fruit Salad

Serve with poppy seed muffins from the bakery.

- 1 (10-ounce) package Italian-blend salad greens (about 6 cups)
- 2 cups grilled chicken breast strips (such as Louis Rich; about 6 ounces)
- 1 cup blueberries
- 1 cup quartered strawberries
- 1 cup sliced banana
- 1 cup sliced peeled kiwifruit (about 3 kiwifruit)
- 2 tablespoons pine nuts, toasted
- 2 tablespoons herbed goat cheese
- Raspberry Dressing

1. Arrange 1½ cups salad greens on each of 4 plates. Divide remaining ingredients except Raspberry Dressing equally among 4 plates. Drizzle each serving with 3 tablespoons Raspberry Dressing. Yield: 4 servings.

(Totals include Raspberry Dressing) CALORIES 332 (24% from fat); FAT 8.8g (sat 2.4g, mono 3.3g, poly 2.1g); PROTEIN 15.9g; CARB 53.3g; FIBER 5.9g; CHOL 32mg; IRON 2.7mg; SODIUM 699mg; CALC 114mg

You can make and refrigerate this dressing up to a week ahead.

- ⅓ cup honey
- ¼ cup raspberry or red wine vinegar
- ¼ cup plain fat-free yogurt
- 1 tablespoon Dijon mustard
- 2 teaspoons olive oil
- ¼ teaspoon salt
- ¼ teaspoon black pepper

1. Combine all ingredients; stir with a whisk. Yield: ¾ cup (serving size: 3 tablespoons).

CALORIES 120 (20% from fat); FAT 2.6g (sat 0.3g, mono 1.8g, poly 0.3g); PROTEIN 1.2g; CARB 25.1g; FIBER 0.1g; CHOL 0mg; IRON 0.4mg; SODIUM 257mg; CALC 39mg

reader recipes

Thai Standby

You won't have to go halfway around the world for this authentic Spicy Beef Salad.

After a year of teaching junior high in a remote area of southern Thailand, Leanne Abt returned home to Vancouver, British Columbia, hooked on Thai cuisine.

Yam Nuea Yang (Spicy Beef Salad) is just one of Leanne's favorite Thai standbys. "It's easy to whip up for a quick dinner, and it's a terrific way to use leftover steak or roast beef, What's more, the dish is filled with tangy, fresh flavors."

Yam Nuea Yang
Spicy Beef Salad
(pictured on page 293)

- 1 (1-pound) flank steak, trimmed
- Cooking spray
- ⅓ cup sliced shallots
- ¼ cup chopped fresh cilantro
- 3 tablespoons fresh lime juice
- 1 tablespoon fish sauce
- 2 teaspoons sliced Thai red chiles or serrano chiles
- 2 medium tomatoes, cut into ¼-inch-thick wedges (about ¾ pound)

1. Prepare grill or broiler.
2. Place steak on a grill rack or broiler pan coated with cooking spray; cook 6 minutes on each side or until desired degree of doneness.
3. Cut steak diagonally across grain into thin slices; cut each slice into 2-inch pieces.
4. Combine steak, shallots, and remaining ingredients, and toss gently. Yield: 4 servings (serving size: 1 cup).

CALORIES 214 (39% from fat); FAT 9.2g (sat 3.9g, mono 3.6g, poly 0.5g); PROTEIN 25g; CARB 7.6g; FIBER 1.1g; CHOL 59mg; IRON 2.8mg; SODIUM 407mg; CALC 17mg

Balsamic Chicken

"This is a lazy-day dish in my house—reserved for when I really don't feel like cooking or shopping. I keep all the ingredients in the pantry. It's also a good dish to sneak leftover vegetables into. I've used spinach, zucchini, all kinds of mushrooms, and green onions, and they all taste great."

—Erin Ferree, San Mateo, California

- 1 teaspoon olive oil
- ¾ cup coarsely chopped onion
- 4 garlic cloves, sliced
- 2 (4-ounce) skinless, boneless chicken breast halves
- 1 cup sliced green bell pepper
- ½ cup balsamic vinegar
- ¼ cup sliced mushrooms
- 1 teaspoon dried Italian seasoning
- 1 (14½-ounce) can diced tomatoes, undrained
- 1 cup hot cooked long-grain rice

1. Heat oil in a large skillet over medium-high heat. Add onion and garlic; sauté 3 minutes. Add chicken; cook 4 minutes on each side or until browned. Add bell pepper and next 4 ingredients. Reduce heat to medium-low; cook 20 minutes or until chicken is done. Serve over rice. Yield: 2 servings (serving size: 1 chicken breast half, 1 cup bell pepper mixture, and ½ cup rice).

CALORIES 376 (10% from fat); FAT 4.3g (sat 0.8g, mono 2.1g, poly 0.7g); PROTEIN 32g; CARB 52.3g; FIBER 6g; CHOL 66mg; IRON 3.8mg; SODIUM 355mg; CALC 110mg

Barley, Beet, and Feta Salad

"This hearty salad can be eaten warm or cold. It's a delicious balance of sweet beets, rich barley, tangy feta, and slightly bitter arugula. Each of the components can be made ahead and mixed at the last minute, making it great for dinner on busy days."

—Robin Johnson,
Sedro-Woolley, Washington

- 1 pound beets
- 4 cups fat-free, less-sodium chicken broth
- 1½ cups uncooked pearl barley
- 2 cups trimmed arugula
- ¼ cup chopped walnuts, toasted
- 1 (4-ounce) package crumbled feta cheese
- ¼ cup balsamic vinegar
- 2 tablespoons olive oil
- 2 teaspoons fennel seeds
- 3 garlic cloves, minced

1. Leave root and 1-inch stem on beets; scrub with a brush. Place in a medium saucepan; cover with water. Bring to a boil; cover, reduce heat, and simmer 35 minutes or until tender. Drain; rinse with cold water, and cool. Trim off beet roots, and rub off skins. Cut beets into ¼-inch-wide wedges.
2. Bring chicken broth to a boil in a large saucepan. Add barley; cover, reduce heat, and simmer 40 minutes. Remove from heat; cool.
3. Combine barley, arugula, walnuts, and cheese in a large bowl. Combine vinegar and remaining 3 ingredients in a small bowl. Pour vinegar mixture over barley mixture, tossing to coat. Top with beets. Yield: 6 servings (serving size: 1⅓ cups barley mixture and about ½ cup beets).

CALORIES 403 (29% from fat); FAT 13g (sat 3.9g, mono 5g, poly 3.3g); PROTEIN 13.9g; CARB 61.2g; FIBER 12.4g; CHOL 17mg; IRON 3.4mg; SODIUM 653mg; CALC 180mg

Apple-Cranberry Crisp

"I like the fact that this dish includes a lot of fruit and whole grains yet tastes like dessert. It's equally good warm or cold, and low-fat vanilla ice cream is nice on top."
—Betty Matteson, Durham, North Carolina

    3 cups cubed Granny Smith apple
      (about 1 pound)
    2 cups fresh cranberries
    ½ cup sugar
    Cooking spray
    ⅓ cup whole wheat flour
    1 cup regular oats
    ½ cup packed brown sugar
    ¼ cup canola oil

1. Preheat oven to 350°.
2. Combine first 3 ingredients in a medium bowl; spoon mixture into an 8-inch square baking dish coated with cooking spray. Lightly spoon flour into a dry measuring cup, and level with a knife. Combine flour, oats, brown sugar, and oil, stirring with a fork until crumbly. Sprinkle over apple mixture. Bake at 350° for 40 minutes or until bubbly. Yield: 10 servings (serving size: ½ cup).

CALORIES 202 (28% from fat); FAT 6.2g (sat 0.5g, mono 3.4g, poly 1.9g); PROTEIN 2g; CARB 36.5g; FIBER 3g; CHOL 0mg; IRON 0.8mg; SODIUM 5mg; CALC 19mg

Weeknight Family Menu

This entrée is similar to lasagna, with sliced zucchini standing in for the noodles. For the Caesar salad, combine torn romaine lettuce with garlic-flavored croutons, shaved Parmesan cheese, and bottled low-fat Caesar dressing.

Layered Zucchini

Garlic bread

Caesar salad

Layered Zucchini

"My husband and I took on a healthier eating style, and I adapted my mother's recipe to fit. It tastes far too rich to be good for you."

—Gena Dunbar,
Prince George, British Columbia

    4 cups water
    6 cups sliced zucchini (about
      3 medium)
    1 pound ground round
    2 garlic cloves, minced
    2 cups low-fat spaghetti sauce
      (such as Muir Glen Organic)
    ½ teaspoon salt
    ½ teaspoon dried basil
    ½ teaspoon dried oregano
    2 cups fat-free cottage cheese
    1 tablespoon dried parsley
    2 large eggs, lightly beaten
    Cooking spray
    ½ cup dry breadcrumbs
    1¾ cups (3½ ounces) preshredded
      part-skim mozzarella cheese,
      divided

1. Preheat oven to 350°.
2. Bring water to a boil in a large saucepan. Add zucchini; cook 3 minutes or until crisp-tender. Drain and cool.
3. Place beef and garlic in a large nonstick skillet over medium-high heat. Cook until browned, stirring to crumble. Stir in spaghetti sauce, salt, basil, and oregano; cook 1 minute. Remove from heat.
4. Combine cottage cheese, parsley, and eggs in a medium bowl.
5. Arrange zucchini slices in a shallow 3-quart casserole coated with cooking spray. Sprinkle zucchini with half of breadcrumbs. Spread half of cottage cheese mixture over breadcrumbs; cover with half of meat mixture and 1 cup mozzarella. Repeat layers with remaining breadcrumbs, cottage cheese mixture, and meat mixture. Bake at 350° for 40 minutes.
6. Sprinkle with ¾ cup mozzarella, and bake an additional 5 minutes or until cheese melts. Yield: 10 servings.

CALORIES 210 (30% from fat); FAT 7.1g (sat 3g, mono 2.8g, poly 0.5g); PROTEIN 20.9g; CARB 14.8g; FIBER 2.3g; CHOL 69mg; IRON 2.5mg; SODIUM 554mg; CALC 153mg

Spice-Crusted Salmon with Lime-Orange Salsa

"This recipe is best described as fresh, light, and full of flavor. I came up with it for a nutrition class. I knew I would get a good grade. It's easy to prepare, and the salsa can be made a day ahead to give it an extra kick."

—Jenifer Illingworth, Corona, California

SALSA:

    1 (7-ounce) can chipotle chiles in
      adobo sauce
    1½ cups orange sections (about
      4 oranges)
    ½ cup fresh orange juice (about
      2 oranges)
    ⅓ cup finely chopped red onion
    ¼ cup fresh lime juice
    ¼ cup chopped fresh cilantro
    ¼ teaspoon salt
    ¼ teaspoon black pepper
    2 garlic cloves, minced

SALMON:

    1 tablespoon coriander seeds
    1 tablespoon cumin seeds
    1½ teaspoons black peppercorns
    1 teaspoon kosher salt
    4 (6-ounce) salmon fillets (about
      1 inch thick)
    Cooking spray

1. To prepare salsa, remove 1 chile from can; mince. Reserve remaining chiles and adobo sauce for another use. Combine chile, orange sections, and next 7 ingredients in a bowl; toss well.
2. Preheat broiler.
3. To prepare salmon, cook coriander and cumin seeds in a small skillet over medium heat 2 minutes or until toasted. Place seeds, peppercorns, and 1 teaspoon kosher salt in a spice or coffee grinder, and process until coarsely ground. Rub coriander mixture over fillets. Place fillets on a broiler pan coated with cooking spray; broil 10 minutes or until fish flakes easily when tested with a fork. Serve with salsa. Yield: 4 servings (serving size: 1 fillet and ½ cup salsa).

CALORIES 418 (33% from fat); FAT 15.2g (sat 3.4g, mono 6.4g, poly 3.5g); PROTEIN 43.8g; CARB 27.5g; FIBER 5.4g; CHOL 107mg; IRON 2.9mg; SODIUM 745mg; CALC 134mg

Potato and Bean Chowder

"My husband and I enjoy spending time together in the kitchen. He's my chopper and dicer, and we make this soup often. It's a meal with a slice of warm bread and a salad. It's quick and easy to prepare because most of the ingredients are usually on hand."

—Louise Barnhill, Mason, Michigan

    Cooking spray
 1 cup chopped onion
 ½ cup chopped celery
 ½ cup chopped green bell pepper
 ¼ cup chopped red bell pepper
 1 garlic clove, minced
 2¼ cups water
 2 cups (½-inch) cubed peeled
    baking potato
 2 cups canned diced tomatoes and
    green chiles, undrained
 1 cup canned chickpeas (garbanzo
    beans), rinsed and drained
 1 teaspoon ground cumin
 ⅛ teaspoon black pepper
 2 (10½-ounce) cans beef consommé
 1 (16-ounce) can kidney beans,
    rinsed and drained
 1 (16-ounce) can navy beans, rinsed
    and drained
 2½ tablespoons grated fresh Parmesan
    cheese

1. Heat a Dutch oven coated with cooking spray over medium-high heat. Add onion and next 4 ingredients; sauté 5 minutes or until crisp-tender.
2. Add water and next 8 ingredients, and bring to a boil. Reduce heat, and simmer 30 minutes, stirring occasionally. Sprinkle with Parmesan cheese Yield: 9 servings (serving size: about 1¼ cups).

CALORIES 199 (7% from fat); FAT 1.6g (sat 0.4g, mono 0.4g, poly 0.6g); PROTEIN 12.5g; CARB 34.9g; FIBER 7.4g; CHOL 1mg; IRON 2.7mg; SODIUM 905mg; CALC 98mg

Autumn Light

Celebrate the flavors and mood of the season with a savory harvest menu.

Our Harvest Menu is a good choice for autumn entertaining. It combines warming spices and cheeses with such comfort-food staples as potatoes, apples, and breads to create sophisticated dishes that go great with a glass of late-harvest Riesling, a honeyed ham, or a roasted turkey.

Harvest Menu

Curried Butternut Squash Soup

Pears with Goat Cheese and Preserves

Leek and Potato Tart with Gruyère

Pear and Roquefort Strata

Spiced Fig and Walnut Bread

Raisin-Rosemary Rye Bread

Honey-Apple Crumble with Dried Fruit

Curried Butternut Squash Soup

 2 teaspoons vegetable oil
 1 cup thinly sliced leek (about 1 large)
 1 tablespoon curry powder
 1 tablespoon brown sugar
 ¾ teaspoon ground cumin
 ¼ teaspoon ground red pepper
 5 garlic cloves, chopped
 6 cups chopped peeled butternut
    squash (about 3 pounds)
 6 cups water
 4 cups chopped peeled Granny
    Smith apple (about 1 pound)
 ⅓ cup whipping cream
 ¾ teaspoon salt
 ⅔ cup minced fresh cilantro

1. Heat oil in a large Dutch oven over medium heat. Add leek and next 5 ingredients; cook 2 minutes, stirring frequently. Add squash, water, and apple; bring to a boil. Cover, reduce heat, and simmer 25 minutes or until tender.

2. Place half of soup in a blender, and process until smooth. Pour pureed soup into a large bowl. Repeat procedure with remaining soup. Return soup to pan; stir in cream and salt. Cook 1 minute or until thoroughly heated. Sprinkle each serving with about 1 tablespoon cilantro. Yield: 10 servings (serving size: 1 cup).

CALORIES 139 (28% from fat); FAT 4.3g (sat 2g, mono 1.1g, poly 0.8g); PROTEIN 2g; CARB 26.5g; FIBER 6g; CHOL 11mg; IRON 1.5mg; SODIUM 188mg; CALC 87mg

Pears with Goat Cheese and Preserves

Almost any flavor of preserves will work, though fig is divine. And while either Bartlett or Comice pears work with the flavors of the recipe, you'll be in for a special treat if you use Comice.

 4 medium Bartlett or Comice pears,
    peeled, cored, and cut in half
    lengthwise
 ¼ cup lemon juice
 1 cup (4 ounces) crumbled goat
    cheese
 ½ cup fig preserves

1. Toss pears with juice. Thinly slice pear halves, cutting to but not through, stem ends. Fan each pear half. Place on a platter. Sprinkle 2 tablespoons cheese on each pear half; dollop each with 1 tablespoon preserves. Yield: 8 servings.

CALORIES 137 (22% from fat); FAT 3.4g (sat 2.1g, mono 0.7g, poly 0.2g); PROTEIN 2.5g; CARB 26.7g; FIBER 1.6g; CHOL 13mg; IRON 0.4mg; SODIUM 175mg; CALC 83mg

Leek and Potato Tart with Gruyère

Serve warm or at room temperature.

1 (11-ounce) can refrigerated breadstick dough (such as Pillsbury)
Cooking spray
1 teaspoon vegetable oil
1 cup thinly sliced leek (about 1 large)
¼ teaspoon black pepper
1 medium peeled baking potato, halved lengthwise and cut into ¼-inch-thick slices (about 1 cup)
1 cup fat-free milk
½ cup egg substitute
⅓ cup (1½ ounces) grated Gruyère or Swiss cheese
2 tablespoons grated fresh Parmesan cheese
1 tablespoon Dijon mustard

1. Preheat oven to 375°.
2. Unroll dough, and separate strips. Let rest 5 minutes. Working on a flat surface, coil one strip of dough around itself in a spiral pattern. Add second strip of dough to end of first strip, pinching ends together to seal; continue coiling dough. Repeat procedure with remaining dough strips. Let rest 5 minutes. Roll into a 13-inch circle; fit into a 9-inch pie plate coated with cooking spray. Fold edges under; flute.
3. Heat oil in a large nonstick skillet over medium-high heat. Add leek, pepper, and potato; sauté 4 minutes. Spread leek mixture into prepared crust.
4. Place milk, egg substitute, cheeses, and mustard in a blender; process until smooth. Pour milk mixture over leek mixture. Bake at 375° for 40 minutes; let stand 10 minutes. Yield: 8 servings (serving size: 1 wedge).

CALORIES 195 (26% from fat); FAT 5.6g (sat 1.6g, mono 1g, poly 0.7g); PROTEIN 8.9g; CARB 26.4g; FIBER 1.1g; CHOL 8mg; IRON 1.8mg; SODIUM 435mg; CALC 135mg

Pear and Roquefort Strata
(pictured on page 295)

You can substitute other cheeses, such as cheddar, Gouda, or Gruyère, in place of the Roquefort.

Cooking spray
10 (1¾-ounce) slices sturdy white bread
2 cups Riesling or other slightly sweet white wine
¼ teaspoon salt
¼ teaspoon black pepper
1½ cups (6 ounces) crumbled Roquefort or other blue cheese
3 Bartlett pears, peeled, cored, and cut lengthwise into ¼-inch-thick slices (about 4 cups)
3 cups fat-free milk
4 large eggs

1. Coat a 13 x 9-inch baking dish with cooking spray. Arrange 5 bread slices in bottom of dish in a single layer. Pour 1 cup wine over bread. Sprinkle with ⅛ teaspoon salt and ⅛ teaspoon pepper. Top with ¾ cup cheese. Arrange pear slices over cheese; repeat layers of bread, wine, salt, pepper, and cheese.
2. Combine milk and eggs in a bowl; stir well with a whisk. Pour milk mixture over bread mixture. Let stand 20 minutes.
3. Preheat oven to 425°.
4. Cover strata, and bake at 425° for 30 minutes. Uncover and bake an additional 25 minutes or until golden brown. Let stand 10 minutes. Yield: 10 servings.

CALORIES 319 (30% from fat); FAT 10.6g (sat 4g, mono 3.3g, poly 0.6g); PROTEIN 13g; CARB 40.6g; FIBER 1.6g; CHOL 102mg; IRON 2.2mg; SODIUM 701mg; CALC 264mg

Spiced Fig and Walnut Bread

Try this bread with Pears with Goat Cheese and Preserves (recipe on page 303) for a light lunch.

2 cups all-purpose flour
¾ cup sugar
1½ teaspoons baking powder
1½ teaspoons ground cinnamon
1 teaspoon ground ginger
½ teaspoon baking soda
½ teaspoon salt
½ teaspoon ground allspice
¼ teaspoon ground nutmeg
½ cup chopped walnuts
8 dried Black Mission figs, chopped
1 cup low-fat buttermilk
⅓ cup molasses
2 tablespoons vegetable oil
2 large eggs
Cooking spray

1. Preheat oven to 350°.
2. Lightly spoon flour into dry measuring cups; level with a knife. Combine flour and next 8 ingredients in a large bowl; make a well in center of mixture. Stir in walnuts and figs. Combine buttermilk, molasses, oil, and eggs in a bowl; add to flour mixture. Stir just until moist.
3. Spoon batter into an 8 x 4-inch loaf pan coated with cooking spray. Bake at 350° for 1 hour or until a wooden pick inserted in center comes out clean. Cool 10 minutes in pan on a wire rack; remove from pan. Cool completely on wire rack. Yield: 12 servings (serving size: 1 slice).

CALORIES 246 (25% from fat); FAT 6.8g (sat 1.2g, mono 1.8g, poly 3.4g); PROTEIN 5.5g; CARB 42.2g; FIBER 2g; CHOL 37mg; IRON 2.1mg; SODIUM 238mg; CALC 104mg

---

Wine Note

Enhance Pears with Goat Cheese and Preserves with a top Sauvignon Blanc such as Mason Sauvignon Blanc from the Napa Valley (the 2000 is $16).

Leek and Potato Tart with Gruyère is reminiscent of many tarts in France's Alsace region. Try a bold, dramatic white wine from Alsace to counterpoint the richness of this dish. Try Hugel Gewürztraminer.

For Curried Butternut Squash Soup serve two different wines: a Chardonnay and a Riesling. Try the Hogue Cellars' Chardonnay from Washington State's Columbia Valley (the 1999 is about $10). Trefethen Vineyards in the Napa Valley makes a good Riesling (the 2000 is $15).

Raisin-Rosemary Rye Bread

Because rye flour produces a soft dough, we added whole wheat flour, bread flour, and cornmeal to give the loaf body.

```
1    tablespoon sugar
1    package dry yeast
1½   cups warm water (100° to 110°)
1    teaspoon olive oil
2⅓   cups bread flour, divided
1    cup whole wheat flour
½    cup rye flour
⅓    cup nonfat dry milk
¼    cup yellow cornmeal
1    teaspoon salt
¾    teaspoon coarsely ground black
     pepper
1    cup raisins
½    cup chopped walnuts
1½   tablespoons dried rosemary
     Cooking spray
```

1. Dissolve sugar and yeast in warm water in a large bowl; let stand 5 minutes. Stir in oil. Lightly spoon flours into dry measuring cups; level with a knife. Combine 2 cups bread flour, whole wheat flour, and next 5 ingredients in a bowl. Add flour mixture to yeast mixture. Turn dough out onto a lightly floured surface. Knead until smooth and elastic (about 10 minutes); add enough of remaining bread flour, 1 tablespoon at a time, to prevent dough from sticking to hands. Knead in raisins, walnuts, and rosemary.

2. Place dough in a large bowl coated with cooking spray, turning to coat top. Cover and let rise in a warm place (85°), free from drafts, 45 minutes or until doubled in size. (Press two fingers into dough. If indentation remains, dough has risen enough.) Punch dough down; cover and let rest 10 minutes. Form dough into a ball; place in a 9-inch pie plate coated with cooking spray. Cover and let rise 30 minutes or until doubled in size.

3. Preheat oven to 400°.

4. Uncover dough. Score top of loaf in a diamond pattern using a sharp knife. Bake at 400° for 50 minutes or until loaf sounds hollow when tapped. Remove from pan, and cool on a wire rack.

5. To serve bread, cut loaf in half crosswise. Place cut sides down, and cut each half into slices. Yield: 1 loaf (20 servings).

CALORIES 149 (16% from fat); FAT 2.6g (sat 0.3g, mono 0.6g, poly 1.4g); PROTEIN 5g; CARB 27.7g; FIBER 1.9g; CHOL 0mg; IRON 1.5mg; SODIUM 130mg; CALC 39mg

Honey-Apple Crumble with Dried Fruit

In addition to rehydrating the dried apricots and cranberries, the cider deepens the flavor of the apples.

```
1¾   cups apple cider
¼    cup finely chopped dried apricots
¼    cup dried cranberries
½    cup nutlike cereal nuggets
     (such as Grape-Nuts)
½    cup packed brown sugar, divided
5    tablespoons all-purpose flour,
     divided
1    teaspoon ground cinnamon,
     divided
3    tablespoons honey
1    teaspoon vanilla extract
5    medium Rome apples (about 2½
     pounds), each peeled and cut into
     8 wedges
     Cooking spray
```

1. Bring cider to a boil. Remove from heat, and stir in apricots and cranberries. Let stand 20 minutes. Drain dried fruit in a colander over a bowl, reserving cider.

2. Preheat oven to 350°.

3. Combine dried fruit, cereal, ¼ cup sugar, 1 tablespoon flour, and ½ teaspoon cinnamon in a bowl.

4. Combine ¼ cup sugar, ¼ cup flour, and ½ teaspoon cinnamon in a large bowl. Stir in reserved cider, honey, and vanilla. Add apples, tossing gently to coat. Place apple mixture in an 11 x 7-inch baking dish coated with cooking spray; top with cereal mixture.

5. Bake at 350° for 55 minutes. Yield: 6 servings (serving size: 1 cup).

CALORIES 267 (2% from fat); FAT 0.7g (sat 0.1g, mono 0.1g, poly 0.2g); PROTEIN 2.4g; CARB 66.2g; FIBER 4.7g; CHOL 0mg; IRON 1.9mg; SODIUM 79mg; CALC 36mg

back to the best

Fried-Chicken Salad

Fried-Chicken Salad debuted in March 1997. Who would have expected to see fried chicken in Cooking Light?

Fried-Chicken Salad

(pictured on page 294)

```
¼    cup all-purpose flour
¼    cup dry breadcrumbs
1    teaspoon garlic powder
1    teaspoon dried thyme
½    teaspoon salt
½    teaspoon black pepper
¾    pound skinless, boneless chicken
     breast, cut into thin strips
½    cup low-fat buttermilk
1    tablespoon olive oil
     Cooking spray
4    cups thickly sliced romaine lettuce,
     cut across rib
1    (15-ounce) can cut baby beets,
     drained
½    cup fat-free honey-Dijon mustard
     salad dressing
½    cup (2 ounces) crumbled blue cheese
```

1. Combine first 6 ingredients in a shallow dish; set aside. Combine chicken and buttermilk in a zip-top plastic bag; seal and marinate in refrigerator 30 minutes.

2. Remove chicken from bag, and discard marinade. Heat oil in a nonstick skillet coated with cooking spray over medium heat. Dredge a few chicken strips at a time in breadcrumb mixture, tossing to coat. Add chicken to pan, and cook 3 minutes on each side or until done.

3. Arrange 1 cup lettuce on each of 4 plates, and divide chicken and beets evenly among plates. Top each with 2 tablespoons dressing and 2 tablespoons cheese. Yield: 4 servings.

CALORIES 287 (27% from fat); FAT 7.4g (sat 2.2g, mono 3.4g, poly 0.8g); PROTEIN 25.8g; CARB 28.3g; FIBER 2g; CHOL 60mg; IRON 2.9mg; SODIUM 710mg; CALC 116mg

Get What You Need

Women need more nutrients, and we know where to find them.

The following recipes are nutrient-rich, delectable ways to add calcium, folic acid, iron, and soy protein—which provides other female-friendly nutrients—to your diet. And by the way, while they're made for women, they're strong enough for men, too.

Soy Protein

It was big news in the food world when the U.S. Food and Drug Administration recently approved the health claim that 25 grams of soy protein a day can help reduce cholesterol levels. There's also evidence that soy may prevent cancer and ease the effects of menopause. Apparently, a combination of substances found in soy—including isoflavones, soluble and insoluble fiber, and omega-3 fatty acids—act in concert to provide its health benefits. There's no shortage of soy choices today: Soy-infused cereals, snack bars, burgers, soups, and even pizzas fill supermarket aisles. But the best soy bets are more natural—tofu, soy milk, and beans like edamame and soy nuts.

Pumpkin-Praline Custards

Substituting soy milk for dairy milk in custards and puddings is a tasty way to increase beneficial soy protein in your diet. A crunchy topping of crumbled praline adds a festive touch to this homey dessert, but it's just as good without it. Each serving contains 3.5 grams of soy protein.

CUSTARDS:

1½ cups vanilla soy milk
¾ cup canned pumpkin
⅔ cup sugar
1½ teaspoons ground cinnamon
½ teaspoon ground nutmeg
½ teaspoon vanilla extract
¼ teaspoon salt
2 large eggs
2 large egg whites
Cooking spray

PRALINE:

¼ cup sugar
2 tablespoons water
¼ cup chopped pecans

1. Preheat oven to 325°.

2. To prepare custards, combine first 9 ingredients in a bowl; stir well with a whisk. Divide pumpkin mixture evenly among 6 (6-ounce) custard cups coated with cooking spray. Place cups in a 13 x 9-inch baking pan; add hot water to pan to a depth of 1 inch. Bake at 325° for 50 minutes or until a knife inserted in center comes out clean. Remove cups from pan, and cool completely on a wire rack. Cover and chill at least 3 hours.

3. To prepare praline, combine ¼ cup sugar and water in a small skillet. Cook over medium-high heat 4 minutes or until golden, stirring occasionally. Remove from heat, and stir in pecans. Immediately scrape pecan mixture onto a baking sheet coated with cooking spray, spreading evenly; cool completely. Break praline into small pieces. Sprinkle praline over custards. Yield: 6 servings (serving size: 1 custard and about 1 tablespoon praline).

CALORIES 220 (25% from fat); FAT 6.2g (sat 0.9g, mono 2.9g, poly 1.7g); PROTEIN 5.7g; CARB 37g; FIBER 1.7g; CHOL 71mg; IRON 1mg; SODIUM 235mg; CALC 101mg

---

Tofu Steaks with Tomato-Olive Sauce

Round out the meal with steamed broccoli and orzo. Each serving contains about 8 grams of soy protein.

2 teaspoons olive oil
¼ teaspoon crushed red pepper
2 garlic cloves, minced
2 cups canned crushed tomatoes
3 tablespoons chopped pitted kalamata olives
3 tablespoons chopped fresh flat-leaf parsley
⅛ teaspoon freshly ground black pepper
Cooking spray
1 pound extra-firm light tofu, drained and cut lengthwise into 4 slices

1. Heat oil in a medium saucepan over medium heat. Add red pepper and garlic; cook 1 minute. Stir in tomatoes; bring to a boil. Reduce heat, and simmer 10 minutes. Add olives; cook 1 minute. Remove from heat. Stir in parsley and black pepper; keep warm.

2. Heat a nonstick skillet coated with cooking spray over medium-high heat. Add tofu; cook 3 minutes on each side or until browned. Yield: 4 servings (serving size: 1 tofu steak and ½ cup sauce).

CALORIES 115 (49% from fat); FAT 6.2g (sat 0.8g, mono 4.1g, poly 1g); PROTEIN 9.2g; CARB 6.7g; FIBER 1.3g; CHOL 0mg; IRON 1.9mg; SODIUM 363mg; CALC 77mg

---

Iron

"Iron deficiency anemia is the most common nutritional deficiency we see in women, and the symptoms are easy to identify," says Michelle Warren, M.D., professor of obstetrics and gynecology at Columbia University. "These women are tired and even out of breath running for the subway or walking up stairs." Have a 3-ounce serving of iron-rich lean red meat for lunch or dinner a few times a week to ensure you're getting enough iron—18 milligrams per day. Or reach for iron-fortified cereals and breads, kidney beans, and spinach.

Hearty Bean and Barley Soup

This satisfying Italian-style soup features a delicious—and iron-packed—combination of red kidney beans and spinach. It's also high in fiber and calcium. To ensure rich flavor, add garlic and herbs to canned broth for a homemade taste. Mashing a portion of the beans gives the soup extra body.

- 7 cups fat-free, less-sodium chicken broth
- ¼ teaspoon crushed red pepper
- 6 garlic cloves, crushed
- 2 (4-inch) rosemary sprigs
- 1 (19-ounce) can dark red kidney beans, rinsed and drained
- 2 teaspoons olive oil
- 1 cup chopped onion
- 1 cup finely chopped carrot
- ¼ cup chopped celery
- 1 (14½-ounce) can diced tomatoes, undrained
- 1 cup uncooked quick-cooking barley
- 10 cups torn spinach leaves (about 4 ounces)
- ¼ teaspoon freshly ground black pepper
- ½ cup (2 ounces) grated fresh Parmesan cheese

1. Bring first 4 ingredients to a boil in a Dutch oven; reduce heat to medium-low, and cook 15 minutes. Drain in a sieve into a large bowl; discard solids.
2. Measure 1 cup beans, and mash with a fork in a small bowl. Reserve remaining whole beans.
3. Heat oil in pan over medium heat. Add onion, carrot, and celery; cook 4 minutes. Add broth mixture, mashed beans, whole beans, tomatoes, and barley; bring to a boil. Reduce heat; simmer 15 minutes. Stir in spinach and black pepper; cook 5 minutes or until barley is tender. Sprinkle each serving with cheese. Yield: 8 servings (serving size: about 1 cup soup and 1 tablespoon cheese).

CALORIES 208 (15% from fat); FAT 3.4g (sat 1.4g, mono 1.4g, poly 0.4g); PROTEIN 11.4g; CARB 34g; FIBER 8g; CHOL 5mg; IRON 2.3mg; SODIUM 615mg; CALC 156mg

Chinese Hot Pot of Beef and Vegetables

This comforting stew teams beef with spinach, an efficient pairing because the iron in the beef enhances your body's ability to absorb the iron in the spinach. Serve it over plain Chinese noodles or all by itself with some crusty French bread.

- 4 teaspoons vegetable oil, divided
- 1½ pounds beef stew meat, cut into 1-inch pieces
- ½ cup chopped green onions
- 2 tablespoons minced peeled fresh ginger
- 1 teaspoon aniseed, crushed
- 4 garlic cloves, minced
- 1 (14¼-ounce) can low-salt beef broth
- 2¾ cups water
- ¼ cup low-sodium soy sauce
- 1 tablespoon brown sugar
- 3 tablespoons dry sherry
- 2 to 3 teaspoons chile paste with garlic
- 2 (3-inch) cinnamon sticks
- 2 cups (1-inch) cubed peeled turnips (about ¾ pound)
- 1½ cups baby carrots
- 1 tablespoon water
- 2 teaspoons cornstarch
- 8 cups fresh spinach (about ½ pound)

1. Heat 2 teaspoons vegetable oil in a Dutch oven over medium-high heat; add half of beef, browning on all sides. Remove from pan. Repeat procedure with remaining oil and beef. Add onions, ginger, aniseed, and garlic to pan; sauté 30 seconds. Stir in broth, scraping pan to loosen browned bits. Return beef to pan. Add 2¾ cups water and next 5 ingredients, and bring to a boil. Cover, reduce heat, and simmer 1 hour.
2. Add turnips and carrots; simmer 45 minutes or until tender. Combine 1 tablespoon water and cornstarch; add to beef mixture. Bring to a boil; cook 1 minute, stirring frequently. Add spinach; cover and cook 3 minutes or until wilted. Discard cinnamon sticks. Yield: 6 servings (serving size: 1⅓ cups).

CALORIES 359 (30% from fat); FAT 11.9g (sat 3.4g, mono 5.5g, poly 1.5g); PROTEIN 26.4g; CARB 35.8g; FIBER 4.5g; CHOL 71mg; IRON 4.8mg; SODIUM 536mg; CALC 88mg

Folic Acid

"Folic acid is revolutionary," says Michelle Warren, M.D. "It offers a significant advance in preventing birth defects." She encourages all women of child-bearing age to consume the recommended 400 micrograms of folic acid daily. Even after menopause, folic acid helps reduce the risks of impaired concentration, memory, and hearing. And because it may help prevent heart disease, it's great for guys, too.

Get the necessary folic acid in orange juice, greens, grains (including whole wheat bread), and dried beans.

Warm Salad of Mustard Greens and Black-Eyed Peas

- 2 bacon slices, chopped
- 12 cups torn mustard greens, stems removed (about 12 ounces)
- ¼ teaspoon salt
- ¼ teaspoon black pepper
- 1 tablespoon extra-virgin olive oil
- ½ cup chopped green onions
- 2 teaspoons caraway seeds
- 3 garlic cloves, minced
- 1 jalapeño pepper, seeded and chopped
- 1 (16-ounce) can black-eyed peas, rinsed and drained
- ¼ cup balsamic vinegar

1. Cook bacon in a large nonstick skillet over medium heat until crisp. Remove bacon from pan, reserving 1 tablespoon drippings in pan; set bacon aside. Add greens to pan; cook 4 minutes or until wilted. Combine greens, salt, and black pepper in a large bowl; set aside. Add oil to pan. Stir in onions, caraway seeds, garlic, and jalapeño; cook 1 minute. Add peas; cook 1 minute. Stir in vinegar, and bring to a boil. Add pea mixture to greens mixture. Sprinkle mixture with reserved bacon. Yield: 4 servings (serving size: ¾ cup).

CALORIES 168 (43% from fat); FAT 8.1g (sat 2.6g, mono 4g, poly 0.9g); PROTEIN 7g; CARB 18g; FIBER 5.4g; CHOL 8mg; IRON 2.5mg; SODIUM 358mg; CALC 127mg

Lentil Burgers with Tzatziki

Lentils are a significant source of folic acid. Even more folic acid comes from the wheat germ used to bind the burgers, and from the whole wheat buns. These burgers pack 143 micrograms of folic acid—more than one-quarter of a day's recommendation. *Tzatziki*, a garlicky Greek yogurt sauce, is a healthful and tasty alternative to mayonnaise.

TZATZIKI:

    1   cup grated peeled English cucumber
    1½ cups plain low-fat yogurt
    ½   teaspoon salt
    2   garlic cloves, crushed
    ¼   cup chopped green onions
    1   teaspoon extra-virgin olive oil

PATTIES:

    2   teaspoons olive oil
    1   cup chopped onion
    ¾   teaspoon dried oregano
    ⅛   teaspoon crushed red pepper
    2   garlic cloves, minced
    1½ cups fat-free, less-sodium
        chicken broth
    ⅔   cup dried lentils
    ¼   cup sun-dried tomato sprinkles
    ⅔   cup (2½ ounces) crumbled feta
        cheese
    ½   cup grated carrot
    ⅓   cup Italian-seasoned breadcrumbs
    ⅓   cup toasted wheat germ
    3   tablespoons chopped pitted
        kalamata olives
    ¼   cup chopped fresh flat-leaf parsley
    ¼   teaspoon freshly ground black
        pepper
        Cooking spray
    8   (1½-ounce) whole wheat
        hamburger buns, toasted
    12 arugula leaves
    2   tomatoes, cut into ¼-inch-thick
        slices (about ¾ pound)

1. To prepare tzatziki, place cucumber on paper towels, and squeeze until barely moist. Place in a medium bowl. Spoon yogurt onto several layers of heavy-duty paper towels; spread to ½-inch thickness. Cover with additional paper towels, and let stand 5 minutes. Scrape into bowl using a rubber spatula.

Stir in salt, crushed garlic, green onions, and extra-virgin olive oil; chill.

2. To prepare patties, heat 2 teaspoons oil in a medium saucepan over medium-high heat. Add 1 cup onion; sauté 2 minutes or until tender. Stir in oregano, red pepper, and minced garlic; cook 30 seconds, stirring constantly. Stir in broth, lentils, and sun-dried tomatoes; bring to a boil. Cover, reduce heat, and simmer 35 minutes or until lentils are tender; drain. Cool.

3. Place lentil mixture, cheese, and next 6 ingredients in a food processor; pulse until coarsely ground. Divide lentil mixture into 8 equal portions, shaping each into a ½-inch-thick patty.

4. Heat a large nonstick skillet coated with cooking spray over medium-high heat. Add patties, and cook 3 minutes. Turn patties over, and cook over medium heat 3 minutes. Spread 1 tablespoon tzatziki evenly on each bun top and bottom. Arrange arugula, patties, and tomato slices over bottom halves of buns; top with remaining bun halves. Yield: 8 servings.

NOTE: You can freeze any uncooked lentil patties for up to 1 month: Separate patties with wax paper, place in a heavy-duty zip-top plastic bag, remove excess air, seal, and freeze. Thaw in refrigerator before cooking.

CALORIES 328 (27% from fat); FAT 9.8g (sat 3g, mono 4.5g, poly 1.4g); PROTEIN 15.8g; CARB 46.7g; FIBER 9.2g; CHOL 11mg; IRON 4.5mg; SODIUM 891mg; CALC 250mg

---

Calcium

"Ninety percent of women are not taking in enough calcium to prevent osteoporosis," says Connie Weaver, Ph.D., professor of foods and nutrition at Purdue University. "Women know they need it, but most are meeting only half their daily requirement." Weaver, an expert on mineral metabolism, urges women to consume a calcium-rich food every time they eat to get 1,000 milligrams per day (women over 50 need 1,200 milligrams).

While calcium's bone-building role gets top billing, it's also been shown to help control blood pressure and may protect against colon cancer. New research suggests it may even play a role in weight control. A University of Tennessee study showed that a diet high in calcium may actually change how fat cells work, causing them to make less fat.

Banana-Berry Smoothie

Sip this power breakfast—which boasts more than 300 milligrams of calcium—while getting ready for work or on your way there. A scoop of powdered milk boosts the calcium contributed by the yogurt and the calcium-fortified orange juice. Additional nutritional benefits come from potassium-rich banana and antioxidant-rich berries. Frozen berries ensure a thick, creamy consistency, but you can also use fresh ones. Other frozen fruits, such as peaches or mangoes, work well, too.

    1¼ cups calcium-fortified orange juice
    1¼ cups frozen mixed berries (such as
        Cascadian Farm Harvest Berries)
    1   cup sliced ripe banana
    ½   cup vanilla fat-free yogurt
    ⅓   cup nonfat dry milk
    1   tablespoon sugar

1. Combine all ingredients in a blender; process until smooth. Yield: 3 servings (serving size: 1 cup).

CALORIES 204 (3% from fat); FAT 0.6g (sat 0.2g, mono 0.1g, poly 0.2g); PROTEIN 6.6g; CARB 45.6g; FIBER 3.3g; CHOL 2mg; IRON 0.6mg; SODIUM 71mg; CALC 327mg

november

Thanksgiving Classic

Step by step to a traditional holiday menu featuring all of the family favorites.

Sometimes it's best to stick to basics—like when you're preparing a Thanksgiving feast. To help you stay on track, our classic Thanksgiving menu is complete with step-by-step instructions for the trickier tasks and a countdown full of make-ahead tips to take you through every step. You can even start up to a month in advance so you won't feel harried or rushed on Thanksgiving Day.

Classic Thanksgiving Menu
serves 8

Roast Turkey with Classic Pan Gravy

Savory Fruited Stuffing

Spiced Sweet Potato Casserole

Green Beans with Roasted-Onion Vinaigrette

Poppy Seed Twists

Cranberry-Apple Relish

Gingered Pumpkin Pie

Thanksgiving Countdown

One month ahead:
• Make and freeze Poppy Seed Twists.

Three days ahead:
• Prepare and refrigerate Cranberry-Apple Relish.

The day before:
• Make and refrigerate vinaigrette for green beans.
• Steam and chill green beans.
• Mix all stuffing ingredients; refrigerate in baking dish.
• Assemble sweet potato casserole; refrigerate in baking dish.
• Prepare streusel topping for pie; refrigerate.
• Mix pie filling ingredients; refrigerate.

Thanksgiving morning:
• Bake pie (serve chilled or at room temperature).

A few hours ahead:
• Put turkey in oven.
• Simmer stock for gravy while turkey roasts.
• Tent roasted turkey with foil to keep warm.

Last minute:
• Bake stuffing and sweet potato casserole while turkey stands.
• Finish gravy; keep warm.
• Place thawed bread (in foil) in oven during last 15 minutes of casserole's cooking time.

Roast Turkey with Classic Pan Gravy
(pictured on page 330)

There are two ways to thaw a frozen bird. The easiest: Place it on a tray in the refrigerator for three days. The quickest: Submerge the wrapped turkey, breast side down, in cold water for 5 to 6 hours; change the water every half hour to keep it cold.

1   (12-pound) fresh or frozen turkey, thawed
⅓   cup spicy brown mustard
¼   cup packed chopped fresh sage leaves
½   teaspoon freshly ground black pepper
2   garlic cloves, minced
2   cups fat-free, less-sodium chicken broth
Classic Pan Gravy

1. Preheat oven to 450°.
2. Remove giblets and neck from turkey, and reserve for Classic Pan Gravy. Rinse turkey with cold water, and pat dry. Trim excess fat. Starting at neck cavity, loosen skin from breast and drumsticks by inserting fingers, gently pushing between skin and meat. Combine mustard, sage, black pepper, and garlic. Rub mustard mixture under loosened skin. Lift wing tips up and over back; tuck under turkey.
3. Place turkey, breast side up, in a shallow roasting pan. Pour broth over turkey. Insert a meat thermometer into meaty part of thigh, making sure not to touch bone. Place turkey in a 450° oven; immediately reduce oven temperature to 325° (do not remove turkey from oven). Bake 2 hours or until thermometer registers 180°, basting turkey frequently with pan juices. Reserve 3 tablespoons drippings for Classic Pan Gravy; let turkey stand 25 minutes. Discard skin. Serve with Classic Pan Gravy. Yield: 12 servings (serving size: 6 ounces turkey and about 3 tablespoons gravy).

(Totals include Classic Pan Gravy) CALORIES 326 (27% from fat); FAT 9.6g (sat 3.1g, mono 2.2g, poly 2.7g); PROTEIN 51.6g; CARB 3.9g; FIBER 0.9g; CHOL 130mg; IRON 3.4mg; SODIUM 418mg; CALC 58mg

How to Make Classic Pan Gravy

1. *Combine flour and reserved turkey drippings to keep the flour from clumping when you add it to the wine.*

2. *Whisking the flour-wine mixture constantly as it begins to cook ensures a smooth gravy with no lumps.*

CLASSIC PAN GRAVY:

Start the stock 30 minutes into the turkey's cooking time so everything will be ready at the same time.

4   cups water
½   cup parsley sprigs
1   teaspoon black peppercorns
2   medium carrots, each cut into
    3 pieces
1   large onion, cut into 8 wedges
1   bay leaf
1   (14½-ounce) can fat-free,
    less-sodium chicken broth
    Reserved turkey neck and giblets
¾   cup dry white wine
3   tablespoons all-purpose flour
3   tablespoons reserved turkey
    drippings
¼   teaspoon salt
¼   teaspoon freshly ground black pepper

1. Combine first 8 ingredients in a large saucepan. Bring to a boil. Reduce heat; simmer over medium-low heat until reduced to 2½ cups (about 1½ hours). Strain stock through a sieve into a bowl; discard solids.
2. Bring wine to a boil in pan; cook until reduced to ½ cup (about 3 minutes). Combine flour and turkey drippings in a bowl; stir with a whisk until smooth. Add to pan; cook over medium heat 1 minute, stirring constantly. Stir in strained stock, salt, and ground black pepper; cook over medium heat 15 minutes, stirring occasionally. Yield: 2½ cups (serving size: about 3 tablespoons).

CALORIES 20 (45% from fat); FAT 1g (sat 0.3g, mono 0.4g, poly 0.2g); PROTEIN 0.7g; CARB 1.9g; FIBER 0.1g; CHOL 1mg; IRON 0.2mg; SODIUM 118mg; CALC 2mg

Savory Fruited Stuffing

(pictured on page 330)

The stuffing can be refrigerated for up to 24 hours before baking.

3½ cups fat-free, less-sodium chicken
    broth
1   cup dried mixed-fruit bits
2   tablespoons butter
2   cups finely chopped onion
½   cup thinly sliced celery
1   (14-ounce) package cubed
    country-style stuffing mix (such
    as Pepperidge Farm)

1. Combine broth and dried fruit in a small microwave-safe bowl; microwave at HIGH 2 minutes or until hot. Cover and let stand 10 minutes.
2. Melt butter in a large saucepan over medium heat. Add onion and celery; cook 8 minutes or until tender, stirring occasionally. Add broth mixture, and bring to a simmer. Remove from heat; stir in stuffing mix, tossing well.

3. Spoon stuffing into a 13 x 9-inch baking dish; cover and refrigerate 2 hours.
4. Preheat oven to 350°.
5. Cover and bake at 350° for 30 minutes. Yield: 10 servings (serving size: 1 cup).

CALORIES 224 (16% from fat); FAT 4g (sat 1.5g, mono 1.8g, poly 0.1g); PROTEIN 7.2g; CARB 41g; FIBER 3.9g; CHOL 6mg; IRON 2mg; SODIUM 597mg; CALC 58mg

Spiced Sweet Potato Casserole

(pictured on page 330)

Assemble this casserole in its baking dish and store it, covered, in the refrigerator for up to one day.

3   pounds sweet potatoes
⅓   cup packed brown sugar
2   tablespoons butter
2   tablespoons orange juice
    concentrate
1½ teaspoons ground cinnamon
½   teaspoon salt
½   teaspoon ground nutmeg
2   large eggs
¼   cup chopped pecans

1. Preheat oven to 350°.
2. Pierce potatoes with a fork; arrange in a circle on paper towels in microwave oven. Microwave at HIGH 16 minutes or until tender, rearranging potatoes after 8 minutes. Let stand 5 minutes.
3. Cut each potato in half lengthwise; scoop out pulp into a large bowl. Discard skins. Add sugar and next 5 ingredients, and beat with a mixer at low speed until combined. Add eggs; beat until smooth.
4. Spoon mixture into a 1½-quart baking dish; sprinkle with pecans. Bake at 350° for 45 minutes or until thoroughly heated. Yield: 8 servings (serving size: ½ cup).

CALORIES 220 (29% from fat); FAT 7g (sat 2.5g, mono 2.9g, poly 1.1g); PROTEIN 3.8g; CARB 36.8g; FIBER 3.8g; CHOL 61mg; IRON 1.1mg; SODIUM 206mg; CALC 53mg

Green Beans with Roasted-Onion Vinaigrette

(pictured on page 329)

2 red onions, peeled (about 1 pound)
4 teaspoons olive oil, divided
¼ teaspoon salt
¼ teaspoon black pepper
2 sprigs fresh thyme
1 tablespoon chopped fresh dill
3 tablespoons Champagne vinegar or white wine vinegar
1 tablespoon stone-ground mustard
2 pounds green beans, trimmed, steamed, and chilled

1. Preheat oven to 400°.
2. Cut onions in half vertically. Drizzle cut side of each onion half with ¼ teaspoon oil. Sprinkle halves evenly with salt and pepper. Place 1 thyme sprig on 1 onion half; top with other half. Wrap in foil. Repeat procedure with remaining thyme and onion halves. Bake wrapped onions at 400° for 1 hour or until tender. Cool to room temperature. Discard thyme, and chop onions. Combine onion, 1 tablespoon olive oil, dill, vinegar, and mustard in a small bowl.
3. Toss beans with vinaigrette. Yield: 8 servings (serving size: about 4 ounces green beans and ¼ cup vinaigrette).

CALORIES 83 (29% from fat); FAT 2.7g (sat 0.4g, mono 1.7g, poly 0.4g); PROTEIN 2.9g; CARB 14g; FIBER 4.8g; CHOL 0mg; IRON 1.6mg; SODIUM 109mg; CALC 65mg

Preparing Onions

Place a thyme sprig between onion halves; roast in foil. Red onions turn a jewel-like pink and take on a sweet herbal flavor.

Poppy Seed Twists

To serve, thaw completely, wrap in foil, and heat at 350° for 15 minutes.

1 tablespoon butter
1 cup finely chopped onion
1 tablespoon poppy seeds
¼ teaspoon salt
1 (1-pound) loaf frozen white bread dough, thawed
Cooking spray
2 teaspoons fat-free milk
1 large egg

1. Melt butter in a large nonstick skillet over medium heat. Add onion; cook 10 minutes or until tender, stirring occasionally. Cool to room temperature; stir in poppy seeds and salt. Set aside.
2. Roll dough into a 14 x 12-inch rectangle on a lightly floured surface. Spread onion mixture lengthwise over half of rectangle. Fold dough in half lengthwise; press edges of dough firmly to seal. Cut dough into 12 (6-inch-long) strips. Gently lift both ends of each strip, and twist. Place twisted dough strips 1 inch apart on a large baking sheet coated with cooking spray. Cover and let rise in a warm place (85°), free from drafts, 40 minutes or until doubled in size.
3. Preheat oven to 375°.
4. Combine milk and egg; brush over dough. Bake at 375° for 20 minutes or until golden. Remove from baking sheet; cool 10 minutes on a wire rack. Yield: 12 servings.

CALORIES 129 (24% from fat); FAT 3.5g (sat 0.8g, mono 0.5g, poly 0.3g); PROTEIN 4.8g; CARB 20.9g; FIBER 1.5g; CHOL 20mg; IRON 1.6mg; SODIUM 275mg; CALC 26mg

Cranberry-Apple Relish

(pictured on page 330)

1½ cups chopped peeled Granny Smith apple (about ½ pound)
1 cup packed brown sugar
½ cup white grape juice
1 teaspoon ground ginger
1 teaspoon ground cinnamon
1 (12-ounce) package fresh cranberries

1. Combine all ingredients in a medium saucepan. Bring to a boil; reduce heat, and simmer until thick (about 15 minutes), stirring occasionally. Cool completely. Yield: 16 servings (serving size: 3 tablespoons).

CALORIES 75 (1% from fat); FAT 0.1g (sat 0g, mono 0g, poly 0.1g); PROTEIN 0.2g; CARB 19.3g; FIBER 1.2g; CHOL 0mg; IRON 0.5mg; SODIUM 6mg; CALC 16mg

Gingered Pumpkin Pie

A gingersnap streusel topping adds crunch to traditional pumpkin pie. Refrigerated pie dough speeds preparation.

½ (15-ounce) package refrigerated pie dough (such as Pillsbury)
10 gingersnap cookies
2 tablespoons sugar
1 tablespoon all-purpose flour
2 tablespoons chilled butter, cut into small pieces
¾ cup sugar
1½ teaspoons ground cinnamon
½ teaspoon ground ginger
¼ teaspoon salt
¼ teaspoon ground nutmeg
1 (15-ounce) can unsweetened pumpkin
1 (12-ounce) can evaporated fat-free milk
1 large egg
3 large egg whites

1. Roll dough into a 12-inch circle; fit into a 10-inch deep-dish pie plate. Fold edges under, and flute. Freeze 30 minutes.
2. Place cookies, 2 tablespoons sugar, and flour in a food processor; process until cookies are ground. Add butter; pulse until crumbly.
3. Preheat oven to 350°.
4. Combine ¾ cup sugar and remaining 8 ingredients; pour into prepared crust. Bake at 350° for 35 minutes. Sprinkle crumb mixture over pie; bake an additional 20 minutes or until center is set. Cool to room temperature on a wire rack. Yield: 8 servings (serving size: 1 wedge).

CALORIES 338 (31% from fat); FAT 11.5g (sat 5.1g, mono 4.7g, poly 1.1g); PROTEIN 7.2g; CARB 51.7g; FIBER 2.6g; CHOL 41mg; IRON 1.2mg; SODIUM 340mg; CALC 157mg

Don't Settle

Why settle for the same old sandwiches?

Spicy Turkey Soft Tacos

(pictured on page 332)

Mole sauce is easy to prepare and comes together in a flash. Be careful, though: The turkey will spatter from time to time in the pan during the browning process.

TOTAL TIME: 35 MINUTES

QUICK TIP: To easily seed an avocado, cut it lengthwise all the way around; twist gently to separate halves. Firmly hit seed with the blade of a knife; twist knife slightly, and lift out seed. Scoop out avocado from peel with a large spoon.

MOLE:

    1 (7-ounce) can chipotle chiles in
       adobo sauce
    ½ medium onion, peeled and
       quartered
    2 garlic cloves, peeled
    ⅓ cup fat-free, less-sodium chicken
       broth
    ⅓ cup orange juice
    2 tablespoons cider vinegar
    ½ teaspoon ground cumin
    ½ teaspoon dried oregano
    ½ teaspoon ground red pepper
    ¼ teaspoon salt
    ¼ teaspoon ground cinnamon
    ¼ teaspoon black pepper

REMAINING INGREDIENTS:

    1 teaspoon vegetable oil
    2 cups shredded cooked turkey
    8 (6-inch) corn tortillas
    ½ cup diced peeled avocado
    ½ cup bottled salsa
    4 lime wedges

1. Preheat oven to 400°.

2. To prepare mole, drain chipotles in a colander over a bowl, reserving ½ teaspoon adobo sauce. Remove 1 chile; chop to measure 1½ teaspoons. Reserve remaining adobo sauce and chiles for another use.

3. Place onion and garlic in a small, shallow baking dish; bake at 400° for 15 minutes.

4. Combine ½ teaspoon adobo sauce, chopped chile, broth, and next 8 ingredients in a blender; add onion and garlic. Process until smooth.

5. Heat oil in a large nonstick skillet over medium-high heat. Add turkey; sauté 12 minutes or until browned. Add mole; cook 4 minutes or until liquid is absorbed, stirring occasionally.

6. Heat tortillas according to package directions. Spoon ¼ cup turkey mixture onto each tortilla, and roll up. Top each serving with 2 tablespoons avocado and 2 tablespoons salsa. Serve with lime wedges. Yield: 4 servings (serving size: 2 tacos and 1 lime wedge).

CALORIES 318 (29% from fat); FAT 10.1g (sat 2.1g, mono 3.8g, poly 2.7g); PROTEIN 25g; CARB 33.7g; FIBER 3.5g; CHOL 54mg; IRON 2.6mg; SODIUM 532mg; CALC 129mg

Turkey Jambalaya

Andouille sausage adds a kick to this colorful post-Thanksgiving twist on the Cajun classic from Louisiana. Rice and shredded turkey absorb a mixture of tomatoes and spices until they're bursting with flavor.

TOTAL TIME: 40 MINUTES

QUICK TIP: You can substitute cooked chicken for turkey in any of these recipes.

    1   tablespoon olive oil
    1½ cups chopped onion
    1   teaspoon bottled minced garlic
    1   cup chopped green bell pepper
    1   cup chopped red bell pepper
    2½ teaspoons paprika
    ½   teaspoon salt
    ½   teaspoon dried oregano
    ½   teaspoon ground red pepper
    ½   teaspoon black pepper
    1   cup uncooked long-grain rice
    2   cups fat-free, less-sodium
        chicken broth
    1   (14.5-ounce) can diced tomatoes,
        undrained
    2   cups shredded cooked turkey
    6   ounces andouille sausage, chopped
    2   tablespoons sliced green onions

1. Heat oil in a large Dutch oven over medium-high heat. Add chopped onion and garlic; sauté 6 minutes or until lightly browned. Stir in bell peppers and next 5 ingredients; sauté 1 minute. Add rice; sauté 1 minute. Stir in broth and tomatoes; bring to a boil. Cover, reduce heat, and simmer 15 minutes. Add turkey and sausage; cover and cook 5 minutes. Sprinkle with green onions. Yield: 8 servings (serving size: 1 cup).

CALORIES 249 (27% from fat); FAT 7.6g (sat 2.4g, mono 3.4g, poly 1.3g); PROTEIN 17.3g; CARB 27.4g; FIBER 2.7g; CHOL 42mg; IRON 2.7mg; SODIUM 523mg; CALC 37mg

Menu 3

serves 6

Turkey Alfredo Pizza

Herbed tomato-mozzarella
salad*

*Combine 3 cups halved grape tomatoes
and 1 cup cubed fresh mozzarella cheese
in a large bowl. Combine 2 tablespoons
white balsamic vinegar, 1 teaspoon bottled minced garlic, 1 teaspoon olive oil, ¼
teaspoon salt, ¼ teaspoon dried basil, and
¼ teaspoon dried oregano in a small
bowl; stir well with a whisk. Pour dressing
over salad; toss well. Serve chilled or at
room temperature.

Peach sorbet

Turkey Alfredo Pizza

TOTAL TIME: 32 MINUTES

QUICK TIP: Rubbing the pizza crust with a
halved garlic clove imparts lots of flavor
with little effort and no chopping.

- 1 cup shredded cooked turkey breast
- 1 cup frozen chopped collard greens
     or spinach, thawed, drained, and
     squeezed dry
- 2 teaspoons lemon juice
- ½ teaspoon salt
- ¼ teaspoon black pepper
- 1 garlic clove, halved
- 1 (1-pound) Italian cheese-flavored
     thin pizza crust (such as Boboli)
- ½ cup light Alfredo sauce
     (such as Contadina)
- ¾ cup (3 ounces) shredded
     fontina cheese
- ½ teaspoon crushed red pepper

1. Preheat oven to 450°.
2. Combine first 5 ingredients; toss well.
Rub cut sides of garlic over crust; discard
garlic. Spread Alfredo sauce evenly over
crust; top with turkey mixture. Sprinkle
with cheese and red pepper. Bake at
450° for 12 minutes or until crust is
crisp. Cut into 6 wedges. Yield: 6 servings (serving size: 1 wedge).

CALORIES 316 (29% from fat); FAT 10.3g (sat 5.2g, mono 3.5g,
poly 1.1g); PROTEIN 19.2g; CARB 35.6g; FIBER 0.6g; CHOL 39mg;
IRON 2.5mg; SODIUM 837mg; CALC 351mg

Menu 4

serves 4

Asian Turkey Salad

Faux won ton soup*

*Combine 2 cups fat-free, less-sodium
chicken broth; 1 cup water; 1 tablespoon
low-sodium soy sauce; and ½ teaspoon
bottled ground fresh ginger in a
saucepan. Bring to a boil. Add half of a
(9-ounce) package fresh cheese tortellini;
reduce heat, and simmer 6 minutes or
until done. Sprinkle with 2 tablespoons
chopped fresh cilantro.

Rice topped with toasted
sesame seeds

Asian Turkey Salad

This fresh, bright salad takes Thanksgiving
leftovers on a trip East. And after the big
day, you'll welcome its lightness.

TOTAL TIME: 25 MINUTES

QUICK TIP: To speed preparation, use
packaged finely shredded cabbage in
place of the napa cabbage.

DRESSING:

- ¼ cup rice vinegar
- ¼ cup vegetable broth
- 1 tablespoon low-sodium soy
     sauce
- 2 teaspoons bottled ground fresh
     ginger (such as Spice World)
- 2 teaspoons lime juice
- 1 teaspoon bottled minced garlic
- 1 teaspoon peanut oil
- 1 teaspoon sesame oil
- ½ teaspoon salt
- ½ teaspoon sugar
- 1 serrano chile

SALAD:

- 4 cups thinly sliced napa (Chinese)
     cabbage
- 3 cups shredded cooked turkey
- 1 cup red bell pepper strips (about
     1 small pepper)
- ½ cup thinly sliced red onion
- ½ cup chopped fresh cilantro
- ¼ cup sliced green onions
- 1 tablespoon dry-roasted peanuts,
     chopped

1. To prepare salad dressing, place first
11 ingredients in a blender, and process
until smooth.
2. To prepare salad, combine cabbage
and remaining 6 ingredients in a large
bowl, and pour dressing over salad, tossing to coat. Yield: 4 servings (serving
size: 1¾ cups).

CALORIES 250 (30% from fat); FAT 8.3g (sat 2.2g, mono 2.3g,
poly 2.6g); PROTEIN 33.2g; CARB 10.3g; FIBER 3.4g; CHOL 80mg;
IRON 2.8mg; SODIUM 592mg; CALC 80mg

inspired vegetarian

A Feast with No Beast

*No one will miss the bird with this hearty
spread.*

People often imagine that Thanksgiving dinner must pose an insurmountable
problem for vegetarians. But if your favorite part of Thanksgiving has always
been the "fixin's," you can be just as joy-
ful at the feast without the turkey. You
may, however, like to create a centerpiece dish to stand in for the turkey since
side dishes are best appreciated when
they are companions to the main event.

This Thanksgiving menu balances
flavors, colors, textures, and time challenges. Invite nonvegetarians to your
spread without apology—they'll hardly
notice the turkey's absent.

Thanksgiving Menu

serves 8

**Mushroom and
Caramelized-Shallot Strudel**

Marinated Lentil Salad

**Sweet Potato
and Apple Gratin**
or
**Creamy Mashed
Potatoes with Chives**

**Cranberry, Pear,
and Ginger Relish**

**Herb and Onion
Wheat Biscuits**

Mushroom and Caramelized-Shallot Strudel

This recipe makes two strudels; for an eye-catching centerpiece, place them on a large platter, and surround them with fresh thyme sprigs.

  1   teaspoon olive oil
  1½   cups sliced shallots (about 8 ounces)
  ⅛   teaspoon sugar
  1   tablespoon water
  4   (8-ounce) packages presliced
       mushrooms
  2   tablespoons dry Marsala or Madeira
  ⅔   cup low-fat sour cream
  ¼   cup chopped fresh parsley
  ½   teaspoon salt
  ½   teaspoon minced fresh or
       ¼ teaspoon dried thyme
  ¼   teaspoon freshly ground
       black pepper
  8   sheets frozen phyllo dough, thawed
Cooking spray
  ⅓   cup dry breadcrumbs, divided
  1   tablespoon butter, melted

1. Preheat oven to 400°.
2. Heat olive oil in a large skillet over medium heat. Add shallots and sugar; cook 2 minutes, stirring constantly. Sprinkle with water; cover, reduce heat to medium-low, and cook 10 minutes or until shallots are soft, stirring occasionally. Add mushrooms; cook, uncovered, over medium-high heat 20 minutes or until liquid evaporates, stirring frequently. Add Marsala; cook 1 minute. Remove from heat, and cool. Stir in sour cream, parsley, salt, thyme, and pepper.
3. Place 1 phyllo sheet on a large cutting board or work surface (cover remaining dough to keep from drying), and lightly coat with cooking spray. Sprinkle with about 2 teaspoons breadcrumbs. Repeat layers with 3 phyllo sheets, cooking spray, and breadcrumbs, ending with phyllo. Spoon 1¾ cups mushroom mixture along 1 long edge of phyllo, leaving a 1-inch border. Starting at long edge with 1-inch border, roll up jelly roll fashion. Place strudel, seam side down, on a baking sheet coated with cooking spray. Tuck ends under. Repeat procedure with remaining phyllo sheets, cooking spray, breadcrumbs, and mushroom mixture. Brush strudels with butter. Bake strudels at 400° for 20 minutes. Let stand 5 minutes. Cut each strudel into 4 slices. Yield: 2 strudels, 8 servings (serving size: 1 slice).

CALORIES 176 (28% from fat); FAT 5.5g (sat 2.7g, mono 1.6g, poly 0.5g); PROTEIN 7.4g; CARB 24.9g; FIBER 2.1g; CHOL 11mg; IRON 2.6mg; SODIUM 314mg; CALC 60mg

Marinated Lentil Salad

Cooking the lentils for only 15 minutes preserves their shape and texture. Tossed with a little vinaigrette, they make a tasty, satisfying salad.

VINAIGRETTE:
  ¼   cup fresh lemon juice
  ¼   cup red-wine vinegar
  3   tablespoons olive oil
  ½   teaspoon salt
  ¼   teaspoon sugar
  ¼   teaspoon freshly ground black
       pepper

SALAD:
  ½   cup chopped parsnip
  ½   cup chopped carrot
  6   cups boiling water
  1½   cups dried lentils
  ½   cup thinly sliced celery
  ⅓   cup thinly sliced green onions
  3   tablespoons minced fresh parsley

1. To prepare vinaigrette, combine first 6 ingredients in a small bowl, stirring with a whisk. Set aside.
2. To prepare salad, cook parsnip and carrot in 6 cups boiling water 1 minute or until tender; remove vegetables with a slotted spoon. Add lentils to pan; bring to a boil. Reduce heat, and simmer 15 minutes or until tender; drain in a colander. Cool.
3. Combine parsnip, carrot, lentils, celery, onions, and parsley in a bowl; stir in vinaigrette. Marinate at room temperature at least 20 minutes. Yield: 8 servings (serving size: ⅔ cup).

CALORIES 186 (27% from fat); FAT 5.5g (sat 0.7g, mono 3.8g, poly 0.6g); PROTEIN 10.5g; CARB 25.1g; FIBER 12g; CHOL 0mg; IRON 3.5mg; SODIUM 262mg; CALC 32mg

---

Game Plan

Two days ahead:
- Make relish; cover and refrigerate.

One day ahead:
- Cook mushroom and shallot filling for strudel; cover and refrigerate.
- Make lentil salad; cover and refrigerate.

One hour before cooking:
- Remove relish and lentil salad from refrigerator; bring to room temperature.
- Peel and cut potatoes for mashed potatoes; let sit in cold water.
- Make breadcrumbs for sweet potato gratin; set aside.
- Assemble the gratin.
- Assemble strudels, and chill.
- Make biscuits.

Time to cook:
- Bake biscuits; decrease oven temperature to 400°.
- Put gratin in oven.
- Twenty-five minutes later, start mashed potatoes.
- Put strudels in oven when it's time to add breadcrumbs to gratin.

Sweet Potato and Apple Gratin

Sweet but not overly so, this side dish is a delicious accompaniment to a holiday meal. Let it stand for 10 minutes after baking so the juices can thicken.

  3   cups thinly sliced peeled Granny
       Smith apple (about 1¼ pounds)
  1   teaspoon lemon juice
  4   small sweet potatoes, peeled and
       thinly sliced (about 2 pounds)
  ¼   cup maple syrup
  1   tablespoon butter, melted
  ½   teaspoon salt
  ¼   teaspoon black pepper
Cooking spray
  2   (1-ounce) slices white bread
  2   teaspoons olive oil
  ¼   teaspoon ground nutmeg

Continued

1. Preheat oven to 400°.
2. Combine apple and lemon juice in a large bowl. Add sweet potato and next 4 ingredients. Place sweet potato mixture in a 13 x 9-inch baking dish coated with cooking spray. Bake at 400° for 40 minutes, stirring after 25 minutes.
3. Place bread in a food processor; pulse 10 times or until coarse crumbs form to measure 1 cup. Combine breadcrumbs, oil, and nutmeg; sprinkle over sweet potato mixture. Bake an additional 15 minutes or until golden. Let gratin stand 10 minutes before serving. Yield: 8 servings.

CALORIES 214 (14% from fat); FAT 3.4g (sat 1.3g, mono 1.4g, poly 0.4g); PROTEIN 2.6g; CARB 44.3g; FIBER 4.6g; CHOL 3.9mg; IRON 1.1mg; SODIUM 218mg; CALC 42mg

Creamy Mashed Potatoes with Chives

You can substitute 5 ounces less-fat cream cheese, 2 tablespoons fresh chives, and 1 tablespoon chopped onion for the flavored cream cheese.

    3   pounds peeled Yukon gold
        potatoes, quartered
    ⅔   cup fat-free milk
    1   teaspoon salt
    ⅔   cup (5 ounces) light cream cheese
        with chives and onions

1. Place potatoes in a Dutch oven, and cover with water; bring to a boil. Reduce heat, and simmer 10 minutes or until tender. Drain. Return potatoes to pan; add milk and salt. Mash potato mixture with a potato masher to desired consistency. Add cheese, and stir just until blended. Yield: 10 servings (serving size: ⅔ cup).

CALORIES 172 (16% from fat); FAT 3g (sat 2g, mono 0g, poly 0.1g); PROTEIN 6.1g; CARB 30.4g; FIBER 2.8g; CHOL 9mg; IRON 2.4mg; SODIUM 399mg; CALC 70mg

Cranberry, Pear, and Ginger Relish

Improvise with this relish: Add or substitute other dried fruits, such as finely diced dried apple, pear, or apricot.

    3   cups fresh cranberries
    2   cups finely chopped peeled Anjou
        pear (about 3 pears)
    1⅓ cups orange juice
    1¼ cups dried cranberries
    ⅔   cup packed brown sugar
    3   tablespoons dried currants or
        raisins
    3   tablespoons minced crystallized
        ginger
    ⅛   teaspoon ground cardamom

1. Combine all ingredients in a large saucepan; bring to a boil. Reduce heat, and simmer 10 minutes, stirring occasionally. Chill. Yield: 15 servings (serving size: ⅓ cup).

CALORIES 123 (1% from fat); FAT 0.2g (sat 0g, mono 0.1g, poly 0.1g); PROTEIN 0.4g; CARB 30.8g; FIBER 2.3g; CHOL 0mg; IRON 1.6mg; SODIUM 8mg; CALC 29mg

Herb and Onion Wheat Biscuits

(pictured on page 332)

The onion is pureed so that its flavor carries throughout the biscuits. You can make and freeze the biscuits up to a week ahead. When ready to serve, thaw, wrap in foil, and bake at 325° for 10 minutes or until thoroughly heated.

    Cooking spray
    1   cup chopped onion
    ¾   cup fat-free milk
    1½ cups all-purpose flour
    ½   cup whole wheat flour
    2   teaspoons baking powder
    ½   teaspoon salt
    ¼   teaspoon sugar
    ¼   teaspoon dried oregano
    ¼   teaspoon dried basil
    ¼   cup chilled butter, cut into small
        pieces

1. Preheat oven to 425°.

2. Heat a small skillet coated with cooking spray over medium heat. Add onion; cook 6 minutes or until tender, stirring frequently. Spoon onion into a blender. Add milk; process until smooth. Cool.
3. Lightly spoon flours into dry measuring cups, and level with a knife. Combine flours and next 5 ingredients in a large bowl; cut in butter with a pastry blender or 2 knives until mixture resembles coarse meal. Add onion mixture; stir just until moist. Turn dough out onto a heavily floured surface (dough will be sticky), and knead lightly 5 times with floured hands. Roll dough to a ½-inch thickness; cut into 10 biscuits with a 3-inch biscuit cutter. Place on a baking sheet coated with cooking spray. Bake at 425° for 12 minutes or until golden. Yield: 10 servings (serving size: 1 biscuit).

CALORIES 119 (31% from fat); FAT 4.1g (sat 2.4g, mono 1.2g, poly 0.3g); PROTEIN 3.1g; CARB 17.9g; FIBER 1.3g; CHOL 11mg; IRON 1.1mg; SODIUM 227mg; CALC 73mg

cooking light profile

Odds-On Winners

A Las Vegas couple's bet on the good life is paying off.

Married for a little more than a year, Kim and Tim Bavington are a fast-track couple who have to remind themselves to slow down and smell the cactus flowers.

For Kim, that means finding time to cook from a repertoire that includes influences from her own heritage: Greek and Filipino on her father's side, Irish and English on her mother's. Kim enjoys whipping up such traditional Filipino favorites such as *pancit*, Filipino noodles resembling rice vermicelli, or *adobo*, probably the best-known Filipino dish, made by marinating meat or fish in a mixture of palm vinegar, garlic, soy sauce, and cracked peppercorns. But she adds her own touches, throwing in nontraditional ingredients like asparagus, mushrooms, or pine nuts.

Pancit

This traditional Filipino noodle dish is a staple in the Bavington's home. Quick and easy to prepare, it's convenient for two, and it doubles easily when company comes for dinner.

Cooking spray
1 (6-ounce) boneless loin pork chop (about ½ inch thick), thinly sliced
½ cup thinly sliced yellow onion
¼ teaspoon freshly ground black pepper
4 ounces uncooked rice noodles
2 teaspoons vegetable oil
3 tablespoons low-sodium soy sauce
1 cup thinly sliced green cabbage
¼ teaspoon paprika
1 hard-cooked large egg, thinly sliced
2 tablespoons chopped green onions

1. Heat a large nonstick skillet coated with cooking spray over medium-high heat. Add pork; sauté 5 minutes or until browned, stirring frequently. Add sliced onion and pepper; sauté 4 minutes or until onion is soft. Remove pork mixture from pan, and set aside.
2. Soak rice noodles in warm water 5 minutes, and drain. Heat oil in pan over medium-high heat; stir in noodles, and sauté 2 minutes. Stir in soy sauce; cook 2 minutes, tossing to coat. Add cabbage and paprika; sauté 1 minute. Add pork mixture; sauté 4 minutes, tossing frequently. Top with egg and green onions. Yield: 2 servings (serving size: 2 cups).

CALORIES 435 (25% from fat); FAT 12g (sat 2.7g, mono 5.8g, poly 2.3g); PROTEIN 26.6g; CARB 52.8g; FIBER 1.6g; CHOL 153mg; IRON 2.8mg; SODIUM 901mg; CALC 85mg

The Oyster Lover

'Tis the season to savor these splendors from the shell.

Baked Italian Oysters

This hot appetizer is served on the half shell for an elegant presentation. The ground red pepper lends a subtle heat to the breadcrumb topping.

1½ (1-ounce) slices white bread
Cooking spray
⅓ cup sliced green onions
¼ cup chopped fresh parsley
2 garlic cloves, minced
¼ cup Italian-seasoned breadcrumbs
¼ cup (1 ounce) grated fresh Parmesan cheese
1 teaspoon fresh lemon juice
⅛ teaspoon ground red pepper
⅛ teaspoon black pepper
24 oysters on the half shell
8 lemon wedges

1. Preheat oven to 450°.
2. Place bread in a food processor, and pulse 10 times or until coarse crumbs form to measure ¾ cup.
3. Heat a medium nonstick skillet coated with cooking spray over medium heat. Add onions, parsley, and garlic; cook 5 minutes, stirring constantly. Remove from heat; stir in fresh breadcrumbs, Italian breadcrumbs, and next 4 ingredients. Place oysters on a jelly roll pan. Sprinkle breadcrumb mixture evenly over oysters.
4. Bake oysters at 450° for 7 minutes or until edges of oysters curl. Serve with lemon wedges. Yield: 8 servings (serving size: 3 oysters).

CALORIES 76 (30% from fat); FAT 2.5g (sat 1g, mono 0.5g, poly 0.5g); PROTEIN 5.4g; CARB 7.7g; FIBER 0.4g; CHOL 26mg; IRON 3.3mg; SODIUM 234mg; CALC 77mg

Shucking and Cutting

Here's the best and safest way to shuck an oyster. Before you get started, you'll need an oyster knife. OXO Good Grips offers an inexpensive model with an easy-to-hold soft handle ($7.50; www.oxo.com).

1. Wrap a heavy dishcloth around an unshucked oyster. Place it on a flat surface, and hold it in place by applying pressure with your hand. Insert an oyster knife between shells near hinge; gently twist knife to break hinge and pry apart shells.

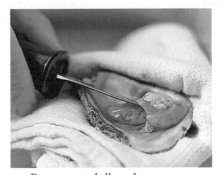

2. Remove top shell, and use oyster knife to cut oyster from bottom shell. Rinse to remove grit and sand.

Oyster Dressing

Corn bread, wild rice, and oysters combine to create the kind of dressing that can transform a holiday dinner—or any other meal of the year.

    1½ cups corn bread stuffing mix (such
          as Pepperidge Farm)
    1   (16-ounce) container standard
          oysters, undrained
    4   hard-cooked large eggs
    Cooking spray
    ½   cup chopped onion
    ½   cup chopped fresh parsley
    ½   cup chopped green bell pepper
    3   cups cooked wild rice
    ½   cup fat-free, less-sodium chicken
          broth
    ½   cup sliced green onions
    ½   teaspoon salt
    ¼   teaspoon black pepper

1. Preheat oven to 350°.
2. Prepare stuffing according to package directions, omitting fat. Set aside.
3. Drain oysters in a colander over a bowl, reserving ⅓ cup oyster liquid.
4. Slice eggs in half lengthwise; discard yolks. Finely chop egg whites.
5. Heat a large nonstick skillet coated with cooking spray over medium heat. Add chopped onion, parsley, and bell pepper; cook 3 minutes or until tender, stirring frequently. Stir in oysters, and cook 2 minutes. Stir in prepared stuffing, ⅓ cup oyster liquid, egg whites, wild rice, and remaining ingredients. Spread dressing in an 8-inch square baking dish coated with cooking spray. Bake dressing at 350° for 30 minutes or until thoroughly heated. Yield: 10 servings (serving size: about ¾ cup).

CALORIES 140 (13% from fat); FAT 2g (sat 0.4g, mono 0.3g, poly 0.8g); PROTEIN 8.2g; CARB 22.3g; FIBER 1.8g; CHOL 25mg; IRON 4.1mg; SODIUM 313mg; CALC 43mg

Creamy Oysters Rockefeller Dip

Mixing oysters with the typical ingredients found in a Rockefeller creates the flavor of that classic dish but eliminates the fuss of topping oyster shells.

    36 (¼-inch-thick) slices diagonally
          cut French bread baguette (about 9
          ounces)
    ½   (1-ounce) slice white bread
    1   (12-ounce) container standard
          oysters, undrained
    1   cup coarsely chopped
          green onions
    1   cup coarsely chopped celery
    ½   cup chopped fresh parsley
    ½   teaspoon butter
    1   (10-ounce) package frozen chopped
          spinach, thawed and drained
    ¼   cup (1 ounce) grated fresh
          Parmesan cheese
    ¼   cup (2 ounces) ⅓-less-fat cream
          cheese
    ¼   cup evaporated fat-free milk
    1   tablespoon fresh lemon juice
    1   tablespoon Worcestershire sauce
    1½ teaspoons anchovy paste
    ¼   teaspoon black pepper

1. Preheat oven to 375°.
2. Arrange baguette slices on 2 baking sheets; bake baguette slices at 375° for 8 minutes or until crisp.
3. Preheat broiler.
4. Place ½ (1-ounce) bread slice in a food processor; pulse 10 times or until coarse crumbs form to measure ¼ cup.
5. Drain oysters in a colander over a bowl, reserving 2 tablespoons oyster liquid. Place oysters on a broiler pan, and broil 7 minutes or until edges of oysters curl. Cool and chop.
6. Place onions, celery, and parsley in a blender or food processor, and process until finely chopped.
7. Melt butter in a Dutch oven over medium-high heat. Add onion mixture; sauté 5 minutes or until tender. Add spinach; cook 2 minutes or until thoroughly heated. Stir in oysters, ¼ cup breadcrumbs, 2 tablespoons oyster liquid, cheeses, and remaining ingredients; cook 2 minutes or until well blended,

stirring constantly. Yield: 18 servings (serving size: 2 tablespoons dip and 2 bread slices).

CALORIES 83 (26% from fat); FAT 2.4g (sat 1.1g, mono 0.6g, poly 0.3g); PROTEIN 4.6g; CARB 11.1g; FIBER 1.3g; CHOL 16mg; IRON 2.3mg; SODIUM 213mg; CALC 80mg

Poached Pepper-Lime Oysters

This recipe from Tony Kischner, owner of the Shoalwater Restaurant in Seaview, Washington, is exceptionally versatile. "The nice thing about this is that it can be served chilled or warm as an appetizer or main course," he says.

    4   cups thinly sliced red onion
    ½   cup white wine vinegar
    ⅓   cup sugar
    7   teaspoons coarsely ground black
          pepper, divided
    3   (12-ounce) containers standard
          oysters, undrained
    ½   cup fresh lime juice (about
          4 limes)
    ½   cup Champagne
    1   tablespoon olive oil
    10 garlic cloves, minced
    ½   teaspoon salt
    3   bay leaves

1. Combine onion, vinegar, sugar, and 1 teaspoon pepper in a medium bowl; marinate in refrigerator 1 hour.
2. Drain oysters in a colander over a bowl, reserving 1 cup oyster liquid. Combine reserved oyster liquid, juice, and Champagne in a large saucepan, and bring to a boil. Add oysters; reduce heat, and simmer 4 minutes or until edges of oysters curl. Drain oysters in a colander over a bowl, reserving 1 cup cooking liquid.
3. Heat oil in a large nonstick skillet over medium-high heat. Add garlic; sauté 1 minute. Add 1 cup reserved cooking liquid, 2 tablespoons pepper, salt, and bay leaves. Bring to a boil, and cook 30 seconds. Remove from heat; cool. Combine oysters and cooking liquid; marinate in refrigerator 30 minutes. Drain oysters, discarding bay leaves;

serve over onion mixture. Yield: 6 servings (serving size: about 9 oysters and ⅓ cup onions).

CALORIES 246 (25% from fat); FAT 6.7g (sat 1.4g, mono 2.1g, poly 1.5g); PROTEIN 13.6g; CARB 29.7g; FIBER 2.1g; CHOL 94mg; IRON 12.5mg; SODIUM 393mg; CALC 114mg

Oyster-Crab Bisque

- 3 (12-ounce) containers standard oysters, undrained
- Cooking spray
- 1 cup chopped onion
- ½ cup chopped celery
- ½ cup chopped green bell pepper
- 2 garlic cloves, minced
- ½ cup all-purpose flour
- 1 (14.5-ounce) can fat-free, less-sodium chicken broth
- ½ teaspoon dried thyme
- 1 bay leaf
- ½ cup sliced green onions
- 1 (12-ounce) can evaporated fat-free milk
- 1 pound lump crabmeat, shell pieces removed
- ¼ teaspoon salt
- ¼ teaspoon black pepper

1. Drain oysters in a colander over a bowl, reserving 1 cup oyster liquid.
2. Heat a large Dutch oven coated with cooking spray over medium-high heat. Add chopped onion, celery, bell pepper, and garlic; sauté 5 minutes. Lightly spoon flour into a dry measuring cup; level with a knife. Add flour to onion mixture; cook 1 minute, stirring constantly. Gradually add reserved oyster liquid and broth, stirring with a whisk until blended. Stir in thyme and bay leaf, and bring to a boil. Add oysters, green onions, and milk; cook 3 minutes or until edges of oysters curl. Gently stir in crabmeat, salt, and ¼ teaspoon black pepper; cook 1 minute or until thoroughly heated. Discard bay leaf. Yield: 7 servings (serving size: about 1½ cups).

CALORIES 263 (18% from fat); FAT 5.3g (sat 1.2g, mono 0.7g, poly 1.8g); PROTEIN 29.5g; CARB 22.2g; FIBER 1.2g; CHOL 147mg; IRON 11.4mg; SODIUM 631mg; CALC 293mg

Oysters over Angel Hair

(pictured on page 330)

It may seem like an unusual combination, but the green onions, garlic, and Parmesan cheese go beautifully with the oysters in this delicate pasta dish. It received raves in our Test Kitchens.

- 3 tablespoons olive oil
- 1 cup sliced green onions
- ½ cup chopped fresh parsley
- 3 garlic cloves, minced
- 4 cups standard oysters (about 3 [12-ounce] containers), drained
- 2 tablespoons fresh lemon juice
- ¼ teaspoon salt
- ⅛ teaspoon ground red pepper
- ⅛ teaspoon black pepper
- 6 cups hot cooked angel hair (about 14 ounces uncooked pasta)
- ½ cup (2 ounces) grated fresh Parmesan cheese

1. Heat oil in a large nonstick skillet over medium heat. Add onions, parsley, and garlic; cook 8 minutes or until tender, stirring frequently. Add oysters; reduce heat, and cook 5 minutes or until edges of oysters curl. Stir in lemon juice, salt, and peppers. Add pasta and cheese, tossing well to coat. Yield: 6 servings (serving size: 1⅓ cups).

CALORIES 470 (28% from fat); FAT 14.5g (sat 3.7g, mono 6.3g, poly 2.3g); PROTEIN 24.4g; CARB 58.9g; FIBER 2.3g; CHOL 100mg; IRON 14.7mg; SODIUM 450mg; CALC 223mg

---

Heaven on the Pacific: Where to Find It

For seafood lovers hoping to experience culinary heaven on earth, there may be no place better than the Long Island Peninsula on Washington State's southern coast. "Our part of the world produces some of the finest seafood there is," says Dobby Wiegardt, a lifelong resident and veteran oyster grower. "Thanks to the Pacific Ocean and the Columbia River, we've got salmon, shrimp, oysters, crabs, clams, sturgeon—you name it, we've got it."

Shelburne Country Inn Oyster, Beef, and Guinness Pie

This recipe from Laurie Anderson, co-owner of the Shelburne Country Inn in Seaview, Washington, is adapted from one she and her husband, David Campiche, have been making for 20 years. "We like it coming hot out of the oven on those rainy winter days we have in the Northwest," David says.

STEW:
- 1½ cups chopped onion, divided
- 3 tablespoons tomato paste
- 3 thyme sprigs
- 2 bay leaves
- 1 (12-ounce) bottle stout beer (such as Guinness Stout)
- 1 (12-ounce) boned sirloin steak, trimmed and cut into ½-inch cubes
- 3 cups quartered small red potatoes (about 1 pound)
- 1½ cups sliced carrot
- Cooking spray
- 2 garlic cloves, minced
- ¼ cup all-purpose flour
- 6 cups chopped fresh spinach (about 12 ounces)
- ¼ teaspoon salt
- ¼ teaspoon black pepper
- 12 shucked oysters

CRUST:
- 1 cup all-purpose flour
- ¼ teaspoon salt
- ¼ cup butter
- ⅓ cup ice water
- 1 tablespoon 1% low-fat milk

1. To prepare stew, combine ¾ cup onion, tomato paste, thyme, bay leaves, and beer in a large zip-top plastic bag. Add beef; seal and marinate in refrigerator 4 to 24 hours, turning bag occasionally. Remove beef from bag, reserving marinade.
2. Cook potato and carrot in boiling water 7 minutes; drain. Rinse with cold water; drain.
3. Heat a Dutch oven coated with cooking spray over medium-high heat.
Continued

Add ¾ cup onion and garlic; sauté 2 minutes. Add beef; cook 3 minutes or until browned. Lightly spoon ¼ cup flour into a dry measuring cup, and level with a knife. Sprinkle ¼ cup flour over beef mixture, stirring to coat. Cook 2 minutes. Gradually add reserved marinade, stirring well, and bring to a boil. Reduce heat, and simmer 20 minutes. Add potato, carrot, spinach, ¼ teaspoon salt, and pepper; cook 20 minutes or until potato is tender. Discard thyme and bay leaves. Remove from heat, and cool slightly. Spoon into a 10-inch deep-dish pie plate coated with cooking spray. Top with oysters.

4. To prepare crust, lightly spoon 1 cup flour into a dry measuring cup, and level with a knife. Combine 1 cup flour and ¼ teaspoon salt in a bowl, and cut in butter with a pastry blender or 2 knives until mixture resembles coarse meal. Sprinkle surface with ice water, 1 tablespoon at a time, tossing with a fork until moist and crumbly (do not form a ball).

5. Press mixture gently into a 4-inch circle on heavy-duty plastic wrap; cover with additional plastic wrap. Chill 15 minutes. Roll dough, still covered, into an 11-inch circle. Place dough in freezer 5 minutes or until plastic wrap can be easily removed.

6. Preheat oven to 350°.

7. Remove 1 sheet of plastic wrap; fit dough over top of beef mixture. Remove top sheet of plastic wrap. Fold edges of dough under beef mixture. Brush surface with milk. Pierce top of dough with a fork; bake at 350° for 40 minutes or until filling is bubbly and crust is browned. Yield: 8 servings.

CALORIES 285 (30% from fat); FAT 9.5g (sat 4.7g, mono 2.8g, poly 1g); PROTEIN 16.1g; CARB 34.6g; FIBER 4.8g; CHOL 53mg; IRON 5.7mg; SODIUM 307mg; CALC 86mg

Oyster Frittata

Adapted from the Shelburne Country Inn, David Campiche's recipe is perfect for just about any meal of the day—especially that first one. "Twenty years ago, we started serving oysters for breakfast, and this dish is the most popular," David says.

12 shucked oysters
¼ teaspoon hot sauce
3 (8-ounce) cartons egg substitute
¼ cup 1% low-fat milk
¼ teaspoon salt
¼ teaspoon black pepper
2 teaspoons olive oil
1 cup fresh or frozen corn kernels (about 2 ears)
½ cup finely chopped onion
¼ cup chopped yellow bell pepper
¼ cup chopped green bell pepper
¼ cup chopped red bell pepper
¼ cup chopped fennel bulb, divided
2 tablespoons chopped seeded jalapeño pepper
¼ cup (1 ounce) grated fresh Parmesan cheese

1. Preheat broiler.

2. Add water to a small saucepan, filling two-thirds full. Bring to a boil; reduce heat, and simmer. Add oysters, and cook 1 minute or until edges of oysters curl. Drain. Place oysters in a small bowl; sprinkle with hot sauce.

3. Combine egg substitute, milk, salt, and black pepper in a medium bowl; stir well with a whisk.

4. Heat oil in a large nonstick skillet over medium heat. Add corn, onion, bell peppers, 2 tablespoons fennel, and jalapeño; cook 3 minutes, stirring frequently. Add oysters, and sauté 1 minute. Add egg mixture; cook 4 minutes or until almost set.

5. Combine 2 tablespoons fennel and cheese. Wrap handle of skillet with foil; broil egg mixture 1 minute. Top with cheese mixture, and broil egg mixture 1 minute or until cheese melts. Serve warm. Yield: 4 servings.

CALORIES 236 (23% from fat); FAT 6g (sat 1.9g, mono 2.5g, poly 0.9g); PROTEIN 26.1g; CARB 20g; FIBER 2.5g; CHOL 29mg; IRON 7mg; SODIUM 596mg; CALC 195mg

Tandoori Oysters

This recipe is our adaptation of a popular offering at Moby Dick Hotel and Restaurant in Nahcotta, Washington.

1 cup plain fat-free yogurt, divided
¼ cup chopped fresh cilantro
1½ tablespoons chopped seeded jalapeño pepper
¼ teaspoon salt
2 teaspoons olive oil
2 teaspoons mustard seeds
1 teaspoon ground cumin
1 teaspoon ground turmeric
1 teaspoon curry powder
½ teaspoon ground red pepper
24 shucked oysters
2 cups hot cooked basmati rice
Cilantro sprigs (optional)

1. Combine ¼ cup yogurt, chopped cilantro, jalapeño, and salt in a blender; process until smooth. Add ¾ cup yogurt; process until just blended.

2. Heat oil in large nonstick skillet over medium-high heat. Add mustard seeds and next 4 ingredients; sauté 1 minute. Stir in oysters; sauté 4 minutes or until edges of oysters curl. Remove from heat; stir in yogurt sauce. Serve over rice. Garnish with cilantro sprigs, if desired. Yield: 4 servings (serving size: 6 oysters, ¼ cup sauce, and ½ cup rice).

CALORIES 239 (20% from fat); FAT 5.4g (sat 1g, mono 2.4g, poly 1g); PROTEIN 12.1g; CARB 34.7g; FIBER 1.2g; CHOL 47mg; IRON 7.8mg; SODIUM 287mg; CALC 185mg

---

Grading Your Oysters

Shucked oysters come in several grades:

West Coast grades: large (less than 8 per pint); medium (8 to 12 per pint); small (12 to 18 per pint); and extra-small (more than 18 per pint).

East Coast grades: extra-large (less than 20 per pint); large or extra-select (20 to 26 per pint); medium or select (26 to 38 per pint); small or standard (38 to 63 per pint); and very small (more than 63 per pint).

Our recipes using shucked oysters are based on the standard size.

cooking class

How to Cook Indian

From curry to tandoori, the flavors of India grow from simple spice blends.

Spices and herbs are the cornerstone of Indian cooking. Indian cooks are masters at using spices to lend an aura of richness and depth to a dish. While other cuisines use spices strictly as aromatics, in Indian cooking they're used for coloring, cooling, heating, souring, thickening, and adding texture as well.

Yet only a handful of seasonings—among them black pepper, cardamom, turmeric, ginger, and *kari*—are indigenous to India. Other spices—including cinnamon, cloves, and nutmeg—were introduced by traders and the migrating ethnic groups that have entered India over thousands of years. While some aspects of the indigenous cuisine—such as the vegetarianism of the Hindu Brahmins—have remained intact, others have intermingled with outside influences and taken on regional identities. Indian cooking today reflects this diversity.

Garam Masala

This homemade spice mixture is much darker and more flavorful than commercial varieties. Toasting the spices is a crucial step that gives the masala a deep, roasted flavor. Cardamom pods are available at Middle Eastern and Indian markets.

- 1 tablespoon cumin seeds
- 1 tablespoon coriander seeds
- 2 teaspoons black peppercorns
- 12 cardamom pods
- 8 whole cloves
- 1 (2-inch) cinnamon stick, broken into pieces
- ½ teaspoon ground nutmeg

1. Place first 6 ingredients in a large skillet over medium-high heat; cook until spices smoke, becoming fragrant and turning dark, shaking pan constantly (about 5 minutes). Stir in nutmeg. Remove from heat; cool completely. Place spice mixture in a spice or coffee grinder; process until finely ground. Store in an airtight container. Yield: ¼ cup.

CALORIES 69 (46% from fat); FAT 3.5g (sat 0.5g, mono 1.6g, poly 0.3g); PROTEIN 2.5g; CARB 11.7g; FIBER 5.9g; CHOL 0mg; IRON 6.3mg; SODIUM 19mg; CALC 149mg

Garam Masala

Toasting spices creates new flavors and aromas that add depth to a dish. When toasting spices, keep them moving in the skillet to prevent burning.

Curry Powder

Compared to a commercial curry powder, this one is dark, slightly bitter, and salt-free. All the ingredients in this version are available at most supermarkets, except the fenugreek seeds, which you can find in Indian and Middle Eastern markets.

- 1½ tablespoons coriander seeds
- 1 teaspoon cumin seeds
- 1 teaspoon yellow mustard seeds
- 1 teaspoon fenugreek seeds
- 1 teaspoon white peppercorns
- 6 whole cloves
- 1 tablespoon ground turmeric
- 1 teaspoon ground red pepper

1. Combine first 6 ingredients in a spice or coffee grinder, and process until finely ground. Place spice mixture in a
Continued

small bowl; stir in turmeric and red pepper. Store in an airtight container. Yield: ¼ cup.

CALORIES 99 (38% from fat); FAT 4.2g (sat 0.5g, mono 2.2g, poly 0.7g); PROTEIN 4.1g; CARB 15.8g; FIBER 7.5g; CHOL 0mg; IRON 7.3mg; SODIUM 17mg; CALC 127mg

Panch Phoron Blend

1   tablespoon cumin seeds
1   tablespoon fennel seeds
1   tablespoon brown mustard seeds
1   tablespoon fenugreek seeds
1   tablespoon nigella seeds

1. Combine all ingredients, and store in an airtight container. Yield: ¼ cup.

CALORIES 134 (44% from fat); FAT 6.5g (sat 0.5g, mono 2.3g, poly 0.5g); PROTEIN 8g; CARB 18.3g; FIBER 9g; CHOL 0mg; IRON 13.4mg; SODIUM 34mg; CALC 245mg

Roasted Cumin Seeds

2   tablespoons cumin seeds

1. Heat a skillet over medium-high heat. Add cumin seeds, and cook until dark (about 1½ minutes), shaking pan constantly. Cool. Store in an airtight container. Yield: 2 tablespoons.

CALORIES 45 (54% from fat); FAT 2.7g (sat 0.2g, mono 1.7g, poly 0.4g); PROTEIN 2.1g; CARB 5.3g; FIBER 1.3g; CHOL 0mg; IRON 8mg; SODIUM 20mg; CALC 112mg

Fat in Spices

Surprisingly, spices do contain some fat. And because they're otherwise calorie-free, their fat percentages are high. But the total amount of fat they contribute to a recipe is minuscule.

Tandoori Chicken

Tandoori cooking is traditionally done using a *tandoor*, a barrel-shaped clay oven. But you'll get great results with a very hot conventional oven. In Indian cooking, poultry is always skinned, as in this recipe, to allow the flavorings to penetrate the meat. Cornish hens are similar to Indian chickens, which tend to weigh no more than 2 pounds. Bread, *raita* (note on page 325), and salad or roasted vegetables are always served alongside tandoori dishes.

⅔   cup plain low-fat yogurt
1   tablespoon ground cumin
1   tablespoon paprika
1   tablespoon grated peeled fresh ginger
3   tablespoons lemon juice
2   teaspoons ground coriander seeds
½   teaspoon ground cardamom
¼   teaspoon ground red pepper
¼   teaspoon black pepper
⅛   teaspoon ground cloves
3   garlic cloves, minced
2   chicken breast halves (about ¾ pound), skinned
2   chicken leg quarters (about 1 pound), skinned
Cooking spray
½   teaspoon salt
4   lemon wedges
Fresh parsley (optional)

1. Combine first 13 ingredients in a large zip-top plastic bag; seal bag, and shake to coat. Marinate in refrigerator 2 hours, turning bag occasionally. Remove chicken from bag, discarding marinade.
2. Preheat oven to 500°.
3. Place chicken on a broiler pan coated with cooking spray; sprinkle with salt. Bake at 500° for 25 minutes or until done. Serve with lemon wedges; garnish with parsley, if desired. Yield: 4 servings (serving size: 3 ounces chicken).

CALORIES 225 (32% from fat); FAT 8g (sat 2.3g, mono 2.6g, poly 1.7g); PROTEIN 29.6g; CARB 8g; FIBER 2g; CHOL 86mg; IRON 2.3mg; SODIUM 404mg; CALC 118mg

Dining, Indian-Style

Traditionally, Indian food is eaten *thali* style. Various dishes are spooned into small bowls called *katori*, which are then arranged neatly on the thali, a large rimmed plate. Thali is also the name for the meal itself.

Indian main dishes, which include variations on grills or curries, are usually accompanied by a grain-based dish such as flatbread, rice, or noodles. Also typically included are a simple stir-fried vegetable and a chutney. To add moisture as well as protein to the meal, *dal* (a bowl of lightly seasoned, creamed lentils) or *raita* (a cool yogurt salad) is served.

Easy alternatives to the thali-style meal include serving stir-fried vegetables wrapped in flatbread. Also, plain rice can be turned into a pilaf simply by folding in some diced lamb and a little gravy.

Spices: The Foundation of Indian Food

With the exception of cinnamon, cloves, and saffron, most spices need to be ground or crushed to release their fragrance. Like perfume, ground spices should be kept in airtight containers. But even under the best of conditions, ground spices retain their fragrance for only about two months. Since spices are so important in Indian cooking, it's best to buy only whole spices and grind them in a spice or coffee grinder as needed. When stored in a cool cupboard, away from light, whole spices will keep for up to two years.

In Indian cooking, some spices are roasted to lend them a distinct caramelized, smoky fragrance. However, cooking removes some of the volatile and essential oils. Raw spice, in pure ground form, has far more fragrance.

Madras Shrimp Molahu Veritadu Curry in Black Pepper Sauce

In south India, this dish is also prepared with chicken, duck, goat, and lamb; vegetarian versions are made with black-eyed peas. Serve this with Spiced Basmati Pilaf with Garden Peas (recipe on page 324).

  1   tablespoon vegetable oil
  1   teaspoon mustard seeds
  1   cup finely chopped onion
1½   tablespoons ground coriander seeds
1½   tablespoons grated peeled fresh ginger
  2   teaspoons black peppercorns, crushed
  ½   teaspoon ground turmeric
  2   garlic cloves, minced
  ½   cup fat-free, less-sodium chicken broth
  2   tablespoons tomato paste
  1   tablespoon fresh lemon juice
  ¾   teaspoon salt
1½   pounds large shrimp, peeled and deveined
  ¼   cup finely chopped fresh cilantro

1. Heat oil in a large nonstick skillet over medium-high heat. Add mustard seeds; cover pan, and cook 2 minutes or until seeds stop popping. Uncover pan. Stir in onion and next 5 ingredients, and cook 5 minutes or until onion is golden, stirring frequently.
2. Reduce heat, and stir in broth, tomato paste, juice, and salt. Cook until thick (about 1 minute), stirring constantly. Add shrimp; cook 4 minutes or until shrimp are done. Sprinkle with cilantro. Yield: 4 servings (serving size: 1 cup).

CALORIES 179 (27% from fat); FAT 5.4g (sat 0.8g, mono 1.2g, poly 2.5g); PROTEIN 23.5g; CARB 8.6g; FIBER 2.9g; CHOL 202mg; IRON 3.9mg; SODIUM 737mg; CALC 77mg

Whole Wheat Chapatis

A typical north Indian flatbread, *chapati* is traditionally made with just two ingredients—flour and water. Its plain flavor complements spicy Indian dishes.

  ¾   cup all-purpose flour
  ¾   cup whole wheat flour
  ½   cup water

1. Lightly spoon flours into measuring cups; level with a knife. Combine flours and water in a large bowl. Press mixture together using a rubber spatula or your hands. (Mixture is dry but will stay together.) Turn dough out onto a lightly floured surface. Knead 3 minutes. Cover and let rest 15 minutes. Divide dough into 12 equal portions, shaping each into a ball. Working with one ball at a time, roll each ball into a 5-inch circle (circles will be very thin) on a lightly floured surface (cover remaining dough while working to prevent it from drying).
2. Heat a large nonstick skillet over medium-high heat until very hot. Place 1 dough round in pan, and cook 30 seconds or until brown spots appear, turning after about 15 seconds. Place bread on a cooling rack over eye of a gas burner. Hold bread over flame with tongs, turning until both sides of bread are puffed and brown spots appear. (Some chapatis will puff more than others.) Repeat procedure with remaining rounds. Yield: 6 servings (serving size: 2 flatbreads).
NOTE: You can use chapati flour in place of all-purpose and whole wheat flours, but we liked bread made with regular flour best. You can also make this dish on an electric stovetop, although bread will take longer to puff.

CALORIES 108 (3% from fat); FAT 0.4g (sat 0.1g, mono 0.1g, poly 0.2g); PROTEIN 3.7g; CARB 22.8g; FIBER 2.3g; CHOL 0mg; IRON 1.3mg; SODIUM 1mg; CALC 7mg

How to Make Chapatis

1. *Combine water and flour in a large bowl, and mix, gathering and pressing until flour stays together. If dough becomes too dry, add a tablespoon or two of water, but no more, or dough will become too soft and sticky to roll.*

2. *Knead dough lightly for 3 minutes; divide into 12 portions, and roll each into a ball. With a rolling pin, roll each ball into a 5-inch circle (they'll be very thin).*

3. *Cook each chapati in a skillet for 15 seconds; turn and cook 15 seconds more. With tongs, remove and place on a cooling rack over eye of a gas burner, or hold directly over eye until chapati is puffed and brown. Don't be discouraged if all of your chapatis don't puff; about half of ours did. (If you prefer, you can skip the second step and cook the chapatis 30 seconds on each side in the skillet, though they won't puff as well.)*

Classic Lamb Curry

Lamb curry is the most popular of all curries. You can create a variety of curries by substituting other ingredients in place of the lamb and adjusting the cooking time. For example, use an equal quantity of beef or veal, a 3-pound skinned and cut chicken, 1½ pounds shelled and deveined shrimp, or 1¼ pounds mixed vegetables, such as cauliflower, potatoes, and carrots.

   Cooking spray
  2 pounds boneless leg of lamb, trimmed and cut into 1-inch pieces
  1 teaspoon vegetable oil
1½ cups chopped onion
  5 whole cloves
  3 cardamom pods
  2 bay leaves
  1 (3-inch) cinnamon stick
  1 tablespoon ground coriander seeds
  1 tablespoon paprika
  2 tablespoons minced peeled fresh ginger
  2 teaspoons Garam Masala (recipe on page 321)
½ teaspoon ground red pepper
½ teaspoon ground turmeric
  2 garlic cloves, minced
  2 cups finely chopped plum tomato (about ½ pound)
1½ cups water
½ teaspoon salt
½ cup chopped fresh cilantro, divided
  4 cups hot cooked long-grain rice

1. Heat a large nonstick skillet coated with cooking spray over medium-high heat. Add lamb; cook 5 minutes on all sides or until browned. Remove lamb from pan.
2. Heat oil in pan over medium-high heat. Add onion and next 4 ingredients; cook 4 minutes or until onion is browned. Stir in coriander and next 6 ingredients; cook 1 minute. Add lamb, tomato, water, and salt; bring to a boil. Cover, reduce heat, and simmer 1½ hours or until lamb is tender. Stir in ¼ cup cilantro. Remove bay leaves. Serve over rice; sprinkle with ¼ cup cilantro. Yield: 4 servings (serving size: 1 cup lamb mixture and 1 cup rice).

CALORIES 457 (22% from fat); FAT 11.2g (sat 3.5g, mono 4g, poly 1.8g); PROTEIN 40.4g; CARB 46.8g; FIBER 4.5g; CHOL 112mg; IRON 5.7mg; SODIUM 477mg; CALC 70mg

Pan-Roasted Vegetables

Serve with Tandoori Chicken (recipe on page 322). This dish is also great with the addition of a fennel bulb, trimmed and thinly sliced.

  5 cups thinly sliced onion (about 1 large)
  1 cup red bell pepper, cut into ⅛-inch strips
  1 cup green bell pepper, cut into ⅛-inch strips
  1 teaspoon olive oil
½ teaspoon salt
¼ teaspoon fennel seeds
  2 tablespoons chopped fresh cilantro

1. Combine first 6 ingredients in a large skillet over high heat. Cook 2 minutes or until vegetables begin to sizzle; reduce heat to medium-low. Cook 20 minutes or until vegetables begin to caramelize, stirring occasionally. Sprinkle with cilantro. Yield: 4 servings (serving size: ½ cup).

CALORIES 78 (17% from fat); FAT 1.5g (sat 0.2g, mono 0.9g, poly 0.2g); PROTEIN 2.1g; CARB 15.4g; FIBER 3.5g; CHOL 0mg; IRON 0.6mg; SODIUM 299mg; CALC 35mg

Lentil Dal with Garlic-and-Cumin-Infused Oil

Dal, the seasoned and often pureed lentil dish, is served with traditional Indian meals. It's either spooned over rice or used as sauce for dipping breads. You can also thin the dal with low-sodium chicken broth or low-fat yogurt to serve as a soup.

1¼ cups dried pink or yellow lentils
½ teaspoon ground turmeric
  4 cups water
  1 cup chopped plum tomato
  1 teaspoon salt
  1 tablespoon vegetable oil
1½ teaspoons cumin seeds
  4 garlic cloves, sliced
¼ teaspoon ground red pepper
⅓ cup minced fresh cilantro, divided
  1 tablespoon fresh lemon juice

1. Place lentils and turmeric in a large saucepan; cover with 4 cups water. Bring to a boil; cover, reduce heat, and simmer 15 minutes, stirring occasionally. Add tomato; cook 5 minutes or until lentils are tender. Stir in salt; keep warm.
2. Heat vegetable oil in a small skillet over medium-high heat. Add cumin seeds and garlic; cook 2 minutes or until garlic is golden, stirring constantly. Stir in red pepper, and remove from heat. Pour oil mixture over lentils, and stir in 2 tablespoons cilantro. Spoon dal into individual bowls, and sprinkle with remaining cilantro and lemon juice. Yield: 5 servings (serving size: 1 cup).

CALORIES 202 (16% from fat); FAT 3.5g (sat 0.5g, mono 0.8g, poly 1.9g); PROTEIN 14.1g; CARB 30.6g; FIBER 15.3g; CHOL 0mg; IRON 5.1mg; SODIUM 479mg; CALC 39mg

Rice—The Indian Way

Indian cooks are serious about cooking rice. Here's their method: Always wash basmati rice before cooking to remove debris and any starch clinging to the grains, which can make the rice sticky and gummy. To wash, place rice in a large bowl, and fill with cold water. After 2 to 3 seconds the water will look cloudy. Pour off the water. Repeat 3 times.

Spiced Basmati Pilaf with Garden Peas

(pictured on page 331)

This flavorful pilaf features an aromatic broth laced with sautéed onion, cardamom pods, cinnamon, and whole cloves. The spices are cooked along with the pilaf (they aren't meant to be eaten), but you can put them in cheesecloth as well.

  1 cup uncooked basmati rice
  2 cups cold water
  1 tablespoon vegetable oil
⅓ cup chopped onion
  8 cardamom pods
  6 whole cloves
  1 (3-inch) cinnamon stick
¾ teaspoon salt
½ cup frozen green peas

1. Wash rice in 3 changes of cold water; drain. Combine rice and 2 cups cold water in a bowl; let stand 30 minutes.
2. Heat vegetable oil in a large saucepan over medium-high heat. Add onion; sauté 3 minutes or until lightly browned. Add rice, soaking liquid, cardamom, cloves, cinnamon, and salt, and bring to a boil. Reduce heat to medium, and cook 5 minutes or until liquid is nearly absorbed. Fold in peas. Cover, reduce heat to low, and cook 8 minutes. Remove from heat; let stand 5 minutes. Remove and discard cardamom, cloves, and cinnamon. Yield: 7 servings (serving size: ½ cup).

CALORIES 126 (16% from fat); FAT 2.2g (sat 0.3g, mono 0.5g, poly 1.2g); PROTEIN 2.6g; CARB 23.4g; FIBER 1.1g; CHOL 0mg; IRON 1.3mg; SODIUM 263mg; CALC 12mg

Raita Salad of Red Grapes and Mint

Raita is a yogurt-mint salad that's a refreshing counterpart to chutney. A variety of raw or cooked vegetables, fruits, nuts, and herbs can be added. Thinned with buttermilk or fruit juice, raitas can also be turned into refreshing cold soups.

1½   cups plain fat-free yogurt
¼   cup raisins
1   teaspoon grated lemon rind
1   teaspoon chopped fresh mint
½   teaspoon salt
½   teaspoon sugar
1   cup seedless red grapes, halved
3   tablespoons chopped pecans, toasted
½   teaspoon Roasted Cumin Seeds (recipe on page 322)
    Mint sprigs (optional)

1. Combine first 6 ingredients in a bowl; stir with a whisk. Cover and refrigerate 15 minutes. Fold in grapes and pecans. Sprinkle with Roasted Cumin Seeds; garnish with mint sprigs, if desired. Yield: 5 servings (serving size: ½ cup).

CALORIES 119 (27% from fat); FAT 3.6g (sat 0.4g, mono 1.9g, poly 1.0g); PROTEIN 5g; CARB 18.3g; FIBER 1.3g; CHOL 1mg; IRON 0.7mg; SODIUM 294mg; CALC 159mg

Cauliflower and Potato Sabzi with Spices

A stir-fried vegetable with spices, *sabzi* is a popular northern dish that can be made with one or more vegetables. It's often cooked with cumin, ginger, cilantro, and garam masala. Make this dish hotter by increasing the red pepper.

1   head cauliflower (about 1½ pounds)
2   tablespoons vegetable oil, divided
2   baking potatoes, peeled, halved lengthwise, and sliced (about 1¾ pounds)
2   teaspoons cumin seeds
4   garlic cloves, minced
⅓   cup water
⅓   cup tomato puree
3   tablespoons chopped peeled fresh ginger
1½   teaspoons salt
¾   teaspoon ground turmeric
½   teaspoon ground red pepper
⅓   cup chopped fresh cilantro
1   teaspoon Garam Masala (recipe on page 321)

1. Separate cauliflower into florets to measure 4 cups, reserving stems. Cut stems into thin slices to measure 1 cup. Heat 1½ tablespoons oil in a Dutch oven over medium-high heat. Add potato, cumin seeds, and garlic; stir-fry 6 minutes or until potato is crisp-tender. Stir in water and next 5 ingredients. Add cauliflower florets and stems, stirring well; cover, reduce heat, and simmer 20 minutes or until vegetables are tender. Uncover, and drizzle with 1½ teaspoons oil, cilantro, and Garam Masala, tossing well. Yield: 6 servings (serving size: 1 cup).

CALORIES 200 (23% from fat); FAT 5.2g (sat 0.8g, mono 1.2g, poly 2.8g); PROTEIN 4.9g; CARB 36.2g; FIBER 4.8g; CHOL 0mg; IRON 1.8mg; SODIUM 676mg; CALC 43mg

Salmon Kalia in Panch Phoron Sauce

A favorite of the Bengalis in eastern India, *kalia* is traditionally made with the local, strong-tasting, freshwater fish called *rui* or *katla*, which belongs to the carp family. We made this dish with salmon, but you can also use sea bass, shrimp, lobster, or crab.

6   (6-ounce) salmon fillets (about 1 inch thick)
1   teaspoon salt, divided
¾   teaspoon ground turmeric
1   tablespoon vegetable oil, divided
2   teaspoons Panch Phoron Blend (recipe on page 322)
4   cups thinly sliced onion (about 1 large)
8   ounces peeled Yukon gold potato, cut into ¼-inch strips
1   pound tomatoes
2   cups (½-inch) cubed zucchini
1   cup water
2   teaspoons paprika
1   teaspoon minced peeled fresh ginger
3   garlic cloves, minced
2   tablespoons plain low-fat yogurt
5   serrano chiles, halved and seeded
1   medium tomato, cut into ½-inch-thick wedges (about 8 ounces)
1   teaspoon Garam Masala (recipe on page 321)
3   tablespoons chopped fresh cilantro

1. Rub salmon fillets with ½ teaspoon salt and turmeric; cover and refrigerate 5 minutes. Heat 1 teaspoon oil in a large nonstick skillet over medium-high heat. Add fillets; cook 1 minute on each side. Remove fillets; cover and set aside. (Fish need not be fully cooked.)
2. Combine 2 teaspoons oil and Panch Phoron Blend in pan; cover and cook 30 seconds, shaking pan constantly. Add onion and potato; stir-fry 6 minutes or until vegetables begin to brown, stirring frequently.
3. Place 1 pound tomatoes in a food processor; process until pureed. Add ½ teaspoon salt, tomato puree, zucchini, and next 4 ingredients to pan; bring to a boil. Cover, reduce heat, and simmer 10

Continued

minutes or until vegetables are tender. Stir in yogurt until well blended.

4. Return fillets to pan, carefully nestling them into vegetable mixture. Arrange chiles and tomato wedges on top of vegetable mixture; cover and cook 20 minutes or until fish flakes easily when tested with a fork. Sprinkle with Garam Masala and cilantro. Yield: 6 servings (serving size: 1 cup).

CALORIES 443 (43% from fat); FAT 20.9g (sat 4.7g, mono 8.3g, poly 5.1g); PROTEIN 37.8g; CARB 22.1g; FIBER 4.4g; CHOL 113mg; IRON 2.8mg; SODIUM 493mg; CALC 89mg

Tomato-Garlic Chutney

Of all the cooked chutneys in India, tomato chutneys are by far the most popular. This version includes loads of garlic and mustard seeds.

  1 tablespoon vegetable oil
  1 teaspoon mustard seeds, crushed
  8 garlic cloves, sliced
  2 cups chopped seeded plum tomato
1½ teaspoons curry powder
 ½ teaspoon salt

1. Heat oil in a large nonstick skillet over medium-high heat. Add mustard seeds and garlic; cover pan immediately, and cook 10 seconds, shaking pan constantly (mustard seeds will pop once they hit the hot pan, causing oil to spatter). Stir in chopped plum tomato, curry powder, and salt; cook 2 minutes. Reduce heat to medium; cook 6 minutes, stirring occasionally. Yield: 2 cups (serving size: ¼ cup).

CALORIES 32 (56% from fat); FAT 2g (sat 0.3g, mono 0.5g, poly 1g); PROTEIN 0.7g; CARB 3.4g; FIBER 0.7g; CHOL 0mg; IRON 0.4mg; SODIUM 151mg; CALC 12mg

Herald of the Holidays

A Colorado clan gives thanks that a favorite pre-Yule tradition can stay in the family.

The day after the big Thanksgiving feast, Gina Doherty and family of Colorado Springs, Colorado, ring in the Yuletide season with a brunch served on holiday china. A big part of this festive tradition is a cranberry-studded upside-down cake.

They all love the great flavor of the cake, but are mindful of their waistlines, too.

By significantly reducing the butter, we cut 14 grams of fat per slice. And we shaved another 19.6 grams of fat from each serving by switching from whipping cream to fat-free whipped topping. Other small changes, such as slightly reducing the amount of nuts and using fat-free milk instead of whole, brought the fat down by more than three-fourths—yet the cake remains moist and flavorful.

Cranberry Upside-Down Cake with Cognac Cream

  2 tablespoons butter, melted
Cooking spray
 ½ cup packed brown sugar
 ¼ cup chopped pecans, toasted
  1 (12-ounce) package fresh cranberries
1⅓ cups all-purpose flour
1½ teaspoons baking powder
 ⅛ teaspoon salt
 ¾ cup granulated sugar
  3 tablespoons butter, softened
  2 large egg yolks
  1 teaspoon vanilla extract
 ½ cup fat-free milk
  2 large egg whites
  1 cup frozen fat-free whipped topping, thawed
  1 tablespoon cognac

1. Preheat oven to 350°.

2. Pour melted butter into an 8-inch square baking pan coated with cooking spray; sprinkle with brown sugar. Bake at 350° for 2 minutes. Remove from oven, and top with pecans and cranberries.

3. Lightly spoon flour into dry measuring cups; level with a knife. Combine flour, baking powder, and salt in a bowl; stir with whisk.

4. Place sugar and softened butter in a large bowl; beat with a mixer at medium speed until well blended. Add egg yolks, 1 at a time, beating well after each addition. Stir in vanilla.

5. Add flour mixture and milk alternately to butter mixture, beginning and ending with flour mixture; mix after each addition. Beat egg whites with a mixer at high speed until stiff peaks form using clean, dry beaters; fold into batter.

6. Spread batter over cranberries. Bake at 350° for 45 minutes. Cool in pan 5 minutes on a wire rack. Loosen edges of cake with a sharp knife. Place a plate upside down on top of cake pan; invert onto plate.

7. Combine whipped topping and cognac, and serve with warm cake. Yield: 9 servings (serving size: 1 cake piece and about 2 tablespoons cognac cream).

CALORIES 316 (29% from fat); FAT 10.2g (sat 4.6g, mono 3.7g, poly 1.2g); PROTEIN 4.3g; CARB 51.7g; FIBER 2.4g; CHOL 65mg; IRON 1.5mg; SODIUM 210mg; CALC 88mg

BEFORE	AFTER
SERVING SIZE	
1 cake piece and about 2 tablespoons cognac cream	
CALORIES PER SERVING	
728	316
FAT	
46.6g	10.2g
PERCENT OF TOTAL CALORIES	
58%	29%

. . . And Ready in Just About 20 Minutes

In the time it takes to spin a globe, you can enjoy flavors from around the world with these quick entrées.

Linguine with Clam Sauce

Serve with crusty bread.

- 1 (9-ounce) package fresh linguine
- 4 bacon slices
- 2 teaspoons bottled minced garlic
- 1 teaspoon dried basil
- 1 tablespoon lemon juice
- ⅛ teaspoon crushed red pepper
- ⅛ teaspoon black pepper
- 2 (6½-ounce) cans minced clams, drained
- 1 (8-ounce) bottle clam juice
- ¼ cup (1 ounce) preshredded fresh Parmesan cheese

1. Cook pasta according to package directions, omitting salt and fat. Drain.
2. While pasta cooks, place bacon in a large nonstick skillet over medium heat, and cook until crisp. Remove bacon from pan, and crumble. Reserve 1 tablespoon drippings in pan. Add garlic and basil; sauté 30 seconds. Add bacon, lemon juice, and next 4 ingredients; cook 3 minutes, stirring occasionally.
3. Combine pasta and clam mixture, and toss well. Sprinkle with cheese. Yield: 4 servings (serving size: 1 cup linguine and 1 tablespoon cheese).

CALORIES 290 (24% from fat); FAT 7.7g (sat 2.8g, mono 1.7g, poly 1.2g); PROTEIN 32g; CARB 21.7g; FIBER 1.3g; CHOL 97mg; IRON 26.9mg; SODIUM 415mg; CALC 190mg

Sesame-Crusted Salmon

Serve with roasted or stir-fried asparagus.

- ¼ cup sesame seeds
- 1 tablespoon grated orange rind
- ½ teaspoon salt
- 1 teaspoon dark sesame oil
- 4 (6-ounce) salmon fillets (about 1 inch thick)
- Cooking spray
- 1¼ cups water
- ¾ cup uncooked couscous
- ¼ cup sliced green onions
- 2 tablespoons orange juice
- ¼ teaspoon salt

1. Preheat broiler.
2. Combine first 3 ingredients in a shallow dish. Drizzle oil over fillets. Dredge fillets in sesame mixture. Place fillets on a broiler pan coated with cooking spray. Broil 12 minutes or until fish flakes easily when tested with a fork.
3. While fillets cook, bring water to a boil in a medium saucepan; gradually stir in couscous. Remove from heat, cover, and let stand 5 minutes. Fluff with a fork. Stir in onions, juice, and ¼ teaspoon salt. Serve with fillets. Yield: 4 servings (serving size: 1 fillet and ½ cup couscous).

CALORIES 401 (35% from fat); FAT 15.4g (sat 3.1g, mono 6.4g, poly 4.8g); PROTEIN 33.3g; CARB 30.1g; FIBER 2.8g; CHOL 65mg; IRON 2mg; SODIUM 503mg; CALC 106mg

Pork Chops with Lemon Spinach

Serve with mashed potatoes.

- 3 tablespoons all-purpose flour
- 1 tablespoon brown sugar
- ½ teaspoon salt
- ¼ teaspoon ground nutmeg
- ⅛ teaspoon ground red pepper
- 4 (4-ounce) boneless center-cut loin pork chops (about ½ inch thick)
- 1 teaspoon olive oil
- ½ cup dry white wine
- 2 teaspoons lemon juice
- 1 tablespoon bottled minced garlic
- 1 (10-ounce) package fresh spinach

1. Combine first 5 ingredients in a shallow dish. Dredge pork in flour mixture.
2. Heat oil in a large skillet over medium heat. Add pork, and cook 3 minutes on each side or until done. Remove from pan. Stir in wine and lemon juice, scraping pan to loosen browned bits; cook 1 minute. Add garlic, and cook 1 minute. Add spinach, tossing 1 minute or until spinach wilts. Serve with pork. Yield: 4 servings (serving size: 1 pork chop and ½ cup lemon spinach).

CALORIES 309 (38% from fat); FAT 12.9g (sat 4.3g, mono 6.1g, poly 1g); PROTEIN 36.2g; CARB 11.3g; FIBER 2.2g; CHOL 92mg; IRON 3.2mg; SODIUM 425mg; CALC 114mg

Moroccan Chicken Thighs

Serve over a bed of couscous.

- 2 teaspoons olive oil
- 1 pound skinless, boneless chicken thighs, trimmed and cut into bite-size pieces
- ½ cup chopped fresh cilantro
- ½ cup quartered dried Calimyrna figs (about 2 ounces)
- ¼ cup chopped green olives
- 3 tablespoons sweet Marsala or Madeira
- 2 tablespoons honey
- 1 tablespoon bottled minced garlic
- 2 tablespoons balsamic vinegar
- ½ teaspoon ground coriander
- ½ teaspoon ground cumin
- ¼ teaspoon ground cardamom
- Cilantro sprigs (optional)

1. Heat oil in a large nonstick skillet over medium-high heat. Add chicken; cook 5 minutes or until browned, stirring frequently. Stir in chopped cilantro and remaining ingredients except cilantro sprigs; reduce heat to medium, and cook 8 minutes, stirring occasionally. Garnish with cilantro sprigs, if desired. Yield: 4 servings (serving size: ¾ cup).

CALORIES 275 (29% from fat); FAT 8.9g (sat 1.4g, mono 4.5g, poly 1.8g); PROTEIN 23.1g; CARB 22.7g; FIBER 2.1g; CHOL 94mg; IRON 2mg; SODIUM 324mg; CALC 44mg

Cashew-Crusted Chicken on Basil-Pineapple Rice

Serve with steamed broccoli or snap peas.

- ½ cup unsalted cashews
- 2 tablespoons garlic-seasoned breadcrumbs
- 4 (4-ounce) skinless, boneless chicken breast halves
- 1 large egg white, lightly beaten
- 1 (8-ounce) can crushed pineapple in juice, drained
- Cooking spray
- 1 (3½-ounce) bag precooked long-grain rice (such as Success)
- ⅓ cup finely chopped fresh basil
- ½ teaspoon salt

1. Preheat oven to 450°.
2. Place nuts and breadcrumbs in a food processor, and pulse 10 times or until crumbs measure ⅔ cup. Pour nut mixture into a shallow dish. Brush chicken with egg white; dredge chicken in nut mixture. Spread pineapple in an 11 x 7-inch baking dish coated with cooking spray. Arrange chicken over pineapple; bake at 450° for 14 minutes or until chicken is done, turning after 7 minutes.
3. While chicken cooks, prepare rice according to package directions. Remove chicken from dish. Stir rice, basil, and salt into pineapple. Yield: 4 servings (serving size: 1 chicken breast half and ¾ cup rice).

CALORIES 430 (20% from fat); FAT 9.7g (sat 2g, mono 5.1g, poly 1.8g); PROTEIN 33.6g; CARB 50.4g; FIBER 1.9g; CHOL 66mg; IRON 3.8mg; SODIUM 489mg; CALC 42mg

Polenta with Sausage

- 1 (16-ounce) tube of polenta, cut into ¼-inch slices
- Cooking spray
- 12 ounces hot Italian turkey sausage
- 1 cup chopped green bell pepper
- ½ teaspoon fennel seeds
- 1 teaspoon Italian seasoning
- 2 (14.5-ounce) cans no-salt-added diced tomatoes, drained
- 1 cup preshredded part-skim mozzarella cheese

1. Preheat oven to 450°.
2. Arrange polenta slices in bottom of an 11 x 7-inch baking dish coated with cooking spray. Bake at 450° for 8 minutes, turning once.
3. While polenta bakes, heat a large nonstick skillet coated with cooking spray over medium-high heat. Remove casings from sausage. Place sausage, bell pepper, and fennel seeds in pan; cook 5 minutes or until sausage is browned, stirring to crumble. Add seasoning and tomatoes; cook 2 minutes or until thoroughly heated. Pour sausage mixture over polenta, and top with cheese. Bake at 450° for 3 minutes Yield: 4 servings (serving size: 1½ cups).

CALORIES 327 (19% from fat); FAT 6.9g (sat 3.6g, mono 1.3g, poly 0.2g); PROTEIN 22.7g; CARB 41.3g; FIBER 1.7g; CHOL 39mg; IRON 2.5mg; SODIUM 1,076mg; CALC 296mg

Spicy Chicken Soup

Baked tortilla chips and a garden salad are excellent accompaniments for this soup.

- 1 (7-ounce) can chipotle chiles in adobo sauce
- 1 teaspoon olive oil
- 1 cup chopped green bell pepper
- ½ cup chopped green onions
- 1 tablespoon bottled minced garlic
- 1 teaspoon ground cumin
- 2 cups chopped cooked chicken breast strips (such as Louis Rich; about 12 ounces)
- 2 (14½-ounce) cans fat-free, less-sodium chicken broth
- 1 (14½-ounce) can diced tomatoes and green chiles, undrained (such as Del Monte)
- 1 (11-ounce) can whole-kernel corn with sweet peppers, drained

1. Remove 1 chile from can; reserve remaining chiles and sauce for another use. Mince chile.
2. Heat oil in a large saucepan over medium-high heat. Add bell pepper, onions, garlic, and cumin; sauté 4 minutes or until vegetables are soft. Stir in minced chile, chicken, broth, tomatoes, and corn. Bring to a boil; reduce heat,

and simmer 3 minutes. Yield: 4 servings (serving size: 2 cups).

CALORIES 358 (30% from fat); FAT 11.8g (sat 2.8g, mono 4.4g, poly 2g); PROTEIN 40.6g; CARB 23.3g; FIBER 4.9g; CHOL 95mg; IRON 2.5mg; SODIUM 1,536mg; CALC 65mg

Ham and Spinach Focaccia Sandwiches

Look for focaccia in the bakery section of your grocery store.

- 3 tablespoons low-fat mayonnaise
- 2 tablespoons chopped fresh basil
- 2 teaspoons sun-dried tomato sprinkles
- ¼ teaspoon crushed red pepper
- 1 (8-inch) round focaccia bread (about 8 ounces)
- 8 ounces smoked deli ham, thinly sliced
- 1 (7-ounce) bottle roasted red bell peppers, drained and sliced
- 1 cup spinach leaves

1. Combine first 4 ingredients in a small bowl. Cut bread in half horizontally. Spread mayonnaise mixture over cut sides of bread. Place ham over bottom half of bread. Top with peppers and spinach, and cover with top half of bread. Cut sandwich into 4 wedges. Yield: 4 servings (serving size: 1 wedge).

CALORIES 275 (19% from fat); FAT 5.9g (sat 1.6g, mono 2.4g, poly 1.3g); PROTEIN 17.7g; CARB 36.5g; FIBER 2.3g; CHOL 30mg; IRON 2.7mg; SODIUM 1,190mg; CALC 59mg

Green Beans with Roasted-Onion
Vinaigrette, page 312

Oysters over Angel Hair, page 319

Roast Turkey with Classic Pan Gravy,
page 310, Spiced Sweet Potato Casserole,
page 311, Savory Fruited Stuffing, page 311
and Cranberry-Apple Relish, page 312

Apple and Cream Cheese
Roll-Ups, page 338

Sweet Potato
Streusel Tarts,
page 339

Mini Mocha-Toffee
Crunch Cheesecakes,
page 338

Spiced Basmati Pilaf with
Garden Peas, page 324

Herb and Onion Wheat Biscuits,
page 316

Spicy Turkey Soft Tacos,
page 313

Serendipitous Stew

Veal, onions, wine, and creativity spark this artist's supper.

While Montreal resident Yvonne Callaway Smith picked up a paintbrush only a few years ago, she's been creating culinary masterpieces for years.

As a food-loving college student, she couldn't afford to splurge on extravagant dinners in upscale restaurants, but that didn't stop her from eating well.

"I set about making the glorious foods I craved by replicating the great restaurant meals I did have," she says. To do that, she relied on cookbooks, magazines, and friends—along with her own creativity. Among her collection of time-tested favorites—Osso Buco with Balsamic Onions.

Osso Buco with Balsamic Onions

    4   cups vertically sliced onion
 1½   cups dry white wine, divided
    1   tablespoon sugar
    2   teaspoons dried thyme, divided
    ½   teaspoon black pepper, divided
    3   tablespoons balsamic vinegar
    4   (10-ounce) veal shanks (1½ inches thick)
    3   cups fat-free, less-sodium chicken broth
    ½   teaspoon crushed red pepper
    1   (14.5-ounce) can diced tomatoes with basil, garlic, and oregano
    4   garlic cloves, minced
    ½   cup tubetti (small, tube-shaped pasta)
    1   (19-ounce) can cannellini or other white beans, rinsed and drained
    ¼   cup sliced fresh basil
    2   teaspoons lemon zest

1. Combine onion, ½ cup wine, sugar, 1 teaspoon thyme, and ¼ teaspoon black pepper in a large Dutch oven. Cover and cook over medium heat 20 minutes or until onion is soft, stirring occasionally. Add vinegar; cook, uncovered, 15 minutes or until liquid almost evaporates and onions are caramelized. Remove ¾ cup onion mixture; set aside.

2. Sprinkle veal with ¼ teaspoon black pepper. Add 1 cup wine, 1 teaspoon thyme, veal, broth, red pepper, tomatoes, and garlic to pan; bring to a boil. Cover, reduce heat, and simmer 1 hour and 15 minutes, turning veal occasionally. Uncover and cook 30 minutes. Stir in pasta and beans; simmer 15 minutes or until pasta is tender. Serve with reserved onion mixture, basil, and lemon zest. Yield: 4 servings.

CALORIES 653 (19% from fat); FAT 14g (sat 4.5g, mono 5g, poly 1.7g); PROTEIN 77.7g; CARB 49.2g; FIBER 7.3g; CHOL 264mg; IRON 7.2mg; SODIUM 1,196mg; CALC 216mg

Chicken and Dumplings

"Friends rave every time I make this recipe. I often use a whole chicken cut into pieces and skinned. You can make the store-bought chicken stock taste more home-made by adding some fresh herbs and parsley and simmering until it's reduced by half."

—Charlene Hill, Tustin, California

    Cooking spray
    1   cup chopped onion
    1   garlic clove, chopped
    ¼   cup dry sherry
    ½   teaspoon salt
    ¼   teaspoon black pepper
    2   (14½-ounce) cans fat-free, less-sodium chicken broth
    1   (10¾-ounce) can condensed reduced-fat, reduced-sodium cream of mushroom soup, undiluted
    4   pounds chicken pieces, skinned
    1   cup frozen green peas
    ¼   cup water
    2   tablespoons cornstarch

DUMPLINGS:

    2   cups baking mix (such as Bisquick)
    ⅔   cup fat-free milk

REMAINING INGREDIENT:

    Chopped parsley (optional)

1. Heat a Dutch oven coated with cooking spray over medium-high heat. Add onion and garlic; sauté 5 minutes. Stir in sherry and next 4 ingredients, and bring to boil. Add chicken pieces; bring to a boil. Cover, reduce heat, and simmer 35 minutes or until chicken is tender.

2. Remove chicken pieces from cooking liquid. Place chicken in a bowl, and chill 15 minutes.

3. Remove chicken from bones, and cut meat into bite-sized pieces. Discard bones. Return chicken to pan; stir in peas.

4. Combine water and cornstarch in a small bowl; stir with a whisk. Add cornstarch mixture to pan; stir well.

5. To prepare dumplings, combine baking mix and milk. Drop dough into chicken mixture to form 16 dumplings. Bring to a simmer; cook 20 minutes, stirring occasionally. Cover and cook 10 minutes or until dumplings are done. Garnish with parsley, if desired. Yield: 8 servings (serving size: 1½ cups chicken mixture and 2 dumplings).

CALORIES 373 (24% from fat); FAT 10.1g (sat 2.8g, mono 3.1g, poly 1.5g); PROTEIN 35.9g; CARB 31.7g; FIBER 2.4g; CHOL 99mg; IRON 2.9mg; SODIUM 725mg; CALC 116mg

Potato Lasagna

"I use this recipe as a side dish for special occasions. It goes great with lean, grilled steak or fish. Sometimes I add sliced ham with the potato layers and serve it as a main dish."

—Gretchen Clothier, Wichita, Kansas

SAUCE:

    1   teaspoon olive oil
    ½   cup chopped onion
    ½   cup chopped green bell pepper
 2½   cups chopped tomato (about 1½ pounds)
    3   tablespoons tomato paste
    ¼   teaspoon salt
    ¼   teaspoon dried basil
    ⅛   teaspoon garlic salt
    ⅛   teaspoon black pepper
    1   (14½-ounce) can fat-free, less-sodium chicken broth

Continued

POTATOES:

½ teaspoon salt
½ teaspoon dried basil
½ teaspoon ground red pepper
⅛ teaspoon black pepper
1½ cups thinly sliced peeled baking potato (about 1 large)
1½ cups thinly sliced peeled Yukon gold potato (about 2 large)
1½ cups thinly sliced peeled sweet potato (about 1 large)
1 cup (4 ounces) shredded reduced-fat sharp cheddar cheese
1 cup (4 ounces) shredded part-skim mozzarella cheese
Cooking spray

1. Preheat oven to 350°.

2. To prepare sauce, heat oil in a large saucepan over medium heat. Add onion and bell pepper; sauté 8 minutes or until tender, stirring frequently. Add tomato and next 6 ingredients. Bring to a boil, reduce heat, and simmer 45 minutes, stirring occasionally.

3. To prepare potatoes, combine ½ teaspoon salt, ½ teaspoon basil, red pepper, and ⅛ teaspoon black pepper in a large bowl. Add potatoes; toss well, and set aside. Combine cheeses. Spoon 1½ cups potato mixture into an 11 x 7-inch baking dish coated with cooking spray. Top with 1 cup sauce and ⅔ cup cheese mixture. Repeat layers, reserving ⅔ cup cheese mixture and ending with sauce. Cover and bake at 350° for 1 hour. Uncover and sprinkle with ⅔ cup cheese mixture; bake an additional 10 minutes or until bubbly. Yield 6 servings.

CALORIES 227 (23% from fat); FAT 5.8g (sat 3.1g, mono 1.9g, poly 0.4g); PROTEIN 13.7g; CARB 31g; FIBER 3.9g; CHOL 14mg; IRON 1.2mg; SODIUM 694mg; CALC 239mg

Bean Salad with Artichokes

"This salad is quick to make and can be adapted to include other vegetables you may have on hand. Vary the seasonings to suit your taste. Try it inside a pita pocket for a tasty sandwich."

—Frieda Chodos, Nepean, Ontario

SALAD:

1 cup chopped plum tomato
½ cup chopped red bell pepper
½ cup chopped red onion
¼ cup chopped fresh parsley
1 (19-ounce) can chickpeas (garbanzo beans), drained
1 (19-ounce) can red kidney beans, drained
1 (14-ounce) can quartered artichoke hearts, drained

DRESSING:

¼ cup (1 ounce) feta cheese, crumbled
2 tablespoons fresh lemon juice
1 tablespoon olive oil
1 tablespoon balsamic vinegar
1½ teaspoons spicy brown mustard
1 teaspoon dried basil
1 teaspoon dried oregano
1 teaspoon dried thyme
1 garlic clove, minced

1. To prepare salad, combine first 7 ingredients in a large bowl.

2. To prepare dressing, combine cheese and remaining 8 ingredients in a small bowl, stirring with a whisk. Pour dressing over salad; cover and chill 1 hour. Yield: 6 servings (serving size: 1⅓ cups salad).

CALORIES 294 (15% from fat); FAT 4.9g (sat 1.1g, mono 2.1g, poly 0.7g); PROTEIN 14.1g; CARB 49.2g; FIBER 13.3g; CHOL 4mg; IRON 2.9mg; SODIUM 404mg; CALC 75mg

Italian Meatball Soup

"This recipe is so versatile. I use whatever frozen or fresh vegetables I have on hand and cook a double batch of the meatballs so I can freeze them for next time."

—Heidi Smid,
Travelers Rest, South Carolina

MEATBALLS:

1 cup Italian-seasoned breadcrumbs
½ cup grated Parmesan cheese
¼ cup dried parsley
2 tablespoons water
1 teaspoon dried basil
1 teaspoon black pepper
1 pound ground round
1 large egg
Cooking spray

SOUP:

1½ teaspoons vegetable oil
1 cup chopped onion
1 cup chopped carrot
½ cup chopped celery
2 cups low-sodium tomato juice
½ cup chopped green bell pepper
½ cup frozen green beans
1 teaspoon dried basil
1 teaspoon dried oregano
⅛ teaspoon black pepper
2 (14½-ounce) cans low-salt beef broth

1. Preheat oven to 375°.

2. To prepare meatballs, combine first 8 ingredients in a bowl. Shape beef mixture into 30 (1-inch) meatballs, and place on a broiler pan coated with cooking spray. Bake at 375° for 20 minutes or until done. Drain on paper towels.

3. To prepare soup, heat oil in a Dutch oven over medium heat. Add onion, carrot, and celery, and sauté 10 minutes or until tender, stirring occasionally. Add meatballs, tomato juice, and remaining ingredients. Bring to a boil, reduce heat, and simmer 10 minutes or until vegetables are done. Yield: 6 servings (serving size: 1⅓ cups soup and 5 meatballs).

CALORIES 315 (30% from fat); FAT 10.6g (sat 4.1g, mono 3.9g, poly 1.4g); PROTEIN 28.1g; CARB 25.8g; FIBER 3.6g; CHOL 89mg; IRON 4.4mg; SODIUM 842mg; CALC 206mg

Spicy Pork Tenderloin with Ginger-Maple Sauce

"If you're craving meat, this will hit the spot."
—Cathy Noh, Cerritos, California

2 teaspoons chili powder
1¼ teaspoons salt
1 teaspoon black pepper
1 teaspoon ground cinnamon
1½ pounds pork tenderloin, trimmed
Cooking spray
2 tablespoons butter
1 cup chopped onion
2 tablespoons bottled ground fresh ginger
1 cup fat-free, less-sodium chicken broth
½ cup maple syrup

1. Preheat oven to 375°.

2. Combine first 4 ingredients in a small bowl; rub pork with spice mixture. Refrigerate 30 minutes.

3. Heat a large nonstick skillet coated with cooking spray over medium-high heat; add pork. Cook 6 minutes; brown on all sides. Place on a broiler pan coated with cooking spray. Bake at 375° for 30 minutes or until thermometer registers 155°. Let stand 10 minutes before slicing.

4. While pork bakes, melt butter in a medium saucepan over medium-high heat. Add onion, and cook 10 minutes or until golden brown, stirring frequently. Add ginger, and cook 4 minutes. Stir in broth and syrup, scraping pan to loosen browned bits. Bring broth mixture to a boil; cook until reduced to ¾ cup (about 10 minutes). Cut pork into ¼-inch-thick slices; serve with sauce. Yield: 6 servings (serving size: 3 ounces pork and 2 tablespoons sauce).

CALORIES 263 (28% from fat); FAT 8.2g (sat 3.9g, mono 2.8g, poly 0.6g); PROTEIN 25g; CARB 21.7g; FIBER 1.1g; CHOL 78mg; IRON 2mg; SODIUM 663mg; CALC 39mg

in season

Finding Fennel

Often unrecognized or misunderstood, fennel has culinary versatility worth exploring.

Native to the Mediterranean region, fennel is a licorice-flavored member of the parsley family.

The type you'll find in America—Florence, or bulb, fennel (sometimes labeled "fresh anise")—has a bulbous base, stalks like celery, and feathery leaves that resemble Queen Anne's lace. Like celery, the entire plant is edible. The crisp and slightly sweet bulb is especially delicious served raw in salads. Whether braised, sautéed, roasted, or grilled, the bulb mellows and softens with cooking.

Look for small, heavy, white bulbs that are firm and free of cracks, browning, or moist areas. The stalks should be crisp, with feathery, bright-green fronds.

Waste Not

- Fennel seeds don't come from bulb fennel but from common, or wild, fennel. The seeds are slightly nutty, with the expected licorice flavor, and are widely used in sausages, stews, soups, and curries.

- Fennel stalks can take the place of celery in soups and stews and can be used as a "bed" for roasted chicken and meats.

- Use fronds as a garnish, or chop them and use as you would other herbs, like dill or parsley. Chopped fennel works especially well in Italian tomato sauces, but add it late in the cooking process so the flavor isn't diluted.

Bulb Basics

- Trim the stalks about an inch above the bulb.

- If you want pieces to stay together for grilling, keep the root end intact. Otherwise, trim about a half inch off the root end before cooking.

- To slice fennel, stand the bulb on the root end and cut vertically.

Braised Fennel with Onion and Sweet Pepper

Serve with roast lamb, chicken, or fish.

    2   teaspoons olive oil
    4   cups thinly sliced fennel bulb
        (about 4 small bulbs)
    3   cups vertically sliced onion
    1   cup red bell pepper strips
    ⅔   cup vegetable broth
    ¼   teaspoon salt
    ¼   teaspoon fennel seeds
    ⅛   teaspoon coarsely ground black
        pepper
    1   garlic clove, minced
    2   tablespoons thinly sliced basil
   1½   tablespoons chopped fennel fronds
        or fresh flat-leaf parsley

1. Heat oil in a large nonstick skillet over medium-high heat. Add sliced fennel, onion, and bell pepper; sauté 6 minutes. Add broth and next 4 ingredients. Cover, reduce heat, and simmer 20 minutes or until vegetables are tender. Stir in basil and fennel fronds. Yield: 4 servings (serving size: ¾ cup).

CALORIES 92 (27% from fat); FAT 2.8g (sat 0.3g, mono 1.7g, poly 0.3g); PROTEIN 2.8g; CARB 16.3g; FIBER 4.9g; CHOL 0mg; IRON 1.1mg; SODIUM 363mg; CALC 69mg

Beef Stew with Fennel Gremolata

Gremolata, a garnish for meat dishes, is traditionally made with chopped parsley, garlic, and lemon rind. This variation substitutes fennel fronds for the parsley, chopped fennel bulb in place of the garlic, and orange rind in place of lemon. Serve over mashed potatoes.

STEW:
    Cooking spray
   1½   pounds eye-of-round roast,
        trimmed and cut into 1-inch cubes
    2   cups thinly sliced fennel bulb
        (about 2 small bulbs)
   1½   cups chopped red bell pepper
    1   large onion, cut into ¼-inch-thick
        wedges (about 1½ cups)
    1   garlic clove, minced
    2   cups (1-inch) diagonally cut
        carrot (about ¾ pound)
    1   cup water
    2   tablespoons tomato paste
    1   teaspoon fennel seeds
    ¾   teaspoon salt
    ¾   teaspoon dried thyme
    ¼   teaspoon coarsely ground black
        pepper
    3   orange rind strips
    1   (14.5-ounce) can diced tomatoes,
        undrained
    1   (10½-ounce) can beef broth
   2½   cups (1-inch) diagonally cut
        parsnip (about ¾ pound)

GREMOLATA:
    ½   cup finely chopped fennel bulb
    2   tablespoons finely chopped fennel
        fronds or fresh flat-leaf parsley
    2   teaspoons grated orange rind
                                   Continued

1. To prepare stew, heat a large Dutch oven coated with cooking spray over medium-high heat. Add beef; cook 6 minutes, browning on all sides. Remove from pan.

2. Add 2 cups fennel bulb, bell pepper, onion, and garlic to pan; reduce heat to medium, and cook 10 minutes, stirring occasionally. Add beef, carrot, and next 9 ingredients. Cover and reduce heat to low; simmer 1 hour, stirring occasionally. Add parsnip; cover and simmer 30 minutes or until beef is tender, stirring occasionally.

3. To prepare gremolata, combine ½ cup fennel bulb, fennel fronds, and grated orange rind in a small bowl.

4. Spoon 1⅓ cups beef stew into each of 6 bowls, and top each serving with 1½ tablespoons fennel gremolata. Yield: 6 servings.

CALORIES 271 (29% from fat); FAT 8.8g (sat 3.2g, mono 3.6g, poly 0.5g); PROTEIN 23.4g; CARB 26g; FIBER 7.5g; CHOL 54mg; IRON 3.2mg; SODIUM 652mg; CALC 97mg

Chicken with Fennel, Tomatoes, and Zucchini

This dish is good served with egg noodles or rice.

> 6 (4-ounce) skinless, boneless
>   chicken breast halves
> 2½ tablespoons Italian-seasoned
>   breadcrumbs
> 5 teaspoons olive oil, divided
> 2 cups thinly sliced fennel bulb
>   (about 2 small bulbs)
> 2 cups finely chopped zucchini
> 1½ cups thinly sliced leek
>   (about 2 large)
> ½ cup fat-free, less-sodium
>   chicken broth
> 2 tablespoons tomato paste
> ¼ teaspoon salt
> ¼ teaspoon fennel seeds
> ¼ teaspoon dried tarragon
> ⅛ teaspoon coarsely ground
>   black pepper
> 1 (14.5-ounce) can diced tomatoes,
>   undrained
> 2 tablespoons chopped fennel fronds
>   or fresh flat-leaf parsley

1. Dredge chicken in breadcrumbs. Heat 3 teaspoons oil in a large nonstick skillet over medium-high heat. Add chicken; sauté 3 minutes on each side or until golden brown. Remove from pan.

2. Heat 2 teaspoons oil in pan over medium heat. Add fennel bulb, zucchini, and leek; cook 5 minutes, stirring occasionally. Add broth and next 6 ingredients. Cover, reduce heat, and simmer 15 minutes or until vegetables are tender, stirring occasionally.

3. Return chicken to pan; cover and cook 12 minutes or until chicken is done. Sprinkle with fennel fronds. Yield: 6 servings (serving size: 1 chicken breast half, ⅔ cup vegetables, and 1 teaspoon fennel fronds).

CALORIES 221 (23% from fat); FAT 5.7g (sat 1g, mono 3.2g, poly 0.8g); PROTEIN 28.9g; CARB 13.5g; FIBER 3.1g; CHOL 66mg; IRON 2.4mg; SODIUM 429mg; CALC 78mg

Fennel, Leek, and Potato Soup

This warm take on vichyssoise makes a fine appetizer.

> 1 tablespoon butter
> 2 cups chopped fennel bulb
>   (about 2 small bulbs)
> 2 cups thinly sliced leek (about 2 large)
> 1¾ cups (1-inch) cubed peeled baking
>   potato
> 1¼ cups water
> ½ teaspoon salt
> ¼ teaspoon fennel seeds
> ⅛ teaspoon black pepper
> 2 (14½-ounce) cans fat-free,
>   less-sodium chicken broth
> Fennel fronds (optional)

1. Melt butter in a Dutch oven over medium-high heat. Add fennel bulb and leek; sauté 4 minutes. Add potato and next 5 ingredients, and bring to a boil. Cover, reduce heat, and simmer 20 minutes or until potato is tender. Place half of soup in a blender; process until smooth. Pour pureed soup into a bowl. Repeat procedure with remaining soup. Return pureed soup to pan; simmer 5 minutes or until slightly thick. Garnish

with fennel fronds, if desired. Yield: 7 servings (serving size: 1 cup).

CALORIES 85 (31% from fat); FAT 2.9g (sat 1.6g, mono 0.5g, poly 0.1g); PROTEIN 3.4g; CARB 12.7g; FIBER 1.7g; CHOL 7mg; IRON 0.8mg; SODIUM 193mg; CALC 39mg

Pizza with Caramelized Fennel, Onion, and Olives

While the dough rises, prepare the topping.

DOUGH:
> 1½ teaspoons dry yeast
> ⅔ cup warm water (100° to 110°)
> 2 cups all-purpose flour, divided
> ½ teaspoon salt
> Cooking spray
> 2 teaspoons yellow cornmeal

TOPPING:
> 1 tablespoon olive oil
> 4 cups thinly sliced fennel bulb
>   (about 4 small bulbs)
> 2 cups thinly sliced onion
> ½ teaspoon salt
> ¼ teaspoon dried oregano
> ¼ teaspoon dried thyme
> ¼ teaspoon black pepper

REMAINING INGREDIENTS:
> 1 cup bottled tomato-basil pasta
>   sauce (such as Classico)
> 1 cup (4 ounces) shredded
>   part-skim mozzarella cheese
> ¼ cup coarsely chopped pitted
>   kalamata olives

1. To prepare dough, dissolve yeast in warm water in a large bowl, and let stand 5 minutes. Lightly spoon flour into dry measuring cups; level with a knife. Add 1¾ cups flour and ½ teaspoon salt to yeast mixture, and beat with a mixer at medium speed until smooth. Turn dough out onto a floured surface. Knead until smooth and elastic (about 10 minutes); add enough of remaining flour, 1 tablespoon at a time, to prevent dough from sticking to hands (dough will feel tacky).

2. Place dough in a large bowl coated with cooking spray, turning to coat top. Cover and let rise in a warm place (85°), free from drafts, 45 minutes or until doubled in size. (Press two fingers into dough. If an indentation remains, dough has risen enough.) Punch dough down; knead 5 times, and let rest 15 minutes. Roll dough into a 12-inch circle on a floured surface. Place dough on a 12-inch pizza pan or baking sheet coated with cooking spray and sprinkled with cornmeal. Crimp edges of dough with fingers to form a rim.

3. To prepare topping, heat oil in a large nonstick skillet coated with cooking spray over medium-high heat. Add fennel and next 5 ingredients, and cook 20 minutes or until golden, stirring frequently.

4. Preheat oven to 450°.

5. Spread pasta sauce over crust, leaving a ½-inch border; sprinkle with fennel mixture, cheese, and olives. Bake at 450° for 18 minutes or until browned. Yield: 6 servings (serving size: 1 wedge).

CALORIES 296 (23% from fat); FAT 7.5g (sat 2.6g, mono 3.7g, poly 0.6g); PROTEIN 11.9g; CARB 45.4g; FIBER 4.5g; CHOL 10mg; IRON 3.1mg; SODIUM 653mg; CALC 220mg

White Bean Spread with Fennel

Use as a sandwich spread on bagels or as a dip for vegetables and bagel chips.

- 2 tablespoons light mayonnaise
- 1 tablespoon fresh lemon juice
- ¼ teaspoon salt
- ⅛ teaspoon black pepper
- 1 (16-ounce) can cannellini beans or other white beans, rinsed and drained
- ¼ cup finely chopped fennel bulb
- 2 tablespoons finely chopped fennel fronds
- 1 tablespoon finely chopped red onion

1. Combine first 5 ingredients in a food processor, and pulse 5 times or until beans are coarsely chopped. Combine bean mixture, fennel bulb, fennel fronds, and onion in a small bowl. Yield: 5 servings (serving size: ¼ cup).

CALORIES 130 (16% from fat); FAT 2.3g (sat 0.4g, mono 0g, poly 0.1g); PROTEIN 6.8g; CARB 21.3g; FIBER 4.6g; CHOL 2mg; IRON 2.9mg; SODIUM 172mg; CALC 72mg

No Forks Required

These bite-sized desserts are big on glamour—and flavor.

Here is our offering of bite-sized, party-friendly pastries. They all pack the flavor of a full-sized dessert into a package that you can pick up and eat in just a couple of fork-free bites.

Sweet Plantain and Chocolate Empanaditas

Empanaditas—small sweet or savory turnovers—are popular throughout Spain and Latin America.

FILLING:

- 1 cup (1-inch-thick) sliced soft black plantain (about ½ pound)
- 2 tablespoons fat-free sweetened condensed milk

DOUGH:

- 2 cups all-purpose flour, divided
- 6 tablespoons ice water
- 1 teaspoon cider vinegar
- 2 tablespoons powdered sugar
- ½ teaspoon salt
- ½ cup vegetable shortening
- Cooking spray

REMAINING INGREDIENTS:

- 5 teaspoons 2% reduced-fat milk, divided
- ¼ cup granulated sugar
- ¼ cup semisweet chocolate minichips

1. Preheat oven to 400°.

2. To prepare filling, cook plantain in boiling water 10 minutes or until tender; drain. Combine plantain and condensed milk in a bowl, and mash with a potato masher. Set aside.

3. To prepare dough, lightly spoon flour into dry measuring cups; level with a knife. Combine ½ cup flour, ice water, and vinegar, stirring with a whisk until well blended to form a slurry. Combine 1½ cups flour, powdered sugar, and salt

in a bowl; cut in shortening with a pastry blender or 2 knives until mixture resembles coarse meal. Add slurry, tossing with a fork until moist.

4. Slightly overlap 2 lengths of plastic wrap on a slightly damp surface. Place dough on plastic wrap. Gently press dough into a 4-inch circle; cover with 2 additional lengths of overlapping plastic wrap. Roll dough, still covered, into an 18 x 12-inch rectangle; freeze 10 minutes or until wrap can be easily removed. Remove wrap; place dough on a lightly floured surface. Cut dough into 24 circles using a 3-inch round cutter.

5. Place circles on a baking sheet coated with cooking spray, and lightly moisten edges of dough with water. Spoon 2 teaspoons plantain mixture into each circle. Fold dough over filling; pinch edges together to seal. Brush tops of dough evenly with 1 tablespoon 2% milk; sprinkle evenly with granulated sugar.

6. Bake at 400° for 17 minutes or until lightly browned. Combine chips and 2 teaspoons 2% milk in a small bowl, and microwave at HIGH 30 seconds; stir until smooth. Drizzle melted chocolate over empanaditas. Serve warm. Yield: 2 dozen (serving size: 1 empanadita).

CALORIES 111 (41% from fat); FAT 5g (sat 1.4g, mono 2.1g, poly 1.2g); PROTEIN 1.5g; CARB 15.8g; FIBER 0.6g; CHOL 0mg; IRON 0.6mg; SODIUM 52mg; CALC 9mg

Apple and Cream Cheese Roll-Ups

(pictured on page 331)

These desserts resemble small strudels.

FILLING:
     1   cup dried apples, chopped
    ⅓   cup thawed apple juice
         concentrate, undiluted
    ¼   teaspoon ground cinnamon
        Dash of ground nutmeg
    ¼   cup sugar
    ¼   cup (2 ounces) ⅓-less-fat cream
         cheese
     1   large egg

PASTRY:
    12   sheets frozen phyllo dough,
         thawed
        Cooking spray
    ½   cup graham cracker crumbs,
         divided
    ¼   cup sugar, divided

TOPPING:
    1½ teaspoons sugar
    ½   teaspoon ground cinnamon

1. To prepare filling, combine first 4 ingredients in a small saucepan over medium-high heat. Bring apple mixture to a boil; cover, reduce heat, and simmer 5 minutes or until most of liquid is absorbed. Cool to room temperature. Combine ¼ cup sugar and cream cheese; beat with a mixer at low speed until blended. Add egg; beat until blended. Fold in apple mixture; cover and set aside.

2. Preheat oven to 350°.

3. To prepare pastry, place 1 phyllo sheet on a large cutting board or work surface (cover remaining dough to keep from drying), and lightly coat with cooking spray. Sprinkle phyllo with 2 teaspoons graham cracker crumbs and 1 teaspoon sugar. Repeat layers twice, ending with crumbs and sugar. Cut phyllo stack lengthwise into 6 (2¾-inch-wide) strips using a sharp knife. Spoon 1 rounded teaspoon apple mixture ½ inch from end of each phyllo strip. Roll up each strip, beginning with apple mixture end; place strips, seam sides down, on a

baking sheet coated with cooking spray, and lightly coat each roll with cooking spray. Repeat procedure 3 times.

4. To prepare topping, combine 1½ teaspoons sugar and ½ teaspoon cinnamon; sprinkle evenly over phyllo rolls. Bake at 350° for 10 minutes, and cool on a wire rack. Yield: 24 servings (serving size: 1 roll-up).

CALORIES 81 (18% from fat); FAT 1.6g (sat 0.6g, mono 0.6g, poly 0.2g); PROTEIN 1.4g; CARB 15.4g; FIBER 0.6g; CHOL 11mg; IRON 0.5mg; SODIUM 77mg; CALC 6mg

Polenta-Blueberry Cakes

If you're using frozen blueberries, there's no need to thaw them before folding them into the batter.

     1   cup all-purpose flour
     3   tablespoons yellow cornmeal
    ¼   teaspoon salt
    ¼   teaspoon baking powder
    ¼   teaspoon baking soda
    ½   cup granulated sugar
    ¼   cup butter, softened
     1   large egg
     2   teaspoons grated lemon rind
    ⅔   cup low-fat buttermilk
    ½   cup fresh or frozen blueberries
     1   tablespoon all-purpose flour
        Cooking spray
    ½   cup powdered sugar
     1   tablespoon fresh lemon juice

1. Preheat oven to 350°.

2. Lightly spoon 1 cup flour into a dry measuring cup; level with a knife. Combine 1 cup flour and next 4 ingredients, stirring well with a whisk. Place granulated sugar and butter in a large bowl, and beat with a mixer at medium speed until well blended (about 2 minutes). Add egg and lemon rind; beat until well blended. Add flour mixture and buttermilk alternately to sugar mixture, beginning and ending with flour mixture. Mix after each addition. Toss blueberries with 1 tablespoon flour, and fold into batter.

3. Spoon batter into 24 miniature muffin cups coated with cooking spray. Bake at 350° for 14 minutes or until cakes spring back when touched lightly in center.

Combine powdered sugar and juice, and drizzle over warm cakes. Yield: 2 dozen (serving size: 1 cake).

CALORIES 75 (28% from fat); FAT 2.3g (sat 1.3g, mono 0.7g, poly 0.1g); PROTEIN 1.2g; CARB 12.6g; FIBER 0.3g; CHOL 15mg; IRON 0.4mg; SODIUM 73mg; CALC 13mg

Mini Mocha-Toffee Crunch Cheesecakes

(pictured on page 331)

Look for prebaked miniature phyllo dough shells in your supermarket's freezer section or at Middle Eastern markets. (There are usually 15 shells in a package.) Place the shells in miniature muffin cups to prevent overbrowning.

    36   commercial prebaked miniature
         phyllo dough shells
    1½ teaspoons instant coffee granules
     1   teaspoon hot water
     1   teaspoon Kahlúa (coffee-flavored
         liqueur)
    ½   cup sugar
    ½   cup (4 ounces) ⅓-less-fat cream
         cheese
    ½   cup (4 ounces) block-style
         fat-free cream cheese
     1   tablespoon all-purpose flour
    ¼   teaspoon vanilla extract
     1   large egg
     3   tablespoons toffee bits (such as
         Skor)

1. Preheat oven to 350°.

2. Place 1 phyllo shell into each of 36 miniature muffin cups.

3. Combine coffee granules, hot water, and Kahlúa in a small bowl. Place coffee mixture, sugar, and next 5 ingredients in a food processor; process until smooth. Spoon about 1 tablespoon cheese mixture into each shell; discard remaining filling. Sprinkle cheesecakes evenly with toffee bits.

4. Bake at 350° for 15 minutes or until set. Remove from pans, and cool on a wire rack. Yield: 3 dozen (serving size: 1 cheesecake).

CALORIES 55 (38% from fat); FAT 2.3g (sat 0.8g, mono 0.9g, poly 0.6g); PROTEIN 1.5g; CARB 6.5g; FIBER 0g; CHOL 10mg; IRON 0.1mg; SODIUM 47mg; CALC 10mg

Sweet Potato Streusel Tarts

(pictured on page 331)

These pies feature a topping made with hazelnuts, although any nut will work.

CRUST:

- 1 cup all-purpose flour
- 2 tablespoons granulated sugar
- ⅛ teaspoon salt
- 2 tablespoons chilled butter, cut into small pieces
- 2 tablespoons vegetable shortening
- 3 tablespoons ice water
- Cooking spray

FILLING:

- ¼ cup maple syrup
- 2 tablespoons brown sugar
- ¾ teaspoon ground cinnamon
- ½ teaspoon ground allspice
- ¼ teaspoon salt
- 1 large egg
- 1 cup mashed cooked sweet potatoes
- ¼ cup evaporated fat-free milk

STREUSEL:

- 2 tablespoons finely chopped hazelnuts
- 2 tablespoons brown sugar
- 1½ teaspoons chilled butter, cut into small pieces

1. To prepare crust, lightly spoon flour into a dry measuring cup, and level with a knife. Place flour, granulated sugar, and ⅛ teaspoon salt in a food processor; pulse 2 times or until combined. Add 2 tablespoons butter and shortening, and pulse 4 times or until mixture resembles coarse meal. With processor on, add ice water through food chute, 1 tablespoon at a time, processing just until combined (do not form a ball). Shape mixture into a 6-inch log; wrap in plastic wrap coated with cooking spray. Freeze 30 minutes.

2. Preheat oven to 425°.

3. Shape dough into 24 balls; place 1 ball in each of 24 miniature muffin cups coated with cooking spray. Press dough into bottoms and up sides of muffin cups.

4. To prepare filling, place syrup and next 5 ingredients in a bowl; beat with a mixer at medium speed 1 minute or until well blended. Add sweet potatoes and milk; beat until well blended. Spoon about 4 teaspoons filling into each muffin cup.

5. To prepare streusel, combine hazelnuts and 2 tablespoons brown sugar in a small bowl; cut in 1½ teaspoons butter with a pastry blender or 2 knives until mixture resembles coarse meal. Sprinkle streusel evenly over tarts; bake at 425° for 10 minutes. Reduce heat to 350° (do not remove tarts from oven); bake 12 minutes or until filling is set. Cool 5 minutes on a wire rack. Run a knife around outside edges. Remove tarts, and cool completely on wire rack. Yield: 2 dozen (serving size: 1 tart).

CALORIES 81 (32% from fat); FAT 2.9g (sat 1.1g, mono 1.2g, poly 0.4g); PROTEIN 1.3g; CARB 12.6g; FIBER 0.5g; CHOL 12mg; IRON 0.5mg; SODIUM 57mg; CALC 18mg

---

Tackling Tarts

A batonlike device called a "tamper" makes pressing dough evenly into muffin cups easy and fast. Buy one at www.cookswares.com ($3.70 each) or www.kitchenkrafts.com ($5.25 each).

Apricot-Cranberry Tarts

Made with store-bought pie dough and a filling of dried fruit, these tarts couldn't be more simple. And you can easily cut the recipe in half.

- 1 (15-ounce) package refrigerated pie dough (such as Pillsbury)
- 1 cup chopped dried apricots
- 1 cup golden raisins
- ½ cup sweetened dried cranberries
- ½ cup dark rum
- ½ cup pineapple juice
- 3 tablespoons honey
- 1 tablespoon butter
- ¼ teaspoon ground cinnamon
- ⅛ teaspoon salt

1. Preheat oven to 425°.

2. Roll each dough portion into a 12-inch circle on a lightly floured surface. Cut dough into 36 circles with a 2½-inch round cutter. Place 1 dough circle in each of 36 miniature muffin cups, pressing into bottoms and up sides. Bake at 425° for 7 minutes or until lightly browned. Remove from pans; cool on wire racks.

3. Combine apricots and next 4 ingredients in a small saucepan; bring to a boil. Reduce heat; simmer 10 minutes or until liquid is absorbed. Stir in honey and remaining 3 ingredients. Cool. Spoon about 2 teaspoons apricot mixture into each pastry shell. Yield: 3 dozen (serving size: 1 tart).

CALORIES 94 (38% from fat); FAT 4g (sat 1.1g, mono 1.7g, poly 1g); PROTEIN 1g; CARB 14.2g; FIBER 1.1g; CHOL 1mg; IRON 0.6mg; SODIUM 69mg; CALC 7mg

---

Mini Peppermint and Chocolate Chip Cheesecakes

You can make the cheesecakes ahead—cover and store them in the refrigerator. Add the topping before serving.

CRUST:

- 1 cup chocolate wafer crumbs (such as Nabisco's Famous Chocolate Wafers; about 22 cookies)
- 2 tablespoons sugar
- 2 tablespoons butter, melted
- Cooking spray

FILLING:

- 12 hard peppermint candies, divided
- ⅔ cup (5 ounces) block-style fat-free cream cheese, softened
- ½ cup (4 ounces) ⅓-less-fat cream cheese, softened
- ¼ cup sugar
- 2 tablespoons flour
- 2 large egg whites
- 1 large egg
- 1 (8-ounce) carton low-fat sour cream
- ¼ cup semisweet chocolate minichips
- ¼ teaspoon peppermint extract
- 1 cup frozen fat-free whipped topping, thawed
- 2 tablespoons chocolate sprinkles

Continued

1. Preheat oven to 325°.

2. To prepare crust, combine first 3 ingredients in a small bowl. Press about 1½ teaspoons crumb mixture into bottom of each of 48 miniature muffin cups coated with cooking spray. Bake at 325° for 5 minutes.

3. To prepare filling, place 6 candies, fat-free cream cheese, and next 6 ingredients in a food processor; process until smooth. Stir in minichips and peppermint extract. Divide filling evenly among prepared crusts. Bake at 325° for 12 minutes or until done. Cool in pans on a wire rack 30 minutes. Remove cheesecakes from pans; cool completely. Top each mini cheesecake with 1 teaspoon whipped topping. Crush 6 candies; sprinkle crushed candies and chocolate sprinkles over cheesecakes. Yield: 4 dozen (serving size: 1 cheesecake).

CALORIES 54 (37% from fat); FAT 2.2g (sat 1.3g, mono 0.6g, poly 0.1g); PROTEIN 1.6g; CARB 6.9g; FIBER 0.2g; CHOL 10mg; IRON 0.2mg; SODIUM 62mg; CALC 15mg

Peanut Butter-Fudge Cups

With their peanut butter cookie crusts and their chocolaty cake centers, these diminutive desserts offer a festive twist on the traditional peanut butter cup.

CRUST:

¼ cup chunky peanut butter
3 tablespoons brown sugar
2 tablespoons chilled butter, cut into small pieces
1½ tablespoons corn syrup
1 cup all-purpose flour
⅛ teaspoon salt
3 tablespoons cold water
Cooking spray

FILLING:

⅔ cup packed brown sugar
2 tablespoons unsweetened cocoa
2 tablespoons semisweet chocolate chips
1 tablespoon butter
3 tablespoons 1% low-fat milk
2 tablespoons all-purpose flour
1 large egg
2 teaspoons powdered sugar

1. Preheat oven to 350°.

2. To prepare crust, place first 4 ingredients in a large bowl; beat with a mixer at medium speed until smooth. Lightly spoon 1 cup flour into a dry measuring cup; level with a knife. Add 1 cup flour and salt to peanut butter mixture; cut in flour with a pastry blender or 2 knives until mixture resembles coarse meal. Sprinkle surface with cold water, 1 tablespoon at a time; toss with a fork until combined.

3. Shape flour mixture into 24 balls. Place 1 ball in each of 24 miniature muffin cups coated with cooking spray. Press dough into bottoms and up sides of muffin cups.

4. To prepare filling, combine ⅔ cup brown sugar and next 4 ingredients in a small saucepan over medium-low heat. Cook 3 to 4 minutes or until smooth, stirring frequently. Remove from heat; stir in 2 tablespoons flour and egg until well blended. Divide chocolate mixture evenly among muffin cups. Bake at 350° for 10 minutes or until pastry is lightly browned; cool in pan on a wire rack 5 minutes. Run a knife around outside edges of cups. Remove cups from pan; cool completely on wire rack. Sprinkle with powdered sugar. Yield: 2 dozen (serving size: 1 cup).

CALORIES 92 (33% from fat); FAT 3.4g (sat 1.4g, mono 1.3g, poly 0.5g); PROTEIN 1.7g; CARB 14.6g; FIBER 0.5g; CHOL 13mg; IRON 0.6mg; SODIUM 48mg; CALC 13mg

back to the best

Cheddar Chicken Chowder

Senior Food Editor Jill Melton developed this easy, rich, and creamy chowder to combine two of her favorites—corn chowder and chicken soup.

The recipe first appeared in our November-December 1996 issue, in a story titled "In from the Cold."

Cheddar Chicken Chowder

2 bacon slices
1 pound skinless, boneless chicken breast, cut into bite-size pieces
1 cup chopped onion
1 cup chopped red bell pepper
2 garlic cloves, minced
4½ cups fat-free, less-sodium chicken broth
1¾ cups chopped peeled red potato
2¼ cups frozen whole-kernel corn
½ cup all-purpose flour
2 cups 2% low-fat milk
¾ cup (3 ounces) shredded cheddar cheese
½ teaspoon salt
¼ teaspoon black pepper

1. Cook bacon in a Dutch oven over medium-high heat until crisp. Remove bacon from pan; crumble. Set aside. Add chicken, onion, bell pepper, and garlic to drippings in pan; sauté 5 minutes. Add broth and potato, and bring to a boil. Cover, reduce heat, and simmer 20 minutes or until potato is tender. Add corn; stir well.

2. Lightly spoon flour into a dry measuring cup, and level with a knife. Place flour in a bowl. Gradually add milk, stirring with a whisk until blended; add to soup. Bring to a boil over medium-high heat. Reduce heat to medium, and simmer 15 minutes or until thick, stirring frequently. Stir in cheddar cheese, salt, and black pepper. Top with crumbled bacon. Yield: 7 servings (serving size: 1½ cups).

CALORIES 306 (22% from fat); FAT 7.5g (sat 4g, mono 2.2g, poly 0.6g); PROTEIN 25g; CARB 33.7g; FIBER 2.9g; CHOL 58mg; IRON 1.6mg; SODIUM 376mg; CALC 193mg

Look Who's Coming to Dinner

Six famous foodies. Five different backgrounds. One remarkable Thanksgiving feast.

For this Thanksgiving menu, *Cooking Light* decided on a potluck dinner. As host, we supplied the turkey and the dessert. To round out the meal, we invited a diverse group of chefs and cookbook authors to be our guests and bring a dish. From Curtis Aikens' down-home goodness to Norman Van Aken's flamboyant Nuevo Latino bravado to Ying Compestine's compelling fusion of Oriental and Occidental, the menu offers both comfort and surprise.

Thanksgiving Potluck Menu 2001

serves 6

Cooking Light's
Ultimate Roasted Turkey

Mama's Corn Bread Dressing
by Curtis Aikens

Crunchy Autumn Vegetable Salad
by Carole Peck

Plantains in Temptation Sauce
by Norman Van Aken

Millionaire Salad
by Jane and Michael Stern

Harmony Holiday Delight
by Ying Compestine

Cooking Light's **Pear Galette**
with Brandied Cranberries
and Raisins

Cooking Light's Ultimate Roasted Turkey

This recipe—developed by *Cooking Light* Contributor Elizabeth Taliaferro—is nearly perfect, having won the highest rating in our Test Kitchens.

¾ cup apple cider
5 tablespoons dark corn syrup, divided
1 (12-pound) fresh or frozen turkey, thawed
1 tablespoon poultry seasoning
1 tablespoon dried rubbed sage
1 teaspoon salt
¼ teaspoon black pepper
4 garlic cloves, sliced
2 onions, quartered
2 Golden Delicious apples, cored and quartered
Cooking spray
1 teaspoon butter
1 (14½-ounce) can fat-free, less-sodium chicken broth
1 tablespoon cornstarch

1. Preheat oven to 375°.

2. Combine cider and 4 tablespoons corn syrup in a small saucepan; bring to a boil. Remove from heat; set aside.

3. Remove and reserve giblets and neck from turkey. Rinse turkey with cold water; pat dry. Trim excess fat. Lift wing tips up and over back; tuck under turkey. Combine poultry seasoning, sage, salt, and pepper. Rub seasoning mixture into skin and body cavity. Place half each of garlic, onion quarters, and apple quarters into body cavity. Place turkey, breast side up, in a shallow roasting pan coated with cooking spray. Arrange remaining garlic, onion, and apple around turkey in pan. Insert a meat thermometer into meaty part of thigh, making sure not to touch bone. Bake at 375° for 45 minutes. Baste turkey with cider syrup; cover with foil. Bake at 375° an additional 2 hours and 15 minutes or until meat thermometer registers 180°, basting with cider syrup 4 times at regular intervals. Let stand 10 minutes. Discard skin. Remove turkey from pan, reserving drippings for sauce. Place turkey on a platter; keep warm.

4. Strain drippings through a colander into a bowl; discard solids. Place a zip-top plastic bag inside a 2-cup glass measure. Pour drippings into bag; let stand 10 minutes (fat will rise to top). Seal bag; carefully snip off 1 bottom corner of bag. Drain drippings into a bowl, stopping before fat layer reaches opening; discard fat.

5. While turkey bakes, melt butter in a medium saucepan over medium-high heat. Add reserved giblets and neck; sauté 2 minutes on each side or until browned. Add broth, and bring to a boil. Cover, reduce heat, and simmer 45 minutes. Strain mixture through a colander into a bowl, discarding solids. Reserve ¼ cup broth mixture. Combine remaining broth mixture with drippings in roasting pan on stovetop over medium heat, scraping pan to loosen browned bits. Combine ¼ cup reserved broth mixture and cornstarch; add to roasting pan. Add 1 tablespoon corn syrup, stirring with a whisk. Bring to a boil; cook 1 minute. Serve gravy with turkey (gravy will be dark and thin). Yield: 12 servings (serving size: 6 ounces turkey and about 3 tablespoons gravy).

CALORIES 331 (24% from fat); FAT 8.8g (sat 3g, mono 1.9g, poly 2.5g); PROTEIN 50.4g; CARB 9.4g; FIBER 0.1g; CHOL 130mg; IRON 3.2mg; SODIUM 396mg; CALC 52mg

Dear Dressing

Mama's Corn Bread Dressing

Get a head start by making the corn bread a day or two ahead.

    5   cups Mama's Corn Bread, crumbled
    3   cups (1-inch) cubed, toasted white
        bread (about 5 [1-ounce] slices)
    1   cup crushed saltine crackers (about
        20 crackers)
    3   cups vegetable broth
    2   cups chopped celery
    2   cups chopped onion
    ¼   cup butter
    1½ teaspoons dried rubbed sage
    ¼   teaspoon salt
    ¼   teaspoon black pepper
    2   large eggs
    1   large egg white
    Cooking spray

1. Preheat oven to 375°.
2. Combine first 3 ingredients in a large bowl. Combine broth, celery, onion, and butter in a large saucepan; bring to a boil. Reduce heat, and simmer 10 minutes. Add broth mixture to corn bread mixture, stirring well. Add sage and next 4 ingredients; stir well to combine.
3. Pour mixture into an 11 x 7-inch baking dish coated with cooking spray. Bake at 375° for 45 minutes; cover and bake an additional 30 minutes or until golden. Yield: 12 servings.

CALORIES 243 (39% from fat); FAT 10.5g (sat 3.7g, mono 3g, poly 2.5g); PROTEIN 7.1g; CARB 30.4g; FIBER 2.6g; CHOL 65mg; IRON 1.9mg; SODIUM 622mg; CALC 68mg

MAMA'S CORN BREAD:
    1¾ cups yellow cornmeal
    ¼   teaspoon baking powder
    ¼   teaspoon baking soda
    ¼   teaspoon salt
    1   cup 1% low-fat buttermilk
    1   cup water
    1   large egg
    1   large egg white
    Cooking spray
    3   tablespoons vegetable oil

1. Preheat oven to 375°.
2. Combine first 8 ingredients in a large bowl; stir well. Coat a 9-inch cast-iron skillet with cooking spray; add oil, and place in oven 5 minutes. Remove from oven; stir oil into batter. Pour batter into pan. Bake at 375° for 35 minutes or until golden. Yield: 9 servings (serving size: 1 wedge).

CALORIES 161 (32% from fat); FAT 5.8g (sat 1.1g, mono 1.4g, poly 2.9g); PROTEIN 4.4g; CARB 22.4g; FIBER 2g; CHOL 25mg; IRON 1.2mg; SODIUM 157mg; CALC 42mg

New England Style

Crunchy Autumn Vegetable Salad

To simplify preparation, you can substitute 2½ cups of sliced canned beets.

SALAD:
    1   pound beets
    ½   pound green beans, trimmed and
        cut in half
    3   cups shredded peeled celeriac
        (celery root; about ½ pound)
    1½ cups shredded fennel bulb
        (about 1 small bulb)
    ⅓   cup chopped fresh chives

DRESSING:
    ½   cup plain low-fat yogurt
    ¼   cup lemon juice
    3   tablespoons prepared horseradish
    1   tablespoon honey
    1   tablespoon Dijon mustard
    ¾   teaspoon freshly ground black
        pepper
    ¼   teaspoon kosher salt

1. To prepare salad, leave root and 1 inch stem on beets, and scrub with a brush. Place beets in a medium saucepan; cover with water. Bring to a boil; cover, reduce heat, and simmer 35 minutes or until tender. Drain and rinse with cold water. Drain; cool. Trim off beet roots, and rub off skins. Cut into ¼-inch-thick slices. Set aside.
2. Cook green beans in boiling water 4 minutes or until crisp-tender. Drain and rinse with cold water; drain well. Combine beans, celeriac, fennel bulb, and chopped chives in a large bowl.
3. To prepare dressing, combine yogurt and remaining 6 ingredients, and stir well with a whisk. Pour over green bean mixture, tossing to coat. Divide beets evenly among 6 salad plates; top each serving with 1 cup green bean mixture. Yield: 6 servings.

CALORIES 99 (9% from fat); FAT 1g (sat 0.3g, mono 0.2g, poly 0.3g); PROTEIN 4.1g; CARB 21g; FIBER 4.3g; CHOL 1mg; IRON 1.7mg; SODIUM 286mg; CALC 103mg

Tropical Tastes

Norman Van Aken, chef and owner of Norman's in Coral Gables, Florida, and creator of "New World Cuisine," looked beyond the Pilgrims' landing at Plymouth Rock to Christopher Columbus' arrival on the continent. He tapped his passion for sun-drenched seasonings and developed Plantains in Temptation Sauce (recipe below) for this menu. "I was interested in sharing the wonderful Latin-Caribbean flavors of this dish that express Native American and European roots."

Plantains in Temptation Sauce

Serve this sweet side in place of the usual sweet potatoes. Unlike regular bananas, which ripen in two or three days, plantains take much longer. Look for fairly ripe black (rather than green) plantains.

PLANTAINS:
2   teaspoons vegetable oil, divided
Cooking spray
2   cups (1-inch-thick) slices soft black plantains (about 1 pound), divided

SAUCE:
¾   cup sugar
¾   cup water
¾   cup sherry or balsamic vinegar
2   teaspoons grated lime rind, divided
1   teaspoon ground cinnamon
¼   teaspoon ground cloves
1   tablespoon butter

1. To prepare plantains, heat 1 teaspoon oil in a medium skillet coated with cooking spray over medium heat. Add 1 cup plantains; cook 2 minutes on each side or until golden brown. Remove plantains; repeat procedure with 1 teaspoon oil and 1 cup plantains. Set aside.
2. To prepare sauce, place sugar in a heavy saucepan over medium heat; cook until sugar dissolves, stirring to dissolve sugar evenly (about 9 minutes). Combine water and vinegar; carefully add vinegar mixture to sugar, stirring constantly (mixture will bubble vigorously).

Cook 2 minutes or until sugar dissolves. Add 1½ teaspoons rind, cinnamon, and cloves; increase heat to medium-high. Cook 25 minutes or until mixture is reduced to 1 cup. Stir in plantains; cook 2 minutes or until thoroughly heated, spooning sauce over plantains. Stir in butter, and heat until melted. Garnish with ½ teaspoon rind. Yield: 8 servings (serving size: ½ cup).

CALORIES 145 (17% from fat); FAT 2.7g (sat 1.1g, mono 0.7g, poly 0.7g); PROTEIN 0.5g; CARB 32.2g; FIBER 1.1g; CHOL 4mg; IRON 0.4mg; SODIUM 17mg; CALC 7mg

Salad Deluxe

Jane and Michael Stern agree that Thanksgiving is made memorable by the company. "Cold turkey roll on saltines is a great Thanksgiving meal if it's shared with people you love," Michael says. For their menu contribution, these tireless culture preservers, authors, and "road food" experts took a classic Americana route with the retro Millionaire Salad (recipe below). "When we think of big celebration meals, we think of the heartland and of deluxe salads," Michael explains.

Millionaire Salad

Sometimes known as five-cup salad, this sweet, creamy dish is a recipe that many Americans grew up with.

2   cups miniature marshmallows
1   cup flaked sweetened coconut
2   (11-ounce) cans mandarin oranges in light syrup, drained
1   (20-ounce) can crushed pineapple in juice, drained
1   (8-ounce) carton low-fat sour cream
1   (8-ounce) carton plain fat-free yogurt

1. Combine all ingredients in a large bowl. Cover and chill. Yield: 12 servings (serving size: ½ cup).

CALORIES 151 (30% from fat); FAT 5g (sat 4.2g, mono 0.2g, poly 0.1g); PROTEIN 2.9g; CARB 24.8g; FIBER 1g; CHOL 6mg; IRON 0.5mg; SODIUM 60mg; CALC 67mg

Season for Sharing

"All Chinese holidays are surrounded with food and a focus on sharing," says **Ying Compestine,** author of several cookbooks on Chinese cuisine. She wrote her latest book, *The Runaway Rice Cake,* to help children understand the importance of generosity, especially when it comes to sharing food with the hungry. Her Eastern-inspired contribution, a vegetable medley called Harmony Holiday Delight (recipe below), draws from that wholesome spirit—it's appropriate (and filling) as a side, a salad, or a main dish.

Harmony Holiday Delight

3   tablespoons vegetable oil
1   cup coarsely chopped shiitake mushroom caps
1½   tablespoons minced peeled fresh ginger
5   garlic cloves, minced
1   jalapeño pepper, seeded and minced
2   cups fresh or thawed frozen shelled edamame (green soybeans)
1   cup frozen whole-kernel corn
½   cup fat-free soy milk or milk
1   tablespoon rice vinegar
1   cup dried cherries
¼   teaspoon salt
⅛   teaspoon white pepper
16   slices English cucumber
16   slices plum tomato
2   tablespoons black sesame seeds, toasted (optional)

1. Heat oil in a large nonstick skillet over medium-high heat. Add mushrooms, ginger, garlic, and jalapeño; stir-fry 2 minutes. Add edamame; stir-fry 1 minute. Stir in corn, soy milk, and vinegar; cook until liquid almost evaporates (about 3 minutes). Remove from heat, and stir in cherries, salt, and white pepper.
2. Spoon edamame mixture into center of a large platter; arrange cucumber and tomato slices alternately around mixture. Garnish with sesame seeds, if desired. Yield: 8 servings (serving size: ½ cup
Continued

edamame mixture, 2 slices cucumber, and 2 slices tomato).

CALORIES 251 (38% from fat); FAT 10.6g (sat 1.4g, mono 2.4g, poly 5.5g); PROTEIN 11.3g; CARB 29.6g; FIBER 5.7g; CHOL 0mg; IRON 3.3mg; SODIUM 96mg; CALC 187mg

Cooking Light's Pear Galette with Brandied Cranberries and Raisins

5 cups peeled Bartlett pears, cored and cut lengthwise into ¼-inch-thick slices (about 2 pounds)
1 cup brandy
6 tablespoons golden raisins
6 tablespoons dried cranberries
1½ cups all-purpose flour
6 tablespoons granulated sugar, divided
⅛ teaspoon salt
⅓ cup chilled butter, cut into small pieces
5 tablespoons ice water
Cooking spray
3 tablespoons brown sugar
2½ tablespoons cornstarch
2 teaspoons powdered sugar
1¼ cups frozen reduced-calorie whipped topping, thawed

1. Combine first 4 ingredients in a medium bowl; cover and let stand 1 hour. Drain.
2. Preheat oven to 425°.
3. Lightly spoon flour into dry measuring cups, and level with a knife. Place flour, 1 tablespoon granulated sugar, and salt in a food processor, and pulse 2 times or until combined. Add chilled butter, and pulse 4 times or until mixture resembles coarse meal. With processor on, add ice water through food chute, processing just until combined (do not form a ball). Gently press dough into a 4-inch circle on plastic wrap, and cover. Chill dough 15 minutes.
4. Slightly overlap 2 lengths of plastic wrap on a slightly damp surface. Unwrap chilled dough, and place on plastic wrap. Cover dough with 2 additional lengths of overlapping plastic wrap. Roll dough, still covered, into a 14-inch circle. Place dough in freezer 10 minutes or until plastic wrap can be easily removed. Remove top sheets of plastic wrap; fit dough, plastic wrap side up, into a 10-inch round removable-bottom tart pan coated with cooking spray. Press dough against bottom and sides of pan, allowing dough to extend over edges of pan; remove remaining sheets of plastic wrap.

5. Combine 3 tablespoons granulated sugar, brown sugar, and cornstarch; stir with a whisk. Sprinkle ⅓ cup cornstarch mixture into pastry shell; cover with half of fruit mixture. Repeat layers with remaining cornstarch mixture and fruit mixture. Fold edges of dough over fruit mixture (dough will only partially cover fruit). Sprinkle 2 tablespoons granulated sugar over fruit mixture; bake at 425° for 20 minutes. Reduce oven temperature to 350° (do not remove galette from oven), and bake an additional 45 minutes or until pastry is golden. Cool 10 minutes on a wire rack, and sift powdered sugar over top of galette. Serve galette warm or at room temperature with whipped topping. Yield: 10 servings (serving size: 1 wedge and 2 tablespoons whipped topping).

CALORIES 303 (23% from fat); FAT 7.7g (sat 4.9g, mono 1.9g, poly 0.4g); PROTEIN 2.6g; CARB 50.6g; FIBER 3.3g; CHOL 17mg; IRON 1.3 mg; SODIUM 95mg; CALC 21mg

Three Bonus Holiday Menus

Here are three additional Thanksgiving menus to choose from when planning your special holiday. Each menu pairs recipes from our November chapter. Recipe yields may vary within the menus.

Epicure's Thanksgiving Menu
serves 7

Oyster-Crab Bisque
(recipe on page 319)

***Cooking Light's* Ultimate Roasted Turkey**
(recipe on page 341)

Mushroom and Caramelized-Shallot Strudel
(recipe on page 315)

Herb and Onion Wheat Biscuits
(recipe on page 316)

Mini Mocha-Toffee Crunch Cheesecakes
(recipe on page 338)

The Adventurer's Menu
serves 6

Salmon Kalia in Panch Phoron Sauce (recipe on page 325)

Long-grain white rice

Braised Fennel with Onion and Sweet Pepper
(recipe on page 335)

Cranberry Upside-Down Cake with Cognac Cream
(recipe on page 326)

Traditionalist's Thanksgiving Menu
serves 8

Roast Turkey with Classic Pan Gravy (recipe on page 310)

Cranberry, Pear, and Ginger Relish (recipe on page 316)

Oyster Dressing
(recipe on page 318)

Sweet Potato and Apple Gratin
(recipe on page 315)

Gingered Pumpkin Pie
(recipe on page 312)

december

The New Holiday Cookbook

Table of Contents

S ince this is the season for giving, we present you with our holiday cookbook with more than 40 recipes tailored to the season. The collection incorporates updated classics, fresh takes on familiar favorites, and intriguing new ideas.

You'll find new twists on old standbys, like hot chocolate that's doubly warming when ginger livens it up, or a retro party mix charged with sizzling Asian flavors.

You may recognize the standing rib roast, but sides of Madeira sauce and herbed Yorkshire pudding transform it from familiar to fantastic. Ham follows suit with glazes of Champagne and vanilla, or bourbon and cranberries.

There are also old-world traditions: *fougasse*, a pull-apart French bread, and *sformato*, the regal Italian version of down-home mashed potatoes.

Whatever holiday you're celebrating this season, we know food will be a big part of the festivities. There's plenty here to share.

Appetizers, Snacks, and Beverages

Warm up your holiday guests with tasty bites and mugs full of good cheer.

Hot Chocolate with Ginger

Ginger spices up the traditional snowy-night favorite. Serve it with marshmallows and a dusting of cocoa powder.

⅓ cup chopped peeled fresh ginger
2 tablespoons sugar
2 tablespoons water
4 cups 1% reduced-fat milk
½ cup fat-free chocolate syrup

1. Combine first 3 ingredients in a medium saucepan; cook over medium-high heat until sugar dissolves and is golden (about 5 minutes), stirring frequently. Remove from heat; cool slightly. Stir in milk and syrup; cook over medium-low heat, stirring with a whisk. Heat to 180° or until tiny bubbles form around edge of pan, stirring frequently (do not boil). Strain milk mixture through a sieve; discard solids. Yield: 4 servings (serving size: ¾ cup).

CALORIES 190 (13% from fat); FAT 2.7g (sat 1.6g, mono 0.6g, poly 0g); PROTEIN 9.8g; CARB 32g; FIBER 0.9g; CHOL 15mg; IRON 0mg; SODIUM 179mg; CALC 275mg

Tahitian Coffee

Melted ice cream forms a sweet, foamy top layer for this drink.

2¾ cups hot strong brewed coffee
¼ cup dark rum
1 tablespoon sugar
½ cup vanilla low-fat ice cream
4 (3-inch) cinnamon sticks (optional)

1. Combine first 3 ingredients in a pitcher, stirring until sugar dissolves. Pour into mugs, and top with ice cream. Garnish with cinnamon sticks, if desired. Yield: 4 servings (serving size: ¾ cup coffee and 2 tablespoons ice cream).

CALORIES 75 (6% from fat); FAT 0.5g (sat 0.3g, mono 0g, poly 0g); PROTEIN 0.9g; CARB 8.5g; FIBER 0.3g; CHOL 1.3mg; IRON 0.1mg; SODIUM 15mg; CALC 28mg

Mulled Cranberry-Orange Cider

4 whole cloves
4 whole allspice
2 star anise
1 (3-inch) cinnamon stick, broken in half
5 cups apple cider
3 cups cranberry juice cocktail
¼ cup packed brown sugar
4 orange slices
8 star anise (optional)
8 small orange slices (optional)

1. Place first 4 ingredients on a cheesecloth square. Gather edges of cheesecloth together; tie securely. Combine spice bag, cider, cranberry juice, sugar, and 4 orange slices in a Dutch oven. Bring to a boil. Reduce heat; simmer, partially covered, 10 minutes. Remove from heat; let stand 30 minutes. Discard spice bag and orange slices. Serve with additional anise and orange slices, if desired. Yield: 8 servings (serving size: 1 cup).

CALORIES 155 (1% from fat); FAT 0.1g (sat 0g, mono 0g, poly 0.1g); PROTEIN 0.6g; CARB 38.5g; FIBER 0.1g; CHOL 0mg; IRON 0.3mg; SODIUM 20mg; CALC 21mg

Curried Crab Cakes

    2   teaspoons curry powder
   ½   teaspoon salt
   ¼   teaspoon dry mustard
   ¼   teaspoon black pepper
   ⅛   teaspoon ground red pepper
   Cooking spray
    1   cup minced onion
    1   cup chopped red bell pepper
   ½   cup chopped celery
    2   teaspoons minced peeled ginger
    1   garlic clove, minced
  1¼ cups dry breadcrumbs, divided
   ¼   cup light mayonnaise
    1   teaspoon grated lemon rind
    1   pound lump crabmeat, shell pieces
        removed
    1   large egg, lightly beaten
    2   tablespoons butter, divided
   Parsley sprigs (optional)

1. Combine first 5 ingredients in a small bowl; stir well.
2. Heat a large nonstick skillet coated with cooking spray over medium-high heat. Add onion, bell pepper, and celery; cover, reduce heat to medium-low, and cook 10 minutes, stirring occasionally. Add curry powder mixture, ginger, and garlic; cook, uncovered, 5 minutes, stirring frequently. Spoon mixture into a large bowl; cool. Wipe skillet clean with a paper towel.
3. Add ¾ cup breadcrumbs, mayonnaise, rind, crabmeat, and egg to onion mixture; stir well. Divide crabmeat mixture into 24 equal portions, shaping each into a ½-inch-thick patty. Place ½ cup breadcrumbs in a shallow dish; dredge crab cakes in breadcrumbs.
4. Melt 2 teaspoons butter in pan over medium heat. Add 8 patties, and cook 2 minutes on each side or until browned. Remove crab cakes from pan, and keep warm. Repeat procedure with remaining butter and patties. Garnish with parsley sprigs, if desired. Yield: 12 servings (serving size: 2 crab cakes).

CALORIES 124 (30% from fat); FAT 4.2g (sat 1.8g, mono 1g, poly 0.3g); PROTEIN 10.4g; CARB 11.2g; FIBER 1g; CHOL 51mg; IRON 1.2mg; SODIUM 377mg; CALC 65mg

Asian Party Mix

(pictured on page 368)

Sesame rice crackers and wasabi peas add crunch and fire to this old favorite. Dried green peas coated with wasabi are available by the pound in some supermarkets, often in the bulk foods department. Don't worry if you can't find them; the mix is fine without them. Rice crackers are crunchy and airy, with the mild taste of rice. Look for them in the snack or Asian section of your grocery store.

    2   cups crispy corn cereal squares
        (such as Corn Chex)
    2   cups crispy rice cereal squares
        (such as Rice Chex)
    2   cups sesame rice crackers, broken
    1   cup tiny fat-free pretzel twists
   ¾   cup wasabi peas
   ¼   cup lightly salted dry-roasted
        peanuts
    3   tablespoons unsalted butter
    1   tablespoon sugar
    1   tablespoon curry powder
    1   tablespoon low-sodium soy sauce
    1   teaspoon Worcestershire sauce
   ½   teaspoon garlic powder
   ½   teaspoon ground cumin
   ¼   teaspoon salt
   ¼   teaspoon ground red pepper
   Cooking spray

1. Preheat oven to 200°.
2. Combine first 6 ingredients in a large bowl; set aside. Melt butter in a small saucepan over medium heat. Add sugar and next 7 ingredients, stirring with a whisk. Pour butter mixture over cereal mixture, tossing gently to coat. Spread mixture on a jelly roll pan coated with cooking spray. Bake at 200° for 45 minutes. Cool completely before serving. Yield: 8 cups (serving size: ½ cup).

CALORIES 116 (29% from fat); FAT 3.7g (sat 1.6g, mono 1.3g, poly 0.6g); PROTEIN 2.9g; CARB 18.6g; FIBER 1.2g; CHOL 6mg; IRON 2.8mg; SODIUM 269mg; CALC 38mg

Mini Frittatas with Ham and Cheese

Bake these bite-sized frittatas in a miniature muffin pan. They taste great hot or at room temperature, so you can make them in advance.

   Cooking spray
   ½   cup finely chopped onion
   ⅔   cup chopped reduced-fat ham
        (about 2 ounces)
   ⅓   cup (about 1½ ounces) shredded
        reduced-fat extra-sharp cheddar
        cheese
    2   tablespoons chopped fresh chives
   ⅛   teaspoon dried thyme
   ⅛   teaspoon black pepper
    4   large egg whites
    1   large egg

1. Preheat oven to 350°.
2. Heat a large nonstick skillet coated with cooking spray over medium-high heat. Add onion; sauté 2 minutes or until crisp-tender. Add ham; sauté 3 minutes. Remove from heat; cool 5 minutes. Combine cheese and remaining 5 ingredients in a large bowl; stir with a whisk. Add ham mixture, stirring with a whisk. Spoon ham mixture into 24 miniature muffin cups coated with cooking spray. Bake at 350° for 20 minutes or until set. Yield: 8 servings (serving size: 3 frittatas).

CALORIES 39 (30% from fat); FAT 1.3g (sat 0.5g, mono 0.2g, poly 0.1g); PROTEIN 4.4g; CARB 2.3g; FIBER 0.4g; CHOL 32mg; IRON 0.2mg; SODIUM 121mg; CALC 80mg

Soups and Salads

Round out your meal with dishes that are sophisticated in flavor yet in sync with the season.

Apple and Smoked Salmon Salad

This salad combines Thai flavorings with apples and kumquats. The recipe is adapted from one of our favorite Thai cookbooks, *Cracking the Coconut* by Su-Mei Yu.

DRESSING:

- ¼ cup granulated sugar
- ¼ cup Thai fish sauce
- 2 tablespoons light brown sugar
- ¼ teaspoon kosher or sea salt
- ½ cup fresh lime juice

SALAD:

- 3 cups thinly sliced Granny Smith apple (about ¾ pound)
- ½ cup thinly sliced shallots
- ½ cup thinly sliced kumquats or 1 cup pomegranate seeds
- 1 teaspoon minced serrano chile
- 4 ounces thinly sliced smoked salmon, cut into ¼-inch-wide strips

1. To prepare dressing, combine first 4 ingredients in a small saucepan. Bring to a boil; cook 1 minute or until sugars dissolve. Cool; stir in lime juice.

2. To prepare salad, combine apple and remaining 4 ingredients in a medium bowl. Drizzle dressing over salad, and toss gently to coat. Yield: 8 servings (serving size: ½ cup).

CALORIES 100 (7% from fat); FAT 0.8g (sat 0.2g, mono 0.3g, poly 0.2g); PROTEIN 3.6g; CARB 21.2g; FIBER 1.4g; CHOL 3mg; IRON 0.4mg; SODIUM 868mg; CALC 18mg

Triple-Ginger Butternut Squash Soup

Ground, fresh, and crystallized ginger converge in this pungent vegetarian soup. While the soup is pureed until silky, it's given textural contrast with a chopped-peanut garnish. Cooking the squash in the microwave speeds preparation.

- 2 butternut squash (about 1¾ pounds)
- 1 teaspoon olive oil
- 1 cup chopped onion
- 3 tablespoons chopped crystallized ginger
- 1 teaspoon ground ginger
- 1 (1-inch) piece peeled fresh ginger
- 2 (14½-ounce) cans vegetable broth
- ¼ cup thinly sliced green onions
- 4 teaspoons chopped dry-roasted peanuts
- 4 teaspoons low-fat sour cream

1. Pierce each squash with a fork. Microwave at HIGH 20 minutes or until tender, and cool. Cut each squash in half lengthwise, discarding seeds and membrane. Remove pulp.

2. Heat oil in a Dutch oven over medium heat. Add chopped onion, and cook 5 minutes or until golden. Place onion, squash, and gingers in a blender, and process until smooth. Return squash mixture to pan. Stir in vegetable broth, and cook 5 minutes or until thoroughly heated. Spoon 1½ cups soup into each of 4 individual soup bowls. Top each serving with 1 tablespoon green onions, 1 teaspoon chopped peanuts, and 1 teaspoon sour cream. Yield: 4 servings.

CALORIES 164 (21% from fat); FAT 3.9g (sat 0.7g, mono 1.4g, poly 0.5g); PROTEIN 5g; CARB 33.1g; FIBER 8g; CHOL 3mg; IRON 1.7mg; SODIUM 905mg; CALC 117mg

Peeling Beets

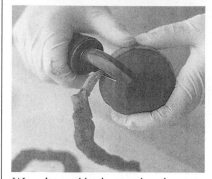

Wear disposable gloves to keep beet juice from staining your hands.

Beet and Black-Eyed Pea Salad

Add black-eyed peas to your Christmas table with this colorful salad that combines them with beets, feta cheese, and toasted pecans. To save time, substitute 3 cups of canned black-eyed peas, rinsed and drained, for the dried peas. You could also use canned beets instead of fresh.

- 1 cup dried black-eyed peas
- ⅓ cup rice vinegar
- 2 tablespoons olive oil
- 2 tablespoons spicy brown mustard
- 2 teaspoons sugar
- 1 teaspoon grated orange rind
- ½ teaspoon salt
- 7 cups coarsely chopped peeled beets (about 2½ pounds)
- ¼ cup (1 ounce) crumbled feta cheese
- 2 tablespoons chopped pecans, toasted
- 2 tablespoons chopped fresh parsley

1. Sort and wash black-eyed peas; place in a small saucepan. Cover with water to 2 inches above peas; bring to a boil. Cook 2 minutes. Remove from heat; cover and let stand 1 hour. Drain peas, and return to pan. Cover with water to 2 inches above peas. Bring to a boil; cover, reduce heat, and simmer 30 minutes or until tender. Drain.

2. Combine vinegar and next 5 ingredients in a small bowl; stir well with a whisk.

3. Steam beets, covered, 25 minutes or until done. Arrange beets on a platter, and top with peas. Sprinkle with cheese, pecans, and parsley. Drizzle vinaigrette over salad. Yield: 8 servings (serving size: 1 cup).

CALORIES 184 (29% from fat); FAT 6g (sat 1.2g, mono 3.5g, poly 0.9g); PROTEIN 5.2g; CARB 28.6g; FIBER 7.8g; CHOL 3mg; IRON 2.1mg; SODIUM 359mg; CALC 127mg

Mushroom Salad with Maple Dressing

Maple syrup and lime juice meld in a sweet-sour dressing for sautéed mushrooms and gourmet salad greens. This salad works well with a dinner featuring ham or pork.

  2 tablespoons lime juice
  2 tablespoons maple syrup
  ¼ teaspoon low-sodium soy sauce
  ¼ teaspoon sesame oil
  ⅛ teaspoon black pepper
1½ teaspoons vegetable oil
Cooking spray
  1 (8-ounce) package button mushrooms, quartered
  6 cups gourmet salad greens
  ⅓ cup chopped green onions
  1 tablespoon finely chopped fresh cilantro

1. Combine first 5 ingredients in a small bowl, and stir well with a whisk.
2. Heat vegetable oil in a large nonstick skillet coated with cooking spray over medium-high heat. Add mushrooms; sauté 6 minutes or until tender. Remove from heat; add maple mixture, tossing to coat. Combine greens, onions, and cilantro in a large bowl. Add mushroom mixture, tossing to coat. Serve salad immediately. Yield: 4 servings (serving size: 1½ cups).

CALORIES 78 (28% from fat); FAT 2.4g (sat 0.4g, mono 0.5g, poly 1.3g); PROTEIN 3g; CARB 12.9g; FIBER 2.9g; CHOL 0mg; IRON 1.8mg; SODIUM 37mg; CALC 56mg

Spicy Turkey and Sweet Potato Gumbo

Use some leftover holiday bird in this flavorful gumbo.

  1 (6-ounce) box long-grain and wild rice mix (such as Uncle Ben's)
  2 (4-ounce) links hot turkey Italian sausage
  1 cup chopped onion
  1 cup chopped celery
  1 cup chopped green bell pepper
  4 garlic cloves, minced
  ½ cup all-purpose flour
  2 cups (¼-inch) cubed peeled sweet potato
  1 teaspoon dried thyme
  1 teaspoon dried oregano
  2 (14½-ounce) cans fat-free, less-sodium chicken broth
  1 (14½-ounce) can diced tomatoes with green pepper and onion, undrained
  1 bay leaf
  2 cups chopped cooked dark-meat turkey
  ½ teaspoon hot sauce

1. Cook rice according to package directions, omitting seasoning packet.
2. Remove casings from sausage. Cook sausage in a Dutch oven over medium heat until browned, stirring to crumble. Add onion, celery, and bell pepper; cook 4 minutes, stirring frequently. Add garlic; cook 1 minute. Lightly spoon flour into a dry measuring cup; level with a knife. Stir in flour; cook 6 minutes or until lightly browned, stirring constantly. Add sweet potato and next 5 ingredients; bring to a boil. Cover, reduce heat, and simmer 15 minutes. Add turkey and hot sauce; cook, uncovered, 3 minutes. Discard bay leaf. Serve over rice. Yield: 6 servings (serving size: 1⅓ cups gumbo and ½ cup rice).

CALORIES 379 (18% from fat); FAT 7.5g (sat 2.3g, mono 2.2g, poly 2.3g); PROTEIN 27.3g; CARB 48.9g; FIBER 4.8g; CHOL 72mg; IRON 3.8mg; SODIUM 804mg; CALC 68mg

Pear, Walnut, and Blue Cheese Salad with Cranberry Vinaigrette

Cranberry sauce, the base for the vinaigrette, lends a holiday flavor to this salad. You can make and refrigerate the dressing up to a week ahead.

VINAIGRETTE:
  ½ cup canned whole-berry cranberry sauce
  ¼ cup fresh orange juice (about 1 orange)
  1 tablespoon olive oil
  2 tablespoons balsamic vinegar
  1 teaspoon sugar
  1 teaspoon minced peeled fresh ginger
  ¼ teaspoon salt

SALAD:
  18 Bibb lettuce leaves (about 2 heads)
  2 cups sliced peeled pear (about 2 pears)
  2 tablespoons fresh orange juice
  1 cup (⅛-inch-thick) slices red onion, separated into rings
  ⅓ cup (2 ounces) crumbled blue cheese
  2 tablespoons coarsely chopped walnuts, toasted

1. To prepare vinaigrette, place first 7 ingredients in a medium bowl; stir well with a whisk.
2. To prepare salad, divide lettuce leaves evenly among 6 salad plates. Toss pear with 2 tablespoons orange juice. Divide pear and onion evenly among leaves. Top each serving with about 1 tablespoon cheese and 1 teaspoon walnuts. Drizzle each serving with about 2½ tablespoons vinaigrette. Yield: 6 servings.

CALORIES 148 (38% from fat); FAT 6.3g (sat 1.8g, mono 2.5g, poly 1.5g); PROTEIN 2.7g; CARB 22.3g; FIBER 2.4g; CHOL 5mg; IRON 0.4mg; SODIUM 205mg; CALC 60mg

Quick Chicken-Corn Chowder

You can have this soup on the table in less than 30 minutes.

2 tablespoons butter
¼ cup chopped onion
¼ cup chopped celery
1 jalapeño pepper, seeded and minced
2 tablespoons all-purpose flour
3 cups 2% reduced-fat milk
2 cups chopped roasted skinless, boneless chicken breasts (about 2 breast halves)
1½ cups fresh or frozen corn kernels (about 3 ears)
1 teaspoon chopped fresh or ¼ teaspoon dried thyme
¼ teaspoon ground red pepper
⅛ teaspoon salt
1 (14¾-ounce) can cream-style corn

1. Melt butter in a large Dutch oven over medium heat. Add onion, celery, and jalapeño; cook 3 minutes or until tender, stirring frequently. Add flour; cook 1 minute, stirring constantly. Stir in milk and remaining ingredients. Bring to a boil; cook until thick (about 5 minutes), stirring frequently. Yield: 6 servings (serving size: about 1 cup).

CALORIES 257 (28% from fat); FAT 8.1g (sat 4.4g, mono 2.4g, poly 0.8g); PROTEIN 19.1g; CARB 28.6g; FIBER 1.9g; CHOL 52mg; IRON 0.4mg; SODIUM 668mg; CALC 165mg

Flour Tip

Stir flour into sautéed vegetables to keep it from clumping when liquid is added.

Golden Oyster Bisque

Saffron colors this holiday favorite a rich yellow-gold. You won't miss it if you omit it, though; the bisque will simply look paler, like oyster stew or chowder.

2 (8-ounce) containers standard oysters, undrained
1 (8-ounce) bottle clam juice
1 tablespoon hot water
¼ teaspoon saffron threads, crushed
1 teaspoon butter
1 cup coarsely chopped red onion
1 cup coarsely chopped celery
¼ cup all-purpose flour
¾ teaspoon ground coriander seeds
3 cups 2% reduced-fat milk
¼ cup chopped fresh flat-leaf parsley
¼ teaspoon salt
⅛ teaspoon ground red pepper

1. Drain oysters in a colander over a bowl, reserving liquid. Add enough clam juice to oyster liquid to equal 1 cup, and set aside. Reserve remaining clam juice for another use. Coarsely chop oysters.
2. Combine water and saffron in a small bowl; set aside.
3. Melt butter in a large saucepan over medium heat. Add onion and celery; cook 5 minutes, stirring frequently. Lightly spoon flour into a dry measuring cup; level with a knife. Stir in flour and coriander; cook 1 minute. Add oyster liquid, saffron water, and milk, stirring with a whisk. Cook until thick (about 12 minutes), stirring frequently. Add oysters, parsley, salt, and pepper. Cook 3 minutes or until edges of oysters curl. Yield: 6 servings (serving size: 1 cup).

CALORIES 153 (30% from fat); FAT 5.1g (sat 2.4g, mono 1.1g, poly 0.7g); PROTEIN 10.6g; CARB 16.2g; FIBER 1.2g; CHOL 53mg; IRON 5.7mg; SODIUM 313mg; CALC 205mg

Main Dishes

For a come-as-you-are brunch or a showstopper supper, your holiday entertaining just got easier.

Standing Rib Roast with Madeira Sauce and Herbed Yorkshire Puddings
(pictured on page 366)

Yorkshire pudding, a holiday classic for generations, derives its name from the Yorkshire region of northern England. Let the roast rest while you finish the sauce and make the puddings; the roast will be easier to carve.

ROAST:
1 (5-pound) French-cut rib-eye roast, trimmed
1 garlic clove, halved
½ teaspoon salt
½ teaspoon freshly ground black pepper
Cooking spray

SAUCE:
1 cup water
2 tablespoons all-purpose flour
½ cup Madeira
½ cup beef broth
½ teaspoon black pepper

PUDDINGS:
1½ cups all-purpose flour
1 teaspoon salt
¾ teaspoon freshly ground black pepper
1½ cups 1% low-fat milk
1 tablespoon chopped fresh or 1 teaspoon dried thyme
1 tablespoon chopped fresh parsley
1 teaspoon grated lemon rind
5 large egg whites
2 large eggs

1. Preheat oven to 450°.
2. To prepare roast, rub roast on all sides with garlic. Sprinkle with ½ teaspoon

salt and ½ teaspoon pepper. Place roast, fat side up, on a broiler pan coated with cooking spray. Insert meat thermometer into thickest portion of roast. Bake at 450° for 25 minutes. Reduce oven temperature to 300° (do not remove roast from oven); bake an additional 1½ hours or until thermometer registers 145° (medium) or desired degree of doneness. Place roast on a platter; let stand while finishing sauce and Yorkshire puddings. Reserve 1½ tablespoons drippings from pan for puddings; set aside.

3. To prepare sauce, wipe remaining drippings from pan with paper towels, leaving brown bits on bottom of pan. Combine water and 2 tablespoons flour in a small bowl. Add Madeira to pan, and bring to a boil over medium-high heat, scraping bottom of pan with a wooden spoon to loosen brown bits. Add flour mixture; cook 1 minute or until slightly thick. Stir in broth and ½ teaspoon pepper; cook 2 minutes. Keep warm.

4. Preheat oven to 450°.

5. To prepare puddings, coat 12 muffin cups with reserved pan drippings. Lightly spoon 1½ cups flour into dry measuring cups, and level with a knife. Combine 1½ cups flour, 1 teaspoon salt, and ¾ teaspoon pepper in a medium bowl. Gradually add milk, stirring with a whisk until smooth. Add thyme and remaining 4 ingredients, stirring with a whisk until smooth. Spoon batter into prepared cups. Bake at 450° for 15 minutes. Reduce oven temperature to 375° (do not remove puddings from oven); bake an additional 15 minutes or until golden. Yield: 12 servings (serving size: 3 ounces beef, 2 tablespoons sauce, and 1 pudding).

WINE SUGGESTION: For centuries, the British have enjoyed red Bordeaux wines (also called "claret") with hearty, warming fare such as this classic roast. If price is no object, a luscious, sophisticated, beautifully structured Bordeaux to consider is Château Lynch-Bages (about $60). For a more modest price, try the Château Greysac Cru Bourgeois (about $15).

CALORIES 304 (38% from fat); FAT 12.8g (sat 5g, mono 5.2g, poly 0.6g); PROTEIN 29g; CARB 16.1g; FIBER 0.6g; CHOL 106mg; IRON 3.5mg; SODIUM 410mg; CALC 58mg

Deglazing the Pan

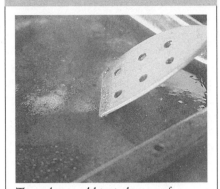

To use browned bits in bottom of a pan to flavor gravy, deglaze the pan by pouring broth into it and scraping flavorful bits into the liquid. Reducing the liquid intensifies the flavor.

Ham with Champagne and Vanilla Glaze

Much of the flavor from the Champagne and vanilla bean seeds ends up in the pan drippings, which are then used to create a simple sauce.

  1 (11-pound) 33%-less-sodium smoked, fully cooked bone-in ham
24 whole cloves
    Cooking spray
1½ cups Champagne or sparkling wine, divided
  1 (2-inch) piece vanilla bean, split lengthwise
  1 cup apple jelly

1. Preheat oven to 350°.

2. Trim fat and rind from ham. Score outside of ham in a diamond pattern, and stud with cloves. Place ham, bone end up, in a roasting pan coated with cooking spray. Pour 1 cup Champagne over ham. Bake at 350° for 45 minutes.

3. Scrape seeds from vanilla bean into a small saucepan. Add vanilla bean and ½ cup Champagne to pan. Bring to a boil; cook 2 minutes. Stir in apple jelly; cook 3 minutes or until jelly dissolves, stirring constantly. Remove from heat. Discard vanilla bean. Pour half of Champagne mixture over ham. Bake 30 minutes; pour remaining Champagne mixture over

ham. Bake an additional 30 minutes or until ham is thoroughly heated. Place ham on a platter; cover loosely with foil. Let stand 15 minutes.

4. Place a zip-top plastic bag inside a 2-cup glass measure. Pour drippings into bag; let stand 10 minutes (fat will rise to top). Seal bag; carefully snip off 1 bottom corner of bag. Drain drippings into measure, stopping before fat layer reaches opening; discard fat. Serve sauce with ham. Yield: 30 servings (serving size: 3 ounces ham and about 1½ teaspoons sauce).

WINE SUGGESTION: Pairing ham with wine takes some care. But this recipe, oriented as it is to vanilla and apple flavors, takes the ham in a Chardonnay direction. And like this ham dish, Chardonnay has vanilla and apple flavors, and its light sweetness mirrors that of the ham. Opt for a Chardonnay that's not too oaky. Try the Gloria Ferrer from the Carneros region of California ($22) or, for a steal, the McPherson Chardonnay from South Eastern Australia ($8).

CALORIES 154 (28% from fat); FAT 4.7g (sat 1.5g, mono 2.2g, poly 0.5g); PROTEIN 17.8g; CARB 8.4g; FIBER 0g; CHOL 45mg; IRON 1.3mg; SODIUM 830mg; CALC 8mg

Ham with Cranberry and Bourbon Glaze

  1 (10-pound) 33%-less-sodium smoked, fully cooked bone-in ham
    Cooking spray
¾ cup packed brown sugar
¾ cup canned whole-berry cranberry sauce
¼ cup bourbon
  1 tablespoon prepared horseradish
  1 bay leaf

1. Preheat oven to 325°.

2. Trim fat and rind from ham. Score outside of ham in a diamond pattern. Place ham, bone end up, on a roasting pan coated with cooking spray. Bake at 325° for 1½ hours.

3. Combine sugar and remaining 4 ingredients in a small saucepan. Bring to a boil. Reduce heat; simmer 5 minutes. Remove from heat; discard bay leaf.

Continued

4. Increase oven temperature to 400° (do not remove ham from oven). Brush cranberry mixture over ham. Bake at 400° for 15 minutes. Place ham on a platter, and cover with foil. Let stand 15 minutes. Do not discard drippings.

5. Drain drippings into a colander over a bowl, reserving cranberries and drippings. Place a zip-top plastic bag inside a 2-cup glass measure or bowl. Pour drippings into bag, and let stand 10 minutes (fat will rise to top). Seal bag, and carefully snip off 1 bottom corner of bag. Drain drippings into a bowl, stopping before fat layer reaches opening; discard fat. Add cranberries to drippings. Serve sauce with ham. Yield: 25 servings (serving size: 3 ounces ham and about 2 teaspoons sauce).

WINE SUGGESTION: The tartness of the cranberries, sweetness of the bourbon, and pungency of the horseradish calls for an equally bold and very fruity wine. Gewürztraminers from Alsace, France, fit the bill. Try the current vintage from any of the following producers: Trimbach, Hugel, Domaine Weinbach, or Zind-Humbrecht (about $18 to $22).

CALORIES 146 (26% from fat); FAT 4.2g (sat 1.4g, mono 2g, poly 0.4g); PROTEIN 15.9g; CARB 9.7g; FIBER 0.1g; CHOL 40mg; IRON 1.2mg; SODIUM 741mg; CALC 11mg

Mahogany Turkey Breast with Vegetable Gravy

The glaze gives a dark sheen to the turkey and lends a rich, caramelized flavor to the chunky gravy. Roasting the turkey on vegetables instead of a rack keeps it moist and adds fragrance to the pan drippings, which are the base of the gravy. For a pretty presentation, garnish the platter with a variety of herbs.

    2   cups thinly sliced onion
    1   cup sliced carrot
    ½   cup thinly sliced celery
    Cooking spray
    3   tablespoons low-sodium soy sauce,
        divided
    1   (14½-ounce) can fat-free,
        less-sodium chicken broth, divided
    1   (5- to 6-pound) bone-in turkey breast
    ½   teaspoon black pepper
    ¼   teaspoon salt
    2   tablespoons dry sherry or Madeira
    2   tablespoons molasses
    1   tablespoon all-purpose flour

1. Preheat oven to 350°.
2. Combine onion, carrot, and celery in a roasting pan coated with cooking spray. Add 1 tablespoon soy sauce and ⅔ cup broth; stir to coat. Place turkey breast, skin side up, on vegetables.

Sprinkle with pepper and salt. Insert meat thermometer into turkey breast, making sure it does not touch bone. Bake at 350° for 1 hour; baste turkey with 2 tablespoons broth every 30 minutes. Combine 2 tablespoons soy sauce, sherry, and molasses. Bake turkey an additional 45 minutes or until thermometer registers 180°, brushing with sherry mixture every 15 minutes. Place turkey on a platter. Cover turkey loosely with foil; let stand 15 minutes. Do not discard drippings.

3. Combine remaining chicken broth and flour, stirring with a whisk until well blended to form a slurry. Drain onion mixture and drippings into a colander over a bowl, reserving both. Place a zip-top plastic bag inside a 2-cup glass measure or bowl. Pour drippings into bag; let stand 10 minutes (fat will rise to top). Seal bag; carefully snip off 1 bottom corner of bag. Drain drippings into a medium saucepan, stopping before fat layer reaches opening; discard fat. Add reserved onion mixture to pan; stir in slurry. Bring to a boil; reduce heat and simmer 5 minutes. Serve turkey with gravy. Yield: 8 servings (serving size: 6 ounces turkey and 3 tablespoons gravy).

CALORIES 336 (23% from fat); FAT 8.6g (sat 2.8g, mono 1.8g, poly 2.5g); PROTEIN 51.8g; CARB 9.6g; FIBER 1.2g; CHOL 129mg; IRON 3.6mg; SODIUM 543mg; CALC 70mg

Flavor: It's in the Bag

Our easy plastic-bag method removes fat, not flavor, from drippings.

1. *Place a zip-top plastic bag in a large measuring cup or bowl, fold back opening of bag, and pour drippings into it.*

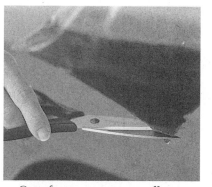

2. *Once fat rises to top, snip off a corner of bag, and drain defatted liquid.*

Coffee-Lacquered Sage Turkey with Redeye Gravy

TURKEY:

    1   (12-pound) fresh or frozen turkey,
        thawed
    3   sage sprigs
    1   large onion, peeled and halved
    ½   cup water
    Cooking spray

GLAZE:

    1   cup strong brewed coffee
    3   tablespoons chopped fresh or
        1 tablespoon dried rubbed sage
    1   tablespoon sugar
    3   tablespoons amaretto
        (almond-flavored liqueur)
    ½   teaspoon salt
    ¼   teaspoon black pepper

GRAVY:

1 cup chopped 33%-less-sodium ham (about 4 ounces)
½ cup fat-free, less-sodium chicken broth
½ cup strong brewed coffee

1. Preheat oven to 350°.
2. To prepare turkey, remove and discard giblets and neck from turkey. Rinse turkey with cold water; pat dry. Trim excess fat. Lift wing tips up and over back; tuck under turkey. Place sage sprigs and onion in body cavity. Tie ends of legs with string. Pour ½ cup water in bottom of a broiler pan. Place turkey on rack of broiler pan coated with cooking spray. Insert meat thermometer into meaty part of thigh, making sure not to touch bone. Bake at 350° for 1 hour.
3. To prepare glaze, combine 1 cup coffee and next 5 ingredients in a small saucepan. Bring to a boil; cook until reduced to ½ cup (about 8 minutes). Brush glaze over turkey. Bake an additional 2 hours or until thermometer registers 180°, basting occasionally with glaze. Place turkey on a platter. Cover turkey loosely with foil; let stand 15 minutes. Do not discard drippings.
4. Place a zip-top plastic bag inside a 2-cup glass measure or bowl. Pour drippings into bag; let stand 10 minutes (fat will rise to top). Seal bag; carefully snip off 1 bottom corner of bag. Drain drippings into a small bowl, stopping before fat layer reaches opening; discard fat. Reserve 1 cup drippings.
5. To prepare gravy, heat a small saucepan over medium-high heat. Add ham; sauté 2 minutes or until browned. Add 1 cup reserved drippings, broth, and ½ cup coffee. Bring to a boil; cook 2 minutes. Remove skin from turkey. Serve turkey with gravy. Yield: 12 servings (serving size: 6 ounces turkey and 2 tablespoons gravy).

CALORIES 315 (25% from fat); FAT 8.8g (sat 2.9g, mono 1.9g, poly 2.5g); PROTEIN 51.8g; CARB 2.7g; FIBER 0g; CHOL 133mg; IRON 3.2mg; SODIUM 334mg; CALC 47mg

Asparagus, Ham, and Fontina Bread Puddings

These savory bread puddings are baked and served in individual custard cups.

1 pound asparagus
1 teaspoon olive oil
1 cup chopped onion
Cooking spray
5 (1.4-ounce) slices firm white sandwich bread (such as Pepperidge Farm Farmhouse), cut into ½-inch cubes
½ cup chopped reduced-fat ham
¾ cup (3 ounces) shredded fontina cheese
1⅔ cups fat-free milk
¾ cup egg substitute
2 teaspoons Dijon mustard
½ teaspoon dried basil
¼ teaspoon salt
¼ teaspoon black pepper

1. Cut a 3-inch tip from each asparagus spear, reserving stalks for another use. Cut asparagus tips into ½-inch pieces.
2. Heat oil in a nonstick skillet over medium-high heat. Add onion; sauté 5 minutes or until tender, stirring frequently. Add asparagus; cover and cook 4 minutes, stirring once. Remove from heat, and set aside.
3. Coat 6 (10-ounce) custard cups or ramekins with cooking spray; place in a large baking pan. Place bread cubes evenly into custard cups. Top evenly with asparagus mixture, ham, and cheese. Combine milk and remaining 5 ingredients, stirring with a whisk. Pour evenly into custard cups; let stand 20 minutes.
4. Preheat oven to 375°.
5. Add hot water to pan to a depth of 1 inch. Cover and bake at 375° for 30 minutes. Uncover and bake an additional 15 minutes. Let stand 10 minutes before serving. Yield: 6 servings.

CALORIES 237 (30% from fat); FAT 7.9g (sat 3.3g, mono 2.4g, poly 0.9g); PROTEIN 16.4g; CARB 26.2g; FIBER 3.9g; CHOL 23mg; IRON 2mg; SODIUM 624mg; CALC 223mg

Southwestern Broccoli Quiche

You can substitute an 11-ounce can of refrigerated breadstick dough for the corn bread twists.

1 (11.5-ounce) can refrigerated corn bread twist dough (such as Pillsbury)
Cooking spray
1 teaspoon vegetable oil
½ cup chopped onion
2 garlic cloves, minced
1 jalapeño pepper, seeded and chopped
½ cup frozen whole-kernel corn
½ cup chopped red bell pepper
½ teaspoon dried oregano
½ teaspoon ground cumin
⅛ teaspoon ground red pepper
1 (10-ounce) package frozen chopped broccoli, thawed, drained, and squeezed dry
1 cup evaporated fat-free milk
3 large egg whites
1 large egg
½ teaspoon salt
¾ cup (3 ounces) reduced-fat sharp cheddar cheese

1. Preheat oven to 350°.
2. Unroll dough; unfold layers (do not separate into strips). Place layers lengthwise, end to end, into an 11 x 7-inch baking dish coated with cooking spray. Pinch ends in middle to seal; press dough up sides of dish. Set aside.
3. Heat vegetable oil in a large nonstick skillet over medium-high heat. Add onion, garlic, and jalapeño; sauté 3 minutes or until soft. Add corn and next 5 ingredients; sauté 5 minutes or until vegetables are soft and liquid evaporates. Remove from heat, and cool 5 minutes.
4. Combine milk, egg whites, egg, and salt; stir well with a whisk. Sprinkle cheese over dough. Spoon broccoli mixture evenly into pan. Pour milk mixture over broccoli mixture. Place dish on a baking sheet. Bake at 350° for 45 minutes; cover and bake an additional 10 minutes or until set. Let stand 10 minutes. Yield 6 servings.

CALORIES 307 (32% from fat); FAT 11g (sat 3.1g, mono 3g, poly 4.2g); PROTEIN 15.6g; CARB 36.9g; FIBER 2.4g; CHOL 40mg; IRON 2.4mg; SODIUM 820mg; CALC 224mg

Breads

Savory or sweet, our loaves or rolls rise to the occasion—be it breakfast, lunch, or a very special dinner.

Parmesan, Garlic, and Basil Twists

Because they begin with refrigerated breadstick dough, these twists are a snap to put together.

- 1 tablespoon olive oil
- 2 garlic cloves, minced
- 1 (11-ounce) can refrigerated breadstick dough
- ¼ cup chopped fresh basil
- ¼ cup (1 ounce) grated fresh Parmesan cheese
- ¼ teaspoon freshly ground black pepper
- Cooking spray

1. Preheat oven to 350°.
2. Heat oil in a small saucepan over medium heat. Add garlic; sauté 30 seconds. Remove from heat.
3. Unroll dough, separating into strips. Brush with garlic mixture. Sprinkle with basil, cheese, and pepper, gently pressing into dough. Twist breadsticks, and place on a baking sheet coated with cooking spray. Gently press ends of breadsticks onto baking sheet.
4. Bake at 350° for 15 minutes or until lightly browned. Yield: 1 dozen (serving size: 1 twist).

CALORIES 94 (30% from fat); FAT 3.1g (sat 0.8g, mono 1.4g, poly 0.6g); PROTEIN 2.9g; CARB 13g; FIBER 0.4g; CHOL 2mg; IRON 0.8mg; SODIUM 231mg; CALC 30mg

Poppy Seed and Onion Crescent Rolls

These soft, fragrant whole wheat rolls are great with roasts or ham—and for sandwiches the next day.

- 1 package dry yeast (about 2¼ teaspoons)
- 1 cup warm water (100° to 110°)
- 1 cup warm 2% reduced-fat milk (100° to 110°)
- 2 tablespoons butter
- 1½ tablespoons sugar
- 1 large egg
- 5½ to 6 cups all-purpose flour, divided
- ½ cup whole wheat flour
- 2 teaspoons salt
- Cooking spray
- 1½ tablespoons olive oil
- 2 cups chopped onion
- 1 large egg
- 1 tablespoon 2% reduced-fat milk
- 1 teaspoon poppy seeds

1. Dissolve yeast in warm water in a large mixing bowl; let stand 5 minutes. Add 1 cup milk, butter, sugar, and 1 egg, and beat with a mixer at medium speed until well blended. Lightly spoon flours into dry measuring cups; level with a knife. Add 3 cups all-purpose flour and whole wheat flour to yeast mixture; beat until blended. Let stand 15 minutes. Add salt, and beat well. Stir in 2 cups all-purpose flour to make a soft dough.
2. Turn dough out onto a floured surface; knead until smooth and elastic (about 10 minutes). Add enough of remaining flour, ¼ cup at a time, to keep dough from sticking to hands (dough will feel tacky). Place dough in a large bowl coated with cooking spray, turning to coat top. Cover and let rise in a warm place (85°), free from drafts, 1 hour or until doubled in size. (Press two fingers into dough. If indentation remains, dough has risen enough.)
3. Heat oil in a large nonstick skillet over medium-high heat. Add onion; cook 10 minutes or until golden.
4. Punch dough down; cover and let rest 5 minutes. Divide in half. Working with 1 portion at a time, roll each portion into a 14-inch circle. Spread half of onion mixture over each portion, and cut each portion into 12 wedges. Roll up each wedge tightly, beginning at wide end. Place, point sides down, on baking sheets coated with cooking spray. Combine 1 egg and 1 tablespoon milk, stirring with a whisk; brush over rolls. Sprinkle evenly with poppy seeds. Let rise, uncovered, 30 minutes or until doubled in size.
5. Preheat oven to 375°.
6. Bake at 375° for 23 minutes or until golden. Yield: 2 dozen (serving size: 1 roll).

CALORIES 159 (16% from fat); FAT 2.9g (sat 1g, mono 1.2g, poly 0.4g); PROTEIN 4.8g; CARB 28.3g; FIBER 1.5g; CHOL 21mg; IRON 1.7mg; SODIUM 217mg; CALC 26mg

Pumpkin-Date Loaf with Cream Cheese Swirl

(pictured on page 367)

White cream cheese batter contrasts with the orange pumpkin in this loaf.

- ½ cup (4 ounces) block-style ⅓-less-fat cream cheese
- 2 tablespoons granulated sugar
- 1 teaspoon vanilla extract
- 1 large egg white, lightly beaten
- 2 cups all-purpose flour
- 1½ teaspoons pumpkin-pie spice
- 1 teaspoon baking powder
- ½ teaspoon salt
- ¼ teaspoon baking soda
- 1 large egg, lightly beaten
- 1 large egg yolk, lightly beaten
- 1¼ cups packed dark brown sugar
- ¾ cup canned pumpkin
- 3 tablespoons vegetable oil
- ¾ cup whole pitted dates, chopped (about 5 ounces)
- Cooking spray

1. Preheat oven to 350°.
2. Combine first 4 ingredients in a small bowl; beat with a mixer at medium speed until blended.
3. Lightly spoon flour into dry measuring cups, and level with a knife. Combine flour and next 4 ingredients in a medium bowl, stirring with a whisk. Combine egg, egg yolk, and brown sugar in a medium bowl; stir with a

whisk until well blended. Add pumpkin and oil; stir well with a whisk. Stir in dates. Add to flour mixture, stirring just until moist.

4. Spoon batter into a 9 x 5-inch loaf pan coated with cooking spray. Spoon cream cheese mixture over batter; swirl batters together using tip of a knife. Bake at 350° for 1 hour or until a wooden pick inserted in center comes out clean. Cool 10 minutes in pan on a wire rack; remove from pan. Cool completely on wire rack. Yield: 16 servings (serving size: 1 slice).

CALORIES 208 (22% from fat); FAT 5.1g (sat 1.7g, mono 1.3g, poly 1.7g); PROTEIN 3.5g; CARB 38.1g; FIBER 1.6g; CHOL 32mg; IRON 1.4mg; SODIUM 167mg; CALC 50mg

How to Make Potato Fougasse

This is a big, impressive loaf. But make 2 (7 x 5-inch) smaller loaves, if you prefer.

1. *Cut 5 diagonal slashes in dough; be sure not to cut to outside border of dough.*

2. *Using your hands, gently pull slits apart so they remain open during baking.*

Potato Fougasse

A *fougasse* (FOO-gass) is a French bread shaped by slashing the dough and stretching it to resemble a ladder or tree-of-life design. It's ideal for an informal supper or a party.

  2 cups cubed peeled Yukon gold or baking potato
  1 package dry yeast (about 2¼ teaspoons)
  1 teaspoon brown sugar
  ½ cup warm water (100° to 110°)
  6 cups all-purpose flour, divided
  2 tablespoons olive oil
  2 tablespoons chopped fresh or 2 teaspoons dried rosemary
  2 teaspoons salt
Cooking spray

1. Place potato in a saucepan; cover with water. Bring to a boil. Reduce heat, and simmer 25 minutes or until tender. Drain in a colander over a bowl, reserving 1 cup cooking liquid. Return potato to pan, and beat with a mixer at medium speed until smooth.

2. Dissolve yeast and sugar in warm water in a large bowl; let stand 5 minutes. Lightly spoon flour into dry measuring cups, and level with a knife. Add 2 cups flour, mashed potato, reserved cooking liquid, oil, rosemary, and salt to yeast mixture; beat with a mixer at medium speed until smooth. Stir in 3½ cups flour. Turn dough out onto a lightly floured surface. Knead until smooth and elastic (about 10 minutes); add enough of remaining flour, 1 tablespoon at a time, to prevent dough from sticking to hands.

3. Place dough in a large bowl coated with cooking spray, turning to coat top. Cover and let rise in a warm place (85°), free from drafts, 45 minutes or until doubled in size. (Press two fingers into dough. If indentation remains, dough has risen enough.) Punch dough down; roll into a 14 x 10-inch rectangle. Place on a large baking sheet coated with cooking spray. Imagine a lengthwise line running through center of rectangle. Cut 5 (4-inch-long) diagonal slits in dough on each side of imaginary line. (Be careful

not to cut through edge of dough.) Gently pull slits open. Cover and let rise 30 minutes or until doubled in size.

4. Preheat oven to 425°.

5. Uncover dough, and bake at 425° for 25 minutes or until browned. Remove from pan. Cool bread on a wire rack. Cut loaf in half lengthwise; cut each half crosswise into 12 pieces. Yield: 1 loaf, 24 servings (serving size: 1 slice).

CALORIES 137 (10% from fat); FAT 1.5g (sat 0.2g, mono 0.9g, poly 0.2g); PROTEIN 3.6g; CARB 26.7g; FIBER 1.1g; CHOL 0mg; IRON 1.6mg; SODIUM 197mg; CALC 7mg

Side Dishes

Mix and match these inventive companions for meals that sparkle with flavor.

Lemon-Scented Broccoli Soufflé

Serve this soufflé straight out of the oven. Plunge the serving spoon in the middle of the dish—the soufflé will fall, but its airy texture will remain.

  ¾ pound finely chopped broccoli
  ⅓ cup all-purpose flour
  1½ cups 1% low-fat milk
  ⅓ cup fat-free sour cream
  1 tablespoon grated lemon rind
  ¾ teaspoon salt
  3 large egg yolks
  1 garlic clove, minced
  6 large egg whites
Cooking spray

1. Preheat oven to 325°.

2. Cook broccoli in boiling water 4 minutes or until tender. Drain. Cool to room temperature on paper towels.

3. Lightly spoon flour into a dry measuring cup; level with a knife. Combine flour and milk in a saucepan; stir well. Bring to a boil over medium heat; cook 1 minute, stirring constantly. Reduce heat to medium-low. Stir in sour cream, rind, salt, yolks, and garlic; cook 1

Continued

minute or until thick, stirring constantly. Pour mixture into a large bowl, and stir in broccoli.

4. Beat egg whites with a mixer at high speed until stiff peaks form. Gently stir one-third of egg whites into broccoli mixture; fold in remaining egg whites. Spoon into a 2-quart soufflé dish coated with cooking spray. Place on middle rack of oven. Bake at 325° for 40 minutes. Serve immediately. Yield: 6 servings (serving size: ¾ cup).

CALORIES 117 (27% from fat); FAT 3.5g (sat 1.3g, mono 1.2g, poly 0.4g); PROTEIN 8.9g; CARB 12.2g; FIBER 0.9g; CHOL 110mg; IRON 0.8mg; SODIUM 398mg; CALC 121mg

Cranberry-Kumquat-Date Relish

Make this relish ahead, and keep it refrigerated. Serve with turkey as an alternative to the usual cranberry sauce.

    1   (12-ounce) package fresh
         cranberries
    1   cup kumquats, quartered
    ¾   cup sugar
    ½   cup chopped pitted dates

1. Combine first 3 ingredients in a food processor, and pulse 10 times or until fruit is coarsely chopped. Add dates, and pulse 5 times or until blended. Cover and let stand at room temperature 1 hour. Yield: 10 servings (serving size: ¼ cup).

CALORIES 111 (1% from fat); FAT 0.1g (sat 0g, mono 0g, poly 0.1g); PROTEIN 0.5g; CARB 29g; FIBER 3.4g; CHOL 0mg; IRON 0.3mg; SODIUM 2mg; CALC 14mg

Orange Beets

    2   large beets (about 1½ pounds)
    1   tablespoon butter
    1   tablespoon grated orange
          rind
    ¾   cup fresh orange juice
    1   teaspoon lemon juice
    ⅛   teaspoon salt
    ⅛   teaspoon black pepper
    1½   tablespoons chopped almonds,
          toasted

1. Leave root and 1 inch stem on beets, and scrub with a brush. Place in a large saucepan; cover with water. Bring to a boil; cover, reduce heat, and simmer 1 hour or until tender. Drain; rinse with cold water. Drain; cool. Trim off beet roots; rub off skins. Cut beets into cubes to measure 3½ cups.

2. Melt butter in a large nonstick skillet over medium heat. Add beets, rind, and next 4 ingredients. Bring to a boil; cook until liquid is the consistency of a thin syrup (about 12 minutes), stirring occasionally. Sprinkle with almonds. Yield: 6 servings (serving size: ½ cup).

CALORIES 89 (29% from fat); FAT 2.9g (sat 1.3g, mono 1.1g, poly 0.3g); PROTEIN 2.4g; CARB 14.8g; FIBER 1.2g; CHOL 5mg; IRON 1mg; SODIUM 157mg; CALC 27mg

Ginger-Lime Sweet Potatoes

    ⅓   cup all-purpose flour
    10   cups thinly sliced peeled sweet
         potato (about 3 pounds)
    ¼   cup butter
    ⅓   cup packed light brown sugar
    1   tablespoon lime rind
    2   tablespoons fresh lime juice
    1   tablespoon grated orange rind
    1   tablespoon grated peeled fresh
         ginger
    1   teaspoon low-sodium soy sauce
    1   teaspoon salt
    ¼   teaspoon black pepper
    Cooking spray

1. Preheat oven to 425°.

2. Lightly spoon flour into a dry measuring cup; level with a knife. Combine flour and potato in a large bowl; toss well.

3. Melt butter in a small saucepan over low heat. Add sugar and next 7 ingredients; cook 4 minutes or until sugar dissolves. Pour over potato mixture; toss well. Spoon mixture into a shallow 2-quart casserole dish coated with cooking spray.

4. Cover and bake at 425° for 55 minutes or until tender. Let stand 10 minutes. Yield: 12 servings (serving size: ⅔ cup).

CALORIES 188 (20% from fat); FAT 4.2g (sat 2.5g, mono 1.2g, poly 0.3g); PROTEIN 2.3g; CARB 36.1g; FIBER 3.6g; CHOL 10mg; IRON 1mg; SODIUM 266mg; CALC 34mg

Corn Bread Stuffing with Sausage and Prunes

Prepare this a day ahead and refrigerate before baking. If you prefer a more savory stuffing, omit the prunes.

    Corn Bread
    2   tablespoons butter
    2   cups chopped onion
    1   cup chopped red bell pepper
    ⅔   cup chopped celery
    1   (14½-ounce) can fat-free,
          less-sodium chicken broth, divided
    1   cup chopped turkey kielbasa
          (about 6 ounces)
    1   cup frozen whole-kernel corn,
          thawed
    1½   teaspoons dried thyme
    1   teaspoon dried sage
    ¾   teaspoon salt
    ¾   teaspoon black pepper
    1   cup coarsely chopped pitted
          prunes
    ¼   cup chopped fresh parsley
    2   large eggs, lightly beaten
    Cooking spray

1. Preheat oven to 400°.

2. Cut corn bread into 1-inch cubes. Place in a large bowl, and set aside.

3. Melt butter in a large nonstick skillet over medium heat. Stir in onion, bell pepper, and celery; cook 5 minutes, stirring frequently. Stir in ¾ cup broth, kielbasa, and next 5 ingredients. Bring to a boil; cover, reduce heat, and simmer 5 minutes. Remove from heat. Pour vegetable mixture over corn bread, stirring well. Stir in prunes and parsley. Combine remaining broth and eggs; pour over corn bread mixture, tossing well. Spoon stuffing into a 13 x 9-inch baking dish coated with cooking spray.

4. Cover and bake at 400° for 15 minutes. Uncover; bake an additional 15 minutes or until browned. Yield: 14 servings (serving size: about ¾ cup).

CALORIES 214 (29% from fat); FAT 6.8g (sat 3.1g, mono 2.2g, poly 0.9g); PROTEIN 8.1g; CARB 31.5g; FIBER 3.3g; CHOL 94mg; IRON 1.6mg; SODIUM 533mg; CALC 107mg

CORN BREAD:

⅔ cup all-purpose flour
1⅓ cups yellow cornmeal
1 tablespoon sugar
2½ teaspoons baking powder
½ teaspoon salt
1¼ cups 1% low-fat milk
3 large eggs, lightly beaten
2 tablespoons butter, melted
Cooking spray

1. Preheat oven to 400°.
2. Lightly spoon flour into dry measuring cups; level with a knife. Combine flour and next 4 ingredients in a large bowl, stirring with a whisk. Make a well in center of mixture. Combine milk, eggs, and butter in a small bowl, stirring with a whisk. Add to flour mixture, stirring just until moist. Spoon batter into a 13 x 9-inch baking pan coated with cooking spray. Bake at 400° for 20 minutes. Cool in pan 10 minutes. Remove from pan; cool completely on a wire rack. Yield: 10 servings.

CALORIES 158 (26% from fat); FAT 4.5g (sat 2.2g, mono 1.4g, poly 0.5g); PROTEIN 5.3g; CARB 23.8g; FIBER 1.6g; CHOL 71mg; IRON 1mg; SODIUM 298mg; CALC 115mg

Sformato

This dish is baked in a springform pan to make a mashed-potato "cake."

3 (1-ounce) slices white bread
7 cups peeled baking potato, cut into 2-inch pieces (about 3 pounds)
2 tablespoons butter
6 cups (¼-inch-thick) sliced onion (about 1¼ pounds)
8 garlic cloves, crushed
¾ cup 2% reduced-fat milk
1½ teaspoons salt
½ teaspoon black pepper
¼ cup chopped fresh parsley, divided
2 large eggs, lightly beaten
Cooking spray
Fresh parsley sprigs (optional)

1. Preheat oven to 350°.
2. Place bread in a food processor; pulse 2 times or until crumbly. Sprinkle crumbs on a baking sheet; bake at 350° for 5 minutes or until golden. (Breadcrumbs should measure 1½ cups.) Set aside. Increase oven temperature to 375°.
3. Place potato in a Dutch oven; cover with water. Bring to a boil. Reduce heat; simmer 15 minutes or until tender. Drain.
4. Melt butter in pan over medium-high heat. Add onion and garlic; sauté 10 minutes or until browned. Add milk, salt, and pepper; bring to a simmer over medium heat, stirring frequently. Reduce heat; simmer 3 minutes. Place onion mixture in a food processor in batches, and process until smooth. Add potato; process until smooth. Add 2 tablespoons chopped parsley and eggs; pulse 10 times or until combined.
5. Combine 1¼ cups breadcrumbs and 2 tablespoons chopped parsley; spread breadcrumb mixture into bottom of a 10-inch springform pan coated with cooking spray. Spread potato mixture over breadcrumb mixture; sprinkle with ¼ cup breadcrumbs. Bake at 375° for 45 minutes or until golden brown. Run a knife around outside edge; cool 10 minutes. Garnish with parsley sprigs, if desired. Yield: 10 servings (serving size: 1 wedge).

CALORIES 217 (18% from fat); FAT 4.3g (sat 2.1g, mono 1.3g, poly 0.4g); PROTEIN 6g; CARB 39.5g; FIBER 3.9g; CHOL 50mg; IRON 1.2mg; SODIUM 456mg; CALC 67mg

Green Beans with Crushed Walnuts

This simple dish relies on freshly ground nutmeg. Look for whole nutmeg in the spice aisle, and store it in the freezer for up to a year.

1¼ pounds green beans, trimmed
2 teaspoons butter
2 tablespoons finely crushed walnuts
½ teaspoon salt
¼ teaspoon freshly ground whole nutmeg

1. Place beans in a large saucepan of boiling water; cook 5 minutes. Drain.

2. Heat butter in a large nonstick skillet over medium-high heat. Add walnuts; sauté 1 minute, stirring constantly. Add beans, salt, and nutmeg; cook 1 minute. Yield: 6 servings (serving size: ⅔ cup).

CALORIES 52 (52% from fat); FAT 3g (sat 1g, mono 0.6g, poly 1.3g); PROTEIN 1.8g; CARB 5.8g; FIBER 2.8g; CHOL 3mg; IRON 0.9mg; SODIUM 213mg; CALC 31mg

Grating Nutmeg

The flavor of freshly ground nutmeg goes a long way. Grating is quick and easy—simply rub whole nutmeg across the grater's surface; the taste of commercially ground and packaged nutmeg doesn't compare.

Brûléed Mashed Sweet Potatoes
(pictured on page 368)

Borrowing from the classic dessert crème brûlée, this dish has a hard candy topping, a crisp contrast to the creamy sweet potatoes.

6 cups hot mashed sweet potatoes (about 4 pounds)
¾ cup whole milk
3 tablespoons butter, softened
½ teaspoon salt
¼ teaspoon ground cinnamon
⅛ teaspoon ground nutmeg
Cooking spray
½ cup packed brown sugar

1. Preheat broiler.
2. Combine first 6 ingredients in a bowl. Spoon potato mixture into an 11 x 7-inch baking dish coated with *Continued*

cooking spray. Sprinkle ½ cup brown sugar evenly over top. Broil 2 minutes or until sugar melts. Let stand until melted sugar hardens (about 5 minutes). Yield: 14 servings (serving size: about ½ cup).

CALORIES 207 (14% from fat); FAT 3.3g (sat 1.9g, mono 0.9g, poly 0.3g); PROTEIN 2.8g; CARB 42.4g; FIBER 2.6g; CHOL 8mg; IRON 1mg; SODIUM 137mg; CALC 53mg

Root Vegetable Latkes

(pictured on page 366)

Latkes are pancakes made from potatoes and are traditionally served as a side dish during Hanukkah. Though they can be made ahead and kept warm in the oven, these latkes are best served immediately.

2½ cups shredded peeled baking
      potato (about 1 large)
1¼ cups shredded parsnips
1¼ cups shredded peeled sweet
      potato
 1   teaspoon salt
 ¼   cup all-purpose flour
1¼ cups chopped onion
 ½   teaspoon black pepper
 2   large egg whites
 2   tablespoons vegetable oil, divided

1. Combine first 4 ingredients in a colander lined with paper towels; let stand 20 minutes. Drain and squeeze excess moisture from potato mixture. Transfer potato mixture to a large bowl. Lightly spoon flour into a dry measuring cup; level with a knife. Add flour, onion, and pepper. Toss well; stir in egg whites.
2. Heat 1 tablespoon oil in a large non-stick skillet over medium-high heat. Spoon ⅓ cup batter for each of 5 latkes into pan; cook 4 minutes on each side or until browned. Repeat procedure with 1 tablespoon oil and remaining batter. Yield: 5 servings (serving size: 2 latkes).

CALORIES 218 (24% from fat); FAT 5.8g (sat 0.9g, mono 1.3g, poly 3.3g); PROTEIN 5g; CARB 37.6g; FIBER 4.1g; CHOL 0mg; IRON 1mg; SODIUM 268mg; CALC 29mg

Leek, Potato, and Caraway Latkes with Spiced Sour Cream

Aromatic caraway seeds—which add a nutty licorice flavor that's a little like that of fennel—may be omitted from the recipe, if you like. The spicy sour cream sauce cools and adds heat at the same time.

LATKES:

 ¼   cup all-purpose flour
 4   cups shredded peeled baking
      potato (about 2 pounds)
 2   cups chopped leek
 1   teaspoon caraway seeds
 ½   teaspoon salt
 ¼   teaspoon black pepper
 1   large egg
 1   large egg white
 4   teaspoons vegetable oil, divided
Cooking spray

SAUCE:

 ¼   teaspoon ground cumin
 ⅛   teaspoon ground red pepper
 ⅛   teaspoon garlic powder
 1   (8-ounce) carton reduced-fat sour
      cream

1. Preheat oven to 350°.
2. To prepare latkes, lightly spoon flour into a dry measuring cup; level with a knife. Combine flour and next 7 ingredients in a large bowl; stir well.
3. Heat 1 teaspoon oil in a large non-stick skillet over medium-high heat.

Spoon ¼ cup batter for each of 4 pan-cakes into pan; cook 3 minutes on each side or until browned. Repeat procedure with remaining oil and batter.
4. Place pancakes on a baking sheet coated with cooking spray. Bake at 350° for 12 minutes or until crisp.
5. To prepare sauce, combine cumin and remaining 3 ingredients, and stir well. Serve sauce over latkes. Yield: 16 serv-ings (serving size: 1 latke and 1 table-spoon sauce).

CALORIES 105 (28% from fat); FAT 3.3g (sat 1.4g, mono 0.4g, poly 0.8g); PROTEIN 2.8g; CARB 16.4g; FIBER 1.2g; CHOL 20mg; IRON 0.6mg; SODIUM 94mg; CALC 36mg

Cran-Apple Relish

Dollop onto Root Vegetable Latkes (recipe at left), or enjoy as a condiment with turkey or ham.

 5   cups chopped peeled cooking
      apple (such as McIntosh or
      Braeburn; 2 pounds)
 2   cups fresh cranberries
 2   cups water
 ¾   cup packed dark brown sugar
 ½   cup white wine vinegar
 ¼   teaspoon ground cloves
 1   (3-inch) cinnamon stick

1. Combine all ingredients in a large, heavy saucepan. Bring to a boil. Reduce heat; simmer 1 hour, stirring occasionally.

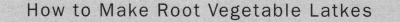

How to Make Root Vegetable Latkes

The key to crisp latkes is removing excess moisture from the vegetables.

1. *Place shredded vegetables in a colander lined with a double layer of heavy-duty paper towels.*

2. *Gather edges of paper towels, and gently squeeze moisture from vegetables.*

Continue to cook until thick (about 30 minutes), stirring frequently. Discard cinnamon. Mash with a potato masher. Cover and chill. Yield: 18 servings (serving size: ¼ cup).

CALORIES 69 (3% from fat); FAT 0.2g (sat 0g, mono 0g, poly 0.1g); PROTEIN 0.1g; CARB 17.8g; FIBER 1.4g; CHOL 0mg; IRON 0.3mg; SODIUM 5mg; CALC 12mg

Glazed Carrots with Candied Chestnuts

Chestnuts are also available canned and can usually be found on the baking aisle of your market.

5 tablespoons brown sugar, divided
4 teaspoons butter, divided
1 cup coarsely chopped bottled chestnuts
2 teaspoons vegetable oil
4 cups baby carrots (about 1 pound)
¼ cup fat-free, less-sodium chicken broth
1 tablespoon chopped fresh parsley
¼ teaspoon salt

1. Combine 2 tablespoons sugar and 2 teaspoons butter in a medium nonstick skillet over medium-high heat; bring to a boil. Add chestnuts; cook 2 minutes or until browned, stirring often. Spread chestnuts in a single layer on wax paper; let stand at room temperature until dry.
2. Heat 2 teaspoons butter and oil in a large nonstick skillet over medium-high heat. Add carrots; sauté 5 minutes. Reduce heat to medium-low. Stir in 3 tablespoons sugar; cook 10 minutes, stirring frequently. Add broth; simmer 2 minutes. Stir in parsley and salt. Top with chestnuts. Yield: 8 servings (serving size: ½ cup).

CALORIES 107 (29% from fat); FAT 3.4g (sat 1.4g, mono 0.9g, poly 0.9g); PROTEIN 1.1g; CARB 19.1g; FIBER 2g; CHOL 5mg; IRON 0.6mg; SODIUM 130mg; CALC 22mg

Caramelized Onion, Green Bean, and Cherry Tomato Tian

This slightly sweet vegetable dish takes its name from the French term *tian* (pronounced tee-AHN) for mixed vegetables prepared gratin-style.

5 cups (1-inch) cut green beans (about 1 pound)
Cooking spray
3 cups thinly sliced onion
6 garlic cloves, minced
2 teaspoons sugar
½ teaspoon salt
¼ teaspoon black pepper
2 tablespoons balsamic vinegar
1 teaspoon dried basil
½ teaspoon dried oregano
4 cups cherry tomatoes, halved
¼ cup (1 ounce) grated fresh Parmesan cheese

1. Preheat oven to 400°.
2. Cook beans in boiling water 3 minutes. Drain and rinse with cold water; set aside.
3. Heat a nonstick skillet coated with cooking spray over medium-high heat. Add onion and next 4 ingredients; sauté 8 minutes or until lightly browned, stirring frequently. Stir in vinegar, basil, and oregano; cook 2 minutes. Remove mixture from heat.
4. Arrange beans in an 11 x 7-inch baking dish coated with cooking spray. Top with onion mixture. Arrange tomatoes on top of onion mixture, and sprinkle with cheese. Bake at 400° for 35 minutes or until cheese is lightly browned. Yield: 6 servings (serving size: 1 cup).

CALORIES 75 (16% from fat); FAT 1.3g (sat 0.6g, mono 0.3g, poly 0.2g); PROTEIN 3.7g; CARB 14g; FIBER 3.7g; CHOL 2mg; IRON 1.3mg; SODIUM 216mg; CALC 86mg

Corn and Parsnip Cakes

Reminiscent of corn fritters, this skillet-cooked side dish features the additional sweetness of parsnips.

1 cup chopped parsnip (about 4 ounces)
1 (15¼-ounce) can whole-kernel corn, drained
⅓ cup all-purpose flour
¼ cup 2% reduced-fat milk
1 tablespoon sugar
½ teaspoon salt
2 large eggs, lightly beaten
1 tablespoon finely chopped fresh chives
1 tablespoon butter, divided

1. Cook parsnip in boiling water 12 minutes or until very tender; drain. Cool to room temperature.
2. Place corn in a food processor; pulse 3 or 4 times or until chopped. Lightly spoon flour into a dry measuring cup; level with a knife. Add parsnip, flour, and next 4 ingredients to food processor. Pulse 3 or 4 times or until combined. Stir in chives.
3. Heat 1 teaspoon butter in a large nonstick skillet over medium-high heat. Drop batter by heaping tablespoonfuls to form 6 cakes. Cook 2 minutes on each side or until golden brown. Repeat procedure with remaining butter and batter. Yield: 6 servings (serving size: 3 cakes).

CALORIES 152 (27% from fat); FAT 4.6g (sat 2g, mono 1.5g, poly 0.6g); PROTEIN 5.2g; CARB 24.8g; FIBER 2.5g; CHOL 77mg; IRON 1.3mg; SODIUM 378mg; CALC 36mg

Chipotle-Cheddar Mashed Potatoes

Chipotle chiles—smoked jalapeños in a vinegar-based sauce—give this dish subtle heat. Vary the amount used in this recipe to suit your taste, or leave them out completely.

  1 (7-ounce) can chipotle chiles in adobo sauce
  4 pounds cubed peeled Yukon gold potato
  6 garlic cloves, peeled
  1½ cups (6 ounces) shredded reduced-fat extra-sharp cheddar cheese
  ¾ cup 1% low-fat milk
  3 tablespoons butter, softened
  1 teaspoon salt

1. Remove 1 chile and 1 tablespoon adobo sauce from can. Chop chile to measure 1 tablespoon. Reserve remaining chiles and adobo sauce for another use.
2. Place potato and garlic in a large Dutch oven; cover with water, and bring to a boil. Cook 15 minutes or until potato is tender. Drain. Return potato mixture to pan. Add chopped chile and adobo sauce, cheese, and remaining ingredients. Mash to desired consistency with a potato masher. Cook 3 minutes over medium heat or until thoroughly heated, stirring constantly. Yield: 12 servings (serving size: ¾ cup).

CALORIES 202 (19% from fat); FAT 4.3g (sat 2.4g, mono 0.9g, poly 0.2g); PROTEIN 5.1g; CARB 36.6g; FIBER 2.8g; CHOL 13mg; IRON 0.6mg; SODIUM 356mg; CALC 158mg

Desserts

These finales, both contemporary and classic, add a festive finish to any menu.

Sweet Potato Bundt Cake with Creamy Orange Glaze

This not-too-sweet cake is a great one to have on hand throughout the holidays—especially since you can serve it for breakfast or dessert.

CAKE:
  Cooking spray
  1 teaspoon flour
  ½ cup fat-free milk
  ½ cup vegetable oil
  1 teaspoon vanilla extract
  3 large eggs
  2 (15-ounce) cans sweet potatoes, drained and mashed (about 2 cups)
  3 cups all-purpose flour
  1 cup granulated sugar
  1 cup packed brown sugar
  1 teaspoon baking soda
  ½ teaspoon salt
  ½ teaspoon ground ginger
  ½ teaspoon ground nutmeg
  ¼ teaspoon ground cinnamon

GLAZE:
  ¾ cup powdered sugar
  ½ cup (4 ounces) ⅓-less-fat cream cheese, softened
  1 teaspoon grated orange rind
  1 tablespoon fresh orange juice
  1 tablespoon fat-free milk

1. Preheat oven to 375°.
2. To prepare cake, coat a 10-inch Bundt pan with cooking spray, and dust with 1 teaspoon flour. Set prepared pan aside.
3. Combine ½ cup milk and next 4 ingredients in a medium bowl.
4. Lightly spoon 3 cups flour into dry measuring cups; level with a knife. Combine 3 cups flour and next 7 ingredients in a large bowl, stirring well with a whisk.
5. Add milk mixture to flour mixture; beat with a mixer at low speed 2 minutes

or until blended. Pour batter into prepared pan. Bake at 375° for 55 minutes or until a wooden pick inserted 1 inch from edge comes out clean. Cool in pan 10 minutes on a wire rack; remove from pan. Cool completely on wire rack.
6. To prepare glaze, combine powdered sugar and remaining 4 ingredients in a bowl; stir well with a whisk. Drizzle glaze over cake. Yield: 18 servings.

CALORIES 300 (26% from fat); FAT 8.7g (sat 2.1g, mono 2.2g, poly 3.8g); PROTEIN 4.7g; CARB 51.5g; FIBER 1.1g; CHOL 40mg; IRON 1.8mg; SODIUM 201mg; CALC 41mg

Kentucky Derby Pie

Pecans, chocolate chips, and bourbon compose the classic filling in this pie. Phyllo dough is layered with breadcrumbs to create a light, crisp crust for this traditionally heavy dessert.

CRUST:
  Cooking spray
  7 sheets phyllo dough, thawed
  2 tablespoons dry breadcrumbs

FILLING:
  ⅔ cup light- or dark-colored corn syrup
  ½ cup packed dark brown sugar
  ⅓ cup bourbon
  ¼ teaspoon salt
  3 large egg whites
  2 large eggs
  ½ cup chopped pecans
  ¼ cup semisweet chocolate chips
  1 teaspoon vanilla extract

1. Preheat oven to 350°.
2. To prepare crust, coat a 9-inch pie plate with cooking spray. Working with 1 phyllo sheet at a time (cover remaining dough to keep it from drying), place phyllo sheet in pie plate with edge overlapping plate rim. Lightly coat phyllo with cooking spray; sprinkle with 1 teaspoon breadcrumbs. Place another sheet of phyllo over first sheet in a crisscross design, and lightly coat with cooking spray. Sprinkle with 1 teaspoon breadcrumbs. Repeat process with 4 phyllo sheets, cooking spray, and 4 teaspoons

breadcrumbs. Top with remaining phyllo sheet, and coat with cooking spray; fold edges over. Set pie plate aside.

3. To prepare filling, combine corn syrup and next 5 ingredients in a large bowl, stirring with a whisk until mixture is well blended. Stir in pecans, chocolate chips, and vanilla. Pour mixture into prepared crust. Bake at 350° for 25 minutes or until lightly browned; cover with foil, and bake an additional 20 minutes or until a knife inserted 1 inch from edge comes out clean. Cool pie on a wire rack. Yield: 8 servings (serving size: 1 wedge).

CALORIES 303 (28% from fat); FAT 9.3g (sat 2g, mono 4.6g, poly 2g); PROTEIN 5.2g; CARB 49g; FIBER 1.4g; CHOL 53mg; IRON 1.5mg; SODIUM 244mg; CALC 32mg

Phyllo Tip

After arranging the phyllo sheets in the pie plate, fold the edges over to form a rim.

Eggnog Semifreddo

Semifreddo, Italian for "half cold," refers to a dessert that's chilled or partially frozen. In this adaptation, traditional Christmas eggnog is transformed from a beverage into a slushy treat you can eat with a spoon. If you don't like rum, substitute vanilla or hazelnut syrup, which you can find with the coffee in most supermarkets.

    ⅔ cup sugar
    1 teaspoon ground nutmeg
    2 large eggs
    2 cups 1% low-fat milk
    ⅔ cup plain low-fat yogurt
    2 tablespoons dark rum
    2 teaspoons vanilla extract

1. Combine first 3 ingredients in a medium bowl, and stir with a whisk.

2. Cook milk in a heavy saucepan over medium-high heat to 180° or until tiny bubbles form around edge (do not boil). Gradually add hot milk to egg mixture, stirring constantly with a whisk. Return milk mixture to pan; cook over medium heat until thick (about 8 minutes), stirring constantly. Remove from heat.

3. Place pan in a large ice-filled bowl until custard cools to room temperature (about 15 minutes), stirring frequently. Stir in yogurt, rum, and vanilla; pour mixture into a glass bowl. Cover and place in freezer 8 hours. Remove mixture from freezer; let stand 15 minutes. Place in a food processor; process until smooth. Serve immediately. Yield: 6 servings (serving size: ½ cup).

CALORIES 181 (15% from fat); FAT 3.1g (sat 1.4g, mono 1g, poly 0.3g); PROTEIN 6.2g; CARB 28.6g; FIBER 0.1g; CHOL 76mg; IRON 0.3mg; SODIUM 82mg; CALC 159mg

Pear Mincemeat Turnovers

These pastries are small enough for the buffet table. You can prepare the filling up to 8 hours ahead, then store covered in the refrigerator.

FILLING:

    ¾ cup bottled mincemeat
    ½ cup coarsely chopped peeled ripe pear
    1½ teaspoons pear nectar or apple juice
    ¼ teaspoon grated lemon rind
    ½ teaspoon lemon juice

PASTRY:

    2 cups all-purpose flour, divided
    6 tablespoons ice water
    1 teaspoon cider vinegar
    2 tablespoons powdered sugar
    ½ teaspoon salt
    ½ cup vegetable shortening

REMAINING INGREDIENTS:

    2 tablespoons 1% low-fat milk, divided
    1 tablespoon granulated sugar

1. To prepare filling, combine first 5 ingredients; set aside.

2. To prepare pastry, lightly spoon flour into dry measuring cups; level with a knife. Combine ½ cup flour, ice water, and vinegar, stirring with a whisk until well blended to form a slurry. Combine 1½ cups flour, powdered sugar, and salt in a bowl; cut in shortening with a pastry blender or 2 knives until mixture resembles coarse meal. Add slurry; toss with a fork until moist. Gently press mixture into a 4-inch circle.

3. Place dough on 2 sheets of slightly overlapping plastic wrap on a slightly damp surface. Cover dough with 2 additional sheets of plastic wrap. Roll dough, still covered, into a 16 x 12-inch rectangle. Slide dough onto a baking sheet; place in freezer 10 minutes or until plastic wrap can be easily removed. (Keep chilled until ready to use.)

4. Preheat oven to 400°.

5. Remove top sheets of plastic wrap. Place dough, plastic wrap side up, on a flat surface. Remove remaining sheets of plastic wrap. Cut pastry into 12 (4-inch) squares. Place about 1 tablespoon filling into center of each square. Moisten edges of squares with 1 tablespoon milk; bring 2 opposite corners together. Press edges together with a fork to seal, forming triangles. Place triangles on a large baking sheet. Brush tops with 1 tablespoon milk; sprinkle evenly with granulated sugar. Bake at 400° for 18 minutes or until golden. Serve warm or at room temperature. Yield: 12 servings (serving size: 1 turnover).

CALORIES 211 (38% from fat); FAT 8.8g (sat 2.2g, mono 3.8g, poly 2.3g); PROTEIN 2.4g; CARB 30.2g; FIBER 0.7g; CHOL 0mg; IRON 1mg; SODIUM 155mg; CALC 7mg

Maple-Bourbon Pumpkin Pie

Maple syrup and brown sugar give this pumpkin pie a rich, molasses-like flavor.

- ½ (15-ounce) package refrigerated pie dough (such as Pillsbury)
- ¾ cup evaporated fat-free milk
- ½ cup maple syrup
- ⅓ cup packed dark brown sugar
- 3 tablespoons bourbon
- 2 teaspoons pumpkin pie spice
- 1 teaspoon vanilla extract
- ¼ teaspoon salt
- 2 large eggs
- 1 large egg white
- 1 (15-ounce) can unsweetened pumpkin
- ¼ cup (2 ounces) ⅓-less-fat cream cheese, softened
- 1 tablespoon maple syrup

1. Preheat oven to 350°.
2. Fit dough into a 9-inch pie plate. Fold edges under; flute. Place pie plate in freezer until ready to use.
3. Combine milk and next 9 ingredients in a large bowl. Stir well with a whisk. Combine cheese and 1 tablespoon syrup in a small bowl; stir with a whisk until smooth. Pour pumpkin mixture into crust. Drop cream cheese mixture by small spoonfuls onto filling; swirl with a knife. Bake at 350° for 55 minutes or until a knife inserted in center comes out clean; cool completely on a wire rack. Yield: 8 servings (serving size: 1 wedge).

CALORIES 297 (30% from fat); FAT 10g (sat 4.3g, mono 4.1g, poly 1g); PROTEIN 5.8g; CARB 44.3g; FIBER 2.3g; CHOL 64mg; IRON 1.1mg; SODIUM 258mg; CALC 125mg

Egg White Tip

Slowly beating the hot sugar syrup into stiff egg whites creates what's called an Italian meringue, yielding a dense, glossy, smooth frosting. Heating the sugar syrup to 238° cooks the whites.

Double-Coconut Cake

(pictured on page 365)

Coconut milk, found with the Asian foods in the supermarket, makes this cake moist and rich.

- Cooking spray
- 1 tablespoon cake flour
- 2¼ cups sifted cake flour
- 2¼ teaspoons baking powder
- ½ teaspoon salt
- 1⅔ cups sugar
- ⅓ cup butter, softened
- 2 large eggs
- 1 (14-ounce) can light coconut milk
- 1 tablespoon vanilla extract
- Fluffy Coconut Frosting
- ⅔ cup flaked sweetened coconut, divided

1. Preheat oven to 350°.
2. Coat 2 (9-inch) round cake pans with cooking spray; dust with 1 tablespoon flour.
3. Combine 2¼ cups flour, baking powder, and salt, stirring with a whisk. Place sugar and butter in a large bowl; beat with a mixer at medium speed until well blended (about 5 minutes). Add eggs, 1 at a time, beating well after each addition. Add flour mixture and milk alternately to sugar mixture, beginning and ending with flour mixture. Stir in vanilla.
4. Pour batter into prepared pans. Sharply tap pans once on countertop to remove air bubbles. Bake at 350° for 30 minutes or until a wooden pick inserted in center comes out clean. Cool in pans 10 minutes on wire racks, and remove from pans. Cool completely on wire racks.
5. Place 1 cake layer on a plate; spread with 1 cup Fluffy Coconut Frosting. Sprinkle with ⅓ cup coconut. Top with remaining cake layer; spread remaining frosting over top and sides of cake. Sprinkle ⅓ cup coconut over top of cake. Store cake loosely covered in refrigerator. Yield: 14 servings.

(Totals include Fluffy Coconut Frosting) CALORIES 298 (24% from fat); FAT 7.9g (sat 5g, mono 1.7g, poly 0.3g); PROTEIN 3.4g; CARB 53.8g; FIBER 0.4g; CHOL 42mg; IRON 1.6mg; SODIUM 273mg; CALC 52mg

FLUFFY COCONUT FROSTING:

- 4 large egg whites
- ½ teaspoon cream of tartar
- Dash of salt
- 1 cup sugar
- ¼ tablespoon water
- ½ teaspoon vanilla extract
- ¼ teaspoon coconut extract

1. Place egg whites, cream of tartar, and salt in a large bowl; beat with a mixer at high speed until stiff peaks form. Combine sugar and water in a saucepan; bring to a boil. Cook, without stirring, until candy thermometer registers 238°. Pour hot sugar syrup in a thin stream over egg whites, beating at high speed. Stir in extracts. Yield: about 4 cups (serving size: about ¼ cup).

CALORIES 54 (0% from fat); FAT 0g; PROTEIN 0.9g; CARB 12.7g; FIBER 0g; CHOL 0mg; IRON 0mg; SODIUM 32mg; CALC 1mg

Coconut-Almond Macaroons

Two classic macaroons are combined in this recipe. Almonds add crunch, while coconut gives the cookies some chewiness.

- 4 large egg whites
- ½ teaspoon cream of tartar
- ¼ teaspoon salt
- 1 cup sugar
- ½ cup flaked sweetened coconut
- ¼ cup finely chopped almonds

1. Preheat oven to 300°.

2. Place first 3 ingredients in a large bowl; beat with a mixer at high speed until soft peaks form. Add sugar, 1 tablespoon at a time, beating until stiff peaks form. Fold in coconut and almonds.

3. Cover baking sheets with parchment paper; secure with masking tape. Drop coconut mixture by level tablespoonfuls onto baking sheets. Bake at 300° for 40 minutes or until dry. Cool on pans on wire racks. Yield: 4½ dozen cookies (serving size: 1 cookie).

NOTE: Store in an airtight container.

CALORIES 22 (20% from fat); FAT 0.5g (sat 0.3g, mono 0.2g, poly 0g); PROTEIN 0.4g; CARB 4.2g; FIBER 0.1g; CHOL 0mg; IRON 0mg; SODIUM 17mg; CALC 1mg

Peppermint Ice Cream

Crushed peppermint candies turn the ice cream a soft pink. This is a great make-ahead dessert; if it's frozen solid, remove it from the freezer 30 minutes before serving, so it can soften.

2½ cups 2% reduced-fat milk, divided
2 large egg yolks
2 teaspoons vanilla extract
1 (14-ounce) can fat-free sweetened condensed milk
⅔ cup crushed peppermint candies (about 25 candies)

1. Combine 1¼ cups 2% milk and egg yolks in a heavy saucepan over medium heat. Cook until mixture is slightly thick and coats the back of a spoon (about 8 minutes), stirring constantly (do not boil). Cool egg mixture slightly.

2. Combine egg mixture, 1¼ cups 2% milk, vanilla, and condensed milk in a large bowl. Cover and chill completely. Stir in crushed candies. Pour mixture into freezer can of an ice-cream freezer; freeze according to manufacturer's instructions. Spoon ice cream into a freezer-safe container; cover and freeze 1 hour or until firm. Yield: 8 servings (serving size: ½ cup).

CALORIES 268 (10% from fat); FAT 2.9g (sat 1.3g, mono 0.9g, poly 0.2g); PROTEIN 7.6g; CARB 52.2g; FIBER 0g; CHOL 62mg; IRON 0.3mg; SODIUM 99mg; CALC 238mg

Five Holiday Menus

To make holiday meal planning easier, Assistant Food Editor Julie Grimes has created five special menus using recipes from our Holiday Cookbook.

Gift-Opening Breakfast

Asparagus, Ham, and Fontina Bread Puddings
(page 353)

Pumpkin-Date Loaf with Cream Cheese Swirl
(page 354)

Hot Chocolate with Ginger
(page 346)

Open House Brunch

Curried Crab Cakes
(page 347)

Mini Frittatas with Ham and Cheese
(page 347)

Asian Party Mix
(page 347)

Mulled Cranberry-Orange Cider
(page 346)

Shoppers' Light Lunch

Triple-Ginger Butternut Squash Soup
(page 348)

Mushroom Salad with Maple Dressing
(page 349)

Parmesan, Garlic, and Basil Twists
(page 354)

Sweet and Savory Supper

Ham with Champagne and Vanilla Glaze
(page 351)

Cranberry-Kumquat-Date Relish
(page 356)

Corn Bread Stuffing with Sausage and Prunes
(page 356)

Ginger-Lime Sweet Potatoes
(page 356)

Maple-Bourbon Pumpkin Pie
(page 362)

Traditional Holiday Feast

Coffee-Lacquered Sage Turkey with Redeye Gravy
(page 352)

Poppy Seed and Onion Crescent Rolls
(page 354)

Green Beans with Crushed Walnuts
(page 357)

Orange Beets
(page 356)

Sweet Potato Bundt Cake with Creamy Orange Glaze
(page 360)

A Downsizing Success Story

A French-toast brunch recipe fares even better under our supervision.

As a practice manager for a medical group, Kristi Wold of Bloomington, Illinois, knows the value of efficiency, which is why she loves Stuffed French Toast. You can throw it together the night before and pop it into the oven right before brunch—perfect for the hectic holiday season.

With layers of smooth cream cheese stuffing and cinnamon-raisin bread, the bread pudding-like dish wins raves from coworkers whenever Kristi takes it to the office. Boyfriend Randy also receives accolades when he makes the recipe for the guys at the fire station where he works. The dish has only one drawback—its nutritional profile.

We knew this recipe could stand some serious downsizing. By combining fat-free and 1/3-less-fat cream cheeses to replace the regular cream cheese, we trimmed the fat by more than 100 grams without losing any richness. Reducing the half-and-half and making up the difference with 1% milk cut another 60 grams of fat, while using egg substitute instead of eggs brought the number down another 23 grams.

Stuffed French Toast

24 (1-ounce) slices cinnamon-raisin bread
Cooking spray
 3 cups 1% low-fat milk
 2 cups egg substitute, divided
 1 cup half-and-half
 1 cup sugar, divided
 1 tablespoon vanilla extract
 1/8 teaspoon ground nutmeg
 1 (8-ounce) block fat-free cream cheese, softened
 1 (8-ounce) block 1/3-less-fat cream cheese, softened
Bottled cinnamon-sugar (optional)

1. Trim crusts from bread. Arrange half of bread in a 13 x 9-inch baking dish coated with cooking spray.
2. Combine milk, 1 1/2 cups egg substitute, half-and-half, and 1/2 cup sugar in a large bowl, stirring with a whisk. Pour half of milk mixture over bread in dish.
3. Combine 1/2 cup egg substitute, 1/2 cup sugar, vanilla, nutmeg, and cheeses in a food processor or blender; process until smooth. Pour cream cheese mixture over moist bread in dish. Top with remaining bread; pour remaining milk mixture over bread. Cover and refrigerate 8 hours or overnight.
4. Preheat oven to 350°.
5. Uncover and bake at 350° for 55 minutes. Let stand 10 minutes before serving. Sprinkle with cinnamon-sugar, if desired. Yield: 12 servings (serving size: 1 piece).

CALORIES 340 (30% from fat); FAT 11.3g (sat 5.1g, mono 3.3g, poly 0.9g); PROTEIN 16.7g; CARB 43.2g; FIBER 1.5g; CHOL 26mg; IRON 3.7mg; SODIUM 447mg; CALC 197mg

BEFORE	AFTER
SERVING SIZE	
1 piece	
CALORIES PER SERVING	
502	340
FAT	
27.3g	11.3g
PERCENT OF TOTAL CALORIES	
49%	30%

Spicy Apple-Glazed Chick 'n' Grits Gorgonzola

Once a winner, always a winner.

Larry Elder of Charlotte, North Carolina, won $5,000 and a weeklong trip for two to the Disney Institute in Orlando, Florida, with this recipe, which first appeared in our May 1997 issue.

Spicy Apple-Glazed Chick 'n' Grits Gorgonzola

 4 (4-ounce) skinless, boneless chicken breast halves
Cooking spray
 1/4 cup apple butter
 1/4 cup spicy brown mustard
 1/4 teaspoon salt
 1/4 teaspoon ground red pepper
 1/8 teaspoon black pepper
Gorgonzola Cheese Grits
 2 tablespoons chopped green onions

1. Preheat oven to 350°.
2. Place each chicken breast half between 2 sheets of heavy-duty plastic wrap; flatten to a 1/2-inch thickness using a meat mallet or rolling pin. Place chicken in a baking pan coated with cooking spray.
3. Combine apple butter, mustard, salt, red pepper, and black pepper; brush over chicken. Bake at 350° for 20 minutes. Cut chicken into 1/2-inch-thick slices.
4. Spoon Gorgonzola Cheese Grits into each of 4 shallow serving bowls. Top with chicken, and sprinkle with green onions. Yield: 4 servings (serving size: 1 cup grits, 3 ounces chicken, and 1 1/2 teaspoons green onions).

(Totals include Gorgonzola Cheese Grits) CALORIES 371 (30% from fat); FAT 12.4g (sat 6.2g, mono 3.3g, poly 0.9g); PROTEIN 41.8g; CARB 21.5g; FIBER 1g; CHOL 94mg; IRON 6.8mg; SODIUM 1,209mg; CALC 190mg

GORGONZOLA CHEESE GRITS:
 2 (14 1/2-ounce) cans fat-free, less-sodium chicken broth
 3/4 cup uncooked quick-cooking grits
 1 cup (4 ounces) crumbled Gorgonzola cheese
 1/3 cup fat-free sour cream
 1/4 teaspoon ground nutmeg
 1/4 teaspoon freshly ground black pepper

1. Bring broth to a boil in a medium saucepan; gradually add grits, stirring constantly. Reduce heat to low; simmer, covered, 5 minutes or until thick, stirring occasionally. Remove from heat; stir in cheese and remaining ingredients. Yield: 4 cups (serving size: 1 cup).

CALORIES 182 (41% from fat); FAT 8.3g (sat 5.3g, mono 2.2g, poly 0.2g); PROTEIN 14.4g; CARB 11.9g; FIBER 0.7g; CHOL 21mg; IRON 5.6mg; SODIUM 795mg; CALC 154mg

Double-Coconut Cake, page 362

Standing Rib Roast with
Madeira Sauce and Herbed
Yorkshire Puddings, page 350

Root Vegetable Latkes, page 358

Pumpkin-Date Loaf with Cream Cheese
Swirl, page 354

Roasted-Poblano Guacamole with
Garlic and Parsley, page 373

Salsa de Molcajete,
page 373

Asian Party Mix, page 347

Brûléed Mashed Sweet Potatoes,
page 357

Play It Again Ham

What to do with leftover holiday ham? Use it in these creative dishes.

Menu 1

serves 4

Spaghetti Carbonara

Steamed broccoli tossed with grated lemon rind

Mini ice-cream sandwiches*

*Spoon about 1 tablespoon strawberry low-fat ice cream onto each of 12 vanilla wafers; top each with 1 vanilla wafer. Freeze until ready to serve.

Spaghetti Carbonara

Chopped ham replaces the bacon in this version of the classic Italian dish.

TOTAL TIME: 30 minutes

QUICK TIP: The water for the pasta will come to a boil faster if covered.

- 8 ounces uncooked spaghetti
- 1 cup chopped cooked ham
- ⅓ cup (1½ ounces) grated Parmigiano-Reggiano or Parmesan cheese
- ¼ cup reduced-fat sour cream
- ½ teaspoon salt
- 2 large eggs, lightly beaten
- 1 garlic clove, minced
- ¼ teaspoon coarsely ground black pepper

1. Cook pasta according to package directions, omitting salt and fat. Drain pasta in a colander over a bowl, reserving ½ cup liquid.
2. Heat a large nonstick skillet over medium heat. Add ham, and cook 2 minutes or until thoroughly heated. Add pasta, and stir well. Combine cheese and next 4 ingredients, stirring with a whisk. Add reserved pasta liquid to egg mixture, stirring with a whisk. Pour egg mixture over pasta mixture; stir well. Cook over low heat 5 minutes or until sauce thickens, stirring constantly (do not boil). Sprinkle with pepper. Yield: 4 servings (serving size: 1 cup).

CALORIES 352 (25% from fat); FAT 9.6g (sat 4.6g, mono 2.2g, poly 0.9g); PROTEIN 21g; CARB 45g; FIBER 1.4g; CHOL 139mg; IRON 1.7mg; SODIUM 748mg; CALC 179mg

Menu 2

serves 4

Warm Lentil-Ham Salad with Dijon Cream

Sautéed Swiss chard*

*Heat 1 tablespoon olive oil in a large nonstick skillet over medium-high heat. Add 12 ounces torn Swiss chard; sauté 3 minutes or until chard begins to wilt. Stir in 1 teaspoon sugar, 1 teaspoon white wine vinegar, and ¼ teaspoon salt; sauté 1 minute or until done.

Crusty French rolls

Warm Lentil-Ham Salad with Dijon Cream

You can serve this main-dish salad at room temperature or chilled.

TOTAL TIME: 35 minutes

QUICK TIP: Dried lentils are ideal for weeknight dinners because they require no soaking and cook in about 20 minutes.

- 1 cup dried lentils
- ½ cup reduced-fat sour cream
- 2 tablespoons Dijon mustard
- 2 tablespoons fat-free milk
- 1 tablespoon white wine vinegar
- 1 teaspoon chopped fresh or ¼ teaspoon dried thyme
- ¼ teaspoon black pepper
- 1⅓ cups chopped cooked ham
- ¾ cup chopped celery
- ¾ cup chopped red onion

1. Place lentils in a large saucepan, and cover with water to 2 inches above lentils. Bring lentils to a boil; cover, reduce heat, and simmer 20 minutes or until tender. Drain well.
2. Combine sour cream and next 5 ingredients in a large bowl. Add lentils, ham, celery, and onion, and toss well. Yield: 4 servings (serving size: about 1⅓ cups).

CALORIES 291 (20% from fat); FAT 6.6g (sat 3.1g, mono 1.2g, poly 0.6g); PROTEIN 24.4g; CARB 35.6g; FIBER 15.8g; CHOL 37mg; IRON 5.5mg; SODIUM 649mg; CALC 114mg

Menu 3

serves 4

Ham and Gruyère-Stuffed Potatoes

Green bean salad*

*Cook 1 pound (1-inch) cut green beans in boiling water 5 minutes or until crisp-tender; drain and rinse with cold water. Combine 2 tablespoons fresh lemon juice, 2 teaspoons olive oil, 1 teaspoon bottled minced garlic, ½ teaspoon dried basil, ¼ teaspoon salt, and ¼ teaspoon pepper in a small bowl; stir well with a whisk. Combine green beans with 2 cups halved cherry tomatoes; toss with vinaigrette.

Garlic bread

Ham and Gruyère-Stuffed Potatoes

Microwaving cooks the potatoes in a flash; briefly baking them at a high temperature once they're stuffed toasts the cheese topping.

TOTAL TIME: 40 minutes

QUICK TIP: Keeping potatoes covered with damp paper towels helps them cook faster and stay moist as they microwave.

- 4 (8-ounce) baking potatoes
- 2 teaspoons butter
- 1 teaspoon bottled minced garlic
- ½ cup fat-free milk
- ½ cup (2 ounces) shredded Gruyère cheese, divided
- ½ cup chopped cooked ham
- 1 tablespoon chopped fresh parsley
- ¼ teaspoon salt
- ¼ teaspoon black pepper

1. Preheat oven to 500°.

Continued

2. Pierce potatoes with a fork, and arrange in a circle on paper towels in microwave oven. Cover potatoes with damp paper towels. Microwave potatoes at HIGH 12 minutes or until done, rearranging after 6 minutes. Let stand 2 minutes. Split open potatoes; scoop out pulp, leaving ¼-inch-thick shells. Reserve shells; set pulp aside.

3. Heat butter in a small skillet over medium-high heat. Add garlic; sauté 30 seconds. Add milk; bring to a simmer. Pour milk mixture over potato pulp. Add ¼ cup cheese, ham, and remaining 3 ingredients, mixing well. Stuff shells with potato mixture. Sprinkle evenly with ¼ cup cheese. Bake at 500° for 8 minutes or until cheese begins to brown. Yield: 4 servings.

CALORIES 358 (19% from fat); FAT 7.5g (sat 4.2g, mono 2.4g, poly 0.5g); PROTEIN 14.1g; CARB 59.8g; FIBER 5.5g; CHOL 30mg; IRON 3.5mg; SODIUM 425mg; CALC 209mg

happy endings

Chocolate Stars

The results of our Chocolate ProAm Recipe Contest are in. The conclusion? Sometimes too much of a good thing really is wonderful.

Chocolate is the Mae West of desserts: over-the-top, glamorous, passionate, and unabashedly decadent. And, like Miss West herself, chocolate can be both naughty and nice. That's what we found when we conducted the first *Cooking Light* Chocolate ProAm Recipe Contest earlier this year. Cosponsored by Hershey's, the competition encouraged both professional and amateur bakers to submit recipes that reveled in chocolate's seductive flavor while holding fat and calories in check. In fact, the only rules were to make the recipe with any Hershey's baking product—and make it light.

Outrageous Warm Double-Chocolate Pudding

This recipe landed first prize in the professional competition for Pam Klink, pastry chef at the Belmont Conference Center in Elkridge, Maryland. She lives in nearby Columbia with her husband, Rob, who's also a chef.

CUSTARD LAYER:
  ¼ cup sugar
  ¼ cup egg substitute
  1 cup plus 2 tablespoons evaporated fat-free milk
  1½ ounces semisweet baking chocolate (such as Hershey's), chopped
Cooking spray

CAKE LAYER:
  3 ounces dark-chocolate candy bar (such as Hershey's), chopped
  ⅓ cup sugar
  ⅓ cup egg substitute
  ¼ cup applesauce
  6 tablespoons frozen fat-free whipped topping, thawed

1. Preheat oven to 325°.
2. To prepare custard layer, combine ¼ cup sugar and ¼ cup egg substitute, stirring well with a whisk. Cook milk in a small, heavy saucepan over medium-high heat to 180° or until tiny bubbles form around edge (do not boil). Remove from heat; add semisweet chocolate, stirring until chocolate melts. Gradually add hot milk mixture to sugar mixture, stirring constantly with a whisk.
3. Pour hot milk mixture into 6 (4-ounce) ramekins or custard cups coated with cooking spray. Place ramekins in a baking pan; add hot water to pan to a depth of 1 inch. Bake at 325° for 30 minutes or until almost set. Remove from oven; cool in pan 30 minutes. Remove ramekins from pan; drain water.
4. To prepare cake layer, place dark chocolate in a small glass bowl. Microwave at HIGH 2 minutes or until almost melted; stir after 1 minute. Set aside. Beat ⅓ cup sugar and ⅓ cup egg substitute with a mixer at medium speed until well blended (about 5 minutes). Add dark chocolate and applesauce; beat

until well blended. Pour evenly over custard layer. Place ramekins in baking pan; add hot water to pan to a depth of 1 inch. Bake at 325° for 20 minutes. Remove ramekins from pan. Top each serving with 1 tablespoon whipped topping. Yield: 6 servings.

CALORIES 257 (26% from fat); FAT 7.5g (sat 4.3g, mono 1.8g, poly 0.5g); PROTEIN 6.9g; CARB 41.1g; FIBER 1.8g; CHOL 4mg; IRON 1.1mg; SODIUM 104mg; CALC 131mg

Light 'n' Creamy Chocolate Cake Roll

Marilyn Smith, whose creation won second place in the professional competition, studied culinary arts at the University of Akron and spent three years working in Italy as a private chef. She now lives in Hudson, Ohio.

CAKE:
  3 tablespoons unsweetened cocoa (such as Hershey's)
  1 (16-ounce) package angel food cake mix (such as Duncan Hines)
Cooking spray
  ½ cup powdered sugar

FILLING:
  2 (1-ounce) bars unsweetened baking chocolate (such as Hershey's)
  1 (8-ounce) block ⅓-less-fat cream cheese, softened
  1 cup powdered sugar
  1 (8-ounce) container frozen fat-free whipped topping, thawed
  1 teaspoon unsweetened cocoa (such as Hershey's)
Chocolate curls (optional)

1. Preheat oven to 350°.
2. To prepare cake, combine 3 tablespoons cocoa and cake mix in a large bowl. Prepare cake mix with added cocoa according to package directions. Coat a 15 x 10-inch jelly roll pan with cooking spray; line bottom with wax paper. Pour batter into pan.
3. Bake at 350° for 25 minutes or until cake springs back when touched lightly in center. Cool cake in pan 5 minutes. Loosen cake from sides of pan, and turn

out onto a dish towel dusted with ½ cup powdered sugar; carefully peel off wax paper. Cool cake 1 minute. Starting at narrow end, roll up cake and towel together. Place, seam side down, on a wire rack; cool completely (about 15 minutes).

4. To prepare filling, place baking chocolate in a glass bowl; microwave at HIGH 2 minutes or until almost melted, stirring after 1 minute. Cool. Place cream cheese in a medium bowl, and beat with a mixer at medium speed until smooth. Gradually add melted chocolate and 1 cup powdered sugar, beating mixture well (mixture will be very thick). Gently stir ½ cup whipped topping into filling, and gently fold in remaining whipped topping.

5. Carefully unroll cake; remove towel. Spread filling over cake, leaving a ½-inch border around outside edges. Reroll cake, and place, seam side down, on a platter. Cover and chill 30 minutes. Sprinkle with 1 teaspoon cocoa. Cut cake into 10 slices; garnish with chocolate curls, if desired. Yield: 10 servings (serving size: 1 slice).

CALORIES 392 (27% from fat); FAT 11.8g (sat 7.2g, mono 3.7g, poly 0.4g); PROTEIN 7.8g; CARB 66.3g; FIBER 2.3g; CHOL 17mg; IRON 1.1mg; SODIUM 377mg; CALC 283mg

Caramel Cloud Bars

Cynthia Clarke, who won third place in the professional category, is a stay-at-home mom to her six sons in Glendora, California. She has written and published one cookbook and has a second in the works.

Cooking spray
1 tablespoon all-purpose flour
1½ cups sugar
¼ cup light margarine, melted
¼ cup evaporated fat-free milk
4 large egg whites
2 cups all-purpose flour
¼ teaspoon salt
¼ teaspoon baking soda
⅔ cup premium white chocolate chips (such as Hershey's)
½ cup chopped macadamia nuts
½ cup caramel sundae syrup (such as Hershey's)

1. Preheat oven to 350°.
2. Coat a 13 x 9-inch baking pan with cooking spray; dust with 1 tablespoon flour.
3. Place sugar, margarine, evaporated milk, and egg whites in a large bowl, and beat with a mixer at medium speed 1 minute. Lightly spoon 2 cups flour into dry measuring cups, and level with a knife. Combine 2 cups flour, salt, and baking soda in a small bowl, stirring well with a whisk. Gradually add flour mixture to sugar mixture, and beat with a mixer at low speed just until blended. Stir in chips and macadamia nuts.
4. Spoon batter into prepared pan. Microwave syrup at HIGH 45 seconds or until warm; stir. Drizzle caramel syrup diagonally across batter. Bake at 350° for 30 minutes or until a wooden pick inserted in center comes out clean. Cool. Yield: 2 dozen bars (serving size: 1 bar).

CALORIES 164 (24% from fat); FAT 4.4g (sat 1.4g, mono 2.3g, poly 0.5g); PROTEIN 2.5g; CARB 28.7g; FIBER 0.5g; CHOL 1mg; IRON 0.6mg; SODIUM 92mg; CALC 23mg

Chocolate-Toffee Puffs

First prize in the amateur division went to Mary Knoblock, a self-taught cook who lives in Omaha, Arizona.

4 large egg whites
⅓ cup granulated sugar
1 cup sifted powdered sugar
½ cup unsweetened cocoa (such as Hershey's)
2 (1.4-ounce) chocolate-covered toffee bars (such as Heath), crushed
Cooking spray

1. Preheat oven to 350°.
2. Beat egg whites in a large bowl with a mixer at high speed until soft peaks form. Gradually add granulated sugar, beating until stiff peaks form.
3. Combine powdered sugar, cocoa, and crushed candy in a small bowl, and mix well. Fold half of cocoa mixture into egg whites (egg whites will deflate quickly). Fold in remaining cocoa mixture until smooth. Drop egg mixture by rounded tablespoonfuls onto a baking sheet coated with cooking spray. Bake at 350° for 15 minutes (puffs will be soft in center). Yield: 2 dozen cookies (serving size: 1 cookie).

CALORIES 52 (24% from fat); FAT 1.4g (sat 0.9g, mono 0.5g, poly 0.1g); PROTEIN 1.1g; CARB 9.9g; FIBER 0.7g; CHOL 1.7mg; IRON 0.3mg; SODIUM 19mg; CALC 7mg

Southwest Chocolate Stack-Ups

Lisa Keys won second prize in the amateur division with this recipe. She works as a physician's assistant in a private pediatric practice and lives in Middlebury, Connecticut.

½ cup semisweet chocolate chips (such as Hershey's)
½ cup (4 ounces) ⅓-less-fat cream cheese, softened
½ cup sugar, divided
½ teaspoon vanilla extract
1 (8-ounce) container frozen fat-free whipped topping, thawed
1 tablespoon unsweetened cocoa (such as Hershey's)
¼ teaspoon ground cinnamon
6 (6-inch) flour tortillas, each cut into 4 wedges
Cooking spray
2 cups sliced fresh strawberries
¼ cup semisweet chocolate minichips (such as Hershey's)
½ cup chocolate syrup (such as Hershey's)

1. Preheat oven to 350°.
2. Place ½ cup chocolate chips in a small glass bowl; microwave at HIGH 2 minutes or until almost melted, stirring after 1 minute. Set aside. Place cream cheese, ¼ cup sugar, and vanilla in a medium bowl, and beat with a mixer at medium speed until well blended. Add melted chips and whipped topping, stirring until well blended. Cover and chill.
3. Combine remaining ¼ cup sugar, cocoa, and cinnamon in a small bowl. Place tortilla wedges on a baking sheet coated with cooking spray. Coat 1 side of each wedge with cooking spray;
Continued

sprinkle evenly with cocoa mixture. Bake at 350° for 10 minutes. Remove from pan, and cool on a wire rack.

4. Spread 1½ tablespoons cream cheese mixture on 1 tortilla wedge, cocoa side up. Top with 1 tortilla wedge, cocoa side up; ¼ cup sliced strawberries; 1½ tablespoons cream cheese mixture; 1 tortilla wedge, cocoa side up; and 1½ tablespoons cream cheese mixture. Sprinkle with 1½ teaspoons minichips. Drizzle tortilla stack with 1 tablespoon syrup. Repeat procedure with remaining tortillas, cheese mixture, strawberries, minichips, and syrup. Yield: 8 servings.

NOTE: Assemble just before serving.

CALORIES 341 (25% from fat); FAT 9.4g (sat 5g, mono 2.4g, poly 0.4g); PROTEIN 4.7g; CARB 60.4g; FIBER 3.6g; CHOL 8mg; IRON 1.6mg; SODIUM 229mg; CALC 49mg

Warm Chocolate Bread Pudding with Turtle Topping

Judges awarded third place in the amateur division to Mary Hawkes. She and her recipe testers—her husband, Reed, and their children, Meghan and Grant—live in Prescott, Arizona.

2½ cups 2% reduced-fat milk
⅔ cup sugar
¼ cup unsweetened cocoa (such as Hershey's)
2 teaspoons vanilla extract
3 large eggs, lightly beaten
1 large egg white
5 cups (1-inch) cubed day-old French bread
Cooking spray
¼ cup caramel sundae syrup (such as Hershey's)
¼ cup chopped pecans
¼ cup milk chocolate chips (such as Hershey's)

1. Preheat oven to 350°.
2. Combine first 6 ingredients in a large bowl, stirring with a whisk. Add bread, pressing down with a spatula to soak. Spoon bread mixture into a 2-quart baking dish coated with cooking spray. Bake at 350° for 50 minutes. Drizzle with

caramel syrup, and sprinkle with nuts. Bake an additional 5 minutes or until caramel syrup is bubbly.

3. Place chocolate chips in a small glass bowl or heavy-duty zip-top plastic bag; microwave at HIGH 30 seconds or until melted. Drizzle over bread pudding. Serve warm. Yield: 6 servings.

CALORIES 403 (28% from fat); FAT 12.4g (sat 4.3g, mono 5.2g, poly 1.9g); PROTEIN 12.7g; CARB 61.8g; FIBER 3.2g; CHOL 116mg; IRON 2.2mg; SODIUM 318mg; CALC 206mg

cooking light profile

A Precious Gift

Welcoming a child challenges one family to keep old traditions while making way for new ones.

As many first-time parents have discovered, having a child brings new meaning to the holidays. But for Magdalena García and her husband, Augusto Torres, last Christmas proved especially meaningful.

After nearly 10 years of marriage, Magdalena, 43, a Presbyterian minister and the managing editor for *¡Exito!* (the Spanish-language newspaper published by the *Chicago Tribune*) and Augusto, 48, a real estate agent and former news anchor for the local Telemundo station, adopted a child from Ecuador.

One of the most important changes wrought by the arrival of their son Miguel Angel ("Miguelito") has been Magdalena's desire to incorporate healthier ways into the family's lifestyle. During the week, she cooks mostly Cuban dishes, making them lighter where she can, particularly by cutting down on fat. Pork fat and frying of any kind have been banned from her kitchen. Heavier Ecuadorean dishes and very sweet traditional desserts haven't been forgotten, just saved for special treats. The following recipe is one of the family's traditional Christmas favorites.

Moros y Cristianos
Moors and Christians

This dish of black beans and rice is a simplified version of the original. It's a Cuban favorite traditionally served at Christmas and on other special occasions. The name—"Moors and Christians"—refers to the Moorish invasion of southern Spain in A.D. 711.

3 tablespoons olive oil
½ cup chopped reduced-fat ham
1 cup chopped onion
3 garlic cloves, minced
½ cup tomato sauce
1 (14½-ounce) can less-sodium, fat-free chicken broth
2 cups long-grain parboiled rice (such as Uncle Ben's)
1 teaspoon ground cumin
1 teaspoon ground oregano
½ teaspoon black pepper
2 (15-ounce) cans black beans, rinsed and drained
1 bay leaf
½ cup finely chopped green bell pepper
Cilantro sprigs (optional)

1. Heat oil in a large Dutch oven over medium-high heat. Add ham; sauté 1 minute. Add onion and garlic; sauté 2 minutes. Stir in tomato sauce and broth; bring to a boil. Add rice and next 5 ingredients; bring to a boil. Cover, reduce heat, and simmer 20 minutes, stirring occasionally. Discard bay leaf. Sprinkle servings evenly with bell pepper. Garnish cilantro sprigs, if desired. Yield: 6 servings (serving size: 1½ cups).

CALORIES 276 (27% from fat); FAT 8.2g (sat 1.4g, mono 5.3g, poly 0.7g); PROTEIN 11.7g; CARB 43.8g; FIBER 8.1g; CHOL 7mg; IRON 2.8mg; SODIUM 870mg; CALC 74mg

The Cooking of Mexico

From roasting chiles to pressing tortillas, learn the techniques that bring Mexican food to life.

Over the years, we've learned a great deal about Mexican cooking and have developed easy-to-follow guidelines for combining commonly available ingredients to make classic dishes. The first fundamental we've learned is that fresh corn tortillas are absolutely essential. They form the all-important foundation of Mexican cooking. Their earthiness provides the background for the flavors that traditionally emerge from the Mexican kitchen.

Roasted fresh chile peppers are also a staple of the Mexican kitchen. The dozens of chiles used in Mexico are relied on more for their taste than for heat. And woven into a luscious guacamole or lively salsa, roasted chiles provide a flavor stamp of authenticity.

What follows is real Mexican food—way beyond Mexican-American inventions such as cheese-covered nachos, big-as-your-head burritos, and U-shaped tacos stuffed with ground beef and iceberg lettuce.

Rustic Jícama Appetizer with Red Chile and Lime

Peel jícama with a knife rather than a vegetable peeler.

- 1 medium jícama (about 1 pound)
- 3 navel oranges, peeled, halved lengthwise, and cut crosswise into ¼-inch-thick slices (about 1½ cups)
- 2 small cucumbers, peeled, halved lengthwise, seeded, and thinly sliced (about 3 cups)
- ½ cup thinly sliced radishes
- ⅓ cup fresh lime juice
- 2 teaspoons dried ground guajillo chile or hot chili powder
- ½ teaspoon salt
- ⅓ cup coarsely chopped fresh cilantro

1. Peel and cut jícama in half. Place halves cut sides down, and cut into ¼-inch-thick slices. Combine jícama, oranges, cucumbers, radishes, and juice in a bowl. Let stand 30 minutes. Add ground chile and salt, and toss well.

Sprinkle with cilantro. Yield: 8 servings (serving size: 1 cup).

CALORIES 53 (5% from fat); FAT 0.3g (sat 0.1g, mono 0g, poly 0.1g); PROTEIN 1.2g; CARB 12.4g; FIBER 4.6g; CHOL 0mg; IRON 0.6mg; SODIUM 153mg; CALC 32mg

Salsa de Molcajete
Roasted Tomato and Green Chile Salsa
(pictured on page 367)

Salsa de molcajete uses centuries-old techniques to combine flavors. Roasting gives tomatoes a sweet and complex taste; rinsing onion under cold water makes it crisp; and crushing roasted garlic and chiles in a mortar releases their full flavor. Though it's typically done in a *molcajete* (Mexican lava rock mortar), you can also make this salsa using a marble mortar and pestle (as we did). Finely chopping the garlic and chiles in a food processor, then adding the tomatoes and pulsing the mixture until everything is coarsely pureed will yield great-tasting results as well.

- 6 plum tomatoes (about 1 pound)
- 3 garlic cloves, unpeeled
- 2 jalapeño peppers
- ⅓ cup chopped fresh cilantro
- ¼ cup finely chopped onion
- 1 teaspoon fresh lime juice
- ¼ teaspoon salt

1. Preheat broiler.
2. Place tomatoes, garlic, and jalapeños on a foil-lined baking sheet. Broil 16 minutes, turning after 8 minutes. Cool and peel tomatoes and garlic. Combine garlic and peppers in a molcajete, mortar, or bowl; pound with a pestle or back of a spoon to form a paste. Add tomatoes, and coarsely crush using pestle or spoon. Combine tomato mixture, cilantro, and remaining ingredients. Yield: 6 servings (serving size: ¼ cup).

CALORIES 23 (12% from fat); FAT 0.3g (sat 0g, mono 0.1g, poly 0.1g); PROTEIN 0.9g; CARB 5g; FIBER 1.2g; CHOL 0mg; IRON 0.5mg; SODIUM 106mg; CALC 10mg

Roasted-Poblano Guacamole with Garlic and Parsley
(pictured on page 367)

You'll find guacamoles in Mexico that range from an intimate gathering of a few ingredients to a big fiesta of tomato, cilantro, onion, green chile, garlic, and lime. In this version, roasted poblanos add spark to the creamy, almost nutty-tasting avocados, especially when bolstered with a little roasted tomato and flat-leaf parsley.

- 2 poblano chiles (about 6 ounces)
- 2 plum tomatoes (about 6 ounces)
- 2 garlic cloves, unpeeled
- 1⅓ cups ripe peeled avocado, seeded and coarsely mashed (about 3)
- 3 tablespoons chopped fresh flat-leaf parsley
- 2 tablespoons fresh lime juice
- ¼ teaspoon salt
- 2 tablespoons grated queso añejo or Parmesan cheese
- 2 tablespoons sliced radishes
- 7 ounces baked tortilla chips (about 7 cups)

Continued

1. Preheat broiler.

2. Cut poblanos in half lengthwise, and discard seeds and membranes. Place poblano halves (skin sides up), tomatoes, and garlic on a foil-lined baking sheet. Broil 12 minutes or until poblanos are blackened, turning tomatoes once. Place poblanos in a zip-top plastic bag, and seal. Let stand 10 minutes. Peel poblanos, tomatoes, and garlic.

3. Place poblanos and garlic in a food processor, and pulse until coarsely chopped. Combine poblano mixture, tomato, avocado, parsley, juice, and salt in a bowl. Sprinkle with cheese and radishes. Serve with tortilla chips. Yield: 8 servings (serving size: ¼ cup guacamole and about ¾ cup chips).

CALORIES 179 (38% from fat); FAT 7.5g (sat 1.3g, mono 4.1g, poly 1.5g); PROTEIN 3.6g; CARB 27g; FIBER 4.8g; CHOL 2mg; IRON 1mg; SODIUM 280mg; CALC 57mg

Pollo Adobado con Papas
Red Chile-Roasted Chicken with Crusty Potatoes

Adobo is a Spanish word that signifies, plainly and simply, "flavoring." A mixture of rehydrated dried red chiles, garlic, spices, and vinegar, it's an essential condiment in the Mexican kitchen. Once the seasoning mixture has done its work—resulting in a light, flavorful, and satisfying dish—the chicken is said to be *adobado*, or marinated (loosely translated). Store leftover marinade in the refrigerator for up to a week or in the freezer for a month. Then use on fish, pork, or lamb chops before grilling.

ADOBO:

  1 tablespoon vegetable oil
  6 dried ancho chiles, seeded and torn (about 3 ounces)
  2 cups hot water
 ¼ cup cider vinegar
1¾ teaspoons salt
  1 teaspoon sugar
  1 teaspoon dried Mexican oregano
 ½ teaspoon freshly ground black pepper
 ¼ teaspoon ground cumin
 ⅛ teaspoon ground cloves
  3 garlic cloves

REMAINING INGREDIENTS:

  1 (3½-pound) whole chicken
 ⅓ cup water
 10 small red potatoes, halved (about 1¼ pounds)
  1 tablespoon vegetable oil
 ¼ teaspoon salt
1¼ cups (¼-inch-thick) sliced onion
  1 tablespoon cider vinegar
  4 watercress sprigs (optional)

1. To prepare adobo, heat 1 tablespoon oil in a large nonstick skillet over medium-high heat. Add anchos; sauté 2 minutes or until anchos are blistered. Combine anchos and 2 cups hot water in a small bowl. Cover and let stand 20 minutes or until tender. Combine ancho mixture, ¼ cup vinegar, and next 7 ingredients in a blender; process until smooth. Strain marinade through a medium-mesh sieve into a bowl; discard solids. (Adobo will have consistency of steak sauce.)

2. To prepare remaining ingredients, remove and discard giblets, neck, and skin from chicken. Rinse chicken with cold water; pat dry. Trim excess fat. Place chicken, breast side down, on a cutting surface. Cut in half lengthwise along backbone. Combine 1 cup marinade and chicken in a large zip-top plastic bag; seal and marinate in refrigerator 4 hours. Reserve remaining marinade for another use.

3. Preheat oven to 375°.

4. Remove chicken from bag, reserving marinade. Place chicken on a broiler pan or rack of roasting pan. Insert meat thermometer into meaty part of thigh, making sure not to touch bone. Pour ⅓ cup water into pan. Combine potatoes, 1 tablespoon oil, and ¼ teaspoon salt in a small bowl. Arrange potatoes around chicken. Bake at 375° for 1 hour or until thermometer registers 160°. Brush reserved marinade over chicken and potatoes, and bake an additional 10 minutes. Place chicken and potatoes on a platter. Combine onion and 1 tablespoon vinegar in a bowl; arrange around chicken and potatoes. Garnish with watercress sprigs, if desired. Yield: 4 servings (serving size: 3 ounces chicken, ¾ cup potatoes, and ½ cup onion mixture).

CALORIES 512 (30% from fat); FAT 17.3g (sat 3.9g, mono 5.5g, poly 6.1g); PROTEIN 46.7g; CARB 42.2g; FIBER 6.5g; CHOL 126mg; IRON 5.2mg; SODIUM 728mg; CALC 58mg

How to Make Pollo Adobado con Papas

1. *Sauté chiles in a skillet over medium heat until they're blistered and smell toasty (about 2 minutes). This adds rustic sweetness and depth to adobo.*

2. *After processing chile mixture, strain it through a medium-mesh sieve; it should have the consistency of steak sauce.*

3. *Place chicken on rack of roasting pan. Arrange potatoes around chicken, and bake until browned.*

Filetes de Pescado a la Veracruzana
Fish Fillets Braised with Tomatoes, Capers, Olives, and Herbs

Though practically any firm, white-fleshed fish would work well, the dish is best made with fresh Gulf snapper.

 1   tablespoon olive oil
1½   cups thinly sliced onion
 4   garlic cloves, minced
 3   pounds ripe tomatoes, chopped
 1   cup sliced pitted manzanilla
     (or green) olives, divided
 ½   cup water
 ¼   cup capers, divided
 ¼   cup sliced pickled jalapeño
     peppers, divided
 3   tablespoons chopped fresh
     flat-leaf parsley
1½   teaspoons dried Mexican oregano
 3   bay leaves
 1   teaspoon salt, divided
 6   (6-ounce) red snapper or other
     firm white fish fillets
 ¼   cup fresh lime juice
     Flat-leaf parsley sprigs (optional)

1. Heat olive oil in a Dutch oven over medium-high heat. Add onion and garlic; sauté 5 minutes or until lightly browned. Add tomato, ½ cup olives, water, 2 tablespoons capers, 2 tablespoons jalapeños, parsley, oregano, and bay leaves. Bring to a boil; reduce heat, and simmer 30 minutes or until reduced to 6 cups. Stir in ½ teaspoon salt. Discard bay leaves.
2. Arrange fillets in a single layer in a 13 x 9-inch baking dish; drizzle with lime juice, and sprinkle with ½ teaspoon salt. Cover and marinate in refrigerator 30 minutes; discard marinade.
3. Preheat oven to 350°.
4. Spoon tomato sauce over fillets. Bake at 350° for 15 minutes or until fish flakes easily when tested with a fork. Sprinkle with ½ cup olives, 2 tablespoons capers, and 2 tablespoons jalapeños. Garnish with parsley sprigs, if desired. Yield: 6 servings (serving size: 1 fillet and about 1 cup sauce).

CALORIES 230 (28% from fat); FAT 7g (sat 1g, mono 3.8g, poly 1.2g); PROTEIN 26.4g; CARB 17g; FIBER 4.3g; CHOL 42mg; IRON 2.5mg; SODIUM 830mg; CALC 88mg

Mango-Lime Ice

Mangoes intense perfume fills your kitchen with the fragrance of the tropics, and their juicy texture makes one of the most appealing fruit ices ever. Focusing the flavors with a little lime juice (and orange rind) makes a simple, refreshing dessert.

 3   cups coarsely chopped peeled
     ripe mango (about 4 mangoes)
1½   cups water
 ½   cup fresh lime juice (about
     6 limes)
 1   cup sugar
 2   teaspoons grated orange rind

1. Combine all ingredients in a blender or food processor, and process until smooth (ingredients may need to be processed in 2 batches).
2. Press mango mixture through a fine sieve over a bowl; discard solids. Pour mixture into an 8-inch square baking dish; cover and freeze 4 hours or until firm. Place mixture in a food processor, and process until slushy. Freeze 3 hours. Soften slightly in refrigerator 30 minutes before serving. Yield: 8 servings (serving size: ½ cup).

CALORIES 142 (1% from fat); FAT 0.2g (sat 0g, mono 0.1g, poly 0.1g); PROTEIN 0.4g; CARB 37g; FIBER 1.2g; CHOL 0mg; IRON 0.1mg; SODIUM 2mg; CALC 9mg

The Mexican Pantry

Ancho chile: When fresh poblano chiles are dried, they're called anchos. Mildly spicy, like their fresh counterparts, anchos give a rich sweetness to marinades or a simmering pot of chili.

Cilantro: This familiar Mexican herb is used only when fresh; it loses all flavor when dried. It provides an explosive sprinkle over lots of street foods, mostly as a component of salsa and guacamole. Store it wrapped in barely damp paper towels in a plastic bag in the warmest part of the refrigerator.

Guajillo chile: These smooth-skinned, brick- or cranberry-red dried chiles are a little spicier than anchos and not nearly as sweet. They're often ground into a powder that gives a tangy jolt to fresh fruits and vegetables; teamed with anchos, they lend multilayered flavor to stews and soups.

Jícama: This root vegetable is the color of a potato, and not much bigger. Sliced or julienned, it adds a slightly sweet, juicy crunch to chicken salads or coleslaw. You can also peel it, slice it, and eat it as a snack, as Mexicans do.

Masa harina: Corn tortillas are made from dried grain (field) corn cooked with mineral lime, then ground into a paste called masa. Several decades ago, a method to dehydrate and powder the perishable masa was discovered; the result became known as masa harina, or masa flour.

Poblano chile: This mildly spicy, dark-green fresh chile resembles a small bell pepper, but with a pointed end, tougher skin, and more compact flesh. The flavor is also similar to that of a bell pepper, only more concentrated and complex.

Queso añejo: This hard, aged cheese, made from cow's milk, adds a salty kick to whatever it touches. Dishes that always get a dusting of grated queso añejo, such as enchiladas, grilled corn on the cob, and street snacks made from corn masa, would be naked without it—like pasta without Romano or Parmesan.

Serrano chile: These bullet-shaped, hot green chiles are about 2½ inches long and ½ inch wide. They have a punchy flavor that is heaven to green-chile lovers—much less sweet than a jalapeño.

How to Make Tortillas de Maíz

Homemade tortillas are simple to make and well worth the effort. They require only masa harina (the ground cornmeal traditionally used to make corn tortillas), a tortilla press, and a skillet. Once you've tasted fresh corn tortillas, you may never want to go back to store-bought. Tortilla presses are available at fine cookware stores (including Williams-Sonoma) and through the Santa Fe School of Cooking and Market (www.santafeschoolofcooking.com) for approximately $24. You can find them for a fraction of that cost at Mexican markets, though.

1. *Combine masa harina and water in a bowl, and stir well. Knead dough until it becomes soft, like cookie dough, but not sticky. The softer the dough, the more moist and tender the tortillas. But don't make it so soft that more than a bit sticks to your hands.*

2. *Divide dough into 12 equal portions. Shape each portion into a ball. Working with 1 portion at a time, place dough between 2 sheets of plastic wrap (cover remaining balls to prevent drying). Place ball, still covered with plastic wrap, on tortilla press. Thicker plastic from food storage bags is easiest to work with and is great for beginners.*

3. *Close press, and move handle from side to side to flatten ball into a 5-inch disk. Open press; turn dough one-half turn. Close press to flatten.*

4. *Remove dough from press; carefully remove plastic wrap. Place dough in a nonstick skillet over medium heat (make sure skillet is hot). Cook 15 to 30 seconds or until tortilla releases itself from pan. Turn tortilla (with spatula or tongs); cook 30 seconds or until brown spots form. Turn tortilla again; cook another 30 to 45 seconds. Tortilla may puff slightly (but you shouldn't worry if it doesn't).*

Tortillas de Maíz
Corn Tortillas

Once you learn how to press and griddle-bake tortillas, they're really quite easy and rewarding. If you'd rather not make your own, search out a locally made brand of tortillas (they'll usually be fresher) in your grocery, and heat them, wrapped in a clean kitchen towel, in a vegetable steamer. Steam 1 minute, turn off heat, and let stand 15 minutes.

1¾ cups masa harina (such as Maseca or Quaker)
1 cup plus 2 tablespoons hot water

1. Lightly spoon masa harina into dry measuring cups; level with a knife. Combine masa harina and water in a large bowl; stir well. Turn dough out onto a surface lightly sprinkled with masa harina; knead lightly 5 times or until soft (consistency should be like soft cookie dough but not sticky). Divide dough into 12 equal portions. Shape each portion into a ball.
2. Working with 1 portion at a time, place dough between 2 sheets of plastic wrap (cover remaining balls to prevent drying). Place ball, still covered, on a tortilla press. Close press to flatten dough, moving handle from side to side. Open press; turn dough one-half turn. Close press to flatten. Remove dough. Carefully remove plastic from dough.
3. Place a nonstick skillet over medium heat. Add dough, and cook 15 to 30 seconds or until tortilla releases itself from skillet. Turn tortilla; cook 30 seconds or until brown spots form. Turn again; cook another 30 to 45 seconds. (At this point, most of tortillas will puff like pita bread.) Remove from pan. Keep warm. Repeat procedure with remaining dough. Yield: 12 tortillas (serving size: 2 tortillas).

CALORIES 129 (11% from fat); FAT 1.6g (sat 0.3g, mono 0.3g, poly 1g); PROTEIN 3.3g; CARB 27.7g; FIBER 3g; CHOL 0mg; IRON 1mg; SODIUM 99mg; CALC 67mg

Tacos de Bistec con Chiles Torreados
Seared Steak Tacos with Blistered Serranos and Browned Onions

In Mexico, the taco is the cultural equivalent of our sandwich—the daily bread with a little something delicious inside. We've used flank steak here since it's readily available, but the author also likes to use *cecina*, *tasajo*, or butterflied skirt steak from a Mexican market, or thinly cut round tip (minute or breakfast steak) from an American market.

- 2½ teaspoons vegetable oil or bacon drippings, divided
- 3 cups (¼-inch-thick) sliced onion, separated into rings (1 medium)
- 6 small serrano chiles, quartered lengthwise
- ¾ teaspoon salt, divided
- 1½ tablespoons fresh lime juice
- 1 (1-pound) flank steak, trimmed and cut into ¼-inch-thick strips
- 12 warm corn tortillas
- ¾ cup bottled green salsa

1. Heat 1 teaspoon oil in a large non-stick skillet over medium-high heat. Add onion and chiles; sauté 6 minutes. Sprinkle onion mixture with ¼ teaspoon salt; stir in lime juice. Remove onion mixture from pan. Add ¾ teaspoon oil to pan. Sprinkle steak with ½ teaspoon salt. Place half of steak in a single layer in pan; cook 2 minutes on each side. Repeat procedure with ¾ teaspoon oil and remaining steak.

2. Arrange steak and onion mixture evenly down centers of tortillas. Top each taco with 1 tablespoon salsa; roll up. Yield: 6 servings (serving size: 2 tacos).

CALORIES 284 (30% from fat); FAT 9.4g (sat 2.9g, mono 3.1g, poly 2g); PROTEIN 19.4g; CARB 31.4g; FIBER 4.3g; CHOL 38mg; IRON 2.5mg; SODIUM 608mg; CALC 113mg

Ceviche de Camarón
Shrimp Ceviche Cocktail

While most of us think of classic ceviche as raw fish marinated in fresh lime juice long enough to give it a cooked texture, in Mexico there are ceviche "cocktails" that combine seafood that's been cooked with fresh vegetables, hot sauce, lime juice, and just a little ketchup. It's an easy, refreshing crowd pleaser, and you don't have to track down the just-off-the-boat fresh fish necessary for classic ceviche. Serve with tostadas, tortilla chips, or saltines.

- ½ cup chopped onion
- 6 cups water
- ¾ cup fresh lime juice, divided
- 1 pound medium shrimp
- 1 cup chopped peeled cucumber
- ½ cup ketchup
- ⅓ cup chopped fresh cilantro
- 2 tablespoons Mexican hot sauce (such as Tamazula)
- 1 tablespoon olive oil
- ¼ teaspoon salt

1. Place chopped onion in a colander, and rinse with cold water. Drain.
2. Bring 6 cups water and ¼ cup juice to a boil in a Dutch oven. Add shrimp; cook 3 minutes or until done. Drain and rinse with cold water; peel shrimp. Combine shrimp and ½ cup juice in a large bowl; cover and chill 1 hour. Stir in onion, cucumber, and remaining ingredients. Serve immediately or chilled. Yield: 6 servings (serving size: ½ cup).

CALORIES 138 (25% from fat); FAT 3.8g (sat 0.6g, mono 1.9g, poly 0.8g); PROTEIN 16.2g; CARB 10.8g; FIBER 0.8g; CHOL 115mg; IRON 2.1mg; SODIUM 483mg; CALC 53mg

Simply Sublime

A reader's Chilean sea bass garnered our Test Kitchens' highest rating.

Because of my addiction to this dish, I was nicknamed 'Chilean sea bass girl' at the fish market," says Catherine Lyet of Lancaster, Pennsylvania. We can understand why. With its freshly ground cumin and delicate, melt-in-your-mouth fillets, her Cumin-Crusted Chilean Sea Bass won raves in our Test Kitchens.

A trained pastry chef who says she shops for food the way many people shop for clothes or music, Catherine recognizes the importance of great-tasting recipes. "The best thing about cooking is how it brings people together," she says. "So many of our rituals and holidays revolve around food—it should be good."

Of course, there's no reason to wait for a special occasion to serve a dish as delicious and easy as Catherine's. "It's a snap," she says. "Little did I know when I first made it how many times I'd be drawn back to this simple recipe to entertain and impress family and friends." And with just a side of steamed asparagus and a good bottle of wine, Catherine explains, you have a meal that'll make a memorable night.

Cumin-Crusted Chilean Sea Bass

Toasting and grinding cumin seeds is a bit more time-consuming than opening a jar, but it makes a big difference in the flavor. Grouper will also work well in this recipe.

- 1 tablespoon cumin seeds
- ½ teaspoon salt
- ¼ teaspoon freshly ground black pepper
- 4 (6-ounce) Chilean sea bass fillets (about 1 inch thick)
- ½ teaspoon olive oil
- 2 tablespoons chopped fresh parsley
- 4 lemon wedges

Continued

1. Preheat oven to 375°.

2. Cook cumin seeds in a large skillet over medium heat 2 minutes or until toasted. Place cumin, salt, and pepper in a spice or coffee grinder; process until finely ground. Rub cumin mixture over both sides of fillets.

3. Heat oil in pan over medium-high heat. Add fillets; cook 2 minutes on each side or until browned. Wrap handle of pan with foil. Bake at 375° for 4 minutes or until fish flakes easily when tested with a fork. Sprinkle with parsley; serve with lemon wedges. Yield: 4 servings (serving size: 1 fillet).

CALORIES 172 (22% from fat); FAT 4.2g (sat 0.9g, mono 1.3g, poly 1.3g); PROTEIN 30.6g; CARB 1.5g; FIBER 0.5g; CHOL 68mg; IRON 1.7mg; SODIUM 408mg; CALC 36mg

Peanut Butter Pie

"My husband loves peanut butter, so I wanted to come up with a dessert recipe using it. The result tastes like eating a peanut butter and chocolate candy bar without a lot of fat. I use this recipe for special occasions and usually make two pies—one to eat and one to keep."

—Mary Frances Noveh,
River Ridge, Louisiana

- 1 cup powdered sugar
- 1 (8-ounce) block light cream cheese, softened
- 1 cup natural-style, reduced-fat creamy peanut butter (such as Smucker's)
- 1 (14-ounce) can fat-free sweetened condensed milk
- 1 (12-ounce) tub frozen fat-free whipped topping, thawed
- 2 (9-inch) ready-made reduced-fat graham cracker shells
- 4 teaspoons fat-free chocolate sundae syrup

1. Combine first 3 ingredients in a large bowl; beat with a mixer at medium speed until smooth. Add condensed milk, and beat until combined. Stir in whipped topping. Divide mixture evenly between shells; chill 8 hours or until set (pies will have a soft, fluffy texture). Cut into

wedges, and drizzle with chocolate syrup. Yield: 20 servings (serving size: 1 wedge).

NOTE: We loved this pie frozen—its texture is more like that of an ice-cream pie.

CALORIES 264 (28% from fat); FAT 8.2g (sat 1.8g, mono 2.2g, poly 1.3g); PROTEIN 7.3g; CARB 40.3g; FIBER 0.8g; CHOL 5mg; IRON 0.6mg; SODIUM 213mg; CALC 69mg

Grilled Fennel-Couscous Salad

"Couscous is a traditional dish from my native country of Morocco, but it isn't typically used in a salad. I developed this recipe one summer when my herb garden produced an unexpected banner crop of fennel. The recipe is a favorite of my wife, who takes leftovers to work for lunch."

—Hakim Agassim, Leesburg, Virginia

Cooking spray
- 1 (8-ounce) fennel bulb, halved
- ¼ cup chopped dry-roasted cashews
- ¼ cup chopped fresh parsley
- 1 tablespoon olive oil
- 1 tablespoon lemon juice
- ½ teaspoon salt
- ½ teaspoon ground cumin
- ⅛ teaspoon black pepper
- 1 navel orange, peeled and cut into ½-inch cubes
- 2 cups water
- 1½ cups uncooked couscous

1. Place a grill pan coated with cooking spray over medium-high heat. Cook fennel 3 minutes on each side or until crisp-tender. Cool 5 minutes, and cut into ½-inch cubes. Combine fennel, cashews, and next 7 ingredients in a large bowl, and set aside. Bring water to a boil in a medium saucepan, and gradually stir in couscous. Remove from heat; cover and let stand 5 minutes. Fluff with a fork. Combine couscous with fennel mixture, and toss well. Serve chilled or at room temperature. Yield: 4 servings (serving size: 1 cup).

CALORIES 360 (20% from fat); FAT 8g (sat 1.3g, mono 4.9g, poly 1.1g); PROTEIN 10.8g; CARB 61.9g; FIBER 6.3g; CHOL 0mg; IRON 2mg; SODIUM 334mg; CALC 69mg

Quick Chicken and Spinach

"I came home from work one day, literally grabbed everything we had in the refrigerator, and invented this recipe using techniques learned from *Cooking Light*. We liked it so much that this is now my Friday night recipe when company comes."

—Brandy Vandergriff, Lexington, Virginia

- 4 (4-ounce) skinless, boneless chicken breast halves
- ⅛ teaspoon salt
- ⅛ teaspoon black pepper
- 1 tablespoon olive oil
- ¾ cup chopped onion
- 1 garlic clove, minced
- 1½ cups fat-free, less-sodium chicken broth
- 2 (14½-ounce) cans diced tomatoes with onions and green peppers, drained
- 4 cups fresh spinach
- 1 tablespoon chopped fresh basil
- 1 tablespoon butter
- 4 cups hot cooked ziti (short, tube-shaped pasta)
- ¼ cup (4 ounces) grated fresh Parmesan cheese

1. Cut chicken into 1-inch pieces, and sprinkle with salt and pepper.

2. Heat oil in a large nonstick skillet over medium-high heat; add chicken, onion, and garlic. Sauté 5 minutes, stirring frequently. Stir in broth and tomatoes. Bring mixture to a boil; reduce heat, and cook 5 minutes, stirring occasionally. Add spinach, basil, and butter; cook 2 minutes.

3. Toss chicken mixture with pasta, and top with cheese. Yield 4 servings (serving size: 2 cups).

CALORIES 431 (23% from fat); FAT 10.8g (sat 4.1g, mono 3.8g, poly 1.3g); PROTEIN 37.8g; CARB 46.3g; FIBER 6.5g; CHOL 80mg; IRON 4mg; SODIUM 911mg; CALC 183mg

...And Ready in Just About 20 Minutes.

So many things to do and so little time— it's a pervasive feeling during the holidays. But with these easy recipes, dinner is one thing you can check off your list.

Once you try Chicken with Eggplant-Pepper Sauce, it's sure to be a favorite in your house. Fruit-based bottled chutney makes a great condiment for Rosemary Pork Tenderloin. And Ham and Pineapple Pizza delivers exotic flavor in mere minutes. Whichever recipe you choose, it will be a welcome—and quick—addition to your table.

Chicken with Eggplant-Pepper Sauce

Serve with crusty bread.

1   medium eggplant (about ½ pound)
2   medium red bell peppers (about 1 pound)
¾   teaspoon salt, divided
¼   teaspoon ground ginger
¼   teaspoon garlic powder
¼   teaspoon ground red pepper, divided
4   (4-ounce) skinless, boneless chicken breast halves
2   teaspoons olive oil, divided
1   teaspoon paprika
4   teaspoons lemon juice

1. Slice eggplant in half lengthwise, and pierce skin with a fork. Cut tops off bell peppers; discard tops, seeds, and membranes. Place eggplant and bell peppers on a microwave-safe plate. Microwave at HIGH 8 minutes or until tender.
2. While eggplant and bell peppers cook, combine ¼ teaspoon salt, ginger, garlic powder, and ⅛ teaspoon red pepper; sprinkle chicken with ginger mixture. Heat 1 teaspoon olive oil in a large nonstick skillet over medium-high heat. Add chicken, and cook 6 minutes on each side or until chicken is done.
3. Combine eggplant and bell peppers in a blender or food processor. Add ½ teaspoon salt, ⅛ teaspoon red pepper, 1 teaspoon oil, paprika, and juice; process until smooth. Serve chicken with sauce. Yield: 4 servings (serving size: 1 chicken breast half and about ⅓ cup sauce).

CALORIES 194 (19% from fat); FAT 4.1g (sat 0.7g, mono 2g, poly 0.7g); PROTEIN 27.9g; CARB 11.8g; FIBER 3.9g; CHOL 66mg; IRON 1.7mg; SODIUM 518mg; CALC 29mg

Rosemary Pork Tenderloin

Pair with boiled red potatoes.

1   tablespoon olive oil
1   (1-pound) pork tenderloin, trimmed and cut crosswise into 12 (1-inch) slices
½   teaspoon salt
½   teaspoon black pepper
½   cup dry white wine
1   tablespoon chopped fresh or 1 teaspoon dried rosemary
2   tablespoons water
1   teaspoon cornstarch
½   cup cranberry chutney (such as Crosse and Blackwell)

1. Heat oil in a large nonstick skillet over medium-high heat. Sprinkle pork with salt and pepper. Add pork to pan; sauté 5 minutes, turning once.
2. Add wine and rosemary to pan; bring to a boil. Cover, reduce heat, and simmer 6 minutes. Combine water and cornstarch in a small bowl. Remove pork from pan; keep warm. Add cornstarch mixture to pan; bring to a boil. Cook 1 minute or until thick, stirring constantly. Serve pork with sauce and chutney. Yield: 4 servings (serving size: 3 slices pork, about 2 tablespoons sauce, and 2 tablespoons chutney).

CALORIES 224 (30% from fat); FAT 7.4g (sat 1.8g, mono 4.3g, poly 0.8g); PROTEIN 24.3g; CARB 14.7g; FIBER 0.9g; CHOL 74mg; IRON 2mg; SODIUM 359mg; CALC 21mg

Chicken-Mushroom-Rice Toss

Steamed snow peas or broccoli tossed with soy sauce and sesame seeds makes a nice side for this dish.

2   (14½-ounce) cans fat-free, less-sodium chicken broth
1   (3½-ounce) bag boil-in-bag long-grain rice
1   tablespoon sesame oil
⅓   cup chopped green onions
1   tablespoon rice vinegar
2   teaspoons bottled minced garlic
1   teaspoon bottled ground fresh ginger
2   cups thinly sliced shiitake or button mushroom caps (about 4½ ounces)
1½ cups chopped cooked chicken breast (about 9 ounces)

1. Bring broth to a boil in a medium saucepan. Add rice; cook, uncovered, 10 minutes. Drain rice in a colander over a bowl, reserving ¼ cup broth; set rice and broth aside.
2. While rice is cooking, heat sesame oil in a large skillet over medium-high heat. Add green onions, vinegar, garlic, and ginger; sauté 1 minute. Add mushrooms; sauté 2 minutes. Stir in rice, reserved broth, and chicken. Cook 3 minutes or until liquid almost evaporates, stirring frequently. Yield: 3 servings (serving size: 1½ cups).

CALORIES 395 (16% from fat); FAT 7.2g (sat 1.4g, mono 2.7g, poly 2.5g); PROTEIN 29.9g; CARB 48g; FIBER 1.7g; CHOL 59.5mg; IRON 3.5mg; SODIUM 568mg; CALC 23mg

Broccoli-Tofu Stir-Fry

This simple meatless stir-fry has a subtle yet addictive sauce. To cut preparation time, use precut broccoli florets. They're near the salad greens in the supermarket.

     1 (3½-ounce) bag boil-in-bag brown rice
     2 tablespoons low-sodium soy sauce
     2 tablespoons oyster sauce
 2½ teaspoons cornstarch
     2 teaspoons rice vinegar
     2 teaspoons dark sesame oil
     2 teaspoons vegetable oil
     1 pound firm tofu, drained and cut into ½-inch cubes
   ¼ teaspoon salt
     2 cups broccoli florets
   ¾ cup water
 1½ tablespoons bottled minced garlic

1. Cook rice according to package directions.
2. While rice cooks, combine soy sauce and next 4 ingredients in a small bowl, stirring with a whisk; set aside.
3. Heat vegetable oil in a large nonstick skillet over medium-high heat. Add tofu, and sprinkle with salt. Cook 8 minutes or until golden brown, tossing frequently. Remove tofu from pan, and keep warm. Add broccoli, water, and garlic to pan. Cover and cook 4 minutes or until crisp-tender, stirring occasionally. Uncover; add soy sauce mixture and tofu, stirring gently to coat. Cook 2 minutes or until sauce thickens, stirring occasionally. Serve broccoli mixture over rice. Yield: 4 servings (serving size: 1 cup stir-fry and ½ cup rice).

CALORIES 451 (17% from fat); FAT 8.3g (sat 1.4g, mono 2.6g, poly 3.8g); PROTEIN 16.2g; CARB 78g; FIBER 4.4g; CHOL 0mg; IRON 2.8mg; SODIUM 581mg; CALC 87mg

Mahimahi with Balsamic-Wine Sauce

Serve with couscous or orzo.

     4 (6-ounce) mahimahi fillets
   ¼ teaspoon salt
   ⅛ teaspoon black pepper
     2 teaspoons olive oil
   ¼ cup finely chopped red onion
     1 cup dry white wine
   ¼ cup balsamic vinegar
     1 tablespoon capers
     1 tablespoon chopped fresh parsley

1. Sprinkle fillets with salt and pepper. Heat olive oil in a large nonstick skillet over medium-high heat. Add fillets and onion; cook 3 minutes. Turn fillets over. Stir in wine, vinegar, and capers; cook 3 minutes. Remove fillets from pan. Cook wine mixture 3 minutes or until reduced to ½ cup. Serve sauce with fillets; sprinkle with parsley. Yield: 4 servings (serving size: 1 fillet and 2 tablespoons sauce).

CALORIES 182 (17% from fat); FAT 3.5g (sat 0.6g, mono 1.9g, poly 0.5g); PROTEIN 31.8g; CARB 4.2g; FIBER 0.3g; CHOL 124mg; IRON 2.4mg; SODIUM 369mg; CALC 39mg

Ham and Pineapple Pizza

Serve with an arugula salad to balance the sweetness of the pineapple and ham.

     1 (10-ounce) Italian cheese-flavored thin pizza crust (such as Boboli)
   ½ cup commercial pizza sauce
   ½ cup (2-inch) julienne-cut cooked ham
     1 (8-ounce) can pineapple tidbits in juice, drained
   ¾ cup (3 ounces) preshredded part-skim mozzarella cheese
   ¼ teaspoon crushed red pepper

1. Preheat oven to 450°.
2. Place pizza crust on a baking sheet. Spread sauce evenly over pizza crust, leaving a ½-inch border. Top with ham, pineapple, and cheese; sprinkle with red pepper. Bake at 450° for 10 minutes or until crust is crisp. Cut into 8 slices. Yield: 4 servings (serving size: 2 slices).

CALORIES 298 (24% from fat); FAT 7.9g (sat 3.7g, mono 3g, poly 0.8g); PROTEIN 16.7g; CARB 39.8g; FIBER 1g; CHOL 21mg; IRON 2.5mg; SODIUM 823mg; CALC 335mg

H O W   T O   U S E   I T   A N D   W H Y   Glance at the end of any *Cooking Light* recipe, and you'll see how committed we are to helping you make the best of today's light cooking. With six chefs, four registered dietitians, four home economists, and a computer system that analyzes every ingredient we use, *Cooking Light* gives you authoritative dietary detail like no other magazine. We go to such lengths so you can see how our recipes fit into your healthful eating plan. If you're trying to lose weight, the calorie and fat figures will probably help most. But if you're keeping a close eye on the sodium, cholesterol, and saturated fat in your diet, we provide those numbers, too. And because many women don't get enough iron or calcium, we can help there, as well. Finally, there's a fiber analysis for those of us who don't get enough roughage.

What it means and how we get there: Besides the calories, protein, fat, fiber, iron, and sodium we list at the end of each recipe, there are a few things we abbreviate for space.

- *sat* for saturated fat
- *mono* for monounsaturated fat
- *poly* for polyunsaturated fat
- *CARB* for carbohydrates
- *CHOL* for cholesterol
- *CALC* for calcium
- *g* for gram
- *mg* for milligram

We get numbers for those categories based on a few assumptions: When we give a range for an ingredient, we calculate the lesser amount. Some alcohol calories evaporate during heating; we reflect that. And only the amount of marinade absorbed by the food is calculated.

Your Daily Nutrition Guide

	WOMEN AGES 25 TO 50	WOMEN OVER 50	MEN OVER 24
Calories	2,000	2,000 or less	2,700
Protein	50g	50g or less	63g
Fat	67g or less	67g or less	90g or less
Saturated Fat	22g or less	22g or less	30g or less
Carbohydrates	299g	299g	405g
Fiber	25g to 35g	25g to 35g	25g to 35g
Cholesterol	300mg or less	300mg or less	300mg or less
Iron	18mg	18mg	10mg
Sodium	2,400mg or less	2,400mg or less	2,400mg or less
Calcium	1,000mg	1,200mg	1,000mg

Calorie requirements vary according to your size, weight, and level of activity. This chart is a good general guide; additional nutrients are needed during some stages of life. For example, children's calorie and protein needs are based on height and vary greatly as they grow. Compared to adults, teenagers require less protein but more calcium and slightly more iron. Pregnant or breast-feeding women need more protein, calories, and calcium. Also, the need for iron increases during pregnancy but returns to normal after birth.

The nutritional values used in our calculations either come from The Food Processor, Version 7.5 (ESHA Research), or are provided by food manufacturers.

Recipe Title Index

*An alphabetical listing of every recipe title that appeared
in the magazine in 2001. See page 397 for the General Recipe Index.*

Month-by-Month Index

A month-by-month listing of every food story with recipe titles that appeared in the magazine in 2001. See page 397 for the General Recipe Index.

General Recipe Index

A listing by major ingredient, food category, and/or regular column
for every recipe that appeared in the magazine in 2001.

Credits

CONTRIBUTING RECIPE DEVELOPERS:

Krista Ackerbloom
Curtis Aikens
Norman Van Aken
Rick Bayless
Peter Berley
Jack Bishop
David Bonom
Maureen Callahan
Penelope Casas
Holly B. Clegg
Katherine Cobbs
Ying Chung Compestine
Martha Condra
Lorrie Hulston Corvin
Dave DiResta
Melissa Dupree
Pàt Earvolino

Linda West Eckhardt
Larry Elder
Jim Fobel
Joanne Foran
Velda de la Garza
Terry Blonder Golson
Alan Gould
Ken Haedrich
Jessica B. Harris
Tamar Haspel
Juli Hasson
Alyson Moreland Haynes
Giuliano Hazan
Lia Mack Huber
Nancy Hughes
Patsy Jamieson
Jeanne Jones
Regan Miller Jones
Barbara Kafka
Jeanne Thiel Kelley

Bharti Kirchner
Aglaia Kremezi
Jean Kressy
Jeanne Lemlin
Karen Levin
Susan Herrmann Loomis
Ronni Lundy
Karen MacNeil-Fife
Don Mauer
Gordon McKnight
Jill Melton
Yvone Ortiz-Haney
Greg Patent
Jean Patterson
Carole Peck
Marge Perry
Maricel Presilla
Steven Raichlen
Leslie Revsin
Victoria Abbott Riccardi

David Ricketts
Claudia Roden
Julie Sahni
Chris Schlesinger
Nina Simonds
Sue Spitler
Jane Stern
Lisë Stern
Michael Stern
Elizabeth J. Taliaferro
Robin Vitetta-Miller
Robyn Webb
Mary Corpening Whiteford
Mike Wilson
Su-Mei Yu

CONTRIBUTING PHOTOGRAPHER:
Jim Bathie, page 332 (bottom)